American Indian Children and the Law

American Indian Children and the Law

Cases and Materials

Kathryn E. Fort
Director of the Indian Law Clinic
Michigan State University College of Law

Carolina Academic Press
Durham, North Carolina

Paperback ISBN 978-1-5310-2826-8
Casebound ISBN 978-1-61163-795-3
e-ISBN 978-1-5310-1461-2
LCCN 2018967080

Carolina Academic Press
700 Kent Street
Durham, North Carolina 27701
(919) 489-7486
www.cap-press.com

Printed in the United States of America

2023 Printing

To David Fort, Thomson Fort, and their friends, who remind me on a daily basis of the awesome responsibility of being the parent and community member every kid deserves.

Annette Nickel, Elizabeth Eggert, Chrissi Nimmo, and all of the tribal in-house ICWA attorneys out there—this is for you. May you encounter lawyers and judges who learned ICWA in law school.

Contents

Table of Cases

Table of Authors

Table of Statutes

Acknowledgments

I would like to thank the entire Fall 2014 Indian Child Welfare Act class at Michigan State University College of Law for being the impetus to finish a first draft of this book, and for having to use it for their class. I would also like to thank the entire Spring 2017 Indian Child Welfare Act class at Michigan State University College of Law for being the impetus to finish the final draft, and for getting to use it for their class. I also thank the MSU Law librarians Jane Meland, Brent Domann, and Allison Eicher, who caught my mistakes—and any left are my own.

I would also like to thank Nicole Adams, Barbara Atwood, Tamera Begay, Nikki Borchardt Campbell, Sarah Donnelly, Anita Fineday, Matthew L.M. Fletcher, Ross Fort, Carrie Garrow, Diane Henningfeld, Ken Henningfeld, Anne Henningfeld, Leah Jurss, Sarah Lawson, Matthew Newman, April Olson, Larry Roberts, Vivek Sankaran, Wenona Singel, Addie Smith, Shannon Smith, Sheldon Spotted Elk, Victoria Sweet, Neoshia Roemer, Crystal Valdez, Peter Vicaire, Kevin Washburn, Ron Whitener, and Monica Williamson.

Introduction

This casebook is the result of years of discussions with Native lawyers, law students, families, tribal leaders, and professors. Because Native children and families continue to be the subject of constant litigation and federal policy changes, this book changed dramatically in the years as it was being written. The actions of federal and state governments against Native children—removing them from their families, culture, language, and communities—has had far ranging implications for generations of families. This casebook discusses the consequences of those actions and the tribal responses to them.

From removing children to boarding, or residential, schools, where Native children lost their language, were subject to abuse, and lost models of traditional parenting before they were returned to their communities, to today's child welfare system, which is incapable of dealing with the poverty, mental health, and chemical dependency issues facing parents today, Native children have felt the brunt of federal and state actions. Today there is not one adult Native person does not have a story of removal—of a cousin, a sibling, a parent, pulled from a community and placed with strangers.

American Indian children make up a small percentage of the total population, and yet are disproportionally impacted by state and federal policies and laws. But Native families are also resilient. For centuries, Native nations worked ingeniously to maintain their culture, language, and families in the face of the full force of the federal government to erase them. And forty years ago, Congress heard years of testimony on this treatment of children and families, and passed one of the most important laws for Native children, and a model of treatment for all children. For perhaps the first time, Congress decided in one law to reverse an entire federal policy dedicated to the destruction of Native families and instead attempt to protect them. The Indian Child Welfare Act guaranteed the right of tribes to make decisions for their own children and families, and when they were unable to due to distance or capacity, that states ensure children stay with their families and communities and receive services to address two hundred years of colonialism.

Scholars write about settler-colonialism, and the historical impacts—but there should be no doubt that individual families continue to feel these very real impacts today. The eight chapters in this casebook attempt to situate those impacts through both primary and secondary sources, including biography, caselaw, articles, and legislative history.

Chapter One provides more detail and context to the history referenced in this introduction. The chapter gives a basic overview of settler-colonial history as it affected American Indian children in particular. It also brings that history into the present, and underscores how recently Congressional policy changed from the destruction to the preservation of American Indian families.

Chapter Two addresses the implications of inherent tribal jurisdiction over children and families. It discusses cases from both before and after the passage of the Indian Child Welfare Act, the effect of Public Law 280 on Indian child welfare, how the best interests of the child standard intersect with jurisdictional decisions, and the role of parental objection and choice in jurisdictional decisions. Finally, it ends with one of the most important modern federal cases in Indian child welfare, which takes on the issue of emergency jurisdiction and the due process rights of parents.

Chapter Three contains the bulk of the casebook—the state case law that has developed over nearly forty years of applying the Indian Child Welfare Act in state court. Regardless of the tribal involvement, when a state court has both an Indian child and a child custody proceeding as defined by the Act, the court must apply the provisions of the law. The provisions addressed in this chapter include notice to tribes, the tribal right of intervention, the heightened standards of proof, the qualified expert witness requirement, the active efforts to prevent the break-up of the Indian family, and the placement preferences for Indian children when they are placed in foster care or for adoption.

Chapter Four contains some of the most contentious materials in Indian child welfare—those surrounding voluntary or direct placement adoptions. The history of coercive removals of children for adoption, the Indian Adoption Project promoted by the Bureau of Indian Affairs, and the casual dismissal of parental rights led to the section of the Indian Child Welfare Act which is designed to provided heightened protections to parents in voluntary situations. However, the push and pull between the tribal interests in the child, the child's right to her identity and stability, and the parent's rights to put a child up for adoption (or the right to rescind that decision) lead to some of the most difficult and high profile cases.

Flowing from Chapter Four, Chapter Five discusses the constitutional issues involved in Indian child welfare, and Indian law generally, including citizenship determinations, federalism, and privacy concerns.

Chapter Six gives a basic overview of juvenile justice and how it applies to American Indian children. Criminal jurisdiction in Indian Country is often described as a maze, but when it applies to children, the intersectionality of children, citizenship, and the effects of settler colonialism is particularly confounding and heartbreaking.

Chapter Seven provides insights into tribal child welfare—how tribes make internal decisions in tribal court and in their tribal codes for children and families. Over and over tribes insist the best policy choice in this area is to allow tribes to make decisions on behalf of their children and families. This chapter shows some of the ways tribes are doing just that.

Finally, Chapter Eight broadens the scope of the question, and looks to other settler-colonial states and the policies for Indigenous children and families. Necessarily a brief overview, this chapter provides a jumping off point for those interested in learning more about the international context in Indigenous family law.

Chapters one, seven, and eight benefitted immeasurably from the work of Leah K. Jurss, who turned very rough ideas and drafts into beautifully written chapters. Her work made this casebook possible.

American Indian Children and the Law

Chapter 1

A Brief History of Federal Child Welfare Policies for American Indian Families

The following case, *Mississippi Band of Choctaw Indians v. Holyfield,* is one of the most important cases interpreting the Indian Child Welfare Act (ICWA). The case is featured later in the casebook for the purpose of exploring its holding and ramifications, but here it offers an introduction and summary to the motivations behind the creation of ICWA.

Mississippi Band of Choctaw Indians v. Holyfield

490 U.S. 30 (1989)

The Indian Child Welfare Act of 1978 (ICWA), 92 Stat. 3069, 25 U.S.C. §§ 1901–1963, was the product of rising concern in the mid–1970's over the consequences to Indian children, Indian families, and Indian tribes of abusive child welfare practices that resulted in the separation of large numbers of Indian children from their families and tribes through adoption or foster care placement, usually in non-Indian homes. Senate oversight hearings in 1974 yielded numerous examples, statistical data, and expert testimony documenting what one witness called "[t]he wholesale removal of Indian children from their homes, . . . the most tragic aspect of Indian life today." Indian Child Welfare Program, Hearings before the Subcommittee on Indian Affairs of the Senate Committee on Interior and Insular Affairs, 93d Cong., 2d Sess., 3 (statement of William Byler) (hereinafter 1974 Hearings). Studies undertaken by the Association on American Indian Affairs in 1969 and 1974, and presented in the Senate hearings, showed that 25 to 35% of all Indian children had been separated from their families and placed in adoptive families, foster care, or institutions. *Id.*, at 15; *see also* H.R. Rep. No. 95–1386, p. 9 (1978) (hereinafter House Report), U.S. Code Cong. & Admin. News 1978, pp. 7530, 7531. Adoptive placements counted significantly in this total: in the State of Minnesota, for example, one in eight Indian children under the age of 18 was in an adoptive home, and during the year 1971–1972 nearly one in every four infants under one year of age was placed for adoption. The adoption rate of Indian children was eight times that of non-Indian children. Approximately 90% of the Indian placements were in non-Indian homes. 1974 Hearings, at 75–83. A number of witnesses also testified to the serious adjustment problems encountered by such children during adolescence, as well as the impact of the adoptions on Indian parents and the tribes themselves. *See generally* 1974 Hearings.

Further hearings, covering much the same ground, were held during 1977 and 1978 on the bill that became the ICWA. While much of the testimony again focused on the harm to Indian parents and their children who were involuntarily separated by decisions of local welfare authorities, there was also considerable emphasis on the impact on the tribes themselves of the massive removal of their children. For example, Mr. Calvin Isaac, Tribal Chief of the Mississippi Band of Choctaw Indians and representative of the National Tribal Chairmen's Association, testified as follows:

> Culturally, the chances of Indian survival are significantly reduced if our children, the only real means for the transmission of the tribal heritage, are to be raised in non-Indian homes and denied exposure to the ways of their People. Furthermore, these practices seriously undercut the tribes' ability to continue as self-governing communities. Probably in no area is it more important that tribal sovereignty be respected than in an area as socially and culturally determinative as family relationships.

1978 Hearings, at 193. *See also id.*, at 62. Chief Isaac also summarized succinctly what numerous witnesses saw as the principal reason for the high rates of removal of Indian children:

> One of the most serious failings of the present system is that Indian children are removed from the custody of their natural parents by nontribal government authorities who have no basis for intelligently evaluating the cultural and social premises underlying Indian home life and childrearing. Many of the individuals who decide the fate of our children are at best ignorant of our cultural values, and at worst contemptful of the Indian way and convinced that removal, usually to a non-Indian household or institution, can only benefit an Indian child.

Id., at 191–192. The congressional findings that were incorporated into the ICWA reflect these sentiments. The Congress found:

> (3) that there is no resource that is more vital to the continued existence and integrity of Indian tribes than their children . . . ;
>
> (4) that an alarmingly high percentage of Indian families are broken up by the removal, often unwarranted, of their children from them by nontribal public and private agencies and that an alarmingly high percentage of such children are placed in non-Indian foster and adoptive homes and institutions; and
>
> (5) that the States, exercising their recognized jurisdiction over Indian child custody proceedings through administrative and judicial bodies, have often failed to recognize the essential tribal relations of Indian people and the cultural and social standards prevailing in Indian communities and families.

25 U.S.C. § 1901.

At the heart of the ICWA are its provisions concerning jurisdiction over Indian child custody proceedings. Section 1911 lays out a dual jurisdictional scheme. Section 1911(a) establishes exclusive jurisdiction in the tribal courts for proceedings concerning an Indian child "who resides or is domiciled within the reservation of such tribe," as well as for wards of tribal courts regardless of domicile. Section 1911(b), on the other hand, creates concurrent but presumptively tribal jurisdiction in the case of children not domiciled on the reservation: on petition of either parent or the tribe, state-court proceedings for foster care placement or termination of parental rights are to be transferred to the tribal court, except in cases of "good cause," objection by either parent, or declination of jurisdiction by the tribal court.

Various other provisions of ICWA Title I set procedural and substantive standards for those child custody proceedings that do take place in state court. The procedural safeguards include requirements concerning notice and appointment of counsel; parental and tribal rights of intervention and petition for invalidation of illegal proceedings; procedures governing voluntary consent to termination of parental rights; and a full faith and credit obligation in respect to tribal court decisions. *See* §§ 1901–1914. The most important substantive requirement imposed on state courts is that of § 1915(a), which, absent "good cause" to the contrary, mandates that adoptive placements be made preferentially with (1) members of the child's extended family, (2) other members of the same tribe, or (3) other Indian families.

The ICWA thus, in the words of the House Report accompanying it, "seeks to protect the rights of the Indian child as an Indian and the rights of the Indian community and tribe in retaining its children in its society." House Report, at 23, U.S. Code Cong. & Admin. News 1978, at 7546. It does so by establishing "a Federal policy that, where possible, an Indian child should remain in the Indian community," *ibid.*, and by making sure that Indian child welfare determinations are not based on "a white, middle-class standard which, in many cases, forecloses placement with [an] Indian family." *Id.*, at 24, U.S. Code Cong. & Admin. News 1978, at 7546.

Notes

1. The Senate Hearing and House Report mentioned in the case excerpt are included with more detail later in this chapter. Do you think the staggering statistics that were presented during the legislative history contributed to the favorable ruling of *Holyfield*? Is there another reason why the Court would choose to include so much background on the motivation for the creation of the Indian Child Welfare Act?

2. As this excerpt explains, much of the motivation for passing ICWA was to ensure that middle class, white standards were not applied in the caretaking of American Indian children. Yet today, the vast majority of judges, lawyers, court advocates, and social workers fall into this category. What is the best method to ensure that these individuals, and every individual working with or learning about Native American child welfare, puts aside their own inherent biases and judges Indian child

welfare situations based only on the practices, history, support, and problems within the family itself?

A. Customary Child-Rearing Practices

The need to create a federal law governing the best interests of American Indian children resulted from a clash between customary tribal child-rearing practices, the legacy of boarding schools and intergenerational trauma, and the continuation of assimilation efforts into the mid-twentieth century. A short description of the customary child-rearing practices of Native American families illustrates why the federal policy of board schools wreaked so much havoc for Indian children

With 573 currently federally recognized tribes, it is impossible and dangerous to theorize about "Native peoples" as a cohesive whole; however, there are some aspects of family life that were generally shared across Turtle Island. Many Native parents relied on the help of their families, extended families, and community members to raise their children. Barbara Ann Atwood, *Tribal Jurisprudence and Cultural Meanings of the Family*, 79 NEB. L. REV. 577, 640-41 (2000). Native children could be left for long periods of time with extended family members, with the trust that the child would be well cared for during the time, and would learn important skills and lessons that the parents could not teach. This practice would be later labeled neglect, but the community considered it necessary for the child to be raised by many relatives, so she would learn the skills, stories, and specializations each family member held. H.R. REP. No. 95-1386, at 20 (July 24, 1978) (report to accompany H.R. 12533).

Native parents and families rarely engaged in corporeal punishment, unlike their colonial counterpoints. Children were allowed to experience mistakes and consequences on their own, rather than being stifled by direct intervention and correction. Children were given the ability to learn freely and openly, while still adhering to a set of community and societal values, such as respecting elders. MARGARET CONNELL SZASZ, INDIAN EDUCATION IN THE AMERICAN COLONIES: 1607-1783, at 1-24 (1988).

Children were also taught community values and social expectations through stories and ceremonies. For example, Ojibwe children would hear the stories of Nanabozho during winter storytelling time. BASIL JOHNSTON, OJIBWAY HERITAGE 122–23 (1976). Nanabozho is both a teacher and a trickster figure in Ojibwe heritage. Stories of Nanabozho making mistakes, causing mischief, and learning from the world around him vividly illustrated to children the proper way to behave within their community. Learning through the experience and stories of others, rather than direct guidance and redirection, leads to a value of non-interference. In ceremonies and other cultural gatherings and problem-solving events, there still exists a practice of deference and non-interference towards others. Jimm G. Good-Tracks, *Native American Non-Interference*, 18:6 SOCIAL WORK 30 (1973).

Native children were also taught to show respect to elders and to support their families and communities in times of need. This meant taking as much time as necessary for an elder to finish speaking, and putting off personal obligations in favor of helping someone in need in the community. MICHAEL D. MCNALLY, OJIBWE SINGERS: HYMNS, GRIEF, AND A NATIVE CULTURE IN MOTION 156 (2000). Today, this traditional ethic competes with the need for children to attend a statutorily mandated number of school days and show up for doctor appointments five minutes early or face cancellation, among the many other rigid requirements of daily life.

B. Boarding Schools and Intergenerational Trauma

After the time of contact and the creation of the United States federal government, the central tenet of child welfare policies in America for Native children centered around education and assimilation. The Cohen Handbook on Federal Indian Law describes education as

> the single most important tool in nineteenth-century assimilation and "civilization" policy. . . . Schooling was intended to provide Indian children with a substitute for a civilized home life. The full brunt of reeducation was directed toward Indian children, who were shipped away from the reservation or brought together at reservation schools. The philosophy was most simply expressed by Richard Henry Pratt, the founder of Carlisle School: "Kill the Indian and Save the Man."

NELL JESSUP NEWTON ET AL, COHEN'S HANDBOOK OF FEDERAL INDIAN LAW 76 (2012 ed).

The atrocities of boarding schools in the United States and Canada have been well documented. *See, e.g.*, BOARDING SCHOOL BLUES (Clifford E. Trafzer et al. eds., 2006); BRENDA J. CHILD, BOARDING SCHOOL SEASONS: AMERICAN INDIAN FAMILIES, 1900–1940 (1998). Children were removed from their homes and communities, forced to speak English and practice Christianity, and forbidden from participating in traditional tribal cultural activities, including religion, dress, language, and food.

The continuing legacy of the boarding school harm exists in the form of intergenerational trauma today. Children taken from their parents and raised in non-Native environments were unable to learn the parenting techniques practiced in their communities since time immemorial. Instead, these children only had experience with the western style of abusive discipline that was practiced in the boarding schools. When these boarding school children in turn had their own children, they lacked the necessary parenting skills to raise their own children into mentally and physically healthy adults. Maria Yellow Horse Brave Horse, *The Impact of Historical Trauma: The Example of the Native Community, in* TRAUMA TRANSFORMED: AN EMPOWERMENT RESPONSE 176, 181-84 (Marian Bussey & Judith Bula Wise eds., 2007); *see also* CAROL A. MARKSTROM, EMPOWERMENT OF NORTH AMERICAN INDIAN GIRLS 44 (2008).

In addition to depriving children from observing, and thereby learning, healthy parenting skills, many boarding schools prepared Native children for jobs that were quickly becoming irrelevant. The need for seamstresses and wheelwrights sharply declined in the twentieth century, especially in the communities to which many Native children would be returning. *See, e.g.*, Robert A. Trennert, *Educating Indian Girls at Nonreservation Boarding Schools, 1878–1920*, 13 Western Hist. Q. 271 (July 1982). Training for jobs that didn't exist left many young adults with an inability to gain employment in the newly industrialized American society. The tribal society that many young adults returned to was unrecognizable due to removal, relocation, and federal policies of allotment. The resulting poverty of American Indian families was used as a justification for removing Native children from their homes. Margaret D. Jacobs, A Generation Removed: The Fostering and Adoption of Indigenous Children 70 (2014).

Boarding schools also had the effect of creating and developing a national sense of Indian identity for many native children. Anishinaabe children were placed into boarding schools with Lakota children, and each learned the culture and language of the other under cover. Even when children were completely separated from their language and culture, they were able to connect with other Native children through the use of their newly learned English language skills. The "pan-Indian" identity that grew out of boarding schools later developed into organizations that were responsible for bringing issues of American Indian sovereignty to the attention of the general public, like the Society of American Indians (SAI), the National Congress of American Indians (NCAI), and the American Indian Movement (AIM). Hazel W. Hertzberg, The Search for an American Indian Identity: Modern Pan-Indian Movements 303 (1971).

Even after the end of the formal boarding school period, many Native children were still sent to receive educations away from their families. When this happened, families were rarely allowed, or had the means available, to visit their children. The legacy of assimilation was still present in the minds of school administrators and others who had power to direct the state of American Indian child welfare; these individuals often urged Native children to leave their families and education in order to perform labor on farms.

While The Locust Slept: A Memoir (2001)

Peter Razor [Excerpts from pages 9–15]

Midwinter 1944 at the State Public School, Dr. Yager, child psychologist at the school, posed a very strange question to me, "Do you think you could call anyone Mother or Father?"

I mumbled, "I wouldn't know what to do in a family."

"It's hard to find a family for an Indian boy, and we have no Indian families listed," Dr. Yager continued. "And you've been here a long time."

"How long?" I asked, without really caring.

"Fifteen years," Dr. Yager replied.

For the first fourteen years of my life, I knew Dr. Yager only as the one who sat blandly behind a desk pointing at tests with assurances that no matter how I did on them, was all right. I worked the tests at another table while he remained at his desk. Dr. Yager loved climbing into the minds of children. It was more than his job, it was his life. Every child had to be somewhere in his text book or he became obsessed with exposing their peculiarity. He recorded that I was very quiet and, before the age of twelve, basically untestable. He might have suspected that cottage life was at least partially responsible for; what he wrote, my *sullen and withdrawn demeanor*, but probably knew little of my experiences with a few employees.

Weeks or a month after Dr. Yager's strange questions about family life, I was interviewed by Mr. Doleman, a social worker under Superintendent Vevle.

"You told Dr. Yager that you would not feel comfortable in a regular family," Mr. Doleman said.

"Well . . . I said maybe I didn't know what it meant to be in a family."

"Perhaps that was it," Mr. Doleman said. "Do you think you would like to work on a farm?"

"The work might be all right," I replied, then mumbled, "Heard it was dangerous. Being on a farm, I mean." Shifting uneasily on my chair, I glanced at documents on the wall, which said collectively that Mr. Doleman was very wise, indeed. I knew he stared at me, *into* me, and, uneasy, I looked around at the floor.

After a long silence, Mr. Doleman spoke, sounding like a preacher, "Everyone has to work for a living."

"A guy died on a farm last year, they said," I persisted. "The farmer beat him up or something." When stubborn, I pursed my mouth while staring at the floor near my shoes.

Mr. Doleman straightened in his chair. "You don't know that for sure," he said. He leaned back, slowly tapping his fingertips together in front of his face. "Unfortunate things might have happened in the past, but we watch things today." He seemed mildly irked.

Who watched Kruger and Beaty or Monson? I wanted to ask, but instead I mumbled, "Do I have to go to a farm?"

"Please understand . . . if you're not placed soon . . . well, you have to go somewhere." Mr. Doleman spoke softly, but I heard his threat.

"Why couldn't I go to relatives up north?" I asked. I squinted at the floor near my shoes. "If I can work for a farmer, I can work for relatives, can't I . . . or myself?"

"You're not old enough to be on your own," Mr. Doleman insisted. "Can't you see? If I remembered correctly, you were quite run down and filthy when I picked you up in St. Paul. Miss Klein"—the C-16 assistant—"also mentioned how terrible you and Dale looked."

Shrugging, I whispered almost to myself, "You made me come back." Then louder, "The State School, I mean."

Mr. Doleman pushed away from his desk. "We'll talk again," he said with a sigh of disappointment. "You may return to Cottage Sixteen."

* * *

Called to the office in early July, I was ushered before Miss Borsch for the first time. She was young and vivacious, smiled nonstop, and her eyes were warm friendly things. Mr. Doleman had called up the big guns. Having no experience with girls or doting women, I'd be a pushover.

"Good morning, Peter. My, isn't the weather simply grand?" Miss Borsch breathed. Her right arm was elevated toward the window, her upturned palm sagged off the wrist with two fingers languidly extended. I watched her hand and reeled from her brilliant smile.

"How have you been?" Her charm was in full gallop.

"All right, I guess," I replied, trying to guess her next move.

"Did you enjoy the outing with Mr. and Mrs. Cory?" Miss Borsch asked.

"Corys? . . . Uh, yea," I replied. More pieces to the puzzle suddenly fell into place.

"Have you thought about what comes after the State School?" she murmured softly.

"Some. I'd rather go on my own or to relatives."

"You became quite ill after your first, ah . . . trip last summer," Miss Borsch said, appearing concerned. "It's not in your file, but Mrs. Steele says your second trip was quite dangerous." She was referring to the two times I had run away from the school.

"I didn't think so."

"Anyway," she murmured, appearing sympathetic, "you can see why you can't be on your own. Just yet."

"Dunno," I mumbled but I knew where it all headed. "Couldn't I go to high school in Owatonna?"

"I'd like to see you in a regular home, if possible," Miss Borsch persisted.

"Older boys go to high school from here," I insisted.

"Perhaps they want to do something else," she replied. "Go into the army, for instance."

"Can I do something else?" I groped. "Besides this farm thing, I mean. Somebody said indenture is slavery."

"It's no longer indenture," Miss Borsch corrected. "It's farm placement." Her smile faded, but she retained composure. "And it's certainly not slavery! I really think you'd like a farm. We'd see that you got a good family, and somebody would visit you to see how things were going." Her smile could against melt steel.

"I don't know." Trapped, hating myself for letting her lead me on, I looked around at the floor. "If I went on a farm, would I go to high school?"

"Absolutely!" she said leaning across her desk toward me. "A farmer has to sign an agreement allowing you to attend school. It's your choice after age sixteen, but the family can't make you quit. And you are to be paid for summer work."

"Oh? Besides food and clothes?"

"That's right. We would leave the amount up to you and the family to decide."

"What do guys get working for farmers?" I asked.

"It depends on age and experience," Miss Borsch replied. "You might start at twenty-five dollars per month for the summer work, but you'd work only for room and board while in school."

"That's a lot of money," I said. It was hard imagining money in amounts over one dollar. My grandmother on my father's side had sent me a one-dollar bill when I was twelve, and I had seldom possessed more than a quarter or fifteen cents at a time, since. Money bought tickets to movies in town or candy and circulated as part of a barter economy. Relatives sent money to children, and older boys, who seemed to always have money for cigarettes, worked in town or ran errands.

"You would get more as you grow older," Miss Borsch pressed. Beaming, she leaned more toward me, but still stared like most office workers.

I shrank back, my head tilted to one side. I wondered what would happen if I held out. I'd probably be sent to Red Wing, the state reformatory for boys.

"Yea, all right," I said. My decision was not sincere and I sagged into the chair looking nervously around. Sighing my defeat, I mumbled, "When would I go?"

"A worker will check with the family."

"Somebody," I cleared my throat, "needs a worker?"

"It's not that you would go just for work," Miss Borsch replied, trying not to sound defensive. "But you'll be expected to help out. Anyway, the family lives near Rushford. We specifically discussed your Indian heritage and they say that's no problem."

Miss Borsch closed her notes. "It's settled then," she said with apparent satisfaction. "We'll call you when the time comes."

For a time it seemed Miss Borsch would make good on her promise to let me attend school. As August faded into September, I started ninth grade, riding with the other boys and girls to Owatonna High School, but the scorching wind of prejudice followed me there. One day the science teacher posed a question to the class. No one raised their hand, so for the first time I mustered the courage to raise mine. The teacher scanned past me a number of times. Finally he stopped and stared at me until I lowered my hand. I never tried to speak in that class again.

Despite the hatred of one teacher, those days were a heady time. I attended football games and pep rallies and, as the weeks passed, began to make friends. I felt better about my life and my future than ever before. Then, in late September, Miss Borsch called me into her office to meet a man and a woman who had come to take me away.

Interview with John Schauls from the records of the State School:

John: *Is anybody interest in Peter? Will they stop to visit him or take him on trips or anything?*

Social worker: *Peter has no visitors at the school. The only one seeming him will be a social worker twice a year.*

John: *Peter is just the boy I want. . . .*

John thanked Miss Borsch and pointed at the outside door. "We's chores to do. Best be going." He started down the hall. Emma followed him and I followed her. We went through the large double doors and down the front steps of the Main Building to their two-tone green 1934 Ford sedan where I sat in the rear sat.

I said goodbye to no one except Miss Borsch, and there was less note of my departure from the school than from the cottage. We drove down the hill and past C-15. A pang of loss and helplessness struck me as I glanced back through the rear window. Then I sagged into the seat and stared out the side.

I was told nothing about a letter than came during the placement process, from relatives in northern Minnesota, nor of this reply: *Peter is well. Social Services is seeing to his welfare. It is important that he has no visitors, as that might disrupt his life with a new family.*

No one would know where I went.

Notes

1. Why do you think Peter's family was not told the truth about his eventual location?

2. Why do you think Peter's family did not come to visit him regularly while he was at school?

3. How do you think Peter ended up at this school in the first place? Do you think it had anything to do with how the "authorities" likely viewed his family and his living situation?

The Testimony of Robert Kewaygoshkum

Grand Traverse Band of Ottawa and Chippewa Indians v. Office of the U.S. Attorney for the Western District of Michigan, 46 F. Supp. 2d 689 (W.D. Mich. 1999)
Trial R. Test. Robert Kewaygoshkum 119, 122-26

[William Rastetter] **Q:** Did you remain with both your grandparents throughout your childhood?

[Robert Kewaygoshkum] **A:** No, I didn't.

Q: At some point did you remain with just one of your grandparents?

A: Yes, as I was growing up with my grandparents there was a situation that my grandmother left and went to Grand Rapids visiting her elder relatives at the time, but I remember when she came back home she came back home in a casket.

Q: And from then you were with your grandfather alone?

A: I was with my grandfather.

Q: And for how long were you with him?

A: It probably was for a short time because this one day a white lady came to the door and knocked on the door and said it was time to go.

Q: How old were you at the time?

A: Oh, I know I was going into the third grade at the time, so probably seven or eight or somewhere in there.

Q: Had you any prior experience with anybody coming to your household suggesting that maybe you should be taken away?

A: No.

Q: What happened that day?

A: Well, that day it probably all sticks in my mind but there was nothing I could do, nothing my grandfather could do. All I had to do is pack my bags and get in this lady's car, which was a little Volkswagen at the time, and off to boarding school I went.

Q: And what was that school?

A: That school is Harbor Springs Holy Childhood.

Q: In retrospect looking back now do you assume that she was a social worker?

A: Yes.

Q: What was it like in boarding school?

A: It was different from everyday life you live at home. You know, the boarding school there's rules, regulations. You got to live under their rules which is no freedom. I guess you can look at it this way, in the Catholic boarding school they pretty much just take away your culture, could not speak your language. They cut your hair. I pretty much had a bush-cut most of my young adult life.

Q: Had you had long hair prior to being taken to the boarding school?

A: Yes, I had.

Q: Is that an important aspect of your culture?

A: Yes, it is.

Q: Did you have any contact with your grandfather when you were at the school?

A: Yes, because it wasn't very far away, you know, Harbor Springs was just across the bay. My grandfather used to come and visit probably at least twice a month at the school on weekends.

Q: Now, were you at the boarding school just for the school year or were you there year around?

A: This boarding school was just for the school year, and usually in the summertime you got out and most of the kids went back to their parents.

Q: Were you able to go back to your grandfather's house?

A: No, I wasn't. I was stuck in a foster home.

Q: And where was that?

A: That was in Petoskey.

Q: How long did you stay at that boarding school?

A: It was from third grade all the way up to eighth grade.

Q: And did they only continue through the eighth grade at that time?

A: Right.

Q: What happened after the eighth grade? Did you go back to your grandfather's house?

A: No, I didn't. I got shipped off to another—the current foster home I was at that took care of me through the summer months did not want me on a full-time basis through my high school years. So they shipped me out to another home way out in the country, way out in the boondocks, and I didn't care for that, and I told them, I said, I didn't want to stay there. So the next thing I knew I was shipped down to Kingsley, which was further away but, you know, there was no choice so I might as well go with the system.

Q: How old were you at the time?

A: I was probably about 13 or 14, I think.

Q: And where is Kingsley located?

A: Kingsley is about 18 miles south of Traverse City, roughly.

Q: In what county?

A: In Grand Traverse.

Q: When you were placed in a foster home in Kingsley, were you able to maintain any contact with your grandfather?

A: No, I didn't. It was too far away.

Q: Did you ever see him again?

A: I never saw him again. And the only thing I heard—three or four months passed that my grandfather had passed away in the fall of '65. I came into Kingsley in the spring of '65.

Q: How long were you placed with that foster family?

A: Through my high school years.

Q: During this time, did you have any contact at all with the Native American culture?

A: None whatsoever.

Notes

1. How does Mr. Kewaygoshkum's story of being removed from his family speak to the notion that Native families historically, and presently, look much different from the nuclear family considered average in the United States?

2. Was there any indication that Mr. Kewaygoshkum was being harmed by living only with his grandfather after his grandmother passed away? Does Mr. Kewaygoshkum give any indication that he felt in danger? Why do you think the "authorities" took Mr. Kewaygoshkum away from his grandfather?

3. What harm do you think happened to Mr. Kewaygoshkum by the fact that he spent much of his adolescence not being raised with his Native American heritage?

4. How did the overwhelming nature of "the system" play out in Mr. Kewaygoshkum's experience?

C. A Grey Market for American Indian Children: Development of the Indian Child Welfare Act

After the formal end of the boarding school period, a new policy appeared regarding child welfare in reservation communities. The "problem" of Indian children as "forgotten children" arose in the consciousness of the American public. In 1958, the Bureau of Indian Affairs and the Child Welfare League of America created a joint partnership to match Native children to white families. The "Indian Adoption Project" placed nearly 400 Native children with white families, as one of the only exceptions to the general "race matching" practices of adoption in that time. Claire Palmiste, *From the Indian Adoption Project to the Indian Child Welfare Act: The Resistance of Native American Communities*, 22(1) Indigenous Pol'y J. 2 (Summer 2011). Similar programs operated throughout the country between the 1950s and 1970s. The Lutheran Social Services of South Dakota, for example, placed over three hundred Native children in white families between 1965 and 1976. Linda R. Rosene, A Follow-up Study of Indian Children Adopted by White Families vi, 19 (1985) (dissertation).

On a much larger scale, the Church of Jesus Christ of Latter-day Saints (LDS) Indian Student Placement Program (IPP) operated as an educational foster-care system for an estimated 70,000 Native children, primarily Navajo, between 1947 and 2000. Jared Farmer, On Zion's Mount: Mormons, Indians, and the American Landscape 367 (2008). Students were placed in LDS homes during the school year, where they attended public schools they would not otherwise have access to, and were assimilated into the LDS religion and American culture during this time. Access to the program was limited to LDS members—Indian children were baptized into the LDS Church before receiving the educational benefits of placements, the main reason many Indian families allowed their children to participate in the program. James V. Allen, *The Rise and Decline of the LDS Indian Student Placement Program, 1947–1996*, *in* Mormons, Scripture, and the Ancient World: Studies in Honor of John L. Sorenson 85-119 (Davis Bitton ed., 1998).

Children were rarely removed from their families because of allegations of actual physical abuse or neglect; instead, social workers and other child advocates often equated single parents, poverty, and community-parenting with abandonment and neglect to parent. The Indian Adoption Project at one point "listed 'unmarried motherhood' as the top social problem—*above* alcoholism, gross neglect of family, criminal record, and mental illness—that social workers should be concerned with in possibly placing an Indian child for adoption." Margaret D. Jacobs, A Generation Removed: The Fostering and Adoption of Indigenous Children in the Postwar World 52 (2014) (quoting "Research Schedule on Indian Adoption Project," ca. 1960, 7, 8, box 17, folder 3, Child Welfare League of America papers via Social Welfare History Archives, Special Collections, University of Minnesota Libraries, Minneapolis). These children were often removed without proper due process accorded to the parents—parents rarely had the process explained to them, and often were not even notified of important court hearings in the foster and adoption process.

Native children who were adopted out of their tribal communities during this era reported higher levels of emotional and identity instability, even though they received better educational and financial opportunities as measured by typical United States benchmark standards. *See* Statement on Behalf of the Association on American Indian Affairs, Inc., Submitted to the Senate Committee on Indian Affairs, Hearing on Legislation to Amend the Indian Child Welfare Act, 303, 306-07 (June 26, 1996). In addition to creating personal instability, the removal of tribal children from their community negates the possibility that they would continue the process of building and maintaining tribal sovereignty as leaders, professionals, and community members.

House Committee on Interior and Insular Affairs Establishing Standards for the Placement of Indian Children in Foster or Adoptive Homes, to Prevent the Breakup of Indian Families, and for Other Purposes

H.R. Rept. No. 95–1386 (1978)

The wholesale separation of Indian children from their familieis [sic] is perhaps the most tragic and destructive aspect of American Indian life today.

Surveys of States with large Indian populations conducted by the Association on American Indian Affairs (AAIA) in 1969 and again in 1974 indicate that approximately 25–35 percent of all Indian children are separated from their families and placed in foster homes, adoptive homes, or institutions. In some States the problem is getting worse: in Minnesota, one in every eight Indian children under 18 years of age is living in an adoptive home; and, in 1971–72, nearly one in every four Indian children under 1 year of age was adopted.

The disparity in placement rates for Indians and non-Indians is shocking. In Minnesota, Indian children are placed in foster care or in adoptive homes at a per capita rate five times greater than non-Indian children. In Montana, the ratio of Indian foster-care placement is at least 13 times greater. In South Dakota, 40 percent of all adoptions made by the State's Department of Public Welfare since 1967–68 are of Indian children, yet Indians make up only 7 percent of the juvenile population. The number of South Dakota Indian children living in foster homes is per capita, nearly 16 times greater than the non-Indian rate. In the State of Washington, the Indian adoption rate is 19 times greater and the foster care rate 10 times greater. In Wisconsin, the risk run by Indian children of being separated from their parents is nearly 1,600 percent greater than it is for non-Indian children. Just as Indian children are exposed to these great hazards, their parents are too.

The Federal boarding school and dormitory programs also contribute to the destruction of Indian family and community life. The Bureau of Indian Affairs (BIA), in its school census for 1971, indicates that 34,538 children live in its institutional facilities rather than at home. This represents more than 17 percent of the Indian school age population of federally-recognized reservations and 60 percent of the children enrolled in BIA schools. On the Navajo Reservation, about 20,000 children or 90 percent of the BIA school population in grades K–12, live at boarding schools. A number of Indian children are also institutionalized in mission schools, training schools, etc.

In addition to the trauma of separation from their families, most Indian children in placement or in institutions have to cope with the problems of adjusting to a social and cultural environment much different than their own. In 16 States surveyed in 1969, approximately 85 percent of all Indian children in foster care were living in non-Indian homes. In Minnesota today, according to State figures, more than 90 percent of nonrelated adoptions of Indian children are made by non-Indian couples. Few States keep as careful or complete child welfare statistics as Minnesota does, but informed estimates by welfare officials elsewhere suggest that this rate is the norm. In most Federal and mission boarding schools, a majority of the personnel is non-Indian.

It is clear then that the Indian child welfare crisis is of massive proportions and that Indian families face vastly greater risks of involuntary separation than are typical of our society as a whole.

Standards

The Indian child welfare crisis will continue until the standards for defining mistreatment are revised. Very few Indian children are removed from their families on the grounds of physical abuse. One study of a North Dakota reservation showed that these grounds were advanced in only 1 percent of the cases. Another study of a tribe in the Northwest showed the same incidence. The remaining 99 percent of the cases were argued on such vague grounds as "neglect" or "social deprivation" and on allegations of the emotional damage the children were subjected to by living with their parents. Indian communities are often shocked to learn that parents they regard as excellent caregivers have been judged unfit by non-Indian social workers.

In judging the fitness of a particular family, many social workers, ignorant of Indian cultural values and social norms, make decisions that are wholly inappropriate in the context of Indian family life and so they frequently discover neglect or abandonment where none exists.

For example, the dynamics of Indian extended families are largely misunderstood. An Indian child may have scores of, perhaps more than a hundred, relatives who are counted as close, responsible members of the family. Many social workers, untutored in the ways of Indian family life or assuming them to be socially irresponsible, consider leaving the child with persons outside the nuclear family as neglect and thus as grounds for terminating parental rights.

Because in some communities the social workers have, in a sense, become a part of the extended family, parents will sometimes turn to the welfare department for temporary care of their children, failing to realize that their action is perceived quite differently by non-Indians.

Indian child-rearing practices are also misinterpreted in evaluating a child's behavior and parental concern. It may appear that the child is running wild and that the parents do not care. What is labelled "permissiveness" may often, in fact, simply be a different but effective way of disciplining children. BIA boarding schools are full of children with such spurious "behavioral problems."

One of the grounds most frequently advanced for taking Indian children from their parents is the abuse of alcohol. However, this standard is applied unequally. In areas where rates of problem drinking among Indians and non-Indians are the same it is rarely applied against non-Indian parents. Once again cultural biases frequently affect decisionmaking. The late Dr. Edward P. Dozier of Santa Clara Pueblo and other observes have argued that there are important cultural differences in the use of alcohol. Yet, by and large, non-Indian social workers draw conclusions about the meaning of acts or conduct in ignorance of these distinctions.

The courts tend to rely on the testimony of social workers who often lack the training and insights necessary to measure the emotional risk the child is running at home. In a number of cases, the AAIA has obtained evidence from competent psychiatrists who, after examining the defendants, have been able to contradict the allegations offered by the social workers. Rejecting the notion that poverty and cultural differences constitute social deprivation and psychological abuse, the Association argues that the State must prove that there is actual physical or emotional harm resulting from the acts of the parents.

The abusive actions of social workers would largely be nullified if more judges were themselves knowledgeable about Indian life and required a sharper definition of the standards of child abuse and neglect.

Discriminatory standards have made it virtually impossible for most Indian couples to qualify as foster or adoptive parents, since they are based on middle-class values. Recognizing that in some instances it is necessary to remove children from their homes, community leaders argue that there are Indian families within the tribe who could provide excellent care, although they are of modest means. While some progress is being made here and there, the figures cited above indicate that non-Indian parents continue to furnish almost all the foster and adoptive care for Indian children.

Due Process

The decision to take Indian children from their natural homes is, in most cases, carried out without due process of law. For example, it is rare for either Indian children or their parents to be represented by counsel to or [sic] have the supporting testimony of expert witnesses.

Many cases do not go through an adjudicatory process at all, since the voluntary waiver of parental rights is a device widely employed by social workers to gain custody of children. Because of the availability of the waivers and because a great number of Indian parents depend on welfare payments for survival, they are exposed to the sometimes coercive arguments of welfare departments. In a recent South Dakota entrapment case, an Indian parent in a time of trouble was persuaded to sign a waiver granting temporary custody to the State, only to find that this is now being advanced as evidence of neglect and grounds for the permanent termination of parental rights. It is an unfortunate fact of life for many Indian parents that the primary service agency to which they must turn for financial help also exercises police powers over their family life and is, most frequently, the agency that initiates custody proceedings.

The conflict between Indian and non-Indian social systems operates to defeat due process. The extended family provides an example. By sharing the responsibility of child rearing, the extended family tends to strengthen the community's commitment to the child. At the same time, however, it diminishes the possibility that the nuclear family will be able to mobilize itself quickly enough when an outside agency acts to assume custody. Because it is not unusual for Indian children to spend considerable time away with other relatives, there is no immediate realization of what is happening—possibly not until the opportunity for due process has slipped away.

Economic Incentives

In some instances, financial considerations contribute to the crisis. For example, agencies established to place children have an incentive to find children to place.

Indian community leaders charge that federally-subsidized foster care programs encourage some non-Indian families to start "baby farms" in order to supplement their meager farm income with foster care payments and to obtain extra hands for farmwork. The disparity between the ratio of Indian children in foster care versus the number of Indian children that are adopted seems to bear this out. For example, in Wyoming in 1969, Indians accounted for 70 percent of foster care placements but only 8 percent of adoptive placements. Foster care payments usually cease when a child is adopted.

In addition, there are economic disincentives. It will cost the Federal and State Governments a great deal of money to provide Indian communities with the means to remedy their situation. But over the long run, it will cost a great deal more money not to. At the very least, as a first step, we should find new and more effective ways to spend present funds.

Social conditions

Low-income, joblessness, poor health, substandard housing, and low educational attainment—these are the reasons most often cited for the disintegration of Indian family life. It is not that clear-cut. Not all impoverished societies, whether Indian or non-Indian, suffer from catastrophically high rates of family breakdown.

Cultural disorientation, a person's sense of powerlessness, his loss of self-esteem—these may be the most potent forces at work. They arise, in large measure, from our national attitudes as reflected in long-established Federal policy and from arbitrary acts of Government.

One of the effects of our national paternalism has been to so alienate some Indian patents from their society that they abandon their children at hospitals or to welfare departments rather than entrust them to the care of relatives in the extended family. Another expression of it is the involuntary, arbitrary, and unwarranted separation of families.

It has already been noted that the harsh living conditions in many Indian communities may prompt a welfare department to make unwarranted placements and that they make it difficult for Indian people to qualify as a foster or adoptive parents. Additionally, because these conditions are often viewed as the primary cause of family breakdown and because generally there is no end to Indian poverty in sight, agencies of government often fail to recognize immediate, practical means to reduce the incidence of neglect or separation.

As surely as poverty imposes severe strains on the ability of families to function—sometimes the extra burden that is too much to bear—so too family breakdown contributes to the cycle of poverty.

Problems that American Indian Families Face in Raising their Children and How these Problems are Affected by Federal Action or Inaction Hearings before the Subcommittee on Indian Affairs of the Senate Committee on Interior and Insular Affairs

93rd Cong. 64–71 (1974) (statement of Cheryl Spider DeCoteau)

Senator Abourezk [A]. The next witness will be Mrs. Cheryl Spider DeCoteau from Sisseton, S. Dak.

Cheryl, I'll leave it up to you about your children coming up with you, perhaps it's better that they don't.

Mr. Hirsch [H]. Senator Abourezk, if you don't mind, Mrs. DeCoteau suggests that I come up with her.

A. Yes; you may.

Cheryl, first of all, I'd like to welcome you to the subcommittee hearings and ask you if this is your first trip into Washington to testify like this?

Mrs. DeCoteau [D]. Yes.

A. Your first time?

D. Yes.

A. Do you have any of the children here with you today?

D. Yes; two.

A. Are they here in the room?

D. Yes.

A. Cheryl, we want to ask you to go ahead and testify any way that you would like to so you don't feel nervous about it. I just want to tell you that we appreciate you coming in all the way from Sisseton to provide testimony.

As I told the other witnesses, we are hopeful that what you have to tell us today will help other people and prevent the things that happened to you from happening to other people.

Your testimony will be very important to the committee and we are very grateful for you coming.

You can tell your story any way that you like.

First, it might be good to give your name, your age, and exactly where you live, and so on.

D. Cheryl Spider DeCoteau, I'm 23.

A. From where?

D. I'm not originally from Sisseton, but from Minnesota.

A. You are living in Minnesota now?

D. Yes.

Herbert John Spider is 5, and Robert Lee is 3, and Joseph there, is 10 months.

A. Ten months?

D. Yes

A. Only the two oldest ones with you today?

D. Yes.

A. Who is keeping the baby?

D. I have a babysitter in Minnesota.

I had a babysitter watching the kids, in 1970, and I went to them and they wouldn't let me take them.

A. I have to stop you for just a minute and tell you that I can hardly hear you, because I suspect that what it is, is you're bashful and a little bit scared because of all the lights, and you're afraid to talk. I know you can talk a lot more clearly than that. I know that's because you're a little bit nervous.

If you just talk as loud as you can.

D. I'll start with my oldest boy, John. I had a babysitter watching him and I went to get him, and they wouldn't give him back to me. So, I went to my social worker and I asked him if he would come with me up there.

A. I have to ask you a couple of questions. When did this take place? Can you tell us the month and the year?

Do you want to wait a minute before you start testifying?

D. Yes.

That was in December 1970, and I asked him—

A. You asked the social worker?

D. Yes. Asked him to meet me at the store. He didn't come. So, I left, and I called from that store, and I said that they already went and they took John, and they took him to a foster home, and that I couldn't get him back.

A. They had taken John without your permission or without you knowledge?

D. Yes.

They took him, and I went back up there, and I tried to get him back, and they said "No", that they couldn't. I don't know if they had a court hearing or something. I didn't get any papers or nothing.

A. Did you go to the court hearing?

D. No, I didn't. I didn't know they had a court hearing.

A. They had a court hearing without your knowledge?

D. They had a petition or something.

I didn't know anything about it, and when I did go, they had to appoint me a lawyer. The welfare appointed me a lawyer, so I went to see him. The judge appointed me a lawyer.

I went to see him, and he didn't try to help me or anything. All he did was just ask me my age, name and address, and the name of my first boy and my other one. Then he asked me how old they were, and that was all. Then he said he was going to talk to the judge and the welfare workers. He didn't do anything because I didn't know anything that happened until July of 1971.

A. Did they keep John all that time?

D. Yes. They had John all that time in a foster home.

A. Did you know where he was?

D. No; I didn't know where he was. I kept asking, but they wouldn't tell me where he was or anything.

A. I'd like to ask you to back up just a minute. Did this happen in South Dakota or Minnesota?

D. It was in Sisseton.

A. Did the welfare department ever, to your knowledge, prove that you weren't being the best mother for that child at all, and perhaps your lawyer, Mr. Hirsch, can answer if you're unable to?

D. The man said that I wasn't a very good mother and everything, and that my children were better off being in a white home where they were adopted out, or in this home, wherever they were. They could buy all this stuff that I couldn't give them, and give them all the love that I couldn't give them.

A. They said that, but did they really prove that in court, or did they give any specific examples of why you weren't a good mother?

H. The answer to that is "No."

A. Did you work on this case?

H. Yes. Mrs. DeCoteau was my client. She became my client after she had already had about two or three other lawyers who weren't able to do anything for her.

It was never proven in court that she was unfit. We had a hearing in the district county court.

A. In Roberts County?

H. In Roberts County.

We had a hearing on two full days and the State, or the county put forward several witnesses and we never completed that hearing. So, a final disposition on the merits was never reached because we took an appeal based on lack of jurisdiction of the court to adjudicate anything with regard to Mrs. DeCoteau's children.

That appeal was lost in the South Dakota Supreme Court which stated that the court did have jurisdiction and a petition for certiorari is now before the U.S. Supreme Court in that case.

Since the time that the appeal was taken on the jurisdictional ground, the proceedings on the merits were suspended, pending the outcome of the jurisdictional appeal.

We were successful in retrieving custody of Mrs. DeCoteau's oldest child, John, during the pendency of the appeal on this issue.

But, there were hearings on the merits and there was testimony in the record from Mrs. DeCoteau's social workers, their opinion that she was unfit and the reasons therefore.

A. Is it true that you found out about the original hearing accidentally and that she was given no notice of the hearing?

H. The original hearing was one of the grossest violations of due process that I have ever encountered. Unfortunately, I find it is quite commonplace when you're dealing with Indian parents and Indian children.

A. Did you get notice?

H. She did not get notice of either the first hearing or the second hearing.

The first hearing was a hearing on the petition of the social worker stating that there was a need for emergency custody in the department of welfare over Mrs. DeCoteau's children.

The judge issued an order placing that child in the custody of the department of public welfare without informing Mrs. DeCoteau that such a hearing was taking place, and without allowing her an opportunity to come before the court and submit testimony that such an order should not be issued.

So, the child was placed in a foster home and the judge appointed an attorney for Mrs. DeCoteau and set a hearing date on the issue of dependency and neglect. Pending the hearing the child was to remain in a foster home.

In other words, you were talking before about burden of proof. They already took the child away from her prior to having any hearing on unfitness and the burden of proof was very clearly shifted on Mrs. DeCoteau to prove that she was fit, rather than the State proving that she was unfit.

Then the hearing was scheduled for about 7 months after the child was originally taken from her.

Then the hearing was scheduled. They notified Mrs. DeCoteau by publication in the local Sisseton paper, despite the fact that her social worker knew exactly where to find her. This is another problem where the State quite frequently uses the publication notice when, in fact, they know very clearly where the person can be found and how to serve that person directly. They use publication notices instead.

Needless to say, these people don't usually make a habit of reading the local paper. She found out entirely by accident that there was a hearing on the merits because another tribal member happened to pick up the paper the day before the hearing and notice that the hearing was scheduled for the next day.

A. All right.

Cheryl, then, did you have a subsequent experience with the welfare people with regard to your second son, Bobby?

D. Yes.

A. I wonder if you could tell us what happened there?

D. I was pregnant with Bobby and the welfare came there and asked me if I would give him up for adoption.

A. While you were pregnant with him?

D. Yes.

A. Before he was even born?

D. Yes.

They just kept coming over to the house. They came every week. On a certain day they come and they kept talking to me and asking if I would give him up for adoption and said that it would be better.

They kept coming and coming and finally when I did have him, he came to the hospital. After I came home with the baby, he would come over to the house. He asked me if I would give him up for adoption and I said no.

He'd go back again and he'd come next week and ask me again and I'd say no.

He let me alone for awhile until I moved into Sisseton and moved in town.

He kept coming over and asking if I would give him up for adoption. Then he called me one afternoon and said if I wanted to give him up, and I said no; and the next morning, real early he came pounding on the door and I let him in and he asked me if I'd come up to the office. He had something to talk to me about.

So, I went up to the office and there were a whole bunch of papers there. I was kind of sick then too and I didn't know what I was signing. He just asked me if I would sign my name on this top paper, and I signed it and he sealed it or something. I signed it and he signed it, and sealed it or something.

A. Do you know what that paper was?

D. No; I didn't know what that paper was. But, then they took the baby and I asked him what he was doing, and he said it was too late now, that I gave him up for adoption. I signed the papers.

Then, they took him. They told me to wait a week. Before all this happened, when I did sign the paper, he told me to come back and see him in a week and he would tell me if I could have him back or not.

When I did go back in 1 week, that's when he told me it was too late, that I had signed the papers for adoption and I couldn't get him back.

A. How old was the baby when he took him?

D. He was 4 months.

A. Can you describe how they came and took him, or how that happened?

D. When they came to the house there, I just had the baby with me. My grandmother took John home the day before. I had the baby with me and then I took him with me when I went up there. Before I signed the paper, one of the social workers came there and took him to the next room. When they did that, I signed the papers and stuff and they wouldn't give him back to me. They wouldn't let me take him home and all that. They told me that they'd give me 1 week and to come back and see him in 1 week.

A. You mean you took the baby with you when you signed the papers and they kept the baby right there?

D. When they took me in the office there, the social worker went and called another lady in to watch the baby in the next room until I got done. When he got through talking with me, when they took the baby and I signed the papers, they just took him right out the doors and they took him right to the foster home the same day.

Afterwards, I went to see an attorney and he said that he would help me, and that was in March 1970. And, it took me until February. No, this all happened in March 1970.

I went to this lawyer and he said that he would help me and I filled out all kinds of papers and answered all the questions he wanted to know and then he said he'd let me know.

I didn't hear nothing from him for awhile and I think it was in August he called me and I went to see him. He said that a date was set in September 1970, to have a court hearing.

We went to that, but I lost that. This was before John was taken away, because they took Robert and then John was taken away. My grandfather notified me and said that I had to go to court for both kids. They were going to give them up for adoption and that's when Bert here, he was my lawyer.

A. Did you eventually get Bobby back?

D. I got him back last April.

A. How long did you and your lawyer have to fight that in court before you got him back?

D. About 10 months, 7 months for Johnny and 10 for Robert.

A. It was almost a year and a half for both kids?

D. Yes.

A. Do you have custody now of all three of the children?

D. Yes.

H. That was 10 months, Senator, after I became involved in the case. She had been trying for quite some time before that to get the kids back.

A. Yes.

Cheryl, do you have anything more to say?

D. No.

A. I want to thank you very much. Senator Bartlett probably has some questions.

Senator Bartlett [B]. Thank you, Mr. Chairman.

I wonder if, Mr. Hirsch, in either case, was there any indication of black market for adoption?

H. As close as I can come to answering affirmatively to that question is to describe to you an incident that occurred in the county welfare office when I went to serve papers for tribal intervention. The tribe felt very strongly about this case and the tribe wanted to intervene in the case on behalf of Mrs. DeCoteau and to assert a tribal right to maintain custody of these children within the tribe.

I went to serve intervention papers upon the State's attorney and he was with one of the supervisors, codirectors of the county welfare department. When I served those papers we had the following exchange: I gave him the papers. He said why is the tribe so interested in this case. What is the big issue here?

I said that the tribe was concerned that if many more of their children were taken, because there's been quite a history of taking these kids from this reservation, that they were afraid that their very survival would be at stake.

And, the codirector of this county welfare office responded to that by shrugging his shoulders and saying, "So, what?"

B. Mr. Hirsch, has there been any indication by the large number of adoptions that there is a black market for children for adoption?

H. I would say you could describe it as a gray market, rather than a black market. Although, there have been in the past, I suppose, quite a few cases that might be more accurately described as black market cases. Recently, they've only had a few of those types of cases that I know of.

I think it is more accurately described as a gray market. I think there's tremendous pressure to adoption Indian children, or have Indian children adopted out. I think that local welfare workers in Indian communities feels this pressure intensely. They have long lists of non-Indian applicants for Indian children, and they feel obligated for a whole variety of social reasons [sic] to comply with the orders that they receive for children.

B. You say long lists for adopting Indian children. Is that a relative term? Is there more interesting adopting Indian children than other children?

H. I think so. I think there's more interest in adopting Indian children primarily because non-Indian potential adoptive parents are white. They do not want to have a black child, as a generalization. White children are unavailable, there are just a few; and they are generally now settling on either Indians or orientals.

B. You mentioned just a moment ago that the tribe took particular interest in Mrs. DeCoteau.

When did they take the interest? At what time in the whole procedures?

H. I first became aware of the tribe's interest, I would say, about 2 to 3 weeks before the proceeding in court the second time. This was the time that Mrs. DeCoteau did not even know of the proceeding. The tribe did not know that Mrs. DeCoteau was going to be there. She was not in his section at that time and they knew where she was but they didn't know whether she had received notice. I was really asked by the tribe to come in and represent the tribe's interest in that proceeding. I was not representing Mrs. DeCoteau.

Mrs. DeCoteau showed up that day and the tribal council and Mrs. DeCoteau. Both asked me if I would represent her. I agreed to represent both the tribe and Mrs. DeCoteau, since there was no conflict of interest between them.

B. Was the Bureau of Indian Affairs contacted by Mrs. DeCoteau or the tribe or anybody connected with the problem?

H. Mrs. DeCoteau says that she did not contact the Bureau of Indian Affairs.

I did contact the Bureau in an effort to obtain some information that they had in their case files on Mrs. DeCoteau and her family situation which I thought would be helpful to my case.

I was told that those files were confidential and I could not get them.

B. Who were you told that by?

H. By the area's social worker.

B. Was the area's social worker connected with the BIA?

H. Yes. He is the chief of social services for the area office.

I was going to pursue that further and make a major effort to get those documents, but because of the turn that these proceedings took, it became unnecessary and I never did pursue it further.

B. Thank you very much.

Thank you very much Mrs. DeCoteau.

A. I want you thank you very much Mrs. DeCoteau, especially for your testimony, which is very revealing and which, again, I hope will be very helpful.

Thanks for coming.

Notes

1. The testimony of Cheryl Spider DeCoteau in the 1974 hearings was only one portion of the vast quantity of material gathered in the movement towards the development of the Indian Child Welfare Act. In 1975, the Senate's American Indian Policy Review Commission began a yearlong campaign, Task Force Four, to investigate Indian child welfare. The Task Force Four project included testimonies from 250 witnesses and participation from ninety tribes. It culminated in a 1976 report calling for comprehensive legislation to address the state of Indian child welfare. *Task Force Four, Report on Federal, State, and Tribal Jurisdiction*, American Indian Policy Review Commission (1976). For a detailed account of the movement to create the Indian Child Welfare Act and its passage, see Margaret D. Jacobs, *Campaign for the Indian Child Welfare Act*, *in* A Generation Removed, *supra* (2014).

2. What impact do you think the personal stories of mothers who had their children removed from them have on the committee members and members of Congress voting on ICWA?

3. Compare the testimony of Cheryl Spider DeCoteau above with the description of the hearing in the *Oglala Sioux v. Van Hunnik* class action suit, featured in Chapter 2. What has changed in the last five decades regarding the experience of tribal members and their children? What has remained the same?

D. Indian Child Welfare Act: An Overview

The Indian Child Welfare Act was passed on November 8, 1978, as Public Law No. 95-608, 92 Stat. 3069; codified at 25 U.S.C. §§ 1901-63. A full text of ICWA is located in the Appendix.

The key components of ICWA are both procedural and substantive in nature. Procedurally, ICWA applies to any Indian child either enrolled, or eligible for enrollment, in a federally recognized tribe. When it applies to a particular child, the tribe must receive notice of any qualified state court custody proceeding involving the child. The tribe has exclusive jurisdiction over Indian children domiciled on the reservation, while it has concurrent jurisdiction over all other Indian children, although the Act favors tribal jurisdiction absent good cause. ICWA also requires a heightened burden of proof to remove an Indian child from her family. Substantively, once a child has been removed, there is a set of mandatory placement preferences designed to keep the child as close as possible to the tribal community.

The following chapters will describe in detail the provisions of ICWA through the use of case law. These cases present many aspects of the Act. Some cases are necessary for a full understanding of the Act because of precedential judicial interpretation. In others, judges display the veiled racism of ignorance and showcase the difficulty of ensuring that state child protection cases comply with ICWA. Other cases reveal the triumph of the Act, when ICWA's procedures are followed and parents are given the time to change their behaviors and situation so their children can be returned to their homes and communities. Passing ICWA was a momentous triumph, but as of this writing in 2018, there is still a long way to go to ensure that Native American children have a child welfare system that supports and protects both them and their tribal families.

Chapter 2

Jurisdiction

A. Introduction

The jurisdiction over child welfare and family law issues in Indian Country has a long history of case law. Though ICWA defines and differentiates between tribal and state jurisdiction in child welfare cases, the Act is a continuation of federal Indian law and policy that recognizes established tribal jurisdiction over internal tribal issues. The jurisdictional issues inherent in juvenile justice issues is covered more fully in chapter six.

Tribes have always had the inherent sovereign jurisdiction "to make their own laws and be ruled by them," *Williams v. Lee*, 358 U.S. 217, 220 (1959), and have long been recognized as "distinct, independent political communities," *Worcester v. Georgia*, 31 U.S. 515, 559 (1832), with the inherent sovereignty to govern their own members. Tribal powers of self-governance are not granted by the federal government, but rather arise from tribal sovereignty that preexisted the United States. *Santa Clara Pueblo v. Martinez*, 436 U.S. 49, 56 (1978). Tribes have a unique government-to-government relationship with the federal government based on agreements, treaties, and the Constitution. NELL JESSUP NEWTON ET AL, COHEN'S HANDBOOK OF FEDERAL INDIAN LAW 1 (2012 ed).

Central to this power of self-governance is the arena of domestic relations, including jurisdiction over Indian children. As the Ninth Circuit has written, "in short Indian tribes are currently recognized as sovereign because they were, in fact, sovereign before the arrival of non-natives on this continent. The practical result of this doctrine is that an Indian tribe need not wait for an affirmative grant of authority from Congress in order to exercise dominion over its members." *Native Village of Venetie I.R.A. Council v. State of Alaska*, 944 F.2d 548, 556 (9th Cir. 1991).

Wisconsin Potowatomies of the Hannahville Indian Community v. Houston

393 F. Supp. 719 (W.D. Mich. 1974)

ENGEL, District Judge.

The Wisconsin Potowatomies of the Hannahville Indian Community are a duly constituted Indian tribe within the meaning of the Indian Reorganization Act of 1934, 25 U.S.C. §461, their charter having been issued on July 23, 1936 by the Secretary of the Interior. Plaintiffs reside on the Hannahville Reservation located near

Wilson in Menominee County, Michigan and within this judicial district. They bring this action against Bernard Houston, individually and as Director of the Michigan Department of Social Services to regain custody and the right to determine the custody, care and control of Leroy Roger Wandahsega, Jr., born July 8, 1967; Veronica Wandahsega, born September 3, 1968, and Tyrone Wandahsega, born October 23, 1969. The suit was commenced on behalf of the tribe following the passage on June 26, 1972 of a resolution of the tribal council of the Hannahville Indian Community authorizing the employment of counsel for such purposes.

* * *

I. Stipulated Facts

Prior to his marriage in 1967, Leroy Wandahsega, now deceased, lived on the Hannahville reservation. He was a full-blooded Potowatomie Indian. In 1967 Leroy Wandahsega married Faye Wandahsega, a white person, and the couple lived on the reservation until they moved to Milwaukee in 1968. None of their three children was born on the reservation. Leroy, Jr. was born in Escanaba, Michigan and Veronica and Tyrone were born in Milwaukee, Wisconsin. The children are Indians of the half-blood.

In 1970 the family retunred [sic] to the reservation with their children and continued to live there together until Faye Wandahsega left the reservation with the three children sometime between October 1 and 9, 1971. In early 1971, Leroy Wandahsega worked for P & S Manufacturing Company in nearby Spalding, Michigan, until he was laid off that spring. Thereafter he worked in the woods. The family, while on the reservation, rented a home from the Public Housing Authority and rental thereof continued until the time of Leroy's death. Sometime prior to October 9, 1971, Faye Wandahsega and her children left Leroy and went first to Escanaba, Michigan. On October 9, the mother and three children left Escanaba to stay with the mother's aunt Mrs. Helen Waldo in Bagley, Michigan where they stayed until October 19, 1971. At that time Mrs. Wandahsega rented a trailer home in Bagley and received direct relief benefits from the Menominee County Department of Social Services during that time. Earlier, when Leroy became unemployed in the spring of 1971, the family had also received public assistance. In the fall of 1971, the oldest child, Leroy, Jr., was enrolled in the Headstart Program on the reservation. On November 22, 1971, Faye Wandahsega left the three children with her niece, Mrs. Roseanne Baumler, at Stephenson, Michigan while she traveled to Menominee to request further assistance from the Department of Social Services in the form of additional funds, ostensibly to move herself and her three children to Milwaukee, Wisconsin. Upon returning to her trailer home on November 22, 1972, in the company of her mother, Leroy came into her home and apparently killed his wife and mother-in-law before killing himself. Other than this last statement taken directly from the stipulation filed by the parties, there is no express determination of who actually survived the other as between the parents, beyond perhaps any inference to be drawn from the probable sequence of the shooting.

The three Wandahsega children, having thus been orphaned, continued to stay with Faye's niece, Mrs. Baumler. On November 29, 1971, Francis Grun, Juvenile Officer for the Menominee County, filed a petition with the Menominee Probate Court alleging that the three children were without legal custody and without guardianship and were, thus, dependent children within the meaning of the Michigan Juvenile Court. The petition requested the court to take "temporary custody of said children to facilitate proper planning for them."

On December 1, 1971 an order was issued by the Menominee County Probate Court making the children temporary wards of the court. On January 6, 1972, a further order was entered providing for the placement of the children in a licensed foster home under the Michigan Department of Social Services pending hearing on the petition filed November 29, which was subsequently held on January 13, 1972. A guardian ad litem, Steven G. Barstow, was appointed to represent the three children at the hearing. Also present were Mr. and Mrs. Jake McCulloch, paternal great uncle of the children, and their attorneys, Mrs. Alice Wandahsega, Mr. and Mrs. William Wilsey, the petitioning juvenile officer Francis Grun, and Gary Curtin, Regional Director of Youth Services with the Department of Social Services. Mr. and Mrs. Jake McCulloch had, on January 4, 1972, filed a petition for adoption of the children, Mr. McCulloch being their paternal great uncle. Mrs. Alice Wandahsega had, on December 1, 1971, filed a petition for guardianship of the children.

Following that hearing and by order dated January 13, 1972, the Menominee County Probate Court directed that the three children be made permanent wards of the court and committed them to the Department of Social Services for admission to the Michigan Childrens Institute for purposes of adoption. The adoption planning and investigations were completed by the Department of Social Services and it was determined by the Department that the best interests of the children dictated that they be transported to Florida, there to be placed for adoption with Mr. and Mrs. William Wilsey, the children's maternal aunt and uncle.

Both sides concede that at the time of determination of these issues before the Menominee County Probate Court, it was found that both Mr. and Mrs. McCulloch and Mr. and Mrs. Wilsey were fit and suitable persons to have custody of the children.

* * *

Plaintiff tribe claims that it has a right under the foregoing facts to determine the custody of the Wandahsega children, and that this right is superior to any right of persons derived from the exercise of jurisdiction by the Probate Court for the County of Menominee. It is the plaintiff's contention that the exercise of jurisdiction of the probate court in determining permanent custody of said children is void, exclusive jurisdiction under federal law resting with the Potowatomie Tribe of the Hannahville Community.

* * *

The case was stipulated to the court for decision upon the foregoing stipulated facts. Upon consideration, however, the court concluded that the stipulated facts were too bleak and skeletal to enable it to reach a full and fair adjudication. Accordingly, the court on its own motion, re-opened the proofs and called upon the parties to offer additional evidence at a hearing held on October 10, 1973. In an order dated September 26, 1973, the court requested proofs, to the extent available, on the following:

1. The existence or lack thereof of Potowatomie tribal customs as respects

a) the status of children of the half-blood born to an Indian father and a white mother,

b) care, custody and control of orphaned Indian children.

2. Attempts, if any, made by the Potowatomie Tribe or any representative of the tribe to have the children after the death of the parents and prior to the filing of this lawsuit.

3. What, if any, public or formal claim was made relating to the children's tribal status between the time of the parents' death and the filing of this lawsuit.

4. Any additional evidence relating to domicile, tribal custom, or tribal status of the children which is deemed relevant to the issues presented in this case.

* * *

The October 10 hearing produced the testimony of four witnesses, which is herein briefly summarized.

James "Jake" McCulloch, Jr.

Jake McCulloch is an uncle of the deceased Leroy Wandahsega, and greatuncle to the three Wandahsega children. Presently, Mr. McCulloch is the President of the Council of the Hannahville Community.

He testified that except for six years, he had spent the entire thirty years of his life on the reservation. He is the brother of Alice, the children's paternal grandmother. Mr. McCulloch testified that he was close to the Wandahsega family, saw them regularly and had a good relationship with the children. He stated that Faye returned at least once to the reservation during the time between October 9 and the date of her death, although he did not know whether she stayed overnight on the reservation.

Mr. McCulloch said that he first heard the news about the three deaths at 11 o'clock on the night they took place, and then immediately went to his sister Alice and niece Sally's house. He had thought the children might be there. Upon discovering that they were not, McCulloch testified that the three decided to get an attorney as soon as possible to obtain custody of the children, which was done the following day. It was agreed that Jack should be guardian. Jake testified that, because of the ineffectiveness of Omar Sagatauk, the then council president, who was later impeached, his attempts to call a meeting of the council regarding the children were unsuccessful.

* * *

Sally Half-a-Day

Sally Half-a-Day, Leroy Wandahsega's older sister, a married woman with seven children, testified that she has been in the tribal council since May of 1972, and is currently the secretary. She testified that she called a June, 1972 meeting which was cancelled because the then-chief Sagatauk did not want to take time for a meeting.

Mrs. Half-a-Day was familiar with the Wandahsegas, seeing them almost daily. She testified that during Faye's absence from the reservation immediately prior to her death, the two women conversed frequently by telephone, and that Faye returned to the reservation several times during that period, and left the children in Sally's care on those occasions. She saw Faye at the Wandahsega house on the Wednesday before Faye's death.

Mrs. Half-a-Day stated that the day after the deaths, she made a number of phone calls in an attempt to locate the children. She also saw Mrs. O'Hara of the Department of Social Services, and said that Mrs. O'Hara informed her that it would be best if she didn't try to locate the children. Sally stated that Mrs. O'Hara did not want the children to be on the reservation. Sally stated that she called the State Police who referred her to Mrs. Bommer. Mrs. Bommer told Sally that the children were receiving good care, but would not tell her where they were.

* * *

Dr. James A. Clifton

Dr. Clifton, a professor of anthropology at the University of Wisconsin at Green Bay, testified as an expert witness regarding Potowatomie history, culture and custom. He had worked among the Potowatomie Indians and had extensively studied Indian culture, and Potowatomie culture in particular. Dr. Clifton's expertise in this area was impressive.

It was Dr. Clifton's testimony that the Hannahville Community of the Potowatomies dates back to 1843, but there is little known history regarding the early years of the Community. Their constitution and by-laws were standard and were drawn up by the Bureau of Indian Affairs.

Dr. Clifton testified that in the social life of the Potowatomies, the traditional and contemporary problems of child care did not arise. The communities are fundamentally "kinship communities", wherein if a child lost both of his parents, other relatives automatically assumed responsibility for his care. The closest relatives were those traced on the father's side, i.e. patrilineal side. The father's line is very important, but the mother's is not ignored. Traditionally, a child would take a name selected from a set of names belonging to the father's side of the family. In Potowatomie culture, responsibility for the day-to-day care of the children was with the grandparents, even when the parents were living. The term "grandfather" also included great-uncles on the father's side. According to Dr. Clifton, under Ptowatomie [sic] culture, Jake McCulloch would have been the customary grandfather since the grandfather himself was deceased.

In Potowatomie traditions, Dr. Clifton testified, adoptions are not referred to in the legal sense. In tribal custom, a person was "adopted" to replace a lost relative. Thus, the child was not adopted by an adult, but was considered to adopt a substitute parent. Formally, the child would pick a parent, and where a minor was involved, the record would reflect the change. Potowatomies recognized the discretion of a child to make his own choice upon reaching a certain age. Dr. Clifton testified that the assumption of jurisdiction in forced adoption by white courts is a matter of great bitterness among the Indian community.

Michael Miketinac, Regional Director of the Department of Social Services for the Upper Peninsula.

He stated that Department studies the families, and files a racial and ethnic line if possible. He said that children on the reservation are treated no differently than those outside. There is apparently no recognition by the Department of any special status attaching to Indians living on reservations.

* * *

Opinion and Conclusions of Law

* * *

Neither party has petitioned this court for appointment of a guardian ad litem on behalf of the children in this action, and upon inquiry by the court, each has asserted that such appointment is not required in view of the narrowness of the issue presented. Under the circumstances here, the court agrees and further finds that no potential advantage would inure to the benefit of the children by such appointment. To the extent the children are properly wards of the State of Michigan, any interest in such status is protected by the defendant and the Attorney General of Michigan appearing on his behalf. To the extent the children are not under this court's ruling properly such wards, the adversary role assumed by defendant and his counsel has adequately precluded any prejudice from failure to appoint a guardian ad litem.

While, therefore, the ultimate question of the best interests of the children is not directly before the court, it does not necessarily follow that the court is thereby precluded from any consideration of the question. Fundamental concepts of justice and humanity, as well as of wardship, impose upon the court the independent obligation to be satisfied that any order entered by it, however proper otherwise, does not result in actual harm or damage to the minor children involved here.

* * *

The court finds that the Wandahsega children were and are full members of the Hannahville Indian Community. They fall clearly within the definition thereof as set forth in the Constitution and Bylaws of the tribe. Membership in an Indian tribe has been variously defined in statute and in caselaw, depending in large part upon the circumstances under which the issue of membership arose. It is clear that in most cases and for most purposes the fact of mixed blood does not destroy the identity of such a person as Indian and, particularly, where the person is the child of an Indian of full blood.

Most cases and statutes which seek to define the term "Indian" define it within the context of a given situation, e.g. for purposes of receiving tribal property (*Waldron v. U.S.*, 143 F. 413 (8 Cir. 1905)), for the purposes of obtaining a census (see Felix Cohen: Federal Indian Law (1958) p. 6 n. 8) or for purposes of preclusion from the purchase of alcoholic beverages (*People v. Gebhard*, 151 Mich. 192, 115 N.W. 54 (1908)), or for the purpose of construction of a particular statute (*U.S. v. Rogers*, 4 How. 567, 45 U.S. 567, 11 L.Ed. 1105 (1846)).

The purpose asserted here is the purpose of exercise of tribal jurisdiction over orphaned minor children who are members of the tribe.

* * *

Under the common law, these children would take the status of their father, and would, therefore, be Indian. Under the tribal custom doctrine, it would be logical to resort to the custom of the tribe involved, rather than to a more general tribal doctrine. No definitive evidence as to Potowatomie custom has been offered this court regarding the status of offspring of a white mother and an Indian father. However, the court, in keeping with the trend discussed above, of defining "Indian" in terms of specific purpose, concludes that the facts of the children's half-blood and their status as enrolled members of the tribe are sufficient to render them Indians for the purpose of this case—that is, determining the extent of tribal jurisdiction over them. Their enrollment is a key element in light of the importance of their relationship to the Potowatomie tribe and its reservation, in resolving the rights of the parties in this case.

* * *

It is the position of the defendant that whatever may be the rights of the plaintiff Indian tribe to govern the conduct and affairs of its members within its reservation, such rights do not extend beyond the geographical confines of the reservation and, particularly where the children involved are half white and are found as orphans outside of the reservation and within territorial jurisdiction of the state court.

It is true that as a general proposition, Indians who find themselves outside the reservation have generally the same rights and are subject to the same responsibilities and are subject to the jurisdiction of state courts in the same manner and to the same extent as other state citizens. *Mescalero Apache Tribes v. Jones*, 411 U.S. 145, 93 S.Ct. 1267, 36 L.Ed.2d 114 (1973). See also, Cohen, *supra*, at pp. 510–511 and cases cited. It is true also that under 8 U.S.C. § 1401, Indians are specifically declared to be citizens of the United States and that under the Fourteenth Amendment they are considered as well to be citizens of the state wherein the reservation is geographically located. *Deere v. State of N.Y.*, 22 F.2d 851 (2 Cir. 1927).

It is also true that under M.S.A. § 27.3178(1) et seq., M.C.L.A. § 701.1 et seq., the probate court is authorized to take custody of neglected or abandoned children, or children otherwise without custody or guardianship, when "found within the county". It appears that these children where found, were covered by the literal language of the statute. The court assumes, therefore, that the initial exercise of jurisdiction for the immediate protection of the health and safety of the children was both proper and laudable.

The issue in this case, however, goes further.

Had the circumstances set forth in the above findings of fact all occurred within the boundaries of the reservation, there can be little doubt that no power or jurisdiction would exist in the probate court for the County of Menominee to take custody of or to determine questions involving the custody of the three Wandahsega children. *Williams v. Lee, supra.* See also *State v. Superior Court*, 57 Wash.2d 181, 356 P.2d 985 (1960) and *In re Colwash*, 57 Wash.2d 196, 356 P.2d 994 (1960), wherein the Supreme Court of Washington held that the state probate court was without jurisdiction over the determination of custody of Indian children, enrolled as members of a tribe, and who resided on the reservation. *Colwash, supra*, so held, notwithstanding the fact that the Indian parents had abandoned the children. Nor would the probate court be in a position to question the procedures or customs by which, within the tribe, the physical custody of the children would be determined, at least in the absence of any compliance with the federal enabling statute. See Cohen, *supra*, at p. 117–118 re marriage and divorce customs, and cases cited. See also *United States v. Quiver*, 241 U.S. 602, 36 S.Ct. 699, 60 L.Ed. 1196 (1916), where the Supreme Court recognized:

"At an early period it became the settled policy of Congress to permit the personal and domestic relations of the Indians with each other to be regulated . . . according to their tribal customs and laws." 241 at 603-604, 36 S.Ct. at 700.

If tribal sovereignty is to have any meaning at all at this juncture of history, it must necessarily include the right, within its own boundaries and membership, to provide for the care and upbringing of its young, a sine qua non to the preservation of its identity. That sovereignty, as the Supreme Court has noted 'predates that of our own government. Indians today are American citizens. They have the right to vote, to use state courts, and they receive some state services. (But they are still) a separate people, with the power of regulating their internal and social relations.' *McClanahan* [*v. State Tax Commission*], [411 U.S.] 172, 93 S.Ct. at 1263 [(1973)].

* * *

Popular notions, both of the rights and customs of Indians as well as of their way of living have notoriously been inaccurate. See Introduction to Handbook of Federal Indian Law 1942 by Felix S. Cohen. Indeed, it is all too easy to assume either that in this latter period, the Indians' status is no different from that of other citizens of the United States, or to the contrary, that Indians and Indian tribes are somehow relegated to that romantic and historic role which fiction has preserved for them. It is apparent from this case, as it must be to anyone aware of Indians and Indian tribes in the 20th century that their way of life has, in fact, taken on many of the aspects of other citizens of the United States in habits, language and dress and that, as did the Wandahsega family, Indians frequently move in and out of reservations in pursuit of employment and for many of the same reasons which motivate other citizens. When they do, it is well established that their rights to mobility and to live outside the reservation temporarily or permanently cannot be impeded by the action of the tribe. See *Standing Bear v. Crook*, 25 Fed (as No. 14891 (1899)). Thus, had Leroy and Faye Wandahsega been legally domiciled in a community outside of the reservation at the time of their deaths, it is the opinion of the court that the tribe, if it was entitled to custody of the children at all, would have been obligated to submit itself to the jurisdiction of the probate court which had lawfully taken custody of the children, to have met the criteria for custody established by Michigan law, and to be governed by proper decision of the probate judge with respect to the best welfare of the children as provided by law. See *Mescalaro, supra*. On the other hand, if Leroy and Faye Wandahsega had been living in their home on the reservation with their children and had, for example, been killed in an automobile accident, off the reservation, occurring while they were on a brief trip to visit friends or returning from a movie in a nearby town, could it then be said that this happenstance would be sufficient to divest the tribe of that right which was otherwise so inherently a part of its retained sovereignty? Or, if Leroy and Faye had themselves died within the reservation, leaving their children orphans and if the children had been abducted from the reservation and removed therefrom, could it be said that such an unlawful act could be interposed to deprive the tribe of such fundamental rights? It would seem to the court that while physical presence within or without the reservation may for most purposes be sufficient to dispose of the issues of jurisdiction, it is not sufficient to resolve the issues presented here. These issues go deeper and ought not to be controlled solely by either the situs of the parents' death or by the situs of the children's presence when they were taken into initial custody by the probate court.

On the contrary, it would appear to the court that the only rational approach is to determine the domicile of the children at the time their physical custody was gained by the probate court. Upon the facts contained in the stipulation in this case, as well as those obtained at the reopening of proofs, the court is of the opinion that at the time the physical possession was acquired by the probate court and subsequently through the probate court the Department of Social Services, the domicile of the children was within the reservation.

The general rule is that the domicile of minor children follows that of the parents and that where the parents are separated, the domicile is that of the parent with whom the child lives. Restatement of Conflicts § 313. It has also been held that the domicile of the wife follows that of her husband, although this rule is breaking down in a time that is increasingly recognizing the rights of married women. The general rule of domicile respecting adults, even notwithstanding special rules for married women, is that domicile requires two elements: intent and physical presence, which must concur in time. See *In re Fox Estate*, 3 Mich.App. 501, 142 N.W.2d 866 (1966). Further, it is generally held that an old domicile is not abandoned until a new one has been established. See Restatement of Conflicts, Section 15 (1934).

* * *

To the extent that intent can be known, there is nothing other than the physical facts themselves to indicate that Faye did not, up to the time of her death, intend to return to the reservation ultimately, or that she intended permanently to abandon the home available to her there. The fact that she lived for a period of time with her mother and again with a friend and again in a rented house trailer, and the fact that she had applied for assistance to enable her to go to Milwaukee evidence an uncertainty as to her future which makes it impossible, under the facts here, to find that she had established any new domicile and abandoned the old.

Even if she had intended to abandon her former domicile (the reservation), she had not done so because she had not established a new one. See Restatement of Conflicts, § 15. Subsequent to Faye's departure from the reservation in October of 1971, there is no evidence that she was ever physically present in Milwaukee or any other place concurrent with an intent to make a home. Having failed to establish a new domicile, her domicile remained that of the reservation, and thus, so did that of her children. It is, therefore, the opinion of the court that, notwithstanding the physical absence of the mother and children from the reservation, that the domicile of both parents and thus of the children remained the reservation at Hannahville.

The court is of the opinion, therefore, that tribal custom ought to have governed the custody of the Wandahsega children, rather than the laws and procedures of the State of Michigan. Upon reopening proofs, the court was concerned with ascertaining the existence of a tradition or custom, and with discovering whether or not such customs had been abandoned, and indeed whether jurisdiction itself might have been waived or abandoned in favor of the probate court. Upon consideration of all the proofs and applicable caselaw, the court concludes that tribal custom existed, was followed in spirit and largely in practice until frustrated by the actions of employees of the Michigan Department of Social Services, and that the tribe has neither conferred jurisdiction upon the Michigan Probate Court, nor waived its right to assert its jurisdiction before the federal court. While the evidence showed that it was quite usual for the community to rely upon state agencies and state courts in matters involving marriage, divorce, law enforcement and guardianship of children, the evidence failed to show that the precise problem facing the Hannahville Community in this situation had arisen before. The court does not find that past reliance on state government for aid in Indian problems constituted a waiver of jurisdiction in this case. See Cohen, *supra*, 402 (1958).

The court finds that the Hannahville Indian Community is comprised of Wisconsin Potowatomies and that the history and customs of the Wisconsin Potowatomies are applicable to members of the Hannahville Community. The court finds, as testified to by Dr. Clifton, that the Potowatomies are patrilineal, that it was in accordance with an unwritten, unarticulated, but nonetheless living custom, for Jake McCulloch to take control and custody of the children. He attempted to do this in all avenues available to him. Although he acted according to a custom, the court finds, and he so testified, that he was acting upon his own family interest in the welfare of the children, when he sought their custody through the probate court. That court had already taken possession of the children under the circumstances. To petition the state court to voluntarily grant him custody of the children was rational, given his interest in the children. In so doing, he submitted himself to the personal jurisdiction of the court as to that case. But the actions of an individual person, even if in accord with custom, cannot create subject matter jurisdiction over Indian affairs in a state court. The tribe itself must have, by some prior act performed through a legally recognized procedure, conferred jurisdiction upon the court. Note that in *Kennerly v. District Court*, 400 U.S. 423, 91 S.Ct. 480, 27 L.Ed.2d 507 (1971), it was held that a vote by a tribal council was insufficient to create jurisdiction over Indian affairs, where the statute (25 U.S.C. § 1326) required a majority vote of the adult Indians of the tribe, voting at a special election.

Indeed, had no one from the tribe made any attempts to locate and care for the Wandahsega Children between the time they became orphaned and the time this lawsuit was filed, this court might be inclined to find, not a conferring of jurisdiction upon the state court, but perhaps a waiver of the right to assert tribal jurisdiction.

But such is not the case. Efforts were made by the parties to whom tribal custom would dictate custody to find and care for the Wandahsega children. The fact that the attempts were made by an individual seeking to assert his personal interest in the children does not mean that the tribe had failed to assert its jurisdiction. Indeed, the tradition of the Potowatomies reveals that it is their custom to act informally, through blood relatives, in affairs of the family. Had Jake McCulloch been successful in finding the children, returning them to the reservation, and commenced caring for them, it well may be that the tribal authorities may have considered that no dispute existed over which to assert jurisdiction and render a decision. Whereas, in white society, orphaned children may always present a question for procedural government intervention, that may not be the case among Indian tribes. It is not for this court or the state court to say that the Hannahville Community must have a formal procedure to determine guardianship. It is sufficient that the tribe has shown that, according to its standards, it did not abandon interest in the children or jurisdiction over them. Relinquishment of Indian rights is not to be lightly inferred. Doubts as to the intent of a law, or a treaty, are to be resolved in favor of the Indians, and are to be construed as the Indians understood their meaning. See *Waldron v. U.S.*, 143 F. 413 (8 Cir. 1905). If this be so, doubts as to existence of a custom or the intent to abandon a custom must likewise be resolved in favor of the Indians.

* * *

The determination of permanent custody of the children, therefore, as a question involving the affairs of reservation Indians residing on the reservation, remained, under settled principles of law, within the exclusive jurisdiction of the tribe. *Worcester* [*v. Georgia*, 31 U.S. (6 Pet.) 515 (1832)], *McClanahan*, *supra*. This being the case, the court is of the opinion that the probate court, while perhaps within its jurisdiction to care for the immediate needs of the children, was without jurisdiction to take permanent custody of them, and is without jurisdiction to enter further orders for the adoption or other custody of the Wandahsega children.

Notes

1. Two years after this decision, in *Fisher v. District Court*, 424 U.S. 382 (1976), the Supreme Court overturned the Montana Supreme Court and found that the Northern Cheyenne Tribe had exclusive jurisdiction over an adoption case where all of the parties were citizens of the tribe, and they all resided on the reservation. In this case, rather than the state attempting to avoid the jurisdiction of the tribe, the adoptive parents attempted to use the state court to instigate adoption proceedings to avoid a tribal court order granting the mother summer visiting time. The Supreme Court held that:

> State-court jurisdiction plainly would interfere with the powers of self-government conferred upon the Northern Cheyenne Tribe and exercised through the Tribal Court. It would subject a dispute arising on the reservation among reservation Indians to a forum other than the one they have established for themselves.

In addition, the Court found that:

> the exclusive jurisdiction of the Tribal Court does not derive from the race of the plaintiff but rather from the quasi-sovereign status of the Northern Cheyenne Tribe under federal law. Moreover even if a jurisdictional holding occasionally results in denying an Indian plaintiff a forum to which a non-Indian has access, such disparate treatment of the Indian is justified because it is intended to benefit the class of which he is a member by furthering the congressional policy of Indian self-government.

2. The Western District noted that if no one from the Tribe had attempted to find the children, it may have found the tribe had waived its jurisdiction. Therefore, the actions of the family in locating the children meant that the tribe *wanted* jurisdiction over the children. What does it mean that the tribe could conceivably create or destroy jurisdiction based on how quickly it attempted to exercise it? Timing of intervention and transfer petitions will be discussed in Chapter 3, but even under ICWA, a tribe's late timing may be used to defeat tribal jurisdiction over tribal children. Alternatively, the *Fisher* case stands for the proposition that the tribe has exclusive jurisdiction over on-reservation children. ICWA codified that jurisdiction in 25 U.S.C. § 1911(a).

3. As noted above, federal involvement in Indian families is a defining element of the relationship between the federal government and tribes. In this case, the tribe asked the federal district court to review the case under 28 U.S.C. § 1362, the

"arising under" provision granting federal jurisdiction over controversies brought by a federally recognized tribe where the controversy "arises under the Constitution, laws, or treaties of the United States."

4. This case presents some interesting inter-sectionality issues with our understanding of domestic violence. The mother's actions in this case followed a classic cyclical abuse pattern. She was murdered as she was trying to leave her abusive husband. Her domicile was in question due to her attempts to leave an abusive situation. Would this have come out differently today? How would our understanding of intimate partner violence inform this case? The most recent major Congressional change to tribal jurisdiction involves the Violence Against Women Act, where in 2013, the Act was amended to allow tribes to exercise jurisdiction over non-Indians who commit acts of violence against their intimate partners on the reservation. The Act does not, however, address how a tribe can exercise certain jurisdiction to protect the *children* of these relationships.

B. Supreme Court Precedent

ICWA governs jurisdiction for Indian children as codified in 25 U.S.C. § 1911, when an Indian child is the subject of a child welfare or voluntary adoption case.

> **§ 1911. Indian tribe jurisdiction over Indian child custody proceedings**
>
> a. Exclusive jurisdiction
>
> An Indian tribe shall have jurisdiction exclusive as to any State over any child custody proceeding involving an Indian child who resides or is domiciled within the reservation of such tribe, except where such jurisdiction is otherwise vested in the State by existing Federal law. Where an Indian child is a ward of a tribal court, the Indian tribe shall retain exclusive jurisdiction, notwithstanding the residence or domicile of the child.
>
> b. Transfer of proceedings; declination by tribal court
>
> In any State court proceeding for the foster care placement of, or termination of parental rights to, an Indian child not domiciled or residing within the reservation of the Indian child's tribe, the court, in the absence of good cause to the contrary, shall transfer such proceeding to the jurisdiction of the tribe, absent objection by either parent, upon the petition of either parent or the Indian custodian or the Indian child's tribe: provided, that such transfer shall be subject to declination by the tribal court of such tribe.

The second provision allows for the concurrent jurisdiction over Indian children not domiciled on the reservation. Sometimes called "transfer jurisdiction," Indian Child Welfare Act Handbook 59 (B. J. Jones et al. eds., 2d ed. 2008), because of the requirement that state courts relinquish jurisdiction when requested by the tribe, this provision is heavily litigated. The questions surrounding what is "good cause" not to transfer the case to tribal court are only slightly illuminated by the federal regulations, and are discussed at length in Section C of this Chapter.

Of the two Supreme Court decisions on ICWA, one of them directly addresses the issue of tribal jurisdiction over Indian children. Much of the decision was presented in Chapter 1. This excerpt directly relates to the question of exclusive tribal jurisdiction.

Mississippi Band of Choctaw Indians v. Holyfield

490 U.S. 30 (1989)

Justice Brennan delivered the opinion of the Court.

This appeal requires us to construe the provisions of the Indian Child Welfare Act that establish exclusive tribal jurisdiction over child custody proceedings involving Indian children domiciled on the tribe's reservation.

I

A

The Indian Child Welfare Act of 1978 (ICWA), 92 Stat. 3069, 25 U.S.C. §§ 1901–1963, was the product of rising concern in the mid-1970's over the consequences to Indian children, Indian families, and Indian tribes of abusive child welfare practices that resulted in the separation of large numbers of Indian children from their families and tribes through adoption or foster care placement, usually in non-Indian homes. Senate oversight hearings in 1974 yielded numerous examples, statistical data, and expert testimony documenting what one witness called "[t]he wholesale removal of Indian children from their homes, . . . the most tragic aspect of Indian life today." Studies undertaken by the Association on American Indian Affairs in 1969 and 1974, and presented in the Senate hearings, showed that 25 to 35% of all Indian children had been separated from their families and placed in adoptive families, foster care, or institutions. Adoptive placements counted significantly in this total: in the State of Minnesota, for example, one in eight Indian children under the age of 18 was in an adoptive home, and during the year 1971–1972 nearly one in every four infants under one year of age was placed for adoption. The adoption rate of Indian children was eight times that of non-Indian children. Approximately 90% of the Indian placements were in non-Indian homes. A number of witnesses also testified to the serious adjustment problems encountered by such children during adolescence, as well as the impact of the adoptions on Indian parents and the tribes themselves. . . .

For example, Mr. Calvin Isaac, Tribal Chief of the Mississippi Band of Choctaw Indians and representative of the National Tribal Chairmen's Association, testified as follows:

> "Culturally, the chances of Indian survival are significantly reduced if our children, the only real means for the transmission of the tribal heritage, are to be raised in non-Indian homes and denied exposure to the ways of their

> People. Furthermore, these practices seriously undercut the tribes' ability to continue as self-governing communities. Probably in no area is it more important that tribal sovereignty be respected than in an area as socially and culturally determinative as family relationships."

Chief Isaac also summarized succinctly what numerous witnesses saw as the principal reason for the high rates of removal of Indian children:

> One of the most serious failings of the present system is that Indian children are removed from the custody of their natural parents by nontribal government authorities who have no basis for intelligently evaluating the cultural and social premises underlying Indian home life and childrearing. Many of the individuals who decide the fate of our children are at best ignorant of our cultural values, and at worst contemptful of the Indian way and convinced that removal, usually to a non-Indian household or institution, can only benefit an Indian child. . . .

At the heart of the ICWA are its provisions concerning jurisdiction over Indian child custody proceedings. Section 1911 lays out a dual jurisdictional scheme. Section 1911(a) establishes exclusive jurisdiction in the tribal courts for proceedings concerning an Indian child "who resides or is domiciled within the reservation of such tribe," as well as for wards of tribal courts regardless of domicile. Section 1911(b), on the other hand, creates concurrent but presumptively tribal jurisdiction in the case of children not domiciled on the reservation: on petition of either parent or the tribe, state-court proceedings for foster care placement or termination of parental rights are to be transferred to the tribal court, except in cases of "good cause," objection by either parent, or declination of jurisdiction by the tribal court.

Various other provisions of ICWA Title I set procedural and substantive standards for those child custody proceedings that do take place in state court. The procedural safeguards include requirements concerning notice and appointment of counsel; parental and tribal rights of intervention and petition for invalidation of illegal proceedings; procedures governing voluntary consent to termination of parental rights; and a full faith and credit obligation in respect to tribal court decisions. See §§ 1901–1914. The most important substantive requirement imposed on state courts is that of § 1915(a), which, absent "good cause" to the contrary, mandates that adoptive placements be made preferentially with (1) members of the child's extended family, (2) other members of the same tribe, or (3) other Indian families. . . .

B

This case involves the status of twin babies, known for our purposes as B.B. and G.B., who were born out of wedlock on December 29, 1985. Their mother, J.B., and father, W.J., were both enrolled members of appellant Mississippi Band of Choctaw Indians (Tribe), and were residents and domiciliaries of the Choctaw Reservation in Neshoba County, Mississippi. J.B. gave birth to the twins in Gulfport, Harrison County, Mississippi, some 200 miles from the reservation. On January 10, 1986,

J.B. executed a consent-to-adoption form before the Chancery Court of Harrison County. W.J. signed a similar form. On January 16, appellees Orrey and Vivian Holyfield filed a petition for adoption in the same court, and the chancellor issued a Final Decree of Adoption on January 28. Despite the court's apparent awareness of the ICWA, the adoption decree contained no reference to it, nor to the infants' Indian background.

Two months later the Tribe moved in the Chancery Court to vacate the adoption decree on the ground that under the ICWA exclusive jurisdiction was vested in the tribal court. On July 14, 1986, the court overruled the motion, holding that the Tribe "never obtained exclusive jurisdiction over the children involved herein . . . ." The court's one-page opinion relied on two facts in reaching that conclusion. The court noted first that the twins' mother "went to some efforts to see that they were born outside the confines of the Choctaw Indian Reservation" and that the parents had promptly arranged for the adoption by the Holyfields. Second, the court stated: "At no time from the birth of these children to the present date have either of them resided on or physically been on the Choctaw Indian Reservation."

The Supreme Court of Mississippi affirmed. 511 So.2d 918 (1987). It rejected the Tribe's arguments that the state court lacked jurisdiction and that it, in any event, had not applied the standards laid out in the ICWA. The court recognized that the jurisdictional question turned on whether the twins were domiciled on the Choctaw Reservation. It answered that question as follows:

> "At no point in time can it be said the twins resided on or were domiciled within the territory set aside for the reservation. Appellant's argument that living within the womb of their mother qualifies the children's residency on the reservation may be lauded for its creativity; however, apparently it is unsupported by any law within this state, and will not be addressed at this time due to the far-reaching legal ramifications that would occur were we to follow such a complicated tangential course."

The court distinguished Mississippi cases that appeared to establish the principle that "the domicile of minor children follows that of the parents," *ibid.*; see *Boyle v. Griffin*, 84 Miss. 41, 36 So. 141 (1904); *Stubbs v. Stubbs*, 211 So.2d 821 (Miss.1968); see also *In re Guardianship of Watson*, 317 So.2d 30 (Miss.1975). It noted that "the Indian twins . . . were voluntarily surrendered and legally abandoned by the natural parents to the adoptive parents, and it is undisputed that the parents went to some efforts to prevent the children from being placed on the reservation as the mother arranged for their birth and adoption in Gulfport Memorial Hospital, Harrison County, Mississippi." 511 So.2d, at 921. Therefore, the court said, the twins' domicile was in Harrison County and the state court properly exercised jurisdiction over the adoption proceedings. Indeed, the court appears to have concluded that, for this reason, none of the provisions of the ICWA was applicable. *Ibid.* ("[T]hese proceedings . . . actually escape applicable federal law on Indian Child Welfare"). In any case, it rejected the Tribe's contention that the requirements of the ICWA applicable in state courts had not been followed: "[T]he judge did conform and strictly adhere to the minimum federal standards governing adoption of Indian children with respect to parental consent, notice, service of process, etc." *Ibid.* . . .

II

Tribal jurisdiction over Indian child custody proceedings is not a novelty of the ICWA. Indeed, some of the ICWA's jurisdictional provisions have a strong basis in pre-ICWA case law in the federal and state courts. See, e.g., *Fisher v. District Court, Sixteenth Judicial District of Montana*, 424 U.S. 382, 96 S.Ct. 943, 47 L.Ed.2d 106 (1976) (per curiam) (tribal court had exclusive jurisdiction over adoption proceeding where all parties were tribal members and reservation residents); *Wisconsin Potowatomies of Hannahville Indian Community v. Houston*, 393 F. Supp. 719 (WD Mich.1973) (tribal court had exclusive jurisdiction over custody of Indian children found to have been domiciled on reservation); *Wakefield v. Little Light*, 276 Md. 333, 347 A.2d 228 (1975) (same); *In re Adoption of Buehl*, 87 Wash.2d 649, 555 P.2d 1334 (1976) (state court lacked jurisdiction over custody of Indian children placed in off-reservation foster care by tribal court order); see also *In re Lelah-puc-ka-chee*, 98 F. 429 (ND Iowa 1899) (state court lacked jurisdiction to appoint guardian for Indian child living on reservation). In enacting the ICWA Congress confirmed that, in child custody proceedings involving Indian children domiciled on the reservation, tribal jurisdiction was exclusive as to the States.

The state-court proceeding at issue here was a "child custody proceeding." That term is defined to include any "'adoptive placement' which shall mean the permanent placement of an Indian child for adoption, including any action resulting in a final decree of adoption." 25 U.S.C. § 1903(1)(iv). Moreover, the twins were "Indian children." See 25 U.S.C. § 1903(4). The sole issue in this case is, as the Supreme Court of Mississippi recognized, whether the twins were "domiciled" on the reservation.

A

The meaning of "domicile" in the ICWA is, of course, a matter of Congress' intent. The ICWA itself does not define it. The initial question we must confront is whether there is any reason to believe that Congress intended the ICWA definition of "domicile" to be a matter of state law. While the meaning of a federal statute is necessarily a federal question in the sense that its construction remains subject to this Court's supervision, Congress sometimes intends that a statutory term be given content by the application of state law. We start, however, with the general assumption that "in the absence of a plain indication to the contrary, . . . Congress when it enacts a statute is not making the application of the federal act dependent on state law." *Jerome v. United States*, 318 U.S. 101, 104, 63 S.Ct. 483, 485, 87 L.Ed. 640 (1943); *NLRB v. Natural Gas Utility Dist. of Hawkins County*, 402 U.S. 600, 603, 91 S.Ct. 1746, 1749, 29 L.Ed.2d 206 (1971); *Dickerson v. New Banner Institute, Inc.*, 460 U.S. 103, 119, 103 S.Ct. 986, 995, 74 L.Ed.2d 845 (1983). One reason for this rule of construction is that federal statutes are generally intended to have uniform nationwide application. Accordingly, the cases in which we have found that Congress intended a state-law definition of a statutory term have often been those where uniformity clearly was not intended. A second reason for the presumption against the application of state law is the danger that "the federal program would be impaired if state law were to control." *Jerome*, *supra*, 318 U.S., at 104, 63 S.Ct., at 486. For this reason, "we look to the purpose of the statute to ascertain what is intended." *Id.*, at 403. . . .

First, and most fundamentally, the purpose of the ICWA gives no reason to believe that Congress intended to rely on state law for the definition of a critical term; quite the contrary. It is clear from the very text of the ICWA, not to mention its legislative history and the hearings that led to its enactment, that Congress was concerned with the rights of Indian families and Indian communities vis-à-vis state authorities. More specifically, its purpose was, in part, to make clear that in certain situations the state courts did not have jurisdiction over child custody proceedings. Indeed, the congressional findings that are a part of the statute demonstrate that Congress perceived the States and their courts as partly responsible for the problem it intended to correct. See 25 U.S.C. § 1901(5) (state "judicial bodies . . . have often failed to recognize the essential tribal relations of Indian people and the cultural and social standards prevailing in Indian communities and families"). Under these circumstances it is most improbable that Congress would have intended to leave the scope of the statute's key jurisdictional provision subject to definition by state courts as a matter of state law.

Second, Congress could hardly have intended the lack of nationwide uniformity that would result from state-law definitions of domicile. An example will illustrate. In a case quite similar to this one, the New Mexico state courts found exclusive jurisdiction in the tribal court pursuant to § 1911(a), because the illegitimate child took the reservation domicile of its mother at birth—notwithstanding that the child was placed in the custody of adoptive parents 2 days after its off-reservation birth and the mother executed a consent to adoption 10 days later. *In re Adoption of Baby Child*, 102 N.M. 735, 737–738, 700 P.2d 198, 200–201 (App. 1985). Had that mother traveled to Mississippi to give birth, rather than to Albuquerque, a different result would have obtained if state-law definitions of domicile applied. The same, presumably, would be true if the child had been transported to Mississippi for adoption after her off-reservation birth in New Mexico. While the child's custody proceeding would have been subject to exclusive tribal jurisdiction in her home State, her mother, prospective adoptive parents, or an adoption intermediary could have obtained an adoption decree in state court merely by transporting her across state lines.[1] Even if we could conceive of a federal statute under which the rules of domicile (and thus of

1. [FN 20] Nor is it inconceivable that a State might apply its law of domicile in such a manner as to render inapplicable § 1911(a) even to a child who had lived several years on the reservation but was removed from it for the purpose of adoption. Even in the less extreme case, a state-law definition of domicile would likely spur the development of an adoption brokerage business. Indian children, whose parents consented (with or without financial inducement) to give them up, could be transported for adoption to States like Mississippi where the law of domicile permitted the proceedings to take place in state court.

jurisdiction) applied differently to different Indian children, a statute under which different rules apply from time to time to the same child, simply as a result of his or her transport from one State to another, cannot be what Congress had in mind....

It is undisputed in this case that the domicile of the mother (as well as the father) has been, at all relevant times, on the Choctaw Reservation. Thus, it is clear that at their birth the twin babies were also domiciled on the reservation, even though they themselves had never been there. The statement of the Supreme Court of Mississippi that "[a]t no point in time can it be said the twins ... were domiciled within the territory set aside for the reservation," 511 So.2d, at 921, may be a correct statement of that State's law of domicile, but it is inconsistent with generally accepted doctrine in this country and cannot be what Congress had in mind when it used the term in the ICWA.

Nor can the result be any different simply because the twins were "voluntarily surrendered" by their mother. Tribal jurisdiction under § 1911(a) was not meant to be defeated by the actions of individual members of the tribe, for Congress was concerned not solely about the interests of Indian children and families, but also about the impact on the tribes themselves of the large numbers of Indian children adopted by non-Indians. See 25 U.S.C. §§ 1901(3) ("[T]here is no resource that is more vital to the continued existence and integrity of Indian tribes than their children"), 1902 ("promote the stability and security of Indian tribes"). The numerous prerogatives accorded the tribes through the ICWA's substantive provisions, e.g., §§ 1911(a) (exclusive jurisdiction over reservation domiciliaries), 1911(b) (presumptive jurisdiction over nondomiciliaries), 1911(c) (right of intervention), 1912(a) (notice), 1914 (right to petition for invalidation of state-court action), 1915(c) (right to alter presumptive placement priorities applicable to state-court actions), 1915(e) (right to obtain records), 1919 (authority to conclude agreements with States), must, accordingly, be seen as a means of protecting not only the interests of individual Indian children and families, but also of the tribes themselves.

In addition, it is clear that Congress' concern over the placement of Indian children in non-Indian homes was based in part on evidence of the detrimental impact on the children themselves of such placements outside their culture. Congress determined to subject such placements to the ICWA's jurisdictional and other provisions, even in cases where the parents consented to an adoption, because of concerns going beyond the wishes of individual parents. As the 1977 Final Report of the congressionally established American Indian Policy Review Commission stated, in summarizing these two concerns, "[r]emoval of Indian children from their cultural setting seriously impacts a long-term tribal survival and has damaging social and psychological impact on many individual Indian children." Senate Report, at 52.

These congressional objectives make clear that a rule of domicile that would permit individual Indian parents to defeat the ICWA's jurisdictional scheme is inconsistent with what Congress intended. The appellees in this case argue strenuously that the twins' mother went to great lengths to give birth off the reservation so that her children could be adopted by the Holyfields. But that was precisely part of Congress' concern. Permitting individual members of the tribe to avoid tribal exclusive jurisdiction by the simple expedient of giving birth off the reservation would, to a large extent, nullify the purpose the ICWA was intended to accomplish. The Supreme Court of Utah expressed this well in its scholarly and sensitive opinion in what has become a leading case on the ICWA:

> To the extent that [state] abandonment law operates to permit [the child's] mother to change [the child's] domicile as part of a scheme to facilitate his adoption by non-Indians while she remains a domiciliary of the reservation, it conflicts with and undermines the operative scheme established by subsections [1911(a)] and [1913(a)] to deal with children of domiciliaries of the reservation and weakens considerably the tribe's ability to assert its interest in its children. The protection of this tribal interest is at the core of the ICWA, which recognizes that the tribe has an interest in the child which is distinct from but on a parity with the interest of the parents. This relationship between Indian tribes and Indian children domiciled on the reservation finds no parallel in other ethnic cultures found in the United States. It is a relationship that many non-Indians find difficult to understand and that non-Indian courts are slow to recognize. It is precisely in recognition of this relationship, however, that the ICWA designates the tribal court as the exclusive forum for the determination of custody and adoption matters for reservation-domiciled Indian children, and the preferred forum for nondomiciliary Indian children. [State] abandonment law cannot be used to frustrate the federal legislative judgment expressed in the ICWA that the interests of the tribe in custodial decisions made with respect to Indian children are as entitled to respect as the interests of the parents.

In re Adoption of Halloway, 732 P.2d 962, 969–970 (1986).

We agree with the Supreme Court of Utah that the law of domicile Congress used in the ICWA cannot be one that permits individual reservation-domiciled tribal members to defeat the tribe's exclusive jurisdiction by the simple expedient of giving birth and placing the child for adoption off the reservation. Since, for purposes of the ICWA, the twin babies in this case were domiciled on the reservation when adoption proceedings were begun, the Choctaw tribal court possessed exclusive jurisdiction pursuant to 25 U.S.C. § 1911(a). The Chancery Court of Harrison County was, accordingly, without jurisdiction to enter a decree of adoption; under ICWA § 104, 25 U.S.C. § 1914, its decree of January 28, 1986, must be vacated.

III

We are not unaware that over three years have passed since the twin babies were born and placed in the Holyfield home, and that a court deciding their fate today is not writing on a blank slate in the same way it would have in January 1986. Three years' development of family ties cannot be undone, and a separation at this point would doubtless cause considerable pain. Whatever feelings we might have as to where the twins should live, however, it is not for us to decide that question. We have been asked to decide the legal question of who should make the custody determination concerning these children—not what the outcome of that determination should be. The law places that decision in the hands of the Choctaw tribal court. Had the mandate of the ICWA been followed in 1986, of course, much potential anguish might have been avoided, and in any case the law cannot be applied so as automatically to "reward those who obtain custody, whether lawfully or otherwise, and maintain it during any ensuing (and protracted) litigation." *Halloway*, 732 P.2d, at 972. It is not ours to say whether the trauma that might result from removing these children from their adoptive family should outweigh the interest of the Tribe—and perhaps the children themselves—in having them raised as part of the Choctaw community. Rather, "we must defer to the experience, wisdom, and compassion of the [Choctaw] tribal courts to fashion an appropriate remedy." *Ibid.*

Justice STEVENS, with whom THE CHIEF JUSTICE and Justice KENNEDY join, dissenting.

The ICWA was passed in 1978 in response to congressional findings that "an alarmingly high percentage of Indian families are broken up by the *removal*, often unwarranted, of their children from them by nontribal public and private agencies," and that "the States, exercising their recognized jurisdiction over Indian child custody proceedings through administrative and judicial bodies, have often failed to recognize the essential tribal relations of Indian people and the cultural and social standards prevailing in Indian communities and families." 25 U.S.C. §§ 1901(4), (5) (emphasis added). The Act is thus primarily addressed to the unjustified removal of Indian children from their families through the application of standards that inadequately recognized the distinct Indian culture....

The Act gives Indian tribes certain rights, not to restrict the rights of parents of Indian children, but to complement and help effect them. The Indian tribe may petition to transfer an action in state court to the tribal court, but the Indian parent may veto the transfer. § 1911(b). The Act provides for a tribal right of notice and intervention in involuntary proceedings but not in voluntary ones. §§ 1911(c), 1912(a). Finally, the tribe may petition the court to set aside a parental termination action upon a showing that the provisions of the ICWA that are designed to protect parents and Indian children have been violated. § 1914....

The interpretation of domicile adopted by the Court requires the custodian of an Indian child who is off the reservation to haul the child to a potentially distant tribal court unfamiliar with the child's present living conditions and best interests. Moreover, it renders any custody decision made by a state court forever suspect, susceptible to challenge at any time as void for having been entered in the absence of jurisdiction. Finally, it forces parents of Indian children who desire to invoke state-court jurisdiction to establish a domicile off the reservation. Only if the custodial parent has the wealth and ability to establish a domicile off the reservation will the parent be able to use the processes of state court. I fail to see how such a requirement serves the paramount congressional purpose of "promot[ing] the stability and security of Indian tribes and families." 25 U.S.C. § 1902.

Notes

1. This case is a ringing endorsement of the principles of ICWA, and a statement to the states of the intended uniformity of the law. However, as is illustrated throughout the following chapters, states continued to chip away at ICWA using state law. The Supreme Court did not take another ICWA case until 2013, so while *Mississippi Choctaw* still governs, state decisions have varied wildly. Is it even possible for states to have uniform definitions of family law, or is it inherently local?

2. The Court quotes from *In re Adoption of Halloway*, 732 P.2d 962 (Utah 1986), a very early ICWA jurisdictional decision. In that case, a maternal aunt of a Navajo child removed him from the reservation where he was living with his grandmother and put him up for adoption in Utah to a non-Indian couple. The aunt acknowledged that she did so to avoid the Nation's social services, and to avoid tribal jurisdiction. Nearly two years after the adoption petition, the Navajo Nation intervened in the proceedings and moved to dismiss them because the Nation had jurisdiction over the case. The case turned on the child's domicile and whether his mother abandoned him.

The Utah Supreme Court wrote, "[i]n determining the correctness of the trial court's assumption of jurisdiction over Jeremiah, we must look to federal law, for the ICWA grants state courts jurisdiction to act regarding Indian child custody and adoption matters under only limited circumstances, while it grants tribal courts broad jurisdiction over such matters." *Halloway*, 732 P.2d at 965. While ICWA does not so much grant jurisdiction over Indian children to Indian tribes as divide up preexisting jurisdiction, the Court's reading of the law is one of the reasons the *Mississippi Choctaw* case came out the way it did.

3. In Mississippi, there was a six month waiting period between the first interlocutory decree and final decree, with the discretion of the chancellor to waive the requirement. How much of ICWA is a federally enforced scheme to ensure *standard* family law protections are applied to Indian people? The Mississippi courts essentially changed their own state definition of domicile to get around the requirements of ICWA. If the state's common law definition of domicile had matched the lower court's decision, would the Supreme Court have overturned the decision? Why did the lower court distinguish the usual domicile rule from this case?

4. In her chapter in *Family Law Stories*, Solangel Maldonado recounts background information on the case through interviews, including one with the adoptive mother, Joan Holyfield. After the Supreme Court decision, the Choctaw Social Services did a home study, and based on that and the recommendation of the guardian ad litem, the Choctaw judge allowed the children to stay in the adoptive home. He did order the children to remain in contact with their tribe and extended family members.

Solangel Maldonado, *The Story of the Holyfield Twins: Mississippi Band of Choctaw Indians v. Holyfield, in* FAMILY LAW STORIES (Carol Sanger ed., 2008).

5. The Court cites to a fairly well-known pre-ICWA jurisdiction case, *Fisher v. District Court*, 424 U.S. 382 (1976), which held that the Northern Cheyenne Tribe had exclusive jurisdiction over an adoption dispute involving all tribal members living on the reservation. Interestingly, in that case, the state district court certified a question to the Northern Cheyenne Appellate court, asking for an interpretation of Northern Cheyenne code. The tribal appellate court responded:

> "It is the opinion of this Court, and this Court so rules, that the Tribal Court has exclusive jurisdiction of all adoptions of members of the Northern Cheyenne Tribe of Indians where it appears that the minor who is being adopted and all other parties to the adoption proceedings, which is to say, the parent and/or parents of the minor and the person and/or persons adopting said minor are each and all members of the Northern Cheyenne Tribe and each and all reside within the exterior boundaries of the Northern Cheyenne Indian Reservation.
>
> "This Court has not been called upon to decide any issue involving non-members of the Northern Cheyenne Tribe or non-Indians or both, who wish to adopt a member of the Northern Cheyenne Tribe. Therefore, this Court does not make any opinion or interpretation as to the provisions of the last (3rd) paragraph of said Section 1 of Chapter III of the Tribal Code." *In re Firecrow*, at 5 (filed Apr. 12, 1975).

424 U.S. at 384 n.6. The district court agreed, and dismissed the case. The Montana Supreme Court reversed, and the U.S. Supreme Court reversed the Montana Supreme Court, upholding the tribal appellate court's original opinion.

C. Public Law 83-280's Jurisdictional Effect

The jurisdictional provision of ICWA includes a reference to when jurisdiction has been otherwise vested in the state by federal law. This is a reference to Public Law 83-280 (P.L. 280), passed in 1953 during what is known as the "Termination Period." *See* GETCHES ET AL., CASES AND MATERIALS ON FEDERAL INDIAN LAW 200-15 (6th ed. 2011). Congress's attempt to end its political relationship with Indian tribes and assimilate tribal citizens has since been formally repudiated, but P.L. 280 remains on the books.

P.L. 280 allowed six states to assume both criminal and civil jurisdiction over Indian country within its borders. The states include Alaska (except the Metlakatla Indian Community for criminal), California, Minnesota (except the Red Lake Reservation), Nebraska, Oregon (except the Warm Springs Reservation), and Wisconsin. *See* WILLIAM C. CANBY JR., AMERICAN INDIAN LAW IN A NUTSHELL 232-58 (4th ed. 2004). Though P.L. 280 purported to place jurisdiction on the reservation in the hands of the state, courts and commentators have come to agree that state civil jurisdiction on reservations is to be construed narrowly. *Bryan v. Itasca County*, 426 U.S. 373 (1976); COHEN'S HANDBOOK OF FEDERAL INDIAN LAW, *supra* at 546. The Wisconsin Attorney General found that P.L. 280 did not grant the state "general jurisdiction over child custody matters." Jurisdictional Questions Relating to the Implementation of the Indian Child Welfare Act Discussed, 70 Op. Att'y Gen. Wisc. 237 (1981). Carole Goldberg, *Public Law 280: The Limits of State Jurisdiction Over Reservation Indians*, 22 UCLA L. REV. 535, 541 (1975). However, P.L. 280 was not a divestiture statute, nor a removal of jurisdiction *from* tribes. *See California v. Cabazon Band of Mission Indians*, 480 U.S. 202, 207-12 (1987). In other words, tribes in P.L. 280 states with tribal courts, such as the White Earth Band, Leech Lake Band, and Mille Lacs Band, continue to maintain concurrent jurisdiction over family law issues, and may have exclusive jurisdiction over some family law issues. B.J. JONES ET AL., THE INDIAN CHILD WELFARE ACT HANDBOOK 54 (2d ed. 2008); BARBARA ANN ATWOOD, CHILDREN, TRIBES, AND STATES: ADOPTION AND CUSTODY CONFLICTS OVER AMERICAN INDIAN CHILDREN 80 (2010).

Native Village of Venetie I.R.A. Council v. State of Alaska

944 F.2d 548 (9th Cir. 1991)

We must decide whether federal law requires the state of Alaska to accord "full faith and credit" to child-custody determinations made by the tribal courts of native villages.

The native villages of Venetie and Fort Yukon lie on or above the Arctic Circle in Alaska's frozen tundra. Venetie has a population of 132, according to the 1980 census, all but three of whom are native. Five hundred and eighty-six people reside in Fort Yukon; 442 are native.

The native villages are organized under the Indian Reorganization Act ("I.R.A."). *See* 25 U.S.C. § 476 (1988). The villages' I.R.A. councils, two of the plaintiffs in this action, are the duly organized and elected governing bodies of the native villages.

Plaintiff Margaret Solomon is an Athabascan Indian from the Native Village of Fort Yukon. In the fall of 1985, Solomon was asked whether she would adopt a child born on September 28, 1985. She went to Fairbanks to pick up the infant, then eight days old. On May 27, 1986, the tribal court of the Native Village of Fort Yukon purported to formalize the adoption. Subsequently, in October 1986, Alaska denied Solomon benefits under the Aid to Families with Dependent Children program. State welfare officials informed Solomon that the state would not recognize the purported adoption and that the child was therefore not eligible for AFDC benefits.

Nancy Joseph is also an Athabascan Indian from the Native Village of Fort Yukon. One of Joseph's relatives, an expectant mother, asked Joseph to adopt the baby following the child's birth. Joseph agreed, and took the child home from the hospital shortly after his birth on February 24, 1986.

As the child's natural mother was from Venetie, she consented to the adoption in the tribal court of the Native Village of Venetie. Joseph subsequently requested a substitute birth certificate showing her to be the child's mother. However, the Bureau of Vital Statistics of the state of Alaska denied the request, observing that the Bureau "does not give recognition to native or tribal council adoption orders at this time."

In June 1986, Joseph was laid off her job at the University of Alaska. After she had exhausted her unemployment benefits, she applied for AFDC benefits. On October 20, 1986, the Division of Public Assistance denied Joseph's application, informing her that "the courts have not recognized the Tribal adoption of the child. You should reapply when you can prove that you are the mother of the child."

Ms. Joseph, Ms. Solomon, the Native Village of Venetie I.R.A. Council, and the Native Village of Fort Yukon I.R.A. Council brought this suit in the United States District Court for the District of Alaska. They sought to enjoin the state of Alaska and certain of its officials from refusing to recognize the tribal court adoptions. The plaintiffs asserted that under the Indian Child Welfare Act of 1978 ("Act"), 25 U.S.C. §§ 1901–1963 (1988), Alaska was required to give full faith and credit to the native-village adoption decrees. *See id.* § 1911(d). . . .

Congress enacted the Indian Child Welfare Act in 1978 pursuant to the national policy "to protect the best interests of Indian children and to promote the stability and security of Indian tribes." 25 U.S.C. § 1902 (1988). To promote this policy, Congress established in the Act "minimum Federal standards for the removal of Indian children from their families" and sought to ensure "the placement of such children in foster or adoptive homes which will reflect the unique values of Indian culture." *Id.*

As the primary mechanism for advancing its objectives in the Act, Congress created a comprehensive jurisdictional scheme for the resolution of custody disputes involving Indian children. This scheme expanded the role of tribal courts and correspondingly decreased the scope of state court jurisdiction. Indeed, state courts are powerless to resolve child-custody disputes concerning Indian children who reside on their tribal reservations; jurisdiction is exclusive in the tribe. *See id* § 1911(a). In the case of Indian children who do not reside or are not domiciled on their tribe's reservation, state courts may exercise jurisdiction concurrent with tribal courts. However, the state court must refer the dispute to the appropriate tribal court unless good cause is shown for the retention of state court jurisdiction. *See id.* § 1911(b); *see also Mississippi Band of Choctaw Indians v. Holyfield*, 490 U.S. 30, 35, 109 S.Ct. 1597, 1601, 104 L.Ed.2d 29 (1989) ("Section 1911(b) . . . creates concurrent but presumptively tribal jurisdiction in the case of children not domiciled on the reservation . . . ."). Most importantly, whether such tribal jurisdiction is concurrent with or exclusive of state jurisdiction, all courts in the United States must give full faith and credit to the child-custody determinations of tribal courts to the same extent that full faith and credit are given to the decisions of any other entity. *See* 25 U.S.C. § 1911(d) (1988).

For some tribes, the exclusive and referral jurisdiction provisions of sections 1911(a) and (b) became effective automatically following the enactment of the

Act. However, tribes located within so-called Public Law 280 states, which include Alaska, can invoke such jurisdiction only after petitioning the Secretary of the Interior. *See id.* § 1918(a). Upon receipt of a proper petition, the Secretary has several options. He may grant the tribe exclusive jurisdiction over the entire reservation as provided in section 1911(a), allow the tribe to exercise exclusive jurisdiction only over limited community or geographic areas, or permit the tribe to exercise only referral jurisdiction pursuant to section 1911(b). *See id.* § 1918(b)(2).

The Indian Child Welfare Act includes Alaska natives within its definition of "Indians." *See id.* § 1903(3). Similarly, Alaska native villages are "Indian tribes" within the meaning of the Act. *See id.* § 1903(8); 43 U.S.C. § 1602(c) (1982). The parties agree that Venetie and Fort Yukon come within the meaning of "Alaska Native Village" as defined by this Act. Similarly, both Ms. Joseph and Ms. Solomon are members of such an Alaska Native Village. Alaska, however, is a Public Law 280 state. Accordingly, the state contends that these native villages cannot exercise *any* child-custody jurisdiction unless and until they apply to the Secretary of the Interior and receive his approval as described above. The villages, on the other hand, maintain that they have, at the very least, concurrent jurisdiction by virtue of their inherent sovereignty.

In order to resolve this dispute, we must confront two issues. First, we must inquire whether the native villages are inherently sovereign, at least insofar as domestic relations or child-custody issues are concerned. Second, if such villages are possessed of such sovereignty, we must determine whether Congress has stripped the villages of that aspect of sovereign authority which encompasses child-custody determinations. We address each question in turn. . . .

In accordance with this doctrine of inherent tribal sovereignty, it follows that the Indian groups to be recognized as sovereigns should be those entities which historically acted as bodies politic, particularly in the periods prior to their subjugation by non-natives. There is, however, an additional prerequisite that an Indian group must meet in order to achieve present-day recognition as a sovereign: the modern-day group must demonstrate some relationship with or connection to the historical entity. *See United States v. State of Washington,* 641 F.2d 1368, 1372–73 (9th Cir.1981), *cert. denied,* 454 U.S. 1143, 102 S.Ct. 1001, 71 L.Ed.2d 294 (1982); *Mashpee Tribe v. New Seabury Corp.,* 592 F.2d 575, 585–87 (1st Cir.), *cert. denied,* 444 U.S. 866, 100 S. Ct. 138, 62 L.Ed.2d 90 (1979). In *United States v. State of Washington,* we held that in order for a group of Indians to enjoy the benefits of a treaty between the federal government and the tribe from which the Indians descended, the "group [of Indians] must have maintained an organized tribal structure." *State of Washington,* 641 F.2d at 1372. "[T]ribal status is preserved," we held, "if some defining characteristic of the original tribe persists in an evolving tribal community." *Id.* at 1372–73.

With these fundamental concepts in mind, we turn to Alaska. Following the United States' purchase of Alaska in 1867, Congress paid little heed to the region's natives and was content to leave their legal status unresolved. The courts, however, could not escape the issue so easily. In a series of cases, Judge Matthew Deady, a federal district judge with chambers in the Pioneer Courthouse in Portland, Oregon, but occasionally sitting on the circuit court with jurisdiction extending to Alaska, held that Alaska was not "Indian country" for purposes of either the Indian Intercourse Act or the Revised Statutes of the United States. *See United States v. Seveloff,* 27 F.Cas. 1021, 1022 (D.Or.1872) (No. 16,252); *Waters v. Campbell,* 29 F. Cas. 411, 411–12 (C.C.D.Or.1876) (No. 17,264); *Kie v. United States,* 27 F. 351, 352–55 (C.C.D.Or.1886). Ultimately, a newly-created federal district court for Alaska expanded Judge Deady's view and declared that Alaska native groups were not independent sovereigns. The Alaska district court concluded that "[t]he United States has at no time recognized any tribal independence or relations among these Indians, . . . [and that] they have been and now are regarded as dependent subjects." *In re Sah Quah,* 31 F. 327, 329 (D.Alaska 1886); *see also id.* ("their system is essentially patriarchal, and not tribal").

As a result of these decisions, Alaska natives were treated as divorced from the rules of Indian law which applied to lower-forty-eight tribes. *See Native Village of Venetie [v. Alaska],* 687 F.Supp. at 1393 ("The law of aboriginal peoples in Alaska has remained distinct from Indian law for the continental United States, because of the different historical path taken in Alaska."); Harring, [*The Incorporation of Alaskan Natives Under American Law: United States and Tlingit Sovereignty, 1867–1900,* 31 Ariz. L. Rev. 279, 283–84 (1989)], at 293 n. 103 ("The cumulative effect of Deady's opinions was to deprive Alaska natives of the same right to sovereignty over their political affairs that Indians in the rest of the United States had."). The district court in the case at bar believed that a partial reconciliation had occurred: "Since *Sah Quah,* Alaska has been partially assimilated to the national body of Indian law." 687 F.Supp. at 1393.

The district court erred, however, in believing that reconciliation was even necessary. Judge Deady's superannuated views of tribal sovereignty notwithstanding, such notions are not the law of the land today. Rather, if native groups in Alaska were sovereign prior to the incorporation of the land mass into the United States, they could lose their sovereignty only by express act of Congress or assimilation by the natives into non-native culture.

Indian sovereignty flows from the historical roots of the Indian tribe. *See* [*United States v.*] *Wheeler,* 435 U.S. at 322–23, 98 S.Ct. at 1085–86 [(1978)]. Tribal sovereignty exists unless and until affirmatively divested by Congress. *See id.* at 323, 98 S.Ct. at 1086. Thus, to the extent that Alaska's natives formed bodies politic to govern domestic relations, to punish wrongdoers, and otherwise to provide for the general welfare, we perceive no reason why they, too, should not be recognized as having been sovereign entities. If the native villages of Venetie and Fort Yukon are the modern-day successors to sovereign historical bands of natives, the villages are to be afforded the same rights and responsibilities as are sovereign bands of native Americans in the continental United States.

V

Our inquiry cannot end here, however, as all is for naught if Congress has divested the villages of any inherent authority or sovereignty to make child-custody determinations. The state of Alaska contends that such a statutory divestiture exists. Public Law 83–280, the state asserts, stripped the villages of whatever authority they may have had to make child-custody determinations. Alaska contends, and the district court apparently agreed, that Public Law 280 vested the enumerated states with exclusive, not merely concurrent, jurisdiction over civil and criminal matters involving Indians. *See Native Village of Venetie,* 687 F.Supp. at 1382 ("Some states, called 'Public Law 280 states,' operate under federal statutes stripping tribal courts of most of their traditional jurisdiction, and giving state courts jurisdiction over Indian country in most respects.").

Alaska buttresses this contention by invoking section 1918 of the Indian Child Welfare Act, which provides that "[a]ny Indian tribe which became subject to State jurisdiction pursuant to [Public Law 280] . . . may reassume jurisdiction over child custody proceedings" by following certain procedures. 25 U.S.C. § 1918(a) (1988). Alaska contends that section 1918 would be a meaningless provision if Public Law 280 did not vest exclusive jurisdiction in the states; if jurisdiction is not exclusive in the states, Alaska asks, what is there for the native villages to "reassume" under section 1918?

We must begin our analysis of Alaska's argument with a brief overview of Public Law 280. Enacted in 1953, Public Law 280 mandated the transfer of civil and criminal jurisdiction over "Indian country" from the federal government to the governments of five states, and permitted other states to assume such jurisdiction voluntarily. In 1958, Alaska was added to the list of mandatory Public Law 280 jurisdictions. See Act of Aug. 8, 1958, Pub.L. No. 85–615, § 2, 72 Stat. 545. The civil portion of Public Law 280 provides as follows:

> Each of the [mandatory Public Law 280] States . . . shall have jurisdiction over civil causes of action between Indians or to which Indians are parties which arise in the areas of Indian country listed opposite the name of the State to the same extent that such State has jurisdiction over other civil causes of action, and those civil laws of such State that are of general application to private persons or private property shall have the same force and effect within such Indian country as they have elsewhere within the State.

It is not disputed that private adoption cases are included within this transfer of civil jurisdiction from the federal government to the states.

Although Public Law 280 was enacted during Congress's so-called "termination era" methodology of dealing with Indians, the law "plainly was not intended to effect total assimilation of Indian tribes into mainstream American society." *California v. Cabazon Band of Mission Indians,* 480 U.S. 202, 208, 107 S.Ct. 1083, 1087, 94 L.Ed.2d 244 (1987). The legislative history behind Public Law 280 is sparse, but Congress's primary motivation in enacting the legislation seems to have been a desire to remedy the lack of adequate criminal-law enforcement on some reservations. *See, e.g.*, S.Rep. No. 699, 83d Cong., 1st Sess., *reprinted in* 1953 U.S. Code Cong. & Admin. News 2409, 2412 ("[T]here has been created a hiatus in law-enforcement authority that could best be remedied by conferring criminal jurisdiction on States indicating an ability and willingness to accept such responsibility."); *see also Bryan v. Itasca County,* 426 U.S. 373, 379, 96 S.Ct. 2102, 2106, 48 L.Ed.2d 710 (1976) ("The primary concern of Congress in enacting Pub. L. 280 . . . was with the problem of lawlessness on certain Indian reservations, and the absence of adequate tribal institutions for law enforcement."); Goldberg, *Public Law 280: The Limits of State Jurisdiction Over Reservation Indians,* 22 U.C.L.A. L. Rev. 535, 540–44 (1975). In fact, certain tribes were exempted from the provisions of Public Law 280 because these tribes had a "'tribal law-and-order organization that function[ed] in a reasonably satisfactory manner.'" *Bryan,* 426 U.S. at 385, 96 S.Ct. at 2109, (quoting H.R.Rep. No. 848, 83d Cong., 1st Sess. 7, *reprinted in* 1953 U.S. Code Cong. & Admin. News 2413). In short, Public Law 280 was designed not to supplant tribal institutions, but to supplement them.

The Supreme Court has also adopted the view that Public Law 280 is not a divestiture statute. *See Cabazon Band of Mission Indians,* 480 U.S. at 207–12, 107 S.Ct. at 1087–90; *Bryan,* 426 U.S. at 383–90, 96 S.Ct. at 2108–12; *see also Walker v. Rushing,* 898 F.2d 672, 675 (8th Cir.1990) ("Public Law 280 did not itself divest Indian tribes of their sovereign power to punish their own members for violations of tribal law. Nothing in the wording of Public Law 280 or its legislative history precludes concurrent jurisdiction."). In *Bryan,* the Court observed that "nothing in [Public Law 280's] legislative history remotely suggests that Congress meant the Act's extension of civil jurisdiction to the States should result in the undermining or destruction of such tribal governments as did exist and a conversion of the affected tribes into little more than 'private voluntary organizations.'" 426 U.S. at 388, 96 S.Ct. at 2111 (quoting *United States v. Mazurie,* 419 U.S. 544, 557, 95 S.Ct. 710, 717, 42 L.Ed.2d 706 (1975)). The Court has rejected all interpretations of Public Law 280 which would result in an undermining or destruction of tribal governments. *See, e.g., Cabazon Band of Mission Indians,* 480 U.S. at 222, 107 S.Ct. at 1095 ("[s]tate regulation [of tribal bingo operation] would impermissibly infringe on tribal government" and therefore is not within Public Law 280's jurisdictional grant); *Bryan,* 426 U.S. at 388, 96 S.Ct. at 2110 ("[U]ndermining or destruction of such tribal governments . . . [is] a possible result if tribal governments and reservation Indians were subordinated to the full panoply of civil regulatory powers, including taxation, of state and local governments.").

In addition, the so-called mandatory Public Law 280 states have, to the extent that they have addressed the issue, considered jurisdiction to be concurrent under Public Law 280. The Wisconsin Attorney General has opined that "[f]or nonregulatory proceedings, such as voluntary termination of parental rights, the tribal courts, and state courts pursuant to Pub.L. 280, have concurrent jurisdiction." 70 Op. Att'y Gen. Wisc. 237, 243 (1981). Likewise, the Attorney General for the State of Nebraska has written: "[U]nder Public Law 280 the tribe retained substantial inherent tribal authority over civil matters arising in Indian country. While some of this tribal jurisdiction and authority may have been concurrent with state jurisdiction (i.e., existing together with it), or while the Tribe may have chosen not to exercise all of its authority and jurisdiction, nonetheless that tribal jurisdiction and authority was always there." Opinion No. 48, Opinion Letter from Robert M. Spire, Attorney General (Charles E. Lowe, Ass't Att'y General) to State Senator James E. Goll (March 28, 1985).

Finally, we note that Congress was aware, while drafting the Indian Child Welfare Act, that the U.S. Department of Justice viewed Public Law 280 as providing for concurrent jurisdiction among state and tribal courts. Then-Assistant Attorney General for Legislative Affairs Patricia M. Wald wrote to Interior and Insular Affairs Committee Chairman Morris K. Udall: "As you may be aware, the courts have consistently recognized that tribal governments have exclusive jurisdiction over the domestic relationships of tribal members located on reservations, *unless a State has assumed concurrent jurisdiction pursuant to Federal legislation such as Public Law 83–280.*" Letter from Assistant Attorney General Patricia M. Wald to Hon. Morris K. Udall (Feb. 8, 1978), included in H.R.Rep. No. 1386, 95th Cong., 2d Sess. 35, *reprinted in* 1978 U.S. Code Cong. & Admin. News 7530, 7558 (emphasis added).

In spite of the foregoing, Alaska suggests that section 1918 of the Indian Child Welfare Act would be rendered meaningless by any non-divestiture interpretation of Public Law 280. However, the two statutes can be harmonized without construing Public Law 280 as a divestiture statute. *See Ruckelshaus v. Monsanto Co.*, 467 U.S. 986, 1018, 104 S.Ct. 2862, 2880, 81 L.Ed.2d 815 (1984) (statutes capable of being harmonized should be so construed). The relevant portions of the Indian Child Welfare Act enable the Secretary of the Interior to grant to a tribe, upon receipt of a proper petition, exclusive jurisdiction (over all or a portion of the appropriate "Indian country") or referral jurisdiction of child-custody proceedings. *See* 25 U.S.C. § 1918(b)(2) (1988). Each of these types of jurisdiction is broader than any tribal jurisdiction which is concurrent with the states. Exclusive jurisdiction, of course, is clearly broader than concurrent jurisdiction. Likewise, referral jurisdiction is broader in scope than concurrent jurisdiction, in that referral jurisdiction is concurrent *but presumptively tribal* jurisdiction. *See id.* § 1911(b). Thus, there is something for a tribe to "reassume" under section 1918—namely, exclusive or referral jurisdiction—even if Public Law 280 is read as not divesting the tribes of concurrent jurisdiction.

In sum, giving the benefit of doubt to Alaska, we conclude that Public Law 280 and the Indian Child Welfare Act are, at best, ambiguous as to whether states have exclusive or concurrent jurisdiction over child custody determinations where the tribe has not petitioned for exclusive or referral jurisdiction. Of course, ambiguities are to be resolved to the benefit of Indians. *Montana v. Blackfeet Tribe,* 471 U.S. 759, 766, 105 S.Ct. 2399, 2403, 85 L.Ed.2d 753 (1985). Accordingly, resolving the jurisdictional ambiguities in favor of the villages, we hold that neither the Indian Child Welfare Act nor Public Law 280 prevents them from exercising concurrent jurisdiction. If the native villages of Venetie and Fort Yukon are sovereign entities which may exercise dominion over their members' domestic relations, Alaska must give full faith and credit to any child-custody determinations made by the villages' governing bodies in accordance with the full faith and credit clause of the Indian Child Welfare Act.

Notes

1. In 2005, the Ninth Circuit again considered the interaction between P.L. 280 and ICWA in *Doe v. Mann*, 415 F.3d 1038 (9th Cir. 2005). The case addressed the issue of an involuntary termination of parental rights, rather than a voluntary adoption. The court determined that Congress "intended Public Law 280 states to have jurisdiction over Indian child dependence proceedings unless tribes availed themselves of § 1918 in order to obtain *exclusive* jurisdiction." *Id.* at 1064 (emphasis added). While Section 1918 of ICWA is titled "Resumption of jurisdiction over child custody proceedings" and states that a tribe subject to P.L. 280 must petition the Secretary of the Interior to reassume jurisdiction, and provide a "suitable plan to exercise such jurisdiction," the question is one of exclusive jurisdiction, not concurrent.

2. In addition, at the time of the *Mann* decision, no tribal court in California had petitioned for such resumption of jurisdiction. *See* Barbara Ann Atwood, Children, Tribes, and States 171 (2010). California tribal courts were still exercising jurisdiction over child welfare issues prior to the *Mann* decision, because tribes do not lose jurisdiction under P.L. 280. How does the *Venetie* case explain this?

D. Transfer to Tribal Court

Under § 1911(b), upon petition by the tribe or the parent, a state court shall transfer the case to tribal court absent good cause to the contrary. ICWA does not define good cause, which leads to some of the most difficult litigation under ICWA. Even the Bureau of Indian Affairs Guidelines good cause examples give limited useful guidance for courts. The Guidelines, promulgated in 1979, and completely revised in 2015, and again in 2016, are not federal regulations, and are therefore not binding on state courts. 80 Fed. Reg. 10,146 (Feb. 25, 2015). However, the 2016 federal regulations are binding. In the case of transfer to tribal court, the regulations state:

§ 23.117 What are the criteria for ruling on transfer petitions?

Upon receipt of a transfer petition from an Indian child's parent, Indian custodian, or Tribe, the State court must transfer the child-custody proceeding unless the court determines that transfer is not appropriate because one or more of the following criteria are met:

(a) Either parent objects to such transfer;

(b) The Tribal court declines the transfer; or

(c) Good cause exists for denying the transfer.

§ 23.118 How is a determination of "good cause" to deny transfer made?

(a) If the State court believes, or any party asserts, that good cause to deny transfer exists, the reasons for that belief or assertion must be stated orally on the record or provided in writing on the record and to the parties to the child-custody proceeding.

(b) Any party to the child-custody proceeding must have the opportunity to provide the court with views regarding whether good cause to deny transfer exists.

(c) In determining whether good cause exists, the court must not consider:

(1) Whether the foster-care or termination-of-parental-rights proceeding is at an advanced stage if the Indian child's parent, Indian custodian, or Tribe did not receive notice of the child-custody proceeding until an advanced stage;

(2) Whether there have been prior proceedings involving the child for which no petition to transfer was filed;

(3) Whether transfer could affect the placement of the child;

(4) The Indian child's cultural connections with the Tribe or its reservation; or

(5) Socioeconomic conditions or any negative perception of Tribal or BIA social services or judicial systems.

(d) The basis for any State-court decision to deny transfer should be stated orally on the record or in a written order.

25 C.F.R. § 23.117-8 (2016)

While the federal regulations replace and supersede the 1979 Guidelines, it is worth comparing the two in order to understand precedent in transfer cases.

1979 Guidelines:

C.3 Determination of Good Cause to the Contrary

a. Good cause not to transfer the proceeding exists if the Indian child's tribe does not have a tribal court as defined by the Act to which the case can be transferred.

b. Good cause not to transfer this proceeding may exist if any of the following circumstances exists:

i. The proceeding was at an advanced stage when the petition to transfer was received and the petitioner did not file the petition promptly after receiving notice of the hearing.

ii. The Indian child is over twelve years of age and objects to the transfer.

iii. The evidence necessary to decide the case could not be adequately presented in the tribal court without undue hardship to the parties or the witnesses.

iv. The parents of a child over five years of age are not available and the child has had little or no contact with the child's tribe or members of the child's tribe.

c. Socio-economic conditions and the perceived adequacy of tribal or Bureau of Indian Affairs social services or judicial systems may not be considered in a determination that good cause exists.

d. The burden of establishing good cause to the contrary shall be on the party opposing the transfer.

1979 BIA Guidelines, 44 Fed.Reg. 67,583, 67,591

Unfortunately, there was no consistent understanding of "advanced stage" of the proceedings across the states. Timeliness depended on which court was making the determination. The federal regulations now make clear that the right to request transfer is available at any stage in the proceedings. 25 C.F.R. § 23.118.

In re Tavian B.

292 Neb. 804 (2016)

Assignments of Error

Appellant assigns, summarized and consolidated, that the juvenile court erred in finding good cause to deny his motion to transfer based on the advanced stage of the proceeding.

* * *

Analysis

The issue is whether the juvenile court abused its discretion in denying Appellant's motion to transfer the proceeding to tribal court. A judicial abuse of discretion exists when a judge, within the effective limits of authorized judicial power, elects to act or refrain from action, which results in a decision which is untenable and unfairly deprives a litigant of a substantial right or a just result in matters submitted for disposition. See *In re Interest of L.V.*, 240 Neb. 404, 482 N.W.2d 250 (1992).

We apply ICWA to the case at bar. Neb. Rev. Stat. § 43–1504(2) (Reissue 2008) governs motions to transfer jurisdiction to tribal courts under ICWA. At the time this case commenced, § 43–1504 provided:

> (2) In any state court proceeding for the foster care placement of, or termination of parental rights to, an Indian child not domiciled or residing within the reservation of the Indian child's tribe, the court, *in the absence of good cause to the contrary*, shall transfer such proceeding to the jurisdiction of the tribe, absent objection by either parent, upon the petition of either parent or the Indian custodian or the Indian child's tribe, except that such transfer shall be subject to declination by the tribal court of such tribe.

(Emphasis supplied.)

At a hearing on a motion to transfer a proceeding to tribal court, the party opposing the transfer has the burden of establishing that good cause not to transfer exists. *In re Interest of Zylena R. & Adrionna R., supra* [284 Neb. 834, 825 N.W.2d 173 (2012)]. In *In re Interest of Zylena R. & Adrionna R.*, we held that a proceeding for termination of parental rights should be regarded as a separate and distinct proceeding from foster care placement. In the case at bar, the Tribe accepted jurisdiction and neither parent objected to the transfer. Thus, absent the State's showing of good cause, the juvenile court was required to transfer the proceeding to tribal court.

The juvenile court found that the State had met its burden of showing good cause because the proceeding was at an advanced stage. It reasoned that usually, the date for determining whether the case was at an advanced stage would be the date of the filing of a motion to terminate parental rights. Because the State withdrew its motion for termination of parental rights on January 6, 2015, the court concluded that May 16, 2013, was the date of the State's petition for adjudication. Using May 16, 2013, as the starting date, it concluded that the proceeding was at an advanced stage.

The juvenile court expressed concern that an Indian parent could play "an ICWA trump card at the eleventh hour" to transfer the case to tribal court. But we point out that the State's dismissal of its motion to terminate parental rights to avoid a transfer leaves an Indian child suspended in uncertainty. If the State sought a termination of parental rights, the party seeking transfer could file a new motion to transfer and the State could again dismiss the termination proceeding. The juvenile court's conclusion that the matter was in an advanced stage stemmed from the State's voluntary dismissal of the termination proceeding.

Good cause to overrule Appellant's motion to transfer to tribal court is not defined in ICWA. But the guidelines published by the Bureau of Indian Affairs (BIA guidelines) provide a basis for determining what constitutes good cause to deny motions to transfer. Previously, this court and other courts have looked to the BIA guidelines in making such determinations. See, *In re Interest of Zylena R. & Adrionna R.*, 284 Neb. 834, 825 N.W.2d 173 (2012); *In re Interest of C.W. et al.*, 239 Neb. 817, 479 N.W.2d 105 (1992), overruled on other grounds, *In re Interest of Zylena R. & Adrionna R., supra*. See, also, *People ex rel. T.I.*, 707 N.W.2d 826 (S.D.2005); *In re Adoption of S.W.*, 41 P.3d 1003 (Okla.Civ.App.2001); *In re A.P.*, 25 Kan.App.2d 268, 961 P.2d 706 (1998). The BIA guidelines provide guidance to state courts and child welfare agencies implementing ICWA and promote compliance with ICWA's stated goals by providing a framework and best practices for compliance.

At the time of the juvenile court ruling, the BIA guidelines provided that good cause not to transfer may exist if the proceeding was "at an advanced stage" when the petition to transfer was received and the petitioner failed to "file the petition promptly" after receiving notice. See Guidelines for State Courts; Indian Child Custody Proceedings, 44 Fed.Reg. 67,584, 67,591, C.3(b)(i) (Nov. 26, 1979) (not codified). While this appeal was pending, the BIA guidelines were amended. They now provide that in determining whether good cause exists to deny a motion to transfer to tribal court, the state court may not consider whether the case is at an advanced stage. See Guidelines for State Courts and Agencies in Indian Child Custody Proceedings, 80 Fed.Reg. 10,149 and 10,156 (Feb. 25, 2015) (not codified). This amendment compels us to reconsider our prior adherence to the advanced stage of the proceedings as a basis for good cause, and on which the juvenile court relied in denying the transfer.

The BIA guidelines state that there may be valid reasons for waiting to transfer a proceeding until it reaches an advanced stage. A tribe might decline to intervene during foster care placement proceedings when the goal is reunification with the parents, whereas the tribe would likely be much more concerned with removal of Indian children in termination proceedings. The BIA guidelines note that denial of motions to transfer because a proceeding is at an advanced stage undermines the presumption of tribal jurisdiction over proceedings involving Indian children not residing or domiciled on the reservation. We note that ICWA seeks to protect not only the rights of the Indian child as an Indian, but also the rights of Indian communities and tribes in retaining Indian children.

In our consideration of whether good cause existed to overrule the motion to transfer, we find the amended BIA guidelines persuasive and instructive. The BIA guidelines were amended during this appeal, and we find them applicable to the case at bar. We hold that a determination that the proceeding is at an advanced stage is no longer a valid basis for finding good cause to deny a motion to transfer jurisdiction to a tribal court. We conclude that the overruling of the motion to transfer denied Appellant a just result

* * *

STACY, J. concurring in part, and in part dissenting:

* * *

Role of Bia's Guidelines

The majority finds the 2015 BIA guidelines are "persuasive and instructive" on what constitutes good cause, and, on the facts of this case, I agree. But because the BIA's guidelines are nonbinding and do not have the force of federal regulations, it is appropriate to explain why we find the guidelines instructive, and clarify why we are, in this case, relying on the 2015 BIA guidelines to change established law.

As the majority recognizes, the BIA's guidelines are designed to promote compliance with the stated goals of the federal Indian Child Welfare Act of 1978 (ICWA) and are intended to provide a framework of best practices for state agencies and courts.6 But the advisory guidelines are simply the Department of the Interior's interpretation of certain provisions of ICWA. In other words, the guidelines are interpretive rather than legislative, and we are under no obligation to follow the guidelines if we conclude they are not in accord with the language or intent of ICWA on a particular point.

The guidelines were first published in 1979 and were not amended until 2015. The 2015 BIA guidelines, which became effective February 25, 2015, attempt to respond to national developments in ICWA jurisprudence. While the 2015 BIA guidelines are instructive, it is important to emphasize that this court does not change its jurisprudence simply because an executive agency has made amendments to nonbinding guidelines. Rather, this court should determine whether to follow the 2015 BIA guidelines on a particular issue only after carefully considering them and judicially determining they are in accord with both ICWA and the Nebraska Indian Child Welfare Act (NICWA) on that issue.

On the issue of the advanced stage of the proceedings, I note there is no language in ICWA or NICWA which expressly or impliedly limits the timeframe for making a motion to transfer to a tribal court. And it is significant that with the enactment of 2015 Neb. Laws, L.B. 566, the Legislature amended NICWA in several respects, one of which was to expressly recognize that Indian tribes have a "continuing and compelling" governmental interest in an Indian child. Particularly given the Legislature's strong language, I think it is apparent that denying a transfer merely because the proceedings are at an advanced stage when the motion is made would frustrate the purpose underlying ICWA and NICWA, and would undermine the presumption of tribal jurisdiction inherent in ICWA. But I leave for another day the question of whether the advanced stage of proceedings, if coupled with other compelling circumstances properly considered under ICWA and NICWA, can constitute good cause for denying a transfer.

Because the 2015 BIA guidelines' interpretation is more consistent with the language and intent of ICWA and NICWA on the advanced stage issue than was our precedent to the contrary, I agree that the mere advanced stage of the proceeding cannot provide good cause to deny a motion to transfer to tribal court. And because the advanced stage of the proceeding was the sole basis for the juvenile court's denial of the transfer to tribal court, I agree the juvenile court's decision cannot be upheld.

* * *

Good Cause

By choosing not to statutorily define "good cause" in the context of transfers under ICWA and NICWA, Congress and the Nebraska Legislature have left to state courts the primary responsibility for interpreting the term. This is not a simple task.

In the past, we have been called upon to interpret the undefined phrase "good cause" in statutory contexts outside ICWA, and we have recognized the complicated nature of such an exercise. We have defined good cause, in the context of a statute dealing with probate, as "a logical reason or legal ground, based on fact or law" and emphasized that the meaning of good cause is to be determined "in light of all of the surrounding circumstances." In the context of a criminal case considering an extension of time to prepare a bill of exceptions for good cause shown, we defined good cause as the intervention of something beyond the control of the litigant. We also have cited to Webster's Third New International Dictionary to define good cause as "'a cause or reason sufficient in law; one that is based on equity or justice or that would motivate a reasonable man under all the circumstances.'" Most recently, we examined the entirety of the relevant statute in determining the meaning of the phrase "good cause." Based on the foregoing, I would hold that good cause to deny a transfer under ICWA and NICWA means a compelling reason, based in law or fact, which is not contrary to the provisions or purposes of ICWA and NICWA and is sufficient to overcome the strong presumption of tribal jurisdiction. And I think having a general definition of good cause in the context of transfers would assist litigants and courts in analyzing factual situations not otherwise addressed in BIA's guidelines.

Historically, when interpreting good cause under ICWA, we have relied primarily on BIA's guidelines, rather than applying more traditional rules of statutory construction. But continued reliance on BIA's guidelines is problematic, because the 2015 BIA guidelines do not undertake to define good cause, and instead focus exclusively on identifying that which is not good cause. This has not always been the case.

Under the 1979 BIA guidelines, good cause to deny a transfer was recognized under four specific scenarios: (1) the proceeding was at an advanced stage when the motion to transfer was filed; (2) the Indian child was over 12 years of age and objected to the transfer; (3) the evidence necessary to decide the case could not be adequately presented in the tribal court without undue hardship to the parties or the witnesses; or (4) the parents of a child over 5 years of age are not available, and the child has had little or no contact with the child's tribe or members of the child's tribe. The 1979 BIA guidelines specifically noted that the third scenario, undue hardship, was included because 25 U.S.C. § 1911(b) of ICWA was "'intended to permit a State court to apply a modified doctrine of forum non conveniens, in appropriate cases, to [e]nsure that the rights of the child as an Indian, the Indian parents or custodian, and the tribe are fully protected.'"

For reasons which are not clear, the 2015 BIA guidelines omit all four of the good cause factors identified in the 1979 BIA guidelines, and instead list only those things the BIA has determined courts may not consider in determining whether good cause exists. As for what may still constitute good cause under ICWA, the 2015 BIA guidelines merely recite that good cause may be found if "the State court otherwise determines that good cause exists." The 2015 BIA guidelines explain why some of the 1979 good cause factors were omitted (including the factor regarding advanced proceedings) but are silent regarding why two of the 1979 factors (the factor addressing the preference of an Indian child over age 12, and the factor addressing undue hardship) were omitted from the 2015 BIA guidelines. Because there was no explanation given for omitting these factors, it is not possible to judicially determine whether the BIA's rationale for omitting these factors is in accord with ICWA and NICWA. But certainly, the lack of guidance from the Department of the Interior on this issue should not preclude state courts from considering whether these remain viable factors when determining good cause under ICWA and NICWA. And something must constitute good cause to deny a transfer to tribal court, because both ICWA and NICWA expressly authorize it:

> In any State court proceeding for the foster care placement of, or termination of parental rights to, an Indian child not domiciled or residing within the reservation of the Indian child's tribe, the court, in the absence of good cause to the contrary, shall transfer such proceeding to the jurisdiction of the tribe, absent objection by either parent, upon the petition of either parent or the Indian custodian or the Indian child's tribe: Provided, That such transfer shall be subject to declination by the tribal court of such tribe.

Statutory language is to be given its plain and ordinary meaning, and an appellate court's duty in discerning the meaning of a statute is to determine and give effect to the purpose and intent of the Legislature. Recognizing this, we must look beyond the notable silence of the 2015 BIA guidelines in order to determine and give effect to the good cause language in ICWA and NICWA.

In determining whether there is good cause to deny a transfer, I think it remains appropriate for courts to consider whether the evidence necessary to decide the case could be adequately presented in the tribal court without undue hardship to the parties or the witnesses. I note the 1979 BIA guidelines addressed this specifically:

> Consideration of whether or not the case can be properly tried in tribal court without hardship to the parties or witnesses was included [as a good cause factor] on the strength of the section-by-section analysis in the House Report on [ICWA], which stated with respect to the § 1911(b), "The subsection is intended to permit a State court to apply a modified doctrine of forum non conveniens, in appropriate cases, to [e]nsure that the rights of the child as an Indian, the Indian parents or custodian, and the tribe are fully protected." Where a child is in fact living in a dangerous situation, he or she should not be forced to remain there simply because the witnesses cannot afford to travel long distances to court.

The 1979 BIA guidelines went on to observe that "[a]pplication of this criterion will tend to limit transfers to cases involving Indian children who do not live very far from the reservation." It was suggested that problems with an inconvenient forum might be alleviated by "having the court come to the witnesses" or requiring the "tribal court meet in the city where the family lived."

I find persuasive the rationale provided in the comments to the 1979 BIA guidelines that the undue burden factor is actually a modified forum non conveniens analysis, and I note that prior to the 2015 BIA guidelines, Nebraska recognized this as a valid factor in the good cause analysis. I see no principled basis under the operative statutes or our jurisprudence to depart from that precedent. When determining whether the doctrine of forum non conveniens should be invoked, we have said the trial court should consider practical factors that make trial of the case easy, expeditious, and inexpensive, such as the relative ease of access to sources of proof, the cost of obtaining attendance of witnesses, and the ability to secure attendance of witnesses through the compulsory process. Particular factors to consider in ICWA and NICWA cases may include whether alternative methods of participation, such as by telephone or videoconferencing, are available. I note the juvenile court in this case made specific reference in its order to the fact that the tribal court was more than 430 miles from Lincoln, Nebraska.

By specifically mentioning forum non conveniens, I do not mean to suggest it is the only "good cause" factor which remains viable in the wake of the 2015 BIA guidelines. I note that when the Legislature amended NICWA in 2015, it added both a definition and a standard of proof for "good cause" in the context of placement preferences for Indian children:

> Good cause to deviate from the placement preferences in subsections (1) through (3) of this section includes: (a) The request of the biological parents or the Indian child when the Indian child is at least twelve years of age; (b) the extraordinary physical or emotional needs of the Indian child as established by testimony of a qualified expert witness; or (c) the unavailability of suitable families for placement after a diligent search has been completed for families meeting the preference criteria. The burden of establishing the existence of good cause to deviate from the placement preferences and order shall be by clear and convincing evidence on the party urging that the preferences not be followed.

This new definition of good cause appears instructive on the related task of determining good cause to deny a transfer request and illustrates several possible factors supporting a good cause finding which the Legislature has concluded are not contrary to the provisions or purpose of ICWA and NICWA.

Notes

1. By only stating what a court cannot consider good cause, did the 2015 Guidelines (and now federal regulations) open the door for courts to consider anything outside of that list good cause?

2. The reason behind the change in the Guidelines had to do with different interpretations of late stage by different states, as well as the tribal motivations for transfer. For example, sometimes tribes wait until the termination of parental rights has been completed at the state level before moving to transfer the case. *In re R.M.B.*,

724 N.W.2d 300, 309 (Minn. 2006); *In re A.L.*, 442 N.W.2d 233 (S.D. 1989); *In re* D.M., 685 N.W.2d 768, 772 (S.D. 2004); *In re S.G.V.E.*, 634 N.W.2d 88, 93 (S.D. 2001). ICWA defines four separate types of "proceedings": foster care, termination of parental rights, preadoptive placement, and adoptive placement. 25 U.S.C. § 1903(1)(i-iv) (2012). ICWA specifies transfer is available for both foster care placement and termination of parental rights, 25 U.S.C. § 1911(b), though some states have broadened that to include "any state court child custody proceeding" their statutes. *See* Mich. Comp. Laws § 712B.7(3) (2016). While a petition to transfer might be filed late in a foster care proceeding, it would be considered early for a termination proceeding. Because the federal definitions of proceedings do not map onto each individual state proceeding neatly, there is room for confusion in the state courts. Second, tribes may be in agreement with state proceedings prior to termination, and work with the state for reunification of the family. However, when the parental rights are terminated, the tribe then has a reason to transfer jurisdiction and ensure the child stays within the community. What is to the tribe a reasonable decision making process appears as indifference to the state court. *In re D.M.*, 685 N.W.2d 768, 772 (S.D. 2004).

3. The federal regulations now qualify the late stage of the proceedings by adding the requirement that "the Indian child's parent, Indian custodian, or Tribe did not receive notice of the child-custody proceeding until an advanced stage," tying the notice to the late stage. What if a tribe receives notice at the start of the proceeding, but still choses to petition for transfer later?

In re M.S.

237 P.3d 161 (Okla. 2010)

This case began as a deprived child proceeding in August, 2004, when an emergency petition was filed by the State of Oklahoma, ex rel. Department of Human Services, to remove M.S. and K.S. ("the children"), and their two older half-siblings, A.H. and K.H., from their parents' home. M.S. and K.S. are registered members of the Puyallup Tribe of Indians (the Tribe), as is their father. All of the children have the same mother, who is of Cherokee descent, but the two older children have a different father. All four children were placed in a foster home together, but the oldest child, A.H., an enrolled Cherokee member, moved to Texas to live with her biological father. M.S. and K.S. remained in the foster home with their older brother, K.H., also a Cherokee member, for approximately two years. On June 21, 2006, the parental rights of M.S.'s and K.S.'s parents were terminated. The Tribe then filed a petition to transfer the case to its tribal court in Tacoma, Washington, or alternatively, for placement of M.S. and K.S. with their great aunt in Florida, in compliance with the placement preferences in subchapter one of the Indian Child Welfare Act (ICWA), 25 U.S.C. §§ 1901–1923, specifically 25 U.S.C. § 1915(b). The trial court denied its requests, and the Tribe appealed. The Court of Civil Appeals ("COCA") affirmed.

The foster parents (the Simmons) have expressed an interest in adopting K.H., M.S. and K.S., although no petition for adoption had been filed as to M.S. and K.S.

at the time this appeal was commenced on October 26, 2006. During the pendency of this appeal, M.S. and K.S. were placed with their great aunt in Tampa, Florida. . . .

At issue in this case is whether COCA correctly interpreted the ICWA when it affirmed the trial court's order denying the Tribe's motion to transfer jurisdiction to tribal court and its alternative motion for relative placement during the pre-adoption stage of these proceedings. We hold COCA erred: (a) by interpreting the ICWA to preclude tribal court jurisdiction after the parental rights to two Indian children were terminated, (b) by finding "good cause" not to transfer, and (c) by failing to use the "clear and convincing" evidence standard in its review of the trial court's finding of "good cause" to deny the Tribe's requests. We previously granted the Tribe's petition for certiorari. We reverse and remand.

[I]t is undisputed that neither M.S., K.S., nor their parents, resided on the reservation. We must therefore consider 25 U.S.C. § 1911(b) which concerns jurisdiction over "child custody proceedings" for non-domiciliary Indian children. The Tribe contends transfer to tribal court may occur in this case, absent good cause to the contrary. The State responds that although § 1911(a) applies to "***any*** child custody proceeding" involving an Indian child, § 1911(b) applies only to transfers of "foster care placement" or "termination of parental rights" proceedings. [emphasis added]. . . .

At issue then is whether § 1911(b) should be construed so narrowly and whether this construction complies with Congressional intent and the purpose of the ICWA. In arguing that the specific inclusion in § 1911(b) of only "foster care placement" and "termination of parental rights" proceedings indicates an intent to exclude transfers of the other "child custody proceedings" defined by 25 U.S.C. § 1903, the State promotes the rule of "expressio unius est exclusio alterius," i.e., the mention of one thing in a statute implies exclusion of something else. However, the rule should be applied only as an aid in arriving at intention and should never be followed when doing so would override the intended purpose of the act. COCA agreed with the State that a transfer to tribal court at the "preadoptive placement" stage was precluded because § 1911(b) does not mention it. We acknowledge § 1911(b) mentions transfers of only "foster care placement" and "termination of parental rights" proceedings "in the absence of good cause to the contrary. . . ." We must therefore determine whether Congress intended to exclude transfers of "pre-adoptive placement" and "adoptive placement" proceedings to tribal court.

We must read § 1911(b) as it is written. The court "shall transfer" foster care placement and termination of parental rights proceedings absent objections and a showing of good cause to the contrary. Reading what **is** contained in the statute, however, does not require us to read into the statute what **is not** there, i.e., that transfers may **only be granted** if requested before a termination of parental rights proceeding is concluded. . . .

Unfortunately, "good cause" is not defined by the ICWA. Under the Bureau of Indian Affairs (BIA) Guidelines, 44 Fed.Reg. 67584 (1979), "good cause" is defined by a non-exclusive list. In this case, the trial court's findings of "good cause not to transfer" to tribal court were: (a) the length of time that the State of Oklahoma has exercised jurisdiction prior to the tribe's motion; (b) the relationships established between the children and their foster parents, their attorney, their CASA representative, DHS social workers, and medical providers; and (c) the most relevant evidence regarding the children is located in the State of Oklahoma.

The length of time in which the State exercised jurisdiction before the Tribe's request for transfer must be addressed because it affects the timeliness issue under § 1911(b), i.e., whether transfer may be approved following the termination proceeding. Resolution of this issue will resolve the other two reasons for denying transfer, i.e., the children's relationships and the availability of the evidence in Oklahoma.

The Tribe was not initially given notice on September 8, 2004, when the State filed its petition resulting in the removal of the children from the home. The State placed the children with the Simmons. The Tribe sought to intervene in this case on December 16, 2004, within three months after the petition was filed. It appears from the record that the State and the Tribe had an agreement that if reunification efforts failed and the State sought the termination of parental rights, the State would place M.S. and K.S. in a Puyallup foster home. When it became obvious that reunification would not occur, the State moved to terminate parental rights on March 28, 2006. Parental rights were terminated on June 21, 2006, by order filed June 23, 2006.

In apparent compliance with its agreement with the Tribe, the State gave notice of removal of placement on June 26, 2006. The Simmons objected to removal on July 5, 2006, and filed a request for hearing through the children's attorney. However, the attorney did not serve a copy on the Tribe. In an affidavit by the Tribe's counsel, Sandra Cooper, dated July 27, 2006, we learn that a copy of the motion was luckily included in a packet of other materials mailed to the Tribe, but with insufficient time to prepare for the hearing. The affidavit also provides that the Tribe's efforts to participate in the hearing by telephone conference were attempted in vain. The objection to removal was granted, and the children remained in foster care with the Simmons.

The Tribe's witness, Tara Reynon, social worker and director of children's services for the Tribe, testified as to the alleged "24 month gap" which had passed since the children were removed from their home. She also spoke about the Tribe's initial support for reunification of M.S. and K.S. with their parents. She stated:

> The first 12 months the Tribe was under the understanding that the children would remain here so that they could try to reunite with their parents. That was the first 12 months. And then since May of 2005 when we knew that they were—when we were getting the information that possibly that they wouldn't be reunited that the children would be moved to Florida with a relative, which was our wishes from the beginning. So 12 months, we look at to where it was hopefully reunification. So truly after it has only been 12 months, we're looking for permanency. And not only that, but termination

> didn't even occur until this year. So it hasn't even been 12 [months] since the children were free for adoption. . . . We were very hopeful [the parents] would get their children back.

Delay also occurred due to the untimely death of the children's great aunt, Gabriella Morely, the sister of Michelle Smith-Valdez, the current custodian. After plans were made for the children to be placed with Gabriella and her husband in Florida, she developed breast cancer and died shortly thereafter. Subsequent to Morely's death, Smith-Valdez expressed an interest in becoming the custodian of the children. Visits were made with the children, and evidence showed that the children seemed happy around her and her grown children. . . .

COCA interpreted the Tribe's actions as inadequate to overcome the requisite "good cause to the contrary" to justify denial of transfer under § 1911(b). The timeliness issue was decided against the Tribe because transfer was not requested at the time of the "foster care placement" or "termination of parental rights" proceedings as a matter of law under § 1911(b). The appellate court appears to have satisfied itself that good cause to deny transfer existed on the basis of a lack of diligence.

However, we see the Tribe's actions in a different light. We see delays caused through circumstances outside the Tribe's control. Supporting the State's reunification efforts should not result in allegations of a Tribe's lack of diligence in requesting transfer. Evidence shows the Tribe's interest in these children through the letters admitted into evidence, the agreement with the State for placement with a tribal member or family member if termination was sought, and the availability of not one, but two, great aunts wishing to take the children permanently. The record shows the Tribe was effectively prevented from attending a hearing which resulted in placement with the Simmons. The Tribe believed their agreement with the State for placement with tribal members or relatives would be honored, and because of this, waited to request transfer. It appears the Tribe was unfairly penalized for entering into that agreement. Moreover, the unfortunate circumstances of the death of the Children's great aunt, Gabriella Morely, led to further delays. . . .

In the instant case, it cannot be said that the Tribe's delay in requesting transfer "was not prevented by the actions of the State. . . ." In fact, the evidence supports a finding that the Tribe's actions were consistent with its belief that, when reunification failed, the State would proceed to satisfy its agreement with the Tribe. The record shows the motion to terminate parental rights was filed on March 28, 2006, but the order of termination was not filed until June 23, 2006. Next, the State's notice to remove the children from the foster home was filed on June 27, 2006. The Simmons' objection was then filed on July 5, 2006, but the Tribe only inadvertently received a copy of it and was, in effect, prevented from participating in a meaningful way. On July 27, 2006, the trial court sustained the Simmons' objection to removal of the children. Then, on August 4, 2006, the Tribe filed its motion to transfer, followed by its petition to transfer on September 21, 2006. In summary, the Tribe had no reason to file a motion to transfer until sometime between July 5, 2006, when the Simmons objected to removal, and July 27, 2006, when the trial court sustained their objection. In other words, the longest the Tribe waited from the time of the objection until the petition to transfer was filed was **seven weeks.** We note that in [*In re*] *A.B., supra*, [2003 ND 98, 663 N.W.2d 625,] the Referee would have denied transfer under § 1911(b) even **during** the proceeding to terminate parental rights, which is apparently allowed by the statute. Thus, the "case-to-case" basis for finding "good cause" is the approach we must follow, and of which we approve, when considering the long-term consequences of the jurisdiction of the tribal court in cases under the ICWA.

The finding of "good cause" not to transfer was against the clear and convincing evidence in this case. The factual circumstances in this case should have worked in favor of the Tribe, not against it. COCA's holding that transfer was not allowed under § 1911(b), as a matter of law, violated the purpose and intent of the ICWA to preserve the bond between Indian tribe and child. Construing the statute in the manner it did, COCA effectively made the Tribe's protections under the ICWA unavailable to it. The order denying the Tribe's motion to transfer jurisdiction to the tribal court and COCA's ruling affirming it are reversed.

Notes

1. The distinction in ICWA regarding what is required of the state in which proceeding is sometimes confusing. For example, notice is not required in a voluntary adoption proceeding, but the state or private agency is required to follow the placement preferences. Those placement preferences would be nearly impossible to follow without the involvement of the tribe. Some courts follow the Oklahoma model, taking a broad reading of Congress's intent. Others, such as the Minnesota Supreme Court, take a more cribbed reading of the law:

> The court of appeals concluded that 25 U.S.C. § 1911(b) is ambiguous with respect to the transfer to tribal court of preadoptive placement proceedings, and therefore the question of transfer of preadoptive proceedings to tribal court is to be resolved based on state law. We conclude that 25 U.S.C. § 1911(b) is not ambiguous on the subject of transfer to tribal court of preadoptive proceedings involving an Indian child not residing or domiciled on the child's tribe's reservation. Rather, we conclude that ICWA does not permit the transfer of such proceedings. We further conclude that, even if 25 U.S.C. § 1911(b) were ambiguous, state law cannot create jurisdiction in the tribal court where federal law has not.

In re R.S., 805 N.W.2d 45, 50 (Minn. 2011).

Who "creates" jurisdiction? What is inherent jurisdiction? Can the federal government create inherent tribal jurisdiction? How does this decision square with other federal decisions in this chapter?

2. Given ICWA's necessarily broad language as a federal statute governing state proceedings, written more than thirty years ago, state courts are often able to construct an outcome that may be at odds with the intent, or spirit, of ICWA.

Congress attempted to address this in § 1902, the Congressional declaration of policy, which states

> The Congress hereby declares it is the policy of this Nation to protect the best interests of Indian children and to promote the stability and security of Indian tribes and families by the establishment of minimum Federal standards for the removal of Indian children from their families and the placement of such children in foster or adoptive homes which will reflect the unique values of Indian culture, and by providing for assistance to Indian tribes in the operation of child and family service programs.

Though originally applied in the treaty context, and therefore used primarily in federal courts, the Indian law canons of construction have been used to interpret statutes. *See* Cohen's Handbook of Federal Indian Law 113 (Nell Jessup Newton et al. eds., 2012 ed.). The canons require that ambiguities be resolved in favor of Indians, and liberally construed to their benefit, unless Congress clearly intends otherwise. *Id.* at 113-15. According to the Supreme Court, "When we are faced with these two possible constructions, our choice between them must be dictated by a principle deeply rooted in this Court's Indian jurisprudence; 'Statutes are to be construed liberally in favor of the Indians, with ambiguous provisions interpreted to their benefit.'" *County of Yakima v. Confederated Tribes & Bands of the Yakima Indian Nation*, 502 U.S. 251, 269 (1992). Rarely relied on in state court, the canons plus the Act itself ought to mean ambiguities that arise are found in favor of Indian children and Indian tribes.

E. The Best Interests of the Indian Child

Some courts incorporated a "best interests" standard into the jurisdictional decision-making process, which assumes that the children's best interests will not be adequately accounted for in tribal court and that the state court knows best about making decisions for the Indian child.

In re A.B.

663 N.W.2d 625 (N.D. 2003)

Vande Walle, Chief Justice.

Norean Hoots, a social worker with Cass County Social Services, ("Cass County") appealed from a juvenile court order granting a motion by the Turtle Mountain Band of Chippewa Indians ("Turtle Mountain Tribe") under the Indian Child Welfare Act ("ICWA"), 25 U.S.C. § 1901 et seq., to transfer jurisdiction of a parental termination proceeding from state juvenile court to the Turtle Mountain Tribal Court ("Tribal Court"). We affirm the transfer, holding the juvenile court did not commit reversible procedural error in overturning a judicial referee's recommendation to deny the motion to transfer, holding the juvenile court did not err in transferring jurisdiction of the child custody proceeding to Tribal Court, and holding the application of ICWA to the minor child is not unconstitutional.

A.B. was born in 1993. A.B.'s biological father, F.B., and her paternal grandmother, H.L., are enrolled members of the Turtle Mountain Tribe, and A.B. is eligible for membership in the Turtle Mountain Tribe. A.B. is therefore an "Indian child" under ICWA....

In a motion filed on February 20, 2002, the Turtle Mountain Tribe moved under ICWA to transfer jurisdiction of child custody proceedings involving A.B. from the state juvenile court to Tribal Court. K.B. objected, and the juvenile court refused to transfer jurisdiction to Tribal Court. See 25 U.S.C. § 1911(b) (providing, in part, state court shall transfer proceeding to jurisdiction of tribe, absent objection by either parent).

On June 3, 2002, Cass County petitioned the juvenile court to terminate the parental rights of K.B. and F.B. In a motion dated July 17, 2002, and filed on July 23, 2002, the Turtle Mountain Tribe moved under ICWA to transfer jurisdiction of the proceeding involving A.B. from state juvenile court to Tribal Court. K.B. did not object to this motion to transfer jurisdiction. After a September 23, 2002 hearing, a judicial referee recommended denying the motion to transfer jurisdiction, concluding it was not timely because the proceeding was at an advanced stage and a transfer of jurisdiction to Tribal Court would create a forum inconveniens. The Turtle Mountain Tribe sought review of the referee's decision under N.D. Sup.Ct. Admin. R. 13. The juvenile court reversed the referee's recommendation, concluding the Turtle Mountain Tribe's motion to transfer was made within seven weeks after Cass County's petition to terminate parental rights was filed and was timely. The juvenile court also concluded the Tribal Court was not an inconvenient forum. The juvenile court granted the Turtle Mountain Tribe's motion to transfer jurisdiction to Tribal Court and dismissed the state court petition to terminate parental rights....

Cass County argues the juvenile court erred in reversing the referee's decision because there was good cause under ICWA to deny the Turtle Mountain Tribe's motion to transfer jurisdiction to the Tribal Court. Cass County contends the Turtle Mountain Tribe's motion to transfer was not timely and the Tribal Court is an inconvenient forum.

Congress enacted ICWA in 1978 as the product of a rising concern for the consequences of state welfare practices which resulted in the separation of many Indian children from their families and tribes through adoption or foster care placement in non-Indian homes. See *Mississippi Band of Choctaw Indians v. Holyfield*, 490 U.S. 30, 32 (1989). In enacting ICWA, Congress declared a national policy to

> protect the best interests of Indian children and to promote the stability and security of Indian tribes and families by the establishment of minimum Federal standards for the removal of Indian children from their families and the placement of such children in foster or adoptive homes which will

> reflect the unique values of Indian culture, and by providing for assistance to Indian tribes in the operation of child and family service programs....

ICWA defines an "Indian child" as "any unmarried person who is under age eighteen and is either (a) a member of an Indian tribe or (b) is eligible for membership in an Indian tribe and is the biological child of a member of an Indian tribe." 25 U.S.C. § 1903(4). Under 25 U.S.C. § 1903(1), a "child custody proceeding" means and includes foster care placement, termination of parental rights, preadoptive placement, and adoptive placement. A.B. is the biological minor child of F.B., an enrolled member of the Turtle Mountain Tribe, and is an "Indian child" under 25 U.S.C. § 1911(b). Absent good cause to the contrary, 25 U.S.C. § 1911(b) thus creates presumptive Tribal Court jurisdiction over any child custody proceeding involving A.B., including a foster care placement proceeding or a termination of parental rights proceeding.

ICWA does not define "good cause to the contrary," but the Bureau of Indian Affairs has issued guidelines which, although not binding, are helpful for determining good cause. Department of the Interior, Bureau of Indian Affairs, Guidelines for State Courts; Indian Child Custody Proceedings—Part III, 44 Fed.Reg. 67583 et seq. (1979) ("BIA Guidelines"). The burden of establishing good cause to deny a transfer is upon the party opposing the transfer. BIA Guidelines, at 67591. As relevant to this case, the BIA Guidelines state that good cause to deny transfer of a child custody proceeding to tribal court exists if the proceeding is at an advanced stage when the petition to transfer is received, or if the evidence to decide the case could not be adequately presented in the tribal court without undue hardship to the parties or the witnesses. BIA Guidelines, § C.3(b)(i) and (iii) at 67591.

A

Here, the referee decided the relevant time period for determining whether the Turtle Mountain Tribe's motion to transfer jurisdiction was timely was when Cass County initiated the foster care proceeding in March 2001. The referee effectively decided the foster care proceeding was part of the termination proceeding and concluded the July 2002 motion to transfer jurisdiction was filed at an advanced stage of the child custody proceeding and was untimely. The juvenile court disagreed, concluding the relevant time for deciding whether the July 2002 motion to transfer was timely was after Cass County filed the June 3, 2002 petition to terminate parental rights, because a foster care placement proceeding and a termination of parental rights proceeding are two separate proceedings under the definition of "child custody proceeding." See 25 U.S.C. § 1903(1). The juvenile court decided the Turtle Mountain Tribe filed its motion to transfer jurisdiction approximately seven weeks after the petition to terminate parental rights was filed, and the termination proceeding was not at an advanced stage when the transfer motion was filed.

Under 25 U.S.C. § 1903(1), a "child custody proceeding" means and includes foster care placement, termination of parental rights, preadoptive placement, and adoptive placement. Foster care placement means "any action removing an Indian child from its parent or Indian custodian for temporary placement in a foster home or institution or the home of a guardian or conservator where the parent or Indian custodian cannot have the child returned upon demand, but where parental rights have not been terminated." 25 U.S.C. § 1903(1)(i). A termination of parental rights proceeding means "any action resulting in the termination of the parent-child relationship." 25 U.S.C. § 1903(1)(ii). The plain language of those definitions distinguishes between a foster care placement proceeding and a termination of parental rights proceeding. By definition, a foster care placement proceeding seeks to temporarily remove an Indian child from the child's parent or Indian custodian without terminating parental rights, while a termination of parental rights proceeding seeks to end the parent-child relationship. Those proceedings have different purposes in the realm of a "child custody proceeding." The plain language of 25 U.S.C. § 1911(b) authorizes transfer motions for either foster care placement proceedings or for termination of parental rights proceedings, and the judicial referee's interpretation of 25 U.S.C. § 1911(b) would subsume an Indian tribe's right to request transfer of a termination proceeding into its right to request transfer of an earlier foster care placement proceeding. The juvenile court's interpretation of "child custody proceeding" correctly distinguishes between proceedings for "foster care placement" and "termination of parental rights" and recognizes the different purposes that may trigger each proceeding. We conclude, as a matter of law, the juvenile court correctly interpreted ICWA to measure the relevant time period for a motion to transfer jurisdiction in this case from the filing of the petition to terminate parental rights.

Cass County's petition to terminate parental rights was filed on June 3, 2002. In a motion dated July 17, 2002, and filed on July 23, 2002, the Turtle Mountain Tribe moved to transfer jurisdiction of the proceeding to Tribal Court. The Turtle Mountain Tribe's motion to transfer was some seven weeks after the petition to terminate parental rights was filed, and the transfer motion was filed about one week before a pre-trial conference and about two weeks before the scheduled trial. . . .

Whether a motion for transfer jurisdiction is timely is determined on a case-by-case basis, and some courts have held that transfer petitions are not timely if filed on the morning of trial, or after trial has commenced. Other courts have held that transfer motions filed after the final disposition of the case are not timely.

Here, we reject Cass County's characterization that the Turtle Mountain Tribe filed the transfer motion on the "eve of trial." Rather, the transfer motion was filed about seven weeks after the termination petition was filed and two weeks before the scheduled trial. Although the requirement for a timely motion encourages the prompt exercise of the right to transfer jurisdiction and the Turtle Mountain Tribe's motion to transfer could have been made earlier, under the circumstances of this case we agree with the juvenile court that the transfer motion was not at an advanced stage of the proceeding to terminate parental rights. We therefore conclude the motion to transfer jurisdiction was not untimely.

B

The judicial referee also decided the Tribal Court would be a forum inconveniens, stating if the Turtle Mountain Tribe's motion to transfer jurisdiction was granted, the proceeding would be terminated and there would be no forum in which to present evidence related to the long term deprivation of A.B. and her best interests. The referee also stated all the evidence relating to the child's best interest was in the juvenile court's jurisdiction. The juvenile court rejected the referee's determination, concluding there was no hardship in transferring jurisdiction to the Tribal Court because the Tribal Court had offered to hear the case in Fargo. The juvenile court said a dismissal of the state termination proceeding was a procedural formality to allow the Tribal Court to take jurisdiction.

The referee's decision reflects an erroneous conclusion that there would be no forum in which to present evidence related to the deprivation of A.B. and her best interests if the transfer was granted. The referee's conclusion ignores that ICWA gives the Tribal Court presumptive jurisdiction over child custody proceedings involving an Indian child and there is no reason to believe the Tribal Court will not fulfill its obligations regarding A.B. Moreover, the commentary to the BIA Guidelines states that application of a modified doctrine of "forum non conveniens" may limit transfers to cases involving Indian children who do not live very far from a reservation, but the problem may be alleviated by having tribal courts come to the witnesses and a transfer may be conditioned on having a tribal court meet in the city where the family lives. BIA Guidelines, at 67591. Because the Tribal Court has offered to sit in Fargo for proceedings relating to A.B., we see no reason for concluding the Tribal Court is unable to adequately deal with issues pertaining to A.B. We affirm the juvenile court's decision granting the transfer of jurisdiction to the Tribal Court. . . .

Cass County argues the judicial referee and the juvenile court erred in refusing to consider evidence regarding A.B.'s best interest in the context of the motion to transfer jurisdiction.

Although one of the goals of ICWA is to protect the best interests of an Indian child, see 25 U.S.C. § 1902, the issue here is the threshold question regarding the proper forum for that decision. See *Holyfield*, 490 U.S. at 53, 109 S.Ct. 1597 (stating Supreme Court asked to decide legal question of who makes custody determination of Indian child, not the outcome of the decision, which is placed in the hands of tribal court). We agree with those courts that have concluded the best interest of the child is not a consideration for the threshold determination of whether there is good cause not to transfer jurisdiction to a tribal court.

Notes

1. There has been an ongoing national litigation strategy to incorporate the best interests into the jurisdictional determination of good cause. Courts continue to be split on this issue. *See* Barbara Ann Atwood, Children, Tribes and States: Adoption and Custody Conflicts over American Indian Children 202

(2010). In *In re Zylena R.*, the state held that "[p]ermitting a state court to deny a motion to transfer based upon its perception of the best interests of the child negate the concept of 'presumptively tribal jurisdiction' over Indian children who do not reside on a reservation and undermines the federal policy established by ICWA . . . . Stated another way, recognizing best interests as 'good cause' for denying transfer permits state courts to decide that it is not in the best interests of Indian children to have a tribal court determine what is in their best interests." 825 N.W.2d 173, 186 (Neb. 2012) (overruling *In re C.W.*, 479 N.W.2d 105 (1992)).

However, in *Thompson v. Fairfax County Department of Family Services*, the court slightly modified a best interests standard when finding:

> The focus in a transfer decision under 25 U.S.C. § 1911(b) must remain on the immediate serious emotional or physical damage flowing from the transfer itself. This inquiry is not the same as a determination of a child's best interests in a proceeding to terminate parental rights. The statutory structure makes clear Congress's presumption that, in the event of a transfer, tribal courts are fully competent to consider the child's best interests in adjudicating the termination of parental rights proceeding. Thus, ICWA presumes jurisdiction rests with the tribe, and the transfer inquiry must center on whether a compelling reason exists not to transfer the case, based in part on the immediate effect of a transfer of jurisdiction on the child.
>
> A relevant consideration in this regard is whether the Tribe is willing to allow the child to stay in her current environment, pending adjudication of the case on the merits of termination and/or placement. When the "serious emotional or physical damage" aspect of the good cause determination becomes an issue, good cause to deny transfer does not exist if the tribe agrees to maintain the status quo until it completes its adjudication on the merits. Only if the tribe does not agree or fails to present evidence of its agreement to preserve the status quo does good cause exist not to transfer.

747 S.E.2d 838, 851 (Va. App. 2013).

How can the state court make tribal jurisdiction conditional on the tribe's actions? Isn't the point of jurisdiction the right to make decisions for and on behalf of a child?

2. What do the courts and attorneys arguing these cases mean by the "best interest of the child"? Where does the standard come from? Today, the best interest of the child standard permeates all of child welfare decision making, not only in abuse and neglect cases, but also in custody and guardianship determinations. As we have seen above, state court judges have injected it into jurisdictional determinations for Indian children. The Department of the Interior, in the 2016 Guidelines, attempted to explain how it applies to ICWA and Indian children:

> In a child-custody proceeding, a party might argue that an aspect of ICWA or the rule is in tension with what is in the "best interests of the child." In most cases, this argument lacks merit. First, ICWA was specifically designed by Congress to protect the best interests of Indian children.

> In order to achieve that general goal, Congress established specific minimum Federal standards for the removal of Indian children from their families that are designed to protect children and their relationship with their parents, extended family, and Tribe.
>
> One of the most important ways that ICWA protects the best interests of Indian children is by ensuring that, if possible, children remain with their parents and that, if they are separated, that support for reunification is provided. This is entirely consistent with the "best interests" standard applied in state courts, which recognizes the importance of family integrity and the preference for avoiding removal of a child from his or her home. If a child does need to be removed from her home, ICWA's placement preferences continue to protect her best interests by favoring placements within her extended family and Tribal community. Other ICWA provisions also serve to protect a child's best interests by, for example, ensuring that a child's parents have sufficient notice about her child-custody proceeding and an ability to fully participate in the proceeding (25 U.S.C. 1912(a), (b), (c)) and helping an adoptee access information about her Tribal connections (25 U.S.C. 1917).
>
> Congress enacted ICWA specifically to address the problems that arose out of the application of subjective value judgments about what is "best" for an Indian child. Congress found that the unfettered subjective application of the "best interests" standard often failed to consider Tribal cultural practices or recognize the long-term advantages to children of remaining with their families and Tribes. By providing courts with objective rules that operate above the emotions of individual cases, Congress was facilitating better State-court practice on these issues and the protection of Indian children, families, and Tribes.

U.S. Dept. of the Interior, Guidelines for Implementing the Indian Child Welfare Act, 89 (Dec. 2016) available at https://www.bia.gov/sites/bia.gov/files/assets/bia/ois/pdf/idc2-056831.pdf ("BIA Guidelines").

But what does this standard entail in practice, and how is it different for Indian and non-Indian children? How has the standard developed to establish state jurisdiction over families? Are there problems inherent with the standard, or only as it applies to jurisdictional decisions?

Foster Care— In Whose Best Interest?

43 Harv. Educ. Rev. 599 (1973)
Robert H. Mnookin

[...] Even though state coercion can occur outside of court, judges usually have been responsible for deciding whether or not to remove children over parental objections. Law provides the principal framework to inform and constrain judicial action. This paper therefore addresses two basic questions. First, what legal standards should govern the judicial decision to remove a child over parental objections and place the child in foster care? And second, how can the law ensure developmental continuity and stability for children who must be so removed?

As background, the present legal standards for removing children, the process of intervention, and what is known about foster children and the foster care system are briefly described. I think three principles, currently violated, should govern its operation:

> 1. Removal should be a last resort, used only when the child cannot be protected within the home.
>
> 2. The decision to require foster care placement should be based on legal standards that can be applied in a consistent and even-handed way, and not be profoundly influenced by the values of the particular deciding judge.
>
> 3. If removal is necessary the state should actively seek, when possible, to help the child's parents overcome the problems that led to removal so that the child can be returned home as soon as possible. In cases where the child cannot be returned home in a reasonable time, despite efforts by the state, the state should find a stable alternative arrangement such as adoption for the child. A child should not be left in foster care for an indefinite period of time.

Current legal standards for removal, under which courts increasingly purport to make individualized determinations of what is in the best interests of the child, contribute significantly to the failings of the present foster care system. My criticism is not that present standards fail to give adequate weight to parental interests, as compared to the child's interests; indeed, the focus of social concern probably should be on the child. Nor do I believe that it is always inappropriate to remove a child from parental custody for placement in foster care; in some circumstances nothing less drastic will protect a child from abusing or neglectful parents. Instead, what is wrong with the existing legal standards is that they call for individualized determinations based on discretionary assessments of the best interests of the child, and these determinations cannot be made consistently and fairly. They result in the unnecessary placement of children in foster care and do little to protect children against remaining in foster care for too long. Accordingly, substantial changes in the legal standards are needed, designed to make it more difficult to remove children initially and to provide more continuity and stability for children if removal is necessary. These changes will entail more than added procedural safeguards.

How the State Removes Children from their Parents

Source of the Power

* * *

Today, every state has a statute allowing a court to intervene into the family to protect a child; this authority is usually conferred on the juvenile or family court. Apart from situations where the child has engaged in wrongful behavior of some sort, the statutes in most states allow the court to intrude into the child's life if, for whatever reason, he or she lacks a parent or guardian (dependent or abandoned children), if the parent has neglected properly to care for or to support him or her (neglected children), or if the parent has willfully injured the child (abused children). Frequently the terms "dependent" and "neglected" are used to describe all children subject to a juvenile court's jurisdiction who have not engaged in any wrongful behavior. In this paper, the term "neglected" is so used, and is meant to include dependent and abused children as well.

* * *

[. . .] Typical statutory provisions allow court intrusion to protect a child who is not receiving "proper parental care," "proper attention," "whose home is an unfit place for him by reason of neglect, cruelty, depravity, or physical abuse," or whose parents neglect to provide the "care necessary for his health, morals or well being."

* * *

The Process of Removal

* * *

[. . .] Today a case usually reaches court after weaving through a complicated social welfare bureaucracy where numerous officials including social workers, probation officers, and court personnel, may have had contact with the family.

Unfortunately, very little is known about how the discretion of these various administrative officers is exercised before a case reaches court. The process is usually initiated by a report from a social worker or the police, or less frequently from a neighbor, medical professional, or school staff member. Although practices vary, a member of a special unit of the social welfare or probation department is usually responsible for an initial investigation of the report. Customarily this investigation is not extensive; often it will only involve a visit to the home and a telephone conversation with the person who turned in the report. The investigator, sometimes together with a supervisor, then must decide whether to close the case, to suggest that the welfare agency informally (and non-coercively) provide services or supervision, or to file a petition in court.

Filing a petition initiates a judicial inquiry that usually has two stages. First, the court must determine whether it has jurisdiction over the child. This involves deciding on the basis of exceedingly broad and ill-defined statutory provisions whether the parents have failed to live up to acceptable social standards for child rearing. If it is determined that they have, then such jurisdiction empowers the court to intervene into the family. In the words of one juvenile court judge, "It is the ultimate finding of neglect which releases the court's wide discretionary powers of disposition, a discretion beholden to and circumscribed by the law's most challenging aphorism, 'the best interests of the child.'" The second stage involves a dispositional hearing, where the judge decides the manner of intervention. Removal from the home is by no means mandatory. The court can instead require supervision within the child's own home, psychological counseling for the parents and/or the child, or periodic home visits by a social worker, probation officer, or homemaker.

* * *

What is Wrong with the Best Interests Standard?

We now turn to a close examination of the "best interests of the child" test, the legal standard usually employed by courts to decide whether a child should be removed from parental custody in the dispositional stage of neglect proceedings. This standard has long been used to decide matters of child custody, particularly in disputes between parents. In an opinion written nearly fifty years ago, Benjamin Cardozo described as follows the role of the judge in any child custody proceeding brought before a court of equity:

> He acts as *parens patriae* to do what is best for the interest of the child. He is to put himself in the position of a 'wise, affectionate, and careful parent' . . . and make provision for the child accordingly. He may act at the intervention of a kinsman, if so the petition comes before him, but equally he may act at the instance or on the motion of any one else. He is not adjudicating a controversy between adversary parties, to compare their private differences. He is not determining rights 'as between a parent and a child'; or as between one parent and another. . . . He 'interferes for the protection of infants, *qua* infants, by virtue of the prerogative which belongs to the Crown as *parens patriae*.'

Cardozo's description appears in a decision involving a dispute between estranged parents over who should have custody of the children. Today some version of the best interests standard is incorporated in the divorce legislation of nearly every state. But Cardozo's expansive language makes it easy to understand how the test could be applied not only in disputes between parents, but also in neglect proceedings. Presently, the best interests test is widely used to decide what should be done for a child over whom a juvenile court has assumed jurisdiction; indeed it is sometimes used to decide whether jurisdiction should be assumed.

For the dispositional decision in neglect cases, the best interests test would appear to have much to commend it. It focuses principally on the child rather than on arbitrary legal rights of parents. It implicitly recognizes that each child is unique, and that parental conduct and home environments may have substantially different effects on different children. It also seems to require that the judge find out as much as possible about the child, the child's circumstances, the parents, and the available alternative arrangements. In fact, the best interests standard embodies what David Matza has described as a basic precept of juvenile court philosophy: the principle of "individualized justice." This principle requires each dispositional decision, in Matza's words, "to be guided by a *full understanding* of the client's personal and social characteristics and by his 'individual needs.'"

Nonetheless, a careful analysis reveals serious deficiencies in the best interests test when it is used to decide whether the state should remove a child from parental custody and place the child in foster care. I will discuss some of the test's shortcomings as it is applied in foster care cases.

Conceptual Problems with the Test

One obvious objection to the best interests of the child test is that by its very terms it ignores completely the interests of the parents. Obviously a child's parents have important interests at stake when the state seeks to intervene; a parent can derive important satisfactions and pleasures from a relationship with a child, and the destruction of this relationship can have an enormous effect on the parent quite apart from benefits or losses to the child. I doubt whether courts ignore the effects of judicial action on parents, but the best interests of the child test disallows explicit consideration of parental interests, making the process more highsounding, perhaps, but less honest.

But even if we assume that it is appropriate to focus attention exclusively on the child's interests, there remain conceptual difficulties with the best interests test. Its application assumes the judge will compare the probable consequences for the child of remaining in the home with the probable consequences of removal. How might a judge make this comparison? He or she would need considerable information and predictive ability. The information would include knowledge of how the parents had behaved in the past, the effect of this parental behavior on the child, and the child's present condition. Then the judge would need to predict the probable future behavior of the parents if the child were to remain in the home and to gauge the probable effects of his behavior on the child. Obviously, more than one outcome is possible, so the judge would have to assess the probability of various outcomes and evaluate the seriousness of possible benefits and harms associated with each. Next, the judge would have to compare this set of possible consequences with those if the child were placed in a foster home. This would require predicting the effect of removing the child from home, school, friends, and familiar surroundings, as well as predicting the child's experience while in the foster care system. Such predictions involve estimates of the child's future relationship with the foster parents, the child's future contact with natural parents and siblings, the number of foster homes in which the child ultimately will have to be placed, the length of time spent in foster care, the potential for acquiring a stable home, and myriad other factors.

Obviously one can question whether a judge has the necessary information. In many instances he or she lacks adequate information even about a child's life with his or her parents. Moreover, at the time of the dispositional hearing, the judge typically has *no* information about where the child will be placed if removal is ordered; he or she usually knows nothing about the characteristics of the foster family, or how long that family will want or be able to keep the child. In deciding who should raise a particular child, the court in a neglect proceeding is comparing an existing family with a largely unknown alternative. [. . .]

* * *

The Problem of Fairness

* * *

A judge's reliance on personal values is especially risky when class differences confound the problem. The foster care system is frequently accused of being class biased, one "in which middle-class professionals provide and control a service used mostly by poor people, with upper-lower and lower-middle class foster parents serving as intermediaries." The fact that most foster children come from poor families does not, of course, prove that there is an inherent class bias in the system. There are other plausible explanations for the high proportion of poor children. The condition of poverty may lead to family breakdown and a greater likelihood that children are endangered in times of crisis. Alternatively, since poor families are more subject to scrutiny by social workers who administer welfare programs, their faults, even if no more common, may be more conspicuous. Finally, since poor families have access to few resources in the event of family crisis, their children may be forced into the foster care system because other forms of substitute care, such as babysitters, relatives, and day care centers, are not available.

Although these other explanations are plausible, the fact remains that the best interests standard allows the judge to import his personal values into the process, and leaves considerable scope for class bias. [. . .]

* * *

Finally, there are cases where a child is removed from his parental home because the court determines the *physical conditions* in the home are unsuitable for the child. In a recent California case, an appellate court affirmed a juvenile court decision removing children from a dirty home. The parents claimed there was no evidence showing that the children had been harmed, but the appeals court maintained that the state "was not required, as appellants assert, to prove that the conditions of the above cause 'sickness and disease of mind or body' in order to establish 'neglect' . . . the welfare of the child is of paramount concern, and a purpose of the juvenile court law is to secure for each minor such care and guidance as will serve the spiritual, emotional, mental, and physical welfare of the minor and the best interests of the state." Some "dirty homes" may seriously endanger a child's growth and well-being, but most may merely offend middle-class sensibilities. One suspects courts may sometimes be enforcing middle-class norms of cleanliness where both economic and cultural circumstances make it both unfair and inappropriate.

During the past ten years there have been several appellate court decisions rejecting extreme attempts by trial court judges to use neglect laws "to impose middle-class mores upon families and to punish a parent's undesirable conduct unless that conduct can be shown to result in damage to the child." For two reasons, however, these cases do not significantly limit the discretion of the judge who hears the case. First, the appellate decisions suggesting that specific factors are not appropriate for consideration also emphasize the continuing need for individualized determinations and wide latitude for trial judges. Second, juvenile court judges can often disguise a decision based on an "improper" factor by vague recitation of general language. The real reasons may be very different than the stated ones.

* * *

Present Legal Standards Fail to Make Removal a Last Resort

* * *

Placing a child away from home is often referred to as a "last resort," but in fact most communities offer few preventive or protective services for children within the home while a family is helped through a crisis. Day care or baby sitting services, along with parental counseling, might make removal unnecessary in a wide variety of circumstances; such services typically are unavailable. A national survey conducted by the American Humane Association in 1967 concluded that "*no state* and *no community* has developed a child protective service program adequate in size to meet the service needs of all *reported* cases of child neglect, abuse, and exploitation." Even when such services are available, neglect statutes and the best interest standard do not require that before ordering removal a court conduct an inquiry into whether the child can be protected if left in parental custody. Anecdotal evidence strongly suggests that children are often placed in foster care without a careful analysis of whether less drastic forms of intervention might be preferable. Thus, for instance, children have been placed in foster care because their parents' home is filthy even though a homemaker's services might have remedied the situation and done so at far less cost to the state. Also, an undernourished child may be taken from the home without any prior effort to educate the parents about nutritional needs. Even in child abuse cases, where removal from the home is very likely, many experts believe that the child can often be left safely at home if the parents receive appropriate treatment and support.

Removal would seem appropriate only when there are no means to protect the child within the home. Given the size and quality of present institutional arrangements for children who are removed, and given the widely shared view that parents, not the state, should ordinarily be responsible for child rearing, any legal standard should incorporate a substantial presumption favoring a parent who has expressly indicated that he or she wishes to retain custody. Because of the importance of the parent-child relationship and because of the risks of removal, I believe the state should not be allowed to remove children unless less drastic means of intervention cannot protect the child.

Notes

1. This article was written five years before the passage of ICWA. While some things have changed in child welfare, the application of the best interest of the child standard to abuse and neglect proceedings have not. The individualized and relatively informal nature of child welfare proceedings that judges fiercely defend should lend themselves to individualized solutions for families. Instead, we know that many counties hold routine and short hearings where children are removed.

In a case discussed below, the initial removal hearings were 30 seconds long. While Mnookin offers a best practices way of considering the best interest of the child, many child welfare court systems would be overwhelmed by these standards in their current states.

2. The previous article focused on economic inequality bias in the standard rather than racial bias. In the next article, Evelyn Blanchard, a Native social worker from Laguna Pueblo and Pasqua Yaqui, whose work was instrumental to the passage of ICWA, looks at the best interest standard from the point of view of Native children and families.

The Question of Best Interest, *in*

The Destruction of American Indian Families (Steven Ungar ed., 1977)
Evelyn Blanchard

In recent years the concern of Indian people with the status of child welfare services in their communities, both rural and urban, has greatly magnified. No longer are many Indian people willing to stand mute while various agencies and authorities exercise powers over the lives of Indian children and families, and the tribal community itself.

Hearings before the U.S. Senate Subcommittee on Indian Affairs in April 1974 were the first national public expression of concern by Indian people. While the statements and positions expressed at the hearings received broad attention from Indian people in the field, the larger society, for the most part, remains uninformed. Two years later, the overall picture remains the same. It is very clear from the experience of many Indian workers that the position and intention of the powerful non-Indian social services network in this country has not changed, nor does it appear that change is intended. This serves to complicate and frustrate the work in Indian child welfare. It serves to preserve an adversary position which has no place in the development of a healthy life design for an Indian child or any other child. It becomes clear that protecting one's ideological position remains more important than the preservation of life of a people through the safeguarding of their children.

The testimony of our tribal leaders and Indian child-welfare workers clearly demonstrated the ability of Indian people to care for their own. The statements lucidly revealed the intentional blocks that were placed in the way to prevent this from occurring. Many words were spoken, many tears were shed, many voices were broken with hurt. Yet the response has been minimal. It is difficult to understand how the cited tragedies of Indian children and their families have not moved a people to an expression of human caring.

Not one of the national child-welfare agencies, either public or private, was moved to respond. At best the words were not heard; at worst no attention was paid to them. The only moves of national scope were a request from Senator James Abourezk to the Association on American Indian Affairs, Inc. to prepare an Indian child-welfare bill

(The Indian Child Welfare Act of 1976 [S.3777], introduced by Senator Abourezk on August 27, 1976), and a resolution passed at the 1974 convention of the National Congress of American Indians, Inc. Other national Indian and non-Indian organizations remained noticeably silent.

Within the context of this national attitude and position another ominous block to good Indian child-welfare practice has reared its ugly head. Like other destructive and deceptive visitors to Indian country it is clothed in finery of good words and good intentions. It speaks to the best interests of the child. The position that the concern of the child is paramount in decisions made which effect his life is well-taken. The difficulty arises when the powerful decision-makers interpret this position only within the context of their own value system. The position as developed and interpreted provides the justification for the removal of Indian children from their families and tribes. It provides an opportunity for the decision-makers to look only at a small segment of the Indian child's life experience. It protects child-welfare workers who have not done a responsible job. It sets up a situation in termination of parental right hearings that makes it difficult to determine whose best interests are in reality being considered.

Too many Indian workers witness the rights of Indian parents being terminated because they received no help or encouragement in their rehabilitative efforts. It is heart-breaking to watch the volumes of case record notes being used against parents by workers and department attorneys whose attitudes are never questioned. Yet it is obvious from their own words that their prejudicial attitudes have influenced all of their contacts with the Indian client. This important aspect of the work which should be considered in any decision is overlooked. It appears the department's position is unassailable. After all, are not these people of good will who are concerned with the best interest of every child? It becomes the burden of the Indian family to prove in this "Catch 22" atmosphere that they love and can provide care to their child. But unfortunately the scales of justice have been weighted against them from the very beginning.

Indian children who are recovered from their families are kept in substitute care for long periods before termination is sought. Their parents, like those described in the hearings, often do not know where their children are and, when they do, receive little or no help in the delicate practice of visitation. If their child is upset after return from a visit the behavior is seen as being caused by the uncaring attitude of the parents. The thought that the child is upset because he is again placed away from his parents is given little or no attention. The upsets are carefully reported by foster parents and recorded by caseworkers to use as ammunition against parents when the decision to terminate is made.

The upset behavior exhibited by the child is some of the most damaging evidence presented to the court. The department points out in terms that are not clearly substantiated that the visits with the parents are the cause for this behavior. The workers are not asked to explain how this disruption has gone on so long if they have, in fact, been working to reunite this family. The question of the child's best interest is transformed into a question of case management, and the workers then think that it is time to close this case by moving the child into "permanent" placement. The department's workers can then devote these same efforts to other cases; too many of which unfortunately involve Indian children.

The case planning for Indian children is biased from the beginning. Workers tend to place Indian children in non-Indian substitute homes where there is the likelihood that they can remain a long time either through permanent foster care or adoption. This becomes an important factor in the department's case. It can demonstrate that a permanent, loving, caring home has already been found, and also claim that removal of this child to the questionable home of his Indian parents or relatives would inflict severe, long lasting and traumatic damage to the child. Experts are brought in to testify to the traumatic effects of separation and placement. Parents unwittingly submit themselves to psychiatric or psychological testing paid for by the department to prove that they are unfit, troubled people and parents. The referrals to these psychological experts are made by the department workers who in their letters of referral painstakingly list the parents' failures. No mention is made of strengths.

And the parents' rights are terminated.

Indian families are more than a mother, father and children—they are a large network of relationships. Non-Indian families used to be this way, too. In spite of this known fact many departments fail or consciously decide to disregard it.

Indian children's rights to live with their families and tribes are not considered. Departments and courts do not have the capability or sensitivity to see beyond the next several months of the Indian child's life. Much of the hearing testimony dealt with children whose rights to their family and tribe had been terminated and whose had been placed in good, loving homes. It has been found that many of these children never gained the feeling of permanence and security that was intended. When they grew old enough to wander they left these homes in search of themselves and their people.

Unfortunately for many Indian parents and relatives the long experience of disservice left open wounds of hurt and anger that eventually consumed them. Many gave up hope and incorporated the sentence of worthlessness that was handed down by the court.

The question of best interest is much broader in Indian country than it is elsewhere. Termination hearings sever not only rights of parents but rights of children and rights of tribes. How department workers and the courts perform their work denies the Indian community the opportunity to strengthen old and develop new indigenous social service networks. How the courts define "best interest" negates the right of an Indian person to look for strength and assistance from his tribal identity by denying it as a resource, keeps the Indian parent, child and tribe in a dependent position in this era of self-determination and individual rights, and effectively kills more Indian people through the smothering arms of the helping process. The most learned scholars in child development, after examination of the facts, would not reach a different conclusion.

Indian people have much experience at healing the wounds of forced separation. Many Indian workers complain that only the worst Indian cases are referred to them. These people who are referred have a long history of intimidation from the departments and come to Indian agencies unwilling and unafraid to trust even their own people. Indian agencies are temporary and sometimes unstable because of their funding base. What money is provided is sent with a message daring Indian agencies to prove that they can do better with these clients in an atmosphere of programmed handicaps.

It is frustrating and denigrating to continue to have to demonstrate one's need by digging out the dirty linen. It keeps a whole corps of Indian personnel concentrated on the negative features of Indian child welfare. It takes away from the time and energy they could use to enhance the strengths that exist. It keeps Indian parents in the column of troubled parents rather than healthy, successful ones. It keeps the trouble of Indian people paramount in the view of younger Indians. In this way it consistently and continually inflicts damage on their developing self-identity. It raises the question of self-worth while at the same time it provides damaging answers to the questions. It thwarts the efforts of many adult Indian people to become and present themselves as strong, healthy models to Indian you.

It is an insidiously programmed process that must be stopped.

Indian people share in the concern that the best interest of all children be provided for and recognized. For Indian children they see that the best interest must also include recognition and appreciation for the persons they are. The best interest of the Indian child must be defined within the context of the child's whole life.

Notes

1. Are there different or additional best interests for Indian children? Do Indian children's best interest include being kept with their culture and community? To understand their language and religion? Can non-Indian judges and social workers protect Indian children, and their best interest? A best interest standard is generally understood as centering the child in the court's considerations. How do these interests actually center adult's wishes and biases? Are there other ways children's voices could enter into a conversation about where they should be placed?

2. Various international law standards include a child's right to her community, language, culture, and religion as a human right, which is discussed at length in chapter eight. How can those rights be incorporated into the best interest of the Indian child? The following case is not a child welfare case, but rather considers the best interest of the child in the context of child support.

Sharpe v. Sharpe

366 P.3d 66 (Alaska 2016)

I. Introduction

A non-custodial parent moved to modify a child support order after she quit her job in Anchorage, moved to a remote village, and adopted a subsistence lifestyle. Although the parent acknowledged that she was voluntarily unemployed, she argued that her decision was reasonable in light of her cultural, spiritual, and religious needs. The superior court disagreed and denied the motion.

The parent appeals, arguing that the superior court gave inadequate weight to her cultural and religious needs and that the child support order violates her right to the free exercise of her religion. But the superior court adequately considered all relevant factors in deciding not to modify the child support order. And there was no plain error in the court's failure to anticipate the free exercise claim, which the parent raises for the first time on appeal. Therefore, we affirm the judgment of the superior court

II. Facts and Proceedings

Jolene Lyon and Jyzyk Sharpe divorced in July 2012. The superior court awarded Jyzyk primary physical custody of the parties' only child and ordered Jolene to pay Jyzyk $1,507.00 per month in child support.

Jolene is a Yup'ik Eskimo who was raised in Nome and has family ties to the native village of Stebbins. When the child support order was issued, Jolene was "living in Anchorage, working at Alyeska Pipeline Service Company, and earning approximately [$]120,000 a year." In April 2013, she left Anchorage and took up a subsistence lifestyle in Stebbins.

Soon after relocating to Stebbins, Jolene moved to modify the child support order. She alleged that she was "no longer employed," that she was "a full time stay at home mother," and that her only income was her annual Permanent Fund Dividend. These developments, she argued, constituted a material change in circumstances warranting a modification of the child support order. She requested that the court reduce her monthly child support payment to $50 per month, the minimum allowed under Alaska Civil Rule 90.3(c)(3).

Jyzyk opposed the motion, arguing that modification of the child support order was not warranted because Jolene was "voluntarily and unreasonabl[y] unemployed." Although he acknowledged that Jolene was entitled to quit her job and move to a remote community, he argued that the parties' "ten year old daughter . . . should not be required to fund [Jolene's] lifestyle choice."

The superior court held a motion hearing in July 2013. During the hearing, Jolene testified about her life in Stebbins and the benefits she derived from her subsistence lifestyle. She expressed her desire to expose the parties' child to traditional life in

Stebbins. And she said that living in Stebbins, a dry community, provided reprieve from an alcohol abuse issue she had experienced during her marriage.

Jyzyk also testified at the hearing. He expressed his belief that the parties' child would benefit from receiving child support from Jolene at its existing amount and noted that these monthly payments "helped with everything [including] rent, groceries, [and] clothes." Jyzyk testified that "[i]n a dream world [he] would bring [the parties' child] to Kotzebue [in the area where he was raised] and raise her on the river," but he recognized that financial constraints prevented him from prudently fulfilling this dream.

After the hearing the superior court denied Jolene's motion. Although the court acknowledged that "[Jolene] is finding sort of a spiritual awakening or reconnecting with Native dance, Native culture, [and] subsistence lifestyle" and that life in Stebbins is "rehabilitative for her," it concluded: "[G]iven [Jolene's] background and her previous earnings I do not agree that . . . she does not have any income capacity simply because she chose to relocate to the village of Stebbins and earn nothing . . . ."

Jolene appeals.

IV. Discussion

A. The Superior Court Properly Considered The Financial Impact Of Jolene's Decision To Move To Stebbins And Adopt A Subsistence Lifestyle On Her Child.

* * *

In recent cases, we have repeatedly stated that the "relevant inquiry" when imputing income is "whether a parent's current situation and earnings reflect a voluntary and unreasonable decision to earn less than the parent is capable of earning." And the commentary to Alaska Civil Rule 90.3 specifically requires the superior court to examine the financial impact on the child in deciding whether to impute income: "When a parent makes a career change, [the totality of the circumstances] consideration should include the extent to which the children will ultimately benefit from the change." This directive implies that a court may consider the financial impact of a career change on a child, because the amount of child support inevitably affects the child's well-being.

There are certainly cases where we have affirmed child support modifications when a career change was partly motivated by personal factors. But these cases simply illustrate that the superior court has a wide range of discretion when addressing this issue. The fact that some cases have treated relocation decisions as reasonable does not free the superior court from the obligation to consider the financial impact of a career change on the obligor's child. Jolene does not cite any cases where we have held that the consideration of this impact was an abuse of discretion.

In this case, Jolene moved to Stebbins and adopted a subsistence lifestyle without any intention of seeking employment to meet her child support obligation. In support of her request for reduction of her child support obligation, she specifically stated that she had "no intention to return to the work force." The record thus supports the superior court's conclusion that Jolene's decision to leave her employment and move to Stebbins would have an unreasonable financial impact on the resources available to care for her daughter.

* * *

B. The Superior Court Adequately Considered Jolene's Religious And Cultural Needs.

Jolene argues that the superior court "direct[ed] nearly total focus on [her] past income history" and gave short shrift to Jolene's religious and cultural needs. It is true that "the parents' needs" is one of the factors the superior court must consider in evaluating the totality of the circumstances. But the superior court did adequately consider Jolene's needs, and after considering these needs it found that they did not outweigh other concerns, including her daughter's need for financial support:

> [Jolene] finds that [living in Stebbins] is sort of rehabilitative for her from the standpoint of her eliminating . . . some of the poisons of urban life. . . . She is finding sort of a spiritual reawakening or reconnecting with Native dance, Native culture, subsistence lifestyle, all of which is . . . admirable in an abstract sense.
>
> Then again . . . she effectively is . . . taking a vacation from the financial responsibilities that she assumed when she had a child, and the result of her not working and providing financial assistance is that it's going to impose . . . a greater burden on [Jyzyk], but, more importantly, it's going to have an impact over time on the opportunities . . . and resources that are available to take care of [the parties' daughter].
>
> * * *
>
> I do find it a difficult choice in this case because [Jolene] does seem to derive some very valid benefits from being in Stebbins, and I'm sure that for the summers [her daughter] derives some benefits there, too, but then there's the other nine months of the year when [the parties' daughter] lives in Anchorage and she'd be getting $50 a month, if that, instead of . . . $1500 a month, which could go a long way toward providing for necessities and also toward . . . providing for her future needs, educational needs, and to help give her a good start in life.

Despite this consideration, the dissent worries that the superior court "trivialize[s] Alaska Natives' way of life" and "devalues Alaska Natives' cultural, spiritual, and religious connections to their villages and their subsistence lifestyle." Yet in reality the dissent's desired outcome would have enormous financial implications for Alaska Native children. "The primary purpose of Rule 90.3 is to ensure that child support orders are adequate to meet the needs of children, subject to the ability of parents to pay." Granting either parent absolute freedom to exit the workforce would undermine this purpose.

* * *

The judgment of the superior court is AFFIRMED.

Notes

1. Marcia Zug notes in her article, *Your Money or Your Life: Indian Parents, and Child Support Modifications*, 29 J. of Am. Academy of Matrimonial Lawyers 409 (2017), there are two tests courts use to modify child support—a strict rule, which the court applied here, and good faith. In both cases, courts allow exceptions for a child's best interest:

> It is easy to presume that maximizing child support is in a child's best interest, but . . . there are exceptions. When the benefits of modification outweigh the negatives, modification should be permitted. This is true for all child support cases, but especially those pertaining to American Indian families. When considering modification requests made by Indian obligors, family courts must be particularly sensitive to the effects of income imputation on individual Native families as well as the effects of imputation on their tribes more broadly. If the benefit of modification relates to the child's or the parent's unique status as a member of a federally recognized tribe, this fact should be given substantial, perhaps even decisive, weight in the court's modification decision. As discussed in Part I, courts applying the strict rule test have permitted modification when it benefits the child or the greater community. Supporting native subsistence lifestyles does both.

Id. at 419.

In this case, however, the court specifically stated child support determinations did not consider a child's best interest, but that it is a based on a strict formula set by court rule.

2. The dissent lays out additional facts including the main reason Jolene was denied primary custody was due to her issues with alcohol, the fact that she had a baby boy with her in Stebbins from a relationship with a man from that community, and Jolene's testimony about the importance of her culture and community in Stebbins. The dissent went on to state:

> The fundamental flaw in the superior court's analysis is its conflation of the legitimacy of Jolene's move with the reasonableness of her unemployment in Stebbins and the manner in which the court imputed income to Jolene: "[T]he choice that I'm presented with is between treating [Jolene] as having zero income or . . . having imputed to her the income that she had at Alyeska . . . ." This was a false choice. The questions that should have been posed and answered at the hearing were: (1) whether Jolene's move to Stebbins was for legitimate reasons; (2) whether Jolene was in fact unreasonably unemployed in Stebbins; and if so, (3) what level of income should have been imputed to Jolene based on her work history, her qualifications, and her job opportunities in Stebbins.

3. While not a child welfare or adoption case, this opinion demonstrates the fundamental conflict between western courts and maintaining tribal cultural connections. Whether the Alaska Supreme Court states the determination does not include a best interest analysis or not, the courts are putting their thumb on the side of income over culture and sobriety. Is income more in a child's best interest than a sober and culturally connected mother?

What about a mother who may have also been escaping domestic violence? Two years after the Sharpe's divorce but two years before this opinion was issued, Jyzyk Sharpe was charged with the murder of his girlfriend's nearly 2 year old child. Megan Edge, *Wasilla man charged in toddler's death*, Anchorage Daily News, April 5, 2014. Based on the limited information available, it does not seem that he had full custody of the child in question in this case. See also, *State v. Sharpe*, Opinion, No. 7326 (Alaska, Jan. 4, 2019).

4. Various states have attempted to define the Indian child's best interest in their state ICWA statutes. Note what elements they share and where they differ.

Washington Indian Child Welfare Act

Wash. Rev. Code Ann. § 13.38.040 (West 2011)

2) "Best interests of the Indian child" means the use of practices in accordance with the federal Indian child welfare act, this chapter, and other applicable law, that are designed to accomplish the following: (a) Protect the safety, well-being, development, and stability of the Indian child; (b) prevent the unnecessary out-of-home placement of the Indian child; (c) acknowledge the right of Indian tribes to maintain their existence and integrity which will promote the stability and security of their children and families; (d) recognize the value to the Indian child of establishing, developing, or maintaining a political, cultural, social, and spiritual relationship with the Indian child's tribe and tribal community; and (e) in a proceeding under this chapter where out-of-home placement is necessary, to prioritize placement of the Indian child in accordance with the placement preferences of this chapter.

Nebraska Indian Child Welfare Act

Neb. Rev. Stat. § 43-1503 (2015)

(2) Best interests of the Indian child shall include:

(a) Using practices in compliance with the federal Indian Child Welfare Act, the Nebraska Indian Child Welfare Act, and other applicable laws that are designed to prevent the Indian child's voluntary or involuntary out-of-home placement; and

(b) Whenever an out-of-home placement is necessary, placing the child, to the greatest extent possible, in a foster home, adoptive placement, or other type of custodial placement that reflects the unique values of the Indian child's tribal culture and is best able to assist the child in establishing, developing, and maintaining a political, cultural, and social relationship with the Indian child's tribe or tribes and tribal community.

Minnesota Indian Family Preservation Act

Minn. Stat. Ann. § 260.755 (West 2017)

Subd. 2a. Best interests of an Indian child. "Best interests of an Indian child" means compliance with the Indian Child Welfare Act and the Minnesota Indian Family Preservation Act to preserve and maintain an Indian child's family. The best interests of an Indian child support the child's sense of belonging to family, extended family, and tribe. The best interests of an Indian child are interwoven with the best interests of the Indian child's tribe.

Notes

1. All of the states that define the best interests of the Indian child include the child's connection to her tribe. *See also,* Mich. Comp. Laws Ann. § 712B.5 (2012). When possible, that includes having the tribe make the final decision on the permanent placement of the child.

2. If a court is using the best interest standard to prevent a case from being transferred to tribal court, how is that protecting the child? What considerations is the court using to determine that tribal court jurisdiction is not in the best interest of the child? Are they the child's interest, or the court's? ICWA allows for the party who may best understand the child's interest to object to transfer to tribal court—the parent.

F. Parental Objection

In re Appeal in Maricopa County

922 P.2d 319 (Ariz. App. Div. 1 1996)

Weisberg, Judge.

The Tohono O'odham Nation (the "Nation"), a federally recognized Native American population living within the state, appeals from the trial court's denial of its motion to transfer the underlying dependency proceeding from the superior court to the Nation's Children's Court pursuant to the Indian Child Welfare Act (the "Act"). For the following reasons, we affirm.

Factual and Procedural Background

T.L.M. ("Mother") and A.J.B. ("Father") are the unmarried parents of a child born on July 3, 1993. Mother is not a Native American and Father is an enrolled member of the Nation. Child Protective Services took the child into temporary custody on October 21, 1993. On October 26, 1993, the Arizona Department of Economic Security ("DES") filed a dependency petition in the superior court alleging that Mother was a drug abuser and mentally unstable, and that the child was in danger while in her custody. Father's identity was then unknown to DES. When the petition was filed, Mother and the child were living in Avondale with Mother's relatives, the Clarks. On October 27, 1993, the juvenile court issued temporary orders making the child a ward of the court. Mother then moved out of the Clark home, leaving the child with the Clarks, to whom the court awarded physical custody. . . .

On January 7, 1994, DES filed an amended dependency petition identifying Father and noting that the child is an Indian child as defined by the Act. The Nation then filed a motion to intervene in the dependency proceeding, which was granted. *See* 25 U.S.C. § 1911(c). . . .

Sometime between November 1994 and February 1995, Mother left Arizona and moved to Arkansas. Physical custody of the child remained with the Clarks until August 14, 1995, when the court transferred custody to the child's paternal grandmother who resides within the Nation. Mother neither consented nor objected to this change of custody, and the child remains with his paternal grandmother to date.

On August 22, 1995, pursuant to the Act, the Nation filed a motion to transfer jurisdiction to the Nation's Children's Court. A hearing was held on August 28, 1995, after which the court found the absence of good cause, the presence of which would have prevented the transfer of jurisdiction. Noting that no parental objection (which could also prevent the transfer of jurisdiction) had been filed, the court granted Mother until September 5, 1995, to file an objection through her counsel or GAL. Mother filed a timely objection through counsel.

The court held another hearing on September 28, 1995, at which Mother's counsel stated that he had talked by telephone with Mother, who was still in Arkansas, and that she had objected to the transfer. Mother's GAL, however, stated that he did not object because he felt that the transfer was in Mother's best interest. In addition, Father's counsel, the child's counsel, and DES spoke in favor of the transfer.

The trial court, however, denied the Nation's motion to transfer jurisdiction, relying solely upon Mother's objection. . . .

In the instant case, the trial court specifically found that there was not good cause preventing the transfer of jurisdiction, and this finding remains unchallenged. We therefore consider only whether the trial court correctly denied the motion to transfer because of Mother's objection.

Consistent with uniform authority, this court has held that, under § 1911(b), a parent's "objection mandate[s] the retention of jurisdiction by the Arizona court." *In re Maricopa Juvenile Action No. JS–7359*, 159 Ariz. 232, 235, 766 P.2d 105, 108 (App.1989); see also *In re Adoption of Baby Boy L.*, 231 Kan. 199, 643 P.2d 168, 178 (1982); *In re S.Z.*, 325 N.W.2d 53, 56 (S.D.1982). Such an objection has also been referred to as a "parental veto," *In re S.Z.*, 325 N.W.2d at 56, and an "absolute veto," Guidelines for State Courts: Indian Child Custody Proceedings ("Guideline [s]"), 44 Fed.Reg. 67,584, 67,591 (Nov. 26, 1979). As explained by the Commentary to

Guideline C.2, "[s]ince the Act gives the parents and the tribal court of the Indian child's tribe an absolute veto over transfers, there is no need for any adversary proceedings if the parents or the tribal court opposes transfer." *Id.* A trial court therefore errs when it transfers jurisdiction over a parental veto.

We have found only one reported decision that has affirmed a trial court's transfer over a purported parental objection. In *In re the Welfare of R.I.*, 402 N.W.2d 173 (Minn. App. 1987), relied upon by the GAL, the Court of Appeals of Minnesota held that, although the parent verbally objected, she had by her conduct impliedly consented to transfer. But even assuming arguendo the correctness of *In re the Welfare of R.I.*, we find it to be distinguishable from the instant case....

Mother's failure to object to the child's placement cannot constitute her consent to the transfer of jurisdiction because the issue of the placement of a child is distinct from, and entirely unrelated to, the issue of jurisdiction over the proceeding. Moreover, mother never was informed that her failure to object to the child's placement would result in her waiver of the court's jurisdiction. Therefore, her failure to object cannot be taken as a knowing and intentional waiver of her jurisdictional rights. *Arizona Title Guarantee & Trust Co. v. Modern Homes, Inc.*, 84 Ariz. 399, 402, 330 P.2d 113, 114 (1958) (before waiver of a right may be inferred, there "must be an opportunity of choice between the relinquishment and the enforcement of the right in question.").

For the same reasons, the fact that Mother moved to Arkansas after the adjudication of dependency but before the placement of the child on the reservation neither constitutes abandonment of the child in favor of the tribal authorities nor does it reflect upon her wishes with respect to jurisdiction. Assuming Mother's competency to object, therefore, the trial court correctly concluded that it was required to deny the motion to transfer.

There has been one case where the court transferred over the objection of the parent, which the court in *Maricopa County* discussed.

In re R.I.

402 N.W.2d 173 (Minn. App. 1987)

Appellant seeks custody of her children, R.I., M.I. Jr.... R.I. and M.I. Jr. were born during appellant's marriage to M.I. Sr. The father and the children are all enrolled members of the Warm Springs Tribe in Oregon. Appellant is an enrolled member of the Red Lake Indian Reservation in Minnesota. On February 24, 1982, M.I. Sr. and appellant were divorced by order of the Warm Springs Tribe. Appellant was awarded custody of the children. Appellant lived with her children on the Warm Springs Reservation for a short time, but then returned to Minnesota, leaving her children behind with her ex-husband.

On July 23 and 24, 1983, M.I. Sr. left R.I. and M.I. Jr. unattended while he went out drinking. As a result, the Warm Springs Tribal prosecutor filed a neglect petition in the Tribal Court. On July 27, 1983, the Tribal Court issued emergency custody orders making the children wards of the court. . . .

In September of 1984, appellant returned to the Warm Springs Reservation, retrieved R.I. and M.I. Jr., and brought them to live with her and [and another daughter enrolled at Leech Lake] in Minnesota. On October 2, 1984, a social worker with Leech Lake Family Services visited appellant's household and found appellant and three friends intoxicated. . . . Minnesota Deputy Sheriff then took custody of the children under a 72 hour emergency hold. The children were placed in the temporary custody of the Leech Lake Family Services and Cass County Social Services. On October 5, 1984, Cass County commenced a dependency action concerning all three children pursuant to Minn.Stat. § 260.131, alleging that the children were without proper parental care. . . .

Initially, the trial court was not apprised that R.I. and M.I. Jr. were enrolled or eligible for enrollment with the Confederated Tribes of Warm Springs Reservation and, thus, did not give notice to the Warm Springs Tribe until after the February hearing. On March 15, 1985, the Warm Springs Tribe moved the court to intervene pursuant to § 101(c) of the ICWA. The Tribe served notice on all the parties of their request to dismiss the state action and have R.I. and M.I. Jr. transferred to the Warm Springs Reservation pursuant to 25 U.S.C. § 1911(b).

At a review hearing on April 3, 1985, the parties stipulated that the Warm Springs Tribal Court could intervene as a party and preserve its objection to Minnesota's assertion of jurisdiction over R.I. and M.I. Jr. The Tribal Court and the trial court agreed that the trial court would continue to exercise "courtesy supervision" over the case. . . .

In February of 1986, without permission from the trial court, the legal custodians, or her social workers, appellant took R.I. and M.I. Jr. to the Warm Springs Reservation. While on the reservation, appellant was charged with, and pleaded guilty to, possession of amphetamines. The Tribal Court then gave her $300.00 to take the children back to Minnesota. The Tribal Court informed appellant that if she allowed the children to remain on the reservation, custody proceedings would again be instigated. Appellant took the money, but left the children with their paternal aunts. The Tribal Court then issued another emergency custody order. At a subsequent hearing the Tribal Court temporarily placed the children in the custody of their aunts.

On April 30, 1986, the Cass County Attorney moved to dismiss the Minnesota custody proceedings with respect to R.I. and M.I. Jr. . . . The Tribal Court claimed that it had exclusive jurisdiction over R.I. and M.I. Jr. and sought to have the action transferred to Warm Springs. The trial court, finding that appellant had consented to the transfer of jurisdiction to the Tribal Court by bringing the children to the reservation and leaving them there voluntarily, granted the motion to dismiss the action as to R.I. and M.I. Jr., and transferred jurisdiction to the Tribal Court.

Appellant argues that the trial court erred in transferring the proceedings to the Tribal Court, claiming that she objected to the transfer. Section 101(b) of the ICWA provides:

> In any State court proceeding for the foster care placement of, or termination of parental rights to, an Indian child not domiciled or residing within the reservation of the Indian child's tribe, the court, in the absence of good cause to the contrary, shall transfer such proceeding to the jurisdiction of the tribe, *absent objection by either parent,* upon the petition of either parent or the Indian custodian of the Indian child's tribe.

The State argues that under the ICWA, the court *must* transfer the action absent good cause to the contrary or parental objection, but upon parental objection, the trial court may exercise its discretion in determining whether to transfer the proceedings. We have found no authority for the State's assertion that upon receiving a parental objection, the decision to transfer is discretionary. Other jurisdictions have held that parental objection *mandates* retention of the action in state court. *See, e.g., In the Matter of Adoption of Baby Boy L.,* 231 Kan. 199, 643 P.2d 168, 178 (1982); *Matter of S.Z.,* 325 N.W.2d 53, 65 (S.D.1982).

The Tribal Court and the State argue and the trial court found that although appellant verbally objected to the transfer of the proceedings, she impliedly consented to the transfer by voluntarily bringing the children to the Warm Springs Reservation. Appellant argues that the Tribal Court had no right to issue an emergency custody order, claiming that she placed the children with her extended family in accordance with accepted Indian custom. The Tribal Court, however, found that she had abandoned the children. We will not disturb that finding. We hold that the trial court properly concluded that appellant consented to the transfer of jurisdiction by leaving her children on the reservation.

Notes

1. In the second case, the facts drove the decision to overturn what is usually an insurmountable parental veto. The mother objected to the Warm Springs tribal jurisdiction, and the Minnesota court found that the tribal court did have jurisdiction, regardless of mother's objection, because she abandoned the children on the reservation. Should a tribal court be able to overturn a parental veto if the parent abandons the child on the reservation? What about the absolute right of self-government/jurisdiction? Why does a parent have a right to object? What are reasons a parent would want to object?

2. In the first case, given the mother's similar abandonment of her children, what drove the state court to refrain from allowing the Tohono O'odham Nation to exercise jurisdiction over one of its children residing within its borders? Does the fact that the mother in the first case is non-Native and the mother in the second case is Anishinaabekwe make a difference? If it does, does it make a difference that the Warm Springs Indian Reservation is made up of the Wasco, Walla Walla, and Paiute

tribes and not the Red Lake Anishinaabe? In other words, the tribal court that has jurisdiction in the second case is not the tribe of the mother.

3. At least one court has held that parents can veto a transfer to tribal court even after their parental rights are terminated. *People ex rel. K.D.*, 630 N.W.2d 492 (S.D. 2001). Given the otherwise complete end of all legal decision making when a parental rights are terminated, why would a state court allow those same parents to deny the transfer to tribal court?

G. Emergency Jurisdiction

ICWA allows for an emergency removal if the child is in imminent physical danger under § 1922. This provision is specific and states:

> nothing in this subchapter shall be construed to prevent the emergency removal of an Indian child who is a resident of or is domiciled on a reservation, but temporarily located off the reservation, from his parent or Indian custodian or the emergency placement of such child in a foster home or institution, under applicable State law, in order to prevent imminent physical damage or harm to the child. The State authority, official, or agency involved shall insure that the emergency removal or placement terminates immediately when such removal or placement is no longer necessary to prevent imminent physical damage or harm to the child . . . .

However, most states ignore the reservation residency requirements for an emergency removals, and the 1979 BIA Guidelines allow the temporary emergency custody to be continued for up to 90 days without having to follow the provisions of ICWA.

In 2013, two tribes and three parents filed a federal class-action lawsuit in South Dakota based on the actions of the Pennington County courts. The case, *Oglala Sioux v. Hunnick*, survived summary disposition and moved forward into the fact finding stage. Because the judges refused to release the transcripts of the cases, the federal district court forced the court reporters to turn over every third temporary custody hearing (also called a "48 hour" hearing in South Dakota, sometimes called 24-hour hearing, shelter hearing, or emergency hearing in other states).

Oglala Sioux Tribe et al v. Luann Van Hunnik

Plaintiffs' Statement of Undisputed Facts Re: Defendants' Violations of 25 U.S.C. § 1922, No. 13-cv-05020 (D.S.D. July 11, 2014)

1. Approximately one hundred 48-hour hearings involving Indian children are held each year by Defendants. (This figure was computed based on the number of transcripts that Plaintiffs received in discovery.)

2. The transcripts that were produced demonstrate that in at least 90 percent of Defendants' 48-hour hearings, orders were issued removing Indian children from their homes. It appears that in 100 percent of the hearings decided by Defendant Hon. Jeff Davis on the merits, Judge Davis issued orders removing Indian children from their homes.

3. 25 U.S.C. § 1922 requires a prompt hearing whenever an Indian child is removed from the home to determine whether continued out-of-home placement is "necessary to prevent imminent physical damage or harm to the child." However, in not one 48-hour hearing did Defendants determine whether continued out-of-home placement was necessary to prevent imminent physical damage or harm to the child, except in fewer than five cases when the issue was raised by a parent or by an attorney representing an Indian tribe. See Beauchamp Decl. Ex 1. Judge Davis concedes that: (a) not once in any of the 48-hour hearings over which he presided did the court inquire whether the cause of the child's emergency removal had been rectified prior to the hearing; and that (b) he knows of only three 48-hour hearings, Case Nos. A12-571, A12-468, and A12-36, conducted in the Seventh Judicial Circuit since January 2010 in which an inquiry was made by the court into whether the cause of the child's emergency removal had been rectified. Beauchamp Decl. Ex. 4, Davis Am. Interrog. No. 9. Furthermore, in two of those three cases, the inquiry into whether the cause of the child's emergency removal had been rectified was initiated by counsel for an Indian tribe, and not by the court. See Beauchamp Decl. Ex. 1, Case Nos. A12-571 and A12-36

4. One reason why Defendants never complete the mandatory § 1922 inquiry is because Judge Davis believes that § 1922 is a "statute of deferment," that is, that § 1922 authorizes state courts to defer applying the protections contained in ICWA until proceedings that occur after 48-hour hearings are held. Defendant Davis admitted that this is his position in response to a request for admission. See Request for Admission No. 32: "Admit that in your memorandum of law (Docket 34) you state that 25 U.S.C. § 1922 is a 'statute of deferment' and that you continue to believe that is true." Answer: "Admit." (A copy of this Request for Admission is attached to the Beauchamp Decl. as Exhibit 3.) Judge Davis confirmed this point in a recent 48-hour hearing. During that hearing, counsel for an Intervenor Indian Tribe asked Judge Davis to determine whether there was any "pending imminent threat of danger" in returning an Indian child to the mother, who was present in the courtroom. Judge Davis replied: "ICWA doesn't apply to a 48-hour hearing, Mr. Hanna, and I decline your invitation. We'll be in recess." See Beauchamp Decl. Ex. 1-Case No. A14-444 (June 23, 2014), Transcript at 13-14.3

5. Another reason why Defendants never complete the § 1922 inquiry is because as a matter of policy, practice, and procedure, Defendants do not permit testimony to be given during a 48-hour hearing. This fact was admitted by Judge Davis in response to Request for Admission No. 19 (attached to the Beauchamp Decl. as Ex. 4) (Judge Davis admits that "no oral testimony is taken at a 48-hour hearing."); see also

Beauchamp Decl. Ex. 1-Case No. A13-609 (September 9, 2013) (Pfeifle, J.) Transcript at 2 ("We will not take testimony [during a 48-hour hearing]."); Case No. A13-616 (September 12, 2013) (Pfeifle, J.) Transcript at 2 ("we do not take evidence" during a 48-hour hearing); Case No. A14-47 (January 24, 2014) (Mandel, J.) Transcript at 2 ("This is an informal proceeding, and by that I mean that there's no testimony taken."). As a result of the fact that (a) Defendants allowed no testimony at 48-hour hearings, (b) Defendants allowed no cross-examination at 48-hour hearings, (c) often the only questions asked of the parents in a 48-hour hearing were for purposes of identification and to see if they understood their rights, and (d) Defendants never conducted the inquiries required by 25 U.S.C. § 1922, Defendants' 48-hour hearings were completed rather quickly. Judging from the length of the transcripts that were produced, the average length of time it took to complete a 48-hour hearing, Plaintiffs estimate, was under four minutes. A number of these hearings appear to have been completed in about sixty seconds.

* * *

15. Case No. A10-1191 (November 8, 2010) (Davis, J.): The mother and father both attended the hearing. All that is discernable from the transcript is that the mother apparently had been intoxicated and her son was taken from her custody. The father, however, informed Judge Davis "I wasn't intoxicated," and the father requested that the boy be released to his custody. See Transcript at 4. In response, Judge Davis claimed that the court had only two options: "to allow you to work with" DSS to regain custody of his son "or set the matter for a full, formal hearing." *Id.* at 5. The father again asked why he was losing custody of his son, and when Judge Davis did not supply an answer, the father and Judge Davis then had this conversation:

> THE FATHER: I would just like to know what I did wrong that my son is not with me. That's all I'm asking.
>
> THE COURT: That, sir, I honestly can't tell you at this point because noting has been checked out and verified to come to me yet.

Id. at 5. Notably, a representative from DSS was in the courtroom during the hearing. Judge Davis did not explain why the court was unwilling to ask DSS to supply a response to the father's (legitimate) question. What is clear, however, is that Judge Davis did not know whether the emergency had ceased, and saw no need to address that question. Instead, the court granted DSS's request for continued custody for 60 days.

* * *

21. Case No. A11-1075 (December 5, 2011) (Eklund, J.): The transcript of this hearing is fifteen sentences in length. The mother was present but the court did not even ask her to verify her name. The court granted custody to DSS for 60 days without any discussion of the facts, nor did the court advise the mother of her rights.

* * *

35. Plaintiffs received more than 120 transcripts of 48-hour hearings conducted since January 1, 2010. Plaintiffs also received the Temporary Custody Orders that were entered in nearly all of those cases. Every one of these orders contains the following provision:

> The Department of Social Services is hereby authorized to return full and legal custody of the minor child(ren) to the parent(s), guardian or custodian (without further court hearing) at any time during the custody period granted by this Court, if the Department of Social Services concludes that no further child protection issues remain and that temporary custody of the child(ren) is no longer necessary.

36. Thus, DSS was authorized by these orders to return custody of Indian children to their homes when the emergency has terminated but DSS was never ordered to do so. See Beauchamp Decl. Ex. 2.

37. Similarly, in their oral directives during the hearings, presiding judges never ordered DSS to return an Indian child to the home when the emergency ended. At most, the presiding judges indicated a preference for that result, and merely authorized DSS to return the child.

Notes

1. While this excerpt of the class action focuses on § 1922 violations, the petitioners also claimed due process violations. This case was cited in the 2015 BIA Guidelines for State Courts and Agencies in Indian Child Custody Proceedings as the reason for clarifying the section on emergency removals to keep them as short as possible and what the proper standard is (imminent physical damage or harm). While those Guidelines were rescinded and replaced a year later, the federal regulations cited the case as a reason for the need for federal regulations. 81 Fed. Reg. 38,778, 38,782 (June 14, 2016).

2. According to transcripts from the trial court, there are approximately 100 48-hour (or emergency) removal hearings heard every year. In 90-100% of the cases, the children were ordered removed. These hearings followed many of the pre-ICWA removal concerns, happening without due process, and automatically, with no concern for the reason for the removal of the child.

3. Tribal jurisdiction over Indian children is at the very heart of tribal sovereignty and tribal self-determination. ICWA attempts to negotiate that jurisdiction when children do not live on a reservation. In fact, more than half of the population of Native people in the United States live off the reservation, due in part to federal and state Indian Country policies. In cases where it is not feasible for a child to be in tribal court or under tribal court jurisdiction, ICWA requires state courts to act in the place of tribal courts. Those requirements are discussed in detail in the next chapter.

Chapter 3

Requirements of State Courts Under ICWA

When a child welfare case involving an Indian child stays under state jurisdiction, ICWA creates specific legal requirements for both state courts and state agencies. These requirements are spelled out in §§ 1912, 1913, and 1915 of the Act and are the key provisions every attorney working in state courts should be familiar with. Fundamentally, 1) state courts must provide notice to tribes when an Indian child in involved in a child custody proceeding; 2) tribes have the right to intervene in cases involving their children; 3) the standard of proof for ICWA cases is higher than other family law cases; 4) active, rather than reasonable, efforts must be made to maintain family cohesion; 5) there must be a qualified expert witness giving testimony supporting either foster care placement or termination of parental rights; and 6) there are strict placement preferences in place that delineate where, and in what order, individuals have the ability to adopt or foster Indian children.

ICWA was created specifically to ensure the reformation of state court and agency practices, so these provisions form the essence of the proper daily application of the Act. They were designed to slow down the previously wholesale and nearly automatic removal of Indian children, and they trump other certain other federal requirements in child welfare, such as the Multiethnic Placement Act and certain provisions of the Adoption and Safe Families Act. As such, interpretations of these provisions make up the bulk of the litigation surrounding the law.

In some states, the lack of ICWA compliance, and the easily identified areas of ICWA litigation, has led them to pass state laws incorporating ICWA. In some cases, those laws provide heightened protections for Indian families, as contemplated by § 1921 of the federal law. There is further discussion of some of these laws and the cases interpreting them in Chapter Five. However, some cases in this chapter will also refer to state ICWA laws. In addition, cases involving voluntary relinquishments and adoptions are addressed in Chapter Four. This chapter focuses on child welfare proceedings that involve state agencies, and are usually identified as "involuntary" proceedings.

A. Notice

At the start of a child welfare proceeding, the state agency may remove a child from her family and file a petition to establish jurisdiction over a family, or the agency may allow the child to stay in the home but still file a petition. The petition is based on reports of neglect or abuse of the child by her parents. A family may come to the attention of a state agency through a report of a neighbor or family member, or from a "mandated reporter" such as a teacher or medical professional. A mandated reporter must tell the state agency when he suspects abuse or neglect of a child. When a child is removed from the home, the state must have a hearing within a set period of time, which varies by state. That first hearing is to determine whether the state has enough evidence to keep the child out of the home and to set a date for an adjudicatory hearing, to establish state jurisdiction over a family.

The first requirement of state courts and agencies in *all* child welfare proceedings under ICWA is the duty to inquire of all the parties whether the child in the case is an Indian child. As early in the proceedings as a court "knows or has reason to know" there is an Indian child involved in a proceeding that falls under ICWA, the agency seeking foster care placement or termination of parental rights must notify the applicable tribes by registered mail, return receipt requested. The court must then wait ten days after the return of the receipt to hold further proceedings. When a tribe receives a notice inquiry from a state court, generally the enrollment office of the tribe runs a search within its membership database to determine whether the child involved is either a member of the tribe or is eligible for enrollment in the tribe.

While state agencies must notify tribes in involuntary proceedings involving an Indian child or a child presumed to be Indian, there is no similar formal notification requirement for voluntary proceedings. However, there are provisions of ICWA discussed below that apply to voluntary or private adoptions regarding tribal intervention and placement preferences. This ambiguity, allowing a tribe to participate in certain portions of a voluntary adoption, but not requiring notification, is a fairly large omission in the law. However, the federal regulations affirm that an Indian child must be identified on the record, and this may require contacting the tribe to verify her citizenship. 25 C.F.R. § 23.124 (2016). Issues surrounding voluntary relinquishments and adoptions are discussed in Chapter Four

State courts generally fail to comply with the strict notice requirements of the law. Almost forty years after its passage in 1979, out of ignorance, forgetfulness, defiance, and neglect, state courts continue to fail to notify tribes when Indian children enter their courtrooms. Without proper compliance with ICWA's notice provisions, children, parents, and tribes cannot receive the heightened protections that ICWA offers. The following two articles detail several of the reasons that the notice requirement of ICWA is often overlooked.

Why Ißs Notice Under the Indian Child Welfare Act So Hard to Get Right?

Judicial Council of California, Center for Families, Children, & the Courts (2010)

More Indian Child Welfare Act (ICWA) cases are overturned for failure to give proper notice than for any other cause. Given that ICWA has been around since 1978, why is this still such a problem?

The answer is that finding out where to send notice is much more complicated than many people realize. This is particularly true in California. California has more than 100 federally recognized Indian tribes, at least 33 unrecognized tribes, and more individuals with Native American ancestry than any other state in the nation. Many of these individuals trace their Native American ancestry to tribes outside of California; for an individual who does trace his or her ancestry to a historical California Indian tribe, finding out whether or not he or she is "a member or eligible for membership" in a federally recognized tribe, and if so which tribe, can be very difficult.

* * *

If an individual is an enrolled member of a federally recognized tribe, he or she will likely be able to tell you the name of the tribe as it is identified in the federal register. Many people who identify as California Indians, however, may not be able to tell you the name of their tribe as it appears in the federal register. They may instead identify their tribe by its historic tribal name, for instance Pomo or Cahuilla. If someone states they have Pomo ancestry, it will not be possible to go to the federal register list of Agents for Service of ICWA Notice and look under "P" to find Pomo tribes. There are more than 20 federally recognized tribes whose members trace their ancestry to the historic "Pomo" tribe. Not a single one of these tribes' federally recognized tribal names begins with the word "Pomo." Only six of these tribes even have the word "Pomo" in their federally recognized tribal name.

Similarly, if someone states that he or she has Cahuilla ancestry, it is not possible to look up Cahuilla in the federal register and be certain you have found his or her tribe. Although there is a federally recognized tribe named "Cahuilla," it does not include all people of Cahuilla ancestry. There are nine federally recognized tribes whose members trace their ancestry to the historic Cahuilla tribe. Of those, the federally recognized tribal name of only one (the Cahuilla Band of Mission Indians) begins with the word Cahuilla. Only three have the word Cahuilla in their federally recognized tribal name.

To further complicate matters, several tribes have traditional territories and reservation land bases that straddle the California border. For instance, the Colorado River Indian Tribes ("CRIT") are recognized by the federal government as a single federally recognized tribe. CRIT is, however, composed of descendants of four distinct historic tribes—the Mohave, Chemehuevi, Hopi, and Navajo—who had land set aside in common for them by the federal government in 1865. The reserve straddles the California/Arizona border, with a substantial portion of the reservation lying within San Bernardino County. Nevertheless, because the primary community and tribal offices are located in Arizona, the Colorado River Indian Tribes are not even listed as a "California" tribe in the federal register of Designated Agents for Service of ICWA Notice. Instead, they are listed under the Western Region of BIA, which includes Arizona. The same is true of the Chemehuevi Indian Tribe, the Fort Mojave Indian Tribe, and the Fort Yuma Tribe and perhaps others that also have reserve lands that straddle the California/Arizona border.

* * *

State and local agency personnel are sometimes frustrated that people claiming Native American ancestry sometimes have very little information about their potential links to federally recognized tribes. Similarly, sometimes there is frustration that, when notice is sent to tribes, the tribes sometimes take a very long time to determine whether particular individuals are members or eligible for membership in their tribes.

Many of the historical factors discussed above contribute to the problem that people of Native American ancestry are sometimes disconnected from their tribal communities and do not know whether or not they are members of or eligible for membership in a federally recognized tribe. As discussed in the previous section, not all the historic California tribes currently have status as "federally recognized tribes." Reservations were not set aside for all the tribes in California, even the tribes that signed the eighteen 1851–1852 unratified treaties. The idea of a comprehensive "list" of federally recognized tribes is quite recent; one was first published in 1979. The "list" was primarily based on those groups for which the federal government held lands in trust, and thus left out many individuals and families that descend from historic California tribes and identify as Indian even though they might not be eligible for membership in a federally recognized tribe. These people's status as "Indian" has in many ways been confirmed by federal laws and policies. Federal legislation still contains a unique definition of California Indian that more people than just members of federally recognized tribes and that recognizes this broader category as eligible for health and education services from the BIA.

The Cherokee Conundrum

Kathryn E. Fort

MSU Legal Studies Research Paper No. 07-07 (2009)

California has the most number of ICWA cases of any state in the country. Far and away notice noncompliance is the most litigated issue in these California cases. The situation has become so dire a recent California appellate court decision goes so far as to state that the court is "weary" of these lack of notice proceedings. California is doing a poor job of notifying tribes of Indian children in its court system. But why does California have so many notice cases? And which tribes are, or are not, receiving all of these faulty notifications? Without any doubt, the Cherokee tribes have the most number of parents claiming affiliation. Why is this the case? Why are cases involving potential Cherokee children most likely to have bad notice litigation?

* * *

At times, because of the information provided, the child's tribal affiliation may be vague, but if there is any indication of the affiliation, for example, Anishinaabe or Sioux or Cherokee, the state must find all of the information about the child's family and then notify all of the federally recognized tribes which may have an interest in the child. The state must also notify the regional BIA office. Unfortunately, the state does not always collect all of the necessary information, and the parent does not always know the information. In addition, when the state does collect the information, it is not always listed on the forms correctly. For instance, the switching of paternal and maternal grandparent names is a common mistake.

* * *

California has fairly strict notice requirements, codified in both the family code and rules of court. The courts require notice whenever the state agency "knows or has reason to believe the child is an Indian child." In addition, the state has an ongoing, continuing duty of inquiry throughout the case to determine if the child is an Indian child. Every child, parent, Indian custodian or guardianship in certain court actions must be asked by the state if the child may be an Indian child, and the state must fill out the Indian Child Inquiry Attachment form. Every parent, guardian or Indian custodian in certain court actions must themselves fill out an additional form, the Parental Notification of Indian Status. Notice must be send to the tribe to notify the tribe of the case, inquire as to the status of the child, and notify the tribe that it has the right to intervene. Notice must be sent by registered mail, return receipt requested. The parent has the right to bring up ICWA issues at any time during the proceedings, including at the appellate level even if it was not brought up at the trial level.

* * *

In 2007, a California Court of Appeals partially published an ICWA notice decision reprimanding the Department of Children and Family services for its complete lack of ICWA notice compliance. The case, *In re Justin L.*, involved extreme abuse by the mother, but the Court of Appeals was still required to remand the case for the sole purpose of notice under the ICWA statutes. The mother in this case claimed affiliation with Blackfeet, "Chocktaw" and Cherokee tribes. The Court wrote,

> We are growing weary of appeals in which the only error is the Department's failure to comply with ICWA. Remand for the limited purpose of the ICWA compliance is all too common. ICWA's requirements are not new. Yet the prevalence of inadequate notice remains disturbingly high. This case presents a particularly egregious example of the practice of flouting ICWA. The Department concedes it sent no notices, notwithstanding the juvenile court's specific order that it do so. And, we have been given no

> indication that the Department has attempted to mitigate the damage it caused in failing to attend to ICWA's dictates by sending notices while this proceeding was pending.

In an unpublished decision in 2007, the 4th District Appellate Court took the trial court to task for "disparaging" the work of the Appellate Court. In this case the mother claimed Cherokee, Blackfeet, Crow and Algonquin affiliation. The Court found that for the second time, the Department of Public Social Services (DPSS) failed to properly notify the tribes that might be considered Cherokee, Blackfeet, Crow or Algonquin. The Court found that "in the absence of nearly all significant information about MacKenzie's ancestry we must conclude that the tribes were deprived of any meaningful opportunity to determine whether [] is an Indian child." The Court continued to take the trial court to task, stating that "with the myriad cases that have been published on this subject it is virtually incomprehensible and extremely frustrating that this court should find itself in the position of having to reverse an order for a second time to remedy the slap-dash approach to ICWA compliance perpetrated by the DPSS and sanctioned by an imprudent juvenile court."

This unfortunately is not a new development for California. In 2002 the Appellate Court lamented the same problem with notice compliance. In that case, the state sent the wrong forms certified mail rather than registered, did not request a return receipt and sent the notice to the Santa Ynez Tribal Health Clinic. The Court went on to hold that

> Over the years, this court has published repeatedly to emphasize the importance of ICWA notice compliance. Indeed, with one exception, every opinion cited herein comes from this court. Nevertheless, we still encounter deficient records such as the one in this appeal. Therefore, in yet another effort to ensure compliance with the notice requirements of the ICWA, we will set forth our expectations. We hold that a party, such as the Department here, who seeks the foster are placement of or termination of parental rights to a child who may be eligible for Indian child status, must do the following or face the strong likelihood of reversal on appeal to this court.

In a cost benefit analysis, the limited remand used by the California courts may have made it easier for the state not to notify the tribe and comply only when the case comes back on appeal.

* * *

Surveying ICWA cases using the Westlaw database provides some interesting data. Using both published and unpublished cases under the allstates database, searching with the term "Indian Child Welfare Act" and limiting the time frame from January 1, 2007 through February 29, 2008, the result is 414 appellate or state supreme court cases. Of those, 48 do not involve ICWA other than as a citation or case reference. 308 of the 366 relevant cases come out of California, with only 58 relevant cases coming from all other states combined. After sorting every case in to "Notice and Affirm," "Notice and Remand," "Other ICWA Issue and Affirm" and "Other

ICWA Issue and Remand" it is possible to see just how many California ICWA cases deal with notice. Nationwide 235 of the 366 cases dealt with notice issues, 64% of all cases. However, in California, 226 of all cases were notice cases, 73% of the California cases. Notice cases include cases where the parent brings the claim that notice was insufficient; it does not necessarily mean that the notice was insufficient. However, 137 of the 226 California notice cases had to be remanded for compliance with ICWA notice, which means that sixty percent of the time the appellate court considered notice to be insufficient. Conversely, only 14 other California ICWA cases had to be remanded or reversed, usually for inquiry purposes. This is only four percent of the total California ICWA cases.

However, there was something additional of note with the California cases. One tribe more than any other kept appearing in the California cases, whether the case ended up being remanded or not. Out of 308 California cases, the parent or grandparent claimed Cherokee affiliation in 143 cases, in other words, 46% of all California cases. The second closest affiliation was Blackfeet with 41 cases, followed by Apache with 33 cases. Tribal affiliations which might be reasonably expected in the California court system were barely present: "Rancheria" was only in seven cases, Navajo in 12, Hopi in none and Yaqui in 11. There was also a trend toward vague or anglicized tribal names, so while there were 16 Sioux cases, there were only two Lakota cases. There were seven Chippewa cases, though only one Ottawa and two Potawatomi.

In California, parents claiming Cherokee affiliation are litigating ICWA at a far higher rate than any other tribe. However, what these parents are litigating is almost entirely notice. Of the 143 cases dealing with potentially Cherokee Indian children, only twenty cases do not deal with a notice issue. This means that in the subset of California Cherokee ICWA cases, 85% of the time the problem at issue in the case was notice, almost 13% higher than the overall California rate. And while 44% of all California cases are remanded for notice compliance, 57% of California Cherokee cases are remanded for notice compliance.

Notes

1. If the most claimed tribe by parties involved in child welfare cases in California and across the country is "Cherokee," why are state courts continually failing to notify the Cherokee tribes? There are only three federally recognized Cherokee tribes, and the Bureau of Indian Affairs maintains a register of the appropriate addresses to send ICWA notices. Should all new state court employees working in the family division be required to review ICWA's notice provision and be provided with tribal contact lists from the Bureau of Indian Affairs?

2. Different state courts have adopted different ways of handling notice violations in a child welfare proceeding. California and Michigan, two states with the highest number of appealed notice violations, either affirm the decision regardless of notice or do a "conditional reversal," where the case is sent back down to the trial level for proper ICWA notice. If, after the state provides the proper notice, the

tribe wishes to be involved, the state court must re-do the initial proceedings with the tribe's involvement. If, after the state provides the proper notice, the tribe does not wish to be involved, the initial decision remains. Appellate courts have struggled with whether to conditionally affirm, or conditionally reverse decisions where there is notice non-compliance.

In re Francisco W.

43 Cal. Rptr. 3d 171 (Cal. Dist. Ct. App. 4th 2006)

Huffman, J.

In this appeal of the termination of parental rights based on noncompliance with the Indian Child Welfare Act (ICWA) (25 U.S.C. § 1901 et seq.), we are asked to reexamine our practice of limited reversals and remands in which we instruct the juvenile court to correct the ICWA notice defect and reinstate the prior judgment of termination if no Indian tribe chooses to intervene in the proceeding.

Earl W. and appellate counsel for his dependent child, Francisco W., contend that we should depart from our usual practice in ICWA cases and reverse the judgment without limitation, thereby allowing the juvenile court to revisit dependency issues outside ICWA. Francisco's counsel claims such limited reversals (1) violate due process, (2) are inconsistent with a child's best interests, and (3) prevent the juvenile court from considering changes in the child's circumstances concerning his or her adoptability. Earl has joined in and adopted by reference the brief submitted by Francisco's counsel. (Cal. Rules of Court, rule 13(a)(5).)

* * *

On November 6, 2003, the San Diego County Health and Human Services Agency (Agency) filed a dependency petition on behalf of Francisco, alleging he was at substantial risk of harm because his parents failed to adequately supervise and protect him. (Welf. & Inst. Code, § 300, subd. (b).) The original petition listed Earl as an alleged father.

In his paternity questionnaire, Earl indicated he possibly had Cherokee heritage. The court ordered paternity tests and deferred ICWA findings until it received the test results. The paternal grandmother, along with numerous relatives, attended the detention hearing.

Also in November, the social worker sent ICWA notices to the Bureau of Indian Affairs (BIA) and the three federally recognized Cherokee tribes. The boxes in the child family history section of the form were largely left blank, and the social worker did not include any background information (e.g., birth date, birthplace) for the paternal grandmother even though she had made herself available.

* * *

At the six-month review hearing on June 1, 2004, the court ordered six more months of reunification services. The court also ordered Agency to renotice the Cherokee tribes for the scheduled 12–month review hearing in December.

In August 2004, Agency mailed notices to the BIA and the three Cherokee tribes for the second time. The record on appeal contains only a copy of the notice sent to the BIA. The name of the paternal grandfather and his "Cherokee" tribal affiliation were included in this notice, but not his birth date or birthplace. Most of the boxes requesting information were marked "unknown" as opposed to being left blank as they were in the first round of notices. Neither copies of the notices sent to the Cherokee tribes nor certified mail receipts showing when the tribes received the second notices are included in the record. The BIA responded that it needed more information to determine if Francisco was an Indian child. The United Keetoowah Band of Cherokee Indians of Oklahoma and the Eastern Band of Cherokee Indians indicated that based on the information supplied to them, Francisco was not a member of their respective tribes and they would not intervene.

* * *

On January 4, 2005, the court ordered Agency to again send out ICWA notices to the Cherokee tribes because the court file did not contain copies of the notices previously sent. Again, in the new round of notices, most of the boxes requesting information in the pertinent form were marked "unknown." The record indicates the Cherokee Nation received the notice on January 17, and the Eastern Band of Cherokee Indians received the notice on January 18. The record does not contain a certified mail receipt for the United Keetoowah Band of Cherokee Indians.

On January 26, 2005, the court found the Cherokee tribes were properly noticed. On February 2, the court found ICWA did not apply after Agency indicated no tribes had responded to the latest batch of notices.

* * *

On July 19, 2005, the court found, by clear and convincing evidence, that it was likely Francisco will be adopted if parental rights were terminated, none of the statutory exceptions to adoption existed in this case, and adoption was in Francisco's best interest. The court terminated parental rights.

* * *

ICWA notice requirements are strictly construed. (*In re Karla C.* (2003) 113 Cal. App.4th 166, 174, 6 Cal.Rptr.3d 205.) The notice sent to the BIA and/or Indian tribes must contain enough information to be meaningful. The notice must include: if known, (1) the Indian child's name, birthplace, and birth date; (2) the name of the tribe in which the Indian child is enrolled or may be eligible for enrollment; (3) names and addresses of the child's parents, grandparents, great grandparents, and other identifying information; and (4) a copy of the dependency petition. To enable the juvenile court to review whether sufficient information was supplied, Agency must file with the court the ICWA notice, return receipts and responses received from the BIA and tribes.

It is essential to provide the Indian tribe with all available information about the child's ancestors, especially the one with the alleged Indian heritage. (*In re Louis S.* (2004) 117 Cal.App.4th 622, 631, 12 Cal.Rptr.3d 110.) Notice to the tribe must include available information about the maternal and paternal grandparents and great-grandparents, including maiden, married and former names or aliases; birthdates; place of birth and death; current and former addresses; tribal enrollment numbers; and other identifying data.

* * *

Agency concedes that the juvenile court's rulings regarding the adequacy of the ICWA notices were erroneous. We agree. Even though Agency sent three sets of notices, none of them included sufficient information that would allow the tribes or the BIA to determine Francisco's membership or eligibility for membership. These defects persisted even though Agency easily could have contacted the paternal grandmother for additional pertinent information.

* * *

At issue is the propriety of our practice—as well as that of our colleagues in various other districts—in dependency cases with ICWA notice irregularities to issue limited reversals in which we order the judgment to be reinstated if no Indian tribe intervenes after proper notice is given. As explained below, we conclude this practice is legally authorized, consistent with the best interests of children, and in keeping with fundamental principles of appellate practice. Further, contrary to the positions advanced by Earl's and Francisco's appellate counsel, this approach does not infringe upon due process rights and does not—particularly with the recent enactment of statutory provisions—prevent the juvenile court from considering changes in the dependent child's circumstances concerning his or her adoptability.

* * *

The limited reversal approach is well adapted to dependency cases involving termination of parental rights in which we find the only error is defective ICWA notice. This approach allows the juvenile court to regain jurisdiction over the dependent child and determine the one remaining issue. The parties already have litigated all other issues at the section 366.26 hearing, and it is not necessary to have a complete retrial. Thus, the child is afforded the protection of the juvenile court, and, at the same time, his or her case is processed to cure the ICWA error, which is more expeditious than a full rehearing of all section 366.26 issues. Indeed, a new section 366.26 hearing would be subject to another appeal; by not following our practice we could easily age a child out of adoptability into long-term foster care, which is the least favored permanent plan. Further, we know of no rule or law that would prohibit use of this procedure in child dependency cases. (See *In re Zeth S.* (2003) 31 Cal.4th 396, 405, 2 Cal.Rptr.3d 683, 73 P.3d 541 [review of juvenile dependency cases governed by general rules of appellate procedure].)

* * *

The limited reversal disposition in defective notice ICWA appeals is in keeping with the public policy of our child dependency scheme, which favors prompt resolution of cases.

* * *

Francisco's appellate counsel contends a new section 366.26 hearing after remand for ICWA notice is essential to protect a child's fundamental right to maintain his or her biological family; accordingly, our practice of limited reversals in such cases violates substantive due process principles. The contention is without merit.

* * *

Counsel has not raised any adverse consequence to Francisco by reinstating an otherwise valid order, if no tribe intervenes. Francisco was placed with his maternal grandmother, who wants to adopt him, and there is no indication the relevant circumstances have or will change. We see no justification in requiring the juvenile court to revisit the issue of his adoptability when it was not questioned at trial or on appeal. If we view counsel's call for us to drop our practice of limited reversals in all ICWA cases, the dire consequences she predicts are speculative at best. Another problem with counsel's position is that in every case we would have to remand for a new section 366.26 hearing, with the attendant delays for notice, trial and appeal. Counsel has not offered any support for the sweeping general principle she and Earl's counsel advocate.

As indicated above, we adopted our practice of limited reversals because it promotes the child's best interests and the public policy of this state—namely, that when reunification is not feasible, a permanent home should be found for the child in the most expeditious manner possible under the law. If the only error requiring reversal of the judgment terminating parental rights is defective ICWA notice and it is ultimately determined on remand that the child is not an Indian child, the matter ordinarily should end at that point, allowing the child to achieve stability and permanency in the least protracted fashion the law permits.

We acknowledge there very well might be exceptional cases—those in which significant circumstances have changed during the pendency of the appeal and have adversely affected the likelihood of the child being adopted, and for which an alternate disposition would be in order to avoid a result adverse to the child upon remand. However, we reject the argument of Francisco's counsel and Earl's counsel that our practice of limited reversals in ICWA notice cases effectively ties the hands of the juvenile court on remand and prevents it from reacting to such changes in circumstances. Rather, we find the law accommodates the extraordinary case in which a postjudgment change in circumstances makes it unlikely the child will be adopted, and our limited reversal practice does not infringe upon these accommodations.

Notes

1. Is the court convincing in its reasoning? Is there an assumption that the child is almost always non-Indian? How can a court retroactively increase standards? Does this hurt or help the child?

2. Recently the First District Appellate Court in California has started listing out the exact problems with the notice sent out—not simply that it was not sent out, but that the notice was sent to the wrong address or person:

> As to the Chippewa Cree tribe, the notice for G.B.-C. was sent to Chippewa Cree Indians, Brenda Gardiner, ICWA Rep, RR1, P.O. Box 544, Box Elder, Montana 59521. According to the Department's proof of service, the notice for M.B.-C. was sent to the same address. The address specified for the tribe in the Federal Register was Chippewa Cree Tribe of the Rocky Boy's Reservation of Montana, Christina Trottier, ICWA Director, 31 Agency Square, Box Elder, MT 59521. (79 Fed.Reg. 3225 (January 17, 2014).) Although the city, state and zip code were the same, the addresses were completely different.

In re M.B.-C., No. 147812, slip op. at 6-7 (Cal. App. Ct. Nov. 3, 2016). The Federal Register is updated annually with tribal contacts for ICWA notice, but few state social workers know of its existence.

3. The courts also have a difficult time determining what should be the threshold trigger for it to know or have reason to know an Indian child is involved in the case. In 2010, the California Court of Appeals in the Fourth District found that when a parent claimed her great-great grandfather was a "full blooded Cherokee" and her maternal grandmother "participated in an annual Indian pow-wow," that was not "sufficient reason to know" the child "is a member of or eligible for membership in an Indian tribe." The court went on to state that notice is not required "unless there is a reasonable probability the child is an Indian child." *In re Skyler H.*, 112 Cal. Rptr. 3d 892, 897 (Cal. Ct. App. 2010). The court was "mindful of the appropriate use of judicial resources, including the resources of the social service agency in its capacity as an arm of the court." *Id.* at 898.

While state courts have limited resources, sending the notices required by ICWA should not be out of the reach of most judicial budgets. While state case law delineates the specific level of attenuation that requires the issuance of notice to tribes, sending notice even when the tribal claim is attenuated is immeasurably less expensive than re-doing proceedings because of a notice violation. However, many courts face the question of whether to treat attenuated-claim cases as ICWA cases from the very beginning, or only after affirmative involvement is received from the tribe. Treating cases as ICWA cases from the beginning would require, for example, an ICWA-compliant initial foster care placement for a child. There are an extremely limited number of ICWA-compliant placements for Indian children. Should a state court err on the side of caution, and potentially use ICWA-compliant placements for non-Indian children, or should it wait until it has received affirmative notice from a tribe? The federal regulations require the court to treat a child as an Indian child until the state determines otherwise. 25 C.F.R. § 23.107 (2016).

4. Some states add provisions to the notice requirement beyond what ICWA requires. For example, in Michigan, if the state court cannot determine to which

tribe the child belongs, it must send notice to all the tribes in the county where the case arises. MICH. COMP. LAWS § 712B.9(3) (2012). Both Minnesota and Oklahoma state codes also require notice in voluntary relinquishments. MINN. STAT. § 260.761(3) (2017); OKLA. STAT. tit.10, § 40.4 (1994).

5. Using proxies for tribal membership such as attending a pow-wow, or eating traditional food to determine whether a child is an Indian for the purposes of ICWA is a version of the existing Indian family exception, discussed at length in Chapter Five. This is an improper way to determine if ICWA applies, since only a child's tribe can make the final determination as to whether a child is a citizen or eligible for citizenship. Though most states have rejected this judicially created exception to the law, some continue to apply it. *See S.L.C.E. v. Cabinet for Health and Family Services*, 454 S.W.3d 305 (Ky. 2014)

6. As discussed above, state trial courts and social service agencies continually fail to send the statutorily required notice. The problem compounds at the appellate level, where an appellate court must make a determination regarding whether the trial court sent the appropriate notice. The next case details the considerations of one state appellate court in determining whether the trial court notice was sufficient to meet ICWA's standards.

In re Morris

815 N.W.2d 62 (Mich. 2012)

While it is impossible to articulate a precise rule that will encompass every possible factual situation, in light of the interests protected by ICWA, the potentially high costs of erroneously concluding that notice need not be sent, and the relatively low burden of erring in favor of requiring notice, we think the standard for triggering the notice requirement of 25 U.S.C.A. § 1912(a) must be a cautionary one. Therefore, we hold first that sufficiently reliable information of virtually any criteria on which tribal membership might be based suffices to trigger the notice requirement. We hold also that a parent of an Indian child cannot waive the separate and independent ICWA rights of an Indian child's tribe and that the trial court must maintain a documentary record including, at minimum, (1) the original or a copy of each actual notice personally served or sent via registered mail pursuant to 25 U.S.C.A. § 1912(a), and (2) the original or a legible copy of the return receipt or other proof of service showing delivery of the notice. Finally, we hold that the proper remedy for an ICWA-notice violation is to conditionally reverse the trial court and remand for resolution of the ICWA-notice issue.

* * *

We think the "reason to know" standard for purposes of the notice requirement in 25 U.S.C.A. § 1912(a) should set a rather low bar.... Second, we also find instructive *B.H. v. People ex rel. X.H.*, 138 P.3d 299, 303 (Colo., 2006), in which the Colorado Supreme Court examined this same issue and noted:

> Precisely what constitutes "reason to know" or "reason to believe" in any particular set of circumstances will necessarily evade meaningful description. As in other contexts, reasonable grounds to believe must depend upon the totality of the circumstances and include consideration of not only the nature and specificity of available information but also the credibility of the source of that information and the basis of the source's knowledge. In light of the purpose of [ICWA], however, to permit tribal involvement in child-custody determinations whenever tribal members are involved, the threshold requirement for notice was clearly not intended to be high.

The court examined the BIA Guidelines and cases from other jurisdictions before concluding that "[b]ecause membership is peculiarly within the province of each Indian tribe, sufficiently reliable information of virtually any criteria upon which membership might be based must be considered adequate to trigger the notice provisions of the Act." *Id.* at 304 (emphasis added); see also *In re Antoinette S.*, 104 Cal. App.4th 1401, 1407, 129 Cal.Rptr.2d 15 (2002) ("[T]he 'minimal showing' required to trigger notice under the ICWA is merely evidence 'suggest[ing] ' the minor 'may' be an Indian child. . . ."), quoting *Dwayne P. v. Superior Court*, 103 Cal.App.4th 247, 258, 126 Cal.Rptr.2d 639 (2002) (second alteration in original).

Third, we think the burden on the trial court and the DHS of complying with the notice requirement is minimal when compared to the potential costs of erroneously failing to send notice. At most, complying with 25 U.S.C.A. § 1912(a) will extend the proceedings by some 30 days after the date the tribe or the Secretary of the Interior receives notice. If those entitled to notice do not respond within 10 days, the trial court may conduct the foster care placement or termination of parental rights proceedings. If the tribe replies to the notice, indicating that the child is not a member of the tribe and is not entitled to membership then, again, proceedings may resume. Finally, if those entitled to notice request an additional 20 days, then the court may have to wait a total of 30 days beyond the date the notice was received, as shown by the return receipt. An additional 30 days seems a comparatively low burden on the trial court and the DHS, especially when child custody cases generally take well over a year and the Indian heritage question will normally be raised at least by the time of the preliminary hearing. MCR 3.965(B)(2).17 However, if the trial court errs by concluding that no notice is required and proceeds to place the child into foster care or terminate parental rights, the purposes of ICWA are frustrated and the Indian child, the parent or Indian custodian, or the Indian child's tribe may petition to have the proceedings invalidated pursuant to 25 U.S.C.A. § 1914. Thus, the cost of making 25 U.S.C.A. § 1912(a) notice is far less than the potential cost of incorrectly deciding that no notice is required.

* * *

C. 25 U.S.C.A. § 1912(a) Recordkeeping Requirements

In [*In re*] *Gordon*, 490 Mich. 917, 805 N.W.2d 444 [(2011)], we asked the parties to address "whether the Department of Human Services and the family court are under a duty to make a complete record of their compliance with the notice requirements of the ICWA. . . ." While the DHS personnel and the prosecutor made numerous assertions at various hearings that notice had been sent, the record in *Gordon* is devoid of any documentation of the DHS's efforts to notify either the Saginaw Chippewa Indian Tribe or the Secretary of the Interior. There are no copies of the actual notice purportedly sent. Nor does the record include any original or copy of a registered mail return receipt, which is necessary to show not only that notice was received, but also to determine when the 25 U.S.C.A. § 1912(a) waiting period begins. Lastly, while caseworker Smith stated to the trial court on January 5, 2009, that she had received and responded to a request for more family-history information, no documentation of that correspondence appears in the record. This is so even though the court repeatedly instructed both the prosecutor and Smith to ensure that copies of the ICWA-related documents were placed in the court file. It is thus impossible to discern from the record in *Gordon* whether notice was actually sent, to whom it was sent, and whether the notices were received by the appropriate recipients.

While ICWA is silent regarding the recordkeeping requirements of 25 U.S.C.A. § 1912(a) notice compliance, we find it essential that certain documents be included in the record. First, our State Court Administrative Office recently adopted the BIA recommendation that "[t]he original or a copy of each notice sent pursuant to this section shall be filed with the court together with any return receipts or other proof of service." BIA Guidelines B.5(d), 44 Fed Reg at 67588.23 Second, without being able to review the return receipt, the trial court cannot determine whether the proper party actually received the notice sent by registered mail. Third, the trial court cannot determine the date on which the 25 U.S.C.A. § 1912(a) waiting period begins to run without knowing the date on which the tribe or the Secretary of the Interior received the notice, as shown by the registered-mail return receipt. Fourth, with no copy of the actual notice in the record, the trial court cannot determine if the contents of the notice provided sufficient, accurate information to enable the tribal authorities to determine tribal status of the child and the child's parents. Finally, appellate courts cannot fulfill their appellate function without documentation in the record sufficient to allow review of a trial court's efforts to comply with 25 U.S.C.A. § 1912(a).

Indeed, *Gordon* illustrates the necessity for a documentary record of the attempts to comply with the notice requirements of 25 U.S.C.A. § 1912(a). The lack of documentation in the record in *Gordon* prevents us from determining if the contents of the notice were sufficient to apprise the intended recipient of the pending child custody proceeding. We likewise are unable to determine to whom the notices were sent, even though the transcript includes references to both the Saginaw Chippewa Indian Tribe and to "ICWA," the latter of which presumably means the Secretary of the Interior. Further, there is an assertion in the January 5, 2009 hearing transcript that a notice recipient had requested additional family-background information, but we are unable to review either the purported request or any responses made to the request because the record includes neither. Lastly, we cannot determine when or if the notices were actually received by the Saginaw Chippewa Indian Tribe, which would allow us to determine when and if the 25 U.S.C.A. § 1912(a) waiting period began to run.

Therefore, we hold that trial courts have a duty to ensure that the record includes, at minimum, (1) the original or a copy of each actual notice personally served or sent via registered mail pursuant to 25 U.S.C.A. § 1912(a), and (2) the original or a legible copy of the return receipt or other proof of service showing delivery of the notice. In addition, it would be helpful—especially for appellate purposes—for the record to include any additional correspondence between the petitioner, the court, and the Indian tribe or other person or entity entitled to notice under 25 U.S.C.A. § 1912(a).

Having determined that the notice requirement of 25 U.S.C.A. § 1912(a) was triggered in both cases before us and that the trial courts did not fully comply with that statute, we are left to consider the proper remedy for ICWA-notice violations.

Notes

1. *In re Morris* goes on to state, "Despite the best efforts of child-protection authorities and our trial courts, there will inevitably be the occasional, unintentional tribal-notice error." *Id.* at 79. Unfortunately, most of the case law available on notice violations indicates something more is happening than "occasional, unintentional" error. The evidence points more to a systematic failure of education of state social workers and trial court practitioners on this issue.

2. Consider this transcript from a preliminary hearing from Wayne County, Michigan:

> *The Court*: All right, the petition is authorized. The children have been placed with relatives. What else? I guess—is that it? Did anyone ever ask is there any . . . American Indian heritage in this family? American Indian heritage?
>
> *Ms. Safran (attorney for respondent [parent])*: Do you have any Indian heritage in your family?
>
> *The Court*: Cherokee, Chippewa.
>
> *Ms. Safran*: There might be some grand—on the grandmother's side, what was it? Some time—some type; attenuated.
>
> *Ms. Trott (attorney for petitioner [state])*: Ms. Topp was told no at the other—
>
> *Ms. Safran*: Well, we didn't have all the parties.
>
> *Ms. Topp (case worker)*: I talked to [respondent], as well, in the police station[,] and I was told no.
>
> *Ms. Safran*: She doesn't think—

The Court: You don't have any kind—are you sure it's American, or, any idea what we're talking about? I mean, what kind of Indian? Cherokees, Chippewa? I mean, there's a whole bunch.

Unidentified speaker: I don't—I don't know; I can ask.

The Court: And . . . what relative? Grandma? Great-grandma?

Ms. Safran: Your Honor, can we get a date because . . . they want me in [Judge] Slavens[' courtroom] and I can't believe it.

The Court: You've got to wait just one second. All right, you can investigate and see. That's pretty distant; great-grandma is pretty far back. So, I'm not gonna demand that we send notice.

Ms. Trott: This is on the paternal side? Or maternal? Of which father?

The Court: On the mother's side or father? It better be a maternal because right now—all right. You have the right to have this heard by a referee as to all the children . . . or by a judge with or without a jury, and, of course, continued right to an attorney at all hearings. We're setting this for trial?

Ms. Trott: Yes.

In re Harrell, No. 316067, 2014 WL 465718, at *6-7 (Mich. Ct. App. Feb. 4, 2014)

Did the exchange between the attorneys and the court meet the *In re Morris* standard for triggering notice? Was this conversation a "low bar" of "sufficiently reliable information of virtually any criteria on which tribal membership might be based"? The exchange also demonstrates fundamental confusion about Native people, and also shows the hurried nature of child welfare proceedings at the trial level. The court held that the case must be remanded for notice because the trial court "had information, however slight" to suggest the child, the child's parents, or other family members are members of a tribe. *Id.* at *7.

3. The federal regulations require courts to follow the *In re Morris* requirements on recordkeeping, stating that "the original or copy of each notice sent under this section should be filed with the court together with any return receipts or other proof of service." 25 C.F.R. § 23.111(2) (2016).

B. Intervention

Tribes have an absolute right of intervention in ICWA foster care and termination of parental rights proceedings in state court. This means that tribes have the same rights (and responsibilities) as other parties to a case. While this is a fairly straightforward proposition in the law—there is no good cause exception—tribes are still forced to litigate this issue. Tribal intervention also gets directly at the issue of tribal capacity. For example, not every tribe has a lawyer who can intervene in a case. Even if a tribe does have an in-house attorney who can intervene, there may be more cases than is possible for one attorney to cover. In addition, because tribes intervene in cases wherever the tribal children are, in order to intervene, tribal attorneys are forced to appear in states where they are not licensed. While pro hac vice is often offered as solution, it has significant limitations, including the right of the state to deny the application. *See* GA. UNIFORM SUP. CT. R. 4.4(d)(1).

Other barriers of pro hac vice include cost, number of appearances, and requirements of local co-counsel. Many states have significant fees for appearing pro hac vice. S.C. JUD. DEP'T R. 404(e) ($250 for each application); IDAHO B. COMM. R. 227(a)(4) ($325 fee); TEX. GOV. CODE Tit. 2(G)(82)(A), 82.0361(b) ($250 for each case); GA. UNIFORM SUP. CT. R. 2, 3 ($75 for each application plus a $200 annual fee); MISS. R. APP. PROC. 46(5) ($200 for each application). More than one state limits the number of times an attorney can appear pro hac vice. S.C. JUD. DEP'T R. 404(f) (six times in a calendar year); CAL. R. CT. 9.40 ("repeated appearances" cause for denial of application); MICH. CT. R. 8.126 (A)(1)(c) (fewer than five appearances); MISS. R. APP. PROC. 46(b)(1)(iii) (five appearances); IDAHO B. COMM. R. 227(h)(2) (reciprocal to the attorney's home state number). Other states require the local co-counsel to appear at each hearing, S.C. JUD. DEP'T R. 404(i); IND. R.B. ADMISSIONS 3; IDAHO B. COMM. R. 227(b)(2); MISS. R. APP. PROC. 46 (b)(4), which is cost prohibitive for tribes.

Therefore a major issue in this area is whether non-attorneys can intervene on behalf of tribes.

In re Elias L.

767 N.W.2d 98 (Neb. 2009)

The Ponca Tribe of Nebraska (Tribe) appeals from the county court's order denying its motion to intervene in child custody proceedings involving two children who are members of the Tribe. The court denied the motion to intervene because an attorney had not signed the motion. We reverse, and remand because the Tribe's right to intervene under the federal Indian Child Welfare Act (ICWA) preempts Nebraska's laws regulating the unauthorized practice of law.

The Nebraska Department of Health and Human Services filed two separate petitions in the Dakota County Court alleging that Elias L. and Evelyn M., both children of Jennifer M., are children in need of assistance under Neb.Rev. Stat. § 43–247(3)(a) (Reissue 2008). Because the children are "Indian children" under both ICWA and the Nebraska ICWA, the Tribe was notified of the children's custody proceedings. The Tribe moved for intervention under § 1911(c), which provides that "[i]n any State court proceeding for the foster care placement of, or termination of parental rights to, an Indian child, the Indian custodian of the child and the Indian child's tribe shall have a right to intervene at any point in the proceeding."

Jill Holt, the Tribe's ICWA specialist and an employee of the Tribe's Department of Social Services, and the Tribe's representative, filed the motion. No party objected. Yet, on October 9, 2008, the court refused to let the Tribe intervene. It ruled that the motion "is not filed in the Court's files pursuant to . . . § 7–101."

The court recognized that the Tribe had a right to intervene under ICWA and the Nebraska ICWA but determined that Holt was not an attorney licensed by the Nebraska Supreme Court to practice law in the State of Nebraska. The court stated that it "is charged with the duty to enforce the prohibition against the practice of law without a license." Because an attorney licensed to practice in Nebraska had not filed the motion, the court refused to recognize the motion.

The Tribe retained legal counsel and appealed. The Tribe assigns that the county court erred in concluding that § 7–101 prohibits it from intervening in an ICWA and Nebraska ICWA child custody proceeding without being represented by a Nebraska licensed attorney. The Tribe also assigns that the court erred in failing to conclude that § 1911(c), which gives an Indian child's tribe the right to intervene in an ICWA proceeding, preempts § 7–101 under the Supremacy Clause of the U.S. Constitution.

* * *

The federal ICWA and state ICWA are silent regarding whether a tribe may appear in court through a nonlawyer representative. Nebraska law allows plaintiffs "the liberty of prosecuting, and defendants . . . the liberty of defending," themselves. But Nebraska does limit nonlawyer representation. Section 7–101 provides that

> no person shall practice as an attorney or counselor at law, or commence, conduct or defend any action or proceeding to which he is not a party, either by using or subscribing his own name, or the name of any other person, or by drawing pleadings or other papers to be signed and filed by a party, in any court of record of this state, unless he has been previously admitted to the bar by order of the Supreme Court of this state. . . . It is hereby made the duty of the judges of such courts to enforce this prohibition.

Applying § 7–101, the county court refused to recognize the Tribe's motion to intervene because a Nebraska licensed attorney did not file the motion. But the Tribe argues that federal law preempts any Nebraska law which requires an attorney to represent the Tribe in ICWA proceedings.

Generally, federal law preempts state law when it "conflicts with a federal statute," when a state law does "major damage to clear and substantial federal interests," or when the U.S. Congress explicitly declares federal legislation to have a preemptive effect. But that is not the preemption standard here. When the state law affects Indian tribes, courts must make "'a particularized inquiry into the nature of the state, federal, and tribal interests at stake.'" In such cases, state jurisdiction over an action or issue is preempted if "it interferes or is incompatible with federal and tribal interests reflected in federal law, unless the state interests at stake are sufficient to justify the assertion of state authority."

Here, we first determine whether the state law requiring that an attorney represent the Tribe in ICWA proceedings "interferes or is incompatible with" the Tribe's right to intervene. If an interference or incompatibility appears, then we must balance the competing state and tribal interests.

The Tribe argues that conditioning tribal intervention on whether an attorney represents it would significantly interfere with its ability to intervene. The Tribe claims it lacks sufficient financial resources to retain legal counsel to represent it in state court child custody proceedings governed by ICWA. By implication, if the Tribe cannot intervene, its rights and interests in the Indian child would go unrepresented.

* * *

Federally recognized Indian tribes, while possessing unique attributes of sovereignty and self-government, lack many of the revenue-generating options open to federal and state governments. And we must be cognizant of the hardship that would occur if we were to require tribes to hire attorneys in ICWA matters. Requiring legal counsel to represent the Tribe in ICWA proceedings would place additional financial burdens on the Tribe which would directly interfere with its right to intervene. Thus, we conclude that enforcement of § 7–101 in this case interferes and is incompatible with the federally granted tribal right of intervening in child custody proceedings governed by ICWA.

We next address whether the State's interest in enforcement of the representation requirement in ICWA proceedings outweighs tribal interests in intervening in such proceedings. Because requiring legal counsel as a condition of intervention under ICWA would, at a minimum, burden the Tribe's right of intervention, the State can require legal representation only if the State's interests outweigh those of the Tribe and the United States.

Obviously, the State has a legitimate interest in requiring groups and associations to be represented by an attorney. Section 7–101 ensures that those appearing in judicial proceedings are familiar with substantive and procedural requirements and protocols, thus ensuring adequate representation. By limiting the practice of law to only licensed attorneys, the State's goal is to protect the public from any potential harm caused by the actions of nonlawyers engaging in the unauthorized practice of law.

Yet, Nebraska law allows individuals to represent themselves and participate in trials and legal proceedings in their own behalf. And, an employee of an organization can engage in certain acts that would normally constitute the practice of law if done for the sole benefit of the organization. Additionally, a nonlawyer may engage in the authorized practice of law to the extent allowed by a published opinion or rule of this court. So, while the general rule may be that only an individual can appear pro se in his or her own behalf, statutes and court rules provide some exceptions.

Furthermore, the Tribe has significant interests in intervening in ICWA proceedings.

* * *

Moreover, other state courts have concluded that the tribal interests articulated in ICWA are of the highest order, outweighing other state interests. The Utah Supreme Court stated that "[t]he protection of th[e] tribal interest [in its children] is at the core of the ICWA." The Iowa Supreme Court, concluding that an Indian tribe may represent itself in ICWA proceedings, determined that the state's interest in requiring adequate representation "'cannot compare with a tribe's interests in its children and its own future existence.'"

And, in the narrow context of ICWA proceedings, the State's interests are not necessarily compromised by allowing the Tribe to be represented by a nonlawyer. In this case, the Tribe has authorized Holt, its ICWA specialist, to appear on its behalf and has entrusted her with representing its interests in ICWA proceedings. Her responsibilities require familiarity with the procedural and substantive requirements of ICWA, and familiarity with other social service agencies that are a part of the state child custody proceedings. In sum, the Tribe has authorized her to speak for it, and she is familiar with the applicable law and procedures.

We conclude that tribal participation in state custody proceedings involving Indian children is essential to achieving the goals of ICWA. The tribal interests represented by ICWA and the Tribe's right to intervene under § 1911(c) and § 43–1504(3) outweigh the State interests represented by § 7–101. Under the applicable preemption test, the scale tips in favor of tribal interests. Thus, we determine that federal law preempts the requirement of § 7–101 that the Tribe be represented by a Nebraska licensed attorney in these ICWA proceedings. On remand, the court shall allow the Tribe's designated representative to fully participate in further proceedings.

Reversed and remanded with directions.

Notes

1. Since this case was decided, Nebraska has incorporated its holding into state statute:

> In any state court proceeding for the foster care placement of, or termination of parental rights to, an Indian child, the Indian custodian of the child and the Indian child's tribe or tribes shall have a right to intervene at any point in the proceeding regardless of whether the intervening party is represented by legal counsel. The Indian child's tribe or tribes and their counsel are not required to associate with local counsel or pay a fee to appear pro hac vice in a child custody proceeding under the Nebraska Indian Child Welfare Act. Representatives from the Indian child's tribe or tribes have the right to fully participate in every court proceeding held under the act.

Neb. Rev. St. § 43-1504(3) (2015).

In other states (Michigan, Oregon, Wisconsin, Washington, and Minnesota), there are court rules to waive certain pro hac vice requirements for tribal attorneys representing tribes in ICWA cases. MCR 8.126, Oregon UTCR 3.170.

2. In a very early ICWA case, the Supreme Court of Alaska held that a Native Village should be allowed to intervene in an adoption case, even if the strict language of the law only explicitly provides for intervention in foster care and termination of parental rights proceedings. *In re J.R.S.*, 690 P.2d 10 (Alaska 1984). Using a construction that courts often look to in ICWA proceedings, the court found that while Congress might not have specifically authorized intervention, that did not mean Congress explicitly forbade it. *But see In re R.S.*, 805 N.W.2d 44, 50 (Minn. 2011) (stating in a transfer case, "Where a statute is clearly limited to specifically enumerated subjects, we do not extend its application to other subjects by process of construction.").

However, the court in *J.R.S.* held:

> We also hold that intervention was necessary to preserve this interest. An Indian tribe may petition a state court to set aside actions which violate Indian parents' rights or improperly take jurisdiction from a tribal court, but the I.C.W.A. does not provide for the filing of such a petition if a state ignores § 1915's adoptive preferences. See 25 U.S.C. 1914. Procedurally, the tribe must intervene if it is to defend the Act's preference system. In this regard we reject the adoptive parents' argument that Chalkyitsik should have used its presence in the C.I.N.A. action to move for an order requiring the state to withhold its consent from the adoption. This is a needlessly roundabout scheme and the adoptive parents cite no cases requiring it. It is obvious from the record that a "good cause" determination was made at the adoption hearing. This suggests that the appropriate place to oppose such a determination is the hearing itself. By refusing to allow this kind of opposition, the superior court made it inevitable that the Village's interests would be impaired.
>
> Nor were the Village's interests represented by existing parties. State attorneys represented the Division of Family and Youth Services. Adoptive parents M.S.F. and J.J.G. had interests adverse to the Village's. One possible representative of the Village's interests would have been the guardian ad litem. But under Alaska law the guardian's task is to promote the child's best interests. As a practical matter these interests will often differ from the tribe's; the record suggests that they were different here. The guardian represented J.R.S., not the Village. The guardian did not defend the Act's preferences. Only one potential litigant was ready to defend the Act's placement scheme, and the superior court excluded that litigant from the adoption hearing at which these statutory preferences were overridden. We hold that it was error on the superior court's part not to permit Chalkyitsik to intervene and we thus remand for a hearing at which the Village will be a party.

3. While the concept that tribes have the right to intervene and to be represented by non-attorneys is fairly well settled at the appellate level, *see State ex rel Juvenile Dep't of Lane Co. v. Shuey*, 850 P.2d 378 (Or. 1993), trial courts remain inconsistent in their decisions. In addition, *how* a tribe will be allowed to participate is not settled. An Iowa case from 2008 held that a tribe could be represented by a non-attorney, but that it was not abuse of discretion for the trial court to deny a tribe's motion to participate telephonically. *In re N.N.E.*, 752 N.W.2d 1, 13 (Iowa 2008). The federal regulations require states to allow tribes to participate using various types of technology when possible. 25 C.F.R. § 23.133 (2016).

C. Standard of Proof

The standard of proof for ICWA cases is generally higher than other child welfare proceedings. Difficulties arise when trying to determine when the higher standards apply, and to what proceeding. The law states,

> No foster care placement may be ordered in such proceeding in the absence of a determination, supported by *clear and convincing evidence*, including testimony of qualified expert witnesses, that the continued custody of the child by the parent or Indian custodian is likely to result in serious emotional or physical damage to the child.

25 U.S.C. § 1912(e) (2012) (emphasis added).

> No termination of parental rights may be ordered in such proceeding in the absence of a determination, supported by evidence *beyond a reasonable doubt*, including testimony of qualified expert witnesses, that the continued custody of the child by the parent or Indian custodian is likely to result in serious emotional or physical damage to the child.

25 U.S.C. § 1912(f) (2012) (emphasis added).

Because each state has a slightly different naming system for their proceedings, the question becomes when the particular findings must be made, and how often. For example, must the heightened foster care standard be proven at the very first hearing, the hearing when a child is placed in foster care, or the hearing where the court determines if there is enough proof to take jurisdiction over a family?

In re Esther V.

248 P.3d 863 (N.M. 2011)

This case addresses the relationship between the Indian Child Welfare Act of 1978 (ICWA), 25 U.S.C. §§ 1901–1963 (2006), which sets "minimum Federal standards for the removal of Indian children from their families," § 1902, and the New Mexico Abuse and Neglect Act, NMSA 1978, Sections 32A-4-1 to—34 (1993, as amended through 2009), which governs the State's transfer of custody of a child in cases of abuse or neglect. More specifically, we are asked to determine when and how a district court in an abuse and neglect proceeding must make the two factual findings required by § 1912(d) and (e) of ICWA.

* * *

Mother, a member of the Navajo Nation, and Child, who is eligible for enrollment in the Navajo Nation, were living with a Gallup-based family pursuant to a safety contract with CYFD in which the family agreed to provide a residence for Mother and Child and "ensur[e] the child's safety." Child's father (Father) was incarcerated at the time. On August 21, 2007, CYFD received a referral indicating that the safety-contract family no longer wanted to help Mother and Child because Mother "was causing family discord, making [false] allegations, leaving with the baby on foot and in the extreme heat, and bringing items into the home that [were] against [the family's] religious beliefs."

In response to the referral, CYFD immediately faxed to the district court a petition alleging abuse and neglect, a motion for an ex parte custody order with a supporting affidavit, and a proposed ex parte custody order to be signed by the district judge. CYFD's petition alleged that Mother and Father neglected Child, contrary to Section 32A-4-2(E)(4), "in that [they] are unable to discharge their responsibilities to and for [C]hild because of incarceration, hospitalization or other physical or mental disorder or incapacity," and that Mother and Father abused Child, contrary to Section 32A-4-2(B)(1), "in that [C]hild has suffered or is at risk of suffering serious harm because of the action or inaction of the child's parent, guardian or custodian." The petition also noted that ICWA applies to Child because Child is Native American. The supporting affidavit contained facts to establish probable cause that Child was abused or neglected, and it stated that "reasonable and active efforts ha[d] been made to avoid removal of the child from the home."

The district court signed the submitted ex parte custody order within ten minutes of receiving CYFD's request, thereby commanding the immediate removal of Child from Mother's care, granting "legal and physical custody of the child" to CYFD, and appointing a guardian ad litem for Child. The district court's order found that there was "probable cause to believe that ... [C]hild [was] abused or neglected," that CYFD custody was "necessary," and that CYFD had made "active efforts ... to avoid removal of [C]hild from the home."

On August 24, 2007, the district court appointed counsel to represent Mother, and, on August 27, the court set a custody hearing within ten days of the ex parte order as required by Section 32A-4-18(A). In response to CYFD's abuse and neglect petition, Mother's counsel filed a response denying "all allegations of neglect or abuse" and disputing that CYFD made "reasonable efforts ... to avoid removing the child." The temporary custody hearing was postponed several days to accommodate the various parties and the excusal of the district court judge and was ultimately held on September 12, 2007.

At the thirty-minute custody hearing, counsel for Mother asked the court to allow him five minutes to consult with Mother before the hearing began, explaining that he had not had an opportunity to talk to his client. After conferring with counsel, Mother neither renewed her denial of the alleged abuse and neglect nor challenged the portion of CYFD's affidavit that stated CYFD had made active and reasonable efforts to keep the family together. Instead, she stipulated to temporary CYFD custody of Child pending the adjudicatory hearing, which was scheduled for October 5, 2007. The court verified Mother's understanding of the stipulation in open court as follows:

> Judge: ... We are here today for a hearing to determine whether or not reasonable grounds exist to allow the State of New Mexico to keep your child and take legal custody of your child.... If you want a hearing, you can have a hearing to dispute that there is not reasonable grounds for the government to keep your child from you.... Do you understand?
>
> Mother: Yes.
>
> Judge: Are you willing to give up that right?
>
> Attorney: In other words, are you willing to not have a hearing today, but to say okay, they can keep the child on a temporary basis?
>
> Mother: No, I want to get them back.
>
> Attorney: I understand you want to get them back. The question is do you want a hearing today on whether you should have them temporarily back now. Because you're going to have a hearing later on what's called an adjudication. Do you understand that?
>
> Mother: Yes.
>
> Attorney: Temporarily they're going to be with the State, understand? You're going to have visitation. I think she understands, your honor.
>
> Judge: Alright. So with your permission, we will not have a hearing to determine whether or not at this time you should get your kids back. We're not going to have that hearing. Do you understand that?
>
> Mother: Yes....
>
> Judge: And ... down the line we can have a further hearing called an adjudication to see if your child will remain with the State for a longer period of time. We're not going to have that right now. Do you understand that?
>
> Mother: Um-hum.

The court then signed the stipulated order, which stated that "[t]here is probable cause to believe that the [parents] are not able to provide adequate supervision and care for the child" and that "[c]lear and convincing evidence exists to believe that continued custody of the child by the parent or guardian is likely to result in serious emotional or physical damage to the child." Mother did not contest the findings contained in the stipulated order.

The district court held an adjudicatory hearing on October 29 and November 28. Father did not contest the proceedings, but Mother disputed the allegations of abuse and neglect. Relying on Mother's earlier stipulation and the ex parte custody order, CYFD did not present "qualified expert testimony" as required by § 1912(e) of ICWA or otherwise address the § 1912 requirements at the adjudicatory hearing. At the close of the hearing, the judge dismissed the abuse allegation but found neglect on the part of Mother. The judge's written order stated that "[t]he Court finds by clear and convincing [evidence that Mother] has neglected the child . . . in that [she] is unable to discharge [her] responsibilities to and for the child because of incarceration, hospitalization or other physical or mental disorder or incapacity; and a factual basis exists to support this finding."

* * *

CYFD petitioned this Court for review of the Court of Appeals opinion, and Mother cross-petitioned. We granted both petitions for certiorari to review three issues: (1) did the Court of Appeals err by holding that Mother's consent to temporary custody pending the adjudicatory hearing transformed the involuntary custody hearing into a voluntary proceeding governed by § 1913 of ICWA; (2) in a contested adjudication, does the trial court always need to make the factual findings required by § 1912(d) and (e) of ICWA at the adjudicatory hearing on abuse and neglect, or can those findings be made at an earlier stage of the proceedings; and (3) if the § 1912(d) and (e) findings must be made at the adjudication stage, should we reverse the adjudication and dismiss the petition for lack of proof, or should we remand for additional proceedings in which that proof may be presented?

* * *

D. In a Contested Adjudication of Abuse or Neglect of an Indian Child, the Court Always Must Make the Factual Findings Required by § 1912(d) and (e) of ICWA at the Adjudicatory Hearing.

1. Overview of New Mexico Abuse and Neglect Proceedings

The primary issue before this Court is when, within the procedural framework established by New Mexico's Abuse and Neglect Act, the district court should address § 1912(d)'s "active efforts . . . to prevent the breakup of the Indian family" requirement and§ 1912(e)'s "likely to result in serious . . . damage" requirement. To provide context for our discussion, we begin our analysis with a brief overview of the relevant stages of an abuse and neglect proceeding, including the ex parte custody stage, custody hearing, adjudicatory hearing, and dispositional hearing.

CYFD initiates a proceeding by filing a petition alleging abuse or neglect with the district court. See § 32A–4–15; Rule 10–312 NMRA. To obtain immediate custody of the child, CYFD must also file a motion for an ex parte custody order, including an affidavit showing probable cause that custody is necessary and that the child has been abused or neglected. See § 32A–4–16(A)–(B); Rule 10–311(A) NMRA. If the district court finds probable cause, it may issue an order giving CYFD interim legal custody of the child until an initial custody hearing is held. See §§ 32A–4–16(A),—18(A). The rules of evidence do not apply to the issuance of an ex parte custody order. Section 32A–4–16(C); Rule 11–1101(D)(2) NMRA. At the inception of the abuse and neglect proceedings, the district court must appoint counsel for the parent and a guardian ad litem for the child. Section 32A–4–10(B)–(C).

The district court must hold a custody hearing within ten days of the date the petition is filed "to determine if the child should remain in or be placed in [CYFD]'s custody pending adjudication." Section 32A–4–18(A). CYFD must give the parent "reasonable notice of the time and place of the custody hearing." Section 32A–4–18(B). The parent must be informed of the allegations in the petition, potential consequences if those allegations are found true, and the rights to counsel and an adjudicatory hearing. Section 32A–4–10(G); Rule 10–314 NMRA. The rules of evidence do not apply at the custody hearing. Section 32A–4–18(H); Rule 11–1101(D)(2). If the court finds that there is probable cause to believe there has been abuse or neglect, the court determines custody of the child pending the adjudicatory hearing on the merits of the petition. See § 32A–4–18(A), (D).

At the adjudicatory hearing the court determines whether the allegations in the petition are true. The adjudicatory hearing is an evidentiary hearing on the merits of the abuse or neglect case, complete with due process protections.

[A]t a minimum, due process in neglect and abuse proceedings requires timely notice reasonably calculated to inform the person concerning the subject and issues involved in the proceeding; a reasonable opportunity to refute or defend against a charge or accusation; a reasonable opportunity to confront and cross-examine adverse witnesses and present evidence on the charge or accusation; representation by counsel, when such representation is required by constitution or statute; and a hearing before an impartial decisionmaker. *State ex rel. Children, Youth & Families Dep't v. Kathleen D.C. (In re Damion M.C.)*, 2007–NMSC–018, ¶ 12, 141 N.M. 535, 157 P.3d 714 (internal quotation marks and citation omitted). The adjudicatory hearing must be "commenced within sixty days after the date of service" of the petition upon the respondent. Section 32A–4–19(A); see also Rule 10–343 NMRA (detailing triggering events for the sixty-day time limit). If the respondent denies the allegations in the petition, the court must hear evidence on the petition and make findings on whether the child is abused, neglected, or both. Section 32A–4–20(G). Unlike the ex parte and custody hearing stages, the rules of evidence apply at the adjudicatory hearing. Rule 10–141 NMRA; see also Rule 11–1101(A), (D). The court must determine, in the absence of a valid admission, whether the child is abused or neglected "on the basis of clear and convincing evidence, competent, material and relevant in nature." Section 32A–4–20(H).

If the court concludes on the basis of clear and convincing evidence that the child is abused or neglected, the next stage is the dispositional hearing, which can either be included within the adjudicatory hearing or conducted separately within thirty days after the adjudication of abuse or neglect. Sections 32A–4–20(H),—22(A).

At disposition the court makes factual findings relevant to a custody determination, determines custody of the child, and establishes a treatment plan. Section 32A–4–22. The court must make multiple findings regarding the interests of the child, the wishes of the child and parent, and the ability of the potential custodians. Section 32A–4–22(A). The rules of evidence do not apply at disposition; the court is instead allowed to consider "all relevant and material evidence helpful in determining the questions presented, including oral and written reports, . . . even though not competent had it been offered during the part of the hearings on adjudicatory issues." Section 32A–4–20(I); Rule 11–1101(D)(2).

2. The § 1912(d) and (e) Findings in the Context of New Mexico's Procedural Framework

With New Mexico's procedural framework in mind, we consider which procedural stage is best suited for addressing the requirements of § 1912(d) and (e) of ICWA. See *R.A.C.P. v. State (In re Interest of D.S.P.)*, 166 Wis.2d 464, 480 N.W.2d 234, 238 (1992) (noting that state statutes should be read to harmonize with ICWA); *San Diego Cnty. Health & Human Servs. Agency v. Francisco Z. (In re Matthew Z.)*, 80 Cal. App.4th 545, 95 Cal.Rptr.2d 343, 349 (2000) (explaining that the state proceeding best suited for addressing ICWA is the proceeding that requires findings that parallel the ICWA findings). CYFD's regular practice has been to address the findings required by § 1912(d) and (e) at the earliest possible procedural stage. Accordingly, CYFD asserts in this case that the district court, by issuing the ex parte custody order, made the "active efforts" finding required by § 1912(d) and that Mother's stipulation at the temporary custody hearing satisfied § 1912(e)'s "serious . . . damage" requirement. CYFD argues in the alternative that the dispositional hearing is the appropriate procedural stage for addressing the requirements of ICWA. Mother argues that the factual findings required by § 1912(d) and (e) must always be made at the adjudicatory hearing. We agree with Mother that § 1912(d) and (e) findings must be made at the adjudicatory hearing because the adjudicatory hearing is the procedural phase that affords the Indian parent and tribe the most procedural due process protection and best accommodates the requirements of § 1912.

To construe ICWA within the procedural framework of New Mexico's Abuse and Neglect Act, we begin with a textual analysis to determine whether the plain meaning of the relevant ICWA provisions addresses the question at hand. The plain language of § 1912(d) and (e) specifies what is required to be shown: (1) that "active efforts have been made" and (2) that "the continued custody of the child . . . is likely to result in serious emotional or physical damage." But the text gives only a vague indication of when the findings must be made: prior to a "foster care placement," which ICWA defines as "any action removing an Indian child from its parent or Indian custodian for temporary placement in a foster home . . . where the parent or Indian custodian cannot have the child returned upon demand, but where parental rights have not been terminated." § 1903(1)(i). This language does not unambiguously indicate which procedural phase within a foster care placement proceeding is the proper time for the § 1912(d) and (e) findings to be made. Accordingly, we resort to the policy and purpose of ICWA and our tools of statutory construction as we attempt to effectuate Congress's intent.

3. New Mexico's Ex Parte and Custody Hearing Stages Are Unsatisfactory Procedural Stages for Addressing the Requirements of § 1912(d) and (e) of ICWA.

New Mexico's ex parte and custody hearing stages are ill-suited for making the § 1912(d) and (e) findings because they are emergency proceedings that do not provide sufficient due process protections. New Mexico's ex parte and custody hearing stages are expedited emergency proceedings that enable the State to remove a child and take temporary custody in order to ensure the child's safety until a full hearing on the merits is held. See *Yount v. Millington*, 117 N.M. 95, 101, 869 P.2d 283, 289 (Ct.App.1993) ("[W]hen a child's safety is threatened, that is a sufficient basis to justify postponing the parent's hearing until after the child has been taken into protective custody."). Congress has expressly recognized a state's power to implement emergency removal and placement actions for Indian children in § 1922 of ICWA which states, in pertinent part:

> Nothing in this subchapter shall be construed to prevent the emergency removal of an Indian child who is a resident of or is domiciled on a reservation, but temporarily located off the reservation, from his parent or Indian custodian or the emergency placement of such child in a foster home or institution, under applicable State law, in order to prevent imminent physical damage or harm to the child.

Although § 1922 expressly refers only to Indian children who are residents of or domiciled on the reservation, we conclude that CYFD must necessarily have the power to take emergency custody of any Indian child who is physically located off the reservation. ICWA gives an Indian tribe exclusive jurisdiction "over any child custody proceeding involving an Indian child who resides or is domiciled within the reservation of such tribe." § 1911(a). But when an emergency arises with respect to a child who is physically located off a reservation, the time-sensitive nature of the emergency may require CYFD to take immediate action to remove the child from harm's way without first establishing whether the child is subject to exclusive tribal jurisdiction. Once the child is safe, § 1922 requires CYFD to "expeditiously initiate a child custody proceeding subject to the provisions of this subchapter, transfer the child to the jurisdiction of the appropriate Indian tribe, or restore the child to the parent or Indian custodian, as may be appropriate." Section 1922 thus allows CYFD to secure the child first and ask questions about the child's residence and domicile later in order to ensure the child's safety.

* * *

4. The Adjudicatory Hearing Is the Best Procedural Stage in Which to Make the § 1912(d) and (e) Findings.

New Mexico's adjudicatory hearing incorporates procedural due process protections and a stringent standard of proof that parallel those required by ICWA. The adjudicatory hearing must be held within sixty days after the date the petition is served on the parent. Section 32A–4–19(A). This time frame comports with ICWA's requirement that the parent and tribe receive notice at least ten days and up to thirty days before the commencement of a foster care placement proceeding. See § 1912(a). The timing of the adjudicatory hearing allows for the notice required by § 1912(a) while meeting the ICWA requirement that CYFD "expeditiously" initiate a foster care placement proceeding following an emergency removal or placement proceeding. See § 1922. If a parent denies allegations of abuse or neglect at the adjudicatory hearing, the court must hear all evidence bearing on the issue. Section 32A–4–20(G). Because the adjudicatory hearing is an evidentiary hearing, it is a practical time to satisfy the ICWA requirement that CYFD present the "testimony of qualified expert witnesses." See § 1912(e). At a contested adjudication, the State is required to prove abuse or neglect by "clear and convincing evidence, competent, material and relevant in nature." Section 32A–4–20(H). Consistently, § 1912(e) of ICWA requires a showing by "clear and convincing evidence . . . that the continued custody of the child by the parent or Indian custodian is likely to result in serious emotional or physical damage to the child." The similarities between New Mexico's requirements for an adjudicatory hearing and the ICWA requirements for the involuntary placement of an Indian child in foster care make the adjudicatory hearing the best procedural phase for the court to make the findings required by § 1912(d) and (e).

More importantly, requiring courts to make the factual findings prescribed by § 1912(d) and (e) at the adjudicatory hearing furthers the purposes and policies behind ICWA because both the parent and the tribe are able to participate meaningfully in the process. Parents have a fundamental liberty interest in the care and custody of their children; due process of law is required before parents can be deprived of that right. See *Kathleen D.C.*, 2007–NMSC–018, ¶ 12, 141 N.M. 535, 157 P.3d 714. ICWA also protects the interests of both the Indian child and the tribe by preventing the unwarranted removal of Indian children from their unique culture and heritage. See § 1901(3)–(5). Because we must construe ICWA by resolving all ambiguities liberally in favor of the Indian parent and tribe, we conclude that the findings required by § 1912(d) and (e) always must be made at the adjudicatory hearing, which incorporates due process protections.

* * *

6. A Parent Can Admit to the Factual Findings Required by § 1912(d) and (e) Only If the Court Adheres to Procedural Safeguards Protecting the Rights and Interests of the Parent, Child, and Tribe.

Parental stipulations to temporary CYFD custody pending adjudication are not unusual in abuse and neglect proceedings. Our holding does not preclude stipulations to temporary custody pending adjudication, so long as the court ensures that the parent knowingly enters into the stipulation. Although we differ from the view expressed in the Court of Appeals opinion that § 1913(a) controls voluntary stipulations made in involuntary proceedings, we agree that § 1913(a) provides helpful guidance on what should be required for a valid parental stipulation in involuntary proceedings. See [*State ex rel. Children, Youth, & Families Dep't v.*] *Marlene C.*, 2009–NMCA–058, ¶ 15, 146 N.M. 588, 212 P.3d 1142.Under § 1913(a), a parent's consent is valid only if the court ensures "that the terms and consequences of the consent were fully explained in detail and were fully understood by the parent or Indian custodian." It is reasonable that the same underlying principle should govern valid parental consent to temporary custody pending adjudication: A parent must understand what the consent really means.

* * *

Admission to the factual findings required by § 1912 invokes more stringent procedural safeguards than a parental stipulation to temporary custody. Unlike the custody hearing, which is a preliminary emergency proceeding, the adjudicatory hearing addresses the ultimate merits of the case, and a parent's admission to allegations of either abuse or neglect or to the factual findings required by § 1912(d) and (e) has much more serious consequences than a stipulation to temporary custody. The result of a stipulation to abuse or neglect may well be a permanent severance of the relationship between the parent and child. Accordingly, the court must adhere to stricter procedural safeguards at adjudication to ensure that parents do not casually surrender either their fundamental liberty interest in the care and custody of their children or the substantive rights protected by ICWA.

While an abuse and neglect proceeding is designed to protect the best interests of the child and the rights of the parents, ICWA goes further by protecting the unique relationship between a tribe and its children. That relationship is not to be severed casually or without good cause. If a parent wishes to admit to the factual findings required by ICWA without a full adjudicatory hearing, we must require procedural safeguards that meet the standards New Mexico law requires for admissions in ordinary abuse and neglect proceedings. The New Mexico Children's Court Rules provide that a parent can admit to abuse or neglect, by "admitting sufficient facts to permit a finding that the allegations of the petition are true," Rule 10–342(A) NMRA, and give details of the procedural safeguards required for an admission to be valid, Rule 10–342(C)–(D). We hold that similar procedural requirements apply when a parent admits to the factual findings prescribed under § 1912(d) and (e). Before the court accepts a parent's admission to the § 1912(d) and (e) findings, the court must make "such inquiry as shall satisfy the court that there is a factual basis for the admission." Rule 10–342(D). CYFD must be prepared to offer evidence to satisfy the court that such a basis exists. Cf. *State ex rel. Children, Youth & Families Dep't v. Stella P.*,1999–NMCA–100, ¶ 35, 127 N.M. 699, 986 P.2d 495 (explaining that to meet CYFD's burden of proof in a termination of parental rights proceeding, CYFD must present "sufficient testimony to allow the court to make the required statutory findings").

Additionally, before accepting an admission, the court must ensure that the admission is voluntary and that the parent understands (1) the allegations of the petition, (2) the possible dispositions should the allegations of the petition be found true, (3) the right to deny the allegations and have a full adjudicatory hearing, and (4) that the admission waives the parent's right to contest the § 1912(d) and (e) findings in a full adjudicatory hearing. See Rule 10–342(D). In this case, Mother's stipulation to temporary custody pending adjudication did not meet the requirements for a valid evidentiary admission to the factual findings required by § 1912(d) and (e).

* * *

In child abuse and neglect proceedings to which ICWA applies, the findings required by § 1912(d) and (e) always must be addressed at the adjudicatory hearing. They were not in this case. Accordingly, we reverse the adjudication of neglect and remand this case to the district court for a new adjudicatory hearing that satisfies the requirements of § 1912(d) and (e) of ICWA.

Notes

1. A common theme through out this chapter of the book is the nature of the state court proceedings at the trial level. The mother's attorney had to ask the court for a few minutes before the hearing because he had not met with his client. While parents under ICWA (and most state laws) are guaranteed counsel in child welfare proceedings, the quality of that representation varies dramatically. How can attorneys represent clients they have not yet met? What should the balance between a timely initial hearing and a parent's right to meet with counsel be?

2. While each state ultimately makes similar findings regarding exercising jurisdiction (adjudication) over a family, the timing of each hearing in each state varies. The most recent understanding of the law mirrors the reasoning in this case. The federal regulations would have a state court apply the emergency removal standards in 25 U.S.C. § 1922 at the first removal of a child from the home, with the full panoply of ICWA protections occurring at a later adjudication hearing. This also appears to be the intent of the federal regulations, which clarifies that § 1922 does not only apply to children "temporarily residing off" tribal lands. 25 C.F.R. § 23.113 (2016).

3. Is 60 days—or two months—expeditious? How long should a child be removed from her home without the additional findings required by federal law? The federal regulations limit the emergency removal to 30 days, with certain exceptions. *Id.*

4. How does the burden of proof issue apply to other findings required by the law? For example, what is the burden of proof for a finding that active efforts occurred? The law states that the

> Any party seeking to effect a foster care placement of, or termination of parental rights to, an Indian child under State law shall satisfy the court that active efforts have been made to provide remedial services and rehabilitative programs designed to prevent the breakup of the Indian family and that these efforts have proved unsuccessful.

25 U.S.C. § 1912(d) (2012).

What level of proof should be required to satisfy the court that active efforts have happened?

In re England

887 N.W.2d 10 (Mich. Ct. App. 2016)

At the outset, we note that there is no dispute that E.M. [child] is eligible for membership in the Sault Ste. Marie Tribe of Chippewa Indians (the Tribe) and is thus an Indian child, such that the various procedural and substantive provisions of the Indian Child Welfare Act (ICWA),25 USC § 1901 et seq., and the Michigan Indian Family Preservation Act (MIFPA), MCL 712B.1 et seq., applied to these proceedings. See 25 USC § 1903(4); MCL 712B.3(k).

* * *

As the plain language of the above provisions make clear, 25 USC § 1912(e) and MCL 712B.15(2) pertain to removal decisions, while 25 USC § 1912(d) and (f) and MCL 712B.15(3) and (4) pertain to termination decisions. Because this case did not involve the removal of E.M. from the parental home, but instead involved the termination of respondent's parental rights, the latter provisions govern the outcome of this appeal. Stated succinctly, in proceedings involving termination, the ICWA and the MIFPA "require a dual burden of proof." *In re Payne/Pumphrey/Fortson*, [311] Mich.App [49]; [874] NW2d [205] (Docket No. 324813, issued June 11, 2015); slip op at 4 (citation omitted). "That is, in addition to finding that at least one state statutory ground for termination was proven by clear and convincing evidence, the trial court must also make findings in compliance with [the] ICWA [and the MIFPA] before terminating parental rights." *Id.*; slip op at 4.

The specific findings required by the ICWA and the MIFPA in termination proceedings are: (1) proof that active efforts were made to reunify the family, 25 USC § 1912(d); MCL 712B.15(3); MCR 3.977(G)(1); and (2) proof beyond a reasonable doubt that the continued custody of the child by the parent would likely result in serious emotional or physical damage to the child, 25 USC § 1912(f); MCL 712B.15(4); MCR 3.977(G)(2).

Finally, as in all termination proceedings, the trial court has a duty to determine, by a preponderance of the evidence, "that termination is in the child's best interests before it can terminate parental rights." *In re Olive/Metts*, 297 Mich.App 35, 40; 823 NW2d 144 (2012). The clearly erroneous standard of review applies to each of these findings. MCR 3.977(K); *In re SD*, 236 Mich.App 240, 245–246; 599 NW2d 772 (1999). "A finding of fact is clearly erroneous if the reviewing court has a definite and firm conviction that a mistake has been committed[.]" *In re Moss*, 301 Mich.App 76, 80; 836 NW2d 182 (2013).

We proceed by determining whether the trial court properly applied the dual burden of proof required under this statutory framework.

* * *

I. Statutory Grounds/Best Interests

Respondent does not challenge the trial court's findings that a statutory ground for termination was proved or that termination was in E.M.'s best interests. Nevertheless, because the court's findings in these respects are inextricably linked to its findings under the ICWA and the MIFPA, we have reviewed the record and conclude that the trial court did not clearly err in finding statutory grounds for termination and that the termination was in E.M.'s best interests.

* * *

II. Constitutionality of MCL 712B.15(3)

Respondent argues that MCL 712B.15(3) is unconstitutionally vague because it does not provide an evidentiary standard by which the trial court must make its factual findings.

Constitutional issues and issues of statutory construction involve questions of law that we review de novo. *Federal Home Loan Mortgage Ass'n v. Kelley* (On Reconsideration), 306 Mich.App 487, 493; 858 NW2d 69 (2014). "The primary goal of statutory interpretation is to give effect to the Legislature's intent, focusing first on the statute's plain language." *Klooster v. City of Charlevoix*, 488 Mich. 289, 296; 795 NW2d 578 (2011). "[U]nless explicitly defined in a statute, every word or phrase of a statute should be accorded its plain and ordinary meaning, taking into account the context in which the words are used." *Yudashkin v. Holden*, 247 Mich.App 642, 650; 637 NW2d 257 (2001) (quotation marks and citation omitted). Moreover, "under established rules of statutory construction, statutes are presumed constitutional, and courts have a duty to construe a statute as constitutional unless unconstitutionality is clearly apparent." *In re Gosnell*, 234 Mich.App at 326, 334; 594 NW2d 90 (1999) (internal quotations and citation omitted).

As noted above, MCL 712B.15 provides heightened evidentiary requirements in child protective proceedings involving Indian children. Specifically, MCL 712B.15(2) provides that an Indian child may not be removed from the home or placed into foster care absent "clear and convincing evidence" that active efforts were made to provide the family with services, that those efforts were unsuccessful, and that the child is likely to be harmed if not removed. Similarly, with respect to termination, MCL 712B.15(4) provides that parental rights may not be terminated absent evidence to establish, "beyond a reasonable doubt," that the parent's continued custody of the child would likely result in serious physical or emotional harm to the child. Finally, MCL 712B.15(3), the provision specifically challenged by respondent, provides:

> A party seeking a termination of parental rights to an Indian child under state law must demonstrate to the court's satisfaction that active efforts have been made to provide remedial services and rehabilitative programs designed to prevent the breakup of the Indian family and that the active efforts were unsuccessful.

A statute is void for vagueness if "'(1) it is overbroad and impinges on First Amendment Freedoms, (2) it does not provide fair notice of the conduct it regulates, or (3) it gives the trier of fact unstructured and unlimited discretion in determining whether the statute has been violated.'" *Kenefick v. Battle Creek*, 284 Mich. App 653, 655; 774 NW2d 925 (2009), quoting *Proctor v. White Lake Twp Police Dep't*, 248 Mich.App 457, 467; 639 NW2d 332 (2001). In this case, respondent argues that MCL 712B.15(3) is unconstitutionally vague because, unlike MCL 712b.15(2) and (4), which clearly set forth an applicable standard of proof, the former section does not provide any standard of proof. Essentially, respondent argues that MCL 712B.15(3) is unconstitutionally vague in that it provides the trial court with unfettered discretion to determine whether "active efforts" were made.

We are unaware of any published caselaw addressing the applicable burden of proof under MCL 712B.15(3). However, both this Court and our Supreme Court have addressed an identical issue in the context of the analogous "active efforts" provision of the ICWA, 25 USC § 1912(d). That statutory provision provides as follows:

> [a]ny party seeking to effect a foster care placement of, or termination of parental rights to, an Indian child under State law shall satisfy the court that active efforts have been made to provide remedial services and rehabilitative programs designed to prevent the breakup of the Indian family and that these efforts have proved unsuccessful. [25 USC § 1912(d).]

In *In re Roe*, 281 Mich.App 88, 99–101; 764 NW2d 789 (2008), this Court was tasked with determining what standard of proof applied to the "active efforts" requirement in 25 USC § 1912(d). In resolving the issue, this Court found particularly persuasive the Nebraska Supreme Court's decision in *In re Walter W*, 274 Neb 859; 744 NW2d 55 (2008), in which that Court reasoned:

> ... Congress imposed a "beyond a reasonable doubt" standard for the "serious emotional [or] physical damage" element in parental rights termination cases under § 1912(f). Congress also imposed a "clear and convincing" standard of proof for the "serious emotional or physical damage" element in foster care placements under § 1912(e). The specified standards of proof in subsections § 1912(e) and (f) illustrate that if Congress had intended to impose a heightened standard of proof for the active efforts element in § 1912(d), it would have done so. [*In re Roe*, 281 Mich.App at 100, quoting *In re Walter W*, 274 Neb at 864865.]

Relying on the Nebraska Supreme Court's reasoning, the Roe Court held that Congress intentionally chose not to impose a particular standard for 25 USC § 1912(d), and therefore "the proper standard of proof for determinations under § 1912(d) of the ICWA is the default standard applicable to all Michigan cases involving the termination of parental rights. That standard is proof by clear and convincing evidence." *In re Roe*, 281 Mich.App at 100–101.

Our Supreme Court ultimately adopted Roe's holding in *In re JL*, 483 Mich. 300; 770 NW2d 853 (2009). In that case, the Court noted that "[b]ecause Congress did not provide a heightened standard of proof in 25 USC 1912(d), as it did in 25 USC 1912(f), the default standard of proof for termination of parental rights cases, clear and convincing evidence, applies to the determination whether the DHS provided 'active efforts . . . to prevent the breakup of the Indian family' under 25 USC 1912(d)." *In re JL*, 483 Mich. at 318–319, citing *In re Roe*, 281 Mich. App at 100–101.2

As the above authority illustrates, in the face of Congress' failure to articulate a standard of proof in 25 USC § 1912(d), rather than declare the statute unconstitutionally vague, courts have concluded that Congress intended the "default" standard of clear and convincing evidence to apply to the ICWA's "active efforts" determination. We conclude that the same reasoning applies with equal force in this case.

As set forth above, the relevant provisions of the ICWA and the MIFPA are essentially identical; that is, each requires proof by "clear and convincing evidence" to remove an Indian child and place him or her into foster care, 25 USC § 1912(e), MCL 712B.15(2); proof sufficient to satisfy the trial court that active efforts have been made to terminate parental rights, 25 USC § 1912(d), MCL 712B.15(3); and proof "beyond a reasonable doubt" that continued custody will harm the child, 25 USC § 1912(f); MCL 712B.15(4). Thus, as with its federal counterpart, the Legislature, in enacting the MIFPA, set forth specific evidentiary standards in MCL 712B.15(2) and (4), while declining to do so in MCL 712B.15(3). The inevitable conclusion, therefore, is that, like Congress, the Legislature intended for the "default" evidentiary standard applicable in child protective proceedings—i.e. clear and convincing evidence—to apply to the findings required under MCL 712B.15(3) as to whether "active efforts" were made to prevent the breakup of the Indian family. Accord *In re JL*, 485 Mich. at 318–319; *In re Roe*, 281 Mich. at 100–101. Therefore, because a default standard of proof applies to MCL 712B.15(3), it is not unconstitutionally vague.

Notes

1. At least one other state has found there is no standard beyond satisfaction of the court:

> "Congress displayed considered precision in articulating the evidentiary burdens it was imposing." *Matter of Baby Boy Doe*, 127 Idaho at 458, 902 P.2d at 483. The fact that Congress carefully calibrated the evidentiary standard in subsection (e) to provide for a clear and convincing evidence standard, but provided no similar standard in subsection (d), suggests that Congress did not intend to require that courts make a finding with respect to active efforts by clear and convincing evidence.
>
> 25 U.S.C. section 1912(d) requires that a party seeking termination of parental rights with respect to an Indian child "shall satisfy" the court that active efforts to prevent the breakup of the family have been made, not that

> the party show by clear and convincing evidence that such efforts have been made. The magistrate court stated that it was satisfied that DHW made active efforts to prevent the breakup of the family. In doing so, it made the finding required by 25 U.S.C. section 1912(d).

In re Doe, 342 P.3d 632, 637 (Idaho 2015).

2. Most states are "dual burden" states, where the court must ultimately make findings to meet both state requirements and federal requirements. As the case above indicates, to terminate parental rights, a court in Michigan must find beyond a reasonable doubt that continued custody will likely result in serious emotional or physical harm to the child, and also find under a preponderance of the evidence that a child's best interests are served by termination. This interpretation of the law means that both the child's best interests are considered as well as requiring a higher burden for termination. Are these in conflict? Can a court make one finding, but not the other? What if a court believes it is in a child's best interests to terminate parental rights, but the facts to not rise to the standard set forth in ICWA?

3. The federal regulations state that a finding of clear and convincing evidence must be made to deviate from the placement preferences, discussed in section F below. 25 C.F.R. § 23.132(b) (2016). The regulations specifically do not address the burden of proof for either transfer to tribal court or a finding of active efforts.

D. Qualified Expert Witnesses

As part of the burden of proof, certain decisions must be supported by the testimony of a qualified expert witness. Before a child is placed in foster care or parental rights are terminated under ICWA, a qualified expert witness must testify that the "continued custody of the child by the parent or Indian custodian is likely to result in serious emotional or physical damage to the child." 25 U.S.C. § 1912(e), (f) (2012).

States, with no assistance from a tribe, may have a difficult time finding an expert witness that neither the parents nor the tribe will object to due to their lack of cultural knowledge. Often, a tribe needs to assist the state in finding a properly qualified witness. This can be problematic, because the tribe may not agree with the removal of the child from the family unit or the termination of parental rights. For some tribes, termination of parental rights is not an appropriate solution to the need for permanence for the child, and the tribe will not provide a witness.

Qualifying an expert witness in court may be considered a deeply disrespectful or culturally difficult experience for the witness. A state's attorney who has little understanding of what she is asking may ask the witness questions regarding her expertise on deeply cultural matters. The point of having the witness testify is to demonstrate a member of the child's community agrees with the removal or the termination of parental rights. In some cases, this can be a difficult hurdle.

In re M.F.

225 P.3d 1177 (Kan. 2010)

The opinion of the court was delivered by LUCKERT, J.:

The biological mother of M.F. appeals a decision to terminate her parental rights, arguing the district court failed to comply with the Indian Child Welfare Act (ICWA), 25 U.S.C. § 1901 et seq. (2006). The ICWA standard for termination of parental rights is "evidence beyond a reasonable doubt, including testimony of qualified expert witnesses, that the continued custody of the child by the parent or Indian custodian is likely to result in serious emotional or physical damage to the child." 25 U.S.C. § 1912(f) (2006). The mother argues the State failed to present an ICWA qualified expert witness in either the child in need of care (CINC) proceeding or in the subsequent hearing to terminate parental rights. The Court of Appeals agreed with her argument and reversed the district court. *In re M.F.*, 41 Kan.App.2d 927, 206 P.3d 57 (2009).

On review of that decision, we affirm the Court of Appeals, concluding that the ICWA heightens the requirements for an expert's qualifications beyond those normally required in a proceeding governed solely by state statutes. We further hold that Kansas district courts should consider the legislative history of the ICWA and the Department of the Interior, Bureau of Indian Affairs Guidelines for State Courts; Indian Child Custody Proceedings, 44 Fed.Reg. 67,584 (1979), in determining if a witness meets the heightened standard. In this case, there was no evidence that the two social workers who testified were members of the child's tribe, had substantial experience in the delivery of child and family services to Indians, had extensive knowledge of prevailing social and cultural standards and childrearing practices within the child's tribe, or had substantial education and experience in the area of social work. Thus, the witnesses were not qualified expert witnesses under the ICWA, and there was no expert testimony to support the district court's decision as required by the ICWA. Because this error is not harmless, we reverse and remand for new proceedings.

M.F. was born on October 24, 2006, with special medical needs that required an extended hospitalization. His mother, S.F., was discharged after his birth; she then had no further contact with the hospital. Two weeks after M.F.'s birth, the State filed a CINC proceeding. The district court appointed a guardian ad litem (GAL) for M.F. and held a custody hearing the next day. M.F.'s alleged father, D.J., appeared at the hearing; his mother, S.F., did not. At the hearing, the State requested temporary custody of M.F. because of the mother's homelessness, her possible drug use, and her abandonment of M.F. at the hospital. ... Subsequent genetic testing confirmed D.J. was M.F.'s father. D.J., however, informed the court in writing that he was unable to care for M.F. and he did not contest the claim that M.F. was a child in need of care.

After the initial hearing, the State learned that M.F. might be eligible to enroll as a member of the Northern Arapaho Tribe (Tribe). Consequently, the State notified the Tribe of the proceeding. In response, the Tribe sent the State a notice of the

Tribe's intent to intervene in the case and requested notification of all hearings and other actions. The State filed the Tribe's notice with the district court. Included with the Tribe's notice was a document stating a Tribe enrollment technician had determined M.F. was not enrolled with the Tribe but would be eligible for enrollment.

The only witness to testify at the CINC hearing was Lindsay Courtney, a licensed social worker who was M.F.'s case manager. Courtney testified she received her bachelor's degree in May 2006 and obtained her social work license in July 2006, approximately 3 months before M.F.'s birth in October. No other expert qualifications were offered. Courtney testified that M.F. had required surgery and had been hospitalized since May 10, 2007. M.F. continued to require specialized care because of a "trache" and feeding tubes. According to Courtney, once the mother had been discharged from the hospital, she had not called to check on M.F. and did not know M.F. had required surgery and lengthy hospitalization. Courtney indicated there was an element of danger and risk to M.F. by the mother's not responding to the hospital because a potential caregiver would need to learn how to care for M.F. after M.F. was released from the hospital.

The State argued the evidence complied with the ICWA's standard of proof and established that M.F. was in danger and needed immediate placement. The GAL agreed with the State and additionally argued there was good cause for departing from the ICWA's placement preferences because neither parent was capable of handling M.F. or providing for M.F.'s special needs, no extended family members had come forward, and there was nothing more than an indication the Tribe would intervene. The mother's attorney argued the district court should apply the ICWA standard requiring testimony by an ICWA qualified expert, and the social worker who testified was not a qualified expert. The mother's attorney pointed out that Courtney did not testify she had ever "dealt with any Indian issues" or issues involving "Indian children." In addition, the mother's attorney suggested that the Tribe should be contacted because it might have resources available to meet M.F.'s needs.

The district court found the State had met its burden and the social worker had "testified appropriately as an expert in this matter." Additionally, the district court found the evidence was clear and convincing beyond a reasonable doubt that M.F. was in danger and out-of-home placement was immediately necessary. Further, the court found that "returning the child to [the parents] is not in the child's best interest at this time based on the child's special medical circumstances." Finally, the court held there was "good cause" to depart from any Indian placement because neither parent could care for the child; no family had come forward; the Tribe, despite its indication that it desired to intervene, had not done so; and there were no other viable placement options presented. In conclusion, the district court found M.F. was a child in need of care pursuant to K.S.A. 38–1502(a)(2) (repealed January 1, 2007; now K.S.A.2008 Supp. 38–2202[d][2], with nearly identical language) and set the matter over for disposition.

In November 2007, the district court conducted a permanency hearing to review the permanency plan and concluded the plan should be modified. In the journal entry, the court found reintegration of the family was not a viable alternative because M.F. had been in State custody since birth, M.F. had a serious medical condition that had required him to be hospitalized for 6 months and would require further hospitalization, and there was a lack of effort by the parents.

Also in November 2007, the State filed a motion to terminate parental rights. At a pretrial hearing related to the motion, counsel for the mother expressed concern there was no journal entry recording the CINC determination and the district court had heard no qualified expert testimony, which was required for a CINC determination under the ICWA. In response, the district court reiterated that it had found in July 2007, from the bench, that M.F. was a child in need of care pursuant to Kansas statutes based on evidence that "was clear and convincing and beyond a reasonable doubt." The court nevertheless agreed that the CINC finding needed to be journalized and directed the State to do so. Apparently, the State did not comply with the order; no such journal entry is contained in the record on appeal.

* * *

The motion to terminate parental rights was heard in April 2008, when M.F. was approximately 18 months of age. The mother appeared in person. Before evidence was presented, the district court noted a representative from the Tribe had contacted the district court and requested to participate in the hearing by telephone. Counsel for each parent confirmed that they had talked to the Tribe representative who wanted to participate and they had advised her to contact the district court for arrangements. The district court denied the request, indicating that the Tribe's participation by telephone would be "unwieldy and would not work."

During counsels' arguments pertaining to the termination of parental rights, the mother's attorney again argued the district court had not complied with the ICWA in that, during the numerous proceedings, it had failed to make specific findings required under the federal act. The district court disagreed, focusing on whether notice was given to the Tribe and finding the State made "an adequate record [showing] there has been compliance with all notice provisions." Then, testimony was taken from social worker Lindsay Howes, who had been involved in M.F.'s case since M.F. was placed in State custody. Like Courtney, the social worker who testified at the CINC hearing, Howes testified that she had received a bachelor's degree in social welfare in May 2006 and was licensed in July 2006, just months before M.F.'s birth. Howes recited the case history and the limited contacts she had with the parents. In Howes' opinion, M.F. needed permanency through an adoptive home that could provide for M.F.'s medical care and needs. She did not believe the mother could meet M.F.'s needs, which required more than normal parenting due to M.F.'s extreme medical needs. From the time of M.F.'s birth to the termination hearing, his condition had required numerous hospitalizations and medical procedures, and he continued to require the trache and feeding tubes.

The mother testified at the termination hearing that she knew of two family members who were interested in caring for M.F. if the district court determined she could not regain custody of the child. No family members came forward, however. The mother acknowledged that she had only seen M.F. twice since her postpartum discharge from the hospital 18 months earlier. The district court ultimately entered an order terminating the parental rights of both parents.

* * *

There is no dispute that the ICWA applies to this case. M.F. is an Indian child within the meaning of the ICWA, see 25 U.S.C. § 1903(4) (2006) ("'Indian child' means any unmarried person who is under age eighteen and is either (a) a member of an Indian tribe or (b) is eligible for membership in an Indian tribe and is the biological child of a member of an Indian tribe."). Generally, tribal courts have exclusive jurisdiction over proceedings involving children residing on or domiciled within a reservation and concurrent jurisdiction with state courts over foster care or termination of parental rights proceedings involving children not domiciled on a reservation. See 25 U.S.C. § 1911(a); *Kelly v. Kelly*, 759 N.W.2d 721, 724 (N.D.2009); *In re A.P.*, 25 Kan.App.2d 268, 274, 961 P.2d 706 (1998). In this appeal, it is not disputed that the district court had concurrent jurisdiction. And, as previously noted, the issue of whether the case should have been transferred to the tribal court is not before us.

* * *

The minimum federal standard with regard to CINC-type proceedings—i.e., where an Indian child may be placed in foster care—is stated in 25 U.S.C. § 1912(e), which mandates that there must be a "determination, supported by clear and convincing evidence, *including testimony of qualified expert witnesses*, that the continued custody of the child by the parent or Indian custodian is likely to result in serious emotional or physical damage to the child." (Emphasis added.) Similarly, a decision to terminate parental rights must be supported by the "testimony of qualified expert witnesses," but the State has a higher burden of proof; it must prove "beyond a reasonable doubt, including testimony of qualified expert witnesses, that the continued custody of the child by the parent or Indian custodian is likely to result in serious emotional or physical damage to the child." 25 U.S.C. § 1912(f).

At issue here is whether Courtney and Howes, social workers for M.F., were qualified experts under the ICWA and whether their testimony satisfied the standards for the ICWA in the CINC and termination proceedings. The GAL and State argue that the Court of Appeals erred by essentially holding that to be a qualified expert witness under the ICWA, the witness must be knowledgeable in tribal customs or child welfare specifically related to Indian children and must present testimony supporting the State's burden under the ICWA.

* * *

The ICWA does not define "qualified expert witnesses," leaving Congress' intent unclear. A United States House of Representatives Report prepared in conjunction with the ICWA states that the phrase "'qualified expert witnesses' is meant to apply to expertise beyond the normal social worker qualifications." H.R.Rep. No. 95–1386,

95th Cong., 2d Sess. 1978, at 12, reprinted in 1978 U.S.C.C.A.N. 7530, 7545. This statement indirectly instructs that the standard typically applied in Kansas CINC and termination proceedings—qualifying a social worker as an expert if he or she has a degree, is licensed, and has some contact with the CINC case—is contrary to Congress' intent.

Yet, the legislative history does not explain the qualifications that are necessary to meet the heightened standard. Guidance has been provided, however, by the Department of the Interior, Bureau of Indian Affairs, through guidelines published to assist state courts in applying the ICWA. Department of the Interior, Bureau of Indian Affairs Guidelines for State Courts; Indian Child Custody Proceedings, 44 Fed.Reg. 67,584 (1979) (BIA Guidelines).

* * *

The first two types of individuals characterized in the BIA Guidelines, subparts D.4 (b)(i) and (b)(ii), are individuals who possess knowledge of Indian customs and Indian childrearing practices. The Court of Appeals noted these provisions and concluded neither criterion was satisfied. Although the Court of Appeals did not recognize that the social workers testifying at the two hearings were different individuals, the ultimate conclusion that the criteria of subparts D.4 (b)(i) and (b)(ii) were not satisfied is correct; there was no evidence in this case that the two social workers, Courtney and Howes, could have been qualified under the first two subparts. Neither indicated that she was a member of M.F.'s tribe, had substantial experience with tribal family services, or had extensive knowledge of cultural standards and childrearing practices within M.F.'s tribe.

The GAL focuses on this conclusion by the Court of Appeals to argue that the Court of Appeals required all experts in proceedings controlled by the ICWA to have specialized knowledge of Indian culture and society. This argument ignores the fact that the Court of Appeals acknowledged the BIA Guidelines, subpart D.4 (b)(iii), which makes no mention of knowledge of Indian culture. *In re M.F.*, 41 Kan.App.2d at 935, 206 P.3d 57. Granted, the Court of Appeals' discussion blends the two hearings and the two witnesses, but we do not read the decision as reaching the question of whether an expert must always have expertise in Indian social and cultural matters, and conclude this issue is not before us for decision. See Supreme Court Rule 8.03(g)(1) and (h)(3) (2009 Kan. Ct. R. Annot. 66).

The Court of Appeals' holding was merely that: "ICWA requires a witness be qualified as an expert and the witness testify that evidence existed to support the State's burden under the ICWA. 44 Fed.Reg. 67,593 (1979). See *In re S.M.H.*, 33 Kan. App.2d at 434–35, 103 P.3d 976. There was no such testimony in this case." *In re M.F.*, 41 Kan.App.2d at 935, 206 P.3d 57. The Court of Appeals' reliance on *In re S.M.H.* reveals that the court was focused on the witnesses' lack of special expertise or experience.

* * *

[T]he *In re S.M.H.* holding, which was adopted by the Court of Appeals in this case, is consistent with the conclusion of numerous courts in other jurisdictions that have applied the rule that a person is not a qualified expert witness under the ICWA if they do not have expertise beyond the "normal" social worker qualifications. Generally these courts glean guidance from the legislative history of the ICWA, which specifically states that the education and training should be beyond the normal social worker qualifications, and the BIA Guidelines' language, which suggests there must be substantial education and experience. See, e.g., *In re Desiree F.*, 83 Cal.App.4th 460, 466, 99 Cal.Rptr.2d 688 (2000) (ICWA requires more than showing that social worker was assigned to the case); *C.E.H. v. L.M.W.*, 837 S.W.2d 947, 955 (Mo.App.1992) (stating that phrase "qualified expert witness" is not defined by ICWA, but legislative history of ICWA reveals that phrase is meant to apply to expertise beyond normal social worker's qualifications); *Matter of Adoption of H.M.O.*, 289 Mont. 509, 519, 962 P.2d 1191 (1998) (abuse of discretion found where record was silent as to qualifications beyond being a social worker); *In re Interest of Shayla H.*, 17 Neb.App. 436, 449–50, 764 N.W.2d 119 (2009) (abuse of discretion found where social worker had bachelor's degree in human development, had been in position for approximately 11 years, had received regular training, and had worked with families with Native American heritage); *In re Roberts*, 46 Wash.App. 748, 756, 732 P.2d 528 (1987) (no abuse of discretion where witness had attended numerous workshops on Indian child welfare and was a committee member for two organizations involved in drafting ICWA); *In re Vaughn R.*, 770 N.W.2d 795, 807 (Wis.App.2009) (social worker's specialized knowledge as result of bachelor's and master's degrees in criminal justice did not relate to required showing of likely serious damage to child from continued custody by parent, and experience in monitoring conditions imposed on parents for the return of their children did not suggest something beyond normal social work qualifications); cf. *Sandy B. v. State, Dept. of Health*, 216 P.3d 1180, 1191 (Alaska 2009) (expert had substantial education in his specialty of psychology and, thus, met the ICWA's heightened standard for qualification as an expert in a proceeding to terminate parental rights, where expert had earned master's and doctorate degrees in clinical psychology); *In re Interest of Phoebe S. & Rebekah S.*, 11 Neb.App. 919, 927, 935, 664 N.W.2d 470 (2003) (social work professor qualified to testify as expert witness under ICWA where professor had substantial education and experience in area of child welfare, bonding, and attachment and in sociological aspects of childhood, and was experienced and knowledgeable about ICWA); but see *In Re N.N.E.*, 752 N.W.2d 1, 13 (Iowa 2008) (citing Iowa statute which includes within the definition of "qualified expert witness" a "social worker, sociologist, physician, psychologist, traditional tribal therapist and healer, spiritual leader, historian, or elder").

* * *

Applying subpart D.4 (b)(iii) of the BIA Guidelines (having previously found that the other subparts were not met), neither Courtney nor Howes, the social workers who testified in this case, met the standard. Both Courtney, who testified at the CINC hearing, and Howes, who testified at the termination hearing, graduated with bachelor's degrees a mere 5 months before M.F.'s birth and had been licensed by the state of Kansas for only about 3 months when they became M.F.'s case workers. There was no evidence of any other education, experience, or specialized expertise. By the time of the termination hearing, Howes had garnered more experience but still had practiced her profession less than 2 years. These qualifications pale in comparison to those considered in cases from other jurisdictions where appellate courts found an abuse of discretion in qualifying a social worker as an expert. E.g., *In re Interest of Shayla H.*, 17 Neb.App. at 449–50, 764 N.W.2d 119 (11 years of case work experience insufficient). We affirm the Court of Appeals' conclusion that neither Courtney nor Howes qualified as an expert witness as required by the ICWA.

The GAL also takes issue with the Court of Appeals' statement that the qualified expert must "testify that evidence existed to support the State's burden under the ICWA." *In re M.F.*, 41 Kan.App.2d at 935, 206 P.3d 57. The GAL interprets this statement to mean that a qualified expert must offer a specific opinion as to whether or not the State's evidence meets the burden of proof. It seems, rather, that the Court of Appeals' statement is merely a reiteration of the ICWA standard that a decision to terminate parental rights must be based on "evidence beyond a reasonable doubt, including testimony of qualified expert witnesses, that the continued custody of the child by the parent or Indian custodian is likely to result in serious emotional or physical damage to the child." 25 U.S.C. § 1912(f). The expert need not opine on the ultimate issue of whether the State met its burden of proof. But the expert's opinion must support the ultimate finding of the district court that continued custody by the parent will result in serious emotional or physical damage to the child.

* * *

[I]n applying the harmless error standard, it is difficult to conclude a procedural violation of the ICWA can be harmless in light of 25 U.S.C. § 1914 (2006), which provides:

> "Any Indian child who is the subject of any action for foster care placement or termination of parental rights under State law, any parent or Indian custodian from whose custody such child was removed, and the Indian child's tribe may petition any court of competent jurisdiction to invalidate such action upon a showing that such action violated any provision of sections 1911, 1912, and 1913 of this title."

The expert witness provision is found in section 1912, so a lack of qualified expert witness testimony creates the potential of future invalidation of the foster care placement and termination of parental rights. Under those circumstances, the lack of a qualified expert witness cannot be considered harmless. Consequently, we conclude the error in this case requires us to reverse and remand for proceedings consistent with the requirements of the ICWA, beginning with a rehearing of the decision to determine the child is in need of care.

Notes

1. The federal regulations now provide different standards for the qualified expert witness:

> **§ 23.122 Who may serve as a qualified expert witness?**
>
> (a) A qualified expert witness must be qualified to testify regarding whether the child's continued custody by the parent or Indian custodian is likely to result in serious emotional or physical damage to the child and should be qualified to testify as to the prevailing social and cultural standards of the Indian child's Tribe. A person may be designated by the Indian child's Tribe as being qualified to testify to the prevailing social and cultural standards of the Indian child's Tribe.
>
> (b) The court or any party may request the assistance of the Indian child's Tribe or the BIA office serving the Indian child's Tribe in locating persons qualified to serve as expert witnesses.
>
> (c) The social worker regularly assigned to the Indian child may not serve as a qualified expert witness in child-custody proceedings concerning the child.

25 C.F.R. § 23.122 (2016).

2. What about social workers who are employed by the state, but are members of a tribe who also know the child-rearing practices of a tribe? Can those workers be expert witnesses, or does it have to be a third party not employed by the state? The federal regulations do not address state social workers or supervisors who are not regularly assigned to the child.

3. What should be required of the qualified expert witness? Should they be expected to meet with the family? Meet with the child? Make an independent determination, or base their opinion on the state reports? Can the witness submit a letter to the court, or must the witness testify in court? Should a parent have the opportunity to question the witness? The federal guidelines state "it is also recommended that the qualified expert witness be someone familiar with that particular child. If the expert makes contact with the parents, observes interactions between the parent(s) and child, and meets with extended family members in the child's life, the expert will be able to provide a more complete picture to the court." BUREAU OF INDIAN AFFAIRS, GUIDELINES FOR IMPLEMENTING THE INDIAN CHILD WELFARE ACT 54 (Dec. 2016).

4. In at least one case, the parties and Tribe "waived" the qualified expert witness testimony at the trial level. *In re K.E.*, 2015 WL 4467739 (Cal. Ct. App. July 22, 2015). Parties cannot waive testimony required to meet the burden of proof under ICWA. For the parent, that testimony is an independent added protection. For the tribe, it is a time when a person who understands the tribe and its culture and community can respond to the state's case. The state has not met its burden of proof if it cannot provide a qualified expert witness. No party can waive this requirement.

In re S.E.G.

521 N.W.2d 357, 365 (Minn. 1994)

[This case involves a disagreement about where the children involved with the case should be placed: a Native foster home or a non-Native adoptive family. The lower court took testimony from many people, including some expert witnesses. The Minnesota Supreme Court evaluated whether the witnesses were considered expert or not under the law.]

The [1979] BIA guidelines require that a finding of extraordinary physical or emotional needs be "established by testimony of a qualified expert witness." Section D.4 of the BIA guidelines addresses the use of the phrase "qualified expert witness" in the Act. Subsection (b) of this section states:

> (b) Persons with the following characteristics are most likely to meet the requirements for a qualified expert witness for purposes of Indian child custody proceedings:
>
> > (i) A member of the Indian child's tribe who is recognized by the tribal community as knowledgeable in tribal customs as they pertain to family organization and childrearing practices.
> >
> > (ii) A lay expert witness having substantial experience in the delivery of child and family services to Indians, and extensive knowledge of prevailing social and cultural standards and childrearing practices within the Indian child's tribe.
> >
> > (iii) A professional person having substantial education and experience in the area of his or her specialty.

44 Fed.Reg. 67,584, 67,593 (1979).

The comments to this section of the guidelines state, "The second subsection makes clear that knowledge of tribal culture and childrearing practices will frequently be very valuable to the court." *Id.* In Minnesota, it is important to read this section of the guidelines in conjunction with § A.(2), which states:

> (2) In any child custody proceeding where applicable state or other federal law provides a higher standard of protection to the rights of the parent or Indian custodian than the protection accorded under the Indian Child Welfare Act, the state court shall apply the state or other federal law, provided that application of that law does not infringe any right accorded by the Indian Child Welfare Act to an Indian tribe or child.

Id. at 67,586. The Minnesota Department of Human Services Social Services Manual defines a qualified expert witness somewhat more narrowly, requiring expertise about Indian childrearing practices in all three categories. See Minnesota Department of Human Services, Minnesota Social Services Manual, XIII-3586 (1987); *Matter of Welfare of B.W.*, 454 N.W.2d 437, 442 (Minn.App.1990). "The DHS manual adds to paragraph (iii) the requirement that the professional have 'substantial knowledge of prevailing social and cultural standards and child-rearing practices within the Indian community.'" *Matter of Welfare of B.W.*, 454 N.W.2d at 442.

Most of the testimony in this case which tended to establish that the children had extraordinary physical or emotional needs was not presented by qualified expert witnesses. E.C. and C.C. [non-Native adoptive couple] presented only two witnesses whom they attempted to qualify as expert witnesses. By contrast, nearly all of the tribe's expert witnesses qualified under the guidelines and were found to so qualify by the trial court.

The record before the trial court supported its finding that both families adequately met the children's emotional, educational, and physical needs. By all accounts, the children generally had fared very well in E.C. and C.C.'s home, and neither party disputed that they currently were doing well in A.C.'s [Native foster] home. However, the qualified expert witness portion of the record seemed to show that the placement in A.C.'s home met the children's cultural needs and that it was unlikely E.C. and C.C. would have been able to meet those needs as well as A.C., though E.C. and C.C. certainly showed they would make efforts to do so. Only one qualified expert witness, Darrell Auginash, testified that he believed it was "possible" for the children's cultural needs to be met growing up in a non-Native home. Mr. Auginash did not express an opinion as to whether the children had extraordinary emotional needs and he could not have so testified because he had known E.C. and C.C. only a few days at the time of trial.

Of the experts qualified by the trial court, none testified that the children had extraordinary emotional needs which were not being met in their current placement. Rather, these witnesses' testimony tended to show that the children were not ready to be adopted and needed to stabilize before being placed in an adoptive home and that their need for stability was being met in A.C.'s home. Under these circumstances, we believe that the trial court's finding of extraordinary emotional need could not have been based on the testimony of qualified expert witnesses and was therefore clearly erroneous.

Notes

1. The state prosecutor must get the qualified witness to testify to exactly what the law requires. While other testimony might be helpful to the court, for it to meet the burden of proof required by the law, the expert must provide testimony that the continued custody of the children by their parents will cause physical or emotional damage to the children. Right now, there is no regulation or guidance that states that testimony of the witness must establish the extraordinary physical or emotional needs to deviate from the placement preferences.

2. How many qualified expert witnesses must the state produce? The federal guidelines currently state, "ICWA and the rule do not limit the number of expert witnesses that may testify. The court may accept expert testimony from any number of witnesses, including from multiple qualified expert witnesses." Bureau of

Indian Affairs, Guidelines for Implementing the Indian Child Welfare Act 54 (Dec. 2016). Most states, however, have held that one qualified expert witness is sufficient.

3. What, exactly, is the point of the expert witness? What happens when a witness does not agree with the foster care placement or termination of parental rights, but the prosecutor moves ahead anyway?

In re Payne/Pumphrey/Fortson

311 Mich. App. 49, *appeal denied*, 498 Mich. 869 (2015)

I. Factual and Procedural Background

Respondent has a lengthy history with the Department of Human Services (DHS) dating back to 2009, involving allegations of physical abuse, physical neglect, improper supervision, mental instability, and substance abuse. The trial court initially terminated respondent's parental rights to her minor children, AP, DP, KP, and DF, under MCL 712A.19b(3)(c)(i), (c)(ii), (g), and (j) on September 5, 2013. Respondent appealed that termination order as of right, and in In re Payne/Pumphrey/Fortson, 2014 WL 4656647, at *2–3, this Court affirmed the trial court's order in part, reversed in part, and remanded for further proceedings. Subsequently, on November 6, 2014, the trial court conducted an additional termination hearing as instructed by this Court. That same day, the trial court entered an order affirming its original order terminating respondent's parental rights to each of her minor children.

A. Respondent's First Appeal

In respondent's first appeal, she argued that the lower court erred in terminating her parental rights because the court failed to apply the correct evidentiary standard under ICWA with respect to her two Indian children, DP and AP, and failed to render a finding that termination was in her children's best interests. In re Payne/Pumphrey/Fortson, 2014 WL 4656647, at *1–3. This Court concluded that DP and AP were Indian children under ICWA, but that "the trial court did not apply the heightened 'beyond a reasonable doubt' evidentiary standard of proof at the termination hearing as required under ICWA." Id. at 2. The Court further noted that "although a representative of DP and AP's Indian tribe testified at the termination hearing, the witness was never qualified as an expert and, importantly, the witness did not testify that respondents' 'continued custody of' DP and AP was 'likely to result in serious emotional or physical damage to the' Indian children." Id., quoting 25 USC 1912(f). Accordingly, the Court reversed the trial court's termination order regarding DP and AP and remanded for further proceedings. Id.

* * *

B. Lower Court Proceedings on Remand

* * *

Christopher Hillert, a child welfare worker for the Red Cliff Band of Lake Superior Chippewa, was qualified as an expert regarding the customs, family organization, and child-rearing practices of AP and DP's Indian tribe. Hillert testified that DHS made active efforts to reunify the family, and he could not identify any additional services that could have been provided to respondent during the course of the proceedings. However, Hillert opposed terminating respondent's parental rights because it was generally against the tribe's practice to support termination. When asked whether he believed returning AP or DP to respondent's care would present a serious risk of harm to either child, Hillert stated his position in the following exchange:

> Q. Alright. Let me ask you a specific question, Mr. Hillert. Do you feel, either yes or no, that the continued custody of the children by the parent and custodian would likely result in serious emotional or physical damage to either one or both of the children?
>
> A. No, I do not.
>
> Q. Alright. And as it relates to both of the children, sir, why do you feel that way?
>
> A. I feel that [respondent] has completed everything that has been placed in front of her by the Department of Human Services. She continues to pursue her children, would like to visit with them more often and move towards reunification. I believe that [respondent] wants to work towards getting her children back and the Department has not allowed her an opportunity.

Following additional proofs and closing arguments, the trial court issued a ruling on the record. First, the trial court found that Hillert was properly qualified as an expert witness under ICWA. The trial court, quoting 25 USC 1912(f), acknowledged that the evidentiary standard for terminating respondent's parental rights to AP and DP required "a determination, supported by evidence beyond a reasonable doubt, including testimony of qualified expert witnesses, that the continued custody of the child by the parent or Indian custodian is likely to result in serious emotional or physical damage to the child." Respondent argued that the standard of proof required for the Indian children was not met because the only expert witness to testify expressly opined that respondent's custody of AP and DP was unlikely to result in serious emotional or physical damage to the children. In response to respondent's argument, the trial court stated the following:

> That does not, in this Court's mind, mean that if a qualified expert witness being a qualified expert under the Indian Child Welfare Act testifies that they do not think there is any serious harm, that that ends the discussion. The statute specifically says that it is evidence that includes testimony of [a] qualified expert witness and does not specify that the Court must otherwise discard any other evidence in the case in regard to whether or not there is a serious emotional or physical damage that's likely to result to the

> child. So, the Court takes into account all the things that are presented to it, including the testimony of Mr. Hillert, in this case, as to whether continued custody of the children . . . would likely [ ] result in serious emotional or physical damage to the child.

. . . There is, in this Court's opinion, and still is, despite Mr. Hillert's testimony, evidence and I think it is evidence beyond a reasonable doubt, that the return of the children is likely and was likely to result in serious emotional or physical damage to the children, those two children.

The trial court also found that terminating respondent's parental rights was in KP's and DF's best interests. The court noted that the children were benefitting from their current placements, and that respondent had not demonstrated an ability to benefit from the services provided to her throughout the proceedings.

II. Evidentiary Standard Under ICWA

A. Standard of Review

"Issues involving the application and interpretation of ICWA are questions of law that are reviewed de novo." *In re Morris,* 491 Mich. 81, 97, 815 N.W.2d 62 (2012). We review a trial court's factual findings underlying the application of legal issues for clear error. *Id.* A decision is clearly erroneous if the reviewing court is left with a definite and firm conviction that the trial court made a mistake. *In re Olive/Metts,* 297 Mich.App. 35, 41, 823 N.W.2d 144 (2012).

B. Principles of Statutory Interpretation

When interpreting statutes, our primary goal is to discern and give effect to the intent of the Legislature. *Turner v. Auto Club Ins. Ass'n,* 448 Mich. 22, 27, 528 N.W.2d 681 (1995). If statutory language is unambiguous, courts must honor the legislative intent clearly indicated in the language and "[n]o further construction is required or permitted." *Western Mich. Univ. Bd. of Control v. Michigan,* 455 Mich. 531, 538, 565 N.W.2d 828 (1997). In reviewing a statute's language, courts must "give effect to every word, phrase, and clause in a statute, and must avoid an interpretation that would render any part of the statute surplusage or nugatory." *Koontz v. Ameritech Servs., Inc.,* 466 Mich. 304, 312, 645 N.W.2d 34 (2002). When terms are undefined in a statute, courts should assign the terms their plain and ordinary meaning, and may consult a dictionary to accomplish this task. *Id.*

C. Analysis

Congress enacted ICWA in response to concerns over "'abusive child welfare practices that resulted in the separation of large numbers of Indian children from their families and tribes through adoption or foster care placement, usually in non-Indian homes.'" *In re Morris,* 491 Mich. at 97, 815 N.W.2d 62, quoting *Mississippi Band of Choctaw Indians v. Holyfield,* 490 U.S. 30, 32, 109 S.Ct. 1597, 104 L.Ed.2d 29 (1989). ICWA established "minimum Federal standards for the removal of Indian children from their families to protect the best interests of Indian children and to promote the stability and security of Indian tribes and their families." *In re Elliott,*

218 Mich.App. 196, 201, 554 N.W.2d 32 (1996) (citation and quotation marks omitted). Pursuant to ICWA, proceedings involving the termination of parental rights to an Indian child require a dual burden of proof. *In re Elliott,* 218 Mich.App. at 209, 554 N.W.2d 32. That is, in addition to finding that at least one state statutory ground for termination was proven by clear and convincing evidence, the trial court must also make findings in compliance with ICWA before terminating parental rights. *Id.* at 209–210, 554 N.W.2d 32.

Subsection (f) of 25 USC 1912 governs the federal evidentiary standard necessary to terminate parental rights to an Indian child, and provides the following:

> No termination of parental rights may be ordered in such proceeding in the absence of a determination, supported by evidence beyond a reasonable doubt, including testimony of qualified expert witnesses, that the continued custody of the child by the parent or Indian custodian is likely to result in serious emotional or physical damage to the child.

Both MIFPA and the Michigan court rules contain similar requirements. MCL 712B.15(4) states the following:

> No termination of parental rights may be ordered in a proceeding described in this section without a determination, supported by evidence beyond a reasonable doubt, including testimony of at least 1 qualified expert witness as described in [MCL 712B.17], that the continued custody of the child by the parent or Indian custodian is likely to result in serious emotional or physical damage to the child.

MCR 3.977(G)(2) provides that a court may not terminate a parent's rights over an Indian child unless "the court finds evidence beyond a reasonable doubt, including testimony of at least one qualified expert witness," that "continued custody of the child by the parent or Indian custodian will likely result in serious emotional or physical damage to the child."

Respondent first argues that the "beyond a reasonable doubt" standard was not met in this case because only one expert witness testified, and 25 USC 1912(f) requires the "testimony of qualified expert witnesses." She correctly notes that both MCL 712B.15(4) and MCR 3.977(G)(2) vary slightly from 25 USC 1912(f), inasmuch as they merely require the testimony of "at least one qualified expert witness." She argues that to the extent Michigan authority conflicts with 25 USC 1912(f), the federal statute prevails, thus requiring more than one qualified expert witness to testify before a court may terminate her parental rights. However, this Court has repeatedly interpreted the term "witnesses" as used in 25 USC 1912 "to mean that only one 'qualified expert witness' need testify." *In re Elliott,* 218 Mich.App. at 207, 554 N.W.2d 32; see also *In re Kreft,* 148 Mich.App. 682, 690, 384 N.W.2d 843 (1986). Thus, 25 USC 1912(f) does not conflict with MCL 712B.15(4) and MCR 3.977(G)(2), and only one expert witness was required to testify in this case.

Respondent further contends that the trial court failed to comply with the "beyond a reasonable doubt" evidentiary standard because the only expert witness to testify at the termination hearing expressly opined that returning AP and DP to respondent's care would *not* likely result in serious emotional or physical damage to either child. To terminate parental rights to an Indian child, 25 USC 1912(f), MCL 712B.15(4), and MCR 3.977(G)(2) each require that evidence beyond a reasonable doubt, *including* testimony of a qualified expert witness, must establish that the continued custody of the child by the parent will likely result in serious emotional or physical damage to the child. The term "including" is undefined in ICWA, MIFPA, and the Michigan court rules. The word "including" is neither a technical nor a legal term, so consultation of a dictionary is appropriate to determine its plain and ordinary meaning within the context of the statute. *Koontz,* 466 Mich. at 312, 645 N.W.2d 34. *Random House Webster's College Dictionary* (2000) defines "include" as "to contain or encompass as part of a whole[.]" *Black's Law Dictionary* (10th ed.) similarly defines "include" as "[t]o contain as a part of something." Considering these definitions, we conclude that in order to terminate parental rights to an Indian child, a trial court's "beyond a reasonable doubt" finding must "contain" or "encompass" testimony of a qualified expert witness who opines that continued custody of the Indian child by the parent will likely result in serious physical or emotional harm to the child.

To further support this interpretation, we turn to this Court's recent decision in *In re McCarrick/Lamoreaux,* 307 Mich.App. 436, 861 N.W.2d 303 (2014). In that case, this Court interpreted 25 USC 1912(e) and MCL 712B.15(2), two different—but very similar—provisions of ICWA and MIFPA, which govern the evidentiary standards required to place an Indian child in protective custody. *Id.* at 464–466, 861 N.W.2d 303. Subsection (e) of 25 USC 1912 provides the following:

> No foster care placement may be ordered in such proceeding in the absence of a determination, supported by clear and convincing evidence, *including testimony of qualified expert witnesses,* that the continued custody of the child by the parent or Indian custodian is likely to result in serious emotional or physical damage to the child. [Emphasis added.]

Similarly, MCL 712B.15(2) provides that a trial court may only remove an Indian child "upon clear and convincing evidence, *that includes testimony of at least 1 expert witness* who has knowledge of child rearing practices of the Indian child's tribe, that . . . the continued custody of the child by the parent or Indian custodian is likely to result in serious emotional or physical damage to the child." (Emphasis added.)

In *In re McCarrick/Lamoreaux,* 307 Mich.App. at 439–440, 861 N.W.2d 303, DHS petitioned to remove Indian children from their mother's care because she was abusing drugs and alcohol in the home and allowing her children to do the same. At the removal hearing, Stacey O'Neil was qualified as an expert on the child-rearing practices of the children's tribe. *Id.* at 441, 861 N.W.2d 303. O'Neil provided an overview of the services offered to the mother and the success of those efforts, but she "did not testify about the possible damage to the children." *Id.* at 466, 861 N.W.2d 303.

Despite the lack of expert testimony concerning the possibility of damage to the children, the trial court found that probable cause existed to assume jurisdiction over the children. *Id.* at 441–442, 861 N.W.2d 303.

On appeal, this Court concluded that the trial court failed to comply with the evidentiary standards of ICWA and MIFPA, and held the following:

> While it may appear obvious that drug use has the potential to damage children, ICWA and [MIFPA] require the trial court's determination of damage to include the testimony of a qualified expert witness. *Here, there was simply no testimony in that regard, much less testimony by O'Neil, the qualified expert witness.* We conclude that the trial court's determination regarding the damage to the children did not comply with ICWA or [MIFPA] because the trial court's determination of damage did not include the testimony of a qualified expert witness. [*In re McCarrick/Lamoreaux,* 307 Mich.App. at 466–467, 861 N.W.2d 303.]

Notably, in remanding the case for further proceedings, the Court instructed the trial court that if it could not "support its finding with testimony from a qualified expert witness at a hearing, it must return the children" to the mother's care. *Id.* at 469–470, 861 N.W.2d 303.

In this case, the trial court explicitly recognized that Hillert, the only expert witness at the termination hearing, did not support termination and specifically testified that returning AP and DP to respondent's care would *not* likely result in serious emotional or physical damage to either child. Nonetheless, considering the other evidence presented, the trial court determined that returning AP and DP to respondent's care *would* result in such damage beyond a reasonable doubt. In so doing, the trial court essentially disregarded Hillert's testimony, contrary to the plain language of 25 USC 1912(f), MCL 712B.15(4), and MCR 3.977(G)(2). Accordingly, we conclude that the trial court failed to adhere to the requirements of ICWA and its Michigan counterparts, and remand for further proceedings with respect to AP and DP.

Notes

1. The last paragraph of the case is illustrative the tension of ICWA's qualified witness provision—the qualified expert witness testimony is to demonstrate the child's community agrees with the termination. What happens when a tribe fundamentally does not believe in the state's power to terminate parental rights? What alternatives are available to the state? In this case, Michigan has long-term juvenile guardianships available as an alternative to termination. "Strong cultural beliefs that are in opposition to termination of parental rights" is listed as one reason to pursue guardianship as a permanency goal. State of Michigan, Department of Health and Human Services, Child Guardianship Manual 2 (Feb. 2014), available at http://dhhs.michigan.gov/OLMWEB/EX/GD/Public/GDM/600.pdf.

2. What is the job of the state's attorney when eliciting the testimony of the qualified expert witness? What must the witness say on the record for the court to be able to make a finding for termination of parental rights?

E. Active Efforts

One of the most important provisions when a child welfare case stays in state court is the requirement that the state "provide active efforts have been made to provide remedial services and rehabilitative programs designed to prevent the breakup of the Indian family." § 1912(d). In order to place a child in foster care or terminate parental rights, the petitioner must demonstrate to the court that active efforts have both been done *and* proved unsuccessful. Determining what are active efforts is often a balancing test. In contrast, the state must provide "reasonable efforts" for all child welfare cases under the federal requirements of the Adoption and Safe Families Act (ASFA), 42 U.S.C. § 1305 (2012).

People ex rel. J.S.B. Jr.

691 N.W.2d 611 (S.D. 2005)

Under the Adoption and Safe Families Act (ASFA), enacted in 1997, "reasonable efforts" to reunify a family are not required before termination of parental rights when a parent has a pattern of abusive or neglectful behavior constituting an aggravated circumstance. On the other hand, the Indian Child Welfare Act (ICWA), enacted in 1978, provides special rules for the needs of Indian children and families. ICWA requires "active efforts" to reunite families before a parent's rights may be terminated. In this abuse and neglect case, the father, a member of a federally recognized Indian tribe, appeals the termination of his parental rights. During the proceedings, the trial court ruled that ASFA "preempts" the requirements of ICWA, such that "active efforts" were not required in the circumstances. We conclude that ASFA does not override the requirements of ICWA. We affirm the termination of parental rights, however, because despite the court's erroneous ruling, the record reflects that the Department of Social Services (DSS) continued to provide "active efforts" to reunify the family, but such efforts were unsuccessful.

* * *

ICWA and ASFA

In 1978, Congress enacted the Indian Child Welfare Act (ICWA) after concluding that (1) it "has plenary power over Indian affairs;" (2) it "has assumed the responsibility for the protection and preservation of Indian tribes and their resources;" and (3) "an alarmingly high percentage of Indian families are broken up by the removal, often unwarranted, of their children from them by nontribal public and private agencies and that an alarmingly high percentage of such children are placed in non-Indian foster and adoptive homes and institutions." 25 U.S.C. § 1901 (1978).

Congress had a particular concern with the disproportionately higher rates of parental terminations with Indian families caused by an insensitivity to "Indian cultural values and social norms[,]" leading to misevaluations of parenting skills and to unequal considerations of such matters as parental alcohol abuse. American Indian Law Deskbook, p. 463 (3rd ed. 2004) (quoting H.R. Rep. No. 95–1386, at 10 (1978), reprinted in 1978 USCCAN 7530, 7532); see also 25 U.S.C. § 1901(4) (1978).

The declared policy of ICWA is

> *to protect the best interests of Indian children* and to promote the stability and security of Indian tribes and families by the establishment of minimum Federal standards for the removal of Indian children from their families and the placement of such children in foster or adoptive homes which will reflect the unique values of Indian culture, and by providing for assistance to Indian tribes in the operation of child and family service programs.

25 U.S.C. § 1902 (1978) (emphasis added). This policy acknowledges that Indian children should retain familial, tribal, and cultural ties.

* * *

To ensure that the best interests of Indian children are protected, ICWA (1) establishes either exclusive or presumptive jurisdiction in tribal courts; (2) grants special intervention rights to Indian tribes; (3) mandates that before an Indian parent's or custodian's rights to a child can be terminated, a finding must be made that "active efforts have been made to provide remedial services and rehabilitative programs designed to prevent the breakup of the Indian family and that these efforts have proved unsuccessful"; and (4) guarantees that no parental rights will be terminated without a finding beyond a reasonable doubt that "continued custody of the child by the parent or Indian custodian is likely to result in serious emotional or physical damage to the child." 25 U.S.C. § 1911(a) (1978); 25 USC § 1911(c) (1978); 25 U.S.C. § 1912(d) (1978); 25 U.S.C. § 1912(f) (1978); see generally 25 U.S.C. §§ 1901–1963 (1978).

The Adoption and Safe Families Act (ASFA) was enacted in 1997 as a response to congressional concerns that prior legislation "acted as a barrier to the adoption of abused and neglected children." *In re D.B.*, 2003 SD 113, ¶ 10, 670 N.W.2d 67, 70. Under ASFA, in considering reunification of parents with children, "'the balancing formula should tip on the side of protecting children, and not on the side of protecting the rights of parents.'" *Id.* (following *New Jersey Div. of Youth and Family Serv. v. A.R.G.*, 361 N.J.Super. 46, 824 A.2d 213, 233 (N.J.Super.Ct.App.Div.2003)).

ICWA differs from ASFA in its means of promoting Indian children's best interests. ICWA ensures the best interests of Indian children by maintaining their familial, tribal, and cultural ties. It seeks to prevent capricious severance of those ties, whereas ASFA identifies permanency as a major consideration in promoting the best interests of children. A further distinction between the two acts, and at issue here, is the requirement in ICWA that state agencies make "active" efforts to provide services aimed at the prevention of a family breakup. ICWA provides no exception to this mandate. On the other hand, in an attempt to assist states in increasing the speed with which children might achieve the desired goal of permanency, ASFA recognizes certain circumstances under which no "reasonable efforts" may be necessary. ASFA relieves states from making merely perfunctory remedial efforts in cases where a court has found that the parent has subjected the child to aggravated circumstances of abuse or neglect. Does ASFA override ICWA?

The primary question here is whether ICWA's requirement to provide active efforts to prevent the breakup of Indian families is overridden or excused by the provisions of ASFA. The State argues that ASFA relieves DSS of any duty it held under ICWA to provide active efforts to reunite J.S.B. with his father. This is so, the State argues, because ASFA provides that "reasonable efforts . . . shall not be required to be made with respect to a parent of a child if a court of competent jurisdiction has determined that . . . the parent has subjected the child to aggravated circumstances (as defined in State law, which definition may include but need not be limited to abandonment, torture, chronic abuse, and sexual abuse)[.]" 42 U.S.C. § 671(a)(15)(D). The State asserts that either the father "[h]as a documented history of abuse and neglect associated with chronic alcohol or drug abuse" or he "[h]as exposed the child to or demonstrated an inability to protect the child from substantial harm or the risk of substantial harm, and the child or another child has been removed from the parent's custody because the removed child was adjudicated abused and neglected by a court on at least one previous occasion." See SDCL 26–8A–21.1. Thus, the State argues, DSS was under no duty to make active efforts to provide remedial services to the father.

SDCL 26–8A–21.1 provides:

> Nothing in § 26–8A–21 requires reunification of a child with a parent who:
>
> (6) Has a documented history of abuse and neglect associated with chronic alcohol or drug abuse;
>
> (7) Has exposed the child to or demonstrated an inability to protect the child from substantial harm or the risk of substantial harm, and the child or another child has been removed from the parent's custody because the removed child was adjudicated abused and neglected by a court on at least one previous occasion. . . .

SDCL 26–8A–21.1 states that nothing in SDCL 26–8A–21 requires reunification of a child with a parent where the delineated "aggravated circumstances" are present. However, the language of SDCL 26–8A–21.1 specifically limits application of the state-defined "aggravated circumstances" to SDCL 26–8A–21. In no way does the language of SDCL 26–8A–21.1 relieve DSS of its burden to provide "active efforts" as prescribed by ICWA. In sum, while the presence of "aggravated circumstances" may eliminate the need to provide "reasonable efforts" under SDCL 26–8A–21, it does not remove DSS's requirement to provide "active efforts" for reunification under ICWA.

If it is perhaps open to question whether our Legislature understood the terms "reasonable efforts" and "active efforts" to be interchangeable, we do not think Congress intended that ASFA's "aggravated circumstances" should undo the State's burden of providing "active efforts" under ICWA. Three rules of statutory construction dictate otherwise. See, e.g., *Hartford Underwriters Ins. Co. v. Union Planters Bank, N.A.*, 530 U.S. 1, 6, 120 S.Ct. 1942, 1947, 147 L.Ed.2d 1 (2000). First, ICWA clearly offers no exception to its requirement of "active efforts." And ASFA does not mention ICWA, much less state that its exceptions to "reasonable efforts" should apply to ICWA's "active efforts." In fact, no provision in ASFA specifically purports to modify ICWA. It would seem illogical that ASFA would implicitly leave unchanged certain ICWA provisions, like notice to tribes, intervention, and transfer to tribal courts, while modifying others. Second, the rules of statutory construction require that the more specific statute controls. *In re T.H.M.*, 2002 SD 13, ¶ 7, 640 N.W.2d 68, 71. As between the two acts, ICWA is the more specific. ICWA deals with a discrete segment of our population, Native American families, who Congress found were best served by maintaining their relationships with their tribes and extended families. ICWA specifically imposes higher evidentiary standards and different protections for parents whose rights are subject to termination than do termination proceedings under state law. 25 U.S.C. § 1912(d) ("active efforts") and § 1912(f) (proof "supported by evidence beyond a reasonable doubt, including testimony of qualified expert witnesses, that the continued custody of the child by the parent or Indian custodian is likely to result in serious emotional or physical damage to the child."). Third, when interpreting a statute pertaining to Indians, the United States Supreme Court has stated, "statutes are to be construed liberally in favor of the Indians, with ambiguous provisions interpreted to their benefit. . . ." *Montana v. Blackfeet Tribe of Indians*, 471 U.S. 759, 766, 105 S.Ct. 2399, 2403, 85 L.Ed.2d 753 (1985); see, e.g., *Ramah Navajo Sch. Bd. v. Bureau of Revenue of New Mexico*, 458 U.S. 832, 838, 102 S.Ct. 3394, 3399, 73 L.Ed.2d 1174 (1982). As Congress found when it enacted ICWA, it is to the benefit of Indian children to remain within their families and only after "active efforts" to reunite those families have proven unsuccessful should the children be removed. 25 U.S.C. §§ 1901–1963 (1978).

The State argues that the Supreme Court of Alaska's decision in *J.S. v. State*, 50 P.3d 388, 392 (Alaska 2002), lends support to the conclusion that ASFA modifies ICWA. In that case, however, the court wrote, "[a]lthough this case is not governed by ASFA, that act is useful in providing guidance to congressional policy on child welfare issues." *Id.* As the court itself acknowledged, its remarks on this point were dicta. Moreover, we can find no case directly holding that ASFA modifies ICWA, and the parties have cited none. Nonetheless, to the extent that the decision in J.S. can be read to state that ASFA supersedes ICWA, we respectfully disagree with the Alaska Supreme Court.

Notes

1. Congress passed ASFA in 1997, and as the case states, it makes no reference to ICWA. The Act is "aimed at improving the safety of children and promoting

adoption or some other type of permanency for children in long-term foster care. The ASFA mandates the timely placement of children in permanent homes. States are free to adopt more restrictive time restraints, but at a minimum the ASFA requires that any child who has been in foster care for fifteen out of the most recent twenty-two months be reviewed for termination of parental rights and free for adoption." B.J. Jones, *Differing Concepts of "Permanency" The Adoption and Safe Families Act and the Indian Child Welfare Act, in* Facing the Future: The Indian Child Welfare Act at 30, at 141 (Matthew L.M. Fletcher et al. eds., 2009). These provisions are mandated by linking them to the federal funds for foster care—Title IV-E funding. In order to access the funds, states must implement the federal deadlines into their state laws, as South Dakota did.

2. The 2015 BIA Guidelines also explicitly stated that active efforts are "distinct from the requirements" of ASFA and "constitute more than reasonable efforts as required by Title IV-E of the Social Security Act (42 U.S.C. § 671(a)(15))." 80 Fed. Reg. 10,150 (Feb. 25, 2015). *See also New Mexico v. Yodell B.*, 367 P.3d 881 (N.M. Ct. App. 2015) ("We find these authorities [sister state decisions and the BIA Guidelines] persuasive and we agree with the majority view that the term 'active efforts connotes a more involved and less passive standard than that of reasonable efforts.' *In re C.D.*, 2008 UT App 477, ¶ 34, 200 P.3d 194."). However, the federal regulations refuse to make this comparison:

> Unlike the proposed rule, the final rule does not define "active efforts" in comparison to "reasonable efforts." After considering public comments on this issue, the Department concluded that referencing "reasonable efforts" would not promote clarity or consistency, as the term "reasonable efforts" is not in ICWA and arises from different laws (e.g., the Adoption Assistance and Child Welfare Act of 1980, as modified by the Adoption and Safe Families Act (ASFA), see 42 U.S.C. 670, et seq., as well as State laws). Such reference is unnecessary because the definition in the final rule focuses on what actions are necessary to constitute active efforts.

81 Fed. Reg. 38791 (June 14, 2016).

While this reasoning makes sense in the abstract, the truth is that state court judges often compare the two to figure out what qualifies as active efforts. However, the regulations now include a multi-element definition of active efforts. 25 C.F.R. § 23.2 (2016).

ICWA does not define active efforts. The Alaska Supreme Court has said, "ICWA requires that before a court may terminate parental rights, it must find by clear and convincing evidence 'that active efforts have been made to provide remedial services and rehabilitative programs designed to prevent the breakup of the Indian family and that these efforts have proved unsuccessful.' Although 'no pat formula exists for distinguishing between active and passive efforts,' distinctions do exist. For example, active efforts require taking a parent through the steps of a plan and helping the parent develop the resources to succeed; drawing up a case plan and leaving the client to satisfy it are merely passive efforts." *Jon S. v. State*, 212 P.756, 763 (Alaska 2009).

3. Active efforts are provided by the state social workers, but are monitored and ordered by the court. The state social services should be provided in conjunction with any possible tribal services or services from urban Indian organizations. Some states have attempted to define active efforts to give some guidance to state officials and courts, though perhaps none as thoroughly as Michigan.

Michigan Indian Family Preservation Act

Mich. Comp. Laws § 712B.3 (2012)

(a) "Active efforts" means actions to provide remedial services and rehabilitative programs designed to prevent the breakup of the Indian family and to reunify the child with the Indian family. Active efforts require more than a referral to a service without actively engaging the Indian child and family. Active efforts include reasonable efforts as required by title IV-E of the social security act, 42 USC 670 to 679c, and also include doing or addressing all of the following:

(i) Engaging the Indian child, child's parents, tribe, extended family members, and individual Indian caregivers through the utilization of culturally appropriate services and in collaboration with the parent or child's Indian tribes and Indian social services agencies.

(ii) Identifying appropriate services and helping the parents to overcome barriers to compliance with those services.

(iii) Conducting or causing to be conducted a diligent search for extended family members for placement.

(iv) Requesting representatives designated by the Indian child's tribe with substantial knowledge of the prevailing social and cultural standards and child rearing practice within the tribal community to evaluate the circumstances of the Indian child's family and to assist in developing a case plan that uses the resources of the Indian tribe and Indian community, including traditional and customary support, actions, and services, to address those circumstances.

(v) Completing a comprehensive assessment of the situation of the Indian child's family, including a determination of the likelihood of protecting the Indian child's health, safety, and welfare effectively in the Indian child's home.

(vi) Identifying, notifying, and inviting representatives of the Indian child's tribe to participate in all aspects of the Indian child custody proceeding at the earliest possible point in the proceeding and actively soliciting the tribe's advice throughout the proceeding.

(vii) Notifying and consulting with extended family members of the Indian child, including extended family members who were identified by the Indian child's tribe or parents, to identify and to provide family structure and support for the Indian child, to assure cultural connections, and to serve as placement resources for the Indian child.

(viii) Making arrangements to provide natural and family interaction in the most natural setting that can ensure the Indian child's safety, as appropriate to the goals of the Indian child's permanency plan, including, when requested by the tribe, arrangements for transportation and other assistance to enable family members to participate in that interaction.

(ix) Offering and employing all available family preservation strategies and requesting the involvement of the Indian child's tribe to identify those strategies and to ensure that those strategies are culturally appropriate to the Indian child's tribe.

(x) Identifying community resources offering housing, financial, and transportation assistance and in-home support services, in-home intensive treatment services, community support services, and specialized services for members of the Indian child's family with special needs, and providing information about those resources to the Indian child's family, and actively assisting the Indian child's family or offering active assistance in accessing those resources.

(xi) Monitoring client progress and client participation in services.

(xii) Providing a consideration of alternative ways of addressing the needs of the Indian child's family, if services do not exist or if existing services are not available to the family.

Washington Indian Child Welfare Act

Wash. Rev. Code Ann. § 13.38.040 (West 2017)

(1) "Active efforts" means the following:

(a) In any foster care placement or termination of parental rights proceeding of an Indian child under chapter 13.34 RCW and this chapter where the department or a supervising agency as defined in RCW 74.13.020 has a statutory or contractual duty to provide services to, or procure services for, the parent or parents or Indian custodian, or is providing services to a parent or parents or Indian custodian pursuant to a disposition order entered pursuant to RCW 13.34.130, the department or supervising agency shall make timely and diligent efforts to provide or procure such services, including engaging the parent or parents or Indian custodian in reasonably available and culturally appropriate preventive, remedial, or rehabilitative services. This shall include those services offered by tribes and Indian organizations whenever possible. At a minimum "active efforts" shall include:

(i) In any dependency proceeding under chapter 13.34 RCW seeking out-of-home placement of an Indian child in which the department or supervising agency provided voluntary services to the parent, parents, or Indian custodian prior to filing the dependency petition, a showing to the court that the department or supervising agency social workers actively worked with the parent, parents, or Indian custodian to engage them in remedial services and rehabilitation programs to prevent the breakup of the family beyond simply providing referrals to such services.

(ii) In any dependency proceeding under chapter 13.34 RCW, in which the petitioner is seeking the continued out-of-home placement of an Indian child, the department or supervising agency must show to the court that it has actively worked with the parent, parents, or Indian custodian in accordance with existing court orders and the individual service plan to engage them in remedial services and rehabilitative programs to prevent the breakup of the family beyond simply providing referrals to such services.

(iii) In any termination of parental rights proceeding regarding an Indian child under chapter 13.34 RCW in which the department or supervising agency provided services to the parent, parents, or Indian custodian, a showing to the court that the department or supervising agency social workers actively worked with the parent, parents, or Indian custodian to engage them in remedial services and rehabilitation programs ordered by the court or identified in the department or supervising agency's individual service and safety plan beyond simply providing referrals to such services.

(b) In any foster care placement or termination of parental rights proceeding in which the petitioner does not otherwise have a statutory or contractual duty to directly provide services to, or procure services for, the parent or Indian custodian, "active efforts" means a documented, concerted, and good faith effort to facilitate the parent's or Indian custodian's receipt of and engagement in services capable of meeting the criteria set out in (a) of this subsection.

Minnesota Indian Family Preservation Act

Minn. Stat. Ann. § 260.755 (West 2017)

Subd. 1a. Active efforts. "Active efforts" means a rigorous and concerted level of effort that is ongoing throughout the involvement of the local social services agency to continuously involve the Indian child's tribe and that uses the prevailing social and cultural values, conditions, and way of life of the Indian child's tribe to preserve the Indian child's family and prevent placement of an Indian child and, if placement occurs, to return the Indian child to the child's family at the earliest possible time. Active efforts sets a higher standard than reasonable efforts to preserve the family, prevent breakup of the family, and reunify the family, according to section 260.762. Active efforts includes reasonable efforts as required by Title IV-E of the Social Security Act, United States Code, title 42, sections 670 to 679c.

Notes

1. The federal regulations now define active efforts using language similar to Michigan's statute:

> Active efforts means affirmative, active, thorough, and timely efforts intended primarily to maintain or reunite an Indian child with his or her family. Where an agency is involved in the child-custody proceeding, active efforts must involve assisting the parent or parents or Indian custodian through the steps of a case plan and with accessing or developing the resources necessary to satisfy the case plan. To the maximum extent possible, active efforts should be provided in a manner consistent with the prevailing social and cultural conditions and way of life of the Indian child's Tribe and should be conducted in partnership with the Indian child and the Indian child's parents, extended family members, Indian custodians, and Tribe. Active efforts are to be tailored to the facts and circumstances of the case and may include, for example: (1) Conducting a comprehensive assessment of the circumstances of the Indian child's family, with a focus on safe reunification as the most desirable goal; (2) Identifying appropriate services and helping the parents to overcome barriers, including actively assisting the parents in obtaining such services; (3) Identifying, notifying, and inviting representatives of the Indian child's Tribe to participate in providing support and services to the Indian child's family and in family team meetings, permanency planning, and resolution of placement issues; (4) Conducting or causing to be conducted a diligent search for the Indian child's extended family members, and contacting and consulting with extended family members to provide family structure and support for the Indian child and the Indian child's parents; (5) Offering and employing all available and culturally appropriate family preservation strategies and facilitating the use of remedial and rehabilitative services provided by the child's Tribe; (6) Taking steps to keep siblings together whenever possible; (7) Supporting regular visits with parents or Indian custodians in the most natural setting possible as well as trial home visits of the Indian child during any period of removal, consistent with the need to ensure the health, safety, and welfare of the child; (8) Identifying community resources including housing, financial, transportation, mental health, substance abuse, and peer support services and actively assisting the Indian child's parents or, when appropriate, the child's family, in utilizing and accessing those resources; (9) Monitoring progress and participation in services; (10) Considering alternative ways to address the needs of the Indian child's parents and, where appropriate, the family, if the optimum services do not exist or are not available; (11) Providing post-reunification services and monitoring.

25 C.F.R. § 23.2 (2016)

This definition of active efforts may also allow for some leeway in difficult cases where a parent might be also criminally convicted of physical or sexual abuse, and where reunification is not possible. *See In re* S.D., 599 N.W.2d 772, 775 (Mich. App. 1999). Using this definition, the state can provide active efforts by ensuring the child is with her siblings, ensuring cultural connections through the extended family, assisting the extended family in finding resources and support services, and ensuring the child's tribe is involved in her case.

2. There have been concerns with defining active efforts using precise lists, because there are concerns that the state will consider a list exhaustive, and not do anything beyond that definition. Both Minnesota and Washington chose a broader definition, and both Michigan and Minnesota addressed the ASFA conflict directly. The federal regulations list includes the caveat "active efforts are to be tailored to the facts and circumstances of the case and may include, for example," 25 C.F.R. § 23.2 (2016), before listing examples. Determining whether an agency provided active efforts is an intensely fact based determination. Prior to the passage of the Michigan statute defining active efforts, the Michigan Supreme Court engaged in a detailed analysis in the next case of what constituted active efforts under ICWA.

In re J.L.

770 N.W.2d 853 (Mich. 2009)

CORRIGAN, J.

Respondent Cheryl Lee challenges the judgment of the Court of Appeals affirming the termination of her parental rights to her son, JL. *In re Lee*, unpublished opinion per curiam of the Court of Appeals, issued October 16, 2008, 2008 WL 4603740 (Docket No. 283038). Respondent specifically claims error in the interpretation and application of the Indian Child Welfare Act (ICWA), 25 U.S.C. 1901 et seq. She urges us to adopt the interpretation of the ICWA offered by the dissenting Court of Appeals judge. We affirm the judgment of the Court of Appeals because petitioner the Department of Human Services (DHS), provided timely, affirmative efforts that satisfied the ICWA's "active efforts" requirement, 25 U.S.C. 1912(d). We hold that the ICWA requires the DHS to undertake a thorough, contemporaneous assessment of the services provided to the parent in the past and the parent's response to those services before seeking to terminate parental rights without having offered additional services. The ICWA does not, however, categorically require the DHS to provide services each time a new termination proceeding is commenced against a parent.

I. Basic Facts and Procedural History

Respondent and her son, JL, are both members of the Sault Ste. Marie Tribe of Chippewa Indians. Between 1999 and 2006, respondent gave birth to four children: JL, SD, JD, and BP. JL is the oldest child. Respondent's parental rights to SD, JD, and BP were terminated in earlier proceedings that are not at issue here.

JL was born in 1999, when respondent was 16 years old and living in foster care. DHS Child Protective Services (CPS) worker Regina Frazier began working with respondent in 1998, even before respondent had children. Respondent was then both a delinquent and a victim of abuse and neglect. Respondent displayed abusive and neglectful behavior after JL's birth, so he was removed from respondent's care in September 2000. Frazier provided wraparound services until respondent moved to Sault Ste. Marie. The Sault Ste. Marie Tribe of Chippewa Indians Tribal Court assumed jurisdiction over the case in March 2002. The tribal court released JL from its jurisdiction in August 2002, when he was placed in a limited guardianship with his paternal grandmother, Lois Plank. Meanwhile, respondent gave birth to a daughter, SD, on November 24, 2001.

* * *

JL was returned to respondent's care in September 2003. Her third child, JD, was born on January 11, 2004, while Clark was still working with respondent. When Jill Thompson, a caseworker with the Binogii Placement Agency, began working with respondent in July 2004, three children—JL, SD, and JD—lived with respondent and Justin DuFresne, the father of SD and JD. Respondent and DuFresne failed to supervise the children; instead, JL, then five years old, was supervising his younger siblings. SD wandered into the road multiple times. Caseworkers Thompson and Clark tried to remedy this problem. Clark even installed latches on the front door so that the children could not run out. The condition of the home "ran the gamut from poor housekeeping to filthy." Like Clark, Thompson described cigarette butts on the floor and the presence of choking hazards to young children.

Respondent could not manage her finances and never sought employment. A "payee" managed respondent's finances by paying her bills with the money from respondent's social security disability payments and then giving respondent a $50 weekly allowance. Respondent purchased rent-to-own furniture that cost $30 or $35 a week. She could not afford diapers and other necessary items.

Despite the extensive efforts of Thompson and Clark, the children were removed from respondent's home in 2004. At that time, JL again became a ward of the tribal court and was again placed with his grandmother, Lois Plank. In November 2004, the trial court awarded JL's father, Tony Plank, full physical custody of JL and awarded respondent and Tony Plank shared legal custody. The court also granted respondent unsupervised visitation rights.

* * *

When Clark closed respondent's case in 2005, she had provided all the services she could offer "without staying there 24/7." She opined that respondent had not made significant improvement. Clark participated in the termination trial involving SD and JD that was initiated because respondent had failed to supervise them. The tribal court terminated respondent's parental rights to SD and JD on June 30, 2006. Respondent gave birth to another child, BP, on July 20, 2006. BP was removed from respondent's care shortly after her birth. Melissa VanLuven, who was the child placement services supervisor for the Sault Ste. Marie tribe and the caseworker supervisor of Thompson and Clark, participated in the decision to petition for termination of respondent's parental rights to BP. That decision was based on an assessment of the tribe and the caseworkers that, despite the provision of services, respondent's children could not safely live in her home. The tribal court terminated respondent's parental rights to BP on January 8, 2007.

In spring 2007, the trial court granted respondent's motion for parenting time, allowing her weekly unsupervised visitation with JL. In July 2007, however, the DHS petitioned to terminate respondent's parental rights to JL on the basis of respondent's "children's protective service history" beginning on September 12, 2000, specifically citing the termination of her parental rights to SD, JD, and BP. The DHS filed a supplemental petition on August 20, 2007, alleging that proceedings to terminate Michael Plank's parental rights to BP were pending. The supplemental petition also alleged that Michael Plank had a history of physically abusing and neglecting two other children.

* * *

At trial, caseworkers Frazier, Clark, and Thompson described the extensive services they and their agencies provided to respondent from 1999 to 2005. They testified that, despite these services, respondent failed to become an adequate parent. On the basis of her experience with respondent, Clark did not believe that respondent could appropriately care for JL full-time. She opined that termination of respondent's parental rights was in JL's best interests. Testifying as an Indian expert under 25 U.S.C. 1912(f), VanLuven stated that she was satisfied that active and reasonable efforts had been provided to prevent the termination of respondent's parental rights and that respondent's custody of JL would result in serious emotional or physical damage to him.

Respondent testified that she lived in "a cozy little log house" with Michael Plank and that she had recently completed substance abuse counseling. She had also voluntarily attended and completed parenting classes offered by the tribe. In her view, she had learned from the parenting classes how to "safely raise a child in today's society." She also testified that she visited JL as much as possible, at least twice weekly, and celebrated holidays with him. She testified that Michael Plank and JL had a good relationship and that they hunted, fished, and played together. Respondent denied that Michael Plank had ever been violent with her or JL. She acknowledged, however, that Michael Plank had been convicted of assault after the mother of his other children accused him of being violent. Respondent offered to do whatever was necessary to continue her relationship with JL. She was concerned that if her parental rights were terminated she would have to "suck up to Lois [Plank] forever in order to stay in [JL]'s life."

On cross-examination, respondent admitted that she had not worked or sought work in four years. She received social security benefits because she had been diagnosed with fetal alcohol syndrome. She stated that "[t]hey" believe she had a disability and was incapable of working. Although she acknowledged a possible learning disability, she believed herself capable of working. Respondent acknowledged her convictions of operating a motor vehicle while impaired and aggravated assault.

Eight-year-old JL testified that he liked spending time with respondent and that it was "just the usual," explaining that it was "kind of like when I'm with my Grandma, except being with a different person." He loved and missed respondent and said he would like to spend more time with her, but also said that it was difficult to answer whether he would like to live with her because he liked living with his grandmother. He also liked spending time with Michael Plank and had no fear of him.

* * *

The trial court terminated respondent's parental rights to JL. It found that the DHS had established grounds for termination under MCL 712A.19b(3)(i) by clear and convincing evidence by presenting opinions and orders of the Sault Ste. Marie Tribe of Chippewa Indians Tribal Court terminating respondent's parental rights to JL's siblings. The court noted that termination in those cases was based on sections of the tribal code "virtually identical" to MCL 712A.19b(3)(c)(i) and (ii) and (g). It further noted that those opinions "discussed the services that had been provided and the apparent lack of any benefit gained by Respondent from those services." Next, the trial court found insufficient evidence to conclude that termination was not in the best interests of the child. MCR 3.977(F). Finally, the court concluded that the requirements of MCR 3.980(D)10 had been met. The court summarized its reasoning as follows:

This finding is based on: 1) the previous services and lack of benefit from same which raises the likelihood of some form of serious physical injury; 2) the length of time the child has been residing outside the Respondent's home and the emotional damage that would result in requiring a reunification plan; 3) the testimony presented that Respondent's lack of benefit was not due to Respondent's lack of maturity, but rather lack of ability; and 4) Respondent's most recent conduct of operating a motor vehicle while impaired due to alcohol.

* * *

B. Analysis

We agree with the *Roe* majority [*In re Roe*, 281 Mich App 88, 764 NW2d 789 (2008),] that the crux of the "active efforts" requirement is undertaking affirmative, as opposed to passive, efforts:

> Passive efforts are where a plan is drawn up and the client must develop his or her own resources toward bringing it to fruition. Active efforts, the intent of the drafters of the Act, is where the state caseworker takes the client through the steps of the plan rather than requiring that the plan be performed on its own. For instance, rather than requiring that a client find a job, acquire new housing, and terminate a relationship with what is perceived to be a boyfriend who is a bad influence, the Indian Child Welfare Act would require that the caseworker help the client develop job and parenting skills necessary to retain custody of her child.

[*Id.* at 107, 764 N.W.2d 789, quoting *A.A. v. Alaska Dep't of Family & Youth Services*, 982 P.2d 256, 261 (Alaska 1999).]

We also agree that "active efforts" require more than the "reasonable efforts" required under state law. *Roe, supra* at 108, 764 N.W.2d 789, citing *In re Nicole B.*, 175 Md.App. 450, 471, 927 A.2d 1194 (2007), *Winston J. v. Alaska Dep't of Health & Social Services*, 134 P.3d 343, 347 n. 18 (Alaska, 2006), *M.W. v. Alaska Dep't of Health & Social Services*, 20 P.3d 1141, 1146 n. 18 (Alaska, 2001), *In re Walter W.*, 274 Neb. 859, 865, 744 N.W.2d 55 (2008), and *In re J.S.*, 177 P.3d 590, 593 (Okla.Civ. App., 2008).

The version of the DHS's Childrens Foster Care Manual in effect at the time of the termination trial provides an example of this distinction:

> ICWA requires that anytime the DHS is involved with Indian children and their families, culturally Active Efforts must be provided. "Reasonable Efforts" as defined in other parts of current DHS policy are not sufficient.
>
> * * *
>
> Active Efforts require that the caseworker take a more proactive approach with clients and actively support the client in complying with the service plan rather than requiring the service plan be performed by the client alone. Following are examples of appropriate Active Efforts that could serve as a starting point of reference; in collaboration with the child's Tribe:
>
> a. Taking clients to initial appointments and assisting with the intake process OR
>
> b. Transporting client, arranging transportation and child care appointments OR
>
> c. If the client is isolated from other family members who may be in a position to provide positive support, the worker is to provide help to the families to begin conversations with those family members.
>
> d. Assisting with completing applications.
>
> e. Providing phone availability.
>
> * * *
>
> DHS is to make culturally active and appropriate efforts to provide remedial services and rehabilitative programs designed to prevent the breakup of the Indian family before any consideration for removal can be made. DHS policy requires Active Efforts prior to court involvement. Active Efforts must be documented to the court and Tribe.

[Childrens Foster Care Manual, Indian Child Welfare (June 1, 2007), pp. 5–6.]

In addition, the Bureau of Indian Affairs' guidelines explain that

> [t]hese [active] efforts shall take into account the prevailing social and cultural conditions and way of life of the Indian child's tribe. They shall also

involve and use the available resources of the extended family, the tribe, Indian social service agencies and individual Indian care givers.

[Bureau of Indian Affairs, Guidelines for State Courts; Indian Child Custody Proceedings, D.2, 44 Fed. Reg. 67584, 67592 (November 26, 1979), also available at <http://www.nicwa.org/admini strative_regulations/icwa_guidelines.pdf> (accessed June 30, 2009).]

In this case, however, the fundamental disagreement is not about the nature of the required services, but about the timing of those services. Indeed, respondent acknowledges that the DHS and the tribe provided active efforts in the past, but argues that 25 U.S.C. 1912(d) requires current active efforts, which the DHS failed to provide because it did not offer services in connection with the termination of her parental rights to JL. We decline to read the word "current" into 25 U.S.C. 1912(d). This statutory language does not impose a strict temporal component for the "active efforts" requirement.

This is not to say that active efforts provided in the distant past are sufficient. Although we decline to establish an arbitrary threshold beyond which services will not satisfy the requirements of 25 U.S.C. 1912, we direct trial courts to carefully assess the timing of the services provided to the parent. Services provided too long ago to be relevant to a parent's current circumstances do not establish by clear and convincing evidence that active efforts have been made, as required by 25 U.S.C. 1912(d), and raise a reasonable doubt under 25 U.S.C. 1912(f) about whether continued custody is "likely to result in serious emotional or physical damage to the child." The timing of the services must be judged by reference to the grounds for seeking termination and their relevance to the parent's current situation.

Similarly, we decline to hold that active efforts must always have been provided in relation to the child who is the subject of the current termination proceeding. Again, the question is whether the efforts made and the services provided in connection with the parent's other children are relevant to the parent's current situation and abilities so that they permit a current assessment of parental fitness as it pertains to the child who is the subject of the current proceeding. The evidence must satisfy the court "beyond a reasonable doubt" that the parent's continued custody of that child "is likely to result in serious emotional or physical damage to the child," as required by 25 U.S.C. 1912(f).

Some courts, including the Court of Appeals in *Roe*, have adopted a "futility test" to explain that the "active efforts" requirement may be met in certain cases without the provision of additional services. In *K.D.* [*In re K.D.*, 155 P3d 634 (Colo App, 2007)], for example, the child had been removed from his parents in 2001 and 2004. Both times, the parents completed their treatment plans, and the child was returned to them. The termination petition at issue was filed after the respondent father was arrested in 2005 and the mother was incarcerated. *K.D., supra* at 636. In affirming the trial court's decision to terminate the father's parental rights, the appellate court rejected his argument that the active efforts must be part of a treatment plan offered as part of the current "dependency proceedings." *Id.* at 637. It held that the "active efforts" requirement may be met by "formal or informal efforts to remedy a parent's deficiencies before the dependency proceedings begin":

> In other words, the court may terminate parental rights without offering additional services when a social services department has expended substantial, but unsuccessful, efforts over several years to prevent the breakup of the family, and there is no reason to believe additional treatment would prevent the termination of parental rights. [*Id.*]

The court noted that extensive services had been provided to the father during the two prior dependency cases and concluded that the record supported the trial court's findings that it would have been futile to offer additional services. *Id.* Citing *K.D.* and other sister-state authority, the Court of Appeals majority in *Roe* adopted a futility test. *Roe*, *supra* at 103–106, 764 N.W.2d 789.

We decline to adopt a futility test. In *K.D.*, the court concluded that additional services were not required because it saw no indication that additional services would prevent the need for termination. The ICWA obviously does not require the provision of endless active efforts, so there comes a time when the DHS or the tribe may justifiably pursue termination without providing additional services. A futility test does not capture this concept. In addition, we share dissenting Judge Gleicher's concern that, under a such a test, "the circuit court may altogether avoid applying [25 U.S.C. 1912(d)] by simply deciding that additional services would be 'futile.'" *Roe, supra* at 109, 764 N.W.2d 789 (Gleicher, J., concurring in part and dissenting in part).

We further note that the DHS's apparent policy of providing no services when a petition for termination of parental rights is based on a prior termination will not withstand the heightened standard of the ICWA. When the proceedings involve an "Indian child" within the meaning of the ICWA, the DHS or the tribe must, even if services have been provided to the parent in the past, conduct a thorough and contemporaneous review of those services and the parent's progress or lack thereof in response to those services. Only if active efforts have been provided to prevent the breakup of the Indian family, and it does not appear that the provision of additional services is likely to prevent the need for termination, may the DHS or the tribe pursue termination without providing additional services.

Notes

1. Does the timeliness factor change under the Michigan Indian Family Preservation Act, or would the Michigan Supreme Court's analysis remain the same? When are efforts futile? The federal regulations state that active efforts "means affirmative, active, thorough, and timely efforts. . . ." 25 C.F.R. § 23.2 (2016).

2. One of the reasons the active efforts provision is so important is that it requires the state to do more for a Native family. In most cases, it also requires the state to work with the relevant tribe. Active efforts holds state courts accountable to the goals of ICWA—to preserve the Indian family and allow the child to remain or

become a part of the tribal community. Can state social workers provide the kind of services active efforts requires? What are the dual roles of state social workers?

Child Welfare's Paradox

Dorothy Roberts
49 Wm. & Mary L. Rev. 881 (2007)

A. Caseworkers as Investigators and Helpers

The women interviewed in Woodlawn [a predominantly poor and Black neighborhood on the south side of Chicago] poignantly expressed the tension created by caseworkers' dual roles as both investigator and supporter of neighborhood families. The child welfare system employs social workers who are responsible for providing services to families. Yet, these same service providers also investigate parents alleged to have maltreated their children and coerce parents to comply with rehabilitative measures by threatening to take away their children permanently. Social work professor Leroy Pelton emphasized the threat to family integrity created by the child welfare system's dual function of simultaneously coercing parents while trying to help them. In particular, he observed:

> The investigative/coercive/child-removal role diminishes, hampers, and overwhelms the helping role within the dual-role structure of public child-welfare agencies, as huge and increasingly larger portions of their budgets are devoted to investigation and foster care, with little money left over for preventive and supportive services to combat the impermanency of children's living arrangements.

Thus, agencies fail to maintain a balance between coercion and support of families because their intimidating role tends to dominate.

Some Woodlawn residents viewed caseworkers with suspicion and believed that they unnecessarily disrupted family and community life. They felt that caseworkers' investigations were often unwarranted and their responses overzealous. Some portrayed caseworkers as spies who infiltrated the neighborhood to gather evidence against parents. According to twenty-six-year-old Cassie:

> [Y]ou got to watch what you do and what you say and all this, 'cause you don't know who you could be talking to. Out on the street you don't know who you could be talking to.... She could be DCFS, writing down stuff, taking notes, all of that, and you don't know who she is. So you have to be careful. You have to be very careful.

Parents perceive caseworkers' use of a foreign standard to judge neighborhood families as part of the problem. Pearl, a counselor who provided services for DCFS, but who also had relatives and neighbors involved with the agency, said, "I think sometimes the [DCFS caseworkers] who do the interviews come from a different walk of life, you know, and when they come from a different walk of life, they see things a little different than people within the home community."

Additionally, caseworkers' investigative roles spread beyond those performed by DCFS to influence relationships in the neighborhood. Many of the women reported distrust among neighbors created by the pervasive DCFS surveillance of families. Respondents believed that residents often falsely accused others of child abuse to seek retribution against them. Tiara, a twenty-four-year-old whose close friend was the subject of a DCFS investigation, complained:

> Teachers are even using it for revenge too. If you even went to school with these teachers and they made it all right in their career and now they're teaching in your community and your kids is one of their students, that if she didn't like you unknowingly all this time since high school . . . you got teachers that set you up at the end of the school year.

In this fashion, the presence of DCFS has not only bred distrust between residents and caseworkers, but also among residents.

Despite their criticism of caseworker surveillance, however, the women also expressed gratitude for the support caseworkers provided. Francis, a forty-eight-year-old whose daughter was the subject of a DCFS investigation, explained:

> You can get some [caseworkers] that will help you. They helped [my daughter] get an apartment, furniture, you know, everything they did. You have to know how to work these agencies. Like, you know, anything else. . . . She helped us with a lot of programs that a lot of people don't know about. You know, because a lot of workers won't tell you about the different programs that they have for you to help you. . . . A lot of people don't know that if you cooperate with them, they'll help you more.

Francis and her neighbors were well aware of the paradox created by caseworkers' coercive and supportive roles. According to the Woodlawn residents, although caseworkers were often unfair investigators to be feared, they were also potential sources of useful information and material aid for families. Some residents, like Francis, developed strategies for negotiating this paradox to gain the most advantage from the system that is supposed to serve them.

* * *

III. Child Welfare's Paradox and the Flawed Safety Net

Child welfare's dual nature as investigator and service provider has been intensified by the dwindling safety net in poor inner-city neighborhoods. Furthermore, the child welfare system's racial geography is connected to the geography of social service provision. In his three-city study of social service providers in the wake of welfare reform, political scientist Scott Allard discovered a striking mismatch between neighborhood need and access to support services such as substance abuse treatment, food assistance, job training, education, and emergency aid. Residents of poor black neighborhoods like Woodlawn have especially inadequate access to these services.

Allard also found that distance from services had serious consequences for residents' economic opportunities. Spatial proximity to services helped determine utilization of services among those women receiving welfare. Living closer to employment opportunities also increased recipients' chances of finding a job and leaving welfare. According to Allard, under welfare-to-work programs, "the lack of proximity to relevant social service providers is tantamount to being denied aid." Moreover, the neighborhoods that Allard discovered as lacking in social service access were precisely the ones experiencing intense concentrations of child welfare agency involvement. Given this decline in access to social services, it is no wonder that the women interviewed in Woodlawn looked to DCFS for needed financial support.

The increasingly paradoxical relationship between poor families and the child welfare system suggests that we need to change our view of the system's institutional function. In poor African American neighborhoods where most cases are concentrated, child welfare agencies function as much as economic safety nets as child protection services. Unfortunately, social scientists and feminist theorists pay little attention to the public child welfare system's role in supporting caregiving by poor mothers. Although fewer families are involved with child protection services than with TANF, the number of children in state custody is staggering. In 2005 alone, there were more than half a million children in foster care. Indeed, given the astronomical decline in the number of TANF recipients in the last decade, the gap in the size of the two systems of family aid is likely to shrink dramatically. With welfare rolls slashed by the 1996 welfare law, social programs dwindling, and desperate poverty increasing, child welfare agencies are increasingly important sources of aid.

Conclusion

Having stripped Woodlawn, like other inner-city neighborhoods, of social programs, low-income housing, and guaranteed public assistance, the state is relying more than ever on the punitive system of foster care to address the needs of struggling single mothers and their children. The contradictions expressed by the women in my Woodlawn study reflect these tradeoffs, created because foster care constitutes a critical means for addressing parental poverty in their neighborhood. Poor families are left in the bind of resenting child welfare agencies' surveillance and interference, yet wanting the agencies' continued presence as one of the few remaining sources of public aid. Moreover, the child welfare system's racial geography shows that the agencies' role as a safety net will be most prominent in black neighborhoods, where high rates of foster care, unemployment, and inadequate social services converge. As this Essay demonstrates, the growing yet overlooked role of child welfare agencies in the shrinking welfare state only heightens the tensions inherent in the U.S. approach to child welfare.

The paradoxes discussed in this Essay intensify the need for radical reform of the child welfare system. At the heart of these contradictions are the punitive stipulations for receiving aid, including relinquishing custody of children to the state, and the state's unwillingness to provide needed support directly to poor families. Eliminating the source of tension within the child welfare system should be a central focus of change. Devising voluntary ways to address family poverty before a child-endangering crisis occurs-with the aim of generously supporting families' care of children-could accomplish this change. For example, some states and localities have employed strategies to address racial disparities that make communities central partners in developing policies and practices and that include community-building initiatives that expand the resources available to families. Others have implemented programs that provide subsidies and support services to relative caregivers comparable to what they would receive through foster care, but without the "requirement that children remain in or come from state custody." We should work to transform the child welfare system into a community-based institution that generously and non-coercively supports families.

Notes

1. The role of poverty in child welfare cases cannot be understated. Reducing support for families on the margin leads to increased family stress, inability to provide adequate child care, housing instability and food shortage. Federal policies like the ones addressed by Prof. Roberts article directly contribute to the rates of child neglect. See Karrie M. Raissian & Lindsey Rose Bullinger, *Money Matters: Does the minimum wage affect child maltreatment rates?*, 72 Children and Youth Services Rev. 60 (2017). The answer to their question is yes—a one dollar increase in minimum wages lead to nearly a 10% decline in child abuse neglect reports. Given the extraordinary cost of the child welfare system (over $12 billion dollars in federal spending alone in 2012), does a modest increase in the minimum wage make sense?

2. What is properly determined to be active efforts is extremely fact dependent; a description of the efforts can be found to be active, reasonable, or both, depending on the interpretation and parties involved. Courts are dependent on social worker reports to determine whether active efforts occurred. On top of the dynamic Dorothy Roberts writes about, Indian families are also faced with the particular history of federal and state policies of assimilation on Native people through their children. How can state social workers overcome the natural suspicion of Native family members toward the state?

3. Child welfare cases are overwhelmingly due to substance abuse or mental health issues. Can the requirement of active efforts in ICWA cases provide additional support to help parents with these issues?

In re Nicole B.

976 A.2d 1039 (Md. 2009)

John C. Eldridge, J., Retired, Specially Assigned.

This Child in Need of Assistance ("CINA") case concerns a requirement in the federal "Indian Child Welfare Act of 1978," 25 U.S.C. § 1912(d), which provides as follows (emphasis added):

> Any party seeking to effect a foster care placement of, or termination of parental rights to, an Indian child under State law shall satisfy the court

> that active efforts have been made to provide remedial services and rehabilitative programs designed to prevent the breakup of the Indian family and that these efforts have proved unsuccessful.

The Circuit Court for Montgomery County ordered that the paternal aunt of two Native American children, who are brother and sister, "shall have full care, custody and guardianship of the" children, "that the parents shall have reasonable visitation with" the children "under the supervision of the paternal aunt," and that the CINA "case be and hereby is closed."

[The biological father appealed the decision pro se to the Maryland Court of Special Appeals, which accepted the appeal and remanded the case back to Circuit Court to make findings regarding ICWA's requirement of active efforts instead of simply reasonable efforts. The Department appealed the ruling.]

* * *

The mother of the minor children involved in this CINA case, Wendy B., is a Native American and a registered member of the Yankton Sioux Tribe of South Dakota, although she was not raised within the Tribe but was raised by non-tribal adoptive parents. The children are Max B., born on July 20, 1999, and Nicole B., born on February 28, 2002. Max B. is a registered member of the Tribe, and Nicole B. is eligible for membership in the Tribe. The children's father, John B., is not a Native American.

The Child Welfare Services Office of the Montgomery County Department of Health and Human Services, on April 6, 2005, received a report that Max B. and Nicole B. were being neglected by their parents. The Department, upon investigation, discovered that Nicole, then age 3, had not been toilet trained, and that Max, then age 5, had rotten front teeth, refused to eat at school, and had asthma that his mother did not know how to treat. In addition, the family had no regular meal schedule at home. The Department's investigation disclosed that both parents had struggled with drug addiction for many years. The Department was also told by John B. that he was dependent on the drug oxycontin and that he suffered from bi-polar disorder.

* * *

The Department on May 23, 2005, placed the children in emergency shelter care. The Department's staff met with John B. on May 24, 2005, and he acknowledged that he was unable to meet his children's needs. Also on May 24, 2005, the Department filed in the Circuit Court for Montgomery County a CINA petition. The Circuit Court ordered continued shelter care for the two children and granted John visitation with the children up to six times a week. The children were placed in the temporary custody of their paternal aunt, Denise P.

* * *

In accordance with the parties' agreement, the Circuit Court on June 20, 2005, sustained all of the Department's allegations, found that the children "have been neglected by their parents, and . . . the parents are unable and unwilling to give the children the proper care and attention that they need." The court determined that

Max B. and Nicole B. were children in need of assistance. The court further committed the children "to the Department and place[d] them under the jurisdiction of th[e] court, and place[d] them with their aunt," Denise P. Denise was also made a "limited" guardian of the children "for medical and educational purposes."

Since the Department's permanency plan for the children was reunification with a parent, the Circuit Court at the June 20, 2005, hearing imposed various requirements. The children were to "be supervised, under the direction of the Department, at a minimum weekly." Wendy's visitation with the children was to "be under the direction of the Department, minimum weekly, and supervised by the Department." Wendy, however, would not be allowed to visit the children if, with respect to a particular visit, she was not sober. Wendy was also required to "submit to a substance abuse evaluation and follow all treatment recommendations." In addition, the court ordered that she "participate in semi-weekly urine screens and remain substance free."

Similar requirements were imposed upon John. He was ordered to participate "in a substance abuse evaluation under the direction of the Department" and to undergo semi-weekly urinalysis with "urine screens." The Department was to coordinate with the "Another Way Treatment Center" where John was receiving, as an outpatient, methadone treatment for his oxycontin addiction, and to develop a treatment plan. John was ordered to "secure and maintain stable housing" for the family, as he would not be able to remain in his mother's house after it was sold. He was also directed to continue his treatment with a psychiatrist who was then treating him. In addition, John was told to report "to the Office of Child Support Enforcement" for the purpose of establishing a support order for both children. John's visitation with the children was to be supervised under a plan to be worked out by the Department and Denise P.

During the summer of 2005, the Department presented to John and to Wendy a "Case Plan for Children in Out-of-Home Care." John and Wendy each signed their case plans. Both case plans set forth the reasons causing the children to be placed in the Department's care, the goal of reunifying the children with their parents, and a list of "tasks" for the parents with a time frame, such as addressing substance abuse issues and maintaining safe and stable housing.

In addition to the June 20th hearing, there were four other review hearings in this case: September 15, 2005, December 19, 2005, April 27, 2006, and July 21, 2006. Before each hearing, the Department prepared a "Review Report" outlining the Department's interactions with the parents and the progress made by each parent.

Between the June 20, 2005, hearing and the court hearing scheduled for September 15, 2005, Wendy apparently informed a Department social worker that Max was registered with the Yankton Sioux Tribe of South Dakota, and the Department notified the Tribe of the CINA case. Several months later, the Tribe filed a motion to intervene and a separate motion to transfer jurisdiction to the Yankton Sioux Tribal Court. The Circuit Court granted the motion to intervene but denied the motion to transfer jurisdiction.

* * *

John reported that directly after the September 15th hearing, he went to ASC and attempted to enroll in an inpatient treatment program, but no beds were available at that time. Subsequently, John reported to the Department that he had stopped calling the inpatient treatment facility because he did not want to lose his housing. He also reported that on October 12, 2005, he got a job. During this period following the September hearing, John visited his children on a regular basis.

The Review Report prepared for the December hearing noted that Wendy secured employment but that she still did not have stable housing. The social worker reported that, on one occasion, Wendy was late for an appointment to visit the children and appeared to be under the influence of drugs or alcohol, slurring her words and moving in slow motion. She upset the children by telling them that she would be leaving for 28 days to attend a rehabilitation program. She did not, however, attend the program. Late in October, she went to ASC, tested positive for cocaine and benzodiazepines, and was referred for an extended evaluation.

On November 21, 2005, the Department changed the permanency plan from reunification with a parent to placement with a relative. The Department based this decision on the "parents' lack of progress towards Reunification," and on both parents' failure to comply with the Department's recommendations. The Department also considered the parents' substance abuse, their failure to participate in twice-weekly urinalysis and breathalyzer tests, and their failure to provide documentation of a permanent residence.

At the December 19, 2005, hearing, a representative of the Yankton Sioux Tribe of South Dakota was present. The representative stated that he was the Indian Child Welfare Act's "specialist for the Yankton Sioux Tribe" and that, although the Tribe had been looking for relatives to care for the children, the Tribe had not "found any relatives as of yet." The Tribe presented a petition to intervene, but the petition had not been properly filed with the court and copies had not been sent to the other parties. The Circuit Court noted in its order that a motion to intervene by the Yankton Sioux Tribe would subsequently be filed.

Wendy and her attorney attended the December 19th hearing, the first hearing in this case which she attended. Wendy's attorney objected to the Department's change of permanency plan from reunification to placement with a relative, but the trial judge pointed out that Wendy had not completed any kind of in-house drug treatment program and that she had missed several urinalyses. The judge also said that, in order to achieve reunification, the parents needed to demonstrate that they are drug-free. The trial judge explained to the parents:

> That means that you are probably going to have to go through an in-house program, based on your history. And, you are going to have to have a long period of time where your urines are clean. And that you haven't missed any. And, that you've got a place to take the children where they'll be safe, and where they'll be comfortable.

The judge further stated to the parents:

> [I]t's clear to me that the County has made an awful lot of effort, here, to try and get these kids back to you. And, you guys are not doing your, you are not doing your share. You are not keeping up your part of the bargain.

The case was then continued, and the order issued by the court reiterated "that the conditions and requirements of this court's previous Order of September 15, 2005, shall remain in effect."

On January 25, 2006, Wendy was admitted to an inpatient drug treatment program, but she refused to meet with the Department's social worker while participating in the program or verify her completion of the program. Following the inpatient program, Wendy was referred to a continuing program for substance abuse treatment, but she did not attend because, in her view, the $12 per day fee was too expensive. During the period from January 2006 until the Department's next Review Report dated April 13, 2006, Wendy participated in only two urine tests, even though the Circuit Court had ordered her to participate in twice weekly urine screens, and she was informed that missed tests would be considered positives.

* * *

At the start of the April 27, 2006, hearing, an attorney representing the Yankton Sioux Tribe of South Dakota filed the Tribe's motion to intervene. The Tribe also filed a motion to transfer the case to tribal jurisdiction, but the Department opposed that motion, pointing out that the Tribe had been on notice of the children's status since August 2005. As earlier mentioned, the trial judge granted the Tribe's motion to intervene but denied the Tribe's motion to transfer jurisdiction. The trial judge stated that the motion to transfer jurisdiction had been filed "at the eleventh hour," that the "children have been under the jurisdiction of the Department for nearly a year," and that the Department had provided "an incredible amount of information concerning the services that have been provided to these children." The judge also found that transferring jurisdiction "would be contrary to the welfare of these children, given the fact that the services have been in place for such a period of time." The Tribe's attorney participated in the morning portion of the April 27th hearing but left before the afternoon session. Consequently, the Tribe's attorney was not present when Wendy and Denise testified during the afternoon.

At the April 27th hearing, the Department asked the trial judge to leave the children in the relative placement with their aunt, Denise, and to close the case. The attorney for John and the attorney representing Wendy each asked the judge to postpone closing the case because, as they argued, "we are not at the point where this case should be closed." The Tribe joined in the parents' request to leave the case open.

Several witnesses testified at the April 27, 2006, hearing with regard to the activities of the Department, the children's progress, and the parents' efforts towards reunification. A clinical social worker from the "Reginald Lourie Center for Infants and Young Children" testified concerning the therapy which she had provided to

Nicole. The clinical social worker had determined that Nicole suffered from post-traumatic stress disorder. The social worker testified that, when she first began to work with Nicole, the child was "highly restricted in her movements, very pale, . . . looking very afraid and guarded." During the time Nicole lived with Denise, however, the social worker had observed "an incredible improvement with a brighter aspect, less depression."

* * *

A representative of the Avery Road Treatment Center, the inpatient drug treatment program attended by both John and Wendy, testified that John had been discharged from the program for violating program rules. The representative further testified that Wendy successfully completed the Avery Road program and that she was referred to a methadone treatment facility. On discharge, the program recommended that Wendy abstain from alcohol and stay away from others drinking alcohol. The supervisor of the urine monitoring program also testified, stating that the most recent urinalysis of John, conducted on April 14th, tested positive for benzodiazepine, cocaine and opiate. The supervisor also testified that both John and Wendy had multiple "no shows" between January and April.

Denise, the aunt and caretaker of the children, testified that, when Nicole was first placed with her, the child had not had any vaccinations since infancy, that she was not potty trained, and that she was very shy and withdrawn. According to Denise, Nicole also suffered from terror nightmares when she was first placed with Denise. Max was also very shy at first, Denise testified, and "he needed special help in kindergarten" and was behind in reading. Denise also said that she had smelled alcohol on Wendy during some of her visits with the children, but that she never confronted Wendy about it. Denise stated that the last time she spoke to John and Wendy, "they were living at a hotel" and that she had "really no way to reach them, unless I talk to [the social worker]." She also testified that she had received $1,200 from John shortly after the children were placed in her custody, but that the parents had not provided her with any monetary support since then. Vincent B., another brother of John B. and Denise P., also testified regarding the care of the children. He stated that he had seen "an amazing change" in the children since they moved in with Denise.

The Department's social worker, Karen Crist, who had worked directly with John and Wendy, testified at the April 27th hearing that she had attempted to help John find affordable mental health treatment by giving him an application for a pharmacy assistance program and encouraging him to get involved in the substance abuse treatment program that was a prerequisite to most mental health programs. She stated that John had not been forthcoming regarding his participation in the substance abuse treatment program, making it difficult for her to work with him because he never signed the consent forms necessary for her to work with his program facilitators.

John chose not to testify during the April hearing. Wendy did testify that she had attended the Avery Road substance abuse program, which she followed up with a methadone program, "AA meetings, a Bible retreat, and . . . [she also] enrolled in the abused persons program." When the children were living with her, she stated that Max was "doing really good as a kindergartner" and she had taken the children to Title IX Indian Education Programs twice a week. According to Wendy, the death of the children's grandmother had led to the children's post-traumatic stress disorder. Wendy presented the court with certificates of completion for Microsoft courses which she had taken. She also testified that she intended to return to a job with the federal government, that she had recently purchased a car, and that ultimately she wanted the court's permanency plan to be reunification between herself and the children. Her testimony, however, was vague about her living situation, her job prospects, and her substance abuse recovery program. The trial judge later noted that he had "some issues concerning credibility" with Wendy because she failed to provide verification of her activities.

* * *

At the end of the April 27, 2006, hearing, the Department urged the court to close the case and allow the children to stay in the care of Denise. The Department argued that "the parents have had a long time to try to make some changes, and it's just not happening." The Department also pointed out that, although both parents attended the Avery Road treatment program, John had "recently tested positive for a number of different substances" and Wendy "by her own admission, ha[d] not followed through with the recommendations from Avery Road."

The children's attorney endorsed the recommendation of the Department that the custody and guardianship of the children should stay with Denise. The children's attorney, however, agreed with John's and Wendy's position that "maybe another three months" would be appropriate to see if the parents made any other progress. Although the children's attorney noted his concerns with "all the no-shows for the urines, [and] all of the missed visitations," he encouraged the court to establish a definite visitation schedule.

John's attorney argued that the case should not be closed and that the permanency plan should be to reunify John with his children. The attorney pointed out that several of the witnesses recognized that John had a strong bond with his children and that he was a "good father." John's attorney complained that the Department had failed to provide John with the mental health treatment needed. The attorney also highlighted John's concerns for the children's welfare.

Wendy's attorney argued that the permanency plan should remain reunification with the parents and that the court should keep the case open for three more months. The attorney claimed that Wendy had made some progress by successfully completing a substance abuse treatment program and attending AA meetings. The attorney represented that Wendy had attempted to keep in contact with the children by telephoning them and that Wendy wanted additional time to demonstrate to the court that she could do what was necessary to get her children back.

The trial judge was "underwhelmed . . . at what both of you [parents] have done or, more importantly, failed to do" during the course of the Department's involvement with the children. The judge recognized that both John and Wendy had made some progress in addressing their addictions by attending the substance abuse programs, even though their progress was not "phenomenal." The judge decided to keep the case open, although the judge did agree to modify the permanency plan to placement with a relative and, to that effect, ordered that "Max and Nicole remain placed in the custody and guardianship of Denise P." The court also ordered John and Wendy to comply with a variety of recommendations from the Department, including participating in twice weekly urinalyses and finding stable housing and employment. The judge stated that, at the next hearing, he would evaluate the parties' progress, with particular attention toward "any deviation from this Court's order."

Sometime after July 12, 2006, the Yankton Sioux Tribe of South Dakota submitted a written "Objection of Intervenor Yankton Sioux Tribe to the Review Report Submitted to the Court by the Department of Human Services Dated July 12, 2006." In its objection, the Tribe alleged that "the Department has not made active efforts within the meaning of the [federal statute] to prevent the breakup of the Indian family." Specifically, the Tribe pointed out that the Department's placement of the children with the aunt did not reflect "the unique cultur[al] heritage of the Minor Indian Children." The Tribe urged the Circuit Court to keep the case open and to "direct the Department to make active and reasonable efforts to prevent the breakup of the Indian family."

The final hearing in the case was held on July 21, 2006, and both John and Wendy attended. The evidence at the hearing was as follows. Since the April 27th hearing, John had not attended any urinalyses and Wendy had missed nine tests between May 18th and July 10th. On the dates when Wendy was screened, she tested positive for benzodiazepine on nine occasions, and, on three of those tests, she also tested positive for opiates. Wendy generally refused to take breathalyzer tests because of an asthma condition, but, on the one occasion when she was administered an oral litmus-like test, she tested positive for alcohol, though she disputed those results. Despite the Circuit Court's order requiring verification of attendance at AA meetings, John presented no verification slips and Wendy presented only one to the Department.

Neither parent at the July 21, 2006, hearing provided evidence of a stable housing situation or stable employment, and neither had consistently attended the parenting education classes arranged by the Department. Before the Department would arrange psychological and psychiatric evaluations, it had asked each parent to submit three weeks of clean drug tests, a total of "six consecutive negative urines and breathalyzers," but neither John nor Wendy submitted those clean tests.

At the July hearing, both the children's attorney and the Department argued that the court should close the case. The children's attorney said that the parents, at the April hearing, had been given "another chance, and . . . clearly, the parents haven't done anything close to what they needed to do. And I can't imagine that they're going to do it any time in the foreseeable future." He submitted that "it is absolutely not in [the children's] best interests to be reunified with [the parents] in the foreseeable future, and I think that keeping the case open and giving the parents another chance would only make things more unstable for the children."

John, by his attorney, admitted that he was unable to care for the children and stated that "[h]e's not seeking custody of the kids, but he does support Wendy having custody of the children." John also "acknowledge[d] that he is not ready and that he couldn't do it, but he supports Wendy having the children and if not Wendy, . . . he does support Denise."

Wendy's attorney again requested that the case be kept open for "at least 60 more days" to give Wendy "the opportunity to really demonstrate even further that she really would like to have her children back." Wendy showed the court a lease signed on May 26, 2006, for a home in Silver Spring, Maryland, and she provided documentation of her $15-an-hour employment. She also presented several slips verifying her attendance at AA meetings and, attempting to justify some of the positives on the urinalyses, produced pain medication prescriptions from a dentist.

The Tribe joined Wendy's argument that the case should be kept open longer, claiming that the Tribe had not been given the time necessary to evaluate whether the Department had made the "active efforts" necessary under the federal statute. The Tribe also wanted the case open so that it could assist the Department with a relative search in South Dakota. The Tribe argued that the numerous referrals provided to John and Wendy by the Department constituted "a passive activity" and did not amount to "active efforts."

In response to the Tribe's arguments, the Department indicated that its first contact with the Tribe was on August 15, 2005, and that the Tribe had not responded until April 2006. The Department also stated that there were "repeated efforts by the Department to engage the Tribe to file the right papers," but that the Tribe continually filed "procedurally defective" papers. When the court inquired what efforts the Tribe had made to find an Indian relative placement for the children, the Tribe's attorney admitted that she was "not as well informed as I should be and . . . I have not exercised discovery properly." The court commented on the Tribe's objections, noting that

> as far as the County not being able to provide the service themselves, but directing it, that's for the legislature because . . . it's not like they have the psychiatrist on call in their building and they're purposely telling mom to go somewhere else. This is the way that they operate. They provide the services, they let them know where the programs are and then the parents either show up or they don't, or they get something out of it or they don't.

The Tribe conceded that the Department "has made efforts in the best interests of the children," but concluded that those efforts were not "active efforts at this point in time as required by federal law."

* * *

The court stated:

> I won't address John because he's obviously graciously, and quite properly, backed himself out of the consideration, but also consider[ing] his strong substance abuse problems himself, and I consider that when I consider his recommendations as well, that is, that he recommend that the children go live with their mother.

With regard to Wendy, the judge summarized her recent actions as follows:

> Wendy B.'s minimization and denial of her alcohol and prescription abuse is alarming, and seriously jeopardizes her ability to provide a safe and stable home environment for the children, and she's not consistently participated in weekly urinalysis.

The judge continued:

> I don't think for one moment, that, based on the history of this case, that mom is not going to get herself back in another jam, whether it's with Tommy or somebody else. There's no reason to believe that she'll make good choices. She hasn't yet, and is probably unable to because of the substance abuse.
>
> Now Max and Nicole are in a safe and stable living environment, which we all want, with their paternal aunt who is willing and able to provide for the children, and the doctor's reports indicate that ... the kids will be in good hands with [Denise].

The trial judge found that Wendy had "proven to this court that she's chosen drugs over her children.... [T]he record is clear. This is not a hard case to make the decision on." The judge concluded:

> It's an easy decision because we've had over 14 months and you basically haven't gotten any farther, in the court's opinion, along the way towards addressing your substance and alcohol abuse problem, addressing your relationship problem, addressing what the kids need to be exposed to and what they don't need to be exposed to, what you can say to children, what you can't say to children, and what's in the best interests of the children.

* * *

The record in this case establishes that the Department offered numerous services to both John B. and Wendy B. While there were certain pre-conditions to some of these services, such as the requirement that each have six clean urine screens prior to his or her enrollment in mental health counseling, or a demonstrated commitment to sobriety before offering certain assistance, such prerequisites do not make the efforts of the Department insufficient simply because the parents failed to comply. Although not a case under the federal statute, *In re Adoption/Guardianship of Rashawn H. and Tyrese H.*, 402 Md. 477, 937 A.2d 177 (2007), is pertinent. In that case, this Court explained that the services offered by the Department must be "designed to address both the root causes and the effect of the problem," but noted that "[t]here are some limits, however, to what the State is required to do." 402 Md. at 500, 937 A.2d at 191. The Court specified (402 Md. at 500–501, 937 A.2d at 191):

> The State is not obliged to find employment for the parent, to find and pay for permanent and suitable housing for the family, . . . or to cure or ameliorate any disability that prevents the parent from being able to care for the child. It must provide reasonable assistance in helping the parent to achieve those goals, but its duty to protect the health and safety of the children is not lessened and cannot be cast aside if the parent, despite that assistance, remains unable or unwilling to provide appropriate care.

Courts have accepted a wide array of actions by social services organizations as meeting the federal Indian Child Welfare Act's "active efforts" standard. In *In the Matter of A.N.*, 325 Mont. 379, 382, 106 P.3d 556, 559 (2005), the Montana Supreme Court reviewed a case where the father of two Indian children was accused of abuse and neglect, and was given treatment plans by the Department of Public Health and Human Services. The treatment plans included many of the same services offered to John B. and Wendy B., including chemical dependency evaluations, drug screens, counseling sessions, parenting classes, and meetings with the social worker. Where the father completed only three of the thirteen tasks assigned to him and showed up intoxicated outside the foster home, the court concluded that the "Department's efforts were as active as possible" in light of the father's unavailability. *In the Matter of A.N., supra*, 325 Mont. at 385, 106 P.3d at 561.

* * *

The Supreme Court of Alaska, in *E.A. v. State Div. of Family & Youth Services*, 46 P.3d 986, 991 (Alaska 2002), held that "'a parent's demonstrated lack of willingness to participate in treatment may be considered in determining whether the state has taken active efforts.'" The Alaska Supreme Court recognized that where the Department of Family and Youth Services' efforts consisted "largely of failed attempts to contact [the mother] or obtain information from her rather than the provision of services, [the mother's] evasive, combative conduct rendered provision of services practically impossible." 46 P.3d at 990. See also *In re J.S.B, Jr., supra*, 691 N.W.2d at 621 [(S.D. 2004)], where the South Dakota Supreme Court held that the "active efforts" requirement of the federal statute was satisfied when a father continued to abuse alcohol and failed to complete an outpatient treatment program.

In the present case, the Department made extensive active efforts to reunify Nicole and Max with their parents, while still attempting to locate a permanent placement with stability and safety for the children. The Department's efforts extended over 14 months, with five "Review Reports" and five Circuit Court hearings. The active efforts by the Department to help reunify the children with their parents were continually rebuffed or hindered by John B. and Wendy B. John and Wendy continued their substance abuse, failed to follow the Department's recommendations regarding that abuse, failed to secure stable housing for themselves and the children, failed to show up for various scheduled appointments or visitation with the children, could not be located on many occasions, and generally failed to avail themselves of the help offered to them from the Department.

In the language of the Indian Child Welfare Act of 1978, 25 U.S.C. § 1912(d), the record shows "that active efforts" were "made to provide remedial services and rehabilitative programs designed to prevent the breakup of the" family in this case, "and that these efforts have proved unsuccessful."

Notes

1. Five hearings over 14 months means the state court checked in on this family approximately every three months. In alternative courts that deal specifically with substance abuse, participants check in with the court every week or more often. Are true active efforts possible under a traditional child welfare court schedule (hearings every three to six months)? Are child welfare courts equipped to handle parents with significant chemical dependency or mental health issues? How long should children have to wait for their parents to be able to care for them? Are there ways to achieve permanency for children without terminating the parent-child relationship?

2. The opinion describes the mother in this case as "a Native American and a registered member of the Yankton Sioux Tribe of South Dakota, although she was not raised within the Tribe but was raised by non-tribal adoptive parents." There may be no fact that elicits a more fundamentally different reaction from different groups. In the eyes of a judge with little exposure to ICWA cases or the purpose of ICWA, this fact makes the added requirements of ICWA seem unnecessary. Mom is barely connected to her tribe, and yet this law requires so much of an already strapped state system. But in the eyes of a tribal attorney or practitioner who works in this area, this heartbreaking fact is the fundamental reason for ICWA's very existence, and the importance of its protections.

3. While the Maryland Court of Special Appeals (the lower court) primarily discussed the issue of "active efforts" versus "reasonable efforts," the court also appeared concerned by the discussion between the tribal attorney and the judge in the lower court, and included an extensive portion of the transcript in the lower court's opinion. The trial judge's treatment of the tribal attorney and attitude toward both ICWA and the mother's tribal citizenship may cast a different light on the decision. It also demonstrates the particular difficulty tribal ICWA attorneys face in some courtrooms, especially ones with no regular interaction with Indian tribes.

In re Nicole B.

927 A.2d 1194 (Md. App. 2007)

... At the final hearing on July 21, 2006, (at the conclusion of which the CINA case was closed), the following colloquy occurred:

[Attorney for the Yankton Sioux Tribe]: The Indian Child Welfare Act, in Section 25 U.S.C. § 1902(d), I believe, requires the Department to make active efforts. The Adoption and Safe Families Act, which is another Federal Congressional Act, that does provide funding to states through Title IV(e), funding by the, through the Social Security Act, requires states primarily to make reasonable efforts; and that is what the Department has presented to you in its report regarding its "reasonable efforts."

However, the Indian Child Welfare Act does require active effort. Active efforts are recognized by federal law to be applicable to native families, and active efforts require more than just the reasonable efforts that are alleged in the report by the Department.

I do note that on, I believe page 2, of the report, where there is, about halfway down, a section entitled "Reasonable Efforts to Achieve the Permanency Plan," that the Department is primarily engaged in monitoring of the placement, which is not actually a service to the parents, supervising the visitation between the parents and the children, and primarily providing a referral, referral to other sources, referral to parenting, referral to evaluations, referral to mental health treatment, et cetera. And referral is actually a passive activity, where a department tells parents this is where you can go, they hand them a card, it's someplace to go to, and says go do it. You've got this much time to get it done. That's not actually an active effort.

We do have a mother here who obviously has some issues that she has been dealing with, and the Tribe does believe that she has demonstrated some progress. It is true, and the Tribe also acknowledges, that Judge Algeo's finding of being relatively underwhelmed at the last hearing is correct. However, it does appear that even since that time, that the mother, at least—not to be confused with the father's situation—has made some additional progress that has been requested and ordered by the court.

The Tribe is also very concerned about the mother's apparent mental health condition. She does have a panic disorder, and this is recognized on page six of the Department's report. And there's also some illusion there where there is a—the Department is alluding to a communication it had with the mother, who is saying she is even afraid to leave the house on occasion. Well when you're doing a passive effort, go get this help, handing someone a card, for example, and a person has got a panic disorder, is on medication, has apparently some medical issues as well, and is afraid to leave the house, how, really truly, can a native mother get that done?

* * *

Tribes typically come fairly late to these kinds of proceedings, just by the nature of how things go.

THE COURT: By nature of the fact that usually the parents have absolutely nothing to do with the Tribe, other than the fact that there's some type of lineal descendant. That's the reason. It's not like we have an active member in the Tribe that's in South Dakota, and is part of the Tribe, and happened to come in here and had a liaison with someone else and had a child. I mean, that's the reason the Tribe comes late to these proceedings. These women and fathers—in this particular case, as far as the County would know, would have no idea that they're part of the Tribe. I mean they're not active participants in the Tribe. And there's no indication their lifestyle indicates that she's part of the Tribe. I don't think she goes to tribal meetings, I don't think she's involved in any of these tribal celebrations you're talking about.

* * *

THE COURT: I had this case before Judge Algeo, and if she's a very active member of the Tribe, that's news to me.

[Attorney for the Yankton Sioux Tribe]: She's not required under federal law to—

THE COURT: I didn't say that she was.

[Attorney for the Yankton Sioux Tribe]: —be an active member of the Tribe.

THE COURT: I'm just indicating that how would we know? I could be a member of, say the Boy Scouts, but if I didn't tell anybody, no one would know.

[Attorney for the Yankton Sioux Tribe]: Right. The Indian Child Welfare Act imposes an affirmative duty on departments of social services of the different states to investigate, and to find out whether or not—

THE COURT: Right.

* * *

THE COURT: Have they been out there? Is there anyone there that's had visitation with them? What's the Tribe going to do with them, other than come in here and say you didn't do everything you were supposed to do?

[Attorney for the Yankton Sioux Tribe]: One of the things that the Department needs to be doing and—

THE COURT: Forget the Department. They're doing everything wrong. What is the Tribe recommending be—what is this great Tribe going to do for these children? That's what I want to know.

[Attorney for the Yankton Sioux Tribe]: I object to your language, sir.

THE COURT: Well I object to you objecting, because all I'm hearing is indictments of our system, ma'am.

[Attorney for the Yankton Sioux Tribe]: No.

THE COURT: Yes. You haven't said one positive thing. We haven't done one thing right, here in the state court, as far as you're concerned, or the Tribe is concerned.

What I'm saying is what is the Tribe doing for these children, now that they know there is a, that they're part of a tribe where there is a lineal connection? That's what I'm asking you? Because we're looking at the best interests of the children.

* * *

[Attorney for the Yankton Sioux Tribe]: That's why I'm here today. And so the Tribe is specifically recommending that it be allowed to continue with discovery, to see more of what's happening in the file, to work with the Department of Social Services to do a relative search for relatives at the reservation, and to discuss with the aunt ways in which she can, and should, and must, under federal law, assist these children in maintaining contact with the Tribe.

Sir, there's a long history of tribes, tribal members relocating to urban areas for things like employment. It's my understanding that the mother in this case, who is a tribal member, did, in fact, relocate to this area, and was working with the Indian Health Service[.]

Rockville, Maryland is a center for, a federal center for Indian health issues, and apparently that's why the mother is here. Tribes and tribal members are not limited in their rights, in regards to have to, just stay home, to be, to have and exercise your rights. We go all over the place, and rights follow us because we are citizens of our tribal nations. The—

THE COURT: So you want a relative search, that these children may have relatives within the Tribe?

[Attorney for the Yankton Sioux Tribe]: Yes.

* * *

THE COURT: And what I'm telling you is I'd be happy to look at other possibilities, but I only have basically two choices. People are asking me now to close the case and leave the children with their aunt; or keep the case open and leave the children with their aunt.

I mean, those are the only things that anyone is asking me for, would you agree? You're saying keep it open because I haven't had, completed discovery, which I don't know exactly where that's going to take us. And you're saying keep it open, because the County hasn't provided themselves, they don't have the internal programs at their offices to deal with the mother and father's problem, and, number three, the County hasn't done a sufficient relative search within the Tribe. So I'm trying to address those three issues.

Number one, I don't fault the County for not finding a relative. It sounds that they, the Tribe has been on notice, the County has looked into that and there is no one that's come forward saying, I am a Tribe relative of this child and I'd like to be part of this child's life. More importantly, even if someone is out there, they've obviously had no contact with these two children, which is significant.

> Number two, the discovery that you would get, I don't know what that would lead to with respect to assisting the children at this point in their placement. Their files are pretty open. You have everything the other attorneys would have.

The court and counsel then continued, addressing the sufficiency of the Department's efforts in aiding the B. family:

> **THE COURT:** And as far as the County not being able to provide the service themselves, but directing it, that's for the legislature because they don't, it's not like they have the psychiatrist on call in their building and they're purposely telling mom to go somewhere else. This is the way that they operate. They provide the services, they let them know where the programs are and then the parents either show up or they don't, or they get something out of it or they don't.
>
> **[Attorney for the Tribe]:** Well then if that's the case, then I think it's actually a matter that the Department is not complying with the Indian Child Welfare Act that requires active efforts.
>
> **THE COURT:** Well, I guess it's question of —
>
> **[Attorney for the Tribe]:** Now the Department —
>
> **THE COURT:** —definition of active effort. I don't agree with your definition. I think you can be active. I think, for example, a school principal at an elementary school can be active in recommending to a parent that the child go see a child psychiatrist. I don't think the school has to have a psychiatrist, you know, on their staff, and that's still being active.
>
> **[Attorney for the Tribe]:** Well, the school is not held to the IQUA [sic] standards. It's just in child custody proceedings in court.
>
> **THE COURT:** Analogy. What I'm saying is they don't necessarily have to have the parenting program conducted by themselves —
>
> **[Attorney for the Tribe]:** Well —
>
> **THE COURT:** — if, in fact, they have a reputable one.
>
> **[Attorney for the Tribe]:** It's a false analogy, I'm sorry, because the IQUA [sic] doesn't —
>
> **THE COURT:** Well I disagree.
>
> **[Attorney for the Tribe]:** IQUA [sic] doesn't apply to them.
>
> **THE COURT:** All right. You may proceed.

The circuit court filed a written order, finding that "[r]easonable [e]fforts have been made by the Montgomery County Department of Health and Human Services (hereinafter the 'Department') to achieve Reunification with the Child's parents as listed on page 2 of the Department's report dated July 12, 2006[.]" The court did not mention the ICWA in this written order.

Notes

1. Anecdotally, exchanges such as the one in this case happen with some regularity. This case is one of the few times an excerpt from the trial court is included in an appellate decision. While there was no trial level transcript excerpted in a recent Idaho Supreme Court case, reading between the lines, it seems clear that the trial court had real issues with the Shoshone-Bannock Tribes determining their own membership. Being the tribal attorney in that situation can be extraordinarily difficult. *See Doe v. Shoshone-Bannock Tribes*, 367 P.3d 136 (Idaho 2016).

2. The corrosive and racist attitude of the judge toward the tribal attorney is a reoccurring theme throughout ICWA cases. How does the appearance of a tribal attorney upend a state court's expectations of the child welfare process? How do the demands of the tribe to do more or do better by the parents challenge the standard operation procedures in state court? How does the lens of Critical Race Theory (CRT) explain these outbursts by state court judges? For a longer discussion of CRT, see Chapter 5.

F. Placement Preferences

The purpose of placement preferences is to keep a child who has to be removed from her home with her family and community. While other provisions of ICWA are designed to prevent the removal of a child, and to reunify a family, the placement provisions exist to keep the child close when she is removed. Placement preferences apply to both involuntary foster care and adoption placements and to voluntary adoptions. The latter attracts perhaps the most attention of any ICWA cases. This section will focus on involuntary placements, not the least of which because these are far more common scenarios over a voluntary adoption. In addition, voluntary adoptions implicate any number of other parental rights issues, including the right of a parent to place a child, and the right of a parent to remain anonymous, which are discussed fully in Chapter Four. Despite this separation in the materials, the placement preferences apply to *both* voluntary *and* involuntary proceedings.

Outside of Indian child welfare, states are not allowed to consider race or ethnicity when placing a child with a family. Because ICWA is not based on race or ethnicity, but rather on the trust responsibility and political relationship between the federal government and Indian tribes, it is explicitly exempted from the application of the Multiethnic Placement Act of 1994, P.L. 103-382. These issues are discussed further in Chapter Five.

When litigated, the placement provisions of ICWA can be some of the most emotional and difficult cases, as seen in the following excerpts. As discussed at length in Chapter Two, the best interest of the child standard as used by state court judges may, at times, conflict with the application of the preferences, especially if a child has been in a non-compliant home for many years. In an attempt to address this issue, the federal regulations state that a "placement may not depart from the preferences based solely on ordinary bonding and attachment . . . ." 25 C.F.R. § 23.132(e) (2016).

In re S.E.G.

521 N.W.2d 357 (Minn. 1994)

Keith, Chief Justice.

This appeal arises out of a petition by the respondents, non-Indian foster parents, E.C. and C.C., to adopt three Native American children for whom they had provided foster care. At issue is whether the placement preferences provision of the Indian Child Welfare Act (ICWA), 25 U.S.C. § 1915 (1988), provides a "good cause" exception for "extraordinary emotional needs" based on a child's need for permanence in the form of adoption; also at issue is whether the record in this case supports the trial court's findings that these children had extraordinary emotional needs and that there was an "unavailability of suitable families for placement" after a diligent search. We hold, while good cause may include a child's need for stability, this is not equivalent to a need to be adopted. We also hold that, in this case, the record failed to support the trial court's findings that these children have extraordinary emotional needs. We therefore reverse.

* * *

The substantive provisions of the Act include § 1915(a), the provision at issue in this case, which sets forth the adoptive placement preferences. Other requirements include: the tribes' right to intervene in and be notified of custody proceedings involving Native American children, 25 U.S.C. §§ 1911(c) and 1912(a); higher standards of proof to remove Native American children and to terminate Native Americans' parental rights, § 1912(e), (f); a requirement that Native American children be returned to their parent upon the parent's revocation of consent to placement or to voluntary relinquishment of parental rights, § 1913(b), (c); and a provision that Native American parents or tribes may petition to vacate any action involving custody of a Native American child upon a showing that the action violated the Act, § 1914.

* * *

The parents of the children whose placement is at issue in this case are a Chippewa woman and a white man. S.E.G., the oldest child, was born in 1984; A.L.W. was born in 1985 and V.M.G. in 1987. The factors leading to the family's involvement with the child welfare system are not entirely clear from the record. A.L.W. was first placed out of the home for "failure to thrive" in January, 1986. She was moved to a relative's home in September of 1986 and returned to her mother in December, 1986. The family was apparently still being supervised by Cass County when they moved out of Minnesota in violation of a court order. When the family returned to Minnesota, the children lived at the home of their maternal grandmother.

After V.M.G. was born, the mother was unable to care for them and voluntarily placed all three children in foster care. The children have not lived with their parents since February, 1988. A.L.W. and V.M.G. were moved six times—and S.E.G. five—in the next three years, before being placed in E.C. and C.C.'s therapeutic (PATH) foster home in August, 1991. E.C. and C.C. are a non-Indian couple.

The children remained in E.C. and C.C.'s home until January 29, 1992 when they were placed in a Native American pre-adoptive home. Though discussed in advance, the children's move was not well planned and occurred without prior overnight visits. The placement lasted only nine days, after which the children were returned to E.C. and C.C.'s foster home.

On October 8, 1992, the children were placed in a Native American PATH home in Minneapolis. They moved from that placement within two months because the foster mother was "emotionally not ready to handle the children." The children were then placed in A.C.'s Native American PATH home in Cloquet, Minnesota, where they have resided since November 13, 1992.

* * *

Expert and lay witnesses from both sides testified that the children had a strong need for stability in their home environment. All of the witnesses for the Leech Lake Band of Chippewa were recognized as "qualified expert witnesses" by the trial court. E.C. and C.C. presented two witnesses whom the trial court recognized as "qualified Indian experts." All the testimony seemed to show that E.C. and C.C.'s foster home and A.C.'s Native American foster home each provided for the children's physical, emotional, and intellectual needs, but the witnesses disagreed about whether E.C. and C.C. provided for—or could provide for—the children's cultural needs and whether A.C. provided for the children's need for permanence.

Several of the experts identified as "qualified Indian experts" by the trial court testified that Native American children who grow up in non-Native homes suffer from intense identity crises in adolescence. E.C. and C.C.'s friend from church—a white woman married to a Native American man—was qualified as an expert. She testified that she did not observe that traditional Indian parenting techniques were common on the Red Lake Reservation and that she believed the children were bonded and attached to E.C. and C.C. Darrell Auginash, a Native American man who lives and works as a counselor on the Red Lake Reservation, was also qualified as an expert. He testified that he would be willing to work with E.C. and C.C. to educate the children about their culture if E.C. and C.C. were allowed to adopt. He also testified:

> I think as far as identity is concerned, I think that usually comes a little later. The most important thing that most children are concerned about is

> their, is their security, their, their home, their structure and the love that's provided for them by their family and people like that. And the ones that experience the most dysfunction, have a high percentage rates of some of the problems like suicide and alcoholism and drug abuse, delinquency.

When asked whether, in his opinion, cultural identity could be taught to and understood by a child who did not live in a Native American home or on a reservation, he testified: "I believe that as far as this heritage and this culture is concerned, I think that you can learn it just as well in an urban setting or off the reservation.... You learn it where you're at with whomever. And I can take it anywhere and teach it."

E.C. testified that he was unable to describe the difference between the Leech Lake Band of Chippewa and the Minnesota Chippewa Tribe and could not identify the clan of which the children were members. He testified that he tried to learn as much as possible about Native American culture through his friendships with Native Americans and by reading Native American publications. E.C. and C.C. clearly made efforts to expose the children to Native American cultural events; they attended two powwows, a few storytellings and arranged a naming ceremony for S.E.G. at the suggestion of a social worker.

All of the social workers and therapists involved with the family in the A.C. foster home noted that the children had "identity issues" related to their Native American heritage and that these issues showed improvement in A.C.'s care. S.E.G.'s therapist—when S.E.G. was in E.C.'s and C.C.'s home—testified that S.E.G. seemed to be confused about the fact that E.C. and C.C. could not keep her because she was Native American and they were white. She noted that S.E.G. hoped E.C. and C.C. would "fight for her."

Finally, all three Native American social workers—each of whom was qualified as an Indian expert by the trial court—stated that the most important thing for the children at that time was that they "stabilize" in the current home. Fred Isham, a foster care adoption worker with the Minnesota Chippewa Tribe Human Services Division, testified that he was "actively recruiting an adoptive home for the [children]," but that they were not ready for adoption at that time. It seemed clear from the testimony that the workers not only expected the children to remain in A.C.'s home for an unspecified period of time until they "stabilized" but also expected they eventually would be moved to an adoptive home.

Based upon all of the above evidence and the guardian ad litem's recommendation,[1] the trial court held that good cause existed to place the children in a manner inconsistent with § 1915(a). The court held that the children had "extraordinary physical and emotional needs" and that those needs had been established by the testimony

1. [FN 2] The guardian ad litem was a junior at Bemidji State University working on a social work degree. She attended guardian ad litem training and had acted as a guardian in roughly 10-12 cases. She is also Native American. Neither party moved to have her qualified as an expert witness.

of "several qualified experts." The court also held that a suitable family for adoption was unavailable after a diligent search had been completed.

* * *

The issue presented by this case is whether there is good cause not to follow the preference provisions of § 1915(a). Nothing in the ICWA or its legislative history suggests a definition of good cause or describes the factors to be considered in determining whether it exists.

The BIA guidelines, however, offer some structure to state courts interpreting this provision. Guidelines for State Courts; Indian Child Custody Proceedings, 44 Fed.Reg. 67,584-67,595 (1979). Section F.3 of the guidelines describes circumstances which create "good cause" to modify the placement preferences of the Act:

F.3. Good Cause To Modify Preferences

(a) For purposes of foster care, preadoptive or adoptive placement, a determination of good cause not to follow the order of preference set out above shall be based on one or more of the following considerations:

(i) The request of the biological parents or the child when the child is of sufficient age.

(ii) The extraordinary physical or emotional needs of the child as established by testimony of a qualified expert witness.

(iii) The unavailability of suitable families for placement after a diligent search has been completed for families meeting the preference criteria.

(b) The burden of establishing the existence of good cause not to follow the order of preferences established in subsection (b) shall be on the party urging that the preferences not be followed.

Id. at 67,594. The guidelines also state, however, that Congress intended to give state courts some discretion in these cases:

> Primary responsibility for interpreting other language used in the Act, however, rests with the courts that decide Indian child custody cases. *For example, the legislative history of the Act states explicitly that the use of the term "good cause" was designed to provide state courts with flexibility in determining the disposition of a placement proceeding involving an Indian child.*

Id. at 67,584 (emphasis added).

The Supremacy Clause, as well as state law, requires that placement decisions in Minnesota courts meet the "minimum" requirements of ICWA. See U.S. Const. art. VI; 25 U.S.C. § 1902; Minn.Stat. § 256F.07, subd. 2 (1992). Since long before the passage of the ICWA, child custody cases have been decided pursuant to the "best interests of the child" standard. E.g., *State ex rel. Jaroszewski v. Prestidge*, 249 Minn. 80, 81 N.W.2d 705 (1957). ICWA appears to create a presumption that placement of Indian children within the preferences of the Act is in the best interests of Indian children.

* * *

We believe, however, that a finding of good cause cannot be based simply on a determination that placement outside the preferences would be in the child's best interests. The plain language of the Act read as a whole and its legislative history clearly indicate that state courts are a part of the problem the ICWA was intended to remedy. *See Mississippi Band of Choctaw Indians* [*v. Holyfield*], 490 U.S. at 44-45, 109 S.Ct. at 1606-07 [(1989)]. Furthermore, the report from our own Task Force on Racial Bias in the Judicial System indicates that insensitivity to minority cultures remains a problem in child welfare cases. *See* Minnesota Supreme Court Task Force on Racial Bias in the Judicial System, Final Report, 16 Hamline L. Rev. 477, 624–646 (1993). The best interests of the child standard, by its very nature, requires a subjective evaluation of a multitude of factors, many, if not all of which are imbued with the values of majority culture. It therefore seems "most improbable" that Congress intended to allow state courts to find good cause whenever they determined that a placement outside the preferences of § 1915 was in the Indian child's best interests. *Cf. Mississippi Band of Choctaw Indians*, 490 U.S. at 45, 109 S. Ct. at 1606-07.

* * *

In light of the Act, its legislative history, the BIA guidelines and their commentary, it does not seem that a need for permanence or stability cannot be considered in determining whether good cause exists in a particular case. The Supreme Court of Alaska, in *Matter of Adoption of F.H.*, 851 P.2d 1361, 1365 (Alaska 1993) seemed to assume that adoption was the only possible permanent placement available to the child. *Id.* at 1365. The Alaska Supreme Court noted that "F.H.'s situation would be uncertain" if the white foster parents were not allowed to adopt. *Id.* at 1365. In that case, however, F.H.'s natural mother had voluntarily relinquished her parental rights conditioned on the foster parents' adoption. *Id.* The court noted that the natural mother and foster parents had agreed to an open adoption, the natural mother testified that she could more easily visit F.H. in the foster parent's home than in the Native village in which her relatives lived, and the foster mother and F.H. had formed a strong bond. *Id.* This case presents a somewhat different problem, however, in that parental rights have already been terminated and the children would not be subjected to continued attempts at reunification with the biological parents if they were not placed in E.C. and C.C.'s home.

The Commissioner of Human Services argues that the phrase, "unavailability of suitable families for placement" does not refer only to adoptive placement. She argues that adoption is not the only permanent placement option, and preferring adoption over other options, such as permanent foster care, may result in more placements outside Native American communities.

ICWA's § 1915(d) requires that "[t]he standards to be applied in meeting the preference requirements of this section shall be the prevailing social and cultural standards of the Indian community in which the parent or extended family resides or with which the parent or extended family members maintain social and cultural ties." The record of the 1974 United States Senate Hearings supports the Leech Lake Band of Chippewa's claim that permanency is defined differently in Native American cultures. At least one witness before the trial court testified that she believed S.E.G.'s need for permanence could be met through an attachment to her tribe "if that's an ongoing part of her life." The House Report published with the passage of ICWA in 1978 notes: "For example, the dynamics of Indian extended families are largely misunderstood. An Indian child may have scores of, perhaps more than a hundred, relatives who are counted as close, responsible members of the family." H.R.Rep. No. 1386, 95th Cong., 2d Sess. (1978), reprinted in 1978 U.S.C.C.A.N. 7530, 7532. Finally, as the report of the Task Force on Racial Bias noted regarding application of ICWA in Minnesota: "Problems can arise when a system that is largely white, with middle-class values, is called upon to evaluate cultural and racial norms which are neither white nor necessarily middle-class." Minnesota Supreme Court Task Force on Racial Bias in the Judicial System, Final Report, 16 Hamline L. Rev. 477, 631 (1993). Given that a need for permanence is not discussed in the Act or its regulations, it is important that this need not be defined so narrowly as to threaten or substantially reduce placements in Native American homes. *See* 44 Fed. Reg. 67,586 (1979).

Here the trial court found that the children had extraordinary emotional needs but went on to find the present emotional, cultural, educational, and physical needs of the children are currently being met in the home of A.C., except for the need for permanence. In effect, the trial court found that the need for permanence alone was an extraordinary emotional need and that a suitable family for placement must be a family that could meet this need. Implicit in the trial court's findings that the children's need for permanence was not being met at A.C.'s foster home and that A.C.'s home was not a suitable family for placement was an assumption that only adoption could meet a need for permanence. We believe this holding was based on the improper assumption that the need for permanence could only be met through adoption and, therefore, we reverse this holding as a matter of law.

Decisions on the custody of children, even when the cultural values of all the participants are similar, are often the most difficult for our trial and appellate judges. These decisions can be even more difficult when children are born into an Indian community which may view the family and tribal community very differently from our majority culture. Congress, in conjunction with numerous Indian tribal governments and the Bureau of Indian Affairs, has carefully and thoughtfully set out the nation's policy to prevent the destruction of Indian families and Indian tribes and to protect the best interests of Indian children by preventing their removal from their communities.

For the reasons set out above, we do not believe the record in this case shows good cause to deviate from the placement preferences of the Indian Child Welfare Act.

Reversed.

Notes

1. The federal regulations provide significantly different guidance for deviating from the placement preferences:

> (c) A court's determination of good cause to depart from the placement preferences must be made on the record or in writing and should be based on one or more of the following considerations:
>
> > (1) The request of one or both of the Indian child's parents, if they attest that they have reviewed the placement options, if any, that comply with the order of preference;
> >
> > (2) The request of the child, if the child is of sufficient age and capacity to understand the decision that is being made;
> >
> > (3) The presence of a sibling attachment that can be maintained only through a particular placement;
> >
> > (4) The extraordinary physical, mental, or emotional needs of the Indian child, such as specialized treatment services that may be unavailable in the community where families who meet the placement preferences live;
> >
> > (5) The unavailability of a suitable placement after a determination by the court that a diligent search was conducted to find suitable placements meeting the preference criteria, but none has been located. For purposes of this analysis, the standards for determining whether a placement is unavailable must conform to the prevailing social and cultural standards of the Indian community in which the Indian child's parent or extended family resides or with which the Indian child's parent or extended family members maintain social and cultural ties.
>
> (d) A placement may not depart from the preferences based on the socioeconomic status of any placement relative to another placement.
>
> (e) A placement may not depart from the preferences based solely on ordinary bonding or attachment that flowed from time spent in a non-preferred placement that was made in violation of ICWA.

25 C.F.R. § 23.132 (2016).

Would this case fall under section (e) today? Or would the request of the child govern?

2. The length of an appeal may be no more problematic than in the case of a placement preference violation. In this case, the children were in an ICWA-compliant setting two years by the time the decision was issued. What would have been the outcome if the court had decided the other way? Would the trial court reconsider the children's best interests in light of the passage of time in the new foster placement?

3. The question of what is considered "permanence" often arises in placement preference cases. One big question is where the child's case is in process. How often

can a foster child be moved? How often *are* foster children moved? Can a child be considered for adoption before parental rights are terminated? What about foster parents who frame their placement as the only permanent solution for a child?

In re Alexandria P.

228 Cal. App. 4th 1322 (2014)

Kriegler, J.

This case involves the placement preferences set forth in the Indian Child Welfare Act (ICWA) (25 U.S.C. § 1901 et seq.). At issue is whether the dependency court properly applied the ICWA in finding that the foster parents of an Indian child failed to prove good cause to deviate from the ICWA's adoptive placement preferences.

A 17–month–old Indian child was removed from the custody of her mother, who has a lengthy substance abuse problem and has lost custody of at least six other children, and her father, who has an extensive criminal history and has lost custody of one other child. The girl's father is an enrolled member of an Indian tribe, and the girl is considered an Indian child under the ICWA. The tribe consented to the girl's placement with a non-Indian foster family to facilitate efforts to reunify the girl with her father. The girl lived in two foster homes before she was placed with de facto parents at the age of two. She bonded with the family and has thrived for the past two and a half years.

After reunification efforts failed, the father, the tribe, and the Department of Children and Family Services (Department) recommended that the girl be placed in Utah with a non-Indian couple who are extended family of the father. De facto parents argued good cause existed to depart from the ICWA's adoptive placement preferences and it was in the girl's best interests to remain with de facto family. The child's court-appointed counsel argued that good cause did not exist. The court ordered the girl placed with the extended family in Utah after finding that de facto parents had not proven by clear and convincing evidence that it was a certainty the child would suffer emotional harm by the transfer.

De facto parents appeal from the placement order, raising constitutional challenges to the ICWA, which we hold they lack standing to assert. De facto parents also contend that the ICWA's adoptive placement preferences do not apply when the tribe has consented to a child's placement outside of the ICWA's foster care placement preferences. We disagree with their interpretation of the statutory language. De facto parents further contend the court erroneously applied the clear and convincing standard of proof, rather than preponderance of the evidence, a contention we reject based upon the overwhelming authority on the issue. Finally, de facto parents contend the court erroneously interpreted the good cause exception to the ICWA's adoptive placement preferences as requiring proof of a certainty that the child would suffer emotional harm if placed with the Utah couple, and failed to consider the bond between Alexandria and her foster family, the risk of detriment if that bond was broken, and Alexandria's best interests. We agree with this last contention and reverse the placement order because the court's error was prejudicial.

* * *

By the time Alexandria was placed with the P.s in December 2011, her extended family in Utah, the R.s, were aware of dependency proceeding and had spoken to representatives of the tribe about their interest in adopting Alexandria. The tribe agreed to initial foster placement with the P.s because it was close to father at a time when he was working on reunification. If reunification services were terminated, the tribe recommended placement with the R.s in Utah.

* * *

Because Ginger R.'s uncle is Alexandria's paternal step-grandfather, the tribe recognizes the R.s as Alexandria's extended family. The R.s have an ongoing relationship with Alexandria's half-sister, Anna, who visits the R.s on holidays and for a week or two during the summer. Anna and Alexandria have the same paternal grandmother (who has since passed away) and step-grandfather, and the step-grandfather has designated the R.s to care for Anna if he should become unable to care for Anna.

The R.s expressed their interest in adopting Alexandria as early as October 2011. They were initially told that to avoid confusing Alexandria, they should not contact her while father attempted to reunify. If reunification efforts failed, they were the tribe's first choice for adoption. The family has approval for Alexandria to be placed with them under the Interstate Compact on the Placement of Children (ICPC). The R.s first visited Alexandria shortly after the court terminated father's reunification services. Since then, they video chat with Alexandria about twice a week and have had multiple in-person visits in Los Angeles. The P.s refer to the R.s as family from Utah. At one point, when Alexandria asked if she was going to Utah, the P.s responded that they did not know for sure, but it was possible. Russell and Summer P. testified that before and following a recent visit by the R.s, most likely in June 2013, Alexandria was upset and said she did not want to visit with the R.s and did not like it when they came to visit. Russell P. acknowledged that the change in Alexandria's feelings coincided with the birth of a new baby in the P. family and a transition to a new therapist for Alexandria.

Alexandria has lived with the P.s for over two and a half years, beginning in December 2011. By all accounts, they have provided her with clear and consistent rules, and a loving environment. Alexandria is bonded to the P.s, and has a healthy attachment to them. The Department consistently reminded the P.s that Alexandria is an Indian child subject to the ICWA placement preferences. At some point after father's reunification efforts failed, the P.s decided they wanted to adopt Alexandria. They discussed the issue with the Department social worker, who advised them that the tribe had selected the R.s as the planned adoptive placement.

* * *

On July 29, 2013, the court commenced a hearing that spanned five days over the course of three months to determine whether good cause existed to permit Alexandria to remain with the P.s, rather than placing her with the R.s in Utah in accordance with the ICWA's adoptive placement preferences. The court heard testimony from (1) Roberta Javier, the social worker for the Department who was assigned to the case in December 2011, around the same time Alexandria was placed with the P.s; (2) Jennifer Lingenfelter, clinical director at United American Indian Involvement, where she supervised Alexandria's first therapist, Ruth Polcino, until Polcino went on maternity leave; (3) Russell P., Alexandria's foster father; (4) Summer P., Alexandria's foster mother; (5) Ginger R., Alexandria's extended family member and proposed adoptive mother; (6) Genevieve Marquez, Alexandria's current therapist at United American Indian Involvement; (7) Amanda Robinson, a tribal social worker; (8) Lauren Axline, a foster adoption case manager at the foster agency that placed Alexandria with the P.s; and (9) Billy Stevens, a tribal elder.

The social workers and therapists who testified all agreed that Alexandria has a primary attachment and a strong bond with the P.s. She considers Russell and Summer P. her parents and the P. children her siblings. Regarding Alexandria's ability to attach with a new caregiver if her bond with the P.s is broken, Javier and Lingenfelter acknowledged that a change in placement would be potentially traumatic, but that the existence of a primary bond and healthy attachment increases the likelihood that a child will successfully attach to a new caregiver. Marquez believed that with appropriate intervention and support, Alexandria would cope with a transition resiliently, characterizing the possible trauma as a loss, but not the equivalent of the death of a parent.

[The court found the constitutional arguments, including the existing Indian family exception, unavailable to the de facto parents.]

* * *

The P.s and amici curiae make a novel contention that by consenting to Alexandria's placement with a family outside of the foster care placement preferences identified in section 1915(b), the tribe waived the application of the adoptive placement preferences stated in section 1915(a). We reject this contention because the P.s forfeited the issue by failing to raise it before the court and also because it does not comport with the plain statutory language.

* * *

Even if we did not consider the issue forfeited, we are not persuaded that Congress or the California Legislature intended to require tribes to make an election at the time of foster care placement that would prevent a change in placement for adoption, especially when the foster family is informed that they are not being considered as an adoptive placement because of the ICWA's requirements. Section 1903(1) provides separate definitions for "foster care placement" and "adoptive placement."

The ICWA's placement preferences are distinct for each type of placement, and different considerations apply for foster care and adoptive placements. (See § 1915(a) [adoptive placement preferences]; 1915(b) [foster care placement preferences].) For example, foster care placements must be within reasonable proximity to the child's home and must take a child's special needs into account. (§ 1915(b); [*In re*] *Anthony T.*, *supra*, 208 Cal.App.4th at pp. 1029–1032, 146 Cal.Rptr.3d 124 [(2012)] [foster care placement was not in "reasonable proximity" to minor's home].) The same is not true for adoptive placements. (§ 1915(a)). The P.s and amici curiae argue that once an Indian child is placed in foster care under section 1915(b), the only way for a court to consider adoptive placement preferences under section 1915(a) is if the child is "removed" from the foster placement under section 1916(b).

This argument is unsupported by case law and in fact, runs counter to the many published cases where a tribe or Indian parent initially consents to foster care placement that does not comply with the ICWA's placement preferences, and later asserts adoptive placement preferences, usually after reunification efforts have failed. (See, e.g., [*In re*] *Santos Y.*, *supra*, 92 Cal.App.4th 1274, 112 Cal.Rptr.2d 692 [(2001)] [tribe supported placement with foster parents for two years, until it found a suitable individual qualified as a preferred adoptive placement]; *Native Village of Tununak v. State, Dept. of Health & Social Services, Office of Children's Services* (Alaska 2013) 303 P.3d 431, 434 (*Tununak*) [parties stipulated to a foster placement that departed from the ICWA's placement preferences while a search for preferred placements continued].)

* * *

In determining what evidence is required to establish good cause, the court ruled that a moving party could only show good cause by expert testimony and evidence that the child "currently had extreme psychological and emotional problems, or would definitively have them in the future." This extreme standard is not based in California law, but instead is found in an opinion by the Montana Supreme Court, which reversed a lower court's finding of good cause to deviate from the ICWA's placement preferences. ([*In re*] *C.H.*, *supra*, 997 P.2d 776 [(2000)].)

* * *

Instead, we hold that a court may find good cause when a party shows by clear and convincing evidence that there is a significant risk that a child will be suffer serious harm as a result of a change in placement. (See, e.g., *Fresno County* [*Dept. of Children & Family Services v. Superior Court*], *supra*, 122 Cal.App.4th at p. 640, 19 Cal.Rptr.3d 155 [(2004)].)

* * *

The court erroneously relied on [*In re*] *Desiree F.*, *supra*, 83 Cal.App.4th at p. 476, 99 Cal.Rptr.2d 688 [(2000)] and [*Adoption of*] *Halloway*, *supra*, 732 P.2d 962 [(Utah 1986)] to conclude that "while the bonding with the [P.s] is significant to this court, it does not supersede the placement preference under the ICWA." It is impossible to determine from this language whether the court considered the bond between Alexandria and the P.s as a factor, or felt compelled by *Desiree F.* to ignore the bond in determining good cause. To the extent the court relied on Desiree F. to exclude the bond as a factor in the good cause determination, it did so erroneously, because the facts of our case do not warrant such an exclusion. In *Desiree F.*, the social services agency was responsible for the delay in notifying the tribe of the proceedings, and the appellate court clarified that on remand, the trial court could not consider factors flowing from the agency's "flagrant violation" of the ICWA, including any bond the minor developed with the current foster family. (*Desiree F., supra*, at p. 476, 99 Cal.Rptr.2d 688.) In the present case, the Department acted promptly to notify the tribe, and the social worker was in communication with the tribe even before Alexandria was placed with the P.s. Thus, no ICWA violation precludes the court from considering the bond that Alexandria has with her foster family.

* * *

In fact the bond between Alexandria and her caretakers and the trauma that Alexandria may suffer if that bond is broken are essential components of what the court should consider when determining whether good cause exists to depart from the ICWA's placement preferences.

* * *

The court also committed legal error by failing to consider Alexandria's best interests as part of its good cause determination. The court's written statement of decision does not reveal whether the court considered Alexandria's best interests as one of the key factors in determining whether there is good cause to depart from the ICWA's placement preferences. "The ICWA presumes it is in the best interests of the child to retain tribal ties and cultural heritage and in the interest of the tribe to preserve its future generations, a most important resource. (*In re Crystal K.* (1990) 226 Cal.App.3d 655, 661, 276 Cal.Rptr. 619.)" (*Desiree F., supra*, 83 Cal. App.4th at p. 469, 99 Cal.Rptr.2d 688.) But the presumption that following the placement preferences is in a child's best interest is a starting point, not the end of the inquiry into a child's best interests. As an Arizona appellate court recently explained, courts "should start with the presumption that ICWA preferences are in the child's best interest and then balance that presumption against other relevant factors to determine whether placement outside ICWA preferences is in the child's best interest." (*Navajo Nation* [*v. Arizona Dept. of Economic Security* (Ariz.Ct.App. 2012)], *supra*, 284 P.3d at p. 35.)

"'Good cause' often includes considerations affecting the best interests of the child, such as whether the child has had any significant contact with the tribe . . . or the extent of the child's bonding with a prospective adoptive family. [Citations.]." (*Crystal R., supra*, 59 Cal.App.4th 703, 720, 69 Cal.Rptr.2d 414, fn. omitted.) Although we are unaware of any published California case holding that a court must consider a child's best interests when determining good cause, such an approach is consistent with the law in many other states and with California's emphasis on best interests in dependency proceedings. (See, e.g., *In re Lauren R.* (2007) 148 Cal.App.4th 841, 855, 56 Cal.Rptr.3d 151 ["the fundamental duty of the court is to assure the best interests of the child, whose bond with a foster parent may require that placement with a relative be rejected"]; *Tununak*, supra, 303 P.3d at pp. 451–452 [good cause depends on many factors, including the child's best interests]; *In Interest of A.E.* (Iowa 1997) 572 N.W.2d 579, 585 [good cause depends on a fact determinative analysis consisting of many factors, including the best interests of the child]; *In re Interest of Bird Head* (1983) 213 Neb. 741, 331 N.W.2d 785, 791 ["(ICWA) does not change the cardinal rule that the best interests of the child are paramount, although it may alter its focus."]; but see [*Matter of Custody of*] *S.E.G., supra*, 521 N.W.2d at pp. 362–363 [(Minn. Ct. App. 1993)] [holding that the good cause exception does not include the best interests of the child].) Based on the foregoing, we conclude the court erred in failing to consider whether, in light of the presumption that adherence to the placement preferences would usually be in a minor's best interests, Alexandria's best interests supported a finding of good cause.

* * *

A full year has passed since the court began its good cause hearing in July 2013, and circumstances may have changed in the interim. For example, Alexandria may have had additional opportunities to bond more strongly with the R.s, reducing the risk of detriment or trauma. Alternatively, her bond with the P.s may have become even more primary and strong. Because we reverse and remand, we emphasize that in determining whether good cause exists to depart from the placement preferences identified in section 1915(a), the court may consider facts and circumstances that have arisen since the filing of this appeal. (See, e.g., *In re B.C.* (2011) 192 Cal.App.4th 129, 150–151, 121 Cal.Rptr.3d 366 [reversing and remanding with clarification that in determining child's best interests, the court may consider events arising since the filing of the appeal].)

We recognize that a final decision regarding Alexandria's adoptive placement will be further delayed as a result of our determination of the merits of this appeal. That delay is warranted by the need to insure that the correct legal standard is utilized in deciding whether good cause has been shown that it is in the best interest of Alexandria to depart from the ICWA's placement preferences.

Notes

1. How do the cases of S.E.G. and Alexandria P. differ? Does it matter than Alexandria's placement was with a non-Indian family? Should children always be placed with family members regardless of the trauma of separation from a current placement? ICWA places great value on family placement, or kinship placement. What is the right of a child to be with her community? To know her family?

2. What the legal rights do the biological family of a child have to contact with her? This is discussed further in Chapter Four, but generally speaking, once a child is adopted, there are virtually no legal protections regarding her relationship with

any of her biological family. Some states recognize agreements after adoption, but the relationships are generally at the discretion of the adoptive family.

3. The fact pattern of *In re Alexandria P.* is a common one. Many times, the foster family geographically close to the parent is not an ICWA-compliant placement. Moving the child to her family would have meant the foreclosure of her relationship with her father. However, preventing her family from contacting her during reunification efforts seems strange, given that a child not in state care would be allowed to see any or all of her family. Is it in Alexandria P.'s best interests as a four year old to be with her family? What about when she is thirteen years old? What happens when she ages out of foster care? Would it be more beneficial for her to know her family then? In this case, her family was allowed to spend time with the child and introduce themselves as family using visits and technology. States call this practice "concurrent planning" and are supposed to engage in it to help children adjust to potential changes at permanency.

4. Children in foster care often have no rights to ensure that their relationships with their siblings continue when they are removed from their home. For example, only in 2016 did Michigan pass a bill requiring agencies to use "reasonable efforts" to keep siblings together. S. 483, 98th Leg., Reg. Sess. (Mich. 2016). A minority of states have laws guaranteeing that relationship:

> While the Federal Government through the Fostering Connections Act has taken a leadership role in mandating reasonable efforts to maintain sibling relationships, it is up to the States to vigorously support these connections. Between 2009 and 2011, 13 States passed statutes regarding sibling placement and visitation (National Conference on State Legislatures, 2012), and many others already had such statutes. There is often a gap, however, between what is considered best practice or what the law requires and what happens in day-to-day practice. Ultimately, the State courts will help define reasonable efforts by their decisions as to whether the requirement has been met in specific cases (Gustavsson & MacEachron, 2010).

Child Welfare Information Gateway, Sibling Issues in Foster Care and Adoption 3 (Jan. 2013). In the *Alexandria P.* case, by 2016, she had two siblings living with and near her relatives in Utah.

5. The foster parents in this case ultimately garnered extraordinary media attention in the months following a later decision. In that opinion, the court of appeals found that the move to her family in Utah was appropriate and in the girl's best interests. *In re Alexandria P.*, 204 Cal. Rptr. 3d 617 (Ct. App. 2016). The foster family then petitioned for a writ of certiorari to the United States Supreme Court, which was denied.

6. Who should be allowed to appeal these decisions? If every party except the potential, non-ICWA compliant, foster parents agree that an ICWA-compliant home is appropriate for a child, should the foster parents be allowed to appeal? What kind of considerations should a court make about standing in these situations? Does

California's practice of recognizing de facto parents help or hurt children? What is a de facto parent?

In re Brandon M.

63 Cal. Rptr. 2d 671 (Cal. Dist. Ct. App. 1st 1997)

[Three brothers were removed from their mother. An ex-stepfather to the oldest brother and biological father to the younger two wanted to take all three into his family. The mother appealed the court's determination that the stepfather was a de facto parent to the oldest son, and argued that California's de facto parent doctrine was preempted by ICWA. The appellate court held otherwise.]

The mother's appeal from the court's March 29 order granting de facto parent status to Roger H. is based entirely on a single premise: California's de facto parent doctrine is preempted by the federal Indian Child Welfare Act (25 U.S.C. §§ 1901–1923) (ICWA). Addressing this contention requires some brief review of (a) the doctrine of preemption, (b) California's de facto parent doctrine, and (c) the purpose and thrust of the ICWA.

The preemption doctrine derives from the supremacy clause of the United States Constitution which declares that the "Laws of the United States . . . shall be the supreme Law of the Land; and the Judges in every State shall be bound thereby, any thing in the Constitution or Laws of any State to the Contrary notwithstanding." (U.S. Const., art. VI, § 2.)

* * *

Preemption may arise in three ways. "'First, Congress can define explicitly the extent to which its enactments pre-empt state law.' 'Second, in the absence of explicit statutory language, state law is pre-empted where it regulates conduct in a field that Congress intended the Federal Government to occupy exclusively.' 'Finally, state law is pre-empted to the extent that it actually conflicts with federal law." *Smiley v. Citibank, supra*, 11 Cal.4th at p. 147, 44 Cal.Rptr.2d 441, 900 P.2d 690.

California's doctrine of de facto parent status is a judicially created doctrine, but one which is now spelled out in the California Rules of Court. Rule 1401(a)(4) provides: "'De facto parent' means a person who has been found by the court to have assumed, on a day-to-day basis, the role of parent, fulfilling both the child's physical and psychological needs for care and affection, and who has assumed that role for a substantial period." Cal. Rules of Court, rule 1401(a)(4).

Rule 1412(e) explains what this status means: "[De facto parents] Upon a sufficient showing the court may recognize the child's present or previous custodians as de facto parents and grant standing to participate as parties in disposition hearings and any hearing thereafter at which the status of the dependent child is at issue. The de facto parent may: (1) Be present at the hearing; (2) Be represented by retained counsel or, at the discretion of the court, by appointed counsel; (3) Present evidence." Cal. Rules of Court, rule 1412(e).

This doctrine stems from the case of *In re B.G.*, 523 P.2d 244 (Cal. 1974). Justice Baxter, writing almost two decades later in *In re Kieshia E.*, 859 P.2d 1290 (Cal. 1993), summarized the holding of that case as follows:

> "In *In re B.G.* this court established an important rule of procedure for child custody and dependency cases. We held that one who is not the child's parent or legal custodian, but who has become a 'de facto parent' by assuming that daily role over substantial time, may be privileged to participate as a party to the court proceedings."

Id. at pp. 70–71, 23 Cal.Rptr.2d 775, 859 P.2d 1290.

> "Alluding to a recent book on custody policy, we observed that a nonparent who has undertaken the parental role on a day-to-day basis, 'seeking to fulfill both the child's physical needs and his psychological need for affection and care[, may become the child's de facto parent].' We concluded that one who 'assumes the role of parent, raising the child in his own home,' may, in time, acquire an 'interest' which is 'substantial' in the '"companionship, care, custody, and management"' of the child.... Hence, we concluded, de facto parents should be permitted 'to appear as [full] parties,' not mere amici curiae, in a juvenile dependency proceeding. Their standing, we stressed, does not depend upon pending guardianship applications. Rather, we held, the fact of de facto parenthood alone should entitle them to intervene and protect their 'own interest' in the child's care and custody."

(*Id.* at pp. 75–76, 23 Cal.Rptr.2d 775, 859 P.2d 1290.)

Justice Baxter then articulated the present status of the doctrine in the following words:

> "The de facto parenthood doctrine simply recognizes that persons who have provided a child with daily parental concern, affection, and care over substantial time may develop legitimate interests and perspectives, and may also present a custodial alternative, which should not be ignored in a juvenile dependency proceeding. The standing accorded de facto parents has no basis independent of these concerns. Moreover, as we said in *In re B.G., supra*, the key to the privileged status of de facto parenthood is adherence to 'the role of parent,' both physical and psychological."

* * *

With this background, we come to the mother's contention that the ICWA preempts California's de facto parent doctrine as and when a court attempts to apply that doctrine to Indian children. It will be recalled that there are three ways federal law may be found to preempt state law: (1) by virtue of an express preemption clause in the federal law; (2) by "implied preemption," otherwise sometimes referred to as the "occupation of the field" by the federal government; or (3) by virtue of a conflict between the provisions of federal and state law.

It is clear that neither of the first two principles obtains here. In the first place, the federal law contains nothing at all by way of an express preemption provision. Second, it simply cannot be maintained that the ICWA in any way, manner, shape or form "occupies the field" of child custody or adoption, even as to Indian children. As respondent points out, the ICWA is totally devoid of any provisions dealing with, e.g., the bases on which a child may be removed from a parent's custody, when and how often hearings must be held to review a child's status, who is entitled to what reunification services and for how long, or many, many other similar issues.

Appellant's claim of preemption must, therefore, depend, and depend exclusively, upon a showing that there is a "conflict" between the California de facto parent principle and one or more provisions of the ICWA. Appellant asserts that such a conflict indeed exists and that it derives from the fact that, whereas de facto parent status may be conferred upon one who has no "biological or cultural relationship to the minor, such a designation does not fit within any of the categories of caretakers contemplated by the ICWA." She points out, among other things, that 25 United States Code section 1915(b), mandates that "[i]n any foster care or preadoptive placement, a preference shall be given, in the absence of good cause to the contrary, to a placement with—(i) a member of the Indian child's extended family; (ii) a foster home licensed, approved, or specified by the Indian child's tribe ..." etc. From this, appellant argues that "Congress clearly intended to prevent the placement of Indian children with non-Indian, non-biologically-related parties unless there was no alternative."

The United States Supreme Court's basic approach to preemption in alleged conflicts between Indian rights and status and state law was set forth most recently in *New Mexico v. Mescalero Apache Tribe* (1983) 462 U.S. 324, 103 S.Ct. 2378, 76 L.Ed.2d 611, where the court held that the application of New Mexico's hunting and fishing laws to even nonmembers of a tribe present on an Indian reservation was preempted by federal law and by the tribe's own regulatory scheme. It stated the general rule to be: "State jurisdiction is pre-empted by the operation of federal law if it interferes or is incompatible with federal and tribal interests reflected in federal law, unless the state interests at stake are sufficient to justify the assertion of state authority." (*Id.* at p. 334, 103 S.Ct. at p. 2386.) The court went on to recognize, however, that a State's interests "will be particularly substantial if the State can point to off-reservation effects. ..." (*Id.* at p. 336, 103 S.Ct. at p. 2388.)

Our colleagues in the Second District discussed this issue as it applied to the ICWA in the recent and leading case of *In re Bridget R.* (1996) 41 Cal.App.4th 1483, 49 Cal.Rptr.2d 507. They said: "The principles of tribal self-government, grounded in notions of inherent sovereignty and in congressional policies, seek an accommodation between the interests of the tribes and the federal government on the one hand, and those of the states, on the other. [Citation.] Thus, the United States Supreme Court has held nonreservation Indians are generally subject to nondiscriminatory and generally applicable state laws '[a]bsent express federal law to the contrary.' Even on Indian reservations, state laws generally may be applied insofar as they do not interfere with reservation self-government or essential internal tribal affairs, or impair a right reserved by federal law. Jurisdiction over matters of family relations is traditionally reserved to the states. Thus, where it is contended that a federal law must override state law on a matter relating to family relations, it must be shown that application of the state law in question would do '"major damage" to "clear and substantial federal interests."'" (*Id.* at p. 1510, 49 Cal.Rptr.2d 507.)

We do not believe that any "major damage" can or will be done to either federal law or Indian tribal law, custom, status or rights, as the same are posited in the ICWA, from the application of California's de facto parent doctrine in this case. Congress clearly intended that its 1978 statute exist side-by-side with the child custody laws of the 50 states and necessarily understood that the courts of those states would and should attempt to harmonize, not presume conflicts between, the two. The drafters of the California Rules of Court were clearly of a similar frame of mind because, shortly following the very same rules that articulate the de facto parent principle (Cal. Rules of Court, rules 1401(a)(4) and 1412(e)), there appears almost in haec verba the ICWA, reduced to a California court rule. (See Cal. Rules of Court, rule 1439.) We have great difficulty with the proposition that we can or should readily find conflict between one California juvenile court rule and two others.

Nor can we in point of fact. The relevant provision of the ICWA on which appellant relies is section 1915(b) which, as noted above, provides that, "in the absence of good cause to the contrary," preference in foster or preadoptive placement be given to "(i) a member of the Indian child's extended family. . . ." (25 U.S.C. § 1915(b).) Section 1903(2) says the latter term "shall be as defined by the law or custom of the Indian child's tribe or, in the absence of such law or custom, shall be a person who has reached the age of eighteen and who is the Indian child's grandparent, aunt or uncle, brother or sister, brother-in-law or sister-in-law, niece or nephew, first or second cousin, or stepparent." (25 U.S.C. § 1903(2).)

There are several things that are, for present purposes, noteworthy about the combination of these two statutes. First, and referring to the definition of "extended family," it should be noted that Roger H. was once the "stepparent" of Brandon. Thus, although probably not now within the federal act's definition of "extended family," he clearly was in the recent past. Second, nothing in these sections, or any other provision of the ICWA for that matter, says that any of the people to whom preference should be given as custodians of an Indian child must be of Indian heritage themselves. Third, and perhaps most importantly, the language and tenor of section 1915(b) manifestly bespeaks flexibility: it provides only for a "preference," notes that even the preference gives way when there is "good cause to the contrary," and is preceded by an opening sentence which provides that a child "shall be placed in the least restrictive setting which most approximates a family and in which his special needs, if any, may be met." (25 U.S.C. § 1915(b).) This language hardly suggests a congressional intention to mandate maintenance of a connection with the pertinent Indian tribe when all other factors point in the opposite direction.

In any event, the de facto parent doctrine is substantially consistent with the spirit of these provisions and not at all in conflict with their letter. It is, in effect, the ICWA's "extended family" definition made more flexible. Put another way, marrying the de facto parent doctrine and the pertinent ICWA sections means, and means only, that the scope of the persons to whom preference should be given for custody (or, for that matter, for adoption—see 25 U.S.C., § 1915(a)) is expanded from the already broad definition of "extended family" found in section 1903(2) to a group that includes those encompassed by that definition and the persons embraced by the California de facto parent definition. That is not a conflict. It is, at most, a relatively minor expansion of the definition and an expansion that does no violence to any mandate of the ICWA as to the blood line or cultural heritage of the persons who compose the "extended family."

We take special note of the fact that, in this case, the Tribe filed not one but two pleadings specifically endorsing the motion of Roger H. to be declared the de facto parent of Brandon. In one of these pleadings, the Tribe's counsel stated: "In the Tribe's opinion and in keeping with its traditions, the fact that Brandon is not the biological child of Mr. [H.] is not of great importance. If Brandon considers Mr. [H.] his father, then the Tribe will as well." Perhaps, as appellant argues, these statements do not rise to the level of a tribal "resolution" regarding a "different order of preference" (see 25 U.S.C. § 1915(c)), but they are nonetheless significant to us.

Notes

1. Not all states recognize de facto parent status. California is one of the only states that allow foster parents to achieve de facto parent status. In this case, the tribe approved the determination of the de facto parent. In other cases, the appointment of de facto parents have given those parties standing to contest a placement change in compliance with ICWA.

2. As discussed in Chapter Two, a best interests determination can be a particularly difficult one for a state court judge to evaluate. In the earlier case of *In re Alexandria P.*, every party except the foster parents felt it was in the child's best interest to be with her family. The foster parents were convinced it was in her best interests to be with them. The court of appeals later determined that an Indian child's best interest is a constellation of factors including her connection to her family and culture:

> While we reaffirm our earlier holding that a court should take an Indian child's best interests into account as one of the constellation of factors relevant to a good cause determination, we reject the P.s' argument that the best interests inquiry should exclude consideration of her connection to extended family or her cultural identity. We also caution against using the best interests concept as carte blanche to seize upon any showing as sufficient reason to depart from the ICWA's placement preferences.

In re Alexandria P., 204 Cal. Rptr. 3d 617, 634-5 (Ct. App. 2016).

In addition, the court warned that a "a good cause determination should not devolve into a standardless, free-ranging best interests inquiry." *Id.* at 633.

Brief of Amici Curiae National Latina/o Psychological Association, Asian-American Psychological Association, Association of Black Psychologists, and Society of Indian Psychologists in Support of Respondents

Adoptive Couple v. Baby Girl
570 U.S. 637
(March 27, 2013)

C. Petitioners and Their Amici's Narrow and Constrained View of Best Interests Analysis Does Not Comport with the Current State of Psychological Theory and the Statutory Requirements of ICWA.

The arguments of Petitioners and their amici also fail because they take an inappropriately narrow view of bonding and attachment. The proper analysis should not be so narrowly focused. South Carolina courts, for example, recognize that the best interests inquiry must consider a long list of factors. *Woodall v.Woodall*, 471 S.E.2d 154, 157 (S.C. 1996) (requiring a best interests inquiry to include "the character, fitness, attitude, and inclinations on the part of each parent as they impact the child," and the "psychological, physical, environmental, spiritual, educational, medical, family, emotional, and recreational aspects of the child's life"). By inflating the importance of bonding and attachment in best interests analysis, Petitioners and their amici risk missing the forest for the trees. Bonding and attachment are relevant, but only for one aspect of the analysis. See *In re Adoption of Halloway*, 732 P.2d 962, 971-72 (Utah 1986) ("While stability in child placement should be a paramount value, it cannot be the sole yardstick by which the legality of a particular custodial arrangement is judged."). Further, while bonding and attachment are relevant, it is clear, as discussed above, that the position of Petitioners and their amici on the impact of bonding and attachment in this case is not correct under the prevailing scientific literature on child psychology and development.

In light of the fact that Indian culture must play an important role in best interests analysis under ICWA, bonding and attachment, or indeed any other isolated best interests factor, should not by definition be determinative. See *In re C.H.*, 997 P.2d at 783 ("The emotional attachment between a non-Indian custodian and an Indian child should not necessarily outweigh the interests of the Tribe and the child in having that child raised in the Indian community."); see also *In re Adoption of M.T.S.*, 489 N.W.2d 285, 288 (Minn. Ct. App. 1992) ("Under [the ICWA] standards, placing [Indian child] with [Indian grandmother] is presumptively in his best interests. Although the record indicates that the Nelsons provided [Indian child] with a loving foster home, the fact that separation from them will be initially painful to [Indian child] is not good cause to defeat the preference created by the ICWA."). The argument that bonding and attachment should not be afforded undue weight in the best interests analysis is strengthened in the context of Indian child custody determinations. See Judy C. Pearson & Jeffrey T. Child, *A Cross-Cultural Comparison of Parental and Peer Attachment Styles among Adult Children from the United States, Puerto Rico, and India*, 36 J. Intercultural Comm. Res. 15, 16 (2007) ("Attachment does not generalize across all co-cultures: relationships among attachment, and gender, ethnicity, and sexual orientation have been discovered."); see also Neckoway et al., *supra*, at 68 ("A number of researchers have pointed out that attachment theory makes assumptions, based on Western ideologies, regarding ideal dyadic relationships and preferred developmental outcomes based on the mother-infant bond. For instance, not all cultures expect mothers to be the sole caregiver nor do all cultures interpret the child's needs in the same way or have the same reactions to emotional expression, such as the meaning of an infant's cry. What surely must come into question then, is the universal applicability of attachment theory.").

Petitioners and their amici also argue for a reversal of the lower court's opinion on grounds that bonding and attachment should be afforded such weight as to be determinative in child custody cases. See Child Advocacy Organizations Br. 9-13; National Council for Adoption Br. 11-14. Such a reversal of the South Carolina court's decision also risks creating precedent that could lead to absurd results by focusing disproportionately on bonding and attachment. Consider for example, a child kidnapped immediately after birth. The child lives with the kidnapper for seven years, presumably bonding with the kidnapper, who is then discovered. At this point, society would surely say that the child should be taken away from the kidnapper, but the intractable adherence of Petitioners and their amici to bonding and attachment would invalidate any attempts to remove the child from the kidnapper's custody. Furthermore, a reversal of the lower court's decision would create an incentive for parties to deliberately ignore the purposes of ICWA and to engage in protracted litigation. In the present case, Birth Mother and Adoptive Couple declined to observe the requirements of ICWA, and instead moved to place Baby Girl with non-Indian parents in clear contradiction of ICWA preferences, despite Birth Mother's acknowledgement that she knew of Birth Father's Indian heritage. Thus, by failing even the preliminary requirements of ICWA, Adoptive Couple was afforded the opportunity to bond with Baby Girl over the course of the ensuing litigation. It would be an inequitable result to reward Adoptive Couple by relying on any attachment that may have occurred during the pending litigation. Such reliance would promote more and longer lawsuits in an area, child custody and parental rights, where litigation is often least desired. As a result, a reversal would reward parties for turning a blind eye to the requirements of federal law and would encourage more litigation. Surely such an outcome could not be within Congress' intent, and such an outcome would not be a practical and reasonable decision by this Court.

Note

This amicus brief was filed in a case discussed at length in chapter four, *Adoptive Couple v. Baby Girl*, 570 U.S. 637 (2013). That case involved the placement preferences for an adoptive placement. The father argued his child, if not placed with him, should be placed within the adoption placement preferences. 25 U.S.C. § 1915(a) (2012). The Court held that if there is no other party that has "formally sought" to adopt a child, the adoptive placement preferences do not apply. 570 U.S. 637, 654. Unfortunately, the Court did not define what "formally sought" entails. While practitioners have attempted to limit the case to voluntary proceedings, some states have argued it applies to both involuntary and voluntary cases.

Native Village of Tununak v. State of Alaska, Dept. of Health and Social Services

334 P.3d 165 (Alaska 2014)

This is the second appeal in a case that began in July 2008 when the Alaska Office of Children's Services (OCS) assumed custody of four-month-old Dawn from her parents. Dawn was found to be a child in need of aid (CINA). Dawn's parents were Alaska Natives and thus the protections and requirements of the Indian Child Welfare Act (ICWA) applied to the CINA case. One of ICWA's provisions establishes preferences for foster care and adoptive placement of an Indian child with a member of the child's extended family, with other members of the child's tribe, or with other Indian families.

Native Village of Tununak (the Tribe) intervened in Dawn's CINA case and submitted a list of potential placement options for Dawn, including Dawn's maternal grandmother, Elise, who lives in the village. Throughout much of the case, the parents and Tribe agreed there was good cause not to place Dawn with an ICWA preferred placement, and Dawn was eventually placed with the Smiths, non-Native foster parents who live in Anchorage.

The superior court terminated Dawn's parents' parental rights at a September 2011 trial, making Dawn eligible for adoption. The Tribe asserted that, given the termination of parental rights, there was no longer good cause to deviate from ICWA's placement preferences and objected to Dawn's continued placement in Anchorage. In November the Smiths filed a petition to adopt Dawn. At no point in the case did Elise file an adoption petition in the superior court.

The superior court conducted a placement hearing following the Tribe's objection to placement with the Smiths. Following testimony by a number of witnesses, including Elise, the court found that there was continued good cause to deviate from ICWA's adoptive placement preferences and again approved Dawn's placement with the Smiths. The court then granted the Smiths' adoption petition in March 2012. Dawn was almost four years old, and had lived with the Smiths for almost two and a half years.

* * *

We asked the parties to provide supplemental briefing and oral argument on the effect of the Supreme Court's *Baby Girl* [*Adoptive Couple v. Baby Girl*, 133 S. Ct.

2552, 186 L. Ed. 2d 729 (2013),] decision on the adoption appeal currently before us. We now hold that because the United States Supreme Court's decisions on issues of federal law bind state courts' consideration of federal law issues—including the Indian Child Welfare Act—the decision in *Baby Girl* applies directly to the adoptive placement case on remand and to this adoption appeal. We discern no material factual differences between the *Baby Girl* case and this case, so we are unable to distinguish the holding in *Baby Girl*. Because the Supreme Court's holding in *Baby Girl* is clear and not qualified in any material way, and because it is undisputed that Elise did not "formally [seek] to adopt" Dawn in the superior court, we conclude that, as in *Baby Girl*, "there simply is no 'preference' to apply[,] [as] no alternative party that is eligible to be preferred under § 1915(a) has come forward[,]" and therefore ICWA "§ 1915(a)'s [placement] preferences are inapplicable.

* * *

Dawn F. was born in Anchorage in March 2008. When she was four months old OCS assumed emergency custody and placed her in foster care in Anchorage. The Tribe formally intervened in Dawn's CINA case in August 2008 and submitted a list of potential foster placement options under Alaska Child in Need of Aid Rule 8(c)(7) for Dawn, including placement with her maternal grandmother, Elise F., who lived in Tununak. Elise discussed foster placement at meetings with OCS in July and September 2008, but OCS ruled her out as a potential placement because an adult son living with her at the time had a barrier-crime for placement purposes. OCS placed Dawn in a non-Native foster home to facilitate visitation with her mother, Jenn F., who lived in Anchorage.... In August 2009 Elise contacted OCS to report that her son had moved out; she confirmed that she still sought foster placement.

* * *

Also in December 2009 a representative from the Association of Village Council Presidents visited Elise's home in Tununak on OCS's behalf and noted potential hazards in the home that needed to be addressed before placement could occur. These included unsecured guns, cleaning supplies, medicine, and general clutter in the area that Elise planned to use as Dawn's bedroom. In February 2010 Elise assured OCS she would remedy these issues, and OCS asked Elise to arrange for a second home visit once she made the proposed changes.

In May 2010 Elise attended a visit with Jenn and Dawn and told an OCS social worker that she thought Jenn would complete substance abuse treatment; Elise did not seek foster placement at that time and had not remedied the issues in her home. OCS filed two petitions to terminate Jenn's parental rights: the first was denied in November 2010, and a second was filed in April 2011. At a status conference in February 2011 Elise was present telephonically, and she questioned the court about whether Dawn would be returned to Jenn. The court advised her in no uncertain terms that it was not safe for Dawn to return to Jenn's household given Jenn's continuing mental health issues and illegal drug use. The superior court ultimately terminated Jenn's parental rights in September 2011. Following termination the Tribe argued there was no longer good cause to deviate from ICWA's placement preferences, and a placement hearing was scheduled

* * *

All parties agree that we must decide the Tribe's challenge on appeal to the Smiths' adoption of Dawn in light of the Supreme Court's decision in *Baby Girl.* The State contends that "[b]ecause no one other than the Smiths formally sought to adopt Dawn, her adoption should be upheld under the controlling [*Baby Girl*] decision." The Smiths agree. The Tribe urges us to vacate the superior court's adoption decree and remand this matter for an adoptive placement determination based on our decision in Tununak I that required the superior court to find, under a clear and convincing evidence standard, whether there is good cause to deviate from ICWA § 1915(a)'s placement preferences. The Tribe takes the position that: (1) *Baby Girl* is factually distinguishable and inapplicable to state-driven child protection cases; (2) to the extent *Baby Girl* does apply, it merely requires that a specific family be formally identified as desiring placement of the Native child and Elise satisfied that requirement in this case; and (3) the requirement is satisfied in Alaska as soon as a tribe intervenes in the case and makes formal CINA Rule 8(c)(7) disclosures.

Finally, the Tribe contends that, if we interpret *Baby Girl* to mean that ICWA's placement preferences are inapplicable until an alternative adoptive family files a competing adoption petition, this decision will have disastrous results for rural Alaska, placing the largest burden on Native families with the fewest legal and financial resources, and create a dangerous disincentive for OCS, as the agency will place Native children in the first available home, thereby neutering the protections that ICWA originally sought to provide to promote the preservation of the Indian family.

The Tribe's interpretation of *Baby Girl*, as echoed by the dissent, strains the plain wording of a clear, unequivocal, and unqualified decision on a matter of federal law as interpreted by the United States Supreme Court. For the reasons that follow, we conclude that we are required to apply the Supreme Court's bright-line interpretation of ICWA § 1915(a)'s placement preferences to bar from consideration as an adoptive placement an individual who has taken no formal step to adopt the child.

A. ICWA § 1915(a) and *Baby Girl* Do Not Distinguish A State-Initiated Child Custody Proceeding From A Voluntary Private Adoption.

ICWA § 1915(a)'s placement preferences apply to "any adoptive placement of an Indian child under State law," and ICWA defines adoptive placements broadly as "the permanent placement of an Indian child for adoption, including any action resulting in a final decree of adoption." The federal statute does not distinguish between state-initiated child protection cases and voluntary adoptions. The Supreme Court in *Baby Girl* also did not carve out such a distinction. In *Baby Girl*, the Supreme Court held without qualification that § 1915(a), "which provides placement preferences for the adoption of Indian children, does not bar a non-Indian family like Adoptive Couple from adopting an Indian child when no other eligible candidates have sought to adopt the child." The Court emphasized that the "scope" of § 1915(a) has a "critical limitation," namely, that " § 1915(a)'s preferences are inapplicable in cases where no alternative party has formally sought to adopt the child." The Court reiterated, "This is because there simply is no 'preference' to apply if no alternative party that is eligible to be preferred under § 1915(a) has come forward." To make its rationale perfectly clear, the Court again explained that, because Adoptive Couple was the only family that "sought to adopt Baby Girl," § 1915(a)'s "rebuttable adoption preferences [did not] apply [because] no alternative party . . . formally sought to adopt the child." As a policy matter, the Court broadly concluded that while ICWA "was enacted to help preserve the cultural identity and heritage of Indian tribes," to require a placement preference determination for a party who did not seek to adopt "would put certain vulnerable children at a great disadvantage solely because an ancestor—even a remote one—was an Indian." The Court cautioned that such a result may cause "prospective adoptive parents [to] . . . pause before adopting any child who might possibly qualify as an Indian under the ICWA."

* * *

If in *Baby Girl* the Court had intended to limit its holding to voluntary adoptions, it certainly could have articulated such a restriction. But no such limiting language appears in the Court's opinion in *Baby Girl*. Because the Court did not limit its holding in *Baby Girl* to voluntary adoptions, we reject the Tribe's and the dissent's attempt to factually distinguish *Baby Girl* from the case before us where the adoption resulted from state-initiated child protective proceedings.

B. Elise Did Not Formally Seek To Adopt Dawn.

We are "not bound by decisions of federal courts other than the United States Supreme Court on questions of federal law." But in cases where the Supreme Court has decided a question of federal law that is directly applicable to and binding on the case we are to decide, we "owe obedience to the decisions of the Supreme Court of the United States . . . and a judgment of the Supreme Court provides the rule to be followed . . . until the Supreme Court sees fit to reexamine it."

* * *

The critical piece, however, is Elise's failure to formally assert her intent to adopt Dawn as OCS moved toward terminating Jenn's parental rights. The superior court denied OCS's first petition to terminate parental rights in November 2010, and a second petition was filed in April 2011 that ultimately resulted in termination in September 2011. At a status conference in February 2011 the superior court advised Elise that placement with Jenn was not a viable option due to Jenn's continued mental health and drug issues. And when the Smiths filed a formal petition to adopt Dawn on November 3, 2011, Elise did not file a competing adoption petition or any other formal request that might serve as a proxy for such a petition. In other words, knowing that the Smiths had the only legally viable request for adoption before the court at that time, Elise did not file a competing request to be considered an adoptive parent for Dawn prior to the placement hearing.

Elise did appear at the November 14, 2011 placement hearing and testified that she wanted to adopt Dawn. She also testified that she had filed a formal adoption petition herself in Bethel. From the record developed by the parties both in the superior court and in this court, there is no indication that Elise filed an adoption petition or otherwise filed any formal court document demonstrating her intent to adopt Dawn. In its briefing to us the Tribe conceded that no court petition was filed. The superior court found Elise's testimony on her desire to adopt "less than convincing," observing that Elise also said that she wanted to adopt Dawn because the Tribe wanted her to and pointing out that she had maintained almost no contact with Dawn and knew nothing of Dawn's life in Anchorage. The superior court made this credibility determination and our role as the reviewing court is not to reweigh the evidence on this point, but instead to "review a trial court's decision in light of the evidence presented to that court."

In *Baby Girl*, Biological Father displayed a much higher level of involvement, but the Supreme Court nonetheless found his efforts insufficient. Biological Father requested a stay of the adoption proceedings after learning of Adoptive Couple's pending request and sought custody of Baby Girl. He participated in a trial in the South Carolina Family Court and was awarded custody, had that custody order affirmed by the South Carolina Supreme Court, and participated in the appeal before the United States Supreme Court. Notwithstanding this active participation by Biological Father at every level of the state and federal litigation, the Supreme Court still found that "he did not seek to adopt Baby Girl; instead, he argued that his parental rights should not be terminated in the first place." In other words, because Biological Father did not "formally [seek] to adopt" Baby Girl, the Supreme Court held that he could not be an ICWA preferred placement—he was not an "alternative party" that triggered § 1915(a)'s adoptive preferences.

Applying the Supreme Court's controlling precedent to the facts before us, it is clear that this is also a case where "there simply is no 'preference' to apply [as] no alternative party that is eligible to be preferred under § 1915(a) has come forward" to adopt Dawn. Because the Smiths were the only family that, in the words of the Supreme Court, "formally sought to adopt" Dawn, § 1915(a)'s "rebuttable adoption preferences [do not] apply [because] no alternative party has formally sought to adopt [this] child." In short, we are bound by *Baby Girl*'s interpretation of this subsection of ICWA, and cannot ignore the Supreme Court's clear, unqualified ruling on a matter of federal Indian law.

D. The Tribe's Policy Considerations

Finally, the Tribe argues that if we interpret *Baby Girl* to hold that ICWA's placement preferences are inapplicable until an alternative Native adoptive family member files a competing adoption petition, this decision will place a difficult burden on Native families, which have the fewest legal and financial resources, and create a dangerous incentive for OCS to place Native children in the first available home "except in the rare case when a Native family files its own adoption petition." The dissent echoes the Tribe's concerns, noting that "at least one state practice guide" does not read *Baby Girl* to mean an adoption petition must be filed; rather, all the practice guide cautions is that the adoptive candidate "formally" assert his or her intent to adopt the child and take "proper steps" to convey these intentions to the court.

But the dissent misses the point of the practice guide. The practice guide concludes that "[f]or practitioners representing a parent of an Indian child who wants assurances that his or her child will be placed with another family or tribal member if adoption is needed, the lesson is clear: identify early on any family members, relatives, or tribal members who are willing and desirous of custody and take proper steps to formally convey their intentions to the court in this regard." As we have explained, we read *Baby Girl* to mean that filing a petition for adoption is "formally" asserting an intent to adopt using the "proper steps." And while we do not disregard the Tribe's policy concerns, neither may we disregard the holding of the Supreme Court on this matter of federal law.

Having said this, we urge tribes and OCS to enable and assist tribal members to seek placement early in CINA and voluntary adoption cases, accompanied by a formal adoption petition once it appears that OCS's goal for the child is adoption. The Alaska Court System, attorneys representing tribes in Alaska, the CINA bar, the probate bar, and others will work to develop appropriate adoption forms and online information and instructions to assist tribes and potential adoptive parents in navigating this requirement.

We also stress that OCS remains bound to comply with § 1915(a)'s adoptive placement preferences for "(1) a member of the child's extended family; (2) other members of the Indian child's tribe; or (3) other Indian families." And our decision in Tununak I directs that "OCS must prove by clear and convincing evidence that there is good cause to deviate from ICWA § 1915(a)'s adoptive placement preferences." Implicit in this holding is the understanding that before the court entertains argument that there is good cause to deviate from § 1915(a)'s preferred placements, it must searchingly inquire about the existence of, and OCS's efforts to comply with achieving, suitable § 1915(a) preferred placements. Contrary to the dissent's suggestion, today's decision has no bearing on OCS's duty to comply with the express purpose of ICWA "to promote the stability and security of Indian tribes and families." We anticipate that our decisions in Tununak I and today will highlight the importance of OCS identifying early in a CINA case all potential preferred adoptive placements, and the importance of a person claiming preferred placement filing a petition for adoption, in order to effectuate Congress's intent "to protect the rights of the Indian child as an Indian and the rights of the Indian community and tribe in retaining its children in its society."

Notes

1. Is the Alaska Supreme Court's reasoning persuasive? How would a biological father seek to formally adopt his own child? What does it mean to file a formal adoption for a child in foster care? What should a grandmother have to do to express her willingness to care for her grandchild?

2. The distinctions between a voluntary and involuntary proceeding are substantial. In a voluntary proceeding, relatives are not hoping for reunification between a parent and child in the way they might be in an involuntary one. In this case, Elise was hopeful Dawn could be placed back with her mother. Elise's involvement in the case could only happen after the court decided Dawn could not be placed with her mother.

3. Often the facts of life on the ground in Alaska are lost in court opinions. Elise lived in the Village of Tununak while her daughter and granddaughter lived in Anchorage. Tununak is located on Nelson Island in the Bering Sea, which is 511 miles, as the crow flies, from Anchorage. Indeed, flying is the only way to get to Anchorage, as there are no roads to Tununak, other than a trail to the village of Toksook Bay, which is on the same island. Tununak is at least a four hour flight to Anchorage, with two stops, depending on flight schedules. The flight costs between $500-$800. The Tununak airport has one unattended gravel runway. How reasonable is it to compare Elise's involvement in her granddaughter's life in Anchorage with the father's involvement in *Adoptive Couple v. Baby Girl* (involving travel between the states of Oklahoma and South Carolina)? How would Elise, who is not appointed legal counsel, formally seek to adopt her granddaughter?

4. As a result of this case, Alaska passed a law that, among other things, changed its adoption rules regarding a formal petition for adoption:

> LEGISLATIVE FINDINGS AND INTENT.
>
> The legislature finds that
>
> (1) all children in state custody should be close to home and with extended family members whenever possible; and
>
> (2) because of the number of Alaska Native children in state custody, there is a need to provide an individual seeking immediate permanent placement of an Indian child in state custody with additional flexibility to preserve and apply the placement preferences outlined in the Indian Child Welfare Act of 1978 (25 U.S.C. 1901–1963) with respect to that individual.
>
> * * *
>
> "proxy for a formal petition" or "proxy" means
>
> (A) a request by a person who is interested in immediate permanent placement and adoption or legal guardianship of a child, and is an extended family member, member of an Indian child's tribe, or other Indian family

member, made at any court hearing or conveyed to the department by telephone, mail, facsimile, electronic mail, or in person;

(B) in the case of an Indian child, a request made to the department on behalf of a person described in (A) of this paragraph by

(i) the Indian child's biological parent, individually or through counsel; or

(ii) the Indian child's tribe, a tribe in which the Indian child is eligible for enrollment, or a tribe in which the Indian child's biological parent is a member; or

(C) a proxy for a formal petition, as established by the department by regulation.

ALASKA STAT. § 47.10.112(h)(2) (2016).

Chapter 4

Voluntary Proceedings

Voluntary relinquishments, private adoptions, voluntary guardianships—all of these proceedings are governed by different state laws than those governing child abuse and neglect. They are all, however, governed in some ways by ICWA or by state Indian child welfare laws. This area of the law involves some of the most private and intimate interests of the birth parent, adoptive parent, the child, and the tribe. How courts weigh those interests, which are at times diametrically opposed, varies by state. However, a long history of concerns over the level of voluntary-ness to these proceedings has led both tribes and some states to increase protections of children and parents to ensure parents have due process rights and are able to give true consent when giving up their children for others to raise them. For many years, social service agencies used voluntary relinquishments to avoid formal court proceedings to remove children.

Foster Care—In Whose Best Interest?

43 Harv. Educ. Rev. 599 (1973)
Robert H. Mnookin

No national statistics are available to indicate what proportion of the children in foster care have been removed because of state coercion. When parents oppose foster care placement, a court can nevertheless order removal alter a judicial proceeding if the state can demonstrate parental abuse or neglect. But if parents consent to foster care placement, no judicial action is necessary. Many foster care placements, perhaps one-half or more, are arranged by state social welfare departments without any court involvement. In California, for example, the State Social Welfare Board estimated recently that one-half of the children in state-sponsored foster care were "voluntary" placements where the parent(s) consented to relinquish custody without a formal court proceeding. A study in New York City found that 58 percent of the natural parents of foster children had agreed to foster care placement.

A substantial degree of state coercion may be involved in many so-called voluntary placements, making the distinction between voluntary and coercive placement illusory. Many social welfare departments routinely ask parents to agree to give up their children before initiating neglect proceedings in court. Some parents who would have been willing to keep their children may consent to placement to avoid a court proceeding against them. If one were to use the legal standards of voluntariness and informed consent applied in the criminal law to confessions and to the waiver of important legal rights, many cases of relinquishment after state intervention might not be considered voluntary. On the other hand, not all court-ordered foster care placements involve coercion of the parents. Some take place with their full concurrence. In some cases State welfare agencies require even parents who desire to place their children in foster care to go through a court proceeding. There is a financial incentive for the State to do this because under the Social Security Act, a state can be partially reimbursed by the federal government only if a court orders placement. Although it is unrealistic to make precise estimates given the complexities just outlined, I would judge that at least 100,000 children around the country are now in foster care because of coercive state intervention. Whatever their exact number, the state's role in placing them in foster care suggests a significant social responsibility.

Notes

1. Coercive state practices were even worse in Indian country, and were addressed extensively in the legislative record of ICWA:

> The employment of voluntary waivers by many social workers means that many child welfare cases do not go through any kind of a judicatory process at all. The Indian person has to come to a welfare agency for help; that welfare agency is in the position to coerce that family into surrendering the children through a voluntary waiver.
>
> The Indian family is also placed in jeopardy by the fact of going to a welfare department for help, just to get enough money to live on and money that they're entitled to under law. This exposes that family to the investigations of the welfare worker to see how that family conducts itself; and, welfare departments originate most of the complaints against Indian families and exercise a kind of police power.
>
> We think this is an inappropriate way of administering the laws. There are certain economic incentives for removing Indian children. Agencies that are established to place Indian children have a vested interest in finding Indian children to place. It's interesting to note that in many cases, the rate of non-Indian people applying for Indian children for foster care, or especially adoptive care, rises dramatically when there is an Indian claims settlement.

Problems that American Indian Families Face in Raising their Children and how these Problems are Affected by Federal Action or Inaction, 93rd Cong. 5 (1974) (Statement of William Byler, Executive Director, Association on American Indian Affairs).

2. The provisions in ICWA that apply to private or voluntary proceedings are the subject of intense litigation. 25 U.S.C. § 1913 is titled "Parental rights; voluntary termination" and provides basic due process rights to the parents. These rights include a waiting period before they can give consent, the right to have the consent explained by a judge in a language the parents understand, and the right to revoke consent any time prior to the adoption. In addition, if the consent was obtained through fraud or duress, the parents have two years to petition the court to vacate

the adoption. Some of these protections are considerably higher than applicable state laws. In addition, under 25 U.S.C. § 1914, the child's parent and tribe have the right to invalidate any action that violates the protections in § 1913.

However, whether other provisions of ICWA that protect the child's right to her community and culture, or the tribe's right to ensure the safety of tribal children, apply is less clear when it comes to voluntary proceedings. For example, the notice provision is only required in "involuntary" proceedings. However, without any discussion with the child's tribe, it may be impossible to determine if the law applies, or if the state court has proper jurisdiction. In addition, the tribe's right of intervention and the application of the placement preferences is difficult to achieve without letting the tribe know about the case.

Even immediately after the passage of ICWA, there were concerns about these inconsistencies in the federal law.

The 1985 Minnesota Family Preservation Act: Claiming a Cultural Identity

Kathryn A. Carver
4 Law & Ineq. 327 (1986)

* * *

The 1984 Minn. ICWA, introduced in March 1984 and defeated in April of the same year, proposed to give Indian tribes, through Indian courts, an expanded role in voluntary and involuntary child placements. The Act, detailed in section II, addressed the growing problem of Indian children being placed in non-Indian institutions, foster or adoptive homes, primarily due to involuntary foster care removal but also through voluntary foster care and eventually, adoption proceedings. Nationally the removal rate for Indian children has reached alarmingly high proportions. From 1969 to 1974, national statistics showed that 25% to 35% of Indian children were separated from their families. It appears that out-of-home placement is a favored policy in Minnesota. Figures for Minnesota during the same time period reported that one in eight Indian children under age eighteen was in an adoptive placement, and one in four Indian children under the age of one year was adopted. These figures did not improve even with the passage of the federal ICWA in 1978. In 1982 the United States Department of Health and Human Services compiled a report from a national one-day count of children in foster care placements. For Indian children under the age of twenty-one, Minnesota ranked first nationally in out-of-home placement although the state ranked eleventh nationally in the size of its population of Indian children. Despite the small population of Indian children, Minnesota has an Indian foster care placement rate, known as a point prevalence rate, of 345 per 10,000 Indian children. By comparison, Arizona, which had the largest population of Indian children, had a placement rate of only 10 per 10,000 Indian children.

To put Minnesota's placement rate of 345 for Indian children into context, Minnesota's placement rate was 177 for Black children, 37 for white children, and 32 for Hispanic children. Those figures rank Minnesota respectively fifth, ninth, and in the top forty percent nationally.

* * *

II. The 1984 Minnesota Indian Child Welfare Act

* * *

The 1984 Minn. ICWA was the first piece of Minnesota state legislation introduced to deal specifically with the placement of Indian children in non-Indian homes. The Minn. ICWA grew out of concern for the shortcomings of the existing laws. When the Act was considered, two pieces of legislation partially addressed Indian adoption issues in Minnesota: the federal Indian Child Welfare Act (federal ICWA) and the Minnesota Heritage Child Protection Act (Minn. HCPA). The federal statute, passed in 1978, was designed "[t]o establish standards for the placement of Indian children in foster or adoptive homes, [and] to prevent the break up of Indian families." The Minn. HCPA, which became law in 1983, addressed similar issues in the adoption of minority children in Minnesota by requiring consideration of the ethnic background of a child during adoption proceedings. Undoubtedly, the Minn. HCPA, like the federal ICWA, originated from a concern over temporary and permanent removal of minority children from their homes and their placement in nonminority foster or adoptive care.

The federal ICWA was specifically intended to reduce the high rate of removal of Indian children from their homes. The intent of the Act was to change the criteria applied in making the removal decisions by changing the agencies and forums involved in making those decisions. The federal ICWA provided for exclusive Indian tribal jurisdiction over child welfare proceedings involving Indian children who reside or are domiciled on Indian reservations and authorized the transfer of proceedings involving Indian children living off the reservation, from state courts to tribal jurisdiction.

Although the federal ICWA laid important groundwork, the Act did not go far enough because it did not sufficiently cover voluntary foster care, preadoptive, and adoptive placements. In cases of voluntary consent to foster care placement or the termination of parental rights, the Act requires only that the parental consent be in writing and accompanied by the judge's affidavit that the consequences of the consent were explained and understood. If the identity or location of any of the parties is unknown, the court can comply with the Act by sending notice to the Secretary of the Interior. There is no requirement of notice to tribal social service agencies. Many times the parent or parents do not know that prior to a final termination of parental rights, they have the right to withdraw consent and request the return of their child. Once the final decree of adoption has been entered, the parent must prove fraud or duress to have the decree vacated.

Many of the Indian children removed from their homes each year are "voluntary" placements made by the parents. These placements occur when parents are told that unless the child is "voluntarily" turned over to the social welfare agency for a temporary placement, the child will be permanently removed by court proceedings. The welfare agency's rationale is that parents are given a certain period of time to prove they are fit to care for the child. Problems occur because the parents are unaware of their rights and options during the temporary, voluntary placement. For example, parents frequently do not know that they have visiting rights during voluntary placements. Not visiting a child in temporary placement may be viewed by welfare personnel as lack of interest in the child, leading to permanent removal.

The Minnesota Heritage Child Protection Act did not remedy the federal ICWA's narrow notice requirements for voluntary removals and placements. The Minn. HCPA only required that the appropriate state agencies take the child's cultural heritage into account before deciding on a placement. There was no provision for active tribal involvement in the placement decisions of Indian children. More importantly, there was no provision for tribal input prior to making removal decisions.

* * *

The goal of the 1985 Minn. IFPA, and of the 1984 proposed ICWA, was to inform local judges and referees of the federal ICWA and to strengthen that law. The state laws strove to make the federal law more powerful by addressing its shortcomings. The 1984 Minn. ICWA especially strengthened those provisions of the federal law which dealt with voluntary placements leading to adoption. It was this emphasis that defeated the 1984 Minn. ICWA. Therefore, the drafters of the 1985 bill made the strategic decision to remove the language that dealt with adoption. Although this meant a lost opportunity to strengthen the federal Act, this decision did not greatly compromise the goal of the legislation because the federal Act already had language, albeit not as strong as advocates would have liked, which addressed adoption. Instead, the 1985 Act concentrates on strengthening the provisions of the federal ICWA that deal with foster care. The Minn. IFPA sections on foster care are more comprehensive than their earlier counterparts in the federal ICWA. The new Minnesota law distinguishes between voluntary foster care placements and involuntary foster care placements and requires social service agencies and private child placing agencies to provide notice to the child's tribe in cases of any potential out-of-home placement (involuntary foster care), voluntary foster care, or any *potential* preadoptive or adoptive placement.

The effect of these distinctions is to ensure tribal involvement before the decision is made to place the child out of the home. This will prevent culturally biased removals and work toward keeping the Indian family together. In the case of voluntary foster care placement, the notice provision ensures that the parent understands the nature of the out-of-home placement.

The Minn. IFPA also provides for the immediate return of a child in voluntary foster care placement to his or her parents. Where the federal law only permits the parents to withdraw consent anytime prior to the final termination or adoption decree, under state law the parents may secure return of their child within twenty-four hours of their request. This prevents loss of custody due to bureaucracy and ensures that parents receive the information they need to reclaim their children.

Moreover, because the 1985 IFPA regulates foster care, its effects are nearly the same as if it covered adoption. The temporary nature or impermanence of foster care is a myth. Sometimes long-term foster care is the permanent placement goal rather than adoption. In fact, long-term foster care has been a much more common goal for Minnesota children than for children nationwide. Although foster care was originally intended, and is still frequently thought of, as a temporary placement option, the reality is that a substantial number of children will remain in foster care even after it is clear the child cannot return to his or her biological parent. Minority children spend a longer time in foster care than white children. Because of the length of time a child might spend in foster care, an Indian foster care placement can be as important for an Indian child's cultural identity as an Indian adoptive placement.

The 1985 IFPA has an early-notice provision so the tribe becomes involved before the process of termination of parental rights begins. This allows all the tribal resources to be brought to bear in a timely fashion to aid in counseling the family and in making an appropriate foster care placement for the child. This early involvement of the tribe is the most important distinction between the federal ICWA and the 1985 Minn. IFPA. The 1985 Act also makes the identification of extended family members the responsibility of any agency considering placement of an Indian child. It is important to look to the extended family members because they are an integral part of child rearing in Indian communities.

* * *

In their final effort, the proponents sought to meet the objections of those who had opposed the law in 1984. This meant addressing those concerns for race-blind adoptions voiced by Representative Skoglund and his supporters, most notably those adoption agencies which specialize in overseas, interracial adoptions. Some adoption agencies felt threatened by the adoption provisions because there was concern that limiting the interracial adoption of Indian children would open the door to similar restrictions on other racial or ethnic groups. Open-adoption policy advocates felt this was a return to the "segregationist" policies of the 1950's. This approach to Indian adoption ignores North American Indians' unique legal status in the United States and persists in viewing Indians as a racial classification rather than as a political and legal entity. Separate treatment of Indians is not an equal protection violation because it is not based on race, but on political status. Therefore, Indian adoption policy cannot set a precedent for other racial minority children.

Supporters of the Act ascertained the position of adoption agencies early in the push for the 1985 Act, and used a combination of confrontation, compromise, education, and emotional public testimony to counter much of the adoption agency opposition to the law. This process took several forms depending on the activity. The confrontation entailed just that-asking adoption agencies and advocates directly to determine where they stood on the Act and to educate them about the issues involved in Indian adoption so that the agencies would support the Act. Certainly the compromises changing the language and focus from adoption to foster care went a long way in accomplishing that goal.

Nevertheless, the most important and effective tools for educating the public about the 1984 Minn. ICWA and for gaining the adoption agencies' support for the 1985 Minn. IFPA were the Indian speakouts at many of the subcommittee hearings and meetings. In the speakouts, Indian adults recounted what growing up in a non-Indian, white adoptive home had done to them and their sense of self. For many it was a devastating experience to try to come to terms with their Indian status. Indian adults raised in non-Indian homes reported a profound sense of isolation coupled with a complete lack of Indian identity. These feelings are often labeled the "Apple Syndrome," where during adolescence, Indian children raised in white homes as white, come to a sense of their ethnic and racial differences from their adoptive parents. Without any knowledge of their own cultural history and identity, these Indian children feel they have nowhere to belong. As adults they are left knowing they are not white, but do not quite feel they are Indian because they lack any knowledge of the ceremonies, customs, and religion that make up their cultural identity. These Indian children are raised without the sense of tribal affiliation which is an integral part of Indian self-knowledge and identity.

Notes

1. Minnesota was only the second state to pass a state ICWA law. Oklahoma was the first, in 1982. Since then, many states have passed some kind of an ICWA provision into state law, but a few have passed comprehensive state ICWA statutes. The issue of voluntary proceedings in both state and federal law remains a sticking point, primarily between tribes and adoption attorneys, more than thirty years after this article was written. Minnesota changed its law in 1999 to include voluntary proceedings in its notice and intervention provisions. MINN. STAT § 260.761 (2016). During a run of ICWA challenges in 2015–2016, these provisions were challenged by biological parents in Minnesota federal district court as being violative of the biological parent's right to privacy. *Doe v. Piper*, No. 15-cv-02639 (D. Minn. June 3, 2015). The case was dismissed as moot. *Doe v. Piper*, 2017 U.S. Dist. LEXIS 124308 (D. Minn. Aug. 4, 2017).

2. The Indian Adoption Project (IAP) was a federal government program to encourage non-Indian families to adopt Indian children. As Margaret Jacobs writes,

> . . . instead of working with American Indians to define and address the roots of their problems, many liberal Americans turned to the "rescue" of individual Indian children. As in the past, then, many compassionate white Americans unwittingly supported and participated in a devastating government policy and practice—the removal of Indian children from their families and communities.

Margaret Jacobs, A Generation Removed 39-40 (2014).

While the official IAP ultimately affected a relatively small number of Native children, its influence spread rapidly, and encouraged other religiously affiliated groups to "create their own adoption programs for Indian children.... Lutheran Social Services of South Dakota started its own Special Child Placement Project in 1965 and placed 305 Indian children in 240 white families up to 1976." *Id.* at 49. These actions by public, private, and religious agencies have led to extraordinary suspicion of their motives from tribes and their citizens. The increasing cost of domestic private adoption, and the occasional posting from a private adoption agency of the "cost" of a child based on her race, continues to drive suspicion of agency motives.

3. In addition, the "rescue" view of adopting American Indian children led to a pernicious legal argument that views "individual Indian children as the victim of racism, not the Indian family or tribal community . . . [P]olicymakers and welfare workers claimed that Indian children were denied racial equality, not because their communities still suffered from colonial policies on the part of the U.S. government that had deepened poverty and inequality, but because they lacked the opportunity to be adopted." *Id.* at 51. This same reasoning, applied to Native children in foster care, was the legal argument behind *A.D. v. Washburn*, No. 15-cv-01259 (D. Ariz. July 6, 2015), a case arguing ICWA is unconstitutional and discussed further in Chapter Five. The case was dismissed for a lack of standing. *A.D. v. Washburn*, 2017 U.S. Dist. LEXIS 38060, 2017 WL 1019685 (D. Ariz. March 16, 2017).

4. Because of this history, ICWA's provisions on voluntary proceedings primarily protect the due process rights of biological parents, and are sometimes less clear on the rights of tribes. Section 1913 of ICWA is titled "Parental rights; voluntary termination," and provides nation-wide federal protections to birth parents placing their children voluntarily. There are some states that have higher statutory protections than ICWA, but many with much lower protections of birth parents.

> **(a) Consent; record; certification matters; invalid consents**
>
> Where any parent or Indian custodian voluntarily consents to a foster care placement or to termination of parental rights, such consent shall not be valid unless executed in writing and recorded before a judge of a court of competent jurisdiction and accompanied by the presiding judge's certificate that the terms and consequences of the consent were fully explained in detail and were fully understood by the parent or Indian custodian. The court shall also certify that either the parent or Indian custodian fully understood the explanation in English or that it was interpreted into a language that the parent or Indian custodian understood. Any consent given prior to, or within ten days after, birth of the Indian child shall not be valid.
>
> **(b) Foster care placement; withdrawal of consent**
>
> Any parent or Indian custodian may withdraw consent to a foster care placement under State law at any time and, upon such withdrawal, the child shall be returned to the parent or Indian custodian.

> **(c) Voluntary termination of parental rights or adoptive placement; withdrawal of consent; return of custody**
>
> In any voluntary proceeding for termination of parental rights to, or adoptive placement of, an Indian child, the consent of the parent may be withdrawn for any reason at any time prior to the entry of a final decree of termination or adoption, as the case may be, and the child shall be returned to the parent.
>
> **(d) Collateral attack; vacation of decree and return of custody; limitations**
>
> After the entry of a final decree of adoption of an Indian child in any State court, the parent may withdraw consent thereto upon the grounds that consent was obtained through fraud or duress and may petition the court to vacate such decree. Upon a finding that such consent was obtained through fraud or duress, the court shall vacate such decree and return the child to the parent. No adoption which has been effective for at least two years may be invalidated under the provisions of this subsection unless otherwise permitted under State law.

25 U.S.C. § 1913 (2012).

A. Parental Consent

In re Esther V.

248 P.3d 863 (N.M. 2011)

At the thirty-minute custody hearing, counsel for Mother asked the court to allow him five minutes to consult with Mother before the hearing began, explaining that he had not had an opportunity to talk to his client. After conferring with counsel, Mother neither renewed her denial of the alleged abuse and neglect nor challenged the portion of CYFD's affidavit that stated CYFD had made active and reasonable efforts to keep the family together. Instead, she stipulated to temporary CYFD custody of Child pending the adjudicatory hearing, which was scheduled for October 5, 2007. The court verified Mother's understanding of the stipulation in open court as follows:

> Judge: . . . We are here today for a hearing to determine whether or not reasonable grounds exist to allow the State of New Mexico to keep your child and take legal custody of your child. . . . If you want a hearing, you can have a hearing to dispute that there is not reasonable grounds for the government to keep your child from you. . . . Do you understand?
>
> Mother: Yes.
>
> Judge: Are you willing to give up that right?
>
> Attorney: In other words, are you willing to not have a hearing today, but to say okay, they can keep the child on a temporary basis?

Mother: No, I want to get them back.

Attorney: I understand you want to get them back. The question is do you want a hearing today on whether you should have them temporarily back now. Because you're going to have a hearing later on what's called an adjudication. Do you understand that?

Mother: Yes.

Attorney: Temporarily they're going to be with the State, understand? You're going to have visitation. I think she understands, your honor.

Judge: Alright. So with your permission, we will not have a hearing to determine whether or not at this time you should get your kids back. We're not going to have that hearing. Do you understand that?

Mother: Yes....

Judge: And ... down the line we can have a further hearing called an adjudication to see if your child will remain with the State for a longer period of time. We're not going to have that right now. Do you understand that?

Mother: Um-hum.

The court then signed the stipulated order, which stated that "[t]here is probable cause to believe that the [parents] are not able to provide adequate supervision and care for the child" and that "[c]lear and convincing evidence exists to believe that continued custody of the child by the parent or guardian is likely to result in serious emotional or physical damage to the child." Mother did not contest the findings contained in the stipulated order.

* * *

C. A Parent or Custodian's Consent to Temporary Custody Does Not Transform an Involuntary Proceeding into a Voluntary Proceeding to Which § 1913 of ICWA Applies.

Initially, we address the Court of Appeals' characterization of Mother's stipulation at the custody hearing as a "consent to a foster care placement" within the meaning of § 1913(a) of ICWA. See *Marlene C.*, 2009–NMCA–058, ¶¶ 15–18, 146 N.M. 588, 212 P.3d 1142. Section 1913 details the requirements for valid parental consent in situations where a "parent or Indian custodian voluntarily consents to a foster care placement or to termination of parental rights." CYFD argues that this portion of the Court of Appeals opinion is inconsistent with the purpose of § 1913, which is to establish procedures for voluntary proceedings that are distinguishable from those used for involuntary proceedings. For the reasons that follow, we agree with CYFD and hold that § 1913 applies only to circumstances in which the parent or Indian custodian has initiated a voluntary proceeding.

The characterization by the Court of Appeals that Mother's stipulation at the initial custody hearing was a voluntary consent within the meaning of § 1913(a) is problematic because, under § 1913(b), a parent can withdraw consent to a voluntary foster care placement at any time and regain custody of the child. The Court of Appeals' construction relies on the plain language of § 1913(a), which details the requirements for a valid parental consent in situations where "any parent or Indian custodian voluntarily consents to a foster care placement or to termination of parental rights." We decline to adopt the Court of Appeals' construction.

By enacting § 1913, entitled "Parental rights; voluntary termination," we believe that Congress intended to establish a separate set of requirements for cases where a parent or Indian custodian voluntarily initiates a proceeding in order to relinquish parental or custodial rights to a child. [. . .] Our conclusion that § 1913 applies only to voluntary proceedings initiated by the parent harmonizes two otherwise contradictory provisions within ICWA that define the term "foster care placement." Section 1903(1)(i) defines a foster care placement as "any action removing an Indian child from its parent or Indian custodian for temporary placement . . . where the parent . . . cannot have the child returned upon demand." Section 1913(b) provides that a parent "may withdraw consent to a foster care placement under State law at any time and, upon such withdrawal, the child shall be returned to the parent." We conclude that a foster care placement made in a voluntary proceeding is governed by § 1913 and is unaffected by § 1903(1)(i)'s definition, which applies only to involuntary proceedings. See § 1903 (providing that the definitions apply "except as may be specifically provided otherwise").

Notes

1. This case is more fully discussed in Chapter Three regarding burden of proof, but the question of whether a state-initiated case can ever be voluntary under § 1913 is worth considering. What if a parent voluntarily surrenders parental rights in an involuntary case, and then invokes § 1913(c) to retract his consent? Is the state case reinstated? Do the children go back to the parent the state removed them from? Can a parent truly "voluntarily" consent to foster care or termination of parental rights in the face of state action? *See In re S.E.*, 527 S.W.3d 894 (Mo. Ct. App. 2017) (illustrating this fact pattern).

2. Regardless of the right of revocation under the federal statute, courts are loath to overturn initial consent of the parent, usually the mother. Consider the case of *Quinn v. Walters* from Oregon. Minor mother, under pressure from her own parents, contacted adoptive couple, who provided her with an attorney. On the day of the child's birth, the 14-year-old mother signed an irrevocable consent form. Thirteen days later, she revoked her consent, arguing both her father and she are citizens of the Cherokee Nation. *Quinn v. Walters*, 845 P.2d 206 (Or. App. 1993) *rev'd*, 881 P.2d 795 (Or. 1994). The Court of Appeals agreed with the mother, and overturned the trial court. On appeal to the state supreme court, however, the court found there was not sufficient evidence to determine the child is an Indian child for ICWA to apply, and overturned the court of appeals. Regardless of ICWA's application, the statutes in Oregon provide no protection for minor mothers, and allow irrevocable consent with no time limit on when that consent can be given. While ICWA does

not provide specific protections for minor mothers, its 10-day waiting period before a parent can grant consent may have helped the child in this case determine what she wanted to do after she gave birth.

3. ICWA does not distinguish between mothers and fathers regarding consent to adoption. However, a long history of Supreme Court holdings have defined and delineated a biological father's rights (or lack thereof) to their children. Fathers of Indian children may have more rights under ICWA, though it is difficult to find a court holding such.

B. Biological Fathers, Adoptions, and ICWA

The most recent Supreme Court decision interpreting ICWA involved a voluntary adoption. Voluntary adoptions, or relinquishments, happen when a parent (usually a mother) decides to give a child up for adoption. The intersection of ICWA and parental consent to adoption draws the attention of the media, law professors, and the courts. The laws governing voluntary relinquishments vary widely by state. Some states are considered adoption-friendly because of the relative ease for adoption for adoptive couples. What this also means, however, is that consent to the adoption is irrevocable, or that in certain situations, an adoption can happen without the biological father's consent. This is in conflict with the provisions of ICWA protecting certain due process rights of biological parents—mothers *and* fathers. One of these states where ICWA provides higher protections than state law is South Carolina, where the *Adoptive Couple v. Baby Girl*, 570 U.S. 637 (2013), case arose, discussed in Chapter Three. What happens when only one parent is voluntarily giving consent, and the other parent does not, or may not know about the adoption at all?

Adoptive Couple v. Baby Girl

731 S.E.2d 550 (S.C. 2012), *rev'd*, 133 S. Ct. 2552 (2013)

Chief Justice Toal.

This case involves a contest over the private adoption of a child born in Oklahoma to unwed parents, one of whom is a member of the Cherokee Nation. After a four day hearing in September 2011, the family court issued a final order on November 25, 2011, denying the adoption and requiring the adoptive parents to transfer the child to her biological father. The transfer of custody took place in Charleston, South Carolina, on December 31, 2011, and the child now resides with her biological father and his parents in Oklahoma. We affirm the decision of the family court denying the adoption and awarding custody to the biological father.

Father and Mother are the biological parents of a child born in Oklahoma on September 15, 2009 ("Baby Girl"). Father and Mother became engaged to be married in December 2008, and Mother informed Father that she was pregnant in January 2009. At the time Mother became pregnant, Father was actively serving in the

United States Army and stationed at Fort Sill, Oklahoma, approximately four hours away from his hometown of Bartlesville, Oklahoma, where his parents and Mother resided. Upon learning Mother was pregnant, Father began pressing Mother to get married sooner. The couple continued to speak by phone daily, but by April 2009, the relationship had become strained. Mother testified she ultimately broke off the engagement in May via text message because Father was pressuring her to get married. At this point, Mother cut off all contact with Father. While Father testified his post-breakup attempts to call and text message Mother went unanswered, it appears from the Record Father did not make any meaningful attempts to contact her.

It is undisputed that Mother and Father did not live together prior to the baby's birth and that Father did not support Mother financially for pregnancy related expenses, even though he had the ability to provide some degree of financial assistance to Mother.

In June 2009, Mother sent a text message to Father asking if he would rather pay child support or surrender his parental rights. Father responded via text message that he would relinquish his rights, but testified that he believed he was relinquishing his rights to Mother. Father explained: "In my mind I thought that if I would do that I'd be able to give her time to think about this and possibly maybe we would get back together and continue what we had started." However, under cross-examination Father admitted that his behavior was not conducive to being a father. Mother never informed Father that she intended to place the baby up for adoption. Father insists that, had he known this, he would have never considered relinquishing his rights.

Mother testified she chose the adoption route because she already had two children by another father, and she was struggling financially. In June 2009, Mother connected with Appellants (or "Adoptive Mother" or "Adoptive Father") through the Nightlight Christian Adoption Agency (the "Nightlight Agency"). She testified she chose them to be the parents of the child because "[t]hey're stable. . . . they're a mother and father that live inside a home where she can look up to them and they can give her everything she needs when needed." . . .

Mother testified that she knew "from the beginning" that Father was a registered member of the Cherokee Nation, and that she deemed this information "important" throughout the adoption process. Further, she testified she knew that if the Cherokee Nation were alerted to Baby Girl's status as an Indian child, "some things were going to come into effect, but [she] wasn't for [sic] sure what." Mother reported Father's Indian heritage on the Nightlight Agency's adoption form and testified she made Father's Indian heritage known to Appellants and every agency involved in the adoption. However, it appears that there were some efforts to conceal his Indian status. In fact, the pre-placement form reflects Mother's reluctance to share this information:

> Initially the birth mother did not wish to identify the father, said she wanted to keep things low-key as possible for the [Appellants], because he's

registered in the Cherokee tribe. It was determined that naming him would be detrimental to the adoption.

Appellants hired an attorney to represent Mother's interests during the adoption. Mother told her attorney that Father had Cherokee Indian heritage. Based on this information, Mother's attorney wrote a letter, dated August 21, 2009, to the Child Welfare Division of the Cherokee Nation to inquire about Father's status as an enrolled Cherokee Indian. The letter stated that Father was "1/8 Cherokee, supposedly enrolled," but misspelled Father's first name as "Dustin" instead of "Dusten" and misrepresented his birthdate.

Because of these inaccuracies, the Cherokee Nation responded with a letter stating that the tribe could not verify Father's membership in the tribal records, but that "[a]ny incorrect or omitted family documentation could invalidate this determination." Mother testified she told her attorney that the letter was incorrect and that Father was an enrolled member, but that she did not know his correct birthdate. Adoptive Mother testified that, because they hired an attorney to specifically inquire about the baby's Cherokee Indian status, "when she was born, we were under the impression that she was not Cherokee." Any information Appellants had about Father came from Mother.

When Mother arrived at the hospital to give birth, she requested to be placed on "strictly no report" status, meaning that if anyone called to inquire about her presence in the hospital, the hospital would report her as not admitted. Mother testified that neither Father nor his parents contacted her while she was in the hospital.

Adoptive Mother and Adoptive Father were in the delivery room when Mother gave birth to Baby Girl on September 15, 2009. Adoptive Father cut the umbilical cord. The next morning, Mother signed forms relinquishing her parental rights and consenting to the adoption.

Appellants were required to receive consent from the State of Oklahoma pursuant to the Oklahoma Interstate Compact on Placement of Children ("ICPC") as a prerequisite to removing Baby Girl from that state. Mother signed the necessary documentation, which reported Baby Girl's ethnicity as "Hispanic" instead of "Native American." After Baby Girl was discharged from the hospital, Appellants remained in Oklahoma with Baby Girl for approximately eight days until they received ICPC approval, at which point they took Baby Girl to South Carolina. According to the testimony of Tiffany Dunaway, a Child Welfare Specialist with the Cherokee Nation, had the Cherokee Nation known about Baby Girl's Native American heritage, Appellants would not have been able to remove Baby Girl from Oklahoma.

Father was aware of Mother's expected due date, but made no attempt to contact or support Mother directly in the months following Baby Girl's birth.

Appellants filed the adoption action in South Carolina on September 18, 2009, three days after Baby Girl's birth, but did not serve or otherwise notify Father of the adoption action until January 6, 2010, approximately four months after Baby Girl was born and days before Father was scheduled to deploy to Iraq. On that date outside of a mall near his base, a process server presented Father with legal papers entitled "Acceptance of Service and Answer of Defendant," which stated he was not contesting the adoption of Baby Girl and that he waived the thirty day waiting period and notice of the hearing. Father testified he believed he was relinquishing his rights to Mother and did not realize he consented to Baby Girl's adoption by another family until after he signed the papers. Upon realizing that Mother had relinquished her rights to Appellants, Father testified, "I then tried to grab the paper up. [The process server] told me that I could not grab that [sic] because . . . I would be going to jail if I was to do any harm to the paper."

After consulting with his parents and a JAG lawyer at his base, Father contacted a lawyer the next day, and on January 11, 2010, he requested a stay of the adoption proceedings under the Servicemember's Civil Relief Act ("SCRA"). On January 14, 2010, Father filed a summons and complaint in an Oklahoma district court to establish paternity, child custody, and support of Baby Girl. The complaint named Appellants and Mother as defendants. Paragraph 12 of this Complaint stated, "Neither parent nor the children have Native American blood. Therefore the Federal Indian Child Welfare Act . . . and the Oklahoma Indian Child Welfare Act . . . do not apply." Father departed for Iraq on January 18, 2010, with his father acting as power of attorney while he was deployed overseas.

On March 16, 2010, Appellants, with Mother joining, filed a Special Appearance and Motion to Dismiss Father's Oklahoma action on jurisdictional grounds. The motion was granted, thereby ending the Oklahoma custody action.

Meanwhile, in January 2010, the Cherokee Nation first identified Father as a registered member and determined that Baby Girl was an "Indian Child," as defined under the Federal Indian Child Welfare Act, 25 U.S.C. § 1901, et seq. (the "ICWA"). It is not apparent from the Record when Appellants were made aware of this change, but on March 30, 2010, Appellants amended their South Carolina pleadings to acknowledge Father's membership in the Cherokee Nation. Accordingly, on April 7, 2010, the Cherokee Nation filed a Notice of Intervention in the South Carolina action.

On May 6, 2010, the family court ordered paternity testing which conclusively established Father as the biological father of Baby Girl, and Appellants have since acknowledged Father's paternity. Furthermore, the family court issued an order confirming venue and jurisdiction in Charleston County Family Court and lifting the automatic stay of proceedings under the SCRA. On May 25, 2010, Father answered Appellants' amended complaint, stating he did not consent to the adoption of Baby Girl and seeking custody. By temporary order dated July 12, 2011, the family court set a hearing date for the case, and found separately that the ICWA applied to the case.

The trial of the case took place from September 12–15, 2011. A Guardian ad Litem ("GAL") represented the interests of Baby Girl. On November 25, 2011, the family court judge issued a Final Order, finding that: (1) the ICWA applied and it was not unconstitutional; (2) the "Existing Indian Family" doctrine was inapplicable as an exception to the application of the ICWA in this case in accordance with the clear modern trend; (3) Father did not voluntarily consent to the termination of his parental rights or the adoption; and (4) Appellants failed to prove by clear and convincing evidence that Father's parental rights should be terminated or that granting custody of Baby Girl to Father would likely result in serious emotional or physical damage to Baby Girl. Therefore, the family court denied Appellants' petition for adoption and ordered the transfer of custody of Baby Girl to Father on December 28, 2011.

Appellants filed a motion to stay the transfer and to reconsider on December 9, 2011, which the family court denied on December 14, 2011. Appellants then filed a notice of appeal in the court of appeals on December 20, 2011, along with a petition for a writ of supersedeas. Judge Aphrodite Konduras temporarily granted the petition for a writ of supersedeas pending the filing of a return by Father. On December 30, 2011, Judge Konduras issued an order lifting the temporary grant of supersedeas and denying the petition for a writ of supersedeas. On December 31, 2011, Appellants transferred Baby Girl to Father, and Father and his parents immediately traveled with Baby Girl back to Oklahoma.

This Court certified the appeal ....

II. Transfer of Baby Girl to South Carolina

In its rendering of the facts of the case, the final order of the family court stated that if it were not for the misinformation provided to the Cherokee Nation about the birth father during the process of securing the ICPC, "[Appellants] [would not have] received permission to remove the child from Oklahoma and transport the child to their home state of South Carolina just days after her birth." This statement was neither a finding of fact nor a conclusion of law, but rather was part of the factual background provided in the order. Nevertheless, on appeal Respondents argue that South Carolina courts lack jurisdiction to determine the custody issues. In response, Appellants argue that they properly transferred Baby Girl to South Carolina, and if not, the improper transfer was forgivable or understandable. More specifically, Appellants contend the ICPC form, which did not accurately represent Baby Girl's Indian heritage, should not be construed against them because the ICPC does not protect the rights of birth parents but is designed to ensure the child's safe transfer across state lines. Thus, Appellants maintain, they have satisfied the requirements of the ICPC by providing Baby Girl with a safe and loving home. Furthermore, while Appellants do not dispute that the Cherokee Nation was never informed of Baby Girl's status as an Indian child, Appellants argue that the misspelling of Father's name was an obvious mistake, which they subsequently corrected by amending their pleadings to allege Father is a Cherokee Indian....

A. Voluntary Termination

While Father's consent would not have been required under South Carolina law, see S.C.Code Ann. § 63–9–310(A)(5), for a parent to voluntarily relinquish his or her parental rights under the ICWA, his or her

> consent shall not be valid unless executed in writing and recorded before a judge of a court of competent jurisdiction and accompanied by the presiding judge's certificate that the terms and consequences of the consent were fully explained in detail and were fully understood by the parent or Indian custodian. The court shall also certify that either the parent or Indian custodian fully understood the explanation in English or that it was interpreted into a language that the parent or Indian custodian understood. Any consent given prior to, or within ten days after, birth of the Indian child shall not be valid.

25 U.S.C. § 1913(a). Moreover, a parent may withdraw his or her consent "for any reason at any time prior to the entry of a final decree of termination or adoption, as the case may be, and the child shall be returned to the parent." *Id.* § 1913(c).

It is undisputed that the only consent document Father ever signed was a one-page "Acceptance of Service" stating he was not contesting the adoption, which was purportedly presented for Father's signature as a prerequisite to the service of a summons and complaint. Thus, Appellants did not follow the clear procedural directives of section 1913(a) in obtaining Father's consent. Moreover, even if this "consent" was valid under the statute, then Father's subsequent legal campaign to obtain custody of Baby Girl has rendered any such consent withdrawn. Therefore, neither Father's signature on the "Acceptance of Service" document, nor his stated intentions to relinquish his rights, were effectual forms of voluntary consent under the ICWA. . . .

The family court order stated, "[w]hen parental rights and the best interests of the child are in conflict, the best interests of the child must prevail. However, in this case, I find no conflict between the two." Likewise, we cannot say that Baby Girl's best interests are not served by the grant of custody to Father, as Appellants have not presented evidence that Baby Girl would not be safe, loved, and cared for if raised by Father and his family. Moreover, in transferring custody to Father and his family, Baby Girl's familial and tribal ties may be established and maintained in furtherance of the clear purpose of the ICWA, which is to preserve American Indian culture by retaining its children within the tribe. . . .

Notes

1. After this decision, Father took custody of the two-year-old girl around New Years' Eve. Press coverage of the transfer was incendiary from the start. *See* Allyson Bird, *Decades-old federal act removes 2-year-old girl from the only family she's ever known*, The Post and Courier (Jan. 7, 2012). This press coverage only increased in intensity as the case was appealed to the U.S. Supreme Court. Aside from articles by Michael Overall of the *Tulsa World*, and articles in *Indian Country Today*, the coverage was universally anti-biological father and anti-ICWA.

2. The guardian ad litem (GAL) in this case was requested by the Adoptive Couple and was represented by a high profile Supreme Court advocate in the case. The GAL argued against the constitutionality of ICWA as it applied to Baby Girl. The role of GALs in ICWA cases can be difficult. In the case of a GAL who is also a lawyer

(LGAL), the lawyer is supposed to be representing the best interests of the child, even if those best interests are contrary to the child's wishes. In the case of a baby, determining what those wishes are is obviously impossible. However, in passing ICWA, Congress stated that the law was in the best interests of Indian children. The GAL in *Adoptive Couple v. Baby Girl* did not simply argue that a change in placement was not in Baby Girl's best interest, but rather the entire statutory scheme was unconstitutional. *See* Matthew L.M. Fletcher & Kathryn E. Fort, *Indian Children and Their Guardians ad Litem*, 93 B.U. L. Rev. Annex 59 (2013).

Adoptive Couple v. Baby Girl

570 U.S. 637, 133 S. Ct. 2552 (2013)

Justice Alito delivered the opinion of the Court.

This case is about a little girl (Baby Girl) who is classified as an Indian because she is 1.2% (3/256) Cherokee. Because Baby Girl is classified in this way, the South Carolina Supreme Court held that certain provisions of the federal Indian Child Welfare Act of 1978 required her to be taken, at the age of 27 months, from the only parents she had ever known and handed over to her biological father, who had attempted to relinquish his parental rights and who had no prior contact with the child. The provisions of the federal statute at issue here do not demand this result.

Contrary to the State Supreme Court's ruling, we hold that 25 U.S.C. § 1912(f)—which bars involuntary termination of a parent's rights in the absence of a heightened showing that serious harm to the Indian child is likely to result from the parent's "continued custody" of the child—does not apply when, as here, the relevant parent never had custody of the child. We further hold that § 1912(d)—which conditions involuntary termination of parental rights with respect to an Indian child on a showing that remedial efforts have been made to prevent the "breakup of the Indian family"—is inapplicable when, as here, the parent abandoned the Indian child before birth and never had custody of the child. Finally, we clarify that § 1915(a), which provides placement preferences for the adoption of Indian children, does not bar a non-Indian family like Adoptive Couple from adopting an Indian child when no other eligible candidates have sought to adopt the child. We accordingly reverse the South Carolina Supreme Court's judgment and remand for further proceedings.

I

"The Indian Child Welfare Act of 1978 (ICWA), 92 Stat. 3069, 25 U.S.C. §§ 1901–1963, was the product of rising concern in the mid–1970's over the consequences to Indian children, Indian families, and Indian tribes of abusive child welfare practices that resulted in the separation of large numbers of Indian children from their families and tribes through adoption or foster care placement, usually in non-Indian homes." *Mississippi Band of Choctaw Indians v. Holyfield*, 490 U.S. 30, 32 (1989). Congress found that "an alarmingly high percentage of Indian families [were being] broken up by the removal, often unwarranted, of their children from them by nontribal public and private agencies." § 1901(4). This "wholesale removal of Indian children from their homes" prompted Congress to enact the ICWA, which establishes federal standards that govern state-court child custody proceedings involving Indian children. *Id.* at 32, 36; *see also* § 1902 (declaring that the ICWA establishes "minimum Federal standards for the removal of Indian children from their families"). . . .

II

In this case, Birth Mother (who is predominantly Hispanic) and Biological Father (who is a member of the Cherokee Nation) became engaged in December 2008. One month later, Birth Mother informed Biological Father, who lived about four hours away, that she was pregnant. After learning of the pregnancy, Biological Father asked Birth Mother to move up the date of the wedding. He also refused to provide any financial support until after the two had married. The couple's relationship deteriorated, and Birth Mother broke off the engagement in May 2009. In June, Birth Mother sent Biological Father a text message asking if he would rather pay child support or relinquish his parental rights. Biological Father responded via text message that he relinquished his rights.

Birth Mother then decided to put Baby Girl up for adoption. Because Birth Mother believed that Biological Father had Cherokee Indian heritage, her attorney contacted the Cherokee Nation to determine whether Biological Father was formally enrolled. The inquiry letter misspelled Biological Father's first name and incorrectly stated his birthday, and the Cherokee Nation responded that, based on the information provided, it could not verify Biological Father's membership in the tribal records.

Working through a private adoption agency, Birth Mother selected Adoptive Couple, non-Indians living in South Carolina, to adopt Baby Girl. Adoptive Couple supported Birth Mother both emotionally and financially throughout her pregnancy. Adoptive Couple was present at Baby Girl's birth in Oklahoma on September 15, 2009, and Adoptive Father even cut the umbilical cord. The next morning, Birth Mother signed forms relinquishing her parental rights and consenting to the adoption. Adoptive Couple initiated adoption proceedings in South Carolina a few days later, and returned there with Baby Girl. After returning to South Carolina, Adoptive Couple allowed Birth Mother to visit and communicate with Baby Girl.

It is undisputed that, for the duration of the pregnancy and the first four months after Baby Girl's birth, Biological Father provided no financial assistance to Birth Mother or Baby Girl, even though he had the ability to do so. Indeed, Biological Father "made no meaningful attempts to assume his responsibility of parenthood" during this period.

Approximately four months after Baby Girl's birth, Adoptive Couple served Biological Father with notice of the pending adoption. (This was the first notification that they had provided to Biological Father regarding the adoption proceeding.) Biological Father signed papers stating that he accepted service and that he was "not contesting the adoption." But Biological Father later testified that, at the time he signed the papers, he thought that he was relinquishing his rights to Birth Mother, not to Adoptive Couple.

Biological Father contacted a lawyer the day after signing the papers, and subsequently requested a stay of the adoption proceedings. In the adoption proceedings, Biological Father sought custody and stated that he did not consent to Baby Girl's adoption. Moreover, Biological Father took a paternity test, which verified that he was Baby Girl's biological father.

A trial took place in the South Carolina Family Court in September 2011, by which time Baby Girl was two years old. The Family Court concluded that Adoptive Couple had not carried the heightened burden under § 1912(f) of proving that Baby Girl would suffer serious emotional or physical damage if Biological Father had custody. The Family Court therefore denied Adoptive Couple's petition for adoption and awarded custody to Biological Father. On December 31, 2011, at the age of 27 months, Baby Girl was handed over to Biological Father, whom she had never met.

The South Carolina Supreme Court affirmed the Family Court's denial of the adoption and the award of custody to Biological Father. The State Supreme Court first determined that the ICWA applied because the case involved a child custody proceeding relating to an Indian child. It also concluded that Biological Father fell within the ICWA's definition of a "'parent.'" The court then held that two separate provisions of the ICWA barred the termination of Biological Father's parental rights. First, the court held that Adoptive Couple had not shown that "active efforts ha[d] been made to provide remedial services and rehabilitative programs designed to prevent the breakup of the Indian family." § 1912(d). Second, the court concluded that Adoptive Couple had not shown that Biological Father's "custody of Baby Girl would result in serious emotional or physical harm to her beyond a reasonable doubt." Finally, the court stated that, even if it had decided to terminate Biological Father's parental rights, § 1915(a)'s adoption-placement preferences would have applied. We granted certiorari.

III

It is undisputed that, had Baby Girl not been 3/256 Cherokee, Biological Father would have had no right to object to her adoption under South Carolina law. See Tr. of Oral Arg. 49; 398 S.C., at 644, n. 19, 731 S.E.2d, at 560, n. 19 ("Under state law, [Biological] Father's consent to the adoption would not have been required"). The South Carolina Supreme Court held, however, that Biological Father is a "parent" under the ICWA and that two statutory provisions—namely, § 1912(f) and § 1912(d)—bar the termination of his parental rights. In this Court, Adoptive Couple contends that Biological Father is not a "parent" and that § 1912(f) and § 1912(d) are inapplicable. We need not—and therefore do not—decide whether Biological Father is a "parent." *See* § 1903(9) (defining "parent"). Rather, assuming for the sake of argument that he is a "parent," we hold that neither § 1912(f) nor § 1912(d) bars the termination of his parental rights....

Section 1912(f) conditions the involuntary termination of parental rights on a showing regarding the merits of "continued custody of the child by the parent." The adjective "continued" plainly refers to a pre-existing state. As Justice Sotomayor concedes, "continued" means "[c]arried on or kept up without cessation" or "[e]xtended in space without interruption or breach of conne[ct]ion." Compact Edition of the Oxford English Dictionary 909 (1981 reprint of 1971 ed.) (Compact OED); see also American Heritage Dictionary 288 (1981) (defining "continue" in the following manner: "1. To go on with a particular action or in a particular condition; persist. . . . 3. To remain in the same state, capacity, or place"); Webster's Third New International Dictionary 493 (1961) (Webster's) (defining "continued" as "stretching out in time or space esp. without interruption"); *Aguilar v. FDIC*, 63 F.3d 1059, 1062 (C.A.11 1995) (per curiam) (suggesting that the phrase "continue an action" means "go on with . . . an action" that is "preexisting"). The term "continued" also can mean "resumed after interruption." Webster's 493; see American Heritage Dictionary 288. The phrase "continued custody" therefore refers to custody that a parent already has (or at least had at some point in the past). As a result, § 1912(f) does not apply in cases where the Indian parent never had custody of the Indian child. . . .

Our reading of § 1912(f) comports with the statutory text demonstrating that the primary mischief the ICWA was designed to counteract was the unwarranted removal of Indian children from Indian families due to the cultural insensitivity and biases of social workers and state courts. The statutory text expressly highlights the primary problem that the statute was intended to solve: "an alarmingly high percentage of Indian families [were being] broken up by the *removal*, often unwarranted, of their children from them by nontribal public and private agencies." § 1901(4) (emphasis added); *see also* § 1902 (explaining that the ICWA establishes "minimum Federal standards for the *removal* of Indian children from their families") (emphasis added). And if the legislative history of the ICWA is thought to be relevant, it further underscores that the Act was primarily intended to stem the unwarranted removal of Indian children from intact Indian families. See, e.g., H.R.Rep. No. 95–1386, p. 8 (1978) (explaining that, as relevant here, "[t]he purpose of [the ICWA] is to protect the best interests of Indian children and to promote the stability and security of Indian tribes and families by establishing minimum Federal standards for the *removal* of Indian children from their families and the placement of such children in foster or adoptive homes" (emphasis added)); *id.*, at 9 (decrying the "wholesale separation of Indian children" from their Indian families); *id.*, at 22 (discussing "the removal" of Indian children from their parents pursuant to §§ 1912(e) and (f)). In sum, when, as here, the adoption of an Indian child is voluntarily and lawfully initiated by a non-Indian parent with sole custodial rights, the ICWA's primary goal of preventing the unwarranted removal of Indian children and the dissolution of Indian families is not implicated. . . .

Under our reading of § 1912(f), Biological Father should not have been able to invoke § 1912(f) in this case, because he had never had legal or physical custody of Baby Girl as of the time of the adoption proceedings. As an initial matter, it is undisputed that Biological Father never had physical custody of Baby Girl. And as a matter of both South Carolina and Oklahoma law, Biological Father never had legal custody either. *See* S.C.Code Ann. § 63–17–20(B) (2010) ("Unless the court orders otherwise, the custody of an illegitimate child is solely in the natural mother unless the mother has relinquished her rights to the child"); Okla. Stat., Tit. 10, § 7800 (West Cum.Supp. 2013) ("Except as otherwise provided by law, the mother of a child born out of wedlock has custody of the child until determined otherwise by a court of competent jurisdiction"). . . .

Consistent with the statutory text, we hold that § 1912(d) [providing that any party seeking to terminate parental rights to an Indian child under state law shall satisfy the court that active efforts have been made to provide remedial services and rehabilitative programs designed to prevent the breakup of the Indian family and that these efforts have proved unsuccessful] applies only in cases where an Indian family's "breakup" would be precipitated by the termination of the parent's rights. The term "breakup" refers in this context to "[t]he discontinuance of a relationship," American Heritage Dictionary 235 (3d ed. 1992), or "an ending as an effective entity," Webster's 273 (defining "breakup" as "a disruption or dissolution into component parts: an ending as an effective entity"). See also Compact OED 1076 (defining "break-up" as, inter alia, a "disruption, separation into parts, disintegration"). But when an Indian parent abandons an Indian child prior to birth and that child has never been in the Indian parent's legal or physical custody, there is no "relationship" that would be "discontinu[ed]"—and no "effective entity" that would be "end[ed]"—by the termination of the Indian parent's rights. In such a situation, the "breakup of the Indian family" has long since occurred, and § 1912(d) is inapplicable.

Our interpretation of § 1912(d) is, like our interpretation of § 1912(f), consistent with the explicit congressional purpose of providing certain "standards for the removal of Indian children from their families." § 1902. In addition, the BIA's Guidelines confirm that remedial services under § 1912(d) are intended "to alleviate the need to remove the Indian child from his or her parents or Indian custodians," not to facilitate a transfer of the child to an Indian parent. *See* 44 Fed.Reg., at 67592. . . .

Section 1912(d) is a sensible requirement when applied to state social workers who might otherwise be too quick to remove Indian children from their Indian families. It would, however, be unusual to apply § 1912(d) in the context of an Indian parent who abandoned a child prior to birth and who never had custody of the child. The decision below illustrates this point. The South Carolina Supreme Court held that § 1912(d) mandated measures such as "attempting to stimulate [Biological] Father's desire to be a parent." But if prospective adoptive parents were required to engage in the bizarre undertaking of "stimulat[ing]" a biological father's "desire to be a parent," it would surely dissuade some of them from seeking to adopt Indian children. And this would, in turn, unnecessarily place vulnerable Indian children at a unique disadvantage in finding a permanent and loving home, even in cases where neither an Indian parent nor the relevant tribe objects to the adoption. . . .

Section 1915(a) provides that "[i]n any adoptive placement of an Indian child under State law, a preference shall be given, in the absence of good cause to the contrary, to a placement with (1) a member of the child's extended family; (2) other members of the Indian child's tribe; or (3) other Indian families." Contrary to the

South Carolina Supreme Court's suggestion, § 1915(a)'s preferences are inapplicable in cases where no alternative party has formally sought to adopt the child. This is because there simply is no "preference" to apply if no alternative party that is eligible to be preferred under § 1915(a) has come forward.

In this case, Adoptive Couple was the only party that sought to adopt Baby Girl in the Family Court or the South Carolina Supreme Court. Biological Father is not covered by § 1915(a) because he did not seek to adopt Baby Girl; instead, he argued that his parental rights should not be terminated in the first place. Moreover, Baby Girl's paternal grandparents never sought custody of Baby Girl. Nor did other members of the Cherokee Nation or "other Indian families" seek to adopt Baby Girl, even though the Cherokee Nation had notice of—and intervened in—the adoption proceedings. . . .

The Indian Child Welfare Act was enacted to help preserve the cultural identity and heritage of Indian tribes, but under the State Supreme Court's reading, the Act would put certain vulnerable children at a great disadvantage solely because an ancestor—even a remote one—was an Indian. As the State Supreme Court read §§ 1912(d) and (f), a biological Indian father could abandon his child in utero and refuse any support for the birth mother—perhaps contributing to the mother's decision to put the child up for adoption—and then could play his ICWA trump card at the eleventh hour to override the mother's decision and the child's best interests. If this were possible, many prospective adoptive parents would surely pause before adopting any child who might possibly qualify as an Indian under the ICWA. Such an interpretation would raise equal protection concerns, but the plain text of §§ 1912(f) and (d) makes clear that neither provision applies in the present context. Nor do § 1915(a)'s rebuttable adoption preferences apply when no alternative party has formally sought to adopt the child. We therefore reverse the judgment of the South Carolina Supreme Court and remand the case for further proceedings not inconsistent with this opinion.

Justice Sotomayor, with whom Justice Ginsburg and Justice Kagan join, and with whom Justice Scalia joins in part, dissenting.

A casual reader of the Court's opinion could be forgiven for thinking this an easy case, one in which the text of the applicable statute clearly points the way to the only sensible result. In truth, however, the path from the text of the Indian Child Welfare Act of 1978 (ICWA) to the result the Court reaches is anything but clear, and its result anything but right. . . .

[T]he majority begins its analysis by plucking out of context a single phrase from the last clause of the last subsection of the relevant provision, and then builds its entire argument upon it. That is not how we ordinarily read statutes. The third clue is that the majority openly professes its aversion to Congress' explicitly stated purpose in enacting the statute. The majority expresses concern that reading the Act to mean what it says will make it more difficult to place Indian children in adoptive homes, but the Congress that enacted the statute announced its intent to stop "an alarmingly high percentage of Indian families [from being] broken up" by, among other things, a trend of "plac[ing] [Indian children] in non-Indian . . . adoptive homes." 25 U.S.C. § 1901(4). Policy disagreement with Congress' judgment is not a valid reason for this Court to distort the provisions of the Act. Unlike the majority, I cannot adopt a reading of ICWA that is contrary to both its text and its stated purpose. I respectfully dissent. . . .

When it excludes noncustodial biological fathers from the Act's substantive protections, this textually backward reading misapprehends ICWA's structure and scope. Moreover, notwithstanding the majority's focus on the perceived parental shortcomings of Birth Father, its reasoning necessarily extends to *all* Indian parents who have never had custody of their children, no matter how fully those parents have embraced the financial and emotional responsibilities of parenting. The majority thereby transforms a statute that was intended to provide uniform federal standards for child custody proceedings involving Indian children and their biological parents into an illogical piecemeal scheme. . . .

Petitioners and Baby Girl's guardian ad litem devote many pages of briefing to arguing that the term "parent" should be defined with reference to the law of the State in which an ICWA child custody proceeding takes place. These arguments, however, are inconsistent with our recognition in *Holyfield* [*Mississippi Band of Choctaw Indians v. Holyfield*, 490 U.S. 30 (1989), that Congress intended the critical terms of the statute to have uniform federal definitions. It is therefore unsurprising, although far from unimportant, that the majority assumes for the purposes of its analysis that Birth Father is an ICWA "parent."

Second, the Act's comprehensive definition of "child custody proceeding" includes not only "'adoptive placement[s],'" "'preadoptive placement[s],'" and "'foster care placement[s],'" but also "'termination of parental rights'" proceedings. This last category encompasses "any action resulting in the termination of the parent-child relationship." So far, then, it is clear that Birth Father has a federally recognized status as Baby Girl's "parent" and that his "parent-child relationship" with her is subject to the protections of the Act. . . .

These protections are consonant with the principle, recognized in our cases, that the biological bond between parent and child is meaningful. "[A] natural parent's desire for and right to the companionship, care, custody, and management of his or her children," we have explained, "is an interest far more precious than any property right." *Santosky v. Kramer*, 455 U.S. 745, 758–759 (1982). Although the Constitution does not compel the protection of a biological father's parent-child relationship until he has taken steps to cultivate it, this Court has nevertheless recognized that "the biological connection . . . offers the natural father an opportunity that no other male possesses to develop a relationship with his offspring." *Lehr v. Robertson*, 463 U.S. 248, 262 (1983). Federal recognition of a parent-child relationship between a birth father and his child is consistent with ICWA's purpose of providing greater protection for the familial bonds between Indian parents and their children than state law may afford. . . .

Balancing the legitimate interests of unwed biological fathers against the need for stability in a child's family situation is difficult, to be sure, and States have, over the years, taken different approaches to the problem. Some States, like South Carolina, have opted to hew to the constitutional baseline established by this Court's precedents and do not require a biological father's consent to adoption unless he has provided financial support during pregnancy. *See Quilloin v. Walcott*, 434 U.S. 246, 254–256 (1978); *Lehr*, 463 U.S., at 261. Other States, however, have decided to give the rights of biological fathers more robust protection and to afford them consent rights on the basis of their biological link to the child. At the time that ICWA was passed, as noted, over one-fourth of States did so. . . .

Moreover, the majority's focus on "intact" families begs the question of what Congress set out to accomplish with ICWA. In an ideal world, perhaps all parents would be perfect. They would live up to their parental responsibilities by providing the fullest possible financial and emotional support to their children. They would never suffer mental health problems, lose their jobs, struggle with substance dependency, or encounter any of the other multitudinous personal crises that can make it difficult to meet these responsibilities. In an ideal world parents would never become estranged and leave their children caught in the middle. But we do not live in such a world. Even happy families do not always fit the custodial-parent mold for which the majority would reserve ICWA's substantive protections; unhappy families all too often do not. They are families nonetheless. Congress understood as much. ICWA's definitions of "parent" and "termination of parental rights" provided in § 1903 sweep broadly. They should be honored. . . .

The majority's repeated, analytically unnecessary references to the fact that Baby Girl is 3/256 Cherokee by ancestry do nothing to elucidate its intimation that the statute may violate the Equal Protection Clause as applied here. I see no ground for this Court to second-guess the membership requirements of federally recognized Indian tribes, which are independent political entities. *See Santa Clara Pueblo v. Martinez*, 436 U.S. 49, 72, n. 32 (1978). I am particularly averse to doing so when the Federal Government requires Indian tribes, as a prerequisite for official recognition, to make "descen[t] from a historical Indian tribe" a condition of membership. 25 CFR § 83.7(e) (2012). . . .

The majority's hollow literalism distorts the statute and ignores Congress' purpose in order to rectify a perceived wrong that, while heartbreaking at the time, was a correct application of federal law and that in any case cannot be undone. Baby Girl has now resided with her father for 18 months. However difficult it must have been for her to leave Adoptive Couple's home when she was just over 2 years old, it will be equally devastating now if, at the age of 3 ½, she is again removed from her home and sent to live halfway across the country. Such a fate is not foreordained, of course. But it can be said with certainty that the anguish this case has caused will only be compounded by today's decision.

Notes

1. By the time this decision came down, Baby Girl was four years old. In all of the subsequent proceedings to this decision, there was not one best interests hearing for the child, nor an opportunity for the child to tell the court her wishes.

2. Appellate courts often do a bad job at delineating what they think their decision means for the child involved in a case. The difference between a remand and a vacate can make all the difference in the world for the transfer of placement of a child, but state appellate courts are not always clear on what they intend. *See In re JJW*, 902 N.W.2d 901 (Mich. Ct. App. 2017) (affirming in part, vacating in part, and remanding, but not clarifying if the court intended the children to be immediately moved again before the hearing required by the remand).

For example, after the *Baby Girl* decision, there was a jurisdictional nightmare in both state and tribal courts. There were open cases in six Oklahoma courts, the Cherokee tribal court, and one South Carolina court became involved. The Adoptive Couple got an arrest warrant for the biological father for interfering with their custody of Baby Girl. Father was forced to post $10,000 bail. Michael Overall, *Judge releases Brown on bond*, The Tulsa World, Sept. 6, 2013. The families were ordered to mediate and did so for a week, until it was clear they could not come to an agreement. Finally, the biological father surrendered custody of the child to Adoptive Couple. He was concerned for her privacy and stability, and wanted to keep her out of the center of an ongoing legal battle as she grew up. Glenn Smith, *Dusten Brown drops legal efforts to win back custody of 4-year-old Veronica*, The Post and Courier, Oct. 9, 2013 ("Brown wiped his eyes and choked back tears as he described the void in his home since Veronica's departure and the pain of seeing her empty room full of toys she left behind. But Brown said he could no longer stomach the prospect of her caught at the center of a contentious legal fight and in the glare of national media.").

3. After Adoptive Couple took custody of the girl, they sued the Cherokee Nation and the biological father for one million dollars in legal fees. The case remains unresolved. Michael Overall, *One year later, Baby Veronica case still resonates*, The Tulsa World, Sept. 21, 2014.

4. Justice Thomas concurred in the opinion in *Baby Girl*. His concurrences and dissents in recent cases are deeply disturbing to advocates who practice federal Indian law:

> The ICWA recognizes States' inherent "jurisdiction over Indian child custody proceedings," § 1901(5), but asserts that federal regulation is necessary because States "have often failed to recognize the essential tribal relations of Indian people and the cultural and social standards prevailing in Indian communities and families." However, Congress may regulate areas of traditional state concern only if the Constitution grants it such power. Admt. 10 ("The powers not delegated to the United States by the Constitution, nor prohibited by it to the States, are reserved to the States respectively, or to the people"). The threshold question, then, is whether the Constitution grants Congress power to override state custody law whenever an Indian is involved. . . .

> The ICWA asserts that the Indian Commerce Clause, Art. I, § 8, cl. 3, and "other constitutional authority" provides Congress with "plenary power over Indian affairs." § 1901(1). The reference to "other constitutional authority" is not illuminating, and I am aware of no other enumerated power that could even arguably support Congress' intrusion into this area of traditional state authority. . . .
>
> In light of the original understanding of the Indian Commerce Clause, the constitutional problems that would be created by application of the ICWA here are evident. First, the statute deals with "child custody proceedings," § 1903(1), not "commerce." It was enacted in response to concerns that "an alarmingly high percentage of Indian families [were] broken up by the removal, often unwarranted, of their children from them by nontribal public and private agencies." § 1901(4). The perceived problem was that many Indian children were "placed in non-Indian foster and adoptive homes and institutions." Ibid. This problem, however, had nothing to do with commerce.

Adoptive Couple v. Baby Girl, 133 S.Ct. 2552, 2565-67 (2013) (Thomas, J., concurring).

5. The name of the child involved in *Baby Girl* is easily available online, and in citations to articles about the case, as are other personal details. Her privacy continues to be an issue, and will be throughout her life. Both her biological father and her tribal guardian ad litem were particularly concerned about how the child's name and image were used in the public sphere during the on-going case. In the *Holyfield* case, facts about the children involved only became public after an interview with the mother. And even then, the information was only available in a law review article and chapter in a legal book many years later. The child in the *Baby Girl* case will be able to find a huge source of information about this period of her life online, any time she searches for her name.

6. The misspellings of names and locations, and the use of incorrect forms caused a great deal of concern around the *Baby Girl* case, resulting in investigations into adoption practices in Oklahoma and throughout the country. After the case, a member of the Oklahoma legislature introduced the "Oklahoma Truth in Adoption Act," which would "require biological fathers to appear in front of a judge to relinquish rights before an adoption could proceed." Michael Overall, *Young Coweta Father Wins Fight in Missouri Against Adoption of His Son*, Tulsa World, March 30, 2014; Okla. H.B. 1118 (2013). These reforms echo the requirements of ICWA for all birth fathers, not just Indian fathers.

E.T. v. R.K.B. (In re B.B.)

2017 UT 59, 417 P.3d 1 (Utah 2017)

Contested adoptions are gut-wrenching, and the longer they remain in flux, the greater the toll on the biological parents, the prospective adoptive parents, family members, and, most significantly, the child. But no one is better off for "judicial shortcuts, intentional or unintentional, which reach an expeditious result but fail to recognize the fundamental nature of the right of [biological] parents to the care, custody, and management of their child." *In re Adoption of L.D.S.*, 155 P.3d 1, 8 (Okla. 2006), as supplemented on reh'g, No. 250 (Mar. 6, 2007). "In fact, the best interests of the child can be served in no legitimate manner except in obedience to the policies and procedures mandated by law." *Id.* So it is vital that the courts of this state, this court included, take care to ensure that adoption proceedings are as free as possible from fatal defects. Regrettably, this case is septic: Birth Mother admitted to having perpetrated a fraud on the district court and suborning perjury from her brother-in-law, all in an effort to keep Birth Father from intervening in the proceedings, and all against the backdrop of what I believe was untimely and therefore invalid consent.

Procedurally, this case is before us on certification from our court of appeals, the central issue presented by the parties being whether the district court got it right when it denied Birth Father's motion to intervene. Because both Birth Father and Birth Mother are members of the Cheyenne River Sioux Tribe and B.B. is eligible for enrollment in the tribe, the Child is an Indian child.

* * *

The court is not of one mind on the issues. With respect to issue 1, a minority of this court would hold that where, as here, neither biological parent has validly consented to the adoption nor had their parental rights otherwise terminated, our courts lack subject matter jurisdiction to go ahead with adoption proceedings. With respect to issue 2, the minority would further hold that Birth Father has standing under our traditional approach to standing, and the right, under section 1914 of ICWA, to challenge Birth Mother's consent and the termination order and to argue the lack of subject matter jurisdiction. And with respect to issue 3, which is separate from the jurisdictional questions, a majority of this court holds that Birth Father is a "parent" under ICWA and, as such, is entitled to participate in the proceedings below on remand. The decision of the district court is therefore reversed and the matter remanded for proceedings consistent with this opinion.

* * *

B. Birth Father Is a Parent Under ICWA

Section 1914 of ICWA allows a parent to petition a court to invalidate an action terminating parental rights that violated any provision of sections 1911, 1912, and 1913 of ICWA. We hold that Birth Father meets ICWA's definition of a "parent" because he has acknowledged paternity.

"Pursuant to general principles of statutory interpretation, [w]e . . . look first to the . . . plain language [of ICWA], recognizing that our primary goal is to give effect to [congressional] intent in light of the purpose the statute was meant to achieve." *In re Kunz*, 2004 UT 71, ¶ 8, 99 P.3d 793 (first three alterations in original) (internal quotation marks omitted). We consider it obvious that the plain language does not fully answer the question of what is required for an unmarried biological father to be considered a parent for purposes of ICWA. ICWA defines "parent" as "any biological parent or parents of an Indian child" but specifically excludes "the unwed father where paternity has not been acknowledged or established." 25 U.S.C. § 1903(9). ICWA does not, however, define what actions the unmarried father has to take to acknowledge or establish paternity and also does not specify the timing. Because of the lack of a definition, we look instead to the plain meaning of the terms "acknowledge" and "establish." We conclude that the plain meaning of the terms is so broad that it offers little guidance, so we then address the question of whether the procedures and timing for acknowledging or establishing paternity are defined by state law or are subject to a tribal or federal standard.

The district court determined that "Congress intended for ICWA to defer to state and/or tribal law standards for establishing paternity" and that Birth Father failed to comply with Utah or South Dakota requirements for establishing paternity. We disagree. Instead, we hold that Congress intended that a federal standard apply. We also hold that Birth Father's actions were timely and sufficient to acknowledge paternity under ICWA.

1. Interpreting "Acknowledge" and "Establish" Requires a Plain Meaning Approach

* * *

Theoretically, if we were to rely on a plain meaning of the terms for the actions and timing required, a father could acknowledge or establish paternity many years after the completion of the adoption. Because the terms are so broad and vague and because of the lack of a timing element, dictionary definitions alone are inadequate for determining who is a parent under ICWA.

* * *

A term of art may of course have nuanced differences from state to state, but the core meaning must be the same. Contrary to the dissent's assertion, different states' interpretations of "acknowledge" and "establish" do not share a common core. As the dissent itself notes, "standards vary widely across the fifty states," *infra* ¶ 170 n.35, including whether a writing must be signed by the mother for the father to acknowledge paternity. The standard for acknowledging or establishing paternity in Utah is so different from the standard in, for example, New Jersey, that we could not say they share the same common core. See *Bruce L. v. W.E.*, 247 P.3d 966, 978–79 (Alaska 2011) ("Under New Jersey law, 'fil[ing] a written acknowledgement of paternity . . . or initiat[ing] a lawsuit claiming paternity or any other parental rights prior to the final judgment of adoption' would make an unwed father a parent for ICWA purposes." (alterations in original) (quoting *In re Adoption of a Child of Indian Heritage*, 543 A.2d 925, 936 (N.J. 1988))).

* * *

2. Federal Law Applies to Give Context to the Plain Meaning of the Terms

Having found that a plain language analysis of the terms requires more than the dictionary definitions provide, we now turn to the question of whether the procedures and timing for acknowledging or establishing paternity are defined by state law. We reject the notion that courts should rely on state law to determine whether an unmarried biological father has acknowledged or established paternity under ICWA. Instead, we adopt the reasoning in *Mississippi Band of Choctaw Indians v. Holyfield,* 490 U.S. 30, 109 S.Ct. 1597, 104 L.Ed.2d 29 (1989). In *Holyfield*, the Supreme Court stated that

> the purpose of the ICWA gives no reason to believe that Congress intended to rely on state law for the definition of a critical term; quite the contrary. It is clear from the very text of the ICWA, not to mention its legislative history and the hearings that led to its enactment, that Congress was concerned with the rights of Indian families and Indian communities vis-à -vis state authorities.

Id. at 44–45, 109 S.Ct. 1597. "Parent" is a critical term under ICWA. Whether an individual qualifies as a "parent" determines whether he or she may benefit from the heightened protections for parental rights available under ICWA. There is "no reason to believe that Congress intended to rely on state law for the definition of [this] critical term." *Id.* at 44, 109 S.Ct. 1597. Indeed, we must begin "with the general assumption that in the absence of a plain indication to the contrary, . . . Congress when it enacts a statute is not making the application of the federal act dependent on state law." *Id.* at 43, 109 S.Ct. 1597 (alteration in original) (internal quotation marks omitted). And although "Congress sometimes intends that a statutory term be given content by the application of state law," this applies only in the context of fleshing out the federal standard—it does not mean the federal standard is replaced with fifty state standards. *Id.*

Additionally, *Holyfield* notes that Congress can and does expressly state when it wants a state or tribal law definition to apply. *Id.* at 47 n.22, 109 S.Ct. 1597 ("Where Congress . . . intend[s] that ICWA terms be defined by reference to other than federal law, it state[s] this explicitly."). For example, Congress explicitly stated that "extended family member" and "Indian custodian" are defined by reference to tribal law or custom or state law. 25 U.S.C. § 1903(2), (6). This, the *Holyfield* Court stated, is evidence that if Congress "did intend that ICWA terms be defined by reference to other than federal law," "it would have said so." 490 U.S. at 47 n.22, 109 S.Ct. 1597. And this is not merely "another way of saying that the legislature could have spoken more clearly." *Craig v. Provo City*, 2016 UT 40, ¶ 38, 389 P.3d 423. Rather, the explicit use of state or tribal law for "extended family member" and "Indian custodian" but not for other terms such as "acknowledge" and "establish" indicates that Congress "rejected the formulation embodied in the neighboring provision"—i.e., that it declined to incorporate state or tribal standards for acknowledging and establishing paternity. *Id.* ¶ 38 n.9. Because Congress did not mandate a state or tribal law definition for "acknowledge" or "establish," we can and should rely instead on a federal definition.

In determining how to define the procedures for acknowledging and establishing paternity, we have a duty to "harmonize [a statute's] provisions in accordance with the legislative intent and purpose." *Osuala v. Aetna Life & Cas.*, 608 P.2d 242, 243 (Utah 1980); . . . At times, it may be necessary to delve into legislative history to determine what and how many purposes the legislature intended. *Marion Energy, Inc. v. KFJ Ranch P'ship*, 2011 UT 50, ¶ 15, 267 P.3d 863 ("[W]hen statutory language is ambiguous . . . we generally resort to other modes of statutory construction and 'seek guidance from legislative history' and other accepted sources." (citation omitted)). But that is not the case here, where we have a clear directive in the statute itself that drives at a purpose:

> to protect the best interests of Indian children and to promote the stability and security of Indian tribes and families by the establishment of minimum Federal standards for the removal of Indian children from their families and the placement of such children in foster or adoptive homes which will reflect the unique values of Indian culture, and by providing for assistance to Indian tribes in the operation of child and family service programs.

25 U.S.C. § 1902.

The dissent provides no support for its assertion that 25 U.S.C. section 1901(5) states that a "key countervailing purpose at stake under ICWA is the protection of the traditional jurisdiction of state courts over adoption proceedings." *Infra* ¶ 159. And that is an odd statement given that, in context, section 1901(5) states that "the States, exercising their recognized jurisdiction over Indian child custody proceedings through administrative and judicial bodies, have often failed to recognize the essential tribal relations of Indian people and the cultural and social standards prevailing in Indian communities and families." That is, ICWA represents an extraordinary act of federal intervention into family law precisely in response to Congress's concern about state courts' "alarming []" tendency to disregard the interests of Indian parents and tribes. 25 U.S.C. § 1901(4). So, far from being "recognize[d] . . . to a large degree" as a "countervailing purpose," *infra* ¶ 159, state courts' wielding of their traditional jurisdiction is what led to the need for ICWA in the first place.

Notably, nothing in the "Congressional declaration of policy," 25 U.S.C. § 1902, supports the assertion that protection of states' traditional jurisdiction is part of ICWA's purpose. And the fact that "ICWA does not oust the states of that traditional area of their authority," *infra* ¶ 159, is not a reason to read in another purpose—it is simply how federalism works. See *In re Adoption of Halloway*, 732 P.2d 962, 967 (Utah 1986) ("Under general supremacy principles, state law cannot be permitted to operate as an obstacle to the accomplishment and execution of the full purposes and objectives of Congress." (internal quotation marks omitted)).

The dissent also ignores Congress's plenary powers in this arena by asserting that issues of paternity and other family matters have "never been a creature of federal law," *infra* ¶ 163, and that the use of the past tense in section 1903(9) is significant because it means that Congress intended "acknowledged" and "established" to be defined by existing standards—by which it means state standards. *Infra* ¶ 171. This is not correct. First, acknowledgement or establishment of paternity under a federal standard is consistent with the use of the past tense because any action a putative father takes after the enactment of ICWA necessarily looks back to the standard ICWA had—in the past—established. Second, to the extent the dissent is attempting to guard against a perceived intrusion, it ignores the fact that this "intrusion" is taking place within the context of Indian welfare, an area in which Congress has plenary authority. U.S. Const. art. I, § 8(3) ("The Congress shall have Power ... To regulate Commerce ... with the Indian Tribes."); See *Cotton Petroleum Corp. v. New Mexico*, 490 U.S. 163, 192, 109 S.Ct. 1698, 104 L.Ed.2d 209 (1989) ("[T]he central function of the Indian Commerce Clause is to provide Congress with plenary power to legislate in the field of Indian affairs."); *Halloway*, 732 P.2d at 967 ("The Supreme Court has made it clear that where Indian affairs are concerned, a broad test of preemption is to be applied.").

This authority encompasses family matters such as child-raising. *Wakefield v. Little Light*, 276 Md. 333, 347 A.2d 228, 234 (1975) ("We think it plain that child-rearing is an essential tribal relation." (internal quotation marks omitted)); see also 25 U.S.C. § 1901(2)–(3) (stating that Congress has "assumed the responsibility for the protection and preservation of Indian tribes and their resources" and that "there is no resource that is more vital to the continued existence and integrity of Indian tribes than their children"). Indeed, the very point of ICWA is to regulate family law issues. 25 U.S.C. § 1902(stating that the statute's policy is to protect Indian children and families and establish standards for placing those children in foster or adoptive homes). By arguing that the definition of paternity in the context of Indian affairs is a state issue, the dissent's position largely ignores the federal government's plenary powers over Indian affairs, not to mention the purpose and text of ICWA as a whole. We are loath to pour state law back into ICWA when ICWA's whole reason for being is to drain what, in Congress's view, is an inequitable swamp—displacing state law on the matters on which ICWA speaks.

The danger that ICWA "would be impaired if state law were to control" presents an additional, compelling reason "for the presumption against the application of state law." *Holyfield*, 490 U.S. at 44, 109 S.Ct. 1597 (citation omitted). And hewing closely to this presumption in the Indian affairs arena, in which Congress enjoys plenary power, strikes us as particularly appropriate where "the congressional findings that are a part of the statute demonstrate that Congress perceived the States and their courts as partly responsible for the problem it intended to correct." *Id.* at 45, 109 S. Ct. 1597; see also *Halloway*, 732 P.2d at 969 (stating that Utah court's receptivity to placing Indian children in non-Indian homes "is precisely one of the evils at which the ICWA was aimed"); 25 U.S.C. § 1901(4) (indicating "that an alarmingly high percentage of Indian families are broken up by the removal, often unwarranted, of their children from them by nontribal public and private agencies"); *id.* § 1901(5) (expressing concern "that the States . . . have often failed to recognize the essential tribal relations of Indian people and the cultural and social standards prevailing in Indian communities and families"). The U.S. Supreme Court praised our "scholarly and sensitive" decision in *Halloway* for its sensitivity to the risk that state law could "be used to frustrate the federal legislative judgment expressed in the ICWA." *Holyfield*, 490 U.S. at 52–53, 109 S.Ct. 1597 (quoting *Halloway*, 732 P.2d at 970).

Furthermore, ICWA provides that "where State or Federal law applicable to a child custody proceeding under State or Federal law provides a higher standard of protection to the rights of the parent . . . of an Indian child than the rights provided under [ICWA], the State or Federal court shall apply the State or Federal standard," thus ensuring that parents of Indian children enjoy the highest level of protection of their parental rights available. 25 U.S.C. § 1921. Applying state law to determine who is a parent under ICWA would, in some cases, provide a lower level of protection of parental rights than ICWA intends. Utah law serves as the perfect example of this problem. Whereas ICWA provides that an unmarried biological father may "*acknowledge*[] or establish[]" paternity, *id.* § 1903(9) (emphasis added), Utah law provides no viable procedure for acknowledging paternity in cases where the mother wants to place the child for adoption at birth and does not consent to the acknowledgment. For a biological father to acknowledge paternity through a declaration of paternity, Utah law requires the birth mother's signature in addition to the unmarried biological father's signature. Utah Code § 78B-15-302(1)(c). Thus, in cases where the birth mother declines to sign the declaration, the unmarried biological father is precluded from acknowledging paternity under ICWA, if we look to Utah law for the definition of that term. See *In re Adoption of R.M.*, 2013 UT App 27, ¶ 8, 296 P.3d 757 ("If the birth mother declines to acknowledge the unmarried biological father's paternity and refuses to sign the declaration of paternity, he will have to comply with the paternity provisions in order for his consent to be required."). The result is that, when applying Utah law, the unmarried biological father's option to acknowledge paternity is essentially read out of ICWA. The district court's opinion illustrates this result, as it does not seriously analyze whether Birth Father acknowledged paternity under Utah law, instead focusing on whether he complied with the requirements for establishing paternity under Utah law.

Also, as the district court recognized, "Utah's requirements for establishment of paternity by unwed fathers are notoriously strict." See *In re Adoption of Baby E.Z.*, 2011 UT 38, ¶ 40, 266 P.3d 702 ("The Utah legislature has enacted strict requirements for unmarried birth fathers who seek to prevent adoption of their children."). Applying state law to a term as critical as the definition of a parent under ICWA is not in keeping with ICWA's text and purpose. And applying Utah law specifically to eliminate the option of acknowledging paternity—and instead requiring an unmarried biological father of an Indian child to comply with some of the strictest requirements for establishing paternity in order to receive any protection of his parental rights under ICWA—"would, to a large extent, nullify the purpose the ICWA was intended to accomplish." *Holyfield*, 490 U.S. at 52, 109 S.Ct. 1597.

We also conclude that "Congress could hardly have intended the lack of nationwide uniformity that would result from state-law definitions of" who is a parent under ICWA. *Id.* at 45, 109 S.Ct. 1597.23 In *Holyfield*, the U.S. Supreme Court concluded that ICWA did not incorporate state-law definitions of domicile in large part to avoid the anomaly of different results depending on which state the mother traveled to in order to give birth. *Id.* at 46, 109 S.Ct. 1597. It would be similarly anomalous—not to mention unfair and an unwarranted intrusion by states into Indian customs and practices—to make an unmarried biological Indian father's status as a parent under ICWA depend on whether the mother gave birth in one state or another. "[A] statute under which different rules apply from time to time to the same" unmarried biological father, "simply as a result of" the mother's decision to give birth in "one State [or] another, cannot be what Congress had in mind." *Id.* Thus, we conclude that the interpretation of what is required to acknowledge or establish paternity under ICWA is not left up to state law.

* * *

3. A Federal Standard of Reasonableness Applies

Having rejected the application of state law to define the procedures and timing for acknowledging or establishing paternity under ICWA, we hold that a federal standard applies. We acknowledge that ICWA does not explicitly define the procedures and timing required, but in light of the congressional findings and the purpose of ICWA as discussed above, as well as its protectiveness of parental rights pertaining to Indian children, we conclude that the requirements must be less exacting than those for establishing paternity under Utah law. Instead, we conclude that a reasonability standard applies to the time and manner in which an unwed father may acknowledge or establish his paternity. This comports with the canon of interpretation that where a statute is silent as to the time or manner of a subject, we presume a reasonability standard—an approach that is consistent with ICWA case law and has been applied by many states over many years and many different topics of law. ICWA is silent both as to the manner in which an unwed father may acknowledge or establish paternity and as to the time in which he must do so. Applying a reasonability standard here creates obvious stop-gaps and prevents the slippery-slope concerns of the dissent, as it requires more than "any bare acknowledgement by a putative father," *infra* ¶ 198, and would not allow "a putative Indian father [to] come forward months or even years later and assert a right to disrupt even a finalized adoption." *Infra* ¶ 201.27

This approach is consistent with ICWA's liberal administration. Guidelines for State Courts; Indian Child Custody Proceedings, 44 Fed. Reg. 67,584, 67,586 (Nov. 26,

1979) (stating that ICWA "shall be liberally construed"); see also *Brenda O. v. Ariz. Dep't of Econ. Sec.*, 226 Ariz. 137, 244 P.3d 574, 577 (Ariz. Ct. App. 2010) ("ICWA is to be interpreted 'liberally in favor of the Indians' interest in preserving family units.'" (citation omitted)); *In re Esther V.*, 149 N.M. 315,248 P.3d 863, 869 (2011) (noting that ICWA is a remedial statute that must be interpreted "liberally to facilitate and accomplish [its] purposes and intent" (citation omitted)).

* * *

Thus, we hold that Birth Father's actions satisfied the requirements for acknowledging paternity under ICWA using a reasonability standard. Birth Father and Birth Mother resided together at the time of conception and for the first six months of Birth Mother's pregnancy. During that time, Birth Father supported Birth Mother, paying for their rent, utilities, and groceries and Birth Mother's phone bill. When Birth Mother moved to Utah six months into the pregnancy, the plan was for Birth Father to join her later, once she was settled into their new apartment. Birth Father stayed in contact with Birth Mother over the phone for the first few weeks after her move, until Birth Mother cut off communication with him. Birth Father was then told by family friends that Birth Mother was fine and would return to South Dakota soon. Birth Father indicated that he believed Birth Mother needed some space and that she would either return to South Dakota to deliver their baby or that she would return with the baby after the delivery. Instead, Birth Mother placed their child for adoption. Upon learning of the proceedings shortly after the September 25, 2014 order terminating parental rights was issued, Birth Father informed the tribe of the situation and consulted with Dakota Plains Legal Services. After being referred to Utah Legal Services, Birth Father filed a motion to intervene, a motion for paternity testing, and a paternity affidavit expressly acknowledging that he was the Child's biological father. He also filed an Answer, Objection, and Verified Counter-petition to the Verified Petition for Adoption. When new ICWA guidelines were released on the day of the hearing on his motions, Birth Father acted immediately: the very same day, he submitted those guidelines to the court with a motion requesting the court to review them and drawing the court's attention to pertinent provisions in the guidelines. In the April 21, 2015 order denying Birth Father's motion to intervene on the basis that he was not a parent under ICWA, the district court itself stated that Birth Father has filed numerous documents with the Court in this case asserting paternity. In connection with this case, [Birth Father] has filed an affidavit setting forth his willingness and ability to parent the Child, his plans for care of the Child, and his willingness to pay child support and expenses related to the pregnancy and birth. He has filed a notice, with the Utah Department of Health, Office of Vital Records and Statistics, indicating that he has filed a paternity action regarding the Child (identifying this case as the paternity action). Thus, if one construes this action as a 'paternity action,' then [Birth Father] has now accomplished all of the tasks required by Utah's statute.

These actions, we hold, were both timely and sufficient for Birth Father to acknowledge paternity under ICWA, making Birth Father a "parent" for purposes of section 1914.

Notes

1. A question that regularly arises under ICWA is how much of the federal law preempts state law. There is general consensus in the state courts that ICWA does not constitute either express preemption or implied "field preemption" where Congress intended ICWA to occupy the field for Indian child welfare. There are too many holes in the law, including exact timing of hearings, and other details in state child welfare laws that are simply not addressed in the law. There is, however, preemption when state law conflicts with federal law. In *In re Brandon M.*, discussed in Chapter Three, California found that California's state-created de facto parent doctrine did not conflict with ICWA. 63 Cal. Rptr. 2d 671 (Cal. Ct. App. 1997). Interestingly, the court here does not mention preemption. Re-reading the descriptions of preemption in *Brandon M.*, could that discussion have helped this court address the issue of what standard applies for a putative father?

2. Because states have found that both ICWA and their state law must work together, the question of how to reach ICWA's standards and state standards is often up for discussion. When a state court decides the state must meet both the state and ICWA's standards, it is considered a dual burden state. In Chapter Three, the note for *In re England*, 887 N.W.2d 10 (Mich. App. Ct. 2016), discusses the dual burden issue. In this case, the majority recognized there was no way to meet the Utah standard, and also the ICWA standard for a putative father. The 2015 Guidelines stated "to qualify as a parent, an unwed father need only take reasonable steps to establish or acknowledge paternity. Such steps may include acknowledging paternity in the action at issue or establishing paternity through DNA testing." 80 Fed. Reg. 10151 (Feb. 25 2015) (withdrawn and replaced by Guidelines for Implementing the Indian Child Welfare Act, U.S. Dept. of Interior (Dec. 2016)).

3. Unfortunately, neither the federal regulations nor 2016 Guidelines provide similar guidance. The front matter to the Regulations does state,

> The final rule mirrors the statutory definition and does not provide a Federal standard for acknowledgment or establishment of paternity. The Supreme Court and subsequent case law has already articulated a constitutional standard regarding the rights of unwed fathers, see *Stanley v. Illinois*, 405 U.S. 645 (1972); *Bruce L. v. W.E.*, 247 P.3d 966, 978–979 (Alaska 2011) (collecting cases)—that an unwed father who "manifests an interest in developing a relationship with [his] child cannot constitutionally be denied parental status based solely on the failure to comply with the technical requirements for establishing paternity." *Bruce L.*, 247 P.3d at 978–79. Many State courts have held that, for ICWA purposes, an unwed father must make reasonable efforts to establish paternity, but need not strictly

comply with State laws. *Id.* At this time, the Department does not see a need to establish an ICWA-specific Federal definition for this term.

81 Fed. Reg. 38796 (June 14, 2016).

While *Bruce L v. W.E.* says "[t]hese cases demonstrate that to qualify as an ICWA parent an unwed father does not need to comply perfectly with state laws for establishing paternity, so long as he has made reasonable efforts to acknowledge paternity," 247 P.3d 966, 979 (Alaska, 2011), those cases do not establish any kind of federal standard. Rather, most refer back to their state laws.

4. The court mentions that Utah's standards for establishing paternity are particularly onerous. Prof. Kevin Maillard explored the issue of putative father registries in an article in The Atlantic.

> Since the 1970s, 33 states have created Putative Father Registries, designed as a way to link unmarried men to the mother of their child. States expect men to report—voluntarily and honestly—information about all their sexual partners; otherwise, they forfeit their right to be contacted if a partner pursues adoption. The registry is not a petition for custody or a determination of paternity—only a right to notification.
>
> * * *
>
> State registry systems can also seem like bureaucratic afterthoughts. When I asked a staff member at the Alabama Department of Human Resources if all men should register, he said it was a good idea to "cover all your bases." He wasn't entirely sure of the intricacies of the law, but he promised to send me some forms in the mail, since men can't register online in Alabama.
>
> A few days later, I received a thick envelope containing a form labeled "Putative Father Intent to Claim Paternity Registration." It asked for the man's name, race, and social security number. It also asked for the woman's name, race, birthday, and social security number, as well as a "Possible Date(s) of Sexual Intercourse." The form was hand-typed and crooked from what looked like a rushed copy—or even mimeograph—job. The year on the form was listed as "19___."
>
> And every state is different. In Illinois, men can register online. Texas requests a driver's license number. Utah requires an in-person court hearing and an affidavit stating plans for custody, child support, and pregnancy expenses. Illinois demands height, weight, and eye color.

Kevin Maillard, *Sex and the Single Man*, The Atlantic, Apr. 21, 2014.

Why would the father in this case have gone through the trouble and expense of having an in-person hearing to say he might be the father of a woman he had known in South Dakota and intended joining in Utah? What about the fact that the father in this case lived on a reservation, and not under any state jurisdiction?

C. Tribal Rights in Voluntary Proceedings

Cherokee Nation v. Nomura

160 P.3d 967 (Okla. 2013)

Watt, Justice.

This case was previously retained by this Court for disposition. It involves the interaction of the Oklahoma Indian Child Welfare Act (Oklahoma Act) 10 O.S.2001 §§40–40.9, the federal Indian Child Welfare Act of 1978 (Federal Act), 25 U.S.C. §§1901, et seq., and the Oklahoma Interstate Compact on the Placement of Children (Interstate Compact Act), 10 O.S.2001 §§571–576. We consider the right of an Indian mother to place her child voluntarily for adoption with out of state non-Indian adoptive parents without consideration of the placement preferences of the Federal Act, 25 U.S.C. §1915, or utilizing "to the maximum extent possible" the services of the Indian tribe in placement of the child under 10 O.S. §40.6 of the Oklahoma Act. The dispositive issue in this adoption proceeding is whether the Oklahoma Act must be applied to every adoption of Indian children born to an Oklahoma Indian parent, even if the Indian parent chooses out of state non-Indian adoptive parents. We hold that it must and affirm the trial court's declaratory judgment.

Procedural Background

Through an adoption agency, Appellant American Adoptions of Florida, Inc. (Florida Adoption Agency or Agency), the mother chose to have her child adopted by non-Indian parents living in Florida. The child was born in Oklahoma on October 2, 2005. On October 3, 2005, the adoptive parents appeared before the Oklahoma District Court in Rogers County, Oklahoma, with a motion to approve adoption expenses pursuant to 10 O.S.2001 §7505–3.2(B).1 The trial court filed an order granting their motion on the same day. On October 11, 2005, the adoptive parents filed a petition for adoption in Florida, and a Florida court issued an order for preliminary custody to the adoptive parents, although neither the birth mother nor the child was present. On October 13, 2005, the mother went to Florida to consent to Florida law for the adoption and the termination of her parental rights. On October 14, 2005, Florida Adoption Agency filed a petition in Florida to terminate the birth parents' parental rights. On October 14, 2005, the Florida court entered a judgment terminating the parental rights to the mother and to "any known and unknown biological father," finding the putative father's right to consent to the adoption had been waived. In that order, the Florida court made a finding that "[a]ll provisions of the Indian Child Welfare Act have been complied with, and all notices required by federal or state law have been given. This is a voluntary proceeding under the ICWA, and therefore, notice to the tribe is not required under ICWA or state law." Also recited in the October 14 order is the following:

> IT IS ORDERED, based upon the request of the natural mother of the minor child, . . . that good cause exists to waive, and the court does hereby waive, the adoption placement preferences of the Indian Child Welfare Act, 25

> U.S.C. § 1915, to allow the adoptive placement of [the child] born October 2, 2005, with [adoptive parents]. . . .

The Florida court found that a "voluntary" proceeding under the Federal Act requires neither notice to the Tribe nor adherence to the adoption placement preferences of 25 U.S.C. § 1915 of the Federal Act. "Good cause" to waive the placement preferences was found to exist because the birth mother requested it. It is undisputed that notice to the Tribe was not attempted before October 18, 2005, four days after the Florida court's judgment. There is also testimony in the record that notice by certified mail from Florida Adoption Agency's attorney Jeanne Tate was not received by the Tribe until November 8, 2005, twenty-five (25) days after judgment was entered.

After receiving notice of the adoption proceeding in Florida, the Tribe intervened in the Florida case to insure compliance with the Federal Act and to reserve the right to remove it to tribal court. The Tribe then filed this case seeking a temporary restraining order (TRO) against the Administrator of the Oklahoma Interstate Compact on the Placement of Children (Interstate Compact Act), Michael Nomura, Defendant/Appellee (Nomura). The Tribe sought to prevent Nomura from approving the Interstate Compact Act materials and issuing the "100A" in order to prevent removal of the child from Oklahoma.

* * *

Nomura moved to dismiss on grounds of sovereign immunity and alternatively requested a declaratory judgment, pursuant to 12 O.S.2001 § 1652,5 as to the applicability of 10 O.S.2001 § 40.66 to this case. The court denied Nomura's motion to dismiss, stating an order would issue on Nomura's request for declaratory judgment.

* * *

In its order, the trial court found:

> Thus the ICPC provides that *the child at issue shall be treated in the same manner as such child would have been dealt with had the child remained in the sending state.* Then if OICWA would have been applicable had the child been adopted then it must also be complied with under the provisions of the ICPC. [emphasis in original].
>
> . . .
>
> Under the provisions of 10 O.S. § 40.3, 40.4 and 25 U.S.S. (sic) § 1903 this Court finds that such a proceeding would constitute a child custody proceeding as defined by both ICWA and OICWA, regardless of whether the proceeding was determined to be voluntary or involuntary. The Court further finds that the notice requirements of 10 O.S. § 40.4 would apply, and that the placement preference provisions of 25 U.S.C. § 1915 and 10 O.S. § 40.6 would apply to such an adoption proceeding in Oklahoma.
>
> The Court accordingly finds and determines under the facts and circumstances of this case that the Cherokee Nation is entitled to notice of

> adoption proceedings related to the minor child . . . and that the placement preference of 25 U.S.C. § 1915 and 10 O.S. § 40.6 would apply to said child.
>
> It is therefore the Court's determination that Defendant Nomura in his official capacity as administrator of the Oklahoma ICPC does have a duty to see that the placement preference established by OICWA and ICWA are complied with along with the notice provisions therein before approving the adoption placement of [the child] under the provision of the ICPC.

The trial court overruled Florida Adoption Agency's challenge to the court's jurisdiction and rejected its constitutional argument that the mother has a liberty interest to decide who may adopt her child, holding that the parental rights of these parents were terminated at their request. Therefore, the court held that at that point there were no parental rights "except whatever rights the natural parents may retain with regard to the revocations of their consents. . . ."

The trial court's order concluded:

> The Court finds in balancing whatever liberty interest the natural mother may have in making decisions regarding who may adopt the child at issue against the state's compelling interest to recognize and protect the valid governmental interest of Indian Tribes and Nations regarding Indian children, that the statute while intrusive acts to both preserve the integrity of Indian Tribes and people while at the same time addressing the best interest of the Indian child at issue. The Court finds that the governmental interest outweighs whatever parental rights may remain with the natural parents. See *Blevins*, 10 O.S. § 40.1 and 25 U.S.C. § 1915.

* * *

The issue of the Oklahoma court's continuing jurisdiction after the initial order approving adoption expenses, under 10 O.S.2001 § 7505–3.2, was raised in the trial court. The trial court held that jurisdiction continued. We agree. Under the Interstate Compact Act, the sending agency "shall continue to have financial responsibility for support and maintenance of the child during the period of the placement." Article V(a). Jurisdiction over the child continues in Oklahoma until the receiving state notifies the "sending agency" in writing that the proposed placement is in the interests of the child. See 10 O.S.2001 § 571, Article III(d).11 Article V(a) also provides the sending agency shall retain jurisdiction over the child to determine all necessary matters in relation to the child "which it would have had if the child had remained in the sending agency's state, until the child is adopted. . . ."

Florida Adoption Agency appears to acknowledge the authority of the "sending agency" under Article V(a). However, it argues the birth mother, not Administrator Nomura, is designated the "sending agency" on the Form 100A, and that Nomura is required to forward to Florida any information she provided. Agency contends the "receiving state" actually approves whether placement is proper and Nomura has no authority to refuse to sign the 100A and send it to Florida.

We disagree with Agency's contention that Nomura has a duty to "rubber stamp" any information received from the birth mother and forward it to Florida. The Interstate Compact Act allows the proper authorities of the state from which the placement is made to "obtain the most complete information on the basis on which to evaluate a projected placement before it is made." Article I(c). The receiving state may request additional information. Article III(c). In fact, in this case, the Florida Administrator contacted Nomura with concerns about the lack of notice to the Tribe. This led to Nomura's withdrawal of the original Form 100A.

* * *

DISCUSSION

Florida Adoption Agency seeks to challenge the application of the Oklahoma Act to a Florida adoption, the failure to allow Florida law to determine the appropriateness of placement in Florida, and to challenge the failure to acknowledge valid orders of the Florida Court. Also, Agency questions the constitutionality of the Oklahoma Act in voluntary adoptions, claiming it interfered with mother's constitutional and fundamental rights in and to her child, requiring the courts to apply the test of "strict judicial scrutiny" when examining state law. Florida Adoption Agency contends the birth mother selected the Florida family, which is fit and proper to nurture her child, with only the child's best interests in mind. It also contends the Oklahoma Act does not apply unless the Indian child is at risk, or is being endangered by the birth parents and claims that neither the Tribe, nor Nomura, presented any information the child was endangered by the mother or the adoptive family. Agency further contends the only basis for the Tribe's and Nomura's support of the Oklahoma Act is the fact the child is Cherokee, which infringes upon the mother's constitutional rights.

* * *

In *Baby Boy L.*, we considered a case involving the adoption of an Indian child and the application of the Federal Act and the Oklahoma Act. [*In the Matter of Baby Boy L*, 2004 OK 93, 103 P.3d 1099.] A child was born out of wedlock to a non-Indian mother and a noncustodial Indian father who did not live on an Indian reservation. The mother wished to place the child for adoption. She sought an order terminating the father's parental rights and declaring the baby eligible for adoption without the consent of the father. She located a non-Indian family in another state who wished to adopt the child. The mother argued the Federal Act and the Oklahoma Act were inapplicable because the baby was not being removed from an Indian family. Thus, she argued, the placement preferences set out in the Federal Act were not mandatory. The trial court agreed with her, and the Court of Civil Appeals affirmed. This Court reversed.

In doing so, we examined *Mississippi Band of Choctaw Indians v. Holyfield*, 490 U.S. 30, 109 S.Ct. 1597, 104 L.Ed.2d 29 (1989) (*Holyfield*), and the application of the Federal Act to the law of individual states. We held the "existing Indian family exception" to the Federal Act was no longer viable in Oklahoma. In so ruling, we noted the *Holyfield* Court recognized Congress showed concern, through passage of the Federal Act, "not only about the interests of Indian children and families, but also about the impact on the tribes because of the large numbers of Indian children being adopted by non-Indians." *Baby Boy L.*, 2004 OK 93, ¶ 14, 103 P.3d 1099, 1104.14 We determined the Oklahoma Legislature amended the Oklahoma Act in 1994 to abrogate the judicially created "existing Indian family exception" to the Federal Act in Oklahoma. We determined the Legislature so acted, partly "in recognition of the *Holyfield* teaching." *Baby Boy L.*, 2004 OK 93, ¶ 16, 103 P.3d 1099, 1106. We recognized the Federal Act showed Congressional intent to achieve uniformity among the states where the interests of Indian children, parents and tribes are concerned. We find the 1994 amendments of the Oklahoma Act show the Oklahoma Legislature's intent to make clear a parent involved in a voluntary "child custody proceeding" involving an Oklahoma Indian child may not ignore the application of the Federal Act as a matter of personal choice.15 See 10 O.S.2001 §§ 40.3 (B) and (E):

> B. Except as provided for in subsection A of this section [involving divorce and delinquency], the Oklahoma Indian Child Welfare Act applies to all state **voluntary and involuntary** child custody court proceedings involving Indian children, **regardless of whether or not the children involved are in the physical or legal custody of an Indian parent or Indian custodian at the time state proceedings are initiated.** [emphasis added].
>
> . . .
>
> E. The determination of the Indian status of a child shall be made as soon as practicable in order to ensure compliance with the notice requirements of Section 40.4 of this title.

Also amended in 1994 is section 40.416 which provides:

> In all Indian child custody proceedings of the Oklahoma Indian Child Welfare Act, **including voluntary court proceedings and review hearings**, the court shall ensure that the district attorney or other person initiating the proceeding shall send notice to the parents or to the Indian custodians, if any, **and to the tribe that is or may be the tribe of the Indian child**, and to the appropriate Bureau of Indian Affairs area office, by certified mail return receipt requested. The notice shall be written in clear and understandable language .... [emphasis added].

In *Holyfield*, the sole issue before the United States Supreme Court was the domicile of Indian twins whose voluntary adoption was under consideration. Their parents had lived on the reservation until immediately before their birth when they moved to Mississippi. If domiciled on the reservation, the tribal court had jurisdiction. See 25 U.S.C. § 1911(a). The parents argued the domicile of the twins was in Mississippi and the adoption should proceed in state court. The Supreme Court decided "domicile" under § 1911(a) must be given the construction which provides uniformity under federal law for purposes of the Federal Act. **The Court held the result should not be different "simply because the twins were 'voluntarily surrendered' by their mother . . . [because] [t]ribal jurisdiction . . . was not meant to be defeated by the actions of individual members of the tribe. . . ."** *Holyfield*, 490 U.S. 30, 49, 109 S.Ct. 1597, 1608. [emphasis added].

In the instant case, we do not have before us the domicile issue because neither the mother nor the child lived on a reservation. When "child custody proceedings" under the Federal Act take place in state court, certain statutory preferences are mandated under 25 U.S.C. § 1915(A), "absent good cause to the contrary." The *Holyfield* Court stated, at 1602:

> The most important substantive requirement imposed on state courts is that of § 1915(a), which absent "good cause" to the contrary, mandates that adoptive placements be made preferentially with (1) members of the child's extended family, (2) other members of the same tribe, or (3) other Indian families.

Agency contends the Oklahoma Act's requirement of notice to the Tribe in "voluntary" adoptions is unconstitutional because in the Federal Act, under 25 U.S.C. § 1912(a), notice is only required for involuntary state court proceedings. But See 25 U.S.C. § 1913(c) which provides, "In any voluntary proceeding for termination of parental rights to, or adoptive placement of, an Indian child, the consent of the parent may be withdrawn for **any** reason at any time prior to the entry of a final decree of termination or adoption . . . ." [emphasis added]. Clearly, the Federal Act contemplates voluntary proceedings. See also 25 U.S.C. § 1911(c), which provides "In any State court proceeding for . . . termination of parental rights to, an Indian child, . . . the Indian child's tribe shall have a right to intervene at any point in the proceeding." [emphasis added]. It would be difficult indeed to enforce the right to intervene in the proceeding without receiving notice of it.

Agency contends *Holyfield* is inapplicable to this case because of its distinguishing factual scenario. However, we adhered to its teachings in *Baby Boy L.*, despite somewhat different facts, and we recognized *Holyfield*'s influence on our Legislature's amendments to the Oklahoma Act. Congress intended the protections of the Federal Act to extend not only to Indian children and families, but also to the tribes themselves. Although notice to the tribe was not the main issue, the Supreme Court recognized Congress intended the Federal Act to promote uniformity and the protection of individual Indians **and** the Tribes. This persuades us that compliance with the Federal Act is required in voluntary and involuntary "child custody proceedings." Indeed, the "child custody proceeding" in *Holyfield* was a **voluntary** adoption and termination of parental rights case.

Further, the Oklahoma Act does not restrict the Federal Act, but in fact, supports it in state court adoptions. Neither the purpose of the Federal Act nor the Oklahoma Act can be achieved without notice to the tribe or consideration of the placement preferences. We noted in *Baby Boy L., supra*, that the amendments to the Oklahoma Act showed our Legislature was aware of Holyfield and attempted to conform our laws consistently with the Federal Act. See 25 U.S.C. § 1921, which recognizes:

> In any case where State or Federal law applicable to a child custody proceeding under State or Federal law provides a **higher standard of protection** to the rights of the **parent or Indian custodian of an Indian child** than the rights provided under this subchapter, the State or Federal court shall apply the State or Federal standard. [emphasis added].

Since *Holyfield* instructs that the Federal Act was intended to protect the Indian child, the parents and the Tribe, we find the "higher standard of protection" under § 1921 extends to the Tribe as well. While domicile of mother and child is not an issue in this case, Holyfield instructs that a change in domicile merely for the purpose of avoiding the Federal Act was an invalid act. Crossing state lines to avoid the jurisdiction of the tribal courts was held to be ineffective for purposes of the Federal Act.

Conclusion

We hold that the Oklahoma Act does not conflict with the Federal Act in its requirements of notice to the Tribe under 10 O.S. Supp.2006 § 40.419 when **voluntary or involuntary** child custody proceedings are initiated; or under 10 O.S.2001 § 40.6, which provides the placement preferences in 25 U.S.C. § 1915 shall apply to all adoptive placements of Indian children. Section 40.6 adds the further requirement that the placement agency "shall utilize to the maximum extent possible the services of the Indian tribe of the child in securing placement consistent with the provisions of the Oklahoma Indian Child Welfare Act." The Oklahoma Act supports the Federal Act by recognizing the Tribe's interests must be protected in adoption proceedings involving Indian children. The Oklahoma Act is thus consistent with the Federal Act and its purposes as recognized by the United States Supreme Court.

Notes

1. The litigation over tribal rights of intervention, transfer, and the application of the placement preferences arise over the language of the statute. None of these tribal rights are in section 1913 of ICWA, but rather throughout the language of the statute. For example, 25 U.S.C. § 1911(c) states "In any State court proceeding for the foster care placement of, or termination of parental rights to, an Indian child, . . . the Indian child's tribe has a right to intervene at any point in the proceeding." Any direct placement or voluntary adoption necessarily includes a termination of parental rights proceeding. In addition, ICWA defines "termination of parental rights" as "any action resulting in the termination of the parent-child relationship." 25 U.S.C. § 1903(1)(ii) (2012). Neither of these sections is limited to involuntary proceedings. Similarly, section 1911(b) allows for transfer to tribal court of any foster care placement, or termination of parental rights. However, the section governing notice limits notice to the tribe to "any involuntary proceeding in State court," 25 U.S.C.

§ 1912(a) (2012). This means that while a tribe might have a statutorily guaranteed right of transfer and intervention, it is meaningless if the tribe is not aware the child is even the subject of a proceeding.

2. The Interstate Compact on the Placement of Children (ICPC) is a uniform law adopted by each state governing the transfer of children across state lines. What is required regarding ICWA and an ICPC application is an open question, and usually determined on a state-by-state basis.

> Though the ICPC and ICWA have a similar funding source, most state laws are silent as to whether the ICPC provisions apply to ICWA placement preferences. Thus the application of the ICPC in ICWA cases becomes a matter of state administrative procedure. Generally administrative law allows an executive branch agency to fill gaps—within reason—where they exist in substantive law to further the goal of applying the law through rule-making, which includes implementing interpretive measures and procedures.

Neoshia R. Roemer, *Finding Harmony or Swimming in the Void: The Unavoidable Conflict between the Interstate Compact on the Placement of Children and the Indian Child Welfare Act*, 94 N. Dakota L. Rev. 149 (2019).

3. Understanding the ICWA statutory scheme means remembering that parents and tribes have different, yet equal, interests in Indian children. Those interests at times align—for example, both the parent and the tribe should want a qualified expert witness when needed, though perhaps for different reasons. One of the biggest arguments in the voluntary arena is the concern that tribal interests in keeping a child close and in the community might conflict with a parent's wish to place her child wherever she wants. However, because of the history of removing Indian children for "voluntary" adoptions, many tribes are concerned over the actions of adoption agencies in aggressively going after their most vulnerable citizens.

In re T.S.W.

276 P.3d 133 (Kan. 2012)

The opinion of the court was delivered by Moritz, J.:

Cherokee Nation, Intervenor, challenges the district court's decision under the Indian Child Welfare Act (ICWA), 25 U.S.C. § 1901 et seq. (2001), to deviate from ICWA's placement preferences, see 25 U.S.C. § 1915(a) (2001), based upon the biological non-Indian mother's preference that her child be placed with a non-Indian family. Because we conclude that absent a request for anonymity by a biological parent, a parent's placement preference cannot override ICWA's placement factors, we reverse the district court's determination.

Factual and Procedural Background

D.R.W. (Mother) gave birth to T.S.W. on September 14, 2009. Approximately 2 months before T.S.W.'s birth, Mother decided to place her child for adoption. She contacted Adoption Centre of Kansas, Inc. (the Agency) to assist her in that process, and she identified two possible fathers of her child, one of whom was J.A.L.

In early August 2009, J.A.L.'s mother notified the Agency that J.A.L. was a member of Cherokee Nation (the Tribe). Because of the child's potential eligibility for membership in the Tribe, the Agency requested that the Tribe provide profiles of potential adoptive families.

In early September, employees of the Agency exchanged several e-mails with employees of the Tribe. In these e-mails, the Agency advised that because the Tribe had no families that could pay the Agency's $27,500 flat fee, the Agency wished to place Mother's child with one of its own families. However, the Agency expressed concern that the Tribe might seek to remove the child at a later time. The Agency also pointed out that Mother had her own criteria for any adoptive family, including that the couple be Caucasian, childless, financially secure, and open to postadoption visitation.

The Tribe responded that it had identified several certified families that could meet Mother's adoption criteria but that it had no families capable of paying the Agency's $27,500 fee. The Tribe also pointed out that "[a]gency fees are not a reason to deviate from federal law."

Eventually, on September 9, 2009, the Agency's counsel, through an e-mail sent by an Agency employee, advised the Tribe that Mother would consider family profiles that met Mother's "criteria" and the Agency would "base fees and cost on an appropriate sliding scale." However, the Agency's counsel noted that the Agency's fees and costs could not be calculated absent information as to the prospective adoptive family's overall financial condition. The following day, September 10, 2009, the Tribe sent profiles of two potential adoptive families to the Agency.

Mother gave birth to T.S.W. on September 14, 2009. On September 15, 2009, the Agency filed a petition in district court seeking to terminate the parental rights of the two potential biological fathers. The petition specifically noted: "Subsequent to this petition for termination of parental rights, a petition for the adoption of the subject minor child will be filed."

After court-ordered paternity testing conclusively determined that J.A.L. (Father) was T.S.W.'s biological father, the Agency filed an amended petition on October 1, 2009, seeking termination of Father's parental rights. Also on October 1, 2009, the court granted temporary custody of T.S.W. to the Agency.

Father filed a handwritten objection to the petition, noting that although he was in jail, his mother was willing to raise T.S.W. However, the Agency did not contact any of Father's family members regarding T.S.W.'s placement because Mother did not want T.S.W. to be placed with Father's family.

Meanwhile, the Agency had not communicated with the Tribe regarding the Indian family profiles provided by the Tribe. Consequently, on September 28, 2009, the Tribe requested an update from the Agency on T.S.W.'s placement. On

September 30, 2009, the Agency responded that T.S.W. had been born on September 14, 2009; that paternity testing had confirmed that J.A.L. was T.S.W.'s biological father; that J.A.L. planned to contest the adoption; and that Mother had selected one of the two families provided by the Tribe as a possible adoptive family for T.S.W.

Based on T.S.W.'s status as an Indian child, on October 21, 2009, the Tribe moved to intervene in the action to terminate Father's parental rights. The record on appeal contains no ruling on this motion. Nevertheless, on November 5, 2009, the Tribe filed both an answer to the Agency's amended petition to terminate parental rights and a counter-petition requesting application of ICWA to the proceedings.

By November 2, 2009, both of the families proposed by the Tribe had withdrawn from consideration as potential adoptive families for T.S.W. The record reflects somewhat conflicting testimony regarding the reason for their withdrawal. According to testimony of the Tribe employees, one of the families withdrew because it received another placement while the other family withdrew because of concerns about the Agency's fees as well as the cost of potential litigation with Father.

In any event, upon learning of the unavailability of these families, the Agency requested that the Tribe provide profiles of other available adoptive families. But before the Tribe could do so, the Agency reviewed with Mother the profiles of several of its own families. From these profiles, Mother chose a non-Indian family to adopt T.S.W.

Apparently unaware that Mother had selected a non-Indian family, on November 9, 2009, the Tribe provided the Agency with an additional 17 to 20 Indian family profiles. Mother reviewed those profiles, but according to an Agency employee, Mother did not prefer any of the Indian families over the non-Indian family she had already selected. Mother later testified that had she not been permitted to place T.S.W. with the family of her choice, she would have withdrawn her consent to T.S.W.'s adoption.

Meanwhile, on November 18, 2009, the Agency filed a pleading entitled "Petition" seeking to deviate from ICWA's placement preferences in the pending action to terminate Father's parental rights. Although to this point no adoption proceeding had been filed, the Agency recited that it sought to deviate from ICWA's placement preferences. The pleading did not indicate whether the Agency sought to deviate from ICWA's temporary or adoptive placement preferences, nor did it indicate whether an adoption petition had been filed or was forthcoming. Further, although the "petition" mentioned ICWA, it contained no statutory reference to the Act, nor did it identify or discuss ICWA's placement preferences.

The docket sheet indicates the district court conducted a temporary placement hearing on December 4, 2009, although the transcript of the hearing is not included in the record on appeal. The hearing apparently resulted in T.S.W.'s prospective adoptive placement with the non-Indian family selected by Mother. It is unclear from the record whether the district court considered if good cause existed to deviate from ICWA's foster care and preadoptive placement preferences under 25 U.S.C. § 1915(b) before issuing a temporary placement order.

The record on appeal contains a pretrial order filed on January 12, 2010, reflecting a pretrial conference held on December 29, 2009. The pretrial order identifies the "Nature of hearing" as a "Termination of Parental Rights."

Also on January 12, 2010, the district court conducted a hearing on the Agency's petition to terminate Father's parental rights. Again, although the record on appeal contains no transcript of the hearing, it appears that at the conclusion of the hearing, the district court ruled from the bench, terminating Father's parental rights. However, the district court did not issue a written order terminating Father's parental rights until March 11, 2010.

On January 26 and 27, 2010, the district court conducted a hearing on the Agency's petition to deviate from ICWA's placement preferences. At the close of the hearing, the district court orally ruled from the bench, deviating from ICWA's placement preferences based primarily upon Mother's desire that the child be placed with the adoptive couple she had chosen and Mother's threat to withdraw her consent to the adoption if her choice was not approved.

At the close of the hearing, the district court asked the Agency's counsel to draft and circulate a journal entry memorializing the court's finding within 10 days and indicated that if the parties did not sign the journal entry within 4 days after circulation, the court would sign the journal entry without signatures. The court stated: "I wanna make sure that this case keeps moving and it's not sitting around for a couple of months waiting for the journal entry."

However, the journal entry formalizing the district court's decision was not filed until more than 2 months later, on April 15, 2010. In the meantime, as discussed below, counsel for the Agency in this case apparently filed a separate adoption proceeding in district court. In that separate proceeding, counsel represented the adoptive parents chosen by Mother and, without notice to the Tribe, obtained a final decree of adoption of T.S.W.

In its April 15, 2010, journal entry, the district court found good cause existed to deviate from ICWA. Like the "petition" for deviation filed by the Agency, the journal entry contains neither a statutory reference to ICWA nor a description of ICWA's placement preferences. Further, the journal entry does not specify whether the deviation is for temporary or adoptive placement. Nevertheless, in the journal entry the district court held: "Birth parents can revoke their consent at any time for any reason; and the birth Mother has final say." Further, the district court conclusively stated that the "[b]irth mother's preference is good cause under ICWA to deviate from the prescribed placement preferences."

The Tribe appealed the district court's April 15, 2010, order granting a deviation from ICWA's placement preferences. The appeal was transferred from the Court of Appeals to this court pursuant to K.S.A. 20–3018(c).

Prior to oral argument, this court issued a show cause order advising the parties that the record contained insufficient information for the court to verify its jurisdiction to hear the appeal. Specifically, the court noted the record contained no petition for adoption or final adoption decree, and the court directed the parties to address the finality of the order appealed from under K.S.A. 2011 Supp. 59–2401a(a)(1).

In response to the show cause order, the Tribe pointed out that the district court's journal entry finding good cause to deviate from ICWA's placement preferences was the final docket entry in the district court, other than appeal-related filings. The Tribe also noted that while the Agency had advised the Tribe that T.S.W. was adopted "a long time ago," the Tribe received no notice of the adoption and assumed it occurred "under a different case number." Finally, the Tribe advised that it had requested that the Agency provide confirmation of T.S.W.'s final adoption, but the Agency had not responded to its request.

In its "Response [to Show Cause Order] and Motion to Dismiss Appeal," the Agency argued this appeal should be dismissed for lack of jurisdiction because the Tribe did not appeal the termination of Father's parental rights and because the court's decision regarding placement deviation was not an appealable order under "K.S.A. 59–2401 [sic]" or K.S.A. 60–2102. However, the Agency's response did not address whether a separate adoption proceeding had been filed or a final adoption decree issued.

Nevertheless, during oral argument in this appeal, counsel for the Agency conceded that prior to the expiration of the appeal time in this action, he filed a petition to adopt T.S.W. in a separate proceeding and in that proceeding, he represented the adoptive parents chosen by Mother. Counsel represented at argument that the same judge that granted the deviation from ICWA in this case also entered a final adoption decree in the adoption proceeding. Finally, the Agency's counsel conceded he did not notify or communicate with the Tribe about T.S.W.'s adoption until after this court entered its show cause order, when he advised the Tribe's counsel that the adoption "happened a long time ago." . . .

We review a district court's finding that good cause exists to deviate from ICWA's placement preferences for abuse of discretion. *In re Adoption of B.G.J.*, 281 Kan. 552, 564, 133 P.3d 1 (2006) (finding that the district court abuses its "substantial discretion" if it fails to properly apply the ICWA factors).

> "Judicial discretion is abused if judicial action (1) is arbitrary, fanciful, or unreasonable, i.e., if no reasonable person would have taken the view adopted by the trial court; (2) is based on an error of law, i.e., if the discretion is guided by an erroneous legal conclusion; or (3) is based on an error of fact, i.e., if substantial competent evidence does not support a factual finding on which a prerequisite conclusion of law or the exercise of discretion is based." *State v. Ward*, 292 Kan. 541, Syl. ¶ 3, 256 P.3d 801 (2011).

This case also may require interpretation of ICWA. Interpretation of a statute is a question of law over which we exercise unlimited review. *In re A.J.S.*, 288 Kan. 429, 431, 204 P.3d 543 (2009).

ICWA's placement preferences extend to voluntary placements by a non-Indian parent

Before considering whether the district court correctly applied ICWA's placement preferences here, we first briefly consider what appears to be an alternative argument by the Agency. Although not precisely formulated, the Agency contends ICWA's placement preferences should not be applied to the situation presently before us, i.e., where a non-Indian biological parent has voluntarily consented to the placement of her Indian child with a non-Indian family. Without benefit of authority, the Agency reasons:

> "The most troubling aspect to the Cherokee Nation's position is the attempt to use the Act to usurp the prenatal rights of a fit non-Indian mother to determine the best interest of her child. The Act was designed to prevent the unfair forcible removal of Indian children from their own homes and place them with non-Indian adoptive parents. Here, the Cherokee Nation attempts to use the placement preferences in an involuntary removal to overrule the placement desires of the fit non-Indian mother in a voluntary placement."

But the Agency's argument is contrary to the explicit language of 25 U.S.C. § 1915(a), which makes ICWA's placement preferences applicable to "any adoptive placement of an Indian child." Moreover, this issue was resolved, albeit in a different context, by the United States Supreme Court in *Mississippi Choctaw Indian Band v. Holyfield*, 490 U.S. 30 (1989). There, the Mississippi Band of Choctaw Indians argued ICWA's jurisdictional provisions applied to an attempt by the biological Indian parents of twins to consent to their adoption by a non-Indian family. The tribe argued that the twins, like their parents, were "domiciled" on the reservation and the tribe had exclusive jurisdiction over their placement.

In *Holyfield*, the Supreme Court found that at the time of their birth, the twins were domiciled—like their parents—on the reservation. 490 U.S. at 48–49, 109 S. Ct. 1597. In so holding, the Court noted that tribal jurisdiction under ICWA "was not meant to be defeated by the actions of individual members of the tribe, for Congress was concerned not solely about the interests of Indian children and families, but also about the impact on the tribes themselves of the large numbers of Indian children adopted by non-Indians." 490 U.S. at 49, 109 S.Ct. 1597. The Court reasoned:

> "[I]t is clear that Congress' concern over the placement of Indian children in non-Indian homes was based in part on evidence of the detrimental impact on the children themselves of such placements outside their culture. Congress determined to subject such placements to the ICWA's jurisdictional and other provisions, even in cases where the parents consented to

an adoption, because of concerns going beyond the wishes of individual parents." 490 U.S. at 49–50, 109 S.Ct. 1597.

Thus, the Supreme Court in *Holyfield* held ICWA's jurisdictional provisions apply even when both biological parents voluntarily attempt to place their Indian child with a non-Indian family. Further, the Court expressly extended its jurisdictional holding to ICWA's "other provisions," which include the placement provision at issue here, 25 U.S.C. § 1915(a).

We also reject the Agency's implied suggestion that ICWA's placement preferences apply only when the parental rights of Indian parents are at issue. Simply stated, this argument is inconsistent with our recent holding in *In re A.J.S.* There, we abandoned the existing Indian family doctrine and held ICWA's placement preferences applied to the placement of A.J.S., who had both Indian and non-Indian heritage....

In this case, we need not extensively consider whether the Agency followed the placement preferences before seeking a deviation from those preferences. It did not. While the Agency made some effort to satisfy the second placement preference when it requested the Tribe provide available adoptive family profiles, the Agency impermissibly qualified its request in at least two ways. First, the Agency provided the Tribe with Mother's extensive "CRITERIA" for any prospective adoptive family. Second, the agency specified that prospective adoptive families be able to pay the Agency's $27,500 fee requirement. And while the Agency eventually indicated a willingness to modify its fee based on an unspecified sliding scale, the parties never agreed as to the parameters of that scale because Mother chose a non-Indian family based on profiles presented to her from the Agency.

Essentially, the Agency grafted its substantial fee requirement as well as Mother's placement criteria (which ironically specified that the adoptive parents be Caucasian) onto ICWA's placement preferences. Common sense dictates that ICWA's placement preferences cannot be undermined in this manner. In fact, the Agency's actions appear to fly in the face of Congress' intent in enacting ICWA. See *Holyfield*, 490 U.S. at 37, 109 S.Ct. 1597 (ICWA "'seeks to protect the rights of the Indian child as an Indian and the rights of the Indian community and tribe in retaining its children in its society' ... by establishing 'a Federal policy that, where possible, an Indian child should remain in the Indian community'" and ensuring that Indian child welfare determinations are not based on a white, middle-class standard that often forecloses placement with an Indian family).

Moreover, even if we could conclude that the Agency appropriately and thoroughly attempted to comply with ICWA's second placement preference, it is undisputed that it made no effort to comply with ICWA's first and third preferences. Regarding the first preference—placement with the child's extended family—an Agency employee testified that because Mother did not want T.S.W. to be placed with Father's extended family, the Agency did not ascertain whether such placement was possible. Further, it is undisputed that the Agency made no effort to ascertain the availability of placement with other Indian families—the third placement preference.

Instead, the district court found "good cause" under this statute to deviate from the placement preferences, permitting T.S.W.'s placement with a non-ICWA compliant family. Therefore, we are asked to decide whether a biological parent's preference for placement of an Indian child can provide good cause to override ICWA's placement preferences.

This is not an issue of first impression for this court. In *B.G.J.*, we considered whether the district court abused its discretion in finding good cause to deviate from ICWA's adoptive placement preferences in granting a non-Indian family's petition to adopt an Indian child. Both parties here rely on *B.G.J.* to support their opposing positions regarding whether the district court properly found good cause to deviate from ICWA's placement preferences in this case. For reasons discussed below, we conclude *B.G.J.* does not support the district court's deviation from ICWA here....

[I]n this case the district court made no such findings regarding the availability of placement with either natural parent's extended family or the availability of Tribe families. Instead, the court expressly noted that "[n]either of [the birth mother's or birth father's] families were [sic] considered as the birth mother did not want placement with them." And regarding the Cherokee Nation families offered by the Tribe, the court held: "An additional seventeen (17) to twenty (20) families were presented which the birth mother did not like and rejected." Significantly, the court further commented that "[t]here is no evidence to show that any of these families were disqualified for any legal or practical reason."

Thus, the district court in this case did not rely upon the unavailability of either T.S.W.'s extended family or the families offered by the Tribe. Instead, the court permitted Mother's desire not to place T.S.W. with extended family or any of the potential adoptive Tribe families to override these preferences....

In any event, in light of the text of 25 U.S.C. § 1915(c), BIA Guidelines F.1. and F.3., and the commentary to both of those guidelines, we are persuaded that the "parental preference" referred to in § 1915(c) was not intended to permit a biological parent's preference for placement of a child with a non-Indian family to automatically provide "good cause" to override the adoptive placement preferences of 25 U.S.C. § 1915(a). Instead, a parent's request for anonymity with respect to placement of the child must be considered along with other relevant factors, including the best interest of the child, in deciding whether to modify the order of consideration of ICWA's placement references. See *B.G.J.*, 281 Kan. at 565, 133 P.3d 1 (holding that "[t]he best interest of the child remains the paramount consideration, with ICWA preferences an important part of that consideration").

Our holding is consistent with at least one other jurisdiction that has analyzed and considered the confidentiality aspect of 25 U.S.C. § 1915(c)'s parental preference provision. *In Matter of M.B.*, 350 Mont. 76, 82, 204 P.3d 1242 (2009), the Montana Supreme Court concluded the commentary to BIA Guideline F.3. "indicates the purpose of this exception is to protect the biological parents' confidentiality, if they so choose." Because the biological parents did not seek to protect their confidentiality in that case, the court held the exception did not apply to the parents' request that their children be placed with their current foster family. 350 Mont. at 82–83, 204 P.3d 1242. But see *In re B.B.A.*, 224 P.3d 1285, 1287–88 (Okla.App.2009) (holding that the "persuasive language" of BIA Guideline F.3. "authorizes reliance upon only one factor to establish the existence of good cause" and that one factor could be the request of the biological parents).

Returning to the facts of this case, we note that the record contains no indication that Mother requested confidentiality with respect to T.S.W.'s placement. Rather, Mother simply did not want T.S.W. placed with Father's extended family members or members of the Tribe. Applying the above analysis, we conclude the district court erred in permitting Mother's preference to override ICWA's placement factors absent some request for confidentiality. Accordingly, we reverse the district court's decision deviating from ICWA's placement preferences in this case.

Notes

1. Cherokee Nation did not have the information for the appellate court on what order it was trying to appeal because the adoption agency started the adoption proceedings, in front of the same trial judge, without notifying the Nation.

2. Is this case still good law after *Adoptive Couple v. Baby Girl,* 133 S. Ct. 2552 (2013), which held that placement preferences in voluntary adoption cases only apply if there are formal applications for adoption from families who meet the placement preferences?

D. Anonymity

The issue of parental anonymity in a voluntary proceeding is one of the most difficult to weigh. At that point in a case, the interest of the parent in remaining anonymous conflicts with the tribe's interest in keeping a child in the community, and the child's interest as an adult in her records. Courts have come down on this in various ways. If a mother is from a small tribe, as many are, there is no way to achieve the placement preferences without her anonymity being compromised. *See In re Baby Girl Doe*, 865 P.2d 1090 (Mont. 1993):

> On appeal, the Tribe contends that its right to intervene and advocate enforcement of the statutory preferences for placement is meaningless when the first preference is for placement with the child's extended family and the court will not reveal the identity of the child's natural parent.
>
> The DFS, on the other hand, asserts, and the District Court agreed, that the natural parent's interest in anonymity has greater significance and it is binding on the court when it is invoked.
>
> In order to reconcile two provisions of the ICWA, which are potentially in conflict, we must determine how to best effectuate the principal purpose for which the Act was created.

* * *

> It is clear from the legislative findings and expression of policy, and the U.S. Supreme Court's application of the ICWA in Mississippi Choctaw, that the principal purposes of the Act are to promote the stability and security of Indian tribes by preventing further loss of their children; and to protect the best interests of Indian children by retaining their connection to their tribes.
>
> The principal statutory method by which these purposes are achieved is the order of preferences set forth in 25 U.S.C. § 1915(a) and (b), and the Tribe's right to intervene in order to enforce those preferences. While a parent's wish for anonymity can be considered where not otherwise in conflict with the Act's principal purposes, it cannot be allowed to defeat the purposes for which this Act was created.
>
> To give primary importance to the mother's request for anonymity would defeat the Tribe's right to meaningful intervention and possibly defeat application of the clear preference provided by statute for placement of Baby Girl Jane Doe with a member of her extended family.

Id. at 1095.

In the *Holyfield* case discussed in earlier chapters, the Supreme Court did not reach the issue of parental anonymity, but given the actions of the parents—to leave the reservation before the children were born, identify the adoptive parents, and to give birth far away from the tribe—anonymity may have been part of the motivating factor. At the very least, anonymity for tribal mothers may have to mean not involving the tribe. Whether this wish for anonymity reaches the level of a constitutional right to privacy remains unknown. No court as of this writing has held that it is. In addition, that same privacy or anonymity interest of the parents may also be in conflict with the interest, and right, of adopted Indian children to find their records. For children adopted after ICWA's enactment, their right to certain information about their biological parents is guaranteed in § 1917. For children adopted before ICWA, however, getting that information can be more difficult.

In re Hanson

470 N.W.2d 669 (Mich. App. 1991)

Per Curiam.

Petitioner Elaine F. Hanson appeals as of right from a July 10, 1989, order of the Wayne County Probate Court denying her request to make her adoption records available for her inspection. Petitioner seeks to determine her American Indian ancestry by means of those records in order to establish tribal membership. We reverse and remand.

Petitioner was born on March 13, 1960, the illegitimate daughter of a woman of Irish, Dutch, English, and Indian ancestry. Petitioner was adopted by Geraldine and William Hanson through the Wayne County Probate Court in 1961. Through a previous request for information about her biological parents, petitioner was provided with nonidentifying information, from which she learned she was part Indian.

Petitioner filed the present action for disclosure of identifying information, including the names, birth dates, and birthplaces of her biological parents, or copies of any birth certificates or death certificates. Because of her Indian ancestry, petitioner relied on § 107 of the Indian Child Welfare Act (ICWA), 25 U.S.C. § 1917, in support of her request for the information. Petitioner alleged that if she could prove that she is at least one-quarter-blood North American Indian, she would be entitled to benefits under Michigan's tuition waiver program, M.C.L. § 390.1251 et seq.; M.S.A. § 15.2114(1) et seq., as well as be eligible for other social and economic benefits under federal law. Alternatively, petitioner argued that federal law, particularly the ICWA, constituted good cause for release of the information under state law, M.C.L. § 710.67(1); M.S.A. § 27.3178(555.67)(1).

Following a hearing on the matter, the probate court ruled that the ICWA did not apply and that petitioner had not demonstrated good cause for release of the requested information. Accordingly, the petition was denied. . . .

Section 107 of the ICWA, under which petitioner sought access to her adoption records, states:

> Upon application by an Indian individual who has reached the age of eighteen and who was the subject of an adoptive placement, the court which entered the final decree shall inform such individual of the tribal affiliation, if any, of the individual's biological parents and provide such other information as may be necessary to protect any rights flowing from the individual's tribal relationship.

That section is limited by 25 U.S.C. § 1923, which provides:

> None of the provisions of this subchapter, except sections 1911(a), 1918, and 1919 of this title, shall affect a proceeding under State law for foster care placement, termination of parental rights, preadoptive placement, or adoptive placement which was initiated or completed prior to one hundred and eighty days after November 8, 1978, *but shall apply to any subsequent proceeding in the same matter* or subsequent proceedings affecting the custody or placement of the same child. (Emphasis added.)

The trial court summarily concluded that the present action was not a "subsequent proceeding" under the statute. We have not been able to locate any other case, in this or any other jurisdiction, which is directly on point. However, we believe that an adult adoptee's petition to examine her adoption records to establish her Indian heritage is both a "subsequent proceeding" and "a proceeding under State law for foster care placement, termination of parental rights, preadoptive placement, or adoptive placement."

We note that the Supreme Court of Alaska in *E.A. v. Alaska*, 623 P.2d 1210, 1215 (Alas. 1981), interpreted § 1923 in light of its legislative history which revealed that that section was intended to provide an orderly phasing in of the act's effect by making its provisions inapplicable to proceedings still pending on the act's effective date. However, § 1923 would apply to any subsequent, discrete phase of the same matter or to any proceeding involving the same child initiated after enactment.

We find the petition in this case to be just such a "subsequent proceeding" within the meaning of 25 U.S.C. § 1923. However, even if we did not, we hold that, in light of the express policy of the ICWA as set forth in 25 U.S.C. § 1902, "to protect the best interests of Indian children and to promote the stability and security of Indian tribes and families" petitioner has demonstrated good cause as a matter of law for the release of any information regarding her biological mother which could assist in establishing her tribal affiliation.

Our holding also finds support in the "Guidelines for State Courts; Indian Child Custody Proceedings," issued by the Department of the Interior, Bureau of Indian Affairs, which provides in pertinent part:

> G.2. Adult Adoptee Rights
>
> (a) Upon application by an Indian individual who has reached age 18 who was the subject of an adoptive placement, the court which entered the final decree must inform such individual of the tribal affiliations, if any of the individual's biological parents and provide such other information necessary to protect any rights flowing from the individual's tribal relationship.
>
> (b) The section applies regardless of whether or not the original adoption was subject to the provisions of the Act.
>
> (c) Where state law prohibits revelation of the identity of the biological parent, assistance of the Bureau of Indian Affairs shall be sought where necessary to help an adoptee who is eligible for membership in a tribe establish that right without breaching the confidentiality of the record.

However, while we hold that petitioner is entitled to the release of information regarding her biological mother in this case, we would also note that in cases in which the biological parents have not consented the manner in which that information is released should be tailored to best protect the privacy rights of the biological parents. We feel that a procedure similar to that outlined in 25 U.S.C. § 1951(b) would best effectuate that purpose, yet still provide the means by which the adult adoptee's tribal membership can be established. 25 U.S.C. § 1951(b) provides:

> Upon the request of the adopted Indian child over the age of eighteen, the adoptive or foster parents of an Indian child, or an Indian tribe, the Secretary shall disclose such information as may be necessary for the enrollment of an Indian child in the tribe in which the child may be eligible for enrollment or for determining any rights or benefits associated with that membership. *Where the documents relating to such child contain an affidavit*

> *from the biological parent or parents requesting anonymity, the Secretary shall certify to the Indian child's tribe, where the information warrants, that the child's parentage and other circumstances of birth entitle the child to enrollment under the criteria established by such tribe.* (Emphasis added.)

This procedure is echoed in subsection G.2.(c) of the guidelines set forth previously.

Consequently, where the consent of the adult adoptee's living biological parents has not been obtained, the probate court should release the identifying information to the appropriate tribe, not the adoptee, with a request that the tribe keep the information confidential. The court should seek the assistance of the Bureau of Indian Affairs where necessary to accomplish this. It is the tribe, not the adoptee, which needs the information to establish tribal membership.

In this case, we reverse the order of the probate court and remand for a determination whether there is any further information or documentation regarding petitioner's biological mother which the court could provide to assist her in establishing tribal membership. We do not retain jurisdiction.

Notes

1. The court decided this case despite the fact the plaintiff found her biological mother while the case was pending and met with her. Regardless of this meeting, plaintiff still did not have access to the documents she needed to give to the tribe to determine her tribal citizenship. *Id.* at 394-5. An overarching theme to pre-ICWA adoption is the complete lack of paperwork or official adoption proceedings. Agencies gave children to adoptive parents without any paperwork or formal mechanism. *See* Matthew L.M. Fletcher & Wenona T. Singel, *Indian Children and the Federal-Trust Relationship*, 95 Neb. L. Rev. 885, 887 ("[Prof. Singel and her sister's] mother and her sister . . . were taken by Catholic Social Services in Detroit in the early 1950s and placed with their adoptive parents in an adoption in 1958, without any written documentation whatsoever."). For those pre-ICWA adoptees, finding this information can be nearly impossible.

2. Other states have adopted similar reasoning to the Michigan Court of Appeals. *See In re Mellinger*, 672 A.2d 197 (N.J. 1996). It is one thing, however, to have the statute and case law, and quite another to find where the documents are housed. Under § 1917, the court where the adoption took place is supposed to give out the information. Final adoption records are rarely housed at the actual courthouse, especially twenty to thirty years later. Adult adoptees have to negotiate a large state bureaucracy to find their records, assuming they were properly filed in the first place. The new federal regulations state:

> § 23.71 Recordkeeping and information availability.
>
> (a) The Division of Human Services, Bureau of Indian Affairs (BIA), is authorized to receive all information and to maintain a central file on all State Indian adoptions. This file is confidential and only designated persons may have access to it.

(b) Upon the request of an adopted Indian who has reached age 18, the adoptive or foster parents of an Indian child, or an Indian Tribe, BIA will disclose such information as may be necessary for purposes of Tribal enrollment or determining any rights or benefits associated with Tribal membership. Where the documents relating to such child contain an affidavit from the biological parent or parents requesting anonymity, BIA must certify to the Indian child's Tribe, where the information warrants, that the child's parentage and other circumstances entitle the child to enrollment under the criteria established by such Tribe.

Chapter 5

Constitutional Questions

A. Legislative History

Aspects of the Indian Child Welfare Act's application and constitutionality have been questioned from the time of its passage. Time and again, however, Congress, the executive branch, and the court systems have upheld the Act. This is true for many reasons, but not the least because ICWA is firmly grounded in Congress's trust responsibility and its application is limited to those who have that political relationship between a tribe and the federal government. The three areas that come up most often are related to equal protection concerns, supremacy concerns, and parental right to privacy.

Letters to Hon. Morris K. Udall from the Department of Justice

Patricia Wald

H. Rep. 95-1386 (July 24, 1978), pp. 35-41

February 9, 1978

The bill would appear to subject family relations matters of certain classes of persons to the jurisdiction of tribal courts which are presently adjudicated in State courts. The bill would accomplish this result with regard to three distinct categories of persons, all possessing the common trait of having enough Indian blood to qualify for membership in a tribe. One class would be members of a tribe. Another class would be nontribal members living on reservations, and a third would be nonmembers living off reservations. These three classes would be denied access to State courts for the adjudication of certain family relations matters unless "good cause" is shown under 102(c) of the bill.

May 23, 1978

As you know the Department presented at some length its views on one constitutional issue raised by S. 1214 as it passed the Senate in a letter to you dated February 9, 1978. Briefly, that constitutional issue concerned the fact that S. 1214 would have deprived parents of Indian children as defined by that bill of access to State courts for the adjudication of child custody and related matters based, at bottom, on the racial characteristics of the Indian child. We express in that letter our belief that such racial classification was suspect under the fifth amendment and that we saw no compelling reason which might justify its use in these circumstances. This problem has been, for the most part, eliminated in the subcommittee draft which defines "Indian child" as "any unmarried person who is under age 18 and is either (a) a member of an Indian tribe or (b) eligible for membership in an Indian tribe and is the biological child of a member of an Indian tribe."

* * *

A third and more serious constitutional question is, we think, raised in section 102 of the House draft. That section, taken together with sections 103, and 104, deals generally with the handling of custody proceedings involving Indian children by State courts. Section 102 establishes a fairly detailed set of procedures and substantive standards which State courts would be required to follow in adjudicating the placement of an Indian child as defined by section 4(4) of the House draft.

As we understand section 102, it would, for example, impose these detailed procedures on a New York State court sitting in Manhattan where that court was adjudicating the custody of an Indian child and even though the procedures otherwise applicable in this State-court proceeding were constitutionally sufficient. While we think that Congress might impose such requirements on State courts exercising jurisdiction over reservation Indians pursuant to Public Law 83-280, we are not convinced that Congress' power to control the incidents of such litigation involving nonreservation Indian children and parents pursuant to the Indian commerce clause is sufficient to override the significant State interest in regulating the procedure to be followed by its courts in exercising State jurisdiction over what is traditionally State matter. It seems to us that the Federal interest in the off-reservation context is so attenuated that the 10th Amendment and general principles of federalism preclude the wholesale invasion of State power contemplated by section 102. See Hart, "The Relations Between State and Federal Law," 54 Colum. L. Rev. 489, 508 (1954).

House Committee on Interior and Insular Affairs Report

H. Rep. 95-1386 (July 24, 1978), pp. 12-19

The Department of Justice, in its reports to the committee of February 9 and May 23, 1978, raises questions regarding the constitutionality of certain of the provisions of the legislation. While the committee did not agree with the Department on these issues, certain changes were made in the legislation which will meet some of the Department's concerns. Other issues remain, however. In view of the constitutional doubts of the Department, the committee feels compelled to respond.

Supremacy Clause

Clause 2 of article VI of the U.S. Constitution provides:

> This Constitution, and the Laws of the United States which shall be made in Pursuance thereof; and all Treaties made, or which shall be made, under the Authority of United States, shall be the supreme Law of the Land; and the Judges in every State shall be bound thereby any Thing in the Constitution or Laws of any State to the Contrary notwithstanding.

When Congress legislates pursuant to its delegated powers, conflicting State law and policy must yield, *Gibbons v. Ogden*, 22 U.S. 1 (1824); *Hill v. Florida ex rel Watson*, 825 U.S. 588 (1945); *Nash v. Florida Industrial Comm.*, 389 U.S. 235 (1967); *Lee v. Florida*, 392 U.S. 378 (1968); *Perez v. Campbell*, 402 U.S. 637 (1971).

The Constitution, laws, and treaties of the United States are as much a part of the law of every State as its own local laws and constitution. Their obligation "is imperative upon the State judges, in their official and not merely in their private capacities. From the very nature of their judicial duties, they would be called upon to pronounce the law applicable to the case in judgment. They were not to decide merely according to the laws or constitution of the State, but according to the laws and treaties of the United States—'the supreme law of the land.'" *Martin. v. Hunter's Lessee*, 1 Wheat. 304 (1816); State courts have both the power and duty to enforce obligations arising under Federal law. *Claflin v. Houseman*, 23 U.S. 130 (1876); *Second Employer's' Liability Cases*, 223 U.S. 1 (1912); *Testa v. Katt*, 330 U.S. 386 (1947).

* * *

Membership and plenary power

The question occurs, as raised by the Department of Justice in its report: "Is the power of Congress limited, constitutionally, to only those individuals who are formally enrolled as members of an Indian tribe?" Again, the answer is negative.

In 1934, Congress enacted the Indian Reorganization Act of June 18, 1934 (48 Stat. 988). Section 19 defined "Indians" as:

> *** all persons of Indian descent who are members of any recognized Indian tribe now under Federal jurisdiction, and all persons who are descendants of such members who were, on June 1, 1934, residing within the present boundaries of any Indian reservation, and shall further include all other persons of one-half or more Indian blood.

Categories two and three of this definition are clearly not enrolled members of a tribe, by definition: yet Congress conferred the rights and benefits of the act upon this class of Indians, including the right to preference in Federal employment in the Bureau of Indian Affairs and the Indian Health Service. When the Supreme Court was called upon to construe the constitutionality of the Indian preference section of the Indian Reorganization Act in the case of *Morton v. Mancari*, 417 U.S. 535 (1974), it was aware that Indians who were not enrolled members of a tribe were made eligible for this preference by act of Congress, but did not strike the law down as invidiously discriminatory.

The reason it did not was because it was aware of its own past decisions with respect to congressional power over Indians not members of a tribe, Congress may disregard the existing membership rolls and direct that per capita distributions be made upon the basis of a new roll, even though such act may modify prior legislation, treaties, or agreements with the tribe. *Stephens v. Cherokee Nation*, 174 U.S.

445 (1899). Thus, the Supreme Court in the case of *Sizemore v. Brady*, 235 U.S. 441 (1914), said:

> *** Like other tribal Indians, the Creeks were wards of the United States, which possessed full power, if it deemed such a course wise, to assume full control over them and their affairs, to ascertain who were members of the tribe ***.

In *Federal Indian Law*, at page 45 in note 10, it is said:

> It has been held that Congress is not bound by the tribal rule regarding membership and may determine for itself whether a person is an Indian from the standpoint of a Federal criminal statute. *United States v. Rogers*, 4 How. 567 (1846).

In the very recent case of *United States v. Antelope*, 45 U.S.L.W. 4361 (April 19, 1977), the Supreme Court said:

> It should be noted, however, that enrollment in an official tribe has not been held to be an absolute requirement for federal jurisdiction. ***

Federal District Court Judge Battin, in *Dillon v. Montana*, (1978), ordered:

> 2. That for purposes of applying this (Federal) exemption, the class of "Indian persons" *** shall include persons possessing the following qualifications:
>
> (a) that the person possess some quantum of Indian blood;
>
> (b) that the person be recognized as an Indian by the community in which he or she lives, and that the putative taxpayer's wardship status has not been terminated by the government;
>
> (c) that the person be an enrolled member of a federally recognized Indian tribe *or otherwise eligible to be recognized as an Indian ward by the Federal Government.* (Emphasis added.)

If the courts have found that Congress has the power to act with respect to non-enrolled Indians in the foregoing kinds of circumstances, how much more is its power to act to protect the valuable rights of a minor Indian who is eligible for enrollment in a tribe? This minor, perhaps infant, Indian does not have the capacity to initiate the formal, mechanical procedure necessary to become enrolled m his tribe to take advantage of the very valuable cultural and property benefits flowing therefrom. Obviously, Congress has power to act for their protection. The constitutional and plenary power of Congress over Indians and Indian tribes and affairs cannot be made to hinge upon the cranking into operation of a mechanical process established under tribal law, particularly with respect to Indian children who, because of their minority, cannot make a reasoned decision about their tribal and Indian identity.

* * *

Conclusion

Under the rules of the House, this committee has been charged with the initial responsibility in implementing the plenary power over, and responsibility to, the Indians and Indian tribes, In the exercise of that responsibility, the committee has noted a growing crisis with respect to the breakup of Indian families and the placement of Indian children, at an alarming rate, with non-Indian foster or adoptive homes. Contributing to this problem has been the failure of State officials, agencies, and procedures to take into account the special problems and circumstances of Indian families and the legitimate interest of the Indian tribe in preserving and protecting the Indian family as the wellspring of its own future.

While the, committee does not feel that it is necessary or desirable to oust the States of their traditional jurisdiction over Indian children falling within their geographic limits, it does feel the need to establish minimum Federal standards and procedural safeguards in State Indian child custody proceedings designed to protect the rights of the child as an Indian, the Indian family and the Indian tribe.

Notes

1. While the Department of Justice has not been overtly hostile since the passage of ICWA, it had been completely silent on the issue since 1979. After the decision in *Adoptive Couple v. Baby Girl*, 133 S. Ct. 2552 (2013), the Obama Administration asked tribes in a letter to tribal leaders how the federal government could be more supportive of ICWA compliance. That led directly to an increase of Department of Justice involvement in ICWA cases during the latter half of that Administration, from the filing of amicus briefs to the culmination in the publication of federal regulations. Those Regulations contain considerable front matter, or preamble, addressing the comments the government received regarding the regulations. Compare the following to the 1979 Department's concerns:

> The Department ... has reconsidered the statements it made in 1979. While ICWA does not "oust the States of their traditional jurisdiction over Indian children falling within their geographical limits," H.R. Rep. No. 95–1386, at 19, Congress enacted ICWA to curtail State authority in certain respects. At the heart of ICWA are provisions that address the respective jurisdiction of Tribal and State courts. Other important provisions of ICWA require State courts to apply minimum Federal standards and procedural safeguards in child-custody proceedings for Indian children. This rule serves to clarify ICWA's requirements, with the goal of promoting uniform application of the statute across States.
>
> While a few commenters asserted that this rule violates the Tenth Amendment, the Supreme Court repeatedly has reaffirmed the "power of Congress to pass laws enforceable in state courts." *New York v. United States*, 505 U.S. 144, 178 (1992); *Testa v. Katt*, 330 U.S. 386, 394 (1947); *F.E.R.C. v. Mississippi*, 456 U.S. 742, 760–61 (1982). The Court also has

> explained that "[i]f a power is delegated to Congress in the Constitution, the Tenth Amendment expressly disclaims any reservation of that power to the States." *New York*, 505 U.S. at 156. Here, Congress enacted ICWA primarily pursuant to the Indian Commerce Clause, which provides Congress with plenary power over Indian affairs. 25 U.S.C. 1901(1). In clarifying ICWA's requirements, the Department is exercising the authority that Congress delegated to it. Having considered the nature of this rule, the comments received, and the relevant case law, the Department concludes that this rule does not violate the Tenth Amendment for the same reasons that ICWA does not violate the Tenth Amendment.
>
> The Department also has reflected on the Federalism concerns it noted in 1979. The Department does not view this rule as an "extraordinary" exercise of authority involving an assertion of "supervisory control" over State courts. While the Department's promulgation of this rule may override what some courts believed to be the best interpretation of ambiguous provisions of ICWA or how these courts filled gaps in ICWA's requirements, the Supreme Court has reasoned that such a scenario is not equivalent to making "judicial decisions subject to reversal by executives." *Nat'l Cable & Telecomm. Ass'n v. Brand X Internet Servs.*, 545 U.S. 967, 983 (2005). Rather, the Department's rule clarifies a limited set of substantive standards and related procedural safeguards that courts will apply to the particular cases before them. For these reasons, and because Congress unambiguously provided the Department authority to issue this rule, the Department does not view Federalism concerns as counseling against the issuance of this rule.

81 Fed. Reg. 38788-9.

> . . . the Department does not find the equal protection concerns raised by commenters compelling. The transfer [to tribal court] decision should focus on which jurisdiction is best-positioned to make decisions in the child's custody proceeding. ICWA—and the Department's experience—establishes that Tribal courts are presumptively well-positioned to address the welfare of Tribal children. State courts retain limited discretion under the statute but the choice between two court systems does not raise equal protection concerns. See, e.g. *United States v. Antelope*, 430 U.S. 641 (1977).

81 Fed. Reg. 38826.

2. When Congress writes about the trust responsibility and Indian children in its report on the House Bill, what do they mean? What is that responsibility grounded in? Professors Fletcher and Singel write below that it is grounded in the federal government's use of Indian children specifically in negotiating and concluding [coercive] treaties that form the basis of the federal-tribal relationship. What does the federal government owe to Indian children today?

B. The Treaty Relationship

Indian Children and the Federal-Tribal Relationship

Matthew L.M. Fletcher & Wenona T. Singel
95 Neb. L. Rev. 885 (2017)

It is bitterly ironic that ICWA and its state law siblings are currently subject to multiple attacks throughout the country. These suits characterize ICWA as a constitutional outlier—in short, that ICWA provides too much procedural protection to Indian children and Indian nations, and the federal government does not have authority to enact family law. These claims are based on historical assumptions about the limited role of the federal government in family law and in protecting Indian child welfare.

Those assumptions are wrong.

American Indian children were a terrible focus of the Founding Generation that ratified the Constitution and the Bill of Rights. American military strategists empowered by the foreign affairs and war powers targeted Indian children for kidnapping and imprisonment as a means to undermine tribal resistance. Those children the Americans did not capture remained vulnerable to the military strategy to deny food and shelter to Indian nations. Many Indian children became orphans. American diplomats negotiating Indian treaties under the Treaty Power made thinly-veiled threats about the welfare of Indian children if Indian nations continued to resist. Tribal treaty negotiators acknowledged the vulnerability of their people and negotiated with an eye toward their children, and notably, orphans. Ultimately, the United States in the late 18th and early 19th centuries agreed in numerous ratified treaties to guarantee the safety, education, welfare, and land rights of Indian children. These agreements form the earliest basis of a robust federal government trust relationship with Indian children. Numerous federal statutes enacted in accordance with what is now termed the general trust relationship served as the implementation of the federal government's authority under the Indian Commerce Clause, other Constitutional provisions, and the structure of the Constitution.

Indian children remained a focus of American Indian law and policy for the next century and a half, an era we call the Coercive Period, borrowing the phrase from George D. Harmon, mid-20th century historian. This is the period in which the United States asserted a guardianship-type power over Indian nations and people, virtually immune from accountability to anyone, and in which federal law and policy thoroughly became untethered from the Constitution. Despite no Constitutional provision authorizing the federal government to exercise plenary power over tribal domestic and internal affairs, American policy shifted away from using Indian children as targets of military and diplomatic strategy toward the policy of stripping Indian children from their families and cultures. This era, usually called the assimilation era, is a far darker and abysmal period than even the early era of warfare and land dispossession.

In the beginning of the Coercive Period, Indian nations continued to negotiate treaties and other agreements designed to preserve the safety, welfare, education, and land rights of their children, and for a time the United States honored those obligations. But after the Civil War, federal actions turned toward undermining Indian cultures, languages, and religions through the same tools Indian nations negotiated for during the treaty era. Federal, state, and religious officials again turned again to kidnapping and imprisoning Indian children in oppressive boarding schools, isolating them from their families, nations, and lands. These educational abuses continued into the mid-20th century. The boarding school system would eventually be supplemented by state child protective agencies, state courts, and private adoption agencies in the 20th century. Again, there were reports of kidnapping of Indian children into the 1960s and 1970s, but the focus then was the abuse of the legal system to remove Indian children from their families, terminate the parental rights of their parents, and relocate them to off-reservation, non-Indian foster and adoptive parents.

The modern era of the federal government's trust relationship with Indian children began in the 1970s with the enactment of the Indian Child Welfare Act the Indian Self-Determination and Education Assistance Act (ISDEAA), and related statues. Federal law and policy is once again focused on the trust relationship between the United States and Indian children, and again is grounded in the treaty-based obligations and the federal government's Constitutional powers. In particular, the ISDEAA is a manifestation of the federal government's treaty- and international law-based obligations to guarantee health, education, housing, safety, welfare, and other government services. ICWA is a manifestation of the United States' acknowledgment the federal government overstepped its authority under the Constitution to manage internal tribal matters at the expense of individual Indians' rights to due process and freedom of religion. These statutes represent a return of federal Indian law to fidelity to the Constitution.

* * *

A. The Treaty and International Law Basis of the Federal-Tribal Trust Relationship

The modern understanding of the federal-tribal relationship is that the relationship involves federal trust obligations and duties to Indian nations and Indian people. Centuries of federal statutory and judicial precedents provide deep context and specificity to that relationship. However, the Founding Generation understood the federal-tribal relationship more in terms of international law principles, most notably the duty of protection that superior sovereigns owe to consenting inferior sovereigns. The Constitution's provisions and structure relating to Indian affairs makes sense in this context.

The deep political theory behind the origins of the federal-tribal relationship and the origins of the modern trust relationship is best encapsulated in Justice Thompson's dissenting opinion in *Cherokee Nation v. Georgia* [30 U.S. 1 (1831)], an opinion that formed the theoretical basis for Chief Justice Marshall's groundbreaking opinion recognizing tribal sovereignty in *Worcester v. Georgia* [31 U.S. 515 (1832)] the next year. There, the Court held the relationship of Indian tribes to the United States is founded on "the settled doctrine of the law of nations" that when a stronger sovereign assumes authority over a weaker sovereign, the stronger one assumes a duty of protection for the weaker one; the weaker nation does not surrender its right to self-government. "Protection" was a term of art under international law that meant then and now that the United States agreed to a legal duty of preserving Indian and tribal property and autonomy to the maximum extent allowable in the national interest. In numerous treaties with Indian tribes, the United States agreed to take Indians and tribes under the "protection" of the federal government.

The United States Constitution's provisions relating to the federal Indian affairs—including without limitation the Commerce Clause and the Necessary and Proper Clause, the Treaty Power, the Property and Territory Clause, the Foreign Affairs and War Powers, the Indians Not Taxed Clause, and the Supremacy Clause—all point to the conclusion that federal authority over affairs with Indian nations was a nation-to-nation exercise. The Founding Generation's Indian affairs program, exemplified most notably in the Northwest Ordinance, Trade and Intercourse Acts, and early treaties, most notably the Treaty of Greenville, confirms that federal authority largely stopped at Indian country's borders absent a compelling national interest in intervening. This is what Professor Charles Wilkinson referred to as "measured separatism." The details of early federal-tribal interaction included matters of military and economic alliance, criminal jurisdiction, trade with Indians, and Indian children.

* * *

Post-Revolutionary War Era

After the Revolution, the newly independent United States turned to Indian country. At the forefront of the federal government's economic and political concerns were Indian nations, their lands, and their resources. Conflicts naturally arose. American military strategy to deal with

Indian hostilities remained a focus on burning Indian villages and crops and killing, capturing, or enslaving Indian women and children after the Revolution. For example, In 1792, one American general wrote to the governor of South Carolina the way to defeat Indians was to "march light into Creek [and Cherokee] country . . . and destroy the disaffected . . . towns." Indian women and children remained the weak link for Indian nations engaged in warfare with the United States. They required food and shelter, they travelled slowly, and, most importantly, they would not be left behind. Indian leaders would not sacrifice their children. In fact, Indian leaders invoked their children as a primary reason for their actions in resisting American encroachment.

The federal government's focus on the acquisition of Indian lands and resources from the borders of the newly formed States to the Mississippi River required a nation-to-nation relationship with Indian nations. George Washington wrote, "[T]he [settlement] of the Western Country and making a Peace with the Indians [were] so analogous that there [could] be no definition of the one without involving considerations of the other." While the Americans preferred purchase, trade, and diplomacy to be the focus of this acquisition, this early era was punctuated with horrific wars and concluded with brutal human rights violations perpetrated during Indian removal.

In some instances, the United States regular military stepped aside and allowed "frontiersmen" to attack Indian villages and perpetrate abuses on Indian families. In the festering conflict with the Chickamagua Cherokee nation, the Americans allowed citizens to organize and inflict terrible killings on Indian women and children. "Frontier communities had no shortage of men ... who held little compunction about sacking Indian villages and leaving Indian women and children to perish from disease, starvation, and the elements." In the 1813–1814 wars with the Creek Nation, General Jackson employed irregular militias to eradicate Creek villages from the land. In the 1816-18 wars with the Seminole Nation, the American military was "employed to murder women and children. . . ."

Military goals included kidnapping as many Indian children as possible, incarcerating them, and holding them hostage until an Indian nation capitulated to American demands. Early American state papers make note of military plans to capture children, hold them in military jails, and use them as bargaining chips with tribal leaders.

* * *

American diplomats and military treaty commissioners exploited the vulnerability of Indian children, even the ones not being directly held hostage by the government. They also exploited the salience of tribal leaders to protect their children, their futures. The focus on Indian children by both the American and the tribal sides accounts for the hundreds of treaties and even federal statutes that provide for the health, welfare, safety, and land rights of Indian children. This combination of strategies was best exemplified by the Northwest Indian War, the first large scale war prosecuted by the nascent United States, and the resulting Treaty of Greenville.

The Northwest Indian War

The war in the Old Northwest in Ohio country prosecuted by the American General "Mad" Anthony Wayne began in the 1780s and led to the 1794 Battle of Fallen Timbers, a defeat for the Ohio River Valley Indian nations that led to the British to stop backing the Indian war effort. The 1795 Treaty of Greenville exemplifies how the American military used Indian children as pawns to achieve American aims. This was the first American war after the American Revolution, and highlights the original public understanding of the federal government's Indian affairs powers in action.

The Northwest Indian War began as the American Revolution wound down. The federal government turned to the Ohio River Valley, where Indian nations stood in the way of American expansion. George Rogers Clark's expedition into the Old Northwest in the 1780s was the opening volley in this long war. By 1790, the American government had decided upon a war of extirpation against the Ohio River Indians. Secretary of War Henry Knox ordered Brigadier General Josiah Harmar to go to Fort Washington, now the Cincinnati area, and prosecute this war: "To extend a defensive and efficient protection to so extensive a frontier, against solitary, or small parties of enterprising savages, seems altogether impossible. No other remedy remains, but to extirpate, utterly, if possible, the said Banditti." That first expedition was disastrous for the American military.

After that failure, the United States turned to capturing Indian families in order to force a negotiated conclusion to the war. In 1791, Secretary of War Henry Knox gave chilling instructions to Brigadier General Charles Scott to focus guerrilla-style attacks on women and children for the purpose of capturing them. The women and children were not to be harmed, and Knox ordered that Scott should capture more Indian families if Indian resistance continued. General Scott's group captured 41 Indian women and children in the ensuing campaign.

Those Indian women and children became hostages in efforts to force compliance from Indian nations and conclude the war on the United States' terms. That June, General Scott wrote the Piankeshaw Indians on the Wabash after attacking Indian villages and capturing Indian women and children, demanding they make peace or lose their children forever. The letter offers additional threats to continue to attack villages, capture women and children, and to hold them hostages until the Indian nations capitulated:

> The United States have no desire to destroy the red people, although they have the power; but, should you decline this invitation, and pursue your unprovoked hostilities, their strength will against be exerted against you; your warriors will be slaughtered, your towns and villages ransacked and destroyed, your wives and children carried into captivity, and you may be assured that those who escape the fury of our mighty chiefs, shall find no resting place on this side of the great lakes. The warriors of the United States wish not to distress or destroy women and children, or old men, and, although policy obliges them to retain some in captivity, yet compassion and humanity have induced them to set others at liberty, who will deliver you this talk. Those who are carried off will be left in the care of our great chief and warrior, General St. Clair, near the mouth of the Miami and opposite the Licking river, where they will be treated with humanity and tenderness. If you wish to recover them, repair to that place by the first day of July next, determined, with true hearts, to bury the hatchet, and smoke the pipe of peace; they will then be restored to you, and you may again set down in security at your old towns. . . . But should you foolishly persist in your warfare, the sons of war will be let loose against you, and the hatchet will never be buried until your country is desolated, and your people humbled to the dust.

The letter was accompanied by a list of Indian people captured at "Quiatanon town," including four-year old Nepehhequah, and several other sons and daughters of the community, plainly being used as hostages. In August 1791, American military officials again sent a letter to the Indians on the Wabash offering to return Indian families to the tribe in exchange for surrender. Importantly, the letter specifically references the "protection" of the United States, acknowledging the federal government's standard practice to comport with international law principles that allow for Indian nations to retain internal sovereignty in exchange for divesting external sovereignties:

> The arms of the United States are again exerted against you, and again your towns are in flames, and your wives and children made captives; again you are cautioned to list to the voice of reason, to sue for peace, and submit to the protection of the United States, who are willing to become your friends and fathers, but, at the time, are determined to punish you for every injury you may offer to their children. Regard not those evil counsellors who, to secure to themselves the benefits of your trade, advise you to measures which involve you, your women and children, in trouble and distress. The United States wish to give you peace . . . ; but if you foolishly prefer war, their warriors and ready to meet you in battle, and will be not the first to lay down the hatchet. You may find your squaws and your children under the protection of our great chief and warrior General St. Clair, at fort Washington. To him, you will make all applications for an exchange of prisoners or for peace.

* * *

The Treaty of Greenville and the Founding Generation

Executed and ratified in 1795, a mere six years after the ratification of the Constitution, the Treaty of Greenville was the first comprehensive, large-scale Indian treaty negotiated under the new government. The treaty exemplifies the line of sovereignty between the federal government and Indian nations. The federal government accepted a duty of protection over the dozen or more Indian nations that executed the treaty. Within Indian country, however, Indian nations would assert plenary control over their lands, their people, and non-Indians that entered onto their lands without federal or tribal authorization.

Article 5 of the treaty defines the federal-tribal relationship, six years removed from the ratification of the Constitution, in terms of the duty of protection, and of internal and external tribal sovereign authority. According to the treaty, the duty of protection required the tribes to promise they would not sell lands to anyone except the United States. But tribal use of the land until sale was preserved, as was tribal governance. This is a dramatic difference from the Supreme Court's later description of ceded, unreserved Indian lands as being subject to mere sufferance of the federal government in *Johnson v. McIntosh* [21 U.S. 543 (1823)], and far more robust as a property right than the Court would later hold to be noncompensable if condemned by the government in *Tee-Hit-Ton Indians v. United States* [348 U.S. 272 (1955)]. These cases exemplify instances where the Supreme Court's jurisprudence became unmoored from the Constitution and from the Founding Generation's understanding.

Several other provisions in the treaty offer excellent descriptions of how the Founding Generation understood federal-tribal relations. Section 6 left law and order within these lands to tribal authorities, even over non-Indian American citizens. Section 7 reserved hunting and fishing rights on ceded lands to Indian people so long as they "offer no injury to the people of the United States." Article 8 provided for the introduction and regulation of Indian traders. Tribal jurisdiction over non-Indians is hotly contested now, and off-reservation hunting and fishing has been controversial in recent decades. But these sections show the Founding Generation was apparently willing to acknowledge robust tribal authority over internal tribal affairs, and nonmembers that enter Indian country were under tribal jurisdiction

Federal Indian law and policy in the early decades of the American Republic, almost by definition, was grounded in the Constitution, for good or bad. The federal government fought wars, negotiated peace, recognized reservation lands and property rights, and entered into and regulated a robust trade with Indian nations. The Founding Generation understood the duty of protection as the theoretical core of the federal-tribal relationship. And yet, for all the formal, external relations between the tribes and the federal government, Indian children were at the heart of the government-to-government relationship.

Notes

1. How does this article use history of a specific conflict in federal Indian law to ground the conversation about the role of Indian children in the federal-tribal relationship?

2. What is the role of treaties in the trust relationship? How do treaties organize and ground the federal-tribal relationship? In one of the most famous treaty decisions, the Ninth Circuit affirmed a decision that found the treaties with tribes in the Puget Sound governed fishing rights:

> Although the United States dealt from a clearly superior position, the treaties were negotiated at arms' length. The treaties were not dictated to a defeated nation. The United States wished to free most of the land in the Puget Sound area for the impending white migration and settlement. Governor Stevens' task in executing the treaties was to induce the Indians to move onto reservations. The Indians expressed their concern that they would be unable to continue their traditional way of life, centered on the gathering of fish, because of limited fishing opportunities on the proposed reservations.

> The governor overcame their fears by promising them continued access to their traditional fishing areas off the reservations.
>
> The treaties were "not a grant of rights to the Indians, but a grant of rights from them—a reservation of those not granted." *United States v. Winans*, 198 U.S. 371, 381, 25 S.Ct. 662, 664, 49 L.Ed. 1089 (1905). The extent of that grant will be construed as understood by the Indians at that time, taking into consideration their lack of literacy and legal sophistication, and the limited nature of the jargon in which negotiations were conducted. See *id.* at 380, 25 S.Ct. 662. Although ceding their right to occupy the vast territories in which they had been accustomed to roam unimpeded, the Indians reserved their traditional right to fish at their accustomed places. They granted the white settlers the right to fish beside them. In a sense, the treaty cloaks the Indians with an extraterritoriality while fishing at these locations. Although present Indian status is not understood in terms of tribal sovereignty, recalling past acceptance of that concept aids in perceiving the Indians' understanding of the effect of the treaties which they signed. They retained the right to continue to fish as they were accustomed. Certainly, they did not understand that in permitting other citizens access to their traditional fishing areas they were submitting to future regulations calculated to benefit those other citizens.
>
> * * *
>
> In summary, the Indians negotiated the treaties as at least quasi-sovereign nations. They relinquished millions of acres of their lands, retiring to reservations carved out of those lands. But they expressly reserved their indispensable rights to fish at their traditional places. The United States obtained for the settlers and for the subsequently-admitted state only the right of equal access to these fishing grounds.

United States v. Washington, 520 F.2d 676, 684-5 (9th Cir. 1975).

The treaties discussed in that case, signed in 1854 and 1855, continue to govern the fishing in Puget Sound to this day.

3. Many state supreme court ICWA opinions discuss the trust responsibility in their opinions. ICWA is one of the few federal laws that explicitly state the reason for its existence is Congress's relationship with Indian tribes:

> (2) that Congress, through statutes, treaties, and the general course of dealing with Indian tribes, has assumed the responsibility for the protection and preservation of Indian tribes and their resources;
>
> (3) that there is no resource that is more vital to the continued existence and integrity of Indian tribes than their children and that the United States has a direct interest, as trustee, in protecting Indian children who are members of or are eligible for membership in an Indian tribe;

25 U.S.C. § 1901(2), (3) (2012).

B.H. v. People ex rel. X.H.

138 P.3d 299 (Colo. 2006)

B.H., the natural mother of X.H., sought review of the court of appeals unpublished opinion affirming the district court's order terminating the parent-child relationship. The district court proceeded to trial and granted the state's motion to terminate parental rights, despite notice never having been given to any Indian tribe or the Bureau of Indian Affairs that X.H. might be an Indian child within the meaning of the federal Indian Child Welfare Act. The court of appeals affirmed, holding that the applicability of the Act had not been established.

Because the El Paso County Department of Human Services and the district court had reason to believe that a federally recognized Indian tribe could consider X.H. to be a tribal member or the eligible biological child of a member, potentially affected tribes were entitled to notice of the proceedings prior to any determination by the court. The judgment of the court of appeals is therefore reversed and the case is remanded with instructions to order that notice be given in accordance with the provisions of the Indian Child Welfare Act and the Colorado Children's Code. If it is ultimately determined, after proper notice, that X.H. is not an Indian child, the district court's order terminating parental rights shall stand affirmed. If X.H. is determined to be an Indian child, the district court must proceed in accordance with the Act.

* * *

On the following day, just before the termination hearing was to begin, the department brought the possible applicability of the Indian Child Welfare Act to the court's attention, informing the court that the child's grandmother had mentioned her Native American ancestry in a meeting the day before. In response to the guardian's expressed concerns about dilatory tactics and the court's query about an earlier alleged disclaimer by the child's mother, the mother's attorney represented that she disputed ever having been asked about her Native American roots. The attorney further represented that the child's grandmother had disclosed to the department, as early as August or September 2004, the fact that her own grandmother had received tribal scholarships. The court acknowledged that the child's Indian heritage had clearly been reported in the search documents, and it reprimanded the department for failing to investigate further during the ensuing ten months. Nevertheless, rather than postpone the termination hearing until notice could be given according to the Act, which the court felt would interfere with permanency for the child, it took testimony to resolve for itself the applicability of the Act.

The court heard directly from both the department of human services caseworker and the child's grandmother. The caseworker acknowledged that she had never personally discussed the Indian Child Welfare Act with the child's mother and that she was not familiar with tribal enrollment requirements. She also testified, however, that the child's grandmother had expressed concern about X.H. being disconnected from her Native American cultural traditions. The grandmother herself testified that she was of Cherokee descent; that she had been actively researching her heritage for more than a year; and that she was in direct contact with the "Cherokee Nation through Alabama." When questioned about a previous concession that X.H. should remain with the foster family, the grandmother explained that she had since come to realize how difficult it would be for her to maintain the contact with her granddaughter anticipated under the promised arrangement. While she conceded that she had never before brought the issue of her grandchild's Indian status to the court's attention, she maintained that she had raised it numerous times with the department.

* * *

The mother appealed, assigning error to the court's failure to comply with the tribal notice requirements of the federal Indian Child Welfare Act and the Colorado Children's Code. Acknowledging that "it may have been better practice to follow the notice procedures . . . upon learning that there was some contention of Indian ancestry," the court of appeals nevertheless affirmed. The appellate court held that while the tribe's determination of its membership would be conclusive, the trial court must ascertain whether the child is Indian in the absence of such a determination. As it was undisputed that neither X.H. nor her mother was a "registered" member of an Indian tribe, the court of appeals concluded that ICWA applicability had not been proven.

II

In 1978, Congress enacted the Indian Child Welfare Act, 92 Stat. 3069, 25 U.S.C. §§ 1901–1963, out of a mounting concern over child welfare practices resulting in the involuntary separation of alarming numbers of Indian children from their families for placement in non-Indian homes or institutions. *Mississippi Band of Choctaw Indians v. Holyfield*, 490 U.S. 30, 32, 109 S.Ct. 1597, 104 L.Ed.2d 29 (1989). Congress found that "the United States has a direct interest, as trustee, in protecting Indian children who are members of or are eligible for membership in an Indian tribe." 25 U.S.C. § 1901(3). In the Act, it therefore established minimum standards for the removal of Indian children from their families. 25 U.S.C. § 1902.

The clear policy choice of the Act is to place Indian children within the Indian community whenever possible. *Holyfield*, 490 U.S. at 37, 109 S.Ct. 1597. In furtherance of that goal, the Act vests jurisdiction over custody matters, under certain circumstances, in the tribal courts, while prescribing procedural and substantive standards, including a right of intervention by Indian tribes in proceedings that remain in the state courts. E.g., 25 U.S.C. §§ 1911, 1912; See *Holyfield*, 490 U.S. at 36–37, 109 S.Ct. 1597. The Colorado General Assembly has expressly provided for compliance with, and consistent application of, the federal Act in the Colorado Children's Code. See § 19–1–126, C.R.S. (2005).

In the past, the United States Supreme Court has emphasized the unique relationship that exists between the federal government and Indian tribes. See *Montana v. Blackfeet Tribe of Indians*, 471 U.S. 759, 105 S.Ct. 2399, 85 L.Ed.2d 753 (1985).

The United States Constitution vests the federal government with exclusive authority over Indian affairs, U.S. Const. art. 1, § 8, cl. 3, based upon the historical trust relationship between the United States and Indian tribes. *Blackfeet Tribe*, 471 U.S. at 764, 766, 105 S.Ct. 2399. As a result of this unique trust relationship, even standard principles of statutory construction do not have their usual force in matters involving Indian law. *Id.* at 766, 105 S.Ct. 2399. Rather, the Supreme Court has held that statutes enacted for the benefit of Indians, as well as regulations, guidelines, and state statutes promulgated for their implementation, must be liberally construed in favor of Indian interests. *Id.*; See Guidelines for State Courts: Indian Child Custody Proceedings, 44 Fed.Reg. 67584, 67585–86 (Nov. 29, 1979).

The ICWA pertains to various child custody proceedings involving Indian children, including the termination of parental rights. See 25 U.S.C. §§ 1903(1) and (4), 1911, 1912. A state is required by the Act to provide notice to the child's or its parent's tribe, or the Bureau of Indian Affairs if the tribe cannot be identified or located, whenever the court knows or has reason to know that an Indian child is involved. 25 U.S.C. § 1912(a). By Colorado's implementing legislation, in every termination of parental rights proceeding, the petitioning party has an affirmative duty to make continuing inquiries to determine whether the subject child is an Indian child and to identify any particular tribal affiliation, § 19–1–126(1)(a), and to give notice in the manner prescribed by statute whenever the petitioning or filing party knows or has reason to believe that the child who is the subject of the proceeding is an Indian child, § 19–1–126(1)(b). Under the "reason to know" or "reason to believe" standards, the state's obligation to notify potentially concerned tribes or the BIA necessarily arises preliminary to an ultimate determination of the child's Indian status. See *In re Guardianship of J.O.*, 327 N.J.Super. 304, 743 A.2d 341, 346–47 (App.Div.2000) (citing numerous state court opinions reaching this conclusion with regard to the federal Act).

The Act defines an "Indian child" as any unmarried person under the age of eighteen, who is either a member of an Indian tribe or eligible for membership and the biological child of a member. 25 U.S.C. § 1903(4). Tribal membership, however, is not defined by the Act. Membership for purposes of the Act is instead left to the control of each individual tribe. Guidelines, 44 Fed.Reg. at 67586; Cohen's Handbook of Federal Indian Law § 3.03[3] (Nell Jessup Newton, et al. eds., 2005) ("[O]ne of an Indian tribe's most basic powers is the authority to determine questions of its own membership."). Depending upon an individual tribe's criteria for membership, or its process for acquiring or establishing membership, which may or may not include some form of formal enrollment or registration, the ability of a court to ascertain membership in a particular tribe without a tribal determination may vary greatly. See *United States v. Broncheau*, 597 F.2d 1260, 1263 (9th Cir.1979); *In re Baby Boy Doe*, 123 Idaho 464, 849 P.2d 925, 931 (1993); *In re Termination of Parental Rights to Arianna R.G.*, 259 Wis.2d 563, 657 N.W.2d 363, 369 (2003) (while many tribes require registration or enrollment as a condition of membership, some automatically include descendants of members); Guidelines, 44 Fed.Reg. at 67586 (some tribes do not keep written rolls and others have rolls that only list members as of a certain date).

Not only are the tribes themselves therefore the best source of information concerning tribal membership, see Guidelines, 44 Fed.Reg. at 67586, but the Act also recognizes that Indian tribes have a separate interest in Indian children, distinct from, but equivalent to, parental interests, *Holyfield*, 490 U.S. at 52, 109 S.Ct. 1597. Consequently, tribes must have a meaningful opportunity to participate in determining whether the child is Indian, e.g., Arianna R.G., 657 N.W.2d at 368, and to be heard on the issue of ICWA applicability, e.g., *In re H.D.*, 11 Kan.App.2d 531, 729 P.2d 1234, 1239 (1986). An Indian tribe, like an Indian parent from whom custody was removed, is therefore permitted by the Act to petition any court of competent jurisdiction to invalidate an order terminating parental rights upon a showing that notice was not provided as required by the Act. See 25 U.S.C. § 1914.

Precisely what constitutes "reason to know" or "reason to believe" in any particular set of circumstances will necessarily evade meaningful description. As in other contexts, reasonable grounds to believe must depend upon the totality of the circumstances and include consideration of not only the nature and specificity of available information but also the credibility of the source of that information and the basis of the source's knowledge. In light of the purpose of the Act, however, to permit tribal involvement in child-custody determinations whenever tribal members are involved, the threshold requirement for notice was clearly not intended to be high.

* * *

Because membership is peculiarly within the province of each Indian tribe, sufficiently reliable information of virtually any criteria upon which membership might be based must be considered adequate to trigger the notice provisions of the Act. These criteria have included, but are not necessarily limited to, such considerations as enrollment, blood quantum, lineage, or residence on a reservation. See *Broncheau*, 597 F.2d at 1263. Because the protection of a separate tribal interest is at the core of the ICWA, See *Holyfield*, 490 U.S. at 52, 109 S.Ct. 1597, otherwise sufficiently reliable information cannot be overcome by the statements, actions, or waiver of a parent, *id.* at 49, 109 S.Ct. 1597, or disregarded as untimely, *T.L.G.*, 108 P.3d at 162 n. 26 (citing *In re Junious M.*, 144 Cal.App.3d 786, 193 Cal.Rptr. 40 (1983)).

III.

* * *

Whether the child's mother denied applicability of the Act or not, and whether the child's grandmother actually expressed concerns about protecting the child's Indian heritage before the day of trial or not, the petitioning or filing party (the department) was clearly aware of the child's Indian ancestry, imposing upon it a duty of further inquiry and notice pursuant to the Act. In the circumstances of this case, including the identification of a small class of potentially concerned tribes, the department failed to fulfill its statutory obligation. Because it cannot be determined as a matter of law that neither the child nor her mother is a tribal member, the notice requirements of the Act must be met.

Notes

1. Notice is discussed at length in Chapter Three, but this opinion delineates Congress's concern with tribal children, the role of tribes in determining membership, and the fact that a tribe has a separate but equal interest in the children to that of the parent. The analogy that the tribal government has an interest in the child the same as a state government only holds so far. The existence of a tribal community—its language, art, culture, religion, very understanding of itself—can only survive if its children survive as members of that tribe. This is no small interest, and indeed is one reason why the definition of genocide includes "forcibly transferring children of the group to another group." U.N. Convention on the Prevention and Punishment of the Crime of Genocide art. 2, Jan. 12, 1951.

2. The relationship Congress acknowledged in ICWA, established in treaties, is the trust relationship. Over the course of history, the federal government has used the trust relationship in ways both beneficial and detrimental to Indian tribes. Regardless, it is a unique legal relationship not replicated in other areas of federal law. The relationship is one reason the federal government can pass laws specific to Indian tribes, and Indian people, without implicating equal protection issues.

C. Equal Protection Concerns

The Indian Child Welfare Act is an Act that only applies to Indian children as Indian children. The Act defines an Indian child based on his or her membership or eligibility for membership within a federally recognized tribe. The law works on the basis of citizenship, not race. As such, neither children who are citizens of Canadian tribes nor children of non-federally recognized tribes receive the protections of the law. Nor are children who may be racially Native but do not qualify for membership in a federally recognized tribe. This places ICWA squarely as legislation for the benefit of tribes vis a vis their treaty and trust relationship with the federal government, and under the rubric of the *Morton v. Mancari* decision.

Morton v. Mancari

417 U.S. 535 (1974)

Mr. Justice Blackmun delivered the opinion of the Court.

The Indian Reorganization Act of 1934, also known as the Wheeler-Howard Act, 48 Stat. 984, 25 U.S.C. § 461 et seq., accords an employment preference for qualified Indians in the Bureau of Indian Affairs (BIA or Bureau). Appellees, non-Indian BIA employees, challenged this preference as contrary to the anti-discrimination provisions of the Equal Employment Opportunity Act of 1972, 86 Stat. 103, 42 U.S.C. § 2000e et seq. (1970 ed., Supp. II), and as violative of the Due Process Clause of the

Fifth Amendment. A three-judge Federal District Court concluded that the Indian preference under the 1934 Act was impliedly repealed by the 1972 Act. 359 F.Supp. 585 (NM 1973). We noted probable jurisdiction in order to examine the statutory and constitutional validity of this longstanding Indian preference. 414 U.S. 1142 (1974); 415 U.S. 946 (1974).

I

Section 12 of the Indian Reorganization Act, 48 Stat. 986, 25 U.S.C. §472, provides: "The Secretary of the Interior is directed to establish standards of health, age, character, experience, knowledge, and ability for Indians who may be appointed, without regard to civil service laws, to the various positions maintained, now or hereafter, by the Indian Office, in the administration of functions or services affecting any Indian tribe. Such qualified Indians shall hereafter have the preference to appointment to vacancies in any such position."

* * *

[A]ppellees, who are non-Indian employees of the BIA at Albuquerque, instituted this class action, on behalf of themselves and other non-Indian employees similarly situated, in the United States District Court for the District of New Mexico, claiming that the "so-called 'Indian Preference Statutes,'" App. 15, were repealed by the 1972 Equal Employment Opportunity Act, and deprived them of rights to property without due process of law, in violation of the Fifth Amendment. Named as defendants were the Secretary of the Interior, the Commissioner of Indian Affairs, and the BIA Directors for the Albuquerque and Navajo Area Offices. Appellees claimed that implementation and enforcement of the new preference policy "placed and will continue to place [appellees] at a distinct disadvantage in competing for promotion and training programs with Indian employees, all of which has and will continue to subject the [appellees] to discrimination and deny them equal employment opportunity." App. 16.

* * *

II

The federal policy of according some hiring preference to Indians in the Indian service dates at least as far back as 1834. Since that time, Congress repeatedly has enacted various preferences of the general type here at issue. The purpose of these preferences, as variously expressed in the legislative history, has been to give Indians a greater participation in their own self-government; to further the Government's trust obligation toward the Indian tribes; and to reduce the negative effect of having non-Indians administer matters that affect Indian tribal life.

* * *

Congress was well aware that the proposed preference would result in employment disadvantages within the BIA for non-Indians. Not only was this displacement unavoidable if room were to be made for Indians, but it was explicitly determined that gradual replacement of non-Indians with Indians within the Bureau was a desirable feature of the entire program for self-government. Since 1934, the BIA has implemented the preference with a fair degree of success. The percentage of Indians employed in the Bureau rose from 34% in 1934 to 57% in 1972. This reversed the former downward trend, . . . and was due, clearly, to the presence of the 1934 Act. The Commissioner's extension of the preference in 1972 to promotions within the BIA was designed to bring more Indians into positions of responsibility and, in that regard, appears to be a logical extension of the congressional intent. See *Freeman v. Morton*, 162 U.S.App.D.C. 358, 499 F.2d 494 (1974) . . . .

* * *

IV

We still must decide whether, as the appellees contend, the preference constitutes invidious racial discrimination in violation of the Due Process Clause of the Fifth Amendment. *Bolling v Sharpe*, 347 U.S. 497 (1954). The District Court, while pretermitting this issue, said: "[W]e could well hold that the statute must fail on constitutional grounds." 359 F.Supp. at 591.

Resolution of the instant issue turns on the unique legal status of Indian tribes under federal law and upon the plenary power of Congress, based on a history of treaties and the assumption of a "guardian-ward" status, to legislate on behalf of federally recognized Indian tribes. The plenary power of Congress to deal with the special problems of Indians is drawn both explicitly and implicitly from the Constitution itself. Article I, § 8, cl. 3, provides Congress with the power to "regulate Commerce . . . with the Indian Tribes," and thus, to this extent, singles Indians out as a proper subject for separate legislation. Article II, § 2, cl. 2, gives the President the power, by and with the advice and consent of the Senate, to make treaties. This has often been the source of the Government's power to deal with the Indian tribes. The Court has described the origin and nature of the special relationship:

"In the exercise of the war and treaty powers, the United States overcame the Indians and took possession of their lands, sometimes by force, leaving them an uneducated, helpless and dependent people, needing protection against the selfishness of others and their own improvidence. Of necessity, the United States assumed the duty of furnishing that protection, and with it the authority to do all that was required to perform that obligation and to prepare the Indians to take their place as independent, qualified members of the modern body politic. . . ." *Board of County Comm'rs v. Seber*, 318 U.S. 705 (1943). See also *United States v. Kagama*, 118 U.S. 375, 383-384 (1886).

Literally every piece of legislation dealing with Indian tribes and reservations, and certainly all legislation dealing with the BIA, single out for special treatment a constituency of tribal Indians living on or near reservations. If these laws, derived from historical relationships and explicitly designed to help only Indians, were deemed invidious racial discrimination, an entire Title of the United States Code (25 U.S.C.) would be effectively erased and the solemn commitment of the Government toward the Indians would be jeopardized. See *Simmons v. Eagle Seelatsee*, 244 F.Supp. 808, 814 n. 13 (ED Wash.1965), aff'd, 384 U.S. 209 (1966).

It is in this historical and legal context that the constitutional validity of the Indian preference is to be determined. As discussed above, Congress in 1934 determined that proper fulfillment of it trust required turning over to the Indians a greater control of their own destinies. The overly paternalistic approach of prior years had proved both exploitative and destructive of Indian interests. Congress was united in the belief that institutional changes were required. An important part of the Indian Reorganization Act was the preference provision here at issue.

Contrary to the characterization made by appellees, this preference does not constitute "racial discrimination." Indeed, it is not even a "racial" preference.[FN 24] Rather, it is an employment criterion reasonably designed to further the cause of Indian self-government and to make the BIA more responsive to the needs of its constituent groups. It is directed to participation by the governed in the governing agency. The preference is similar in kind to the constitutional requirement that a United States Senator, when elected, be "an Inhabitant of that State for which he shall be chosen," Art. I, § 3, cl. 3, or that a member of a city council reside within the city governed by the council. Congress has sought only to enable the BIA to draw more heavily from among the constituent group in staffing its projects, all of which, either directly or indirectly, affect the lives of tribal Indians. The preference, as applied, is granted to Indians not as a discrete racial group, but, rather, as members of quasi-sovereign tribal entities whose lives and activities are governed by the BIA in a unique fashion. See n. 24, *supra*. In the sense that there is no other group of people favored in this manner, the legal status of the BIA is truly sui generis.[FN 25] Furthermore, the preference applies only to employment in the Indian service. The preference does not cover any other Government agency or activity, and we

---

[FN 24]. The preference is not directed towards a "racial" group consisting of "Indians"; instead, it applies only to members of "federally recognized" tribes. This operates to exclude many individuals who are racially to be classified as "Indians." In this sense, the preference is political, rather than racial in nature. The eligibility criteria appear in 44 BIAM 335, 3.1:

> ".1 Policy—An Indian has preference in appointment in the Bureau. To be eligible for preference in appointment, promotion, and training, an individual must be one-fourth or more degree Indian blood and be a member of a Federally recognized tribe. It is the policy for promotional consideration that, where two or more candidates who meet the established qualification requirements are available for filling a vacancy, if one of them is an Indian, he shall be given preference in filling the vacancy. In accordance with the policy statement approved by the Secretary, the Commissioner may grant exceptions to this policy by approving the election and appointment of non-Indians, when he considers it in the best interest of the Bureau."
>
> "This program does not restrict the right of management to fill positions by methods other than through promotion. Positions may be filled by transfers, reassignment, reinstatement, or initial appointment." App. 92.

[FN 25]. Senator Wheeler described the BIA as "an entirely different service from anything else in the United States." Hearings on S. 2755 and S. 3645 before the Senate Committee on Indian Affairs, 73d Cong., 2d Sess., pt. 2, p. 256 (1934).

need not consider the obviously more difficult question that would be presented by a blanket exemption for Indians from all civil service examinations. Here, the preference is reasonably and directly related to a legitimate, nonracially based goal. This is the principal characteristic that generally is absent from proscribed forms of racial discrimination.

Notes

1. Many parties have tried to argue that ICWA is unconstitutional because it does not protect all children—that the law causes disparate treatment based on race. These cases have failed uniformly. *See In re A.A.*, 176 P.3d 237, 240 (Kan. App. 2008); *In re Adoption of Hannah S.*, 48 Cal. Rptr. 3d 605, 610-11 (Ct. App., 3rd. Dist. 2006); *In re Interest of Phoenix L.*, 708 N.W.2d 786, 797-89 (Neb. 2006), *disapproved of on other grounds In re Destiny A.*, 742 N.W.2d. 758 (Neb. 2007); *Matter of M.K.*, 964 P.2d 241, 244 (Okla. Ct. App. 1998); *In re Marcus S.*, 638 A.2d 1158, 1159 (Maine 1994); *State ex rel. Children's Services Div. v. Graves*, 848 P.2d 133, 134 (Or. Ct. App. 1993); *In re Miller*, 451 N.W.2d 576, 579 (Mich. App. 1990). However, other parties have argued that ICWA is unconstitutional under the Equal Protection Clause for children who do not have ties to their tribal culture, which is discussed below.

2. What is the constitutional basis of ICWA? *Morton* puts ICWA under the rational basis test, rather than the strict scrutiny test. An interesting question would be whether the ICWA scheme could pass a strict scrutiny test. Is it narrowly constructed? Does it achieve governmental goals? How do we measure this? How would the Court? Given Fletcher & Singel's article and subsequent information in other chapters on how the federal government treated Indian children and families, can it be argued that there is a compelling government interest in ensuring the viability of Indian families?

1. Definition of Indian Child

ICWA defines Indian child in 25 U.S.C. § 1903(4) (2006): "'Indian child' means any unmarried person who is under age eighteen and is either (a) a member of an Indian tribe or (b) is eligible for membership in an Indian tribe and is the biological child of a member of an Indian tribe." If an Indian child is in state court in certain proceedings, as defined in 25 U.S.C. § 1903(1) (discussed at length below), the child, the tribe, and the parents will receive the protections of the law in state court.

While a state court must determine if the child is an Indian child for the purposes of ICWA, only an Indian tribe can ultimately determine if the child is a citizen of the tribe, or eligible for citizenship. Each individual tribe will have its own way of determining citizenship, usually through a constitution, though there may be other traditional ways a tribe may make this determination. Regardless of how the tribe defines citizenship, the right to define citizenship is one of the foundational understandings of tribal self-governance and self-determination.

Santa Clara Pueblo v. Martinez

436 U.S. 49 (1977)

This case requires us to decide whether a federal court may pass on the validity of an Indian tribe's ordinance denying membership to the children of certain female tribal members.

Petitioner Santa Clara Pueblo is an Indian tribe that has been in existence for over 600 years. Respondents, a female member of the tribe and her daughter, brought suit in federal court against the tribe and its Governor, petitioner Lucario Padilla, seeking declaratory and injunctive relief against enforcement of a tribal ordinance denying membership in the tribe to children of female members who marry outside the tribe, while extending membership to children of male members who marry outside the tribe. Respondents claimed that this rule discriminates on the basis of both sex and ancestry in violation of Title I of the Indian Civil Rights Act of 1968 (ICRA), 25 U.S.C. §§ 1301–1303, which provides in relevant part that "[n]o Indian tribe in exercising powers of self-government shall . . . deny to any person within its jurisdiction the equal protection of its laws." § 1302(8).

* * *

I

Respondent Julia Martinez is a full blooded member of the Santa Clara Pueblo, and resides on the Santa Clara Reservation in Northern New Mexico. In 1941 she married a Navajo Indian with whom she has since had several children, including respondent Audrey Martinez. Two years before this marriage, the Pueblo passed the membership ordinance here at issue, which bars admission of the Martinez children to the tribe because their father is not a Santa Claran. Although the children were raised on the reservation and continue to reside there now that they are adults, as a result of their exclusion from membership they may not vote in tribal elections or hold secular office in the tribe; moreover, they have no right to remain on the reservation in the event of their mother's death, or to inherit their mother's home or her possessory interests in the communal lands.

* * *

II

Indian tribes are "distinct, independent political communities, retaining their original natural rights" in matters of local self-government. *Worcester v. Georgia*, 6 Pet. 515, 559, 8 L.Ed. 483 (1832); see *United States v. Mazurie*, 419 U.S. 544, 557, 95 S. Ct. 710, 717, 42 L.Ed.2d 706 (1975); F. Cohen, Handbook of Federal Indian Law 122–123 (1945). Although no longer "possessed of the full attributes of sovereignty," they remain a "separate people, with the power of regulating their internal and social relations." *United States v. Kagama*, 118 U.S. 375, 381–382, 6 S.Ct. 1109, 1112–1113, 30 L. Ed. 228 (1886). See *United States v. Wheeler*, 435 U.S. 313, 98 S.Ct. 1079, 55 L.Ed.2d 303 (1978). They have power to make their own substantive law in internal matters, see *Roff v. Burney*, 168 U.S. 218, 18 S.Ct. 60, 42 L.Ed. 442 (1897) (membership); *Jones v. Meehan*, 175 U.S. 1, 29, 20 S.Ct. 1, 12, 44 L.Ed. 49 (1899) (inheritance rules); *United States v. Quiver*, 241 U.S. 602, 36 S.Ct. 699, 60 L.Ed. 1176 (1916) (domestic relations), and to enforce that law in their own forums, see, e.g., *Williams v. Lee*, 358 U.S. 217, 79 S.Ct. 269, 3 L.Ed.2d 251 (1959).

As separate sovereigns pre-existing the Constitution, tribes have historically been regarded as unconstrained by those constitutional provisions framed specifically as limitations on federal or state authority. Thus, in *Talton v. Mayes*, 163 U.S. 376, 16 S.Ct. 986, 41 L.Ed. 196 (1896), this Court held that the Fifth Amendment did not "operat[e] upon" "the powers of local self-government enjoyed" by the tribes. *Id.*, at 384, 16 S.Ct. at 989. In ensuing years the lower federal courts have extended the holding of *Talton* to other provisions of the Bill of Rights, as well as to the Fourteenth Amendment.

* * *

In addressing this inquiry, we must bear in mind that providing a federal forum for issues arising under § 1302 [federal question jurisdiction] constitutes an interference with tribal autonomy and self-government beyond that created by the change in substantive law itself. Even in matters involving commercial and domestic relations, we have recognized that "subject[ing] a dispute arising on the reservation among reservation Indians to a forum other than the one they have established for themselves," *Fisher v. District Court*, 424 U.S. 382, 387–388, 96 S.Ct. 943, 947, 47 L.Ed.2d 106 (1976), may "undermine the authority of the tribal cour[t] . . . and hence . . . infringe on the right of the indians to govern themselves." *Williams v. Lee*, 358 U.S., at 223, 79 S.Ct., at 272.[9] A fortiori, resolution in a foreign forum of intratribal disputes of a more "public" character, such as the one in this case, cannot help but unsettle a tribal government's ability to maintain authority. Although Congress clearly has power to authorize civil actions against tribal officers, and has done so with respect to habeas corpus relief in § 1303, a proper respect both for tribal sovereignty itself and for the plenary authority of Congress in this area cautions that we tread lightly in the absence of clear indications of legislative intent. Cf. *Antoine v. Washington*, 420 U.S. 194, 199–200, 95 S.Ct. 944, 948, 43 L.Ed.2d 129 (1975); *Choate v. Trapp*, 224 U.S. 665, 675, 32 S.Ct. 565, 569, 56 L.Ed. 941 (1912).

* * *

Moreover, contrary to the reasoning of the court below, implication of a federal remedy in addition to habeas corpus is not plainly required to give effect to Congress' objective of extending constitutional norms to tribal self-government. Tribal forums are available to vindicate rights created by the ICRA, and § 1302 has the substantial and intended effect of changing the law which these forums are obliged to apply. Tribal courts have repeatedly been recognized as appropriate forums for the exclusive adjudication of disputes affecting important personal and property interests of both Indians and non-Indians. See, e.g., *Fisher v. District Court*, 424 U.S. 382, 96 S.Ct. 943, 47 L.Ed.2d 106 (1976); *Williams v. Lee*, 358 U.S. 217, 79 S.Ct. 269, 3 L. Ed.2d 251 (1959). See also *Ex parte Crow Dog*, 109 U.S. 556, 3 S.Ct. 396, 27 L.Ed.

1030 (1883). Nonjudicial tribal institutions have also been recognized as competent law-applying bodies. See *United States v. Mazurie*, 419 U.S. 544, 95 S.Ct. 710, 42 L. Ed.2d 706 (1975). Under these circumstances, we are reluctant to disturb the balance between the dual statutory objectives which Congress apparently struck in providing only for habeas corpus relief.

* * *

By not exposing tribal officials to the full array of federal remedies available to redress actions of federal and state officials, Congress may also have considered that resolution of statutory issues under § 1302, and particularly those issues likely to arise in a civil context, will frequently depend on questions of tribal tradition and custom which tribal forums may be in a better position to evaluate than federal courts. Our relations with the Indian tribes have "always been . . . anomalous . . . and of a complex character." *United States v. Kagama*, 118 U.S., at 381, 6 S.Ct., at 1112. Although we early rejected the notion that Indian tribes are "foreign states" for jurisdictional purposes under Art. III, *Cherokee Nation v. Georgia*, 5 Pet. 1, 8 L.Ed. 25 (1831), we have also recognized that the tribes remain quasi-sovereign nations which, by government structure, culture, and source of sovereignty are in many ways foreign to the constitutional institutions of the federal and state governments. See *Elk v. Wilkins*, 112 U.S. 94, 5 S.Ct. 41, 28 L.Ed. 643 (1884). As is suggested by the District Court's opinion in this case, see supra, at 1674–1675, efforts by the federal judiciary to apply the statutory prohibitions of § 1302 in a civil context may substantially interfere with a tribe's ability to maintain itself as a culturally and politically distinct entity.[FN 32]

Notes

1. This case is uniformly cited for the proposition that tribes have the right to determine their own membership. However, it has also had a long history in the discussion of feminism and intersectionality. For further discussion of these issues, see Getches et al., Cases and Materials on Federal Indian Law 442-447 (7th ed. 2017).

2. Because only a tribe can determine its citizenry, when a child is in state court, the state court must inquire as to whether the child may or may not be Indian. In addition, the court must notify the tribe that one of their children may be in state court. Without this notification process, the tribe may never know that a child is subject to state court jurisdiction. In addition, the court may not know whether it has jurisdiction or not. This is why, among other reasons, it is a best practice to

---

[FN 32]. A tribe's right to define its own membership for tribal purposes has long been recognized as central to its existence as an independent political community. See *Roff v. Burney*, 168 U.S. 218, 18 S.Ct. 60, 42 L.Ed. 442 (1897); *Cherokee Intermarriage Cases*, 203 U.S. 76, 27 S.Ct. 29, 51 L.Ed. 96 (1906). Given the often vast gulf between tribal traditions and those with which federal courts are more intimately familiar, the judiciary should not rush to create causes of action that would intrude on these delicate matters.

notify the tribe any time a child is under state court jurisdiction, even though federal law only requires it for emergency and foster care placement proceedings.

3. Limiting the definition to children who are citizens or eligible for citizenship in federally recognized tribes is one way Congress ensured ICWA's constitutionality. The protections of the law are based ultimately on the government-to-government relationship between tribal nations and the federal government. The federal government determines that relationship, however. This means that children of state recognized tribes, or tribes that are treaty tribes but were terminated by either Congress or the Administration, do not receive the protections of ICWA. Neither do children of tribes in other countries, such as Canada or Mexico.

> Congress enacted ICWA in recognition and furtherance of the "special relationship between the United States and the Indian tribes and their members and the Federal responsibility to Indian people." In particular, Congress found that "there is no resource that is more vital to the continued existence and integrity of Indian tribes than their children and that the United States has a direct interest, as trustee, in protecting Indian children who are members of or are eligible for membership in an Indian tribe." Congress accordingly did not apply ICWA to all children with Indian ancestry, but instead limited the Act's scope exclusively to children who are either themselves Tribal members, or are both eligible for membership and the biological child of a Tribal member. Thus, like the preferences at issue in *Mancari*, ICWA does not apply based on a showing of racial ancestry, but rather applies to particular children on the basis of the unique political status of Indian Tribes. And, because ICWA was enacted to provide procedural and substantive safeguards for qualifying children to be placed or remain with Indian families, the Act thus was passed to help fulfill "Congress's unique obligation toward the Indians."

U.S. Dept. of the Interior, Sol. Op., Implementation of the Indian Child Welfare Act by Legislative Rule at 3 (June 8, 2016).

There are, however, times when the state court can be confused by the tribe's citizenship requirements, or when a tribe may not be able to enroll a child as a citizen. Then the question turns on what Congress intended when it included a child "eligible for membership" in the definition of Indian child.

Doe v. Shoshone-Bannock Tribes

367 P.3d 136 (Idaho 2016)

I. Nature of the Case

This case arises out of Appellant's, the Shoshone–Bannock Tribes (Tribes), intervention in the adoption proceedings of a minor child (Child). While the adoption itself is not at issue on appeal, disputes that arose during the adoption proceedings are. Respondents, Jane and John Doe (Does), initiated adoption proceedings for

Child after the rights of Child's parents were terminated. Because Child may qualify for protection under the laws protecting an Indian child's welfare, the Tribes were given notice and intervened in the adoption proceeding. The trial court appointed an independent attorney for the child whose costs were to be split by the Tribes and the Does. Discovery disputes arose during the proceeding and the trial court issued sanctions against the Tribes. The trial court found the facts before it insufficient to establish that Child is an Indian child, and thus concluded that the Indian Child Welfare Act (ICWA) did not govern the proceeding. Despite this conclusion, the court applied the ICWA's placement preferences out of concern for Child's best interests. The Does prevailed in the adoption, and the court granted them attorney fees as the prevailing party. The Tribes contest the discovery rulings, sanctions, failure to find Child an Indian child, and the grant of attorney fees against them, claiming sovereign immunity and a misapplication of the law. The Does request attorney fees on appeal.

* * *

Because the Tribes' petition to intervene alleged that Child is the biological child of a member of the Tribes and that Child is eligible for enrollment in the Tribes, the Does served interrogatories and requests for discovery regarding these issues. The Tribes did not release the father's 1993 enrollment application (the 1993 Application), claiming it was unnecessary because they had provided conclusive proof of Child's father's status as a tribal member, and that their sovereign privacy act prevented its disclosure. On September 19, 2014, the Does filed a motion to compel the Tribes to respond to discovery and interrogatories. The Tribes objected to the motion to compel and requested a protective order regarding the 1993 Application. The trial court denied the protective order and granted the motion to compel, finding that the 1993 Application was directly relevant to the issue of whether Child was the biological child of a tribal member. Despite the order granting the motion to compel, the Tribes continued to refuse to produce the 1993 Application. The Does filed a motion for sanctions.

* * *

In January of 2015, the Does requested depositions of tribal officials, and the Tribes sought a protective order to stop the depositions or limit their scope. On February 9, 2015, the trial court heard arguments on all of the above motions. It held as follows: (1) sanctions were appropriate for the Tribes' failure to comply with discovery; (2) the Tribes still had to disclose the 1993 Application; (3) while depositions regarding Child's eligibility for enrollment were inappropriate in the face of a tribal resolution to that effect, depositions about other topics like Child's paternity were still appropriate; (4) the Tribes have exclusive authority to determine tribal membership; (5) whether Child was the biological child of his purported father was still a proper issue; and (6) the only issue for trial was whether the Does' adoption of Child is in his best interest. The court then issued written orders with respect to the pending motions. It granted $1,000 in sanctions against the Tribes to cover the Does' attorney fees to file the motion to compel. It based this figure on the rate of $250 per hour for an attorney to doa presumed four hours of work to file the motion to compel.

* * *

On August 12, 2015, the trial court granted the Does $863 in costs and $35,000 in attorney fees against the Tribes, and further granted Child's counsel $6,056.25 in fees against the Tribes. The Tribes initially challenged the lower court's discovery and sanction rulings, as well as its ultimate grant of petition for adoption and attorney fees. The Does cross-appealed, challenging the Tribes' intervention in the matter. The Tribes have since dropped their challenge to the adoption and the Does correspondingly dropped their challenge to the Tribes' intervention. What remains now is the Tribes' assertion that the lower court's discovery rulings, injunction, sanctions, grant of fees, and failure to find Child an Indian child were in error.

* * *

B. The trial court's order compelling discovery was an abuse of discretion.

The trial court abused its discretion when it granted the Does' motion to compel discovery of the 1993 Application because it was not relevant to any issue before the court. As discussed above, the Tribes have sole control over member enrollment and eligibility. During discovery, they produced documentation showing that Child's father was an enrolled member. The Does argued for discovery of the 1993 Application in order to show that the father was not eligible for tribal membership. But the determination of the father's eligibility was and remains in the Tribes' sole discretion. It does not matter how the Does, the trial court, or this Court interpret the Tribes' governing documents regarding eligibility for membership. Child's father's tribal status was conclusively established by the Tribes. The 1993 Application would not lead to any further relevant information on the matter. It was therefore an abuse of discretion for the trial court to order disclosure of the 1993 Application.

* * *

C. The monetary sanctions granted by the trial court against the Tribes were improper because they were based on an erroneous interpretation of the law, and the non-monetary sanctions were harmless.

The trial court imposed two types of sanctions against the Tribes: it fined them $1,000 to cover the costs of the Does' motion to compel, and it then later barred the Tribes from presenting evidence regarding Child's tribal status, that of his father, and whether Child is biologically the child of his purported father.

As discussed in the immediately preceding section, one of the underlying bases for the sanctions—the motion to compel—was erroneously granted and an abuse of discretion. Because the underlying order was an abuse of discretion, sanctions for non-compliance with that order are necessarily not consistent with the legal standards applicable to the specific choices available to the trial court and thus the sanctions were also an abuse of discretion. The sanctions are reversed.

While reversal of sanctions preventing a party from presenting evidence may require remand, the reversal of the non-monetary sanctions in this case does not. The Tribes being allowed to present the evidence they sought would not change the outcome of this case. The only effect the Tribes being allowed to present evidence of Child's tribal status would have had was that the ICWA may have been deemed controlling. As discussed in section A, that determination would not have changed the outcome.

D. The trial court's order preventing the Tribes from processing or filing any enrollment for tribal membership on behalf of Child was an abuse of discretion.

The Tribes claim it was error for the trial court to enjoin them from processing or filing any application for Child's tribal membership. The trial court did issue an order to that effect, but that order was not made a part of the final judgment. However, "when an appeal is taken from an appealable order or judgment, [] this [C]ourt has the jurisdiction and authority to review any and all orders and decisions made by the trial court" that were properly preserved. *Utah Ass'n of Credit Men v. Budge,* 16 Idaho 751, 758, 102 P. 390, 392 (1909). Thus, we may review the order preventing the Tribes from enrolling Child because the ultimate judgment in this case was appealable and the Tribes preserved the issue. The Tribes have exclusive power to determine membership and eligibility for membership. Any order by a trial court seeking to limit that power, however temporarily, is an abuse of discretion. Therefore, the order of the trial court preventing the Tribes from processing or filing any application for Child's membership in the Tribes was an abuse of discretion. The Tribes are concerned that the order was never expressly dissolved and thus may still have been in effect. While there is nothing indicating that to have been the case, whatever effect the erroneous order may have had is hereby terminated.

E. The trial court erred by ordering the Tribes to pay for one half of Child's attorney's fees.

A grant of attorney fees in Idaho must be supported by statutory authority or by contract . . . Because the trial court ordered this fee payment well before issuing a final judgment in the case, no party could have been a prevailing party eligible for a grant of fees under Idaho Code section 12–121. Therefore there was no statutory authority under which to impose an order requiring the Tribes to pay for one half of Child's attorney's fees.

The Tribes did not have a statutory right to intervene in the adoption proceedings. The ICWA grants a child's tribe a right to intervene only in "any State court proceeding for the foster care placement of, or termination of parental rights to, an Indian Child." 25 U.S.C. § 1911(c). The trial court recognized that the Tribes did not have a statutory right to intervene, but granted the Tribes' petition to intervene pursuant to Idaho Rule of Civil Procedure 24(b).

In the order granting the petition to intervene, the trial court also determined that it was appropriate to appoint counsel for child and ordered that "[t]he costs and fees incurred by counsel shall be shared equally by the Petitioners and the Tribes." The Tribes filed a motion asking the court to reconsider that order and argued that they had not waived their sovereign immunity. In denying a motion to reconsider that order, the trial court orally stated that "it's very clear that the court, sitting as a court of equity, has the authority to order a party to pay for attorney fees." In its subsequent written order denying the motion, the court held that by failing to withdraw their motion to intervene after knowing the costs associated with litigation, the Tribes "implicitly consented to pay those costs as ordered by the Court." The issue of waiver of immunity need not be addressed here because, regardless of immunity, the trial court had no authority to impose these fees against the Tribes.

This was not an equitable adoption. It was a statutory adoption. More importantly, even if the proceedings had been in equity, that would not have given the trial court authority to require the Tribes to pay the attorney fees. [citations omitted].

With respect to the alleged implicit waiver of sovereign immunity, the trial court is holding that the Tribes' failure to immediately withdraw from the lawsuit after the court had made an order that it has no authority to make (ordering the Tribes to pay one-half of the Child's attorney fees) constituted a waiver of the Tribes' sovereign immunity with respect to that order. The trial court did not cite any authority so holding, nor has any been suggested by the parties. "[T]o relinquish its immunity, a tribe's waiver must be 'clear.'" *C & L Enters., Inc. v. Citizen Band Potawatomi Indian Tribe of Okla.*, 532 U.S. 411, 418, 121 S.Ct. 1589, 1594, 149 L.Ed.2d 623, 631 (2001). "Indian tribes can waive their sovereign immunity. However such waiver may not be implied, but must be expressed unequivocally." *McClendon v. United States*, 885 F.2d 627, 629 (9th Cir.1989) (citations omitted). There was clearly no waiver in this case.

Finally, 25 U.S.C. § 1915 states, "In any adoptive placement of an Indian child under State law, a preference shall be given, in the absence of good cause to the contrary, to a placement with (1) a member of the child's extended family; (2) other members of the Indian child's tribe; or (3) other Indian families." The trial court complied with this requirement and gave the Tribes ample opportunity to offer alternative placements. However, none were found, which may be why the Tribes do not challenge the adoption in this case.

The order requiring the Tribes to pay one half of Child's attorney's fees is reversed. The Does do not challenge their requirement to pay for one half of Child's attorney's fees. That remains in place.

F. The additional order granting attorney fees in the Does' favor as the prevailing party violates the Tribes' sovereign immunity.

Indian tribes are immune from claims brought in both state and federal court unless Congress has authorized the suit or the tribe waived its immunity. *See, e.g., Santa Clara Pueblo v. Martinez*, 436 U.S. 49, 57, 98 S.Ct. 1670, 1676, 56 L.Ed.2d 106, 114 (1978); *Okla. Tax Comm'n v. Citizen Band Potawatomi Indian Tribe*, 498 U.S. 505, 509–10, 111 S.Ct. 905, 909–10, 112 L.Ed.2d 1112, 1119–21 (1991); *United States v. U.S. Fid. & Guar. Co.*, 309 U.S. 506, 512–13, 60 S.Ct. 653, 656–57, 84 L.Ed. 894,

898–99 (1940). Further, any such waiver of immunity must be expressed and cannot be implied; a rule which the United States Supreme Court has extended to mean that even when a tribe initiates proceedings, it does not waive immunity to counterclaims or cross-claims. *Potawatomi,* 498 U.S. at 509–10, 111 S.Ct. at 909–10, 112 L. Ed.2d at 1119–21. A waiver of sovereign immunity is analyzed the same whether the immunity belongs to the federal government or an Indian tribe. *See Santa Clara Pueblo,* 436 U.S. at 58–59, 98 S.Ct. at 1676–77, 56 L.Ed.2d at 114–16 (1978) (citing to a case involving the United States' waiver of sovereignty to analyze a tribe's waiver). Even when a sovereign entity waives immunity with respect to declaratory or injunctive relief claims, that waiver does not extend to awards of monetary damages. *Lane v. Pena,* 518 U.S. 187, 192, 116 S.Ct. 2092, 2096–97, 135 L.Ed.2d 486, 492–93 (1996). To be liable for monetary damages, a sovereign entity must unambiguously and expressly waive its immunity specifically with respect to those damages. *See id.*

Therefore, grants of statutory attorney fees against Indian tribes are barred by sovereign immunity unless the tribes waive immunity with respect to those claims. The Tribes in this case did not waive their immunity with respect to attorney fees, either by agreement or by requesting attorney fees of their own.

* * *

The order of the trial court granting attorney fees against the Tribes is reversed.

The Does and Child request attorney fees on appeal, but the Tribes do not. Sovereign immunity bars any award of attorney fees against the Tribes. Therefore no attorney fees are awarded on appeal.

Notes

1. This case goes to the heart of how a tribe determines its membership, and whether state courts have the ability to go behind that decision. What evidence did the court want to see here? Why did the Idaho Supreme Court say that was an abuse of discretion? This case does not discuss the membership requirements of the Shoshone Bannock Tribes. Why not?

2. In the Tenth Circuit, the federal appeals court considered a Cherokee Nation internal law regarding citizenship. *Neilson v. Ketchum*, 640 F.3d 1117 (10th Cir. 2011). In that case, the Cherokee Nation had passed the Cherokee Citizenship Act in an effort to make sure children who were eligible for Cherokee citizenship would be considered Indian children for the purposes of ICWA. The relevant provision is as follows:

> Notwithstanding any provisions of this title to the contrary, *every newborn child who is a Direct Descendant of an Original Enrollee shall be automatically admitted as a citizen of the Cherokee Nation for a period of 240 days following the birth of the child.* No request or application for Tribal Citizenship or other documentation need be submitted or delivered to the Registrar as a prerequisite to the temporary Tribal Citizenship of a child under this section. Such temporary Tribal Citizenship shall be effective automatically

> from and after the birth of the child for all purposes although the name of the child is not entered on the Cherokee Register.

Id. at 1120.

How would the Idaho Supreme Court have interpreted this provision? What did the court say about the Shoshone Bannock Tribes' right to enroll the child?

There are any number of reasons why a child might not be enrolled at the time of a proceeding subject to ICWA, and tribes often want to ensure their participation in the process if the child is eligible for citizenship. Given the tribes' right to determine its citizenship regardless of federal or state regulation, this provision was not outside the range of possibility. Some tribes even have the protection of children as constitutional provision. *See* Little Traverse Bay Bands of Odawa Indians Constitution, Art I, II.

However, the 10th Circuit Court of Appeals held that "the tribe cannot expand the reach of a federal statute by a tribal provision that extends automatic citizenship to the child of a nonmember of the tribe." 640 F.3d 1117, 1124 (10th Cir. 2011). The court seemed concerned with the automatic nature of the citizenship of a child who might have a nonmember parent, and also with the "temporary" nature of the citizenship.

3. Some states have tried to change the definition of Indian child in their state ICWA statutes. In Michigan, there was a great deal of consideration of how broad to make the definition of Indian child in what became the Michigan Indian Family Preservation Act. Kathryn Fort, *Waves of Education: Tribal-State Court Cooperation and the Indian Child Welfare Act*, 47 Tulsa L. Rev. 529, 541–42 (2012). The law removed the requirement the child be a biological child of an enrolled member, leaving the requirement that the child be a member or eligible for membership in a federally recognized tribe. Much like the Cherokee Nation's Citizenship Act, this is an attempt to protect children whose parents were unable to be enrolled or enroll themselves in their tribe. This definition was an attempt to address the following fact pattern:

> When C.S. was a child, she was adopted by non-tribal members in another state. If not for this adoption, C.S. believes she would have been a member of the Crow Creek Sioux Tribe. And if she were an enrolled member, then L.S. would be eligible for enrollment within the meaning of ICWA. Based on these circumstances, C.S. asserts that the spirit of ICWA is not being followed because L.S. is a child Congress intended to protect in a way she was not.

In re L.S., 812 N.W.2d 505, 508-509 (S.D. 2013).

Iowa, however, had its definition of Indian child struck down as too broad as a violation of the Equal Protection Clause. *In re A.W.*, 741 N.W.2d 793 (Iowa 2007). The Iowa Supreme Court deemed the definition, "a unmarried Indian person who is under eighteen years of age or a child who is under eighteen years of age that an

Indian tribe identifies as a child of the tribe's community," to be too inclusive and did not make the necessary link between self-government and citizenship. *Id.* at 812.

2. The Existing Indian Family Exception

Though ICWA's constitutional foundation is at least as strong as the foundation all of federal Indian law rests on, some courts have taken it upon themselves to hold that ICWA is unconstitutional as applied to a specific child. Those cases rest on the existing Indian family exception, first created in 1982 in Kansas. Underpinning the cases is an assumption that the state court can evaluate a child's connection to her tribe and make a decision regardless of the plain language of ICWA. As in the cases discussed in the voluntary adoption chapter, this case involved a non-Indian mother putting up a child for adoption.

In re Baby Boy L.

643 P.2d 168 (Kan. 1982)

Holmes, Justice:

This is an appeal from sundry trial court rulings and findings and from a decree of adoption entered by the Sedgwick County District Court. Carmon Perciado (Perciado), the putative father of Baby Boy L., an infant born out of wedlock, Quelin and Ernestine Perciado, the baby's paternal grandparents, and the Kiowa Tribe of Oklahoma, are the appellants. The adoptive parents are the appellees. The baby is the illegitimate son of Miss L., a non-Indian and the appellant, Carmon Perciado, a five-eighths by blood relationship Kiowa Indian duly enrolled as a member of the Kiowa Tribe. The appellants contend that the trial court erred in determining that the provisions of the Indian Child Welfare Act of 1978 (ICWA or the Act), 25 U.S.C. s 1901 et seq. (Supp. III 1979), were not applicable to the adoption proceeding and in the alternative assert that if the Act does not apply then the adoption is invalid under state law.

Due to the involved procedural aspects of this case, it is necessary that we set forth the facts in some detail. Baby Boy L. was born at Wichita, January 29, 1981. On the same date his natural mother, an unmarried non-Indian woman, executed a consent to the adoption specifically directed and limited to the adoptive parents named in the consent. The appellees filed their petition for adoption along with the mother's consent the same day and the court entered an order granting them the temporary care and custody of the child. It is not disputed that the appellant Perciado is the father of the child. Notice of the adoption proceedings and time of hearing was personally served on Perciado at the Kansas State Industrial Reformatory where he was incarcerated and upon the State Department of Social and Rehabilitation Services (SRS).

On March 6, 1981, Perciado filed an affidavit of indigency and the court appointed representatives of the Legal Aid Society of Wichita, Inc., to represent him. On

March 9, 1981, appellees filed an amendment to their adoption petition alleging Perciado was "an unfit person to have or assume or be given parental responsibilities" and asked that his parental rights be terminated and severed. On March 11, 1981, SRS filed its report recommending the granting of the adoption. On March 25, 1981, Perciado filed an answer to the amended petition asking that the adoption be denied, that he be found a fit and proper person, that his parental rights not be severed and that he be given permanent custody of his son.

* * *

On April 1, 1981, it was brought to the court's attention that Perciado was an enrolled member of the Kiowa Tribe and that the federal Indian Child Welfare Act of 1978 might apply, and therefore the case was continued for thirty days to allow proper notice to be given to the Kiowa Tribe. Thereafter, notice was given to the Kiowa Business Committee at Anadarko, Oklahoma. On April 14, 1981, an amended or supplemental consent to the adoption was filed by the baby's mother. This consent was also limited strictly to the named appellees. On May 7, 1981, Perciado, through the Legal Aid Society, filed an amended answer in which he alleged that the ICWA applied to the proceedings and asked, among other things, that the child be placed with a member of its extended family, or other members of the Kiowa Tribe, or with other Indian families as defined by the Act. On May 8, 1981, the Kiowa Tribe filed a petition to intervene in the proceedings and on May 29, 1981, a notice of appearance was filed by Bertram E. Hirsch, an attorney from New York, on behalf of the Kiowa Tribe and the paternal grandparents. Mr. Hirsch associated with local counsel in Wichita as required by our rules. On May 16, 1981, the Business Committee of the Kiowa Indian Tribe, over the objections of the baby's mother, enrolled Baby Boy L. as a member of the Tribe with a Kiowa blood degree of 5/16ths.

* * *

At the outset, we are faced with the interpretation of complex federal legislation which is not only confusing but, if applied as requested by the appellants, would also be inconsistent, contradictory, and would accomplish no worthwhile or useful purpose.

* * *

A careful study of the legislative history behind the Act and the Act itself discloses that the overriding concern of Congress and the proponents of the Act was the maintenance of the family and tribal relationships existing in Indian homes and to set minimum standards for the removal of Indian children from their existing Indian environment. It was not to dictate that an illegitimate infant who has never been a member of an Indian home or culture, and probably never would be, should be removed from its primary cultural heritage and placed in an Indian environment over the express objections of its non-Indian mother. Section 1902 of the Act makes it clear that it is the declared policy of Congress that the Act is to adopt minimum federal standards "for the removal of Indian children from their (Indian) families." Numerous provisions of the Act support our conclusion that it was never the intent of Congress that the Act would apply to a factual situation such as is before the court.

* * *

In this case Baby Boy L. is only 5/16ths Kiowa Indian, has never been removed from an Indian family and so long as the mother is alive to object, would probably never become a part of the Perciado or any other Indian family. While it is true that this Act could have been more clearly and precisely drawn, we are of the opinion that to apply the Act to a factual situation such as the one before us would be to violate the policy and intent of Congress rather than uphold them.

* * *

It is undisputed that Baby Boy L. is the biological child of Perciado, who is 5/8ths Kiowa Indian and a member of the Kiowa Tribe. It is also undisputed that the Kiowa Tribe requires that for a person to be eligible for enrollment in the tribe, such person must be at least one-fourth Kiowa Indian by degree of blood relationship. Baby Boy L. is five-sixteenths Kiowa Indian by degree of blood relationship and therefore meets the tribal requirements. Thus, as defined by the Act, Baby Boy L. must be considered an "Indian child" within the definitions of the Act. Appellees make much of the fact that the child's mother objected to his enrollment in the tribe but we find nothing in the record or in the Act that precludes the enrollment of an otherwise qualified child into an Indian tribe because of the opposition of one of its parents.

Continuing with the assumption that the Act does apply to these proceedings we will briefly address appellants' second and third points. Appellants contend it was error to refuse to allow the Kiowa Tribe to intervene. If the Act were applicable we would agree. Section 1911(c) provides:

> "In any State court proceeding for the foster care placement of, or termination of parental rights to, an Indian child, the Indian custodian of the child and the Indian child's tribe shall have a right to intervene at any point in the proceeding."

Thus, it is obvious that if the Act were applicable the trial court was in error in refusing to allow intervention by the Kiowa Tribe. However, even if such were the case, the error would have been harmless at best.

The mother of Baby Boy L. gave a consent to the appellees to adopt her child. The consent was limited to the two named appellees and was for their benefit only. She has made it clear that if this adoption was denied for any reason, or if an attempt was made to place the child for adoption under the terms of the Act, she would revoke her consent and again take custody of her child, and never consent to his placement with his father or with the father's extended Indian family, the Kiowa Tribe, the grandparents or anyone else.

* * *

Under either the Act or Kansas law, any proceedings which the Kiowa Tribe might have undertaken if allowed to intervene would have been useless. Any attempt to effect the preferential placement contemplated by the Act would necessarily result in the removal of the baby from the custody of appellees and thereupon there being no consent by the mother to any such action, the child would be returned to her. We do not believe that the Congress intended such ridiculous results nor do we believe that the Kiowa Tribe could in good faith recommend such a procedure. Any error which might have occurred by refusal of the Kiowa Tribe's petition to intervene would be harmless. It is elementary that the law, including the ICWA, and the courts do not require citizens and litigants to perform useless acts and be subjected to useless court proceedings when there is no possibility of any positive result for anyone.

Notes

1. The Kansas Supreme Court overturned this case in 2009. The fact pattern was essentially the same, though the newborn was going to be adopted by a member of the mother's family.

> From this point in ICWA interpretation and the development of common law, we are persuaded that abandonment of the existing Indian family doctrine is the wisest future course. Although we do not lightly overrule precedent, neither are we inextricably bound by it. *See Crist v. Hunan Palace, Inc.*, 277 Kan. 706, 715, 89 P.3d 573 (2004). *Baby Boy L.* is ready to be retired.
>
> First, the existing family doctrine appears to be at odds with the clear language of ICWA, which makes no exception for children such as A.J.S. See 25 U.S.C. § 1903(4); Jaffke, The *"Existing Indian Family" Exception to the Indian Child Welfare Act: The States' Attempt to Slaughter Tribal Interests in Indian Children*, 66 La. L.Rev. 733, 745–51 (2006).
>
> Further, as recognized by the *Holyfield* decision, 490 U.S. at 36–37, 109 S. Ct. 1597 tribal interests in preservation of their most precious resource, their children, drove passage of ICWA; and its expressly declared policy is
>
> > "to protect the best interests of Indian children and to promote the stability and security of Indian tribes and families by the establishment of minimum Federal standards for the removal of Indian children from their families and the placement of such children in foster or adoptive homes which will reflect the unique values of Indian culture, and by providing for assistance to Indian tribes in the operation of child and family service programs."
>
> 25 U.S.C. § 1902.
>
> As counsel for the Cherokee Nation emphasized at oral argument before us, a child removed now from the tribe cannot later be a voice for the tribe.

In re A.J.S., 204 P.3d 543, 549-550 (Kan. 2009)

2. Voluntary adoption cases such as these often include in the fact pattern that the mother would not allow her child to be adopted by any other party and would take the child back to raise herself. Why does this concern courts so much? If there was a worry about the safety of the child, then state social services should be involved. Otherwise, is the policy of the courts to keep children with their biological parents or encourage adoption?

> We also detect illogic in the *Baby Boy L.* opinion's secondary justification for its result, also invoked by the district judge here, that the non-Indian mother's refusal to consent to adoption of her infant by anyone other than the proposed non-Indian adoptive parents inevitably means a non-Indian upbringing for the child. In *Baby Boy L.*, as here, the mother's testimony was evidence of her intention only. That intention extends only as far as the mother's unilateral control. If ICWA applies, a father's fitness to parent and the child's placement will not be governed solely by the mother's expressed desires. The father and the tribe also will be heard, and ICWA's preferences will apply in the absence of "good cause to the contrary." 25 U.S.C. § 1915(a). Although the result reached may be the same as that dictated by the existing Indian family doctrine, it may not be. See *Baby Boy C.* [*v. Tohono O'odham Nation*], 27 A.D.3d at 52–53, 805 N.Y.S.2d 313; *In re Alicia S.*, 65 Cal.App.4th 79, 88–89, 76 Cal.Rptr.2d 121 (1998). A.J.S.'s unmarried mother's status as a non-Indian or another factor or set of factors may militate in favor of or against a certain ICWA preference or constitute "good cause" to ignore all of the preferences. We cannot know and neither could the members of this court who decided *Baby Boy L.* Simply put, an Indian family may yet be recognized or created if ICWA is not avoided through the existing Indian family doctrine.

In re A.J.S., at 550.

3. A lesser known provision of ICWA allows for tribal court jurisdiction if the child is a "ward of the tribal court." Ward is not defined. In the case of *Rye v. Weasel*, 934 S.W.3d 257 (Ky. 1996), a child who was born at Standing Rock Sioux Reservation was placed with a family where the father was a tribal citizen at Standing Rock and the mother was not. The placement was a tribal court order that maintained the child was a ward of the tribal court. After the couple divorced and the father moved back to the reservation, the state circuit court gave custody of the child to the mother. According to testimony, during the nine years the family lived together with additional biological children, neither the biological mother or father of the child provided any financial support or contact her, nor did the Tribe. The Kentucky Supreme Court held that the existing Indian family exception meant that the tribe could not exercise jurisdiction over the child, even though the original order placing her with the family was a tribal court order establishing a tribal wardship. The Court found that, "[t]he child has grown up in a non-Indian environment involving public schools and religious faith as well

as complete integration in the community. She does not speak the Sioux language and does not practice its religion or customs. The ICWA should not apply to a factual pattern where the Indian parents had no contact or custody with the child for over a decade." *Id.* at 264.

4. In 2015, the Goldwater Institute filed a federal class action suit alleging ICWA is unconstitutional as it applies to children who live off the reservation and have limited contact with their tribe. While the lawsuit made other claims, the equal protection claim echoed that of the existing Indian family exception. The plaintiffs attorneys used a few key lines from the *Adoptive Couple v. Baby Girl* case to illustrate their belief that the Supreme Court has concerns about the ICWA and equal protection. The district court in Arizona dismissed the case for lack of standing.

A majority of states have not adopted the Indian family exception.

In re Baby Boy C.

27 A.D.3d 34 (N.Y. Sup. Ct. 2005)

GONZALEZ, J.

This is an adoption proceeding in which the Tohono O'odham Nation, a federally recognized Indian Tribe, seeks to intervene pursuant to the Indian Child Welfare Act of 1978 (ICWA) (25 USC § 1901 et seq.) upon the ground that this is a "child custody proceeding" involving an "Indian child," as those terms are defined in ICWA. Family Court denied intervention under ICWA, instead adopting the judicially created "existing Indian family" exception (EIF), which avoids the application of ICWA in circumstances where the court determines that the child is not part of an existing Indian family. Family Court also concluded that the EIF exception was necessary to uphold the constitutionality of ICWA where, as here, the child and his family lack significant ties to an Indian tribe or culture.

The EIF exception to ICWA is a matter of first impression in the appellate courts of this State and its validity has been the subject of conflicting decisions from other jurisdictions' courts. Based on our review of these authorities and the submissions of the parties, the law guardian and amici, we conclude that the EIF exception directly conflicts with the express language and purpose of ICWA, as well as the rationale of the United States Supreme Court's decision in *Mississippi Band of Choctaw Indians v. Holyfield*, 490 U.S. 30, 109 S.Ct. 1597, 104 L.Ed.2d 29 [1989]. Therefore, we decline to accept it as the law of New York.

* * *

Facts

Baby Boy C. was born in California on March 22, 2004 to Rita C. (Rita) and her boyfriend Justin W. (Justin). Rita is one-half Native American Indian and is a registered member of the Tohono O'odham Nation tribe (Tribe). Justin is Caucasian and Jewish. On April 13, 2004, Rita and Justin executed extrajudicial consents in

Arizona to the termination of their parental rights and the adoption of the child by petitioners Jeffrey A. and Joshua A., who have been certified as qualified adoptive parents in New York. Included in Rita's executed consent were representations that she was a member of the Tribe, that the child may be an "Indian child" under ICWA and that she was aware of the placement preferences in ICWA but desired that they be waived, and that a finding of good cause entered to permit the child's adoption by petitioners.

On April 26, 2004, the Superior Court of Arizona certified that the consents to the adoption and relinquishment of parental rights were validly made, and it subsequently issued an order terminating Rita's and Justin's parental rights. The Tribe did not appear in the Arizona proceedings, although it apparently had notice of them. Meanwhile, petitioners took custody of the child, returned to New York and commenced this adoption proceeding in April 2004.

On June 23, 2004, the Tribe moved to intervene in the adoption proceeding as a matter of right under ICWA, or, alternatively, pursuant to CPLR 1013.1 The Tribe argued that Rita's relinquishment of her parental rights implicated the Tribe's right under ICWA to protect its relationship with its children, and that 25 USC § 1911(c) conferred standing on the Tribe to intervene in this proceeding. In opposition, petitioners argued that ICWA was not applicable here since, under the EIF exception, ICWA's purpose of preserving Indian families and tribal culture was not served where the Indian child and parents have not maintained a significant relationship with the Tribe. Petitioners also contended that ICWA was constitutionally flawed in the absence of the EIF exception.

* * *

In a post-hearing decision dated October 26, 2004, Family Court found that ICWA did not apply since the Tribe failed to meet its burden of proving that the subject child was part of an "existing Indian family." The court found that Rita's ties to the Tribe were mainly in her childhood and adolescence, but that as an adult she had "divorced herself from the community affairs, politics and social and religious life of the Tribe," thereby demonstrating a "rejection of her Indian heritage." Rita's rejection of her own Indian heritage, in turn, "has acted to break the link between the Tribe and Rita's nuclear family."

* * *

Applicability of ICWA

Preliminarily, we note that the plain language of ICWA makes the act applicable to this adoption proceeding. As noted, ICWA applies to any "child custody proceeding" involving an "Indian child" (25 USC § 1903[1], [4]; see *Michael J., Jr. v. Michael J., Sr.*, 198 Ariz. 154, 156, 7 P.3d 960 [2000]; *In re Alicia S.*, 65 Cal.App.4th 79, 83, 76 Cal. Rptr.2d 121 [1998]). Here, petitioners concede that the subject child is an Indian child and that this is a child custody proceeding. Thus, petitioners' argument that ICWA is inapplicable rests entirely on its claim that the EIF exception removes this proceeding from the Act. We therefore turn to the issue of whether the EIF exception should be accepted as a matter of New York law.

* * *

Following *Baby Boy L.*, the EIF exception gained some acceptance in other state appellate courts that likewise concluded that the doctrine precluded application of ICWA in circumstances where an Indian child was not being removed from an existing Indian family or environment (see *Matter of Adoption of T.R.M.*, 525 N.E.2d 298 [Ind. 1988], cert. denied sub nom. *J.Q. v. D.R.L.*, 490 U.S. 1069, 109 S.Ct. 2072, 104 L.Ed.2d 636 [1989]; *Matter of S.C.*, 1992 OK 98, 833 P.2d 1249 [1992], overruled by statute as stated in *Leatherman v. Yancey* [*In re Matter of Baby Boy L.*], 2004 OK 93, 103 P.3d 1099 [2004]; *Matter of Adoption of Crews*, 118 Wash.2d 561, 825 P.2d 305 [1992]; *Rye v. Weasel*, 934 S.W.2d 257 [Ky. 1996]; *Hampton v. J.A.L.*, 658 So.2d 331 [La.App. 2d Cir.1995], cert. denied 662 So.2d 478 [La. 1995], cert. denied 517 U.S. 1158, 116 S.Ct. 1549, 134 L.Ed.2d 651 [1996]; *In re Morgan*, 1997 WL 716880, 1997 Tenn. App. LEXIS 818 [Ct. App. Tenn. 1997]). The common rationale behind these decisions was that because Congress's primary goal in passing ICWA was to prevent the removal of Indian children from Indian families, that purpose would not be served by applying the Act to children who had never been a part of an existing Indian family.

The legal landscape surrounding the EIF exception changed in 1989, when the United States Supreme Court decided *Mississippi Band of Choctaw Indians v. Holyfield*, 490 U.S. 30, 109 S.Ct. 1597, 104 L.Ed.2d 29, *supra*.

* * *

Although domicile is not a disputed issue in this case, the Supreme Court's discussion in Holyfield regarding the relative interests of the parents, the child and the tribe in the application of ICWA has great significance. In rejecting the notion that ICWA could be avoided by the fact that the parents had "voluntarily surrendered" the child, the *Holyfield* court stated that tribal jurisdiction was not meant to be defeated by the actions of individual tribe members or parents, "for Congress was concerned not solely about the interests of Indian children and families, *but also about the impact on the tribes themselves of the large number of Indian children adopted by non-Indians*" (*id.* at 49, 109 S.Ct. 1597 [emphasis added], citing 25 USC § 1901 [3] ["there is no resource that is more vital to the continued existence and integrity of Indian tribes than their children"]).

The *Holyfield* Court also emphasized that a major concern of Congress was the "detrimental impact" on the Indian children themselves of being placed outside their culture in non-Indian homes (*id.* at 49–50, 109 S.Ct. 1597). To this end, Congress made ICWA's jurisdictional and placement provisions applicable not only to involuntary removals of Indian children, but also to voluntary adoptions involving placement with non-Indian families "because of concerns going beyond the wishes of individual parents" (*id.* at 50, 109 S.Ct. 1597).

In the wake of *Holyfield*, many state courts rejected the EIF exception on the ground that the doctrine was inconsistent with the Holyfield's express recognition of the tribal interests protected by ICWA, as well as ICWA's plain language (see *Matter of Adoption of T.N.F.*, 781 P.2d 973, 977 [Alaska 1989], cert. denied sub nom. *Jasso v. Finney*, 494 U.S. 1030, 110 S.Ct. 1480, 108 L.Ed.2d 616 [1990] [reliance on judicially created EIF exception would undercut the interests of Indian tribes and children that Congress sought to protect]; *Matter of Adoption of Baade*, 462 N.W.2d 485, 489–490 [S.D. 1990] [rejecting EIF in light of *Holyfield*]; *Matter of Baby Boy Doe*, 123 Idaho 464, 849 P.2d 925 [1993], cert. denied sub nom. *Swenson v. Oglala Sioux Tribe*, 510 U.S. 860, 114 S.Ct. 173, 126 L.Ed.2d 133 [1993] [rejecting EIF exception as inappropriate judicially created doctrine to circumvent mandates of Act]).

* * *

Family Court's determination in this case (5 Misc.3d 377, 784 N.Y.S.2d 334, *supra*), in addition to adopting the EIF exception and a narrow reading of Holyfield, also incorporated the constitutional analysis of *Bridget R.* [*In re Bridget R.*, 41 Cal App 4th 1483, 49 Cal Rptr 2d 507 [2d Dist 1996], cert denied sub nom. *Cindy R. v James R.*, 519 US 1060, 117 S Ct 693, 136 L Ed 2d 616 [1997]] in finding ICWA unconstitutional in the absence of the EIF exception (*id.* at 385, 784 N.Y.S.2d 334). The court specifically found that ICWA was not "rationally related" to its goal of promoting stability of Indian tribes where children are born to Indian parents disconnected from their Indian roots (*id.*). The court explained (at 385, 784 N.Y.S.2d 334):

> "[L]osing a child born to parents involved in tribal life is, in effect, losing part of a family that the tribe needs to retain, if it is to extend its current level of cultural growth into the next generation. Conversely, relinquishing control over a child born to parents uninvolved in Indian life, costs the tribe nothing in terms of maintaining a stable level of cultural growth."

Having considered the various arguments and authorities for and against the acceptance of the EIF exception, we reject it as fundamentally inconsistent with both the plain language of ICWA and one of its core purpose of preserving and protecting the interests of Indian tribes in their children. We also conclude that, contrary to Family Court's holding, ICWA is constitutional because it is rationally related to fulfilling this expressed purpose.

The starting point for any case of statutory interpretation must always be the statutory text itself, which is the "clearest indicator of legislative intent" (*Majewski v. Broadalbin-Perth Cent. School Dist.*, 91 N.Y.2d 577, 583, 673 N.Y.S.2d 966, 696 N.E.2d 978 [1998]). Here, the provisions of ICWA clearly and unambiguously provide only two threshold requirements for applicability—the proceeding must be a "child custody proceeding" involving an "Indian child" (25 USC § 1903[1], [4]). Significantly, the statutory definition of an "Indian child" depends on tribal membership or eligibility for membership—not on the degree of connection with tribal culture. Most assuredly, the statute does not require that the Indian child be a part of an "existing Indian family," i.e., one that actively participates in tribal affairs or customs. Indeed, the word "existing" is not found anywhere in ICWA's definitions section and appears to have been supplied by judicial interpretation (see *Matter of Adoption of Baby Boy L.*, 231 Kan. at 205–207, 643 P.2d 168).

Because Congress has clearly delineated the nature of the relationship between an Indian child and tribe necessary to trigger application of the Act, judicial insertion of an additional criteria for applicability is plainly beyond the intent of Congress and must be rejected (see *In re Alicia S.*, 65 Cal.App.4th at 89–90, 76 Cal.Rptr.2d 121 [no threshold requirement in Act that child must have been part of existing Indian family or have particular type of relationship with tribe or heritage]; *In re A.B.*, 663 N.W.2d at 636 [EIF exception ignores plain language of ICWA which does not require child to be part of existing Indian family or family involvement with tribe]; see also *Matter of Baby Boy Doe*, 123 Idaho at 471, 849 P.2d 925 [EIF exception rejected because provisions of ICWA do not contain limitation based on where child is located]).

Another problem with the EIF exception is that its acceptance would undermine the significant tribal interests recognized by the Supreme Court in *Holyfield*. The Supreme Court made it clear in *Holyfield* that Indian tribes have an interest in applying ICWA that is distinct from that of the child's parents, and that such parents may not unilaterally defeat its application by deliberately avoiding any contact with the tribe or reservation (490 U.S. at 51–52, 109 S.Ct. 1597). In many respects, that is what occurred in this case. By divorcing herself from tribal life and by putting her child up for adoption away from the reservation immediately after birth, Rita singlehandedly destroyed the notion of an "existing Indian family." If the EIF exception were applied in this instance, Rita would have succeeded in nullifying ICWA's purpose at the expense of the interests of the Tribe (*id.* at 51, 109 S.Ct. 1597). However, as *Holyfield* recognized, Congress intended otherwise by specifically mandating that tribal interests be considered (*id.* at 52, 109 S.Ct. 1597 ["protection of this tribal interest is at the core of the ICWA, which recognizes that the tribe has an interest in the child which is distinct from but on a parity with the interest of the parents"]; see also *Matter of Baby Boy Doe*, 123 Idaho at 470–471, 849 P.2d 925; *In re A.B.*, 663 N.W.2d at 636).

Nor can we agree with Family Court's statement that "relinquishing control over a child born to parents uninvolved in Indian life costs the tribe nothing." Where, as here, Rita has rejected Indian life and culture and, then, voluntarily relinquished her newborn Indian child to be adopted by a non-Indian couple, the detriment to the Tribe is quite significant—the loss of two generations of Indian children instead of just one.

The EIF exception also conflicts with the Congressional policy underlying ICWA that certain child custody determinations be made in accordance with Indian cultural or community standards (see *Holyfield*, 490 U.S. at 34–35, 109 S.Ct. 1597 [one of the most serious failings of the present system is that Indian children are removed from natural parents by nontribal governmental authorities who have no basis for intelligently evaluating the cultural and social premises underlying Indian home life and child rearing]; 25 USC § 1915[d] [applicable standards "shall be the prevailing social and cultural standards of the Indian community"]). The EIF exception is clearly at odds with this policy because it requires state courts to make the inherently subjective factual determination as to the "Indianness" of a particular Indian child or parent, a determination that state courts "are ill-equipped to make" (*In re Alicia S.*, 65 Cal.App.4th at 90–91, 76 Cal.Rptr.2d 121). Since ICWA was passed, in part, to curtail state authorities from making child custody determinations based on misconceptions of Indian family life, the EIF exception, which necessitates such an inquiry, clearly frustrates this purpose (*Holyfield*, at 34–35, 109 S.Ct. 1597; *Quinn* [*v. Walters*], 117 Or.App. at 584 n. 2, 845 P.2d 206; D.A.C., 933 P.2d at 999 [1993]).

We also find that ICWA is not constitutionally infirm absent the EIF exception. Every act of Congress is entitled to a presumption of constitutionality and courts must refrain from invalidating such enactments unless a clear showing is made that Congress has exceeded its constitutional bounds (*United States v. Morrison*, 529 U.S. 598, 607, 120 S.Ct. 1740, 146 L.Ed.2d 658 [2000]; see also *Dalton v. Pataki*, 5 N.Y.3d 243, 255, 802 N.Y.S.2d 72, 835 N.E.2d 1180 [2005], cert. denied 546 U.S. 1032, 126 S. Ct. 742, 163 L.Ed.2d 571 [2005]; *Matter of Malpica-Orsini*, 36 N.Y.2d 568, 570–571, 370 N.Y.S.2d 511, 331 N.E.2d 486 [1975], appeal dismissed sub nom. *Orsini v. Blasi*, 423 U.S. 1042, 96 S.Ct. 765, 46 L.Ed.2d 631 [1976]).

The decisions finding ICWA unconstitutional without the EIF exception, such as *Bridget R.*, are premised on the existence of a fundamental right or suspect classification. We find that neither exists in this case. No one could seriously dispute the proposition that an Indian child, like any child, has a significant interest in maintaining a stable home environment. However, other than *Bridget R.* and its progeny, we are unaware of any authority holding that a child's "right" to a stable home environment in the context of adoptive placements is one of constitutional dimensions (see generally *San Antonio Independent School Dist. v. Rodriguez*, 411 U.S. 1, 33–34, 93 S.Ct. 1278, 36 L.Ed.2d 16 [1973] [in determining whether a fundamental right exists, test is not relative societal significance or importance as compared to other rights, but whether the right is explicitly or implicitly guaranteed by the Constitution]).

The *Bridget R.* court derived such a "right" from a series of California Supreme Court cases that involved attempts by biological parents to re-assert their parental rights after a finding of unfitness, and at a time when the child had gained a measure of stability in long-term foster care placement .... While we believe that a child's interest in stability and permanency is obviously a critical factor in making custody and placement determinations, we do not agree that this interest is entitled to constitutional protection.

* * *

We have no difficulty reaching the same conclusion regarding the appropriate test for petitioners' equal protection claim. The Supreme Court and other courts have consistently held that federal laws that treat Indians differently from non-Indians do not derive from race, but rather from the political status of the parents or children and the quasi-sovereign nature of the tribe (see *Fisher v. District Court*, 424 U.S. 382, 390, 96 S.Ct. 943, 47 L.Ed.2d 106 [1976]; *Morton v. Mancari*, 417 U.S. 535, 553–554, 94 S.Ct. 2474, 41 L.Ed.2d 290 [1974]; *Matter of Baby Boy L.*, 103 P.3d at 1107; *In re A.B.*, 663 N.W.2d at 636). Accordingly, most courts have rejected claims that legislation specifically directed at Indians or Indian tribes violates equal protection (*United States v. Antelope*, 430 U.S. 641, 97 S.Ct. 1395, 51 L.Ed.2d 701 [1977]; *Fisher v. District Court*, 424 U.S. at 390–391, 96 S.Ct. 943; *Morton v. Mancari*, 417 U.S. at 551–555, 94 S.Ct. 2474).

Having concluded that no fundamental right or suspect classification is implicated by the application of ICWA in this case, petitioners' constitutional claims are properly evaluated under the rational basis test (*Vacco* [*v. Quill*], 521 U.S. at 799, 117 S.Ct. 2293; *Romer* [*v. Evans*], 517 U.S. at 631, 116 S.Ct. 1620). Applying that test, we agree with those courts that have held that ICWA is rationally related to the protection and preservation of Indian tribes and families and to the fulfillment of Congress's unique guardianship obligation toward Indians (*In re A.B.*, 663 N.W.2d at 636; *Matter of Baby Boy L.*, 103 P.3d at 1107; see also *In re Alicia S.*, 65 Cal. App.4th at 88, 76 Cal.Rptr.2d 121).

* * *

Accordingly, we decline to adopt the EIF exception and hold that ICWA is applicable to this adoption proceeding, irrespective of whether the Indian child or his parents had significant connections to the Tribe. Since ICWA applies here, Family Court should have addressed the Tribe's motion to intervene under ICWA.

Notes

1. California courts are still split on this issue, along with the very constitutionality of ICWA itself.

> Notwithstanding *Holyfield*, two districts of the California Court of Appeals not only adopted the EIF exception to ICWA, but also held that ICWA was unconstitutional absent the EIF exception (see *In re Bridget R.*, 41 Cal. App.4th 1483, 49 Cal.Rptr.2d 507 [2d Dist. 1996], cert. denied sub nom. *Cindy R. v. James R.*, 519 U.S. 1060, 117 S.Ct. 693, 136 L.Ed.2d 616 [1997]; *In re Alexandria Y.*, 45 Cal.App.4th 1483, 53 Cal.Rptr.2d 679 [4th Dist. 1996]). In *Bridget R.*, the court held that ICWA does not apply to a voluntary termination of parental rights proceeding respecting an Indian child who is not domiciled on an Indian reservation unless the parents are of American Indian descent and "maintain a significant social, cultural or political relationship with their tribe" (41 Cal.App.4th at 1492, 49 Cal.Rptr.2d 507). Otherwise, the *Bridget R.* court held, ICWA would violate the child's constitutional rights to due process and equal protection, and also usurp a power reserved to the States under the 10th Amendment to the United

> States Constitution (*id.* at 1506–1510, 49 Cal.Rptr.2d 507; see also *In re Santos Y.*, 92 Cal.App.4th 1274, 1314–1322, 112 Cal.Rptr.2d 692 [2d Dist. 2001]).

Baby Boy C., 27 A.D.3d at 44.

2. More recently, Nevada has used the exception when the only person challenging the decision arguing active efforts were not made was the non-Indian mother:

> We hold that the EIF doctrine should be used on a case-by-case basis to avoid results that are counter to the ICWA's policy goal of protecting the best interest of a Native American child. In the present case, we recognize that N.J.'s interest is protected by the ICWA because her putative father is a member of the Ely Shoshone Tribe. Her father, however, is not contesting the termination, nor is the tribe. The termination will not result in the breakup of a Native American family. Indeed, the only person contesting the termination is the non-Native American parent, Dawn.

In re N.J., 221 P.3d 1255, 1264 (Nev. 2009).

In this case, the child was removed by the state. This was not a voluntary adoption. Does applying the exception become more problematic in an involuntary proceeding versus a voluntary one?

D. Federalism Concerns

In addition to constitutional concerns such as equal protection, one of the major questions surrounding ICWA is related to federalism concerns. Can Congress pass a law directing the state agencies and court systems to apply heightened standards? How does ICWA square with the Tenth Amendment? ICWA is a federal law that governs state court decision-making processes. Generally speaking, family law is considered to be a state bastion, without room for either federal or tribal jurisdiction or laws. This issue arose during promulgation of the federal regulations, and the government addressed it directly.

Department of the Interior
Bureau of Indian Affairs
Indian Child Welfare Act Proceedings
4. Tenth Amendment and Federalism

25 C.F.R. Pt. 23
81 Fed. Reg. 38788-38798

Comment: Some commenters asserted that the proposed rule violates the Tenth Amendment of the U.S. Constitution because it commandeers State courts, or for unspecified reasons. Commenters also cited, or made statements that repeated, Federalism concerns that the Department briefly referenced in 1979. These commenters pointed out that the Department stated in 1979 that it would have been extraordinary for Congress to authorize the Department to exercise supervisory authority over State or Tribal courts, or to legislate for them with respect to Indian child-custody matters, in the absence of an express congressional declaration to that effect. See 44 FR 67584. The Department also stated that nothing in ICWA's legislative history indicated that Congress intended to delegate such extraordinary authority. *Id.* Several commenters stated that the rule violates Federalism principles because it tells State-court judges what they may and may not consider, and exactly how to interpret a Federal law.

Response: The Department has reflected on these comments and has reconsidered the statements it made in 1979. While ICWA does not "oust the States of their traditional jurisdiction over Indian children falling within their geographical limits," H.R. Rep. No. 95–1386, at 19, Congress enacted ICWA to curtail State authority in certain respects. At the heart of ICWA are provisions that address the respective jurisdiction of Tribal and State courts. Other important provisions of ICWA require State courts to apply minimum Federal standards and procedural safeguards in child-custody proceedings for Indian children. This rule serves to clarify ICWA's requirements, with the goal of promoting uniform application of the statute across States. While a few commenters asserted that this rule violates the Tenth Amendment, the Supreme Court repeatedly has reaffirmed the "power of Congress to pass laws enforceable in state courts." *New York v. United States*, 505 U.S. 144, 178 (1992); *Testa v. Katt*, 330 U.S. 386, 394 (1947); *F.E.R.C. v. Mississippi*, 456 U.S. 742, 760–61 (1982). The Court also has explained that "[i]f a power is delegated to Congress in the Constitution, the Tenth Amendment expressly disclaims any reservation of that power to the States." *New York*, 505 U.S. at 156. Here, Congress enacted ICWA primarily pursuant to the Indian Commerce Clause, which provides Congress with plenary power over Indian affairs. 25 U.S.C. 1901(1). In clarifying ICWA's requirements, the Department is exercising the authority that Congress delegated to it. Having considered the nature of this rule, the comments received, and the relevant case law, the Department concludes that this rule does not violate the Tenth Amendment for the same reasons that ICWA does not violate the Tenth Amendment. The Department also has reflected on the Federalism concerns it noted in 1979. The Department does not view this rule as an "extraordinary" exercise of authority involving an assertion of "supervisory control" over State courts. While the Department's promulgation of this rule may override what some courts believed to be the best interpretation of ambiguous provisions of ICWA or how these courts filled gaps in ICWA's requirements, the Supreme Court has reasoned that such a scenario is not equivalent to making "judicial decisions subject to reversal by executives." *Nat'l Cable & Telecomm. Ass'n v. Brand X Internet Servs.*, 545 U.S. 967, 983 (2005). Rather, the Department's rule clarifies a limited set of substantive standards and related procedural safeguards that courts will apply to the particular cases before them. For these reasons, and because Congress unambiguously provided the Department authority to issue this rule, the Department does not view Federalism concerns as counseling against the issuance of this rule.

Notes

1. A recent case brought up the issue of the Tenth Amendment and commandeering of state resources. The plaintiffs argued that the 2015 BIA Guidelines commandeered state resources in violation of the Tenth Amendment. The judge in that case held

> Regardless, even if the 2015 Guidelines were legislative rules, rather than interpretive guidelines that do not mandate the state court compliance, the 2015 Guidelines still would not commandeer state entities to comply with its regulations. As stated [*supra*], Congress passed the ICWA pursuant to congressional authority expressly granted in the Constitution. Just as Congress may pass laws enforceable in state courts, Congress may direct state judges to enforce those laws. *New York v. United States*, 505 U.S. 144, 178 (1992). Where a state court is applying the rights and protections provided for by ICWA the federal government can act to prevent state "rules of practice and procedure" from "dig[ging] into substantive federal rights." *Brown v. Western Ry.*, 338 U.S. 294, 296 (1949). Since the 2015 Guidelines would be within Congress' authority to enforce, there is no suggestion that the 2015 Guidelines commandeer state entitles [sic] to comply with its regulations.

Nat's Council for Adoption v. Jewell, Order, No. 15-00675, 2015 WL 12765872, *7 (E.D. Va Dec. 9, 2015) , vacated as moot by *Nat'l Council for Adoption v. Jewell*, Order No. 16–1110, 2017 WL 9440666 (Fourth Cir. Jan. 30, 2017).

2. ICWA applies to state proceedings defined in 19 U.S.C. § 1903(1) (2006):

> (i) "foster care placement" which shall mean any action removing an Indian child from its parent or Indian custodian for temporary placement in a foster home or institution or the home of a guardian or conservator where the parent or Indian custodian cannot have the child returned upon demand, but where parental rights have not been terminated;
>
> (ii) "termination of parental rights" which shall mean any action resulting in the termination of the parent-child relationship;
>
> (iii) "preadoptive placement" which shall mean the temporary placement of an Indian child in a foster home or institution after the termination of parental rights, but prior to or in lieu of adoptive placement; and
>
> (iv) "adoptive placement" which shall mean the permanent placement of an Indian child for adoption, including any action resulting in a final decree of adoption.
>
> Such term or terms shall not include a placement based upon an act which, if committed by an adult, would be deemed a crime or upon an award, in a divorce proceeding, of custody to one of the parents.

These proceedings go under different names in different states. In fact, applying the federal definition to the state proceedings is often itself been the cause for litigation. *See Empson-Laviolette v. Crago*, 760 N.W.2d 793 (Mich. App. 2008) (finding that a voluntary guardianship where the mother could not have her child back upon demand was subject to ICWA standards). Generally speaking, however, most state court judges argue that family law is an inherently state or local law. Having a federal law overlay that creates different and additional requirements at first seems at odds with the nature of family law. Recently, however, family law scholars have begun to question the nature of federalism and family law, arguing that federal laws are implicated in many different ways in family courts.

Family Law Reimagined

Jill Elaine Hasday

17-20, 38-52 (Harv. Univ. Press 2014)

> The whole subject of the domestic relations of husband and wife, parent and child, belongs to the laws of the States and not to the laws of the United States.

- *United States v. Windsor* (United States Supreme Court 2013)

A canonical story in family law describes the field as a rare respite of localism in an era when the federal government regulates virtually every other legal arena. Many judges, legislators, and other lawmakers, as well as scholars, litigants, and advocates, repeatedly tell this story about family law. The localist narrative is premised on family law's exceptionalism. It portrays family law as clearly beyond the federal government's boundaries when the limits on federal power are otherwise murky. It presents family law as an almost pastoral oasis of jurisdictional stability and certainty when the federal government has otherwise dramatically expanded its reach over time.

Localist arguments about family law are sometimes descriptive, sometimes normative, and often both. They purport to describe family law's present character, and they simultaneously contend that family law should preserve its supposed localism into the future.

If localist arguments about family law were consistently deployed and consistently successful, their description of the field would be much more accurate. The arguments would have succeeded in preventing most, albeit not all, federal family law. (As we will see, some federal family law is unavoidable given federal constitutional requirements and areas of extensive federal jurisdiction.)

Instead, however, the localist narrative about family law is employed selectively against specific federal initiatives and not others. Decisionmakers and the people who seek to influence them frequently make arguments grounded in family law localism, insisting that federal family law is unprecedented and categorically inappropriate, no matter how desirable its substantive policy goals might otherwise be. Many legal authorities take such arguments to have real persuasive power. Yet the premise of family law localism is also frequently disregarded. While the weight of state family law remains enormous, federal family law is extensive, wide-ranging, and well established.

Claims that family law is local cannot be evaluated without a working definition of family law. Yet remarkably little attention has focused on the meaning of the term "family law." The assumed and asserted boundaries of the field oscillate widely between contexts without acknowledgment, explanation, clarity, or specificity. Indeed, some of the most vigorous advocates of the notion that family law is local offer only vague, underspecified, shifting, and inconsistent accounts of what they mean by family law.

My working definition is that family law regulates the creation and dissolution of legally recognized family relationships and determines legal rights and responsibilities that turn on family status. This means that family law decides who counts as a legal family member and who does not, how legalized family relationships are begun and ended, and what turns on being a family member—what it means legally to be a spouse, parent, child, sibling, or other relative as one interacts with the government and with other people inside and outsides of one's family. This is not the only possible definition of family law, but it is a reasonable and functional one that provides a starting point for analysis. It helps us to escape the intellectual silos that often isolate family law from other bodies of law and to see family law's reach into numerous legal arenas where family law's presence and significance have routinely been overlooked. Many federal statutes, regulations, and judicial decisions fall squarely within this definition, although they frequently are not recognized as family law.

Moreover, federal law covers all aspects of this definition of family law. Some federal law regulates the creation and dissolution of legal family relationships, determining who counts as kin for federal purposes. This federal law often tracks state law, so that family members and family relationships recognized under state law are recognized under federal law as well. But federal law also sometimes diverges from state law on those issues. In addition, there is an enormous body of federal law establishing legal rights and responsibilities that turn on family status. This proportion between the various functions of federal family law mirrors state family law, which similarly has an enormous body of law setting out rights and responsibilities tied to family status under state law.

The canonical assumption of family law's localism has distorted how legal authorities understand the field, diverted their attention from the real questions that family law faces, and misshaped the judgments they reach. The urgent questions for family law are not about whether the federal government can or should be involved at all. They are about whether any particular family law policy is substantively desirable on its own merits and about which level of government is best situated (or which levels of government working together are best situated) to effectuate that specific policy.

* * *

Proclamations of family law's localism appear across a range of legal materials, including judicial opinions; statements from judicial organizations and judges; legislative debates, reports, and testimony; legal briefs; scholarly and professional books and articles; and family law casebooks and treatises. For instance, the Supreme Court has frequently announced that "the laws of marriage and domestic relations are concerns traditionally reserved to the states," that "[t]he regulation of domestic relations is traditionally the domain of state law," that "domestic relations [is] an area that has long been regarded as a virtually exclusive province of the States," that "there is no federal law of domestic relations," that—even more emphatically—"'[t]he whole subject of the domestic relations of husband and wife, parent and child, belongs to the laws of the States and not to the laws of the United States.'"

The tone of these pronouncements often implies that their correctness is self-evident. Indeed, Chief Justice William Rehnquist went so far as to suggest that courts should not rely on "'logic'" in concluding that family law is for the states alone. He wrote that "[i]f ever there were an area in which federal courts should heed the admonition of Justice Holmes that 'a page of history is worth a volume of logic,' it is in the area of domestic relations. This area has been left to the States from time immemorial, and not without good reason." Rehnquist did not identify that "good reason."

Some (although happily not all) scholarly books and law review articles also present localist accounts of family law. They maintain that "[f]amily law is considered one of the last sacred refuges of states' rights," report that "[s]tates enjoy exclusive authority over family law," advise that "[l]egislative jurisdiction over matters of domestic relations and family law are among the powers reserved to the States," not that "[f]amily law has traditionally been an area of state prerogative," observe that "[i]n the United States, family law has traditionally remained in the domain of the states," explain that "the entire field of child custody and private adoption has always been regarded by Congress and the Supreme Court as each individual state's concern, with virtually no federal interest at stake," contend that "[s]tate court judges, unlike federal judges, have the unique opportunity to hear issues of family law," and declare that "we consider . . . domestic relations to be the province of the states." Some (although again not all) family law treatises and casebooks describing the present contours of the law similarly announce that "the institution of marriage is regulated by the states," proclaim "that family law is inherently local," recount that "state legislatures have traditionally defined the family and enacted the laws that regulate marriage, parentage, divorce, family support obligations, and family property rights," and repeat that "[t]he whole subject of the domestic relations of husband and wife, parent and child, belongs to the laws of the states and not to the laws of United States."

More than declarations, the narrative about family law localism has powerfully shaped family law. As we will see, the narrative has not prevented the development of abundant federal family law, But the Supreme Court has relied on the premise that family law belongs to the states to structure decisionmaking about both family law and many other subjects, reasoning from the starting point of family law localism in areas as disparate as the Court's federalism jurisprudence, its domestic relations exception to federal diversity jurisdiction, and its judgments on civil rights law. Many courts, judges, and legislators, along with advocates and scholars, have similarly drawn on family law's canonical localism narrative to oppose congressional bills and statues, such as the 1994 Violence Against Women Act and the 1996 Defense of Marriage Act, on the ground that they constituted federal family law and were inappropriate for that reason. Let's start with the Supreme Court's jurisprudence.

* * *

Federal Family Law in the Courts and Congress

As we have seen, many courts, judges, legislators, litigants, advocates, and scholars who agree on little else continue to invoke the contention that family law is and should be local, relying on that canonical idea to describe family law's guiding principles and to make arguments and judgments about family law's future course. They frequently assert that federal family law is unprecedented and inappropriate, regardless of the specific substantive merits of the particular law at issue.

Yet despite such declarations, state family law coexists with extensive and far-reaching federal family law. Federal legislators and judges who announce family law's inherent localism have simultaneously created a robust body of federal family law. Of course, it is hardly unusual for lawmakers and jurists to say and even believe one thing, while doing another. The steady and confident repetition of the idea that family law is local may help decisionmakers overlook or not perceive the tensions between their words and their deeds. Moreover, legal authorities committed to the premise that family law belongs to the states may assume without further analysis that what the federal government is doing simply cannot be family law.

Nonetheless, myriad federal statues, regulations, and judicial decisions govern the creation and dissolution of legally recognized family relationships and/or determine the legal rights and responsibilities that are tied to family status. These statues, regulations, and decisions are forms of family law, whatever other legal categories they fall into as well. Just as state family law decides for purposes of state law who counts as a legal family member, how legalized family relationships are begun and ended, and what turns on legal recognition as a family member, federal family law decides these issues for purposes of federal law.

I make these observations for positive and descriptive reasons, rather than for normative or prescriptive ones. I am not arguing that federal family law is necessarily more, or less, desirable than state family law—that the federal government should aggressively intervene to preempt state law or that the federal government should defer to state law to the extent possible. Indeed, I do not believe that the desirability of federal family law can be judged categorically, rather than case by case.

My point instead is that federal family law is already far-reaching and well established. In addition, federal family law is sometimes unavoidable given the demand of the federal Constitution and the existence of exclusive federal jurisdiction. To be sure, family law, like many legal arenas, has never been under predominantly federal control. The weight and persistence of certain forms of state regulation are undeniable. However, the localist story about family law simply misdescribes the field, masking the scope and even the existence of federal family law.

Federal family law is much too voluminous to describe fully in one chapter. But we can review some of the most interesting and important examples to being mapping what the localist narrative about family law obscures.

Most of this survey will focus on congressional statutes and federal regulations implementing those statutes. Lawmakers exercise more control over the subject matter of their work than courts do. Elected legislators also enjoy more of a democratic mandate than appointed judges. However, we can briefly review some of the federal family law that the United States Supreme Court has produced before we consider some of the family law within federal legislation and regulation.

The Supreme Court's Federal Family Law

While the Supreme Court has frequently trumpeted its commitment to remaining uninvolved in family law, the Court regularly creates and administers family law—sometimes in the very same opinions declaring family law's inherent localism and "the Court's duty to refrain from interfering with state answers to domestic relations questions."

Constitutional Law. As an initial matter, family law is a pervasive and significant part of the Court's constitutional jurisprudence interpreting due process, equal protection, and other constitutional principles. Of course, the existence of family law within federal constitutional law should be unsurprising. Although canonical stories premised on family law's exceptionalism describe family law as distinctly set off from other legal fields, the federal Constitution applies to family law just as it applies to any other site of government activity. This is one reason why federal family law is not just extensive, it is unavoidable.

It is worth noting, however, some of the Supreme Court's constitutional decisions that create both constitutional law and family law at the same time. The Court's constitutional jurisprudence has established uniform family law rules for the nation with striking frequency. Indeed, the Court's constitutional case law has transformed family law.

Consider some of the Supreme Court's constitutional decisions regulating the legal creation and dissolution or marriage. The Court has recognized a fundamental right to marry that precludes many restrictions on marriage formation. For instance, *Loving v. Virginia* (1967) outlawed prohibitions on interracial marriage at a time when sixteen states still had such prohibitions. *Zablocki v. Redhail* (1978) prohibited states from requiring people subject to child support orders to obtain judicial approval before marrying. *Turner v. Safley* (1987) struck down a state prison regulation that prevented many prisoners from marrying.

The Court has also reshaped divorce law. *Boddie v. Connecticut* (1971) provided that states cannot deny people access to divorce "solely because of inability to pay" court fees and costs. Supreme Court decisions on alimony and child support awards at divorce have sparked tremendous change. *Orr v. Orr* (1979) established that laws regulating the provision of alimony must apply equally to husbands and wives. *Stanton v. Stanton* (1975) held that laws governing the provision of child support cannot set different ages of majority for males and female children. These decisions pushed states to rewrite virtually all their family law in language that is facially sex-neutral, so that family law codes that once spoke ubiquitously of husbands and wives, fathers and mothers, and sons and daughters, now govern "spouses," "parents," and "children."

In addition to regulating marriage formation and dissolution, the Court's constitutional decisions determine some of the rights that are, and are not, associated with marriage. For example, the Court has held that a husband has no right to notice of his wife's decision to have an abortion, much less the right to override that decision. The Court has decided that a married couple has the right to use contraception without being subject to criminal prosecution.

The Court's constitutional judgments similarly regulate how legally recognized relationships between parents and children are created and dissolved. The Court's case law provides that an illegitimate child must have more than one year in which to establish a legal relationship with her biological father. The Court has held that a biological father has no constitutional right to create a legally recognized relationship with his child if the child is born to another man's wife. The Court has determined that parental rights may be involuntarily terminated only if the parent is proven unfit by at least clear and convincing evidence and that indigent parents in termination proceedings do not always have a right to appointed legal counsel.

The Court's constitutional decisions also regulate the rights and responsibilities that parents and children have when their relationship is legally recognized. As Chapter 4 will discuss in more detail, these decisions constitutionalize a robust and far-reaching vision of parental prerogatives that grants parents enormous power "to direct the upbringing and education of children under their control." For instance, the Court's decisions establish that a parent may place his child in private rather than public school or remove his child from school entirely in some circumstances. The Court's case law gives parents substantial control over the access that third parties, including grandparents, have to a child. The Court has held that a parent's right to the custody of his child is not diminished by the parent's interracial marriage. The Court's jurisprudence regulates a parent's authority to participate in his daughter's decision to have an abortion, determining that parental consent may be required as long as the daughter had the option of seeking judicial authorization instead. At the same time, the Court has held that a child may be subjected to child labor restrictions against his parent's wishes.

Along the same lines, the Court has regulated rights tied to family relationships beyond marriage and parenthood. It held that a housing ordinance may not deny an extended family the right to live together.

* * *

Federal Common Law. The Supreme Court has also created significant family law as a matter of federal common law. Here, the Court has reached beyond its basic responsibilities to interpret the Constitution and federal statutes. The Court's jurisprudence on federal common law holds that the Court itself should create federal rules when no federal constitutional provision, statute, or treaty directly decides a case, if federal rules are needed to protect federal interests against conflicting state interests. The Court has repeatedly created federal common law to govern family rights and responsibilities, recognizing and safeguarding federal interests in family law.

Some of the Court's federal common law decisions create family law governing current or former servicemembers and their relatives. For instance, the Court has held that federal law preempts state community property law on the distribution of proceeds from an army insurance policy, that federal law precludes state courts from dividing military nondisability retirement pay pursuant to state community property laws, and that federal law permitting a servicemember to change the beneficiary of his life insurance policy trumps a state divorce decree requiring the servicemember to name the children from his first marriage as beneficiaries.

Some of the Court's federal common law decisions create family law governing people with no connection to military service. For example, the Court has held that federal law preempts state community property law on survivorship rights to federal bonds purchased with community property, that federal law governs whether a federal bondholder has defrauded his wife under state property law, and that federal law precludes a state court from treating as community property a spouse's expectancy interest in receiving benefits under the Railroad Retirement Act.

* * *

Federal Family Law in Statutes and Regulations

If the Supreme Court is enmeshed in federal family law, congressional and administrative involvement is even more extensive. Federal legislators and regulators have promulgated a wide range of family law governing the creation and dissolution of legally recognized family relationships and/or determining legal rights and responsibilities associated with family status. These lawmakers have produced a far-reaching body of federal family law.

Family Law Within Areas of Special or Exclusive Federal Control

First, federal legislators and regulators have created considerable family law in contexts where the federal government governs exclusively or has special regulatory authority, such as military law, immigration law, citizenship law, international relations law, Native American law, bankruptcy law, intellectual property law, and benefits law for federal employees and veterans. To some degree, federal family law is simply unavoidable in these contexts, suggesting again the implausibility of claims about family law's inherent localism. But federal legislators and regulators have gone far beyond any necessary minimum of regulation, producing federal family law that often diverges from state law to express and enforce the federal government's own family law policies.

Military Law. Consider a few examples from the federal family law governing the military, which regulates servicemembers and their families in ways that frequently differ from state law. Military law criminalizes adultery, and military courts actively and "routinely" enforce that prohibition. This federal criminalization of adultery constitutes an important legal burden tied to marital status. Remarkably, it persists in an era when states have all but ceased to prosecute adultery. Indeed, state adultery prosecutions faded into obscurity decades before the Supreme Court's decision in *Lawrence v. Texas* (2003), which struck down a state law criminalizing same-sex sodomy. *Lawrence* cast as least some doubt on the constitutionality of civilian criminalization of adultery by recognizing "an emerging awareness that liberty gives substantial protection to adult persons in deciding how to conduct their private lives in matters pertaining to sex."

Military law also regulates legal rights tied to parenthood. For instance, military regulations grant servicewomen who are the mothers of newborns the right to avoid deployment for at least four months after their child's birth, while giving servicemen who are new biological fathers no right to avoid deployment. The explicit sex-specificity of these military regulations contrasts starkly with the overwhelming trend in state family law toward policies written in sex-neutral language.

Immigration Law. Federal immigration law is replete with family law and family law policy choices. This body of law prioritizes family unification, especially for spouses, parents, and children. Sometimes this privileging of family ties takes the form of special exceptions that depend on family status. For example, immigration law permits illegal immigrants who have been in the United States for at least ten continuous years, have maintained a "good moral character," and have not been convicted of specified crimes to avoid deportation and become lawfully admitted for permanent residence if deportation "would result in exceptional and extremely unusual hardship to the alien's spouse, parent, or child, who is a citizen of the United States or an alien lawfully admitted for permanent residence."

* * *

Citizenship Law. Federal citizenship law determines legal rights and responsibilities tied to the parent-child relationship. This body of law establishes which children born outside the United States will be granted American citizenship because of their status as the children of citizens. Congress is unwilling to extend that privilege to all children of citizens and sometimes prefers children with citizen mothers over children with citizen fathers.

Consider the citizenship law regulating children born abroad to one citizen parent, which favors children with an unmarried citizen mother, then children with a married citizen parent, and then children with an unmarried citizen father. The child of an unmarried citizen mother is a citizen at birth so long as the child's mother has previously spent one continuous year in the Unites States or its possessions. The child of a married citizen parent is a citizen at birth so long as the citizen parent previously spent a total of at least five years in the United States or its possessions, at least two years of which were after the citizen parent turned fourteen.

Congress has made it much more difficult for children born abroad to unmarried citizen fathers to establish their American citizenship. A child in this situation must establish her biological relationship with her father "by clear and convincing evidence," prove that her father agreed in writing to support her financially until the age of eighteen, and demonstrate that her legal relationship with her father was established before she reached age eighteen, either because she was legally legitimated, her father acknowledged paternity in writing under oath, or a competent court adjudicated paternity. The unmarried citizen father must also have spent a total of at least five years in the United States or its possessions before the child's birth, at least two years of which were after the citizen father turned fourteen. These federal requirements mean that many children born abroad to unmarried citizen fathers are denied United States citizenship, even though it is clear that they are the biological children of citizens.

* * *

International Relations Law. Family law runs through federal international conventions focusing on family law. For instance, Congress has implemented international conventions focusing on family law. The Intercountry Adoption Act (IAA), which implements the Convention on Protection of Children and Co-operation in Respect of Intercountry Adoption, governs international adoptions involving United States residents and other countries that are parties to the convention. The IAA empowers the Secretary of State to regulate these international adoptions, requires federal accreditation or approval before an agency or person in the United States may offer or provide international adoption services, an preempts all inconsistent state law. The International Child Abduction Remedies Act (ICARA), which implements the Convention on the Civil Aspects of International Child Abduction, is designed to stop people from obtaining custody of children by wrongfully removing the children to another country or wrongfully retaining the children in another country. The ICARA establishes procedures for returning a child who "has been wrongfully removed or retained" back to the child's country of "habitual residence."

Native American Law. Family law is also an important part of federal Native American law. The Indian Child Welfare Act creates a unique set of rules to govern the termination of parental rights over Native American children and the adoption of Native American children, which prioritize keeping Native American children with Native American parents. For instance, the act provides that a parent voluntarily terminating his rights to a Native American child must consent to the termination in writing and before a judge who certifies that the parent understands the consequences of his consent. The parent may withdraw his consent to the termination within two years if the consent was obtained through fraud or duress. More strikingly, the act provides that "[i]n any adoptive placement of an Indian child under State law, a preference shall be given, in the absence of good cause to the contrary, to a placement with (1) a member of the child's extended family; (2) other members of the Indian child's tribe; or (3) other Indian families." These federal requirements override state family law, and state courts must comply with them. As the Supreme Court has observed, the Indian Child Welfare Act "establishes federal standards that govern state-court child custody proceedings involving Indian children."

* * *

Veterans' Benefits. Veterans' benefits are also enmeshed in family law. Veterans' benefits law both establishes significant rights that depend on family status and determines who counts as a family member in ways that sometimes diverge from state law. A veteran's surviving spouse, child, or parent is entitled to monthly dependency and indemnity compensation payments if the veteran's death was service-connected, and a veteran's surviving spouse or child is entitled to pension payments if the veteran's death was not service-connected. Some people are surviving spouses for purposes of veterans' benefits law, even though they are not surviving spouses for purposes of state law. If a person married a veteran unaware that there was a legal impediment that made the marriage invalid under state law and then lived with the veteran for at least a year immediately before the veteran's death or lived with the veteran for any period of time if the couple had a child together, that person counts as a surviving spouse under federal veterans' benefits law, so long as there is not another surviving spouse seeking and entitled to benefits who is the veteran's legal widow or widower under state law.

Notes

1. Is Hasday's argument convincing? What is the purpose in continuing the narrative that family law is local? How do federal laws drive state family laws? This section does not discuss how the federal government ties funding to state behavior, but under the Title IV-E program, funding for foster care drives state foster care and termination of parental rights deadlines.

2. How has the federal government chosen to exercise this power over family law for certain groups and not others? Federal involvement in the lives of Indian families is well documented. What about the government's involvement in military family lives? What federal interests are there in governing military family lives? How does the military investigate child abuse on base? What does it mean that military servicemembers choose their involvement in the federal government, if anything?

3. Just as state policies swing in response to public perceptions of the child welfare system, so do federal statutes. While a federal policy leads to ICWA, it can also lead to the Adoption and Safe Families Act.

Is There Justice in Children's Rights: The Critique of Federal Family Preservation Policy

Dorothy Roberts

2 U. Pa. J. Const. L. 112 (1999–2000)

In November 1997 President Clinton signed the Adoption and Safe Families Act ("ASFA" or the "Act"), aimed at doubling the number of children adopted annually by 2002. ASFA represents a dramatic shift in federal child welfare philosophy from an emphasis on the reunification of children in foster care with their biological families toward support for the adoption of these children into new families. The Act's predecessor, the Adoption Assistance and Child Welfare Act of 1980 ("1980 Act"), encouraged states to replace the costly and disruptive out-of-home placements that had dominated child welfare practice with preventive and reunification programs. ASFA amends the 1980 Act to direct state authorities to make the health and safety of children in foster care their top priority.

Support for ASFA was generated largely by focusing on the failure of federal family preservation policies. Critics recounted tragic stories of children who were killed after caseworkers returned them to blatantly dangerous parents. ASFA's reform, however, goes beyond mandating steps to ensure the safety of children who have been removed from violent homes. The Act and the rhetoric surrounding it weaken federal commitment to family preservation and establish a preference for adoption as the means of reducing the exploding foster care population. ASFA's congressional sponsors declared that the legislation "is putting children on a fast track from foster care to safe and loving and permanent [adoptive] homes." ASFA's preference for adoption is implemented through swifter timetables for terminating the rights of biological parents in order to "free" children for adoption, by the provision of technical assistance to states to facilitate such adoptions, and through financial incentives to states to move more children into adoptive homes. Although ASFA retains the requirement that states make reasonable efforts to reunify children with their families, it encourages concurrent efforts to place these children with adoptive parents. These dual purposes of reuniting foster children with their families while preparing them for adoption create conflicting incentives for child welfare agencies that are likely to attenuate their efforts at family preservation. In case of a conflict between reunification and permanency efforts, permanency prevails.

The law's supporters argue that its permanency provisions promote adoptions for the 100,000 children in foster care who cannot return safely to their birth families. While the state should promote adoptions of children who have been abandoned by their parents or who have little chance of being reunited with their families, the Act's practical impact may be broader, as it could permanently separate children from families that might have been preserved with adequate state resources or alternative custody arrangements. Family preservation efforts often fail because they are inadequate: children are returned to troubled homes without assessing parents' problems or providing the level or continuity of services required to solve them. Having never delivered on its promise to support poor families, Congress is now using the failure of family preservation programs to justify taking more poor children from their parents, despite the fact that states are unlikely to find adoptive homes for most of these children.

Prominent family violence scholar Richard Gelles' The Book of David: How Preserving Families Can Cost Children's Lives galvanized support for ASFA on similar grounds. The Book of David reported the startling events that surrounded the suffocation of a little boy by his mother after he was returned to her abusive home. Gelles attributed this tragic lapse in judgment to the priority policymakers placed on families, rather than on children. According to Gelles, family preservation policies encouraged caseworkers to interpret the mandate to use "reasonable efforts" to reunify foster children with their families as a license to risk children's safety. He argued that "the basic flaw of the child protection system is that it has two inherently contradictory goals: protecting children and preserving families," and advocated reinventing the child welfare system "so that it places children first." In short, ASFA supporters placed children's right to be safe at odds with parents' right to custody of their children.

A number of scholars and activists, however, many of whom are children's advocates themselves, have refuted this opposition of children's to families' rights. As Bruce Boyer, the supervising attorney for the Children and Family Justice Center of Northwestern University Law School put it, "[i]n family preservation, to my mind, there's a commonality of interests." Typically, furthering a family's interests will also benefit the children who belong to that family. Children have an interest in maintaining a bond with their parents and other family members and are terribly injured when this bond is disrupted. The reason for limiting state intrusion in the home, therefore, is not only a concern for parental privacy, but also the recognition that children suffer when separated from their parents and community.

* * *

ASFA's promotion of adoption is unlikely to improve the situation of most children in foster care. There are insufficient adoptive homes for the increasing number of children removed from their biological families. Moreover, unnecessarily separating children from their biological parents does not advance children's interests, but rather destroys family bonds that usually benefit children. Beyond expediting the termination of parental rights, ASFA aids in the dissolution of biological families by neglecting to adequately monitor state removal programs and by failing to require that states implement family preservation programs.

* * *

The Act's focus on severing biological ties to make room for adoptive ones overlooks both the diversity of parent-child relationships as well as alternatives to adoption. Before petitioning for termination of parental rights, agencies should consider the strength of the attachment between parent and child and the likelihood of adoption, both of which are probably related to the child's age. It usually makes more sense on both counts to terminate parental rights in the case of abandoned infants than in the case of adolescents or teens, especially those who have maintained contact with their parents.

There are alternatives to adoption that could ensure family stability while preserving the parent-child relationship. For example, children can often be safely placed in the long-term care of relatives or neighbors with parental visitation, leaving open the possibility of parents regaining custody if circumstances improve. In a 1994 survey of children in Illinois state custody who had been living with a relative for more than one year, 85% of relatives reported that the best plan for the children was to remain with them until the children were grown.

Many of these relatives shun adoption, however, because it disrupts customary kinship norms and creates an adversarial relationship with the parents. Programs intended to encourage long-term care of foster children by relatives could promote family preservation and stability while preventing the unnecessary tension within the child's biological support group that would result from termination of parental rights and adoption. ASFA's effect, however, may be to encourage courts to mechanically abide by statutory deadlines even when there is evidence that termination would not be in the child's best interests.

* * *

Even under the Child Welfare Act's reasonable efforts requirement, state agencies continued to make anemic efforts to prevent out-of-home placements and reunify families. Family preservation programs often fail because they do not address the needs of families, are inadequately funded, and do not last long enough. Caseworkers caught in the dual role of supporting families while recruiting foster and adoptive parents sometimes sabotage parents' quest to reunite with their children. A 1997 report issued by the General Accounting Office stated that more than half of the family support programs it surveyed "were not able to serve all families who needed services primarily due to the lack of funds and staff." Services for families in California, for example, are permitted to continue for a maximum of six months and, on average, end after only half this time. How can agencies expect to solve problems arising from any combination of deplorable conditions—chronic poverty, dangerous neighborhoods, shoddy housing, poor health, drug addiction, profound depression, lack of childcare—with a three month parenting course or ephemeral crisis intervention? It is not surprising that 20 to 32% of children returned home in connection with family preservation plans end up back in foster care. "Reunifying these children with families who are not adequately prepared or supported," writes social work professor Marianne Berry, "is equal to setting the family up for yet another crisis, possibly resulting in further abuse, neglect, or even death." The ideology of family preservation is then blamed when inadequate efforts result in tragedy.

* * *

The focus on adoption as the solution to the foster care problem directs attention away from the wide scale removal of poor black children from their homes. When

Congress stated that its aim was "to make sure that every child has the opportunity to live in a safe, stable, loving and permanent home," it had in mind terminating parents' rights, not reducing poverty or building stronger supports for families. Congress' focus on terminating parental rights represents a philosophical flaw in the Act that injures children, their families, and their communities. It violates children's rights as much as the government's failure to protect children from domestic violence.

By promoting adoption so myopically, we forget that our ultimate goal should be to reduce the need for adoptions. In an ideal society we would expect nearly all children to be raised by their biological families in a healthy, safe, and flourishing environment. Adoptions would be a well-accepted but rare alternative for children whose parents are unable or choose not to take care of them. Although adoption is as valuable as biology with respect to forming parent-child relationships, it typically occurs because of an unfortunate circumstance—the death of the biological parents, an unplanned pregnancy, child abuse or neglect. As a result, we can support adoption while working to curtail its causes. By combating poverty and its dangers to children, an ideal society would radically decrease its need for adoption.

* * *

The deference to non-custodial relationships after divorce raises additional questions about ASFA's support for termination of parental rights. Why do many children's rights advocates appreciate the importance of preserving the parent-child bond in the case of divorce, but not foster care? For some, the reason may be economic. Preserving children's ties to non-custodial middle-class fathers helps to guarantee that these children will not need public assistance. In contrast, terminating the rights of poor parents so their children may be adopted by wealthier ones yields a financial gain for the state. For others, the critical distinction may be the parental maltreatment that led to the removal of children in foster care (although divorced parents may also lose custody because of they are unfit). Parental unfitness, however, does not necessarily negate children's bond with their parents, and therefore does not conclusively determine children's interest in maintaining contact with their biological parents.

Perhaps the major reason for preferring extinction of parental ties in foster care is society's centuries-old depreciation of the relationship between poor parents and their children, especially those who are black. Most Americans can grasp a white middle-class child's emotional attachment to her biological father even though she is being raised by a stepfather. No one doubts the immediate re-connection of a wealthy child with his family when he returns from a year at boarding school. The public has a harder time, however, imagining a strong emotional bond between black parents and their children. Jacquelynn Moffett, Executive Director of Homes for Black Children, discovered that the white participants in a workshop on black adoption she conducted in Charleston, West Virginia "really did not have a concept of black families." Moffett explained that "[t]hey really did not believe that Black families exist . . . so they had no concept of Blacks being caring toward children." Poor black mothers are stereotyped as deviant and uncaring; they are blamed for transferring a degenerate lifestyle of welfare dependency and crime to their children. Black fathers are simply thought to be absent. When parents of children in foster care are portrayed as deranged and violent monsters, it becomes even more difficult for the public to believe that their children would want to maintain a relationship with them.

* * *

A. Welfare Reform

Race and class politics are critical to understanding ASFA's impact because ASFA's emphasis on adoption was influenced by concurrent trends in federal welfare reform. ASFA was passed on the heels of the overhaul of federal welfare policy. The Personal Responsibility and Work Opportunity Reconciliation Act of 1996 ("PRA") ended the federal guarantee of cash assistance to America's children and allowed states to implement extensive welfare reform programs. State welfare reform measures hinder the ability of many poor mothers to care for their children: they reduce cash assistance to families, eliminate payments to some families altogether, and require mothers, often without adequate child care, to work and participate in job training, counseling, and other programs. What will happen to the children of mothers who fail to meet new work rules because of child care or transportation problems, who are unable to find work within the two-year time limit, or who leave their children at home without adequate care while they participate in required work programs? It is likely that some of them will be removed from their mother's custody and placed in foster care. A recent New York Times article on Wisconsin's welfare plan reports that 5% of mothers removed from public assistance have been forced to "abandon their children." Welfare-to-work programs may not rescue enough families from poverty to offset the numbers forced into the child welfare system by time limits, sanctions, and working conditions. In short, welfare reform may cause a net increase in the number of children entering foster care.

* * *

B. Trans-Racial Adoption

The shift in federal policy from family preservation toward adoption also corresponded with the change in the federal position on trans-racial adoption. For decades, the federal government permitted public adoption agencies to enforce race-matching policies that sought to place black children exclusively with black adoptive families. In 1994 and 1996, however, Congress prohibited agencies receiving federal funding from placing children according to race or even from taking race into account in placement decisions. Federal support of trans-racial adoption has been championed as a critical step in increasing the numbers of adoptions of black children, the population with the lowest rate of permanent placements. Race-matching policies, it is argued, damage black children by not only denying them placements with white adoptive parents, but also by causing them to languish in foster care.

Adoption policy has historically tracked the market for children, serving the interests of adults seeking to adopt more than the interests of children needing stable homes. For example, child welfare officials abandoned the child rescue philosophy of the 19th century and refrained from terminating parental rights when the supply of newborns available for adoption exceeded demand. In more recent decades, however, the growing demand for adoptable older children helped to generate policies that free children for adoption by terminating parental rights quickly. The modern retreat from family preservation programs, much like the abolition of race-matching rules, can be seen as an effort to increase the supply of children for white adoptive families.

* * *

The de-politicized conception of children's rights leads to uncertain results. It is natural to feel empathy with any suffering child and to seek to end that suffering as soon as possible. In attending to the suffering of one child, however, we may neglect or even harm many others. Our celebration of the "rescue" of a child fortunate enough to find an adoptive home may come at the expense of hundreds of others who have no hope of ever leaving foster care. In focusing on the physical pain of children abused by their parents, we may forget the emotional pain of children who were needlessly removed from their parents and desperately want to return home. As Professor Garrison poignantly observes, for most foster children "loving foster or adoptive parents will not, any more than stepparents, erase the ties that bind parent and child." Once again, the tragic story chosen for broadcast by the media may depend less on the amount of children's suffering than on the political interests at stake.

Notes

1. Given the colonial relationship between tribal nations and the federal government, federal policy has long governed Indian family structures. From boarding schools to the present, Indian families have had to fight the federal government to maintain their relationships. Only relatively recently have states taken over that power. And only after the states were removing Indian children at distressing levels did the federal government step in with ICWA. How else does the federal government owe a duty of responsibility to Indian tribes and families? How does the Dorothy Roberts article illustrate ways the federal government has backed away from supporting Black families, perhaps all families, and not just Native families?

2. ICWA practitioners and scholars were alarmed when AFSA passed, especially given the federally imposed deadlines for parental termination, which are tied to foster care funding for the states. AFSA did not specifically exclude ICWA cases, and there was concern state courts would use AFSA standards instead of ICWA ones. *See* B.J. Jones, *Differing Concepts of "Permanency": The Adoption and Safe Families Act and the Indian Child Welfare Act, in* Facing the Future: The Indian Child Welfare Act at 30 (eds. Matthew L.M. Fletcher, Wenona T. Singel & Kathryn E. Fort). Generally, however, most states have agreed that ICWA standards govern child welfare cases when it applies:

> Because the ICWA establishes "minimum Federal standards for the removal of Indian children from their families," 25 U.S.C. 1902, and nothing in the ASFA indicates a congressional intent to supersede the ICWA, neither the ASFA nor its state law analogues relieve the DHS from the ICWA's "active efforts" requirement, 25 U.S.C. 1912(d), or from the burden of establishing beyond a reasonable doubt "that the continued custody of the child by the parent or Indian custodian is likely to result in serious emotional or physical damage to the child," 25 U.S.C. 1912(f).

In re J.L., 770 N.W.2d 853, 862-3 (Mich. 2009).

3. Critical Race Theory. Critical race theory (CRT) provides a framework for judicial decision making that argues that race is central to the decision making. Richard Delgado identifies three broad themes of CRT as follows:

> The first is a persistent effort to broaden the substantive scope—or sharpen the analytical focus—of the dialogue on justice.... [C]ritical race theorists focus their writings on the struggle for racial justice, on the persistence of racial hierarchy, and on other issues of special importance to minority communities.... A second feature of critical race theory finds expression in the recurring call to modify the form of jurisprudential dialogue in order to accommodate marginalized voices.... A third distinctive feature is the belief that racism is extremely common, much more so than most people think. It is ordinary, not aberrational—the "normal science" of everyday life.... Other themes that most—but not all—crt scholars would subscribe to are: Interest-convergence and economic determinism—the notion that the interests of white elites are what determine the shifts of fortune for groups of color; the social construction of race—the idea that race is not objective, biological, or fixed, but rather conjured up by the majority to serve various purposes; differential racialization—the recognition that Asian Americans, Latinos, blacks, Native Americans, and other groups are understood in different ways at different times, in response to differing social forces and needs; essentialism and intersectionality—the belief that categories such as white and black are not unitary and indivisible, but that the identities of members of these groups are multiple and complex. For example, a Latina may be a single parent, female, with black skin; as such, she may share the characteristics of several groups and differ in her situation and needs from a white woman or professional-class black man.

Robert L. Hayman, Jr., Nancy Levit & Richard Delgado, Jurisprudence: Classical and Contemporary, 616-619 (2nd ed 2002).

What CRT themes Richard Delgado identifies may explain some of this judicial reasoning? How does Dorothy Roberts employ parts of CRT in her work on family law?

E. Privacy and Fundamental Rights

Another area of Constitutional litigation around ICWA involves the right to privacy. This is usually at issue in voluntary adoptions. There is a tension between a parent's right to privacy and the child's right to information. There can also be a tension between that parent's right and the tribe's right to govern its citizens.

Doe v. Piper

Case No. 15-cv-02639
(D. Minn. June 3, 2015)

Complaint

For their Verified Complaint for Declaratory and Injunctive Relief, Plaintiffs state and allege as follows:

1. This is a complaint for declaratory and injunctive relief challenging the constitutionality of certain provisions of the Minnesota Indian Family Preservation Act (MIFPA), Minn. Stat. 260.751 260.835, Minnesota's state corollary and complement to the Indian Child Welfare Act of 1978 (ICWA), 25 U.S.C. 1901-63.

2. Plaintiffs allege that Minn. Stat. 260.761, subds. 3, 6 (2014) are facially unconstitutional, and unconstitutional as applied to Plaintiffs, under the Fourteenth Amendment to the United States Constitution

Parties

3. Plaintiff Jane Doe is over the age of 18, is domiciled in the State of Minnesota, and is enrolled in the Mille Lacs Band of Ojibwe. Jane Doe does not domicile within or reside on an Indian reservation.

4. Plaintiff John Doe is over the age of 18, domiciled in the State of Minnesota, and is also enrolled in an Indian tribe. John Doe does not domicile within or reside on an Indian reservation.

5. Plaintiffs Jane and John Doe are Baby Doe's biological parents and remain his legal guardians pending the completion of Baby Doe's adoption by his "Adoptive Parents." Jane Doe believes Baby Doe is eligible for membership in the Mille Lacs Band of Ojibwe because her other children, also born to John Doe, are enrolled there. Baby Doe is not and has never been domiciled or resided within an Indian reservation.

* * *

19. Voluntary and involuntary termination proceedings are governed in Minnesota by Minn. Stat. 260C.301. A voluntary termination of parental rights occurs "with the written consent of a parent who for good cause desires to terminate parental rights . . ." *Id.*, subd. 1(a). Involuntary proceedings can occur for a number of reasons including abandonment, neglect, or failure to contribute to the support or financial aid of the child. *Id.* at subds. 1(b)(1)-(3). In Minnesota, parents may also voluntarily consent to adoption by signing consents to adoption under Minn. Stat. 259.24.

The Extended Reach of the Minnesota Indian Family Preservation Act

20. The Minnesota Indian Family Preservation Act was originally enacted in 1985, codified at Minn. Stat. 257.35 257.357 (repealed and renumbered 1999).

21. This law provided notice to tribes in cases where an Indian child was in a "dependent" condition that could lead to involuntary out ofhome placements. Minn. Stat. 257.352, subd. 2.

22. But even as originally enacted the law did not mandate notice to Indian tribes of voluntary proceeding where Indian parents desired to place their children for adoption.

23. In 1997, the Minnesota Legislature expanded upon ICWA and enacted notice and intervention provisions pertaining to *voluntary* adoptions:

> In any voluntary adoptive or preadoptive placement proceeding in which a local social services agency, private child-placing agency, petitioner in the adoption, or any other party has reason to believe that a child who is the subject of an adoptive or preadoptive placement proceeding is or may be an "Indian child," as defined in section 260.755, subdivision 8, and United States Code, title 25, section 1903(4), the agency or person shall notify the Indian child's tribal social services agency by registered mail with return receipt requested of the pending proceeding and of the right of intervention under subdivision 6. If the identity or location of the child's tribe cannot be determined, the notice must be given to the United States secretary of interior in like manner, who will have 15 days after receipt of the notice to provide the requisite notice to the tribe. No preadoptive or adoptive placement proceeding may be held until at least ten days after receipt of the notice by the tribe or secretary. Upon request, the tribe must be granted up to 20 additional days to prepare for the proceeding. The agency or notifying party shall include in the notice the identity of the birth parents and child absent written objection by the birth parents. The private child-placing agency shall inform the birth parents of the Indian child of any services available to the Indian child through the child's tribal social services agency, including child placement services, and shall additionally provide the birth parents of the Indian child with all information sent from the tribal social services agency in response to the notice. Minn. Stat. 260.761, subd. 3 (renumbered from 257 to 260 in 1999).

24. Minn. Stat. 260.761, subd. 6, states: "In any state court proceeding for the voluntary adoptive or preadoptive placement of an Indian child, the Indian child's tribe shall have a right to intervene at any point in the proceeding."

25. MIFPA defines an "Indian child" as "an unmarried person who is under age 18 and is: (1) a member of an Indian tribe; or (2) eligible for membership in an Indian tribe." Minn. Stat. 260.755, subd. 8. By contrast, ICWA defines an Indian child as either "(a) a member of an Indian tribe or (b) is eligible for membership in an Indian tribe and is the biological child of a member ofan Indian tribe." 25 U.S.C. 1903(4).

26. Many Indian tribes have only blood quantum or lineage requirements as prerequisites for membership. See, e.g., Paul Spruhan, *The Origins, Current Status, & Future Prospects ofBlood Quantum as the Definition ofMembership in the Navajo Nation*, 8 Tribal L.J. 1, 5 (2007); see also Rev. Const. & Bylaws of the Minnesota Chippewa Tribe, Minnesota, art. II, 1(c) (child eligible if born to a member and child is at least one quarter Minnesota Chippewa Indian blood). The Mille Lacs Band of Ojibwe is a member of the Minnesota Chippewa Tribe. *Id.* at art. III.

27. Unlike ICWA, the Minnesota Indian Family Preservation Act, facially and as applied, gives Indian tribes the right under the color of state law to interfere with voluntary, private adoptions.

Baby Doe's Private Direct Placement Adoption

28. Jane Doe gave birth to Baby Doe in April 2015 in Minneapolis, Minnesota.

29. Jane and John Doe are unmarried but have been a couple and continuously lived together since 2003. There is no possibility that anyone other than John Doe is the father.

30. Jane and John Doe have not had their parental rights terminated. Instead, they reached the difficult decision that adoption would be best for Baby Doe in light of their personal circumstances.

31. Jane and John Doe specifically elected to proceed with a private direct placement adoption through a private child-placing agency. A private direct placement adoption, commencing under Minn. Stat. 259.47, allows Jane and John Doe to specifically elect who Baby Doe's Adoptive Parents will be. No one other than the selected Adoptive Parents is legally able to adopt Baby Doe under this adoption method since they do not have the parents' consent and the child is not otherwise "free" for adoption.

32. Adoptions proceedings are strictly confidential under state law. Minn. Stat. 259.61 (hearings confidential except as to person and entities having right to notice). All adoption records, such as birth certificates (confidential under Minn. Stat. 144.225, subd. 2), detailed social and medical histories on the birth parents (required under Minn. Stat. 259.43, and adoption studies and criminal background checks on adoptive parents (required under Minn. Stat. 259.41), are likewise confidential, open to inspection only by the commissioner of human services or a licensed child placing agency. *Id.*

33. In private "direct adoptive placements" under Minn. Stat. 259.47, where the parent directly places a child with adoptive parents of their choosing, notice is required to be sent only to the child's guardian, if there is one, and parents with notice rights. Minn. Stat. 259.49. No governmental entity has the right to notice in such adoption proceedings unless the child is an Indian child under MIFPA, in which case the tribe must be notified of its right to intervene. Minn. Stat. 260.761, subd. 3. As an intervenor, the tribe has the right to discovery of all reports or other documents filed with the court. 25 U.S.C. 1912(c).

34. The Adoptive Parents selected by Jane and John Doe are not of Indian descent. However, Jane and John Doe chose the Adoptive Parents after learning about them from their adoption profile. They chose the Adoptive Parents because they appeared to be very good people and excellent parents to another adopted boy. Jane and John Doe were particularly happy about the idea that Baby Doe would have an older brother.

35. Jane and John Doe made an open adoption plan, including plans for Baby Doe to learn about and stay connected with his Indian heritage. Jane and John Doe have arranged with the adoptive parents to share pictures, text each other, and meet with Baby Doe from time to time. Adoptive Parents are already in a similar open adoption situation with their older boy.

36. Jane and John Doe are well aware of their rights under ICWA and MIFPA. However, they believe they are making the best decision about Baby Doe's care, custody, control, and future upbringing.

37. Jane and John Doe are also adamant that they do not want their tribes put on notice regarding Baby Doe's adoption. This notice will result in word spreading in the tribal offices of their adoption plan, and if the tribes seek out alternate placements then their families and others in the tribal community will learn of their private adoption plan. John and Jane Doe have intentionally kept Jane Doe's pregnancy and birth a secret, even from their own parents and family. This will result in embarrassment and immense pressure to deviate from what Jane and John Doe have determined to be the best decision for Baby Doe. This will also provide the tribes with the opportunity to intervene and interfere with what Jane and John Doe have determined to be the best decision for Baby Doe.

38. Jane and John Doe are also embarrassed and alarmed at the breach of confidentiality that would ensue if the tribe intervened in their adoption proceeding and obtained discovery of very private adoption files and records, including Baby Doe's confidential birth certificate, their detailed social medical history statements that they have submitted to the state juvenile court, the names and addresses of the Adoptive Parents and their adoption home study and criminal background checks.

* * *

43. The Fourteenth Amendment to the United States Constitution precludes any State from "depriving any person of life, liberty, or property, without the due process of law." U.S. Const. amend. XIV, 1.

44. The privacy interest of parents is a well-established liberty and right protected by the Due Process Clause of the United States Constitution.

45. Plaintiffs have a liberty and privacy interest in their parental rights and should be entitled to the certain rights, responsibilities, benefits and protections regardless of their race.

46. Defendants' infringement upon the Plaintiffs' liberty and right to privately pursue a direct private placement adoption violates the Due Process Clause.

47. Defendants' interference upon Plaintiffs' direct private placement adoption violates the Plaintiffs' fundamental parental rights and fundamental freedom in liberty, dignity, privacy, and family integrity under the Fourteenth Amendment.

48. Minn. Stat. 260.761, subds. 3, 6, facially and as applied to ICWA's preference provisions (25 U.S.C. 1915(a)), deprives Plaintiffs of their Due Process rights under the Fourteenth Amendment and is not narrowly tailored to serve a compelling governmental interest.

49. Defendants, acting under color of state law, are depriving Plaintiffs of their rights secured by the Due Process Clause of the Fourteenth Amendment to the United States Constitution in violation of 42 U.S.C. 1983.

Notes

1. In Chapter Three, you read the article regarding the passage of the Minnesota Indian Family Preservation Act. Given the resistance to the passage of voluntary coverage of the act then, what do you think convinced the legislature to add voluntary proceedings to the law in 1997, more than ten years later?

2. Are open adoption agreements binding in Minnesota?

3. Is it true no government agency except the tribe would get notice of a direct placement adoption? Can anyone in Minnesota place their child with any person? What if that person is a registered sex offender? Can a parent place their child under the privacy argument with someone who does not pass a background check?

4. Is there any established right to privacy for parents giving up their care, custody, and control of their children in an adoption situation? Should there be? Does the complaint cite to any controlling case law?

5. In Oklahoma, the Supreme Court there has said,

> The Attorney General disputes Florida Adoption Agency's contention that this Court is required to apply the standard of "strict judicial scrutiny" to the alleged violation of birth mother's constitutional rights, (i.e., liberty, privacy and the fundamental right to the care and custody of her child). As the Attorney General correctly argues, we held in *In the Matter of Baby Boy L*, 2004 OK 93, 103 P.3d 1099 (*Baby Boy L.*), discussed *infra*, wherein we cited with approval the case of *In re A.B.*, 2003 ND 98, 663 N.W.2d 625, that the "rational basis" analysis is appropriate when dealing with equal protection and substantive due process challenges. In holding the Federal and Oklahoma Acts are constitutional as applied to the cause in *Baby Boy L.*, we recognized the U.S. Supreme Court has consistently rejected claims that laws which treat Indians as a distinct class violate equal protection.

Cherokee Nation v. Nomura, 160 P.3d 967, 973 (Okla. 2007).

In its response to the Complaint, the state of Minnesota took a slightly different tact in explaining why the law was only subject to a rational basis review.

Memorandum in Support of Defendants' Motion for Summary Judgment

Doe v. Piper
Case No. 15-cv-02639
(D. Minn. December 30, 2016)

* * *

A. There Is No Fundamental Substantive Due Process Right To Adoption.

The Fourteenth Amendment's Due Process Clause contains "a substantive component, which forbids the government to infringe certain 'fundamental' liberty interests at all, no matter what process is provided, unless the infringement is narrowly tailored to serve a compelling state interest." *Reno v. Flores*, 507 U.S. 292, 302 (1993). "A fundamental right is one which is, objectively, deeply rooted in this Nation's history and tradition, and implicit in the concept of ordered liberty, such that neither liberty nor justice would exist if [it] were sacrificed." *Gallagher v. City of Clayton*, 699 F.3d 1013, 1017 (8th Cir. 2012) (quoting *Washington v. Glucksberg*, 521 U.S. 702, 720–21 (1997)) (internal citations and quotation marks omitted).

Where a challenged statute does not infringe upon a fundamental liberty interest, however, the statute must only be "rationally related to legitimate government interests." *Id.* at 728. "'Substantive due process' analysis must begin with a careful description of the asserted right, for '[t]he doctrine of judicial self-restraint requires [the court] to exercise the utmost care whenever [the court is] asked to break new ground in this field.'" *Flores*, 507 U.S. at 302.

In their Complaint, Plaintiffs assert that MIFPA should be subject to strict scrutiny. See ECF No. 1 ¶ 48 ("[MIFPA] . . . is not narrowly tailored to serve a compelling governmental interest."). Unlike the rights the Supreme Court has recognized as "fundamental," however, adoption is not "deeply rooted in this Nation's history and tradition." Adoption is a creature of statute, relies on state involvement, and requires the balancing of multiple competing interests. Indeed, federal courts have consistently held that adoption is not a fundamental right. *Lindley for Lindley v. Sullivan*, 889 F.2d 124 (7th Cir. 1989); *Lofton v. Sec. of Dep't of Children and Family Servs.*, 358 F.3d 804, 811 (11th Cir. 2004).

In *Lindley*, for example, the Seventh Circuit declined to extend an individual's fundamental right to parent to the adoption context. In holding that there is no fundamental right to adoption, the court observed that adoption is "entirely a creature of state law, and parental rights and expectations involving adoption have historically been governed by legislative enactment." 889 F.2d at 130. Unlike fundamental familial rights, adoption is not an intrinsic human right recognized in this Nation's history and tradition. *Id.* at 131. "Adoption always involves the weighing and balancing of many competing interests. The rights of a couple to adopt must be reconciled with the state's interest in protecting the existing rights of the natural parents, as well as in securing ultimately the welfare of the child." *Id.*

Analyzing Illinois adoption law, the *Lindley* court observed that "[a]mong the factors a court must consider in determining whether the proposed adoption is in the child's best interest are the religious belief of the adopters and adoptee, as well as the physical and mental health of all individuals involved and the background, race, ethnic heritage, behavior, age and living arrangements of the adopters." *Id.* (citing Ill. Stat. ch. 40, ¶¶ 1519, 1519.1(b)). The court concluded that "[b]ecause the adoption process is entirely conditioned upon the combination of so many variables, we are constrained to conclude that there is no fundamental right to adopt." *Id.*; see also *Lofton*, 358 F.3d at 811 (acknowledging that there is no fundamental right to adopt, be adopted, or apply for adoption).

In Minnesota, like other states, adoption is a creature of statute, and the State has enacted numerous laws governing adoptions. See *Fleming v. Hursh*, 136 N.W.2d 109, 111 (Minn. 1965) ("Adoption was unknown at common law and the right of adoption exists only by virtue of statute."). For example, Minnesota requires that numerous factors be considered when deciding whether adoption is in the best interest of the child, including the child's medical, educational, developmental, religious, and cultural needs; the child's history and past experience; the child's connection with a community, school, and faith community; the child's interests, and talents; and the child's relationship to current caretakers, parents, siblings, and relatives. Minn. Stat. § 259.29, subd. 1.

In addition, before an adoption placement can be completed, an approved adoption home study on the prospective parent(s) must be conducted. Minn. Stat. § 259.41. The adoption study must assess, among other things, the prospective adoptive parent's potential parenting skills, ability to provide adequate financial support for the child, and level of knowledge and awareness of adoption issues. *Id.*, subd. 2. A background study on the adoptive parent(s) must also be conducted. *Id.*, subd. 3.

Furthermore, adoption proceedings and Plaintiffs' desire to choose Baby Doe's adoptive parents do not fit into the parental rights the Supreme Court has recognized as fundamental. See *Troxel v. Granville*, 530 U.S. 57, 65 (2000) ("[T]he interest of parents in the care, custody, and control of their children[] is perhaps the oldest of the fundamental liberty interests recognized by this Court."). Although the Supreme Court has determined that certain parental decisions are fundamental, it has not held that the choice of adoptive parents is fundamental. See, e.g., *Meyer v. Nebraska*, 262 U.S. 390, 399 (1923) (right to control children's education); *Wisconsin v. Yoder*, 406 U.S. 205 (1972) (holding that compulsory education past eighth grade violated parents' fundamental right of parents to direct religious upbringing of their children).

Notes

1. The *Doe v. Piper* case was dismissed as moot. 2017 WL 3381820 (D. Minn. 2017). The adoption happened without the Tribe's intervention. The court, however, stated that the case presented "significant constitutional questions" regarding the parent's

right to care, custody, and control of their children, and whether MIFPA would be reviewed under a rational basis test or strict scrutiny. *Id.* at *5.

2. What does it mean that "adoption is a creature of statute"? Can statutes create fundamental rights? If Minnesota decided to end all adoptions in the state, could it? Are adoptions contractual agreements, or fundamental rights?

3. The federal regulations attempt to balance the rights of the parents with the rights of the tribe, specifically in the area of placement preferences. The regulations state that "good cause" to not follow the placement preferences would include "the request of one or both of the Indian child's parents, if they attest that they have reviewed the placement options, if any, that comply with the order of preference." 25 C.F.R. § 23.132 (2006).

4. The question of the tribe's right to information regarding their citizens comes up frequently in both the area of child welfare and juvenile justice. In the front matter to the regulations, the federal government pointed out that, "[t]ribes are often treated like Federal agencies for the purposes of exchange of confidential information in performance of governmental duties. See, e.g., Indian Child Protection and Family Violence Prevention Act, 25 U.S.C. 3205; Family Rights and Education Protection Act, 20 U.S.C. 1232(g)." 81 Fed. Reg. 38834. However, the Family Rights and Education Protection Act (FERPA) does not give state education agencies explicit coverage to share information with tribes, though it also does not *prohibit* the sharing of information. Recently the question of whether tribes can access information on a child welfare proceeding prior to a "foster care placement" has arisen in at least two states. So far, attempts to address this issue have been both at the legislative level and in tribal-state agreements. *See* 2016 Mich. Pub. Acts No. 56, (March 6, 2018); Government to Government Child Welfare Agreement between the Tulalip Tribes and the State of Washington at 5 (Jan. 13, 2016), available at https://www.dshs.wa.gov/sites/default/files/CA/icw/documents/tulalipAgreement.pdf.

5. *If* parents have a right to privacy, and to direct the placement of their children in an adoption, what are the corresponding rights of the children? Do they have any? Much of the legislative history of ICWA, and subsequent social science, has involved adult adoptees and the effect on their placements outside their communities. *See* Gallegos & Fort, *Protecting the Public Health of Indian Tribes: the Indian Child Welfare Act*, 8 Harv. Pub. Health Rev. __ (2018), *at* http://harvardpublichealthreview.org/protecting-the-public-health-of-indian-tribes-the-indian-child-welfare-act/. Do those adult adoptees have rights? How are those rights protected for newborns or babies? Chapter Four addresses the issue of anonymity and ICWA, but there are no cases on fundamental rights for *children*.

Chapter 6

Juvenile Justice

Understanding juvenile justice in the American Indian law arena means understanding both the maze of criminal jurisdiction in Indian Country along with special considerations about the prosecution of children. Unfortunately, while the former has been subject to a great deal of scholarship and legal decision-making, the latter has not.

Tribal criminal jurisdiction, while dramatically circumscribed by the Supreme Court in 1978 in *Oliphant v. Suquamish Indian Tribe*, 435 U.S. 191, has been area of Congressional action ever since the Major Crimes Act of 1885. However, in recent years, the federal trend has been toward tribal self-governance, to expand tribal sentencing through the Tribal Law and Order Act, and to provide for a limited expansion of tribal jurisdiction over non-Indians under specific circumstances through the Violence Against Women Act. However, the implications of this change are not clear for children. What is clear is that rules for sentencing and prosecuting adults in the federal system are applied with little distinction to Native children who find themselves in the federal jurisdictional trap on a reservation, even if the tribe also prosecutes.

A. Jurisdiction

Untangling the Web: Juvenile Justice in Indian Country

Addie Rolnick

19 NYU J. Leg. & Pub. Pol'y 40 (2016)

Separate juvenile justice systems have existed in most American jurisdictions for nearly a century. The ideas behind and policies governing these systems have shifted several times over the past century. As is the case with federal Indian policy, understanding the historical shifts in thinking about childhood and criminal responsibility that have guided juvenile justice policy is essential to assessing contemporary choices. At a minimum, this history can help tribal governments learn from the mistakes made by other jurisdictions. One lesson from the field of juvenile justice is clear: state and local systems today are struggling with over-incarceration, especially of minority youth.

Separate juvenile courts were first established in the early twentieth century based on the idea that young people were more deserving of and amenable to rehabilitation, and so should not be treated like adult criminals. These courts were founded by activists called "child savers," who viewed crime as a result of incomplete moral and social development and shared a goal of rescuing and rehabilitating poor and minority children. Separate institutions for youth began to appear in the middle of the nineteenth century. These institutions housed dependent and delinquent youth, and children could be committed by parents, police, or others. Called training or reform schools, they were subject to minimal judicial oversight, which allowed caretakers to experiment with discipline, physical punishment, isolation, manual labor, and even resettlement of children in other communities. For Native youth, it is significant that the dominant policy approaches to both misbehaving children and Indian people in the late 1800s favored removing children from their homes, sending them far away, and subjecting them to programming intended to mold them into race- and gender-specific roles. This emphasis on "fixing" children by training them in what was viewed as race- and gender-appropriate roles foreshadowed the use of federally sponsored boarding schools to "fix" Native children by training them in a gender-coded version of white-ness. Courts upheld the legality of these "houses of refuge," affirming the latitude given to the caretakers and the lack of procedural protections, reasoning that the goal was "reformation, not punishment," and invoking the doctrine of *parens patriae*, or the idea that the state has a role as guardian of all children.

The theoretical emphasis on rehabilitation continued to guide juvenile justice through most of the twentieth century, but the paternalism and lack of oversight has been tempered by procedural reforms. The first legislatively established juvenile courts included some procedural protections, but juvenile courts were still viewed as clearly non-criminal, and their rehabilitative goal left judges, probation officers, and treatment facilities with a great deal of latitude to intervene in the lives of young people, often for behavior that would not have been a crime if done by an adult. While formal courts introduced more oversight, nascent juvenile justice systems still struggled with balancing the values of flexibility and oversight.

Further substantive and procedural protections were extended to youth in juvenile courts in the second half of the century, stemming in part from a 1967 report recognizing that, while the goal of a separate juvenile system was to rehabilitate rather than punish, the reality fell far short of the rehabilitative goal, often resulting in children receiving the worst of both worlds: punitive sanctions without the protections accorded to adult offenders. Courts and policymakers began to recognize that children in these systems endured significant deprivations of liberty that could not be wholly justified by good intentions, culminating in a series of Supreme Court decisions extending various due process protections to juvenile courts. These decisions were grounded in the American constitutional framework, and in extending certain protections to juveniles, the Court in effect acknowledged that the juvenile system, like the adult criminal justice system, was characterized by a state-power-versus-individual-rights framework.

Juvenile imprisonment soared in the 1980s and 1990s, part of a nationwide boom in incarceration that began in the 1970s and nearly derailed the theory of the juvenile system as separate from the adult system and supported by principles of rehabilitation. Guided by narratives about high levels of juvenile violent crime, vicious gangs, and a generation of "super-predators," new federal and state legislation mandated a more punitive response to juvenile crime and blurred the boundaries between juvenile and adult courts and corrections. The shift toward punitive policies was especially dramatic for juveniles when compared to the previously dominant rehabilitative justification for the juvenile system.

The past two decades, by contrast, have yielded a budding consensus that juvenile offenders should be treated differently than adult offenders, that punitive sanctions should be reserved for the most serious offenders, and that communities should reduce their reliance on jails, prisons, and other secure facilities. This focus is accompanied by a recognition that different populations of youth have specific needs, and that interventions should be tailored to those needs whenever possible. Drawing on the constitutional rights framework developed in the mid-twentieth century, scholars and policymakers today also emphasize the importance of procedural rights such as access to counsel and a fair trial.

II.
The Multiple Sovereign Problem

Nothing in Indian country is a purely local matter. Under modern principles of federal Indian law, tribal, federal, and state governments all exercise some authority within Indian country. The rules concerning which sovereign has power over which matters are notoriously confusing. They are also in flux: in the last forty years, federal statutes or judicial decisions have resulted in express changes or major reinterpretations of existing principles, shifting the boundaries of tribal, federal, and state jurisdiction in significant ways. Most importantly, they result in a lack of local control over juvenile justice that is unmatched anywhere else in the United States.

In order to determine how the justice system works on any given reservation, one must first discern the precise extent of federal, tribal, and state authority there, and identify any rules governing the interaction between them. Indian country criminal jurisdiction is commonly described as a "maze." This criticism, and the corresponding idea that greater tribal control is the most important solution to practical problems, is a central theme in the two federal reports indicting juvenile justice in Indian country and in scholarly articles on criminal and juvenile justice. While this is an accurate metaphor for the experience of trying to determine who has authority when a specific crime has been committed, the term "web" better captures the top-down picture described in this Article.

Although the web of criminal jurisdiction is the subject of every basic course in federal Indian law, the manner in which jurisdictional rules relate to juvenile jurisdiction has not been clearly set forth by either courts or scholars. A careful explication of the legal rules is important. Solutions to the problem of juvenile justice in Indian country tend to center around increasing tribal autonomy and ensuring that federal and state authorities supplement, rather than overpower, tribal institutions, so it is especially important to understand which laws need to be changed (and which don't) to make this happen. Furthermore, an incomplete understanding can lead courts and legislators to rely on generalizations and may present a particular risk of underestimating the extent of tribal power. Even those articles and reports focused specifically on juvenile justice tend to treat it as a subset of criminal jurisdiction, assuming that the same rules, criticisms, and solutions apply. As described below, criminal and juvenile jurisdiction are not necessarily identical, and the differences have important implications.

Tribes, as sovereign governments, have jurisdiction over their territory and their people, but that jurisdiction has been limited in certain respects by federal law. Generally speaking, tribes retain any power that has not been taken away by federal law, which includes criminal and civil jurisdiction over members of the tribal community. Federal law restricts tribal jurisdiction over certain matters involving non-Indians and also sets some limits on how tribes may choose to exercise their jurisdiction. Individual tribes may exercise this jurisdiction very differently in practice in light of factors such as the respect that the state accords tribal jurisdiction, the governing tribal law, and financial or other resource-related considerations.

The federal government, on the other hand, is one of limited power, so its jurisdiction only extends as far as is authorized by federal statute. Congress, in the exercise of its plenary power over Indian affairs, has enacted two major statutes that authorize federal authorities to investigate and prosecute crimes occurring in Indian country. Because Indian lands are considered federal lands, federal criminal law applies to Indian lands in the same way it applies to other places where there is no intervening state government, such as national parks and the District of Columbia. However, tribal governments serve a role that is analogous to that of a state government, so the statute extending federal jurisdiction to Indian country contains several exceptions intended to ensure space for the exercise of tribal jurisdiction over local matters. A law granting federal authority over certain matters does not necessarily divest tribes of their inherent authority over the same matters, so federal and tribal jurisdiction are often concurrent.

Absent a specific federal law enlarging their authority, states have criminal jurisdiction in Indian country only over matters involving exclusively non-Indian offenders and non-Indian victims and civil jurisdiction over some of the activities of non-Indians, exceptions that are not relevant to the question of how Native juvenile delinquents are handled. Otherwise, the states' jurisdiction ends at the reservation border. More important for purposes of this discussion, certain states are authorized by federal law to exercise criminal and some civil jurisdiction over tribal lands within their borders. For those tribes, the state effectively stands in for the federal government, although the precise scope of state jurisdiction under these laws differs from the scope of federal jurisdiction that would exist in their absence.

Notes

1. The last paragraph of this excerpt is referring to Public Law 83-280 (P.L. 280), discussed in more detail in Chapter Two. While truancy, delinquency, and status offenses should not be considered in the criminal context, P.L. 280 directly affects tribal criminal jurisdiction, and arises in the context of juvenile justice. In P.L. 280, tribes and states have concurrent criminal jurisdiction over Indians, and Indian children, on tribal lands. While P.L. 280 does not strip tribes of their inherent jurisdiction and right to exercise both concurrent civil and criminal jurisdiction over their members, it did lead to a withdrawal of federal support for tribal justice systems in those states. This withdrawal was particularly acute in both Alaska and California. In both cases, many tribes simply do not have access to the resources available to tribes in other states for law enforcement or tribal courts.

2. The excerpt also refers to other federal laws, explained here:

> Native juveniles can also easily fall under federal jurisdiction. For instance, federal courts have jurisdiction over any crime committed in Indian Country that is listed in the Major Crimes Act. Federal courts also have jurisdiction over crimes that fall under the Indian Country Crimes Act or the Assimilative Crimes Act. However, these two Acts only apply when a Native individual commits a crime against a non-Native in Indian Country. Yet even in those circumstances, their applicability is limited and the Native nation retains concurrent jurisdiction. Finally, the Federal Juvenile Delinquency Act (FJDA) allows federal courts to take jurisdiction over Native juveniles who violate any federal law prior to their "eighteenth birthday which would have been a crime if committed by an adult," so long as the Attorney General, after investigation, certifies to a federal district court one of the following: (1) state courts do not have jurisdiction or refuse to assume jurisdiction; (2) the state does not have adequate services for the juvenile in question; or (3) there is a substantial federal interest in adjudicating the juvenile in the federal system. In such cases, the Attorney General's certification need not address the issue of tribal jurisdiction or tribal juvenile services.

Ryan Seelau, *The Kids Aren't Alright: An Argument to Use Nation Building Model in the Development of Native Juvenile Justice Systems to Combat the Effects of Failed Assimilative Policies*, 17 Berkley J. Crim. L.R. 97, 107-108 (2012).

3. The next case describes in detail how those statues interact and lead to problematic outcomes.

U.S. v. Male Juvenile

280 F.3d 1008 (9th Cir. 2002)

This appeal raises difficult and complex questions relating to federal jurisdiction over Native American juveniles. Once again, we must revisit the interplay of two statutes granting federal jurisdiction: those governing criminal jurisdiction over

Native Americans and those governing federal juvenile delinquency. Both grants of jurisdiction, on their own, have provoked concern about the reach of the federal government and the rights of those brought into court via these statutes. Together, the concern is even greater.

Pierre Y. ("Pierre") is a Native American juvenile who was adjudged a juvenile delinquent in federal court for two burglaries committed on the Fort Peck Indian Reservation, after previously being tried and punished in tribal court for one of the two offenses. Pierre raises numerous challenges to his federal prosecution: he contends that federal jurisdiction does not exist over these offenses; that the proceedings violated his rights to due process and equal protection of the laws; that his confession should have been suppressed; and that his right to a jury trial was violated.

Facts

On March 5, 2000, Pierre was taken into custody by Fort Peck Tribal Police as a suspect in the burglary of Kae Spottedbull's house, after Spottedbull reported to the police that she saw Pierre running away from the residence shortly before she discovered a VCR, a Super Nintendo, and some video games missing from her residence. Pierre's mother was called to the police station, and she gave her permission for the police to question him. The tribal police advised Pierre of his Miranda rights, and he signed an advice-of-rights form. After indicating that he understood his rights and was willing to speak with the officers, Pierre admitted breaking into Spottedbull's house. He was released from custody after the interview.

Shortly thereafter, an unrelated investigation by tribal police linked Pierre to the theft of compact discs from the apartment of Derek Bridges. On March 7, 2000, after obtaining Pierre's mother's permission, tribal police contacted Pierre at Poplar Middle School to question him about the missing CDs. Police told him that he was not under arrest, but nonetheless advised him of his Miranda rights and obtained his signature on an advice-of-rights form. Pierre then admitted to the break-in of Bridges' apartment.

On March 13, 2000, a petition was brought against Pierre in Fort Peck tribal youth court for juvenile delinquency based on the first break-in. After a hearing, Pierre was sentenced to 90 days for theft and 90 days for burglary, to be served consecutively.

Two months later, on May 15, 2000, the United States charged Pierre with two counts of juvenile delinquency, relating to both incidents. The jurisdictional certification statement required by 18 U.S.C. § 5032 (the Juvenile Delinquency Act) to establish federal jurisdiction stated that: (1) the state of Montana did not have jurisdiction over the offenses and (2) the offenses involved a crime of violence and there was a substantial federal interest in the offenses to warrant federal jurisdiction.

Pierre filed a pretrial motion, asserting lack of federal jurisdiction, requesting suppression of his confessions and other tribal court records, and demanding a jury trial. The motion was denied without a hearing. After a bench trial, Pierre was adjudged a juvenile delinquent for both offenses and sentenced to 24 months in custody. He timely appeals.

Jurisdictional Overview

The exercise of federal jurisdiction over tribal youth results from the interplay between the General Crimes Act (18 U.S.C. § 1152, also known as the Indian Country Crimes Act), the Major Crimes Act (18 U.S.C. § 1153) and the Federal Juvenile Delinquency Act (18 U.S.C. §§ 5031 et seq.). An overview of how these statutes work together will be helpful in addressing each of Pierre's claims.

Native American tribes generally have exclusive jurisdiction over crimes committed by Indians against Indians in Indian country. However, two federal statutes provide for federal jurisdiction over such crimes. The first statute, 18 U.S.C. § 1152, known as the General Crimes Act, mandates that the "general laws" of the United States, which are applicable in federal enclaves such as military bases, apply in Indian country. However, there are two important limitations on the scope of the Act: it does not extend to offenses committed by an Indian against another Indian or to any Indian who has been punished for that act by the local law of the tribe. The second statute, 18 U.S.C. § 1153, known as the Major Crimes Act ("MCA"), partially abrogated the General Crimes Act by creating federal jurisdiction over fourteen enumerated crimes committed by Indians against Indians or any other person in Indian country, including arson, murder, assault with intent to kill, and burglary. The MCA was enacted in response to "congressional displeasure over the Supreme Court's decision in Ex parte Crow Dog, holding that neither the federal nor territorial courts had jurisdiction to try an Indian for murder of another Indian on a reservation." Felix S. Cohen, Handbook of Federal Indian Law 300–01 (1982). Therefore, the enactment of the MCA "reflected a view that tribal remedies were either nonexistent or incompatible with principles that Congress thought should be controlling." *Keeble v. United States*, 412 U.S. 205, 210, 93 S.Ct. 1993, 36 L.Ed.2d 844 (1973). Significantly, the MCA does not contain an exception for Indians who have already been punished by the tribe.

Jurisdiction over juvenile defendants in the federal system is governed by the Federal Juvenile Delinquency Act ("FJDA"), 18 U.S.C. § 5031 et seq. Although the FJDA creates federal jurisdiction over alleged acts of juvenile delinquency, the alleged crime must be a "violation of a law of the United States" to trigger that jurisdiction. *Id.* § 5032. Also, as a jurisdictional requirement, the Act requires certification by the Attorney General that (1) the juvenile court or other appropriate court of a State does not have, or refuses to assume, jurisdiction over the acts of a juvenile; (2) the State does not have available programs and services adequate for the needs of a juvenile; or (3) the offense charged is a crime of violence that is a felony or one of several enumerated crimes and there is a substantial Federal interest in the offense. *Id.* Because certification requirements are disjunctive, a single basis for certification establishes jurisdiction. *United States v. Juvenile Male*, 864 F.2d 641, 646 (9th Cir.1988). The certification requirements resulted from Congress' desire to keep juveniles out of the federal court system and instead "channel juveniles into state and local treatment programs." *Id.* at 644.

* * *

I. Certification

Proper certification is a jurisdictional requirement. *United States v. Doe*, 170 F.3d 1162, 1165 (9th Cir.1999). Certification under any one of the three provisions of section 5032 is sufficient to commit a juvenile to the federal court system. *Juvenile Male*, 864 F.2d at 646. Whether the government complied with 18 U.S.C. § 5032 is a matter of statutory interpretation which this court reviews de novo. *United States v. Juvenile Male (Kenneth C.)*, 241 F.3d 684, 686 (9th Cir.2001) (citing *United States v. Doe*, 98 F.3d 459, 460 (9th Cir.1996)).

The certification filed in this case asserts two bases for jurisdiction: (1) the state of Montana (in which the Fort Peck Indian Tribe is located) does not have jurisdiction over the offense and (2) the offense involved a "crime of violence that is a felony" and a substantial federal interest exists in the case to warrant federal jurisdiction. Pierre challenges both grounds.

Pierre first argues that the certification is insufficient because the Attorney General failed to certify that the Fort Peck Tribe did not have, or would not assume, jurisdiction to adjudicate Pierre as a juvenile delinquent. Pierre contends that section 5032 requires such tribal certification.

* * *

A reading of section 5032 in its entirety shows that Congress was aware of its option to include tribal governments in the definition of "State," but chose not to do so. In another portion of the statute, relating to whether a juvenile may be charged as an adult, Congress made reference to the "criminal jurisdiction of an Indian tribal government." The reference, in its entirety, reads:

> Notwithstanding sections 1152 [General Crimes Act] and 1153 [Major Crimes Act], no person subject to the criminal jurisdiction of an Indian tribal government shall be subject to the preceding sentence for any offense the Federal jurisdiction for which is predicated solely on Indian country (as defined in section 1151), and which has occurred within the boundaries of Indian country, unless the governing body of the tribe has elected that the preceding sentence have effect over land and persons subject to its criminal jurisdiction.

Although this reference was added to the statute in 1994, after the 1990 change in the definition of "State," it is nonetheless indicative of Congress's general awareness of section 5032's impact on tribal affairs. This reference, in the same statute, indicates that Congress is certainly aware of the interplay between section 5032 and potential tribal jurisdiction. Congress specifically provided for consultation with tribal governments regarding transfer of Indian youth to the adult system. However, Congress did not include "Indian tribal government" in the list of authorities to be consulted in the certification process. Thus, when the definition of "State" is read within the context of § 5032 as a whole, it appears that Congress did not intend to refer to tribal authorities when it included "territory" in the definition of "State." See *Russello v. United States*, 464 U.S. 16, 23, 104 S.Ct. 296, 78 L.Ed.2d 17 (1983) (citation omitted) (noting that the canon expressio unius est exclusio alterius instructs that "[w]here Congress includes particular language in one section of a statute but omits it in another section of the same Act, it is generally presumed that Congress acts intentionally and purposely in the disparate inclusion or exclusion").

* * *

... [W]e hold that section 5032's amended definition of "State" does not include tribal governments and that the Attorney General was not required to consult with tribal authorities before certifying federal jurisdiction under 18 U.S.C. § 5032(1). Because the certification requirements are disjunctive, we need not reach Pierre's alternative argument concerning whether the Attorney General properly certified Pierre under 18 U.S.C. § 5032(3). We conclude that the certification requirement was met here because the Attorney General certified, under 18 U.S.C. § 5032(1), that the state of Montana lacks jurisdiction over Pierre with respect to his alleged act of juvenile delinquency.

* * *

Pierre was charged with burglary under the Major Crimes Act, 18 U.S.C. § 1153, and Montana Criminal Code Title 45, Chapter 6, Section 204. As stated above, the MCA creates federal jurisdiction over fourteen major offenses (including burglary) committed by Indians against Indians or any other person in Indian country. Under the MCA, if an enumerated crime is not defined and punished by federal law, the offense is "defined and punished in accordance with the laws of the State in which [the] offense was committed...." Since Pierre's offense, residential burglary, is not defined by federal statute, it is therefore defined by reference to state law. *United States v. Bear*, 932 F.2d 1279, 1281 (9th Cir.1990). Accordingly, Pierre was charged with burglary under section 1153 by reference to Montana's state burglary statute.

Pierre argues that because his act of delinquency was determined by reference to substantive state law, his violation of section 1153 did not constitute a "violation of the law of the United States."

* * *

... [T]he fact that no federal residential burglary statute exists, thereby requiring the incorporation of Montana's definition of burglary, does not strip the commission of burglary on an Indian reservation in Montana of its federal character. There is a crucial distinction between a statute that merely grants jurisdiction over state law offenses and a statute that creates a federal offense through the incorporation of a state-law definition. Pierre was not charged with, and did not violate, the Montana burglary statute; rather, he violated the Major Crimes Act, which incorporates the state law only for the purpose of definition. The Major Crimes Act is most definitely a law of the United States, regardless of its use of state law for a limited purpose, and we hold that this law creates federal offenses. This view is supported by the fact that this Circuit and others have referred to violations of the Major Crimes Act as "federal offenses" in other contexts. See *United States v. Begay*, 42 F.3d 486, 498 (9th Cir.1994) (noting that section 1153 extended federal jurisdiction over certain "major crimes" even though "those crimes might not otherwise be *federal offenses* if committed by non-Indians. . . .") (emphasis added); see also *United States v. Long Elk*, 565 F.2d 1032, 1040 (8th Cir.1977) ("[T]he offense [under the MCA] remains a federal offense.").

* * *

Finally, the implications of Pierre's narrow reading of the language of the Federal Juvenile Delinquency Act, § 5031, are unsettling. It would effectively extinguish federal jurisdiction over Native American juveniles with respect to all of the major crimes enumerated in the Major Crimes Act, which were not expressly defined in federal statutes. This would certainly be a dramatic and unintended result, contrary to the purpose of both the MCA and the Juvenile Delinquency Act, in light of the fact that state courts do not have concurrent jurisdiction over such crimes and the tribal courts can impose no punishment in excess of one year of imprisonment and a $5000 fine. See 25 U.S.C. § 1302(7).

* * *

Pierre also argues that his prosecution by the federal government for burglary, after his tribal prosecution, violated the constitutional prohibition against double jeopardy contained in the Fifth Amendment. This argument is foreclosed by *United States v. Wheeler*, 435 U.S. 313, 98 S.Ct. 1079, 55 L.Ed.2d 303 (1978). In *Wheeler*, the Supreme Court addressed the question of whether the Double Jeopardy Clause barred the federal prosecution of a tribe member who had previously been convicted in tribal court of an offense arising out of the same incident. *Id.* Answering in the negative, the Court held that, because Indian tribes are not federal agencies, but rather derive their power from their inherent and independent sovereignty, Wheeler's first prosecution was conducted by a sovereign other than the United States. *Id.* at 328. Accordingly, the subsequent federal prosecution did not violate the Double Jeopardy Clause. *Id.* at 329–330, 98 S.Ct. 1079. The situation in *Wheeler* is no different from the instant case.

* * *

VI. Sentencing

Pierre raises two arguments concerning his punishment under the Federal Sentencing Guidelines: first, that the Major Crimes Act required the district court to apply state law juvenile penalty provisions, rather than federal law, and second, that if the Federal Guidelines were correctly applied, then the ambiguity created by the contradictory language in the Major Crimes Act, § 1153(b), which directs district courts to apply state punishment to offenses defined by state law, and the Sentencing Reform Act, § 3351(a), which directs district courts to apply federal sentencing law to offenses located in the Major Crimes Act, violates due process, because it deprives defendants of adequate notice regarding what sentencing scheme will determine their punishment.

Pierre is correct that the Major Crimes Act does contain the directive that any enumerated offense "not defined and punished by federal law . . . shall be defined and punished in accordance with *the laws of the State* in which such offense was committed as are in force at the time of such offense." 18 U.S.C. § 1153(b) (emphasis added). And, it is true that residential burglary is not defined by federal statute. *Bear*, 932 F.2d at 1281.

However, the Sentencing Reform Act was amended in 1990 to ensure that Native Americans prosecuted for any crime under the MCA were sentenced under the Guidelines: "Except as otherwise specifically provided, a defendant who has been found guilty of an offense described in a federal statute, *including sections 13 and 1153 of this title* . . . shall be sentenced in accordance with the provisions of this chapter." 18 U.S.C. § 3551(a) (emphasis added).

Indeed, in the only Ninth Circuit case addressing punishment for crimes listed in the Major Crimes Act, which arose before the amendment to the Sentencing Reform Act, this court acknowledged that "[b]y th[e] amendment [to the Sentencing Reform Act], Congress has made the Guidelines applicable to those convicted pursuant to the Indian Major Crimes Act, 18 U.S.C. § 1153." *Bear*, 932 F.2d at 1282 n. 1. Therefore, there is no question that the Guidelines currently apply to the MCA.

However, a federal sentence for burglary (or other crime defined by state law) under the Major Crimes Act is not subject solely to the Guidelines. Rather, we find that the Guideline range must still be confined by state law, as it must fall within the minimum, if any, and the maximum sentence established by state law. Although we have not previously addressed the cabining of the Guidelines by state law for the purpose of the Major Crimes Act, we find the Eighth Circuit's reading in *United States v. Norquay*, 905 F.2d 1157 (8th Cir.1990), although predating the 1990 amendment, to be instructive. There, the court held that the range of the sentence imposed for burglary is determined by state law, and within that range, is calculated according to the Guidelines. *Id.* at 1161. In doing so, the court compared its interpretation of the sentencing scheme for the MCA to that of the Assimilative Crimes Act, which adopts a similar method.

* * *

We note that the Sentencing Guidelines do not directly apply to juveniles, such as Pierre, who are adjudged delinquent under the Federal Juvenile Delinquency Act. U.S.S.G. § 1B1.12. However, they are relevant to determining the proper sentence under the Act. For instance, in the case of a juvenile adjudged delinquent who is less than 18 years of age, the Act limits the maximum term of official detention to the lesser of the period until the juvenile becomes 21 or the maximum term of imprisonment that would be authorized if the juvenile had been tried and convicted as an adult. 18 U.S.C. § 5037(c)(1). Here, Pierre was sentenced to two years in custody. As the statutory maximum for burglary under Montana law is 20 years, Pierre's sentence was appropriate. See Mont.Code Ann. 45–6–204(3). Pierre was 14 years old at the time he committed the offense. Thus, his sentence to two years of official detention is within the maximum term authorized by 18 U.S.C. § 5037(c)(1).

Notes

1. The previous case indicates the morass of criminal jurisdiction in a non-P.L. 280 state. It further demonstrates the confusion when the rules for adults are applied to children. In this case, the 14-year-old defendant received a two-year federal sentence for burglary. Does this seem like the best solution given the facts of the case? Is the defendant's reading of the Federal Juvenile Delinquency Act unsettling? How might a tribal system address this crime? In this case, is a year detention or a $5,000 fine inappropriate? But what if the defendant's crime had been murder or rape? Does this change your analysis of the case?

2. The Fort Peck Tribe has the codes and ability to prosecute juvenile offenses in tribal court. How does the dual sovereign doctrine end up hurting the child in this case? In addition, recent reports have determined that the federal agencies often under-prosecute certain crimes, such as rape and domestic assault. *See* Amnesty International, Maze of Injustice: The Failure to Protect Indigenous Women from Sexual Violence in the USA 73 (2007); U.S. Dep't of Justice, Indian Country Investigations and Prosecutions 39 (2015). How does the local attorney general make the decision to prosecute this case?

3. Recently, the federal government issued reports on violence and child welfare in Indian country. Both discuss the difficulties with conflicting and overlapping jurisdictions. In addition, the report points out the lack of actual federal juvenile facilities.

A Roadmap for Making Native America Safer, A Report to the President and Congress of the United States

Indian Law and Order Commission Report, pp. 135-137 (Nov. 2013)

At present, Tribal youth who live on reservations, like their adult counterparts, are under the authority of one of several jurisdictional arrangements: they may be subject to many different regimes: Federal, Tribal-Federal, State, or State-Tribal. The same complexities and inadequacies that plague the Indian country adult criminal justice system impair juvenile justice as well. As with adults, Tribes face significant obstacles toward influencing the lives of their young Tribal citizens involved in juvenile justice systems. In addition, features of the Federal and State juvenile justice systems, combined with the special needs of traumatized Native youth, magnify the problems.

The Federal court system has no juvenile division—no specialized juvenile court judges, no juvenile probation system—and the Bureau of Prisons (BOP), a DOJ component, has no juvenile detention, diversion, or rehabilitation facilities. Federal judges and magistrates, for whom juvenile cases represent 2 percent or less of their caseload, hear juvenile cases along with all others. Native youth processed at the Federal level, along with their families and Tribes, face significant challenges, such as great physical distance between reservations and Federal facilities and institutions, and cultural differences with federal personnel involved in Federal prosecution. If juveniles are detained through the Federal system, it is through contract with State and local facilities, which may be several States away from the juvenile's reservation.

Within Federal juvenile detention facilities for misdemeanor violations operated in Indian country by the Office of Justice Services (OJS), a component of the Bureau of Indian Affairs (BIA), secondary educational services are either lacking or entirely non-existent. Officials of the Federal Bureau of Indian Education, which is statutorily responsible for providing secondary educational services and programs within OJS juvenile detention centers, confirmed for the Commission that Congress has not appropriated any Federal funds for this purpose in recent years. This means that Native children behind bars are not receiving any classroom teaching or other educational instruction or services at all.

When one of the situations triggering Federal Indian country juvenile jurisdiction arises, the corresponding U.S. Attorney's Office decides whether to proceed against the Native youth. This decision is based on "seriousness of the crime, age, criminal history, evidence available, and Tribal juvenile justice capacity." As with adults, the U.S. Attorneys often decline to prosecute juvenile cases, even serious ones. As one research study points out, "[t]ribal governments are left to fill this void . . . [and] . . . many youth simply fall through the cracks, getting no intervention at all." Because some Tribes do not currently have the infrastructure or funding to house juveniles, they are unable to address problems with youth in their communities.

Indian country youth may become part of State juvenile justice systems if they commit a crime in a Tribal community where State criminal jurisdiction extends to Indian country under P.L. 83-280, a settlement act, or some other similar Federal law. In State juvenile systems, there is generally no requirement that a child's Tribe be contacted if an Indian child is involved. Thus, "once Native youths are in the system, their unique circumstances are often overlooked and their outcomes are difficult to track." The juveniles effectively "go missing" from the Tribe. Furthermore, State juvenile systems do not adequately provide the cultural support necessary for successful rehabilitation and reentry back into the Tribal community.

Although data about Indian country juveniles in Federal and State systems are limited, the available data reveal alarming trends regarding processing, sentencing, and incarcerating Native youth. Native youth are overrepresented in both Federal and State juvenile justice systems and especially in receiving the most severe dispositions.

While the Federal government does not have a "juvenile justice system," youth do end up in Federal detention, and typically, the majority of these youth are American Indians and Alaska Natives. Between 1999–2008, for example, 43-60 percent of juveniles held in Federal custody were American Indian. In 2008, 72 Native youth were in Federal custody, although the number fell to 49 in 2012. According to the BOP, contracting to place a juvenile costs $259 per day or $94,535 per year.

Many States have significant populations of Native youth within their systems, and there are a disproportionate number of Native juveniles in State juvenile justice systems compared with non-Indian juveniles. Although the State systems data do not separate Indian country youth and offenses from others, there is no reason to believe there are systematic differences. In 2010 in the State systems, American Indians made up 367 of every 100,000 juveniles in residential placement, compared with 127 of 100,000 for White juveniles. This is especially alarming since American Indians make up little more than 1 percent of the U.S. population. In Oregon, a P.L. 83-280 State, Native American youth are over-represented in the State's juvenile justice system and in its detention programs run by the Oregon Youth Authority (OYA). While Native American youth make up approximately 2 percent of the State's 10-17 year olds, they are 5 percent of the youth committed to OYA. In 2008, the average cost for juvenile detention was $240.99 per day or $87,961.35 per year.

Notes

There is perhaps no greater example of the lack of consideration of the effects of jurisdiction decisions on Native youth than the fact that they can and do end up in federal facilities designed for adults with no mitigation. The following case details how that can happen.

United States v. Jerry Paul C.

929 F. Supp. 1406 (D.N.M. 1996)

THIS MATTER is before the Court on the Motion of the United States of America ("Government") to Transfer Proceedings Against the Juvenile, Jerry Paul C., to Adult Criminal Prosecution. The Court having read all the briefs of counsel and considered the testimony and exhibits presented, finds, with reservations, the motion is supported by the law and must be GRANTED.

The Government files its motion to transfer Jerry Paul C. to be tried as an adult pursuant to 18 U.S.C. § 5032. This statute is based on historical antecedents for dealing with juveniles committing crimes under traditional notions of delinquency and is constructed "around a philosophy of rehabilitation." Maj. Richard L. Palmatier, Jr., *Criminal Offenses by Juveniles on the Federal Installation: A Primer on 18 U.S.C. § 5032*, 1994 Army Law. 3 (1994). These remedial procedures must rehabilitate the juvenile so that he can be released on or before his twenty-first birthday in most cases. *United States v. A.W.J.*, 804 F.2d 492 (8th Cir.1986). The jurisdictional basis of this claim, a Native American committing crimes on the reservation, raises a troubling question.

The problem, so graphically portrayed by this case, is that the snare of federal sentences under the United States Sentencing Commission Guidelines catches only a small class of individuals: those who voluntarily enter federal enclaves and facilities, or Native Americans. See Palmatier, *supra* at 3. Significantly, "[m]uch of the federal case law deals with incidents occurring on Indian reservations." See, e.g., *United States v. Juvenile Male*, 864 F.2d 641 (9th Cir.1988); *United States v. Dennison*, 652 F.Supp. 211 (D.N.M.1986); *United States v. Means*, 575 F.Supp. 1068 (D.S.D.1983); *United States v. E.K.*, 471 F.Supp. 924 (D.Or.1979). Cf. Placido G. Gomez, *The Dilemma of Difference: Race as a Sentencing Factor*, 24 Golden Gate U.L.Rev. 357, 376 (1994) (recognizing cases involving Native Americans present unique sentencing problems for federal courts). If juveniles are transferred and tried as adults in state courts, state criminal sentences on average tend to be shorter, often with greater allowances for "good time" and parole, than federal sentences. Eric B. Levine, *Two Views of Offender Characteristics: A Comparative Look at the Federal Sentencing Guidelines and the New Jersey Sentencing Statutes*, 4 Seton Hall Const.L.J. 661, 662 n. 14 (1994); Robert P. Crouch, Jr., *Uncertain Guideposts on the Road to Criminal Justice Reform; Parole Abolition and Truth-In-Sentencing*, 2 Va.J.Soc.Pol'y & L. 419 (1995); see also Symposium, *Violent Crime Control & Law Enforcement Act of 1994*, 20 U.Day.L.Rev. 763, 766 (1995) ("Only the federal government and a few states require that criminals serve at least eighty-five percent of the imposed sentences."). Indian juveniles, therefore, face disproportionate consequences because transfer to adult status in the federal system exposes them to far graver consequences than their non-Indian counterparts transferred for adult prosecution in the state system. This is especially ironic as one of the goals of the Federal Sentencing Guidelines was to address the fact that several earlier studies showed minority defendants received longer sentences than their White counterparts. Elizabeth T. Lear, *Is Conviction Irrelevant?*, 40 U.C.L.A.L.Rev. 1179, 1189–90 (1993)

The handling of the state action involved in the same "night of terror" that brings this juvenile, Jerry Paul C., before this Court highlights the problem. Jerry Paul C. was convicted and sentenced as an adult on two counts of armed robbery with a firearm enhancement; conspiracy to commit armed robbery; and false imprisonment. He was sentenced to a prison term of ten years (one hundred twenty months). Under the Federal Sentencing Guidelines, he would have been subject to a sentence of approximately eighty-seven to one hundred and eight months, plus sixty consecutive months for use of a firearm during a crime of violence. In addition to the fact Jerry Paul C. was subject to a lesser sentence in the State system, at the time of his convictions the State of New Mexico allowed those serving "adult time" to earn good time credits at the rate of thirty days for every month served. NMSA 1978 § 33–2–34 (1990 Repl.Pamp.). Good time in the federal system is limited to fifty-four days per year. The effect, of course, is that Indian youths tried as adults in the federal system serve a substantially larger percentage of their originally longer sentences than non-Indian youths tried as adults in the State courts.

In spite of what appears to be a very disparate impact on those, mostly Indian, juveniles who are subject to the jurisdiction of the federal criminal system, this

Court is obligated to follow federal law and deal with Jerry Paul C. under the six factors enumerated in 18 U.S.C. § 5032.

* * *

1. Age and Social Background

Jerry Paul C. is an enrolled member of the Acoma Pueblo. His mother was fifteen when he was born. Jerry was raised by his maternal grandparents and actually thought his mother was his sister until he was twelve. He never knew his father although he believes his father resides somewhere near the Pueblo where he was raised. He was not a problem until he entered high school. As he got older, Jerry began to violate his curfew, left the house without permission, and skipped school on a regular basis. He also became disrespectful of his elders, increasingly using obscene language toward all authority figures. Along with the adult defendant in this case, Jerry was an admitted member of the "South Side Locos" gang. He was age fifteen at the time of the incident.

The Court finds his age weighs against transferring Jerry to adult status, but the other factors tilt in favor of transfer. Compare, *United States v. M.L.*, 811 F.Supp. 491 (C.D.Cal.1992) (sixteen year old with supportive family background and no prior record not transferred on murder charge).

2. Nature of the Offense

On July 30, 1995, the victim, William Anthony Morris, had hitched a ride outside of Albuquerque. Around 8:00 PM, just outside of Grants, New Mexico, the truck in which Morris was riding broke down on Interstate-40. The owner of the truck went to Grants to get help. He returned but was unable to fix the truck. The truck owner then told Morris that he could stay with the truck or he could hitchhike on to California, his ultimate destination. The owner left and Morris stayed in the truck.

At about this same time, Jerry and two friends, ages 18 and 14, approached Henry Sanchez who was using a phone in front of a convenience store, pointed a rifle in his face, and directed him to a nearby field. Sanchez was tied and gagged, and the three took his keys and his car. They then entered the convenience store, threatened the clerks with their firearms, and robbed the store. The three left the store but were unable to start Sanchez's car. Jerry fired a shotgun as they left.

The three began walking towards Acoma. They came upon the Dodge pickup truck parked on the shoulder of Interstate-40. Morris was asleep inside. The 18-year-old urged Jerry to "f—him [Morris] up." Jerry fired the shotgun once at Morris's head. When investigators asked Jerry how he knew Morris had been shot, Jerry said that he looked inside and saw blood on the window. When asked what he did next, Jerry said he reloaded and shot the victim a second time. When asked why he shot a second time, he said that Morris was flopping around and screaming. When Jerry was asked if he fired a third shot, as indicated by the evidence, he said he could not remember, but that he shot the victim until he was dead.

This factor weighs very heavily in favor of a transfer. *United States v. One Juvenile Male*, 40 F.3d 841 (6th Cir.1994); *United States v. Hemmer*, 729 F.2d 10 (1st Cir.), cert. denied, 467 U.S. 1218, 104 S.Ct. 2666, 81 L.Ed.2d 371 (1984); *United States v. H.M.M.S.*, 838 F.Supp. 30 (D.P.R.1993).

* * *

4. Present Intellectual Development and Maturity

Jerry Paul C. was last enrolled in the ninth grade. At that time, he was below average or failing most of his classes because of his failure to attend school. Earlier records indicated that Jerry was an average student. The Government presented testimony that he had dropped out of the GED program at the Southern New Mexico Correctional Facility where he is serving his ten-year state sentence. Jerry testified he was unable to participate in the program because it conflicted with his work assignment and the infirmary failed to provide him excused absences when appropriate.

The Court also heard fairly extensive testimony from psychologists presented by both the Government and Jerry Paul C. The Government sponsored David C. Miller, Ph.D., Director of Treatment Services at the New Mexico juvenile facility at Springer. Dr. Miller testified that based on his observations, Jerry was antisocial, had little regard for the rights of others, and was resistant to authority. He traced this to lack of appropriate handling during early childhood. It was Dr. Miller's opinion that Jerry's "conduct disorder" had remained fairly consistent and become internalized.

The Government also submitted a psychological report which concluded that in light of Jerry's long history of threats and physical aggression, both to strangers and family members, he posed a serious risk of becoming a repeat offender. It also concluded he was not amenable to treatment.

Counsel for Jerry Paul C. presented Robert Colby, M.A., who had interviewed and tested Jerry on two occasions and who earlier testified in favor of a juvenile sentence in the State court proceedings. He testified Jerry has at least average intelligence but in Colby's opinion had not been exposed to adequate attempts at rehabilitation in either the state or tribal systems. It was his opinion that no adult had ever established appropriate limits during Jerry's early life so that Jerry never learned to respect adult authority. He acknowledged that Jerry had a conduct disorder and needed treatment for drug and alcohol abuse in a secure facility. He also conceded that on the day of the murder if Jerry indeed heard a voice telling him to "hurt White people," he was very dangerous; at least on that day. Robert Colby further testified that Jerry's incarceration at the Southern New Mexico Correctional Facility had produced a sobering effect. This appears to be substantiated by Jerry's participation in a "scared straight" type program with local youthful offenders.

This factor is evenly balanced.

* * *

6. Availability of Programs

The final factor the Court must consider is the availability of programs designed to treat the juvenile's behavioral problems. Little evidence was presented on this topic. Robert Colby testified he had determined there were facilities which in his opinion could provide Jerry rehabilitative counseling designed specifically for Native American youth. Unfortunately, he knew nothing about whether Jerry would be eligible for any or all of these programs given his age and relatively violent history. Jerry's mandatory incarceration in a State prison until after he has turned twenty-one casts further uncertainty on any such prospects.

The Court does not have enough information to intelligently attribute any real significance to this factor in this case.

Conclusion

The Federal Juvenile Delinquency Act is designed to "'remove juveniles from the ordinary criminal process in order to avoid the stigma of a prior criminal conviction and to encourage treatment and rehabilitation.'" *One Juvenile Male*, 40 F.3d at 844 (quoting *United States v. Brian N.*, 900 F.2d 218, 220 (10th Cir.1990)). Jerry Paul C. has already been imprinted with the stigma of "adult criminal" in the State court, and this Court's ability to effect adequate treatment and rehabilitation before his twenty-first birthday is highly doubtful given his ten-year state sentence. See *United States v. Alexander*, 695 F.2d 398, 401 (9th Cir.1982) ("more than a glimmer of hope of rehabilitation" is necessary). Moreover, the Court must balance this priority with the need to protect the public from violent and dangerous individuals. [*United States v.*] *Bilbo*, 19 F.3d at 916 [(5th Cir. 1994)]. "[A] motion to transfer is properly granted where a court determines that the risk of harm to society posed by affording the defendant more lenient treatment within the juvenile justice system outweighs the defendant's chance for rehabilitation." *United States v. T.F.F.*, 55 F.3d 1118, 1121 (6th Cir.1995) (quoting *One Juvenile Male*, 40 F.3d at 844).

In this case, the Court must conclude that Jerry Paul C. will remain a risk to society. This may subject him to a very long, federal prison term on top of his prior state sentence. In this case, the possibility of a disproportionately long, federal prison sentence is largely the unfortunate product of Jerry Paul C.'s jurisdictional status as a Native American.

Now therefore,

IT IS ORDERED that the Government's Motion to Proceed Against Juvenile as Adult be and hereby is GRANTED; that these records and all further proceedings shall be transferred to the regular criminal division of this court; and that the Government may proceed against Jerry Paul C. as an adult.

Notes

1. The statute the judge is referring to has been described by other courts as "dysfunctional":

The Mandatory Transfer Statute—18 U.S.C. § 5032

Mandatory transfer of juveniles to adult criminal prosecution is governed by 18 U.S.C. § 5032. This verbose statute is far from a model of clarity. *Cf. United States v. A.S.R.*, 81 F.Supp.3d 709, 714 (E.D.Wis.2015) ("[T]his is about as dysfunctional . . . a statute . . . [as] you could find.") (internal citations omitted). Nonetheless, the statute provides that the transfer of a juvenile to adult prosecution is mandatory if three requirements are satisfied:

(1) the juvenile defendant is charged in the instant case with committing a crime after his sixteenth birthday;

(2) the charged crime is "a felony offense that has as an element thereof the use, attempted use, or threatened use of physical force against the person of another, or that, by its very nature involves a substantial risk that physical force against the person of another may be used in committing the offense, or would be [one of several enumerated offenses]"; and

(3) the juvenile defendant "has previously been found guilty of an act which if committed by an adult would have been one of the offenses set forth in this paragraph or an offense in violation of a State felony statute that would have been such an offense if a circumstance giving rise to Federal jurisdiction had existed."

18 U.S.C. § 5032.

United States v. D.J.H., 179 F. Supp. 3d 866, 869 (E.D. Wis. 2016).

The statute goes on to list the factors the court in *Jerry Paul C.* considered in the opinion.

2. Commentary in section 2.05.210 of the Model Indian Juvenile Code discussed below states:

> The Model Code does not provide for the transfer of delinquency cases to the tribal court for the initiation of criminal proceedings, because trying children as adults has not been shown to reduce crime, facilitate rehabilitation, or make communities safer. On the contrary, "transferring juveniles for trial and sentencing in adult criminal court has . . . produced the unintended effect of increasing recidivism, particularly in violent offenders, and thereby of promoting lifecourse criminality;" and "the bulk of the empirical evidence suggests that transfer laws, as currently implemented, probably have little general deterrent effect on would-be juvenile offenders." Richard E. Redding, Office of Juvenile Justice and Delinquency Prevention, United States Department of Justice, Juvenile Transfer Laws: An Effective Deterrent to Delinquency? 8 (June 2010) (citations omitted).

3. Recently the United States Supreme Court held that states could not sentence juveniles convicted of homicide could not be sentenced to life without an individualized evaluation. The Court addressed mandatory sentencing schemes and the problems with applying them to juveniles:

> The mandatory penalty schemes at issue here prevent the sentencer from taking account of these central considerations. By removing youth from the balance—by subjecting a juvenile to the same life-without-parole sentence applicable to an adult—these laws prohibit a sentencing authority from assessing whether the law's harshest term of imprisonment proportionately punishes a juvenile offender. That contravenes *Graham*'s (and also *Roper*'s) foundational principle: that imposition of a State's most severe penalties on juvenile offenders cannot proceed as though they were not children.

Miller v. Alabama, 567 U.S. 460, 474 (2012).

> Even when States give transfer-stage discretion to judges, it has limited utility.... [T]he question at transfer [to adult court] hearings may differ dramatically from the issue at a post-trial sentencing. Because many juvenile systems require that the offender be released at a particular age or after a certain number of years, transfer decisions often present a choice between extremes: light punishment as a child or standard sentencing as an adult (here, life without parole). In many States, for example, a child convicted in juvenile court must be released from custody by the age of 21. See, *e.g.*, Ala.Code § 12–15–117(a) (Cum. Supp. 2011); see generally 2006 National Report 103 (noting limitations on the length of juvenile court sanctions). Discretionary sentencing in adult court would provide different options: There, a judge or jury could choose, rather than a life-without-parole sentence, a lifetime prison term *with* the possibility of parole or a lengthy term of years. It is easy to imagine a judge deciding that a minor deserves a (much) harsher sentence than he would receive in juvenile court, while still not thinking life-without-parole appropriate. For that reason, the discretion available to a judge at the transfer stage cannot substitute for discretion at post-trial sentencing in adult court—and so cannot satisfy the Eighth Amendment.

Id. at 488-89.

4. Under ICWA, states are supposed to notify tribes when Native children are involved in status offenses in state court, discussed in section B below. States rarely give this notice, and even more rarely do states involve tribes in decisions about children in juvenile delinquency proceedings. *See In re W.B., Jr.*, 281 P.3d 906 (2012), below. In addition, tribes are almost never involved in the decision-making process at the federal level either. However, during the hearings on Indian child welfare prior to the passage of ICWA, over and over again, Congress and Committees received the recommendation to support tribal solutions for Native children and families:

> Two basic concepts surfaced at the [1974] hearings [on Indian child welfare]. First, Indian people and child welfare experts stressed the need for adequately funded, tribally controlled family development programs which

> would function at the local level and would be able to exhibit a deeper cultural sensitivity toward Indian people they serve. Second, Indian tribal leaders pointed out that Indian tribes were recognized as by the United States as sovereign governmental units and as such the final decision making powers in areas as basic as child welfare should rest within the relm [sic] of tribal jurisdiction.

S. Rep. 95-597, Indian Child Welfare Act of 1977, 12 (Nov. 3, 1977).

Forty years later, the Attorney General's Advisory Committee found the same thing, and their recommendations mirrored those 1974 hearings: allow tribes to operate their own systems and support them doing so.

B. Tribal Solutions

Ending Violence So Children Can Thrive

Attorney General's Advisory Committee on American Indian/Alaska Native Children Exposed to Violence
November, 2014

Many American Indian and Alaska Native (AI/AN) people believe that the Western criminal/juvenile justice system is inappropriate for children, particularly AI/AN children, as it is contrary to AI/AN values in raising children. As Justice Herb Yazzie said in testimony: "I would be blunt in saying that the American criminal justice system is inappropriate to be applied to young people.... You do not apply criminal concepts to young kids.... So I encourage you to seek ways to break the application of criminal law concepts to young people." This concern raised during testimony points to trends in the 1990s away from a juvenile justice system focused on rehabilitation and toward the overuse of secure detention and formal processing of cases in state court systems. As evidence of this concern, a review of the results of twenty-nine randomized controlled trials found no evidence that formal delinquency processing had any positive effect on juvenile crime control, and in fact this review discovered that most of these randomized controlled trials found formal processing actually increases delinquency. The inescapable conclusion is that the standard approach to juvenile justice in state jurisdictions is a failure.

Testimony at public hearings and site visits conducted by the Advisory Committee established that these formal processing systems are often relied upon by tribal juvenile justice systems as well. This is a disturbing trend, when funding for tribal juvenile justice systems is so disproportionately smaller than that for state systems. This failure is compounded for tribal communities that lack the taxation authority and funding streams available to states. The Indian Law and Order Commission arrived at the same conclusion in its recent report as it entitled its chapter on juvenile justice: "Juvenile Justice: Failing the Next Generation."

Over the history of the federal and tribal relationship, federal law and policies have systematically impeded the sovereignty and governing ability of tribes to meaningfully and positively impact the lives of tribal children. The federal boarding school policies at one time resulted in nearly half of all AI/AN children being in residential boarding schools, sometimes hundreds or even thousands of miles away from their families where many experienced physical and sexual trauma, and loss of role models of effective parenting. Likewise, the allotment acts passed by the U.S. Congress were an attempt to assimilate the American Indian into the dominant culture, but instead had the effect of conveying almost 100 million acres of Indian reservation lands into ownership by non-Indians. Later, in 1953, Congress passed PL-280 resulting in states being delegated criminal and limited civil jurisdiction over Indians located on reservations. PL-280 and the Allotment acts have created a patchwork of non-Indian and Indian landownership on most reservations, and a patchwork of criminal federal, tribal, and state jurisdiction over Indians who reside on these reservations or trust lands. AI/AN children accused of delinquent acts or truancy are at risk of becoming involved in the courts of one or more of the juvenile justice systems of these three sovereign entities.

* * *

Three different jurisdictional systems impact AI/AN youth involved in the juvenile justice system: federal, tribal, and/or state. The confusing criminal jurisdictional framework, which is designed for adults, has a significant and oftentimes harmful impact on youth. Depending upon where a delinquent act takes place, the race of the victim, the seriousness of the act, and whether PL-280 or a similar-styled law applies, one or more of the three systems could have jurisdiction over the juvenile. While this jurisdictional maze is problematic for adults, it is far more disastrous for youth caught in the systems and does not allow for notification of their tribes, which might not realize the extent of their youth's involvement in the state or federal juvenile justice systems.

Many tribal communities have no tribal juvenile court system or juvenile code, and oftentimes lack the supporting service delivery system necessary to meet the specific needs of their youth who come in contact with the juvenile justice system. Due to the fact that tribes do not have a tax base, these systems are largely dependent on federal authorizations and appropriation. Tribes in PL-280 states and Alaska Tribes generally receive little to no funding for court services overall, and much less for handling the unique needs posed by juvenile justice cases specifically.

If a tribe is one of the fortunate few to have successful economic enterprises acting as tax base surrogates that can be used to support juvenile justice system infrastructure and staffing, there is still a significant lack of training in best practices to better the lives of juveniles. A few tribes that have funding through successful economic ventures have developed juvenile justice systems that provide services and support to the youth that enter their systems, with strong focus on prevention and rehabilitation in their communities. However, the Advisory Committee also saw, in these examples, a heavy reliance on detention, even in cases of status offenses such as curfew violations. These detention centers were also much more akin to adult correctional facilities than to a place where these children would feel safe and have their needs addressed. While the Advisory Committee understands that this is a very common practice in state and federal jurisdictions, we believe that a tribe's continued common use of detention for children having such extreme rates of exposure to violence is another infliction of violence on these children. As such, there must be strong support for community-based, culturally specific alternatives to detention for AI/AN children.

Over and over again the Advisory Committee heard testimony to the effect that: "We have the answers." "The answers lie within our people, within the communities." "We as Indian people hold the healing ability to heal our communities though our cultural ways." Tribal culture and tribal and family connections play an important role in responding to the effects of exposure to violence through the development of resiliency. The current system does not support that local participation and develop the capacity of the local community. It does not support local practices that work, but rather supports evidence-based practices that worked in Europe or some non-Indian community, not in Indian country, Alaska Native villages or urban Indian communities. The Advisory Committee supports substantial reform of the juvenile justice systems impacting AI/AN youth. A reformed juvenile justice system should be tribally operated or strongly influenced by tribes within the local region. It is a system:

- Where tribes, parents, and families know where their children are and believe they are safe and in good care.
- Where youth are appropriately screened, and services are trauma-informed.
- Where tribal-specific or culturally based traditional healing, understanding, and practices are interwoven with all therapeutic services available for children and their families.
- Where federal, tribal, and state systems coordinate and cooperate ensuring that their AI/AN youths' needs are being met in a seamless and accountable method.
- Where a variety of diversion and reentry programs involving the tribal or local community are available.
- Where there is less reliance on the use of family methods that disrupt families, and where detention and removal from home are utilized as a last resort when there is no other recourse to protect the child or community.
- Where, when detention is necessary to protect public safety youth are placed close to home and family with adequate and effective services.
- Where juvenile justice codes reflect an understanding of children's exposure to violence and reflect local cultural values, and status offenses are treated differently from other juvenile offenses.

- Where successes are tracked so that other nontribal justice systems feel confident in referring Native children to their system and services.

Notes

The issues of capacity and resources to develop a juvenile justice system that meets the recommendations of the Committee remains a major stumbling block to tribally operated systems. In 2016, the federal government released an updated Model Indian Juvenile Code for tribal courts. In 1986, as part of a large piece of legislation passed involving the war on drugs, the Anti-Drug Abuse Act directed the Secretary of the Interior to develop a model Indian juvenile code:

> SEC. 4221. MODEL INDIAN JUVENILE CODE. The Secretary of the Interior, either directly or by contract, shall provide for the development of a Model Indian Juvenile Code which shall be consistent with the Juvenile Justice and Delinquency Prevention Act of 1974 and which shall include provisions relating to the disposition of cases involving Indian youth arrested or detained by Bureau of Indian Affairs or tribal law enforcement personnel for alcohol or drug related offenses. The development of such model code shall be accomplished in cooperation with Indian organizations having an expertise or knowledge in the field of law enforcement and judicial procedure and in consultation with Indian tribes. Upon completion of the Model Code, the Secretary shall make copies available to each Indian tribe.

25 U.S.C. § 2454 (2012).

The 2016 Model Indian Juvenile Code was the first update in nearly thirty years.

Model Indian Juvenile Code and Commentary

§ 1.01.110, § 1.07.190-210

§ 1.01.110 Purpose

This title shall be construed and interpreted to fulfill the following purposes:

(a) to secure the care, protection, and mental and physical welfare of children coming within the provisions of this title;

(b) to preserve and retain the unity of the family and to carry out the other purposes of this title in a family environment whenever possible, separating the child from the child's parents only when necessary for the child's welfare or the safety and protection of the community;

(c) to distinguish, in judicial and other processes affecting children coming within the provisions of this title, between the child who has committed a delinquent act and the child in need of services, and to provide appropriate and distinct dispositional options for these children and their families;

(d) to remove from children committing delinquent acts the legal consequences of criminal behavior, and to substitute therefore programs of supervision, treatment, and rehabilitation which:

(1) hold them accountable for their actions;

(2) provide for the safety and protection of the community; and

(3) promote the development of competencies which will enable them to become responsible and productive members of the community;

(e) to set forth procedures through which the provisions of this title are to be executed and enforced, while ensuring the rights of the parties are recognized and protected; and

(f) to coordinate services for children and their families, with an emphasis on prevention, early intervention, diversion and community-based alternatives.

§ 1.01.110 Commentary

The purposes articulated in this section reflect the goals and principles that have guided the development of the Model Code from its inception.

The specific language of these provisions, meanwhile, has been adapted from a number of sources, including the juvenile codes of various tribal and other jurisdictions. Implementing tribes are encouraged to review this section carefully, and to tailor it to state their purposes as accurately as possible.

Factors which might inform this process include tribal culture and tradition, the resources available in and to the tribal community, and the structural and procedural character of the tribal court.

§ 1.01.110(d) Commentary

This subsection explicitly invokes the core principles—accountability, community safety, and competency development—of the Balanced and Restorative Justice (BARJ) Model. For a thorough discussion of the BARJ approach to juvenile justice, see Office of Juvenile Justice and Delinquency Prevention, United States Department of Justice, Guide for Implementing the Balanced and Restorative Justice Model (December 1998).

§ 1.01.110(e) Commentary

The Model Code attempts to set forth not only a coherent set of goals and principles, but a comprehensive procedural framework for balancing the interests, addressing the needs, and safeguarding the rights of tribal youth and their communities. While keeping these considerations in mind, implementing tribes may wish to modify or supplement this framework based on their particular purposes, needs and resources.

§ 1.07.190 No Derivative Proceedings

(a) Except as provided in subsections (b) and (c), and other provisions of [the tribal code] notwithstanding, the fact that a child has violated an order of the Juvenile Court shall not be the basis for subjecting the child to:

(1) punitive sanctions;

(2) charges of delinquency; or

(3) a finding of contempt.

(b) Where the violation consists of an alleged act which would constitute a delinquent act in the absence of the order violated, the alleged act may the basis for a delinquency petition filed in accordance with the provisions of Chapter 2 of this title.

(c) Where the child is alleged to have violated a no-contact or protection order, and the violation of such an order would constitute a violation of [specific provision(s) of the criminal code], the alleged violation may the basis for a delinquency petition filed in accordance with the provisions of Chapter 2 of this title.

§ 1.07.210 Use of Disposition and Evidence in Other Proceedings

Neither the adjudication nor disposition of any child in accordance with the provisions of this title, nor any evidence admitted in a hearing before the Juvenile Court, shall be admissible as evidence against the child in any proceeding in another court, including the Tribal Court.

§ 1.07.190 Commentary

This section has been drafted in keeping with two principal objectives of the Model Code: first, to ensure that juvenile court proceedings (including delinquency proceedings) are restorative rather than punitive; and second, to address the needs of tribal children and their communities while minimizing youth involvement in the juvenile justice system.

While subsection (a)(2) bars delinquency charges based on the violation of a court order, subsection (b) is included to ensure that the child may still be held accountable for otherwise delinquent acts.

Meanwhile, if the tribal code includes specific provisions making the violation of a no-contact or protection order a crime, the exception in subsection (c) allows the violation of such orders to be the basis for delinquency charges as well.

Note, however, that the Juvenile Court may generally modify its orders, or take other remedial actions, when those orders fail to accomplish their intended purposes. See, e.g., § 2.03.110(a)(2) (custody orders based on violation of conditions of release or disposition orders); § 2.04.210 (modification of conditions of release and review of the need for detention based on violation of conditions of release); § 2.12.310 (modification of disposition orders) and § 2.12.330(a) (motion for modification based on violation of disposition orders).

If the Juvenile Court enters orders intended to protect the child or the community, for instance, and the child violates those orders, the Juvenile Court may find that more restrictive orders are necessary—not to punish the child for noncompliance, but to accomplish the purposes of the original orders.

§ 1.07.210 Commentary

The Model Code has been drafted to maintain a clear and rigorous distinction between juvenile and criminal proceedings, and to ensure that juvenile proceedings are restorative rather than punitive in nature. Allowing evidence and findings from

Juvenile Court proceedings to be used against the child in other proceedings would undermine both of these objectives, and this section therefore prohibits any such use

Notes

1. While tribes are not required to follow the model code or implement any portion of it, having a code dedicated to restorative justice and healing for juveniles drafted does a great deal of work for tribal councils and their attorneys interested exercising juvenile jurisdiction.

2. How does the Code describe its objectives and goals? What are important considerations for a tribe to discuss before implementing a juvenile code? The Code provides a number of places for tribes to consider choices in their juvenile system, with a focus on diversions and due process. Diversions are opportunities for a tribe and child to decide to not continue in a western court process and move to more culturally appropriate services and consequences. The Model Code makes clear, however, that a diversion agreement should be done with proper representation for the child and due process protections. See § 2.06 Diversion Agreement.

In re Bell

3 Am. Tribal Law 305 (Ft. Peck Tribal Court Assiniboine and Sioux Tribes 2001)

Procedural History and Factual Background

Lt. Wade Krohmer received a report of a stolen .243 rifle from John Johnson IV on December 17, 1998 at 6:45 p.m. The victim stated that he had parked his pickup between the Elks Club and the Prairie Cinema and ran into the Elks Club to speak with his girlfriend. Upon returning to his vehicle, Johnson reported seeing a black Mercury Cougar leaving in a hurry. As he climbed into his truck, Johnson also noted that his .243 bolt-action rifle was missing.

Lt. Krohmer knew that the appellant, Mike Bell, drove a black Cougar and had seen Mike driving around Wolf Point on other occasions. Lt. Krohmer started patrolling Wolf Point looking for the black Cougar. Shortly thereafter, he spotted the black Cougar and followed it to the 900 block of West Blaine. After parking across the street, he saw Mike exit the vehicle and proceed to the front door of David Moran's residence. Apparently no one was home and Mike returned to his vehicle. Lt. Krohmer approached Mike and told him of the reported theft of the rifle and he asked whether Mike knew anything about it. He also asked Mike if he could search his vehicle. Mike denied any knowledge of the theft and gave the officer permission to search his vehicle. The officer found a rifle in the back seat of Mike's vehicle, which matched the description of the stolen .243 rifle. Lt. Krohmer subsequently charged Mike with a violation of Title VII CCOJ 2000 § 320 (felony theft) and Mike was referred to the Juvenile Division of the Tribal Court in accord with Title IX CCOJ 2000 § 102(g)1.

Mike, with his mother Deb'e Bell, appeared at the initial hearing on January 26, 1999 and entered a plea of not guilty. At the initial hearing Mike and his mother were both personally served with written notice of a fact-finding hearing to be held on February 23, 1999 at 10:00 a.m., however, none of their rights were expressly stated on that notice. Several prosecution witnesses were summoned for the fact-finding hearing; however, no defense witnesses were summoned due to the defendant's failure to submit a witness list. Mike appeared pro se and was found guilty of felony theft and sentenced to 90 days in the juvenile detention center; sentence to be reviewed in 30 days.

After appearing pro se in the Juvenile Court, Mike retained the services of Lay Advocate Leighton Reum and filed his appeal on February 26, 1999; a stay of sentence was granted the same day. Oral argument was heard on October 8, 1999, during which the appellant argued that his due process rights were violated, stating that he was not given proper notice as required by Title v. CCOJ § 305(b). He further asserts that he had no opportunity to exercise certain discovery procedures, such as exchanging witness lists and attempting to resolve the matter informally. Still further, Mike contends that because he was not furnished with the full content of the notice requirements of § 305(b), he was not given the opportunity to have legal counsel assist in the preparation of his case and that such lack of preparation (such as calling witnesses, etc.) resulted in an unwarranted conviction.

Issue

The facts in this case are not in dispute. The sole question before the court is whether an oral notice of the contents of § 305(b), given in open court by a judge, satisfies the requirements of § 305(b).

Discussion

The appellant asserts he was denied his due process rights under Title v. CCOJ 305(b)2. § 305(b) states:

> (b) *Notice*. The Court *shall serve prior written notice* of the date, time, and place of the hearing upon the youth, any person authorized to represent the youth and the parent(s), legal custodian or guardian. Notice shall be served in person or by certified mail, return receipt requested, or by publication in the local newspaper for a period of three (3) consecutive weeks, if the whereabouts of the parent(s), legal custodian or guardian are unknown. The youth's full name shall not be published when notice is required by publication in any newspaper. *Notice shall also specify that the youth (and any other party served with notice) has a right to retain counsel at his/her own expense, be present, testify, present documentary evidence, call witnesses, and ask questions of all witnesses. (Our emphasis)*

The appellee counters, arguing that Mike and Deb'e Bell had been in the juvenile system before and were well aware of their rights and they were given personal notice at the initial hearing by Judge Christian where he advised them of all the rights provided to juveniles under the code. In short, the appellee maintains, "due process was satisfied."

At the initial hearing on January 26, 1999, Judge Christian read portions of the petition to Mike and his mother, Deb'e Bell. After advising them of the "general procedures" in Juvenile Court and of the specific charges lodged against Mike, Judge Christian stated:

> **Judge Christian:** . . . Deb'e it is the right of the parent or guardian of the child to obtain counsel at your own expense or through the public defender's office. To be present at all hearings pertaining to this matter. To present to this Court, documentary evidence for your child. To call witnesses for your child. And ask (questions) of all witnesses. Do you understand those rights for your child?
>
> **Deb'e Bell:** Un-huh (yes) (See transcript, page 2, lines 12–19)

The appellant relies heavily on *In Re: Gault*, 387 U.S. 1, 87 S.Ct. 1428, 18 L.Ed.2d 527 (1967) wherein the U.S. Supreme Court sets forth the standard for juvenile due process. In *Gault*, a 15-year-old boy was taken into custody for making lewd phone calls. At the time of his detention, both of his parents were at work and neither of them was notified of his detention. The parents did not learn until later that evening that their son had been taken into custody. After visiting the facility that evening, the parents were told by the deputy superintendent of the Detention Home that the boy would have a hearing before a Juvenile Judge the next day (June 9th) at 3:00 p.m. The deputy superintendent, who was also a Probation Officer for the County, filed a petition which did not set forth any factual basis, but made conclusory remarks that the boy needed protection from "this Court". The parents were not given a copy of the petition, nor were they advised of the contents of the petition at the informal hearing. The boy's mother and older brother, along with two probations officers attended the informal hearing the next day. The complaining witness was not present and did not testify. The hearing was held in the Judge's chambers and at the conclusion, the Judge said he would "think about it." The boy was held in custody for another two or three days, without explanation, and then released. Upon the boy's release, the probation officer gave a signed note to the boy's mother. The note was on plain paper, not letterhead, and read as follows:

> "Mrs. Gault:
>
> "Judge McGHEE has set Monday June 15, 1964 at 11:00 A.M. as the date and time for further Hearings on Gerald's delinquency"

At the June 15th hearing, the boy, both of his parents, the two probation officers and the co-defendant and his parents, were all in attendance. A referral report, which listed the charge as "Lewd Phone Call", was filed on the day of the hearing, but was not given to the boy's parents. The complaining witness did not attend, nor did the Judge speak with her at any time. At the conclusion of the hearing, the judge committed the boy as a juvenile delinquent to the State Industrial School "for the period of his minority [that is, until 21], unless sooner discharged by due process of law." State law did not allow an appeal in juvenile cases, so the parents filed a writ of habeas corpus with the Arizona State Supreme Court. The Supreme

Court referred the matter to the Superior Court for hearing. The Superior Court dismissed the writ. The parents then sought review in the Arizona Supreme Court, which affirmed the dismissal of the writ.

In reversing the Arizona Supreme Court, the U.S. Supreme Court held, inter alia, that "due process of law requires that in a juvenile delinquency proceeding the child and his parents or guardian be notified, in writing, of the specific charge or factual allegations to be considered at the hearing, and that such written notice be given at the earliest practicable time, and in any event sufficiently in advance of the hearing to permit preparation. The Court goes on to hold that the child and the parents have a right to be notified of the child's right to be represented by counsel retained by them, or if they are unable to afford counsel, that counsel will be appointed to represent the child."

Our § 305(b) echoes the requirements set forth in *Gault* and further sets forth the additional requirement of advising the youth and parent or guardian of their right to present documentary evidence, to call witnesses, and to ask questions of witnesses. Thus, inasmuch as § 305(b) includes all of the *Gault* requirements, we examine the language of the statute to determine the Court's obligation.

305(b) requires the notice to be in writing and must include the date, time, and place of the hearing. That requirement was met when Mike and his mother was served with a document entitled "Summons" while in court at the initial hearing on January 26th. The summons contained the time, date, and place of the hearing scheduled for February 23rd. 305(b) also requires that "notice shall . . . specify that the youth (and any other party served with notice) has a right to retain counsel at his/her own expense, be present, testify, present documentary evidence, call witnesses, and ask questions of all witnesses". Judge Christian advised Mike and Deb'e of all of those rights directly from the bench on January 23rd. However, the plain language of § 305 requires that these rights be in writing. And it is not up to this Court to re-write the law. Indeed, it falls to us to insure that all litigants are protected to the fullest extent of the law. While we do not believe that the case at bar reaches anywhere near the severity of *Gault* and further, the failure of our Tribal Court in no way can be compared to the state juvenile court in *Gault*, we believe that the statutory requirements of 305(b) were not met and the judgment of our Juvenile Court must be reversed.

Note

There often concerns from federal courts about due process in tribal courts. This case illustrates the different ways tribal codes may address due process concerns. How does this tribe do that? A tribal code may provide *higher* due process protections than the surrounding state courts. As discussed in Chapter 7, tribal constitutions may require higher protections of children specifically.

In re C.T.

8 Am. Tribal Law 386 (Cherokee Court of the Eastern Band of Cherokee Indians 2010)

Findings of Fact

1. The Court has jurisdiction to rule on the Juvenile's Motion to Dismiss, including jurisdiction to determine whether the Court has subject matter jurisdiction.

2. On April 16, 2010, a Juvenile Petition in case number JV 10–20 was filed with the Clerk of Court alleging Juvenile C.T. committed the delinquent offenses of criminal mischief to property, injuring real property, and first degree trespass, upon the Qualla Boundary on or about September 27, 2009.

3. On January 6, 2010, a Juvenile Petition in case number JV 10–07 was filed with the Clerk alleging Juvenile C.T. committed the delinquent offenses of breaking and entering and injuring real property, upon the Qualla Boundary or about September 27, 2009.

4. The delinquency allegations contained in the Juvenile Petitions in case numbers JV 10–20 and JV 10–07 arose out of the same set of alleged factual circumstances on September 27, 2009.

5. The Juvenile Complaint in case number JV 10–07 was drawn by the Juvenile Services intake counselor on November 12, 2009.

6. The Juvenile Petition in case number JV 10–07 was not filed with the Clerk of Court until January 6, 2010.

7. C.C. § 7A–8(a), which governs evaluation decisions and the filing of Juvenile Complaints and Petitions with the Clerk, states in pertinent part that:

> the evaluation of a particular complaint shall be completed within 15 days, with an additional extension of a maximum of 15 days at the discretion of the intake counselor/court counselor. The intake counselor must decide within this time period whether or not a complaint will be filed as a juvenile petition.

8. A total of 55 days passed from the time the Complaint was drawn by the intake counselor and was filed with the Petition with the Clerk in case number JV 10–07.

9. On March 30, 2010, at a hearing in case number JV 10–07, the Juvenile successfully moved to dismiss the Petition, alleging the Petition was improperly verified, thus depriving the Court of subject matter jurisdiction to pass upon the Petition.

10. In light of the dismissal of the Petition for its improper verification, the Court did not reach the Juvenile's Motion to Dismiss the Petition on the grounds the Court lacked subject matter jurisdiction for incongruities with the filing of the Petition under C.C. § 7A–8.

11. On April 5, 2010, in case number JV 10–07, the Juvenile filed Motions for Review, Reconsideration, and Appropriate Relief, requesting the Court to rule on

the arguments contained in the Juvenile's Motion to Dismiss due to violations of C.C. § 7A–8.

12. Prior to a hearing being set on the Motions, on April 16, 2010, the Tribe subsequently filed a second Juvenile Petition against C.T. in case number JV 10–20, which alleged the Juvenile was delinquent based upon the same acts of September 27, 2009 alleged in the Juvenile Complaint and Petition filed in case number JV 10–07.

13. On April 21, 2010, the Juvenile filed five Motions to Dismiss the Juvenile Petition, which were styled as follows: (1) Motion to Dismiss Juvenile Petition (Violation of C.C. § 7A–13(b)); (2) Motion to Dismiss Juvenile Petition (Failure to Properly Verify Petition); (3) Motion to Dismiss Juvenile Petition (Failure to File Complaint); (4) Motion to Dismiss Juvenile Petition (Violation of C.C. § 7A–8 and § 7A–14); (5) Motion to Dismiss Juvenile Petition (Violation of C.C. § 7A–8).

14. On April 26, 2010, the Tribe filed an Answer to the Juvenile's Motions to Dismiss and moved the Court for leave to amend the Juvenile Petition in case number JV 10–20.

15. On April 26, 2010, the Court heard arguments on the Juvenile's Motions to Dismiss.

16. After hearing arguments, the Court denied all of the Juvenile's Motions except for the Juvenile's Motion to Dismiss Juvenile Petition for the violation of C.C. § 7A–8, which the Court took under advisement. The Court granted the Tribe's Motion to Amend.

17. C.C. § 7A–8, which governs evaluation decisions and requirements for filing Juvenile Complaints and Petitions in Juvenile delinquency cases on the Qualla Boundary, tracks closely, but not exactly, the language N.C. Gen.Stat. § 7B–1703, which governs the same in Juvenile delinquency cases in the State of North Carolina.

18. There is no case law in this Court regarding statutory interpretations of C.C. § 7A–8.

19. This Court is not directly bound by decisions of the appellate courts of North Carolina, however C.C. § 7–2(d) directs that the Court shall look to North Carolina case law for guidance when there is no applicable case law in this jurisdiction, and the Court cannot resolve the matter by an examination of Cherokee Tribal norms, customs, or traditions.

* * *

The question before the Court is whether C.C. § 7A–8, which governs the evaluation process in juvenile cases, and the filing requirements of Juvenile Complaints and Petitions, creates a thirty day jurisdictional deadline within which time the Juvenile Petition must be filed with the Clerk of Court after the Juvenile Complaint has been taken by the intake counselor. The Court concludes that the statute by its plain language creates a mandatory jurisdictional requirement.

* * *

Since 2006, the North Carolina Court of Appeals has issued numerous rulings on whether the failure of the court counselor to file a Juvenile Petition with the Clerk within fifteen days after taking the Juvenile Complaint (with an additional fifteen day extension available at the discretion of the court counselor, for a maximum jurisdictional time period of thirty days) deprives the Court of subject matter jurisdiction to adjudicate the Juvenile Petition.

Jurisdiction is the legal power and authority of a court to make a decision that binds the parties to any matter properly brought before it. *Black's Law Dictionary* 856 7th ed. (1999). A court must possess both personal and subject matter jurisdiction to proceed with litigation in a case and to subsequently enter a valid judgment. Personal jurisdiction is the power of a court to enter a judgment against a party to the litigation. *See generally Pennoyer v. Neff,* 95 U.S. 714, 24 L.Ed. 565 (1877). Subject matter jurisdiction is the power of a court to pass on the merits and nature of the case and type of relief sought. *See In re T.R.P.,* 360 N.C. 588, 589, 636 S.E.2d 787, 790 (2006); *Burgess v. Gibbs,* 262 N.C. 462, 465, 137 S.E.2d 806, 808 (1964) ("The issue of jurisdiction . . . involves the determination by the court of its right to proceed with the litigation.").

"A universal principle as old as the law is that the proceedings of a Court without jurisdiction over the subject matter are a nullity." *In re T.R.P.,* 360 N.C. at 590, 636 S.E.2d at 790. "Subject matter jurisdiction is the indispensable foundation upon which valid judicial decisions rest, and in its absence a court has no power to act." *Id.* A jurisdictional defect is "not a matter of form, but substance." *Id.* Whether a court has subject matter jurisdiction over a court proceeding may be raised at any time. *See In re S.E.P.,* 184 N.C.App. 481, 487, 488, 646 S.E.2d 617, 622 (2007). "Subject matter jurisdiction cannot be conferred upon a court by consent, waiver, or estoppel." *In re Sauls,* 270 N.C. 180, 187, 154 S.E.2d 327, 333 (1967); *see also Dorman v. EBCI,* 7 Cher. Rep. 5, 9, n.3,—Am. Tribal Law—,—, 2008 N.C. Cherokee Sup. Ct. LEXIS, 2, 10 (2008).

The first published case from the North Carolina appellate courts to consider whether the failure of the juvenile court counselor to file a timely Petition in a juvenile delinquency case deprived the Court of subject matter jurisdiction to pass judgment on the case is *In re M.C.,* 183 N.C.App. 152, 645 S.E.2d 386 (2007). In *M.C.,* the appellate court vacated orders on adjudication and disposition where the Juvenile Complaint was drawn and verified on November 1, 2005, but "the Juvenile Petition was not filed with the Court on December 2, 2005. The time from the drawing of the Complaint to the filing of the Petition exceeded thirty days and fell afoul of the jurisdictional requirements of North Carolina law. The Court of Appeals held that the juvenile petition must be filed within a maximum of thirty days after the complaint is received by the juvenile court counselor." *Id.* at 153, 645 S.E.2d at 387. With this jurisdictional defect, the only remedy available to the Court was vacating the orders and remanding the case for dismissal of the action.

* * *

The Tribe argues that the reasoning of the North Carolina appellate courts for dismissing Juvenile Petitions filed outside the mandatory thirty day jurisdictional framework for lack of subject matter jurisdiction should not be adopted by this Court. The Tribe contends that the Cherokee Code and the North Carolina General Statutes differ somewhat in language regarding evaluation procedures. The Tribe is correct that the Cherokee Code and the North Carolina General Statutes are not identical.

The language of C.C. § 7A–8(a) is mandatory, using the words shall, maximum, and must. Mandatory statutory language will not be cast aside lightly by the Court. N.C. Gen.Stat. § 7B–1703(b) essentially contains a recitation of the pertinent language found in N.C. Gen.Stat. § 7B–1703(a). Although the Cherokee Code lacks a recitation similar to that is found in N.C. Gen.Stat. § 7B–1703(b), the distinction is one without a difference. Any reading of C.C. § 7A–8(a), other than one which creates a clear statutory jurisdictional deadline within which time the Tribe must file the Juvenile Petition following the taking of the Juvenile Complaint, would reach a result which could, in effect, nullify the mandatory language in C.C. § 7A–8(a). Under well accepted rules of statutory construction, the Court must give the language of the Cherokee Code a plain reading.

The statute's meaning is plain and unambiguous. The Tribe must timely file the Juvenile Petition under the jurisdictional deadline imposed by the plain language of C.C. § 7A–8(a). Failure to meet the deadline is a jurisdictional defect, and it is fatal to the case. *See e.g. In re T.R.P.*, 360 N.C. at 590, 636 S.E.2d at 790.

Here, the Tribe failed to meet the jurisdictional filing deadline clearly spelled out in C.C. § 7A–8(a) by waiting fifty-five (55) days from the time Juvenile Services took the Complaint until the Petition was filed with the Clerk of Court in case number JV 10–07. The jurisdictional defect created by the failure to meet the requirement that the Petition be timely filed deprives the Court of subject matter jurisdiction to adjudicate this case. The Tribe's efforts to breathe new life into the case by filing a new Petition in case number JV 10–20 in an attempt to bypass the jurisdictional defects of the original Complaint and Petition are to no avail.

Finally, the Court notes that C.C. § 7A–1(b) requires that the Juvenile Code shall be construed "To provide procedures for the hearing of juvenile cases that ensure fairness and equity and that protect the constitutional rights of the juveniles and parents[.]" The lesson learned for this Juvenile today is that the Tribal government must follow and uphold the law in the same way that any individual enrolled member or other resident of Tribal trust lands is required to do.

The law is clear. C.C. § 7A–8 has not been followed. The defect with the Juvenile Petition is jurisdictional in nature, and is thus deprives the Court of subject matter jurisdiction over the allegations in this Petition. The only remedy available to the Court is dismissal of the Juvenile Petition with prejudice. *In re M.C.*, 183 N.C.App. at 153, 645 S.E.2d at 387.

Note

Is this the correct outcome? What is the responsibility of a government to follow its procedures? Does the tribal court hold the tribal government to a higher standard than the state court?

C. ICWA and Juvenile Justice

ICWA applies to children charged with status offenses—or offenses that would not be considered a crime if committed by an adult. These offenses include things like truancy, incorrigibility, and curfew violations. Crimes that are crimes because of age, but that may not lead to a removal from the home, include minor in possession and similar statutes, to which ICWA would arguably apply, but that remains an open legal question. However, even given the statute's clear requirement on status offenses, the states apply ICWA to these cases inconsistently.

Reclaiming the Promise of the Indian Child Welfare Act: A Study of State Incorporation and Adoption of Legal Protections for Indian Status Offenders

Thalia González
42 N.M. L. Rev. 131 (2012)

In an ideal legal world, ICWA would apply whenever Indian children are involved in state child custody proceedings. Unfortunately, ICWA's jurisdictional and procedural protections for Indian status offenders are not equally applied across the states. As the studies discussed in Part II reveal, less than half the states have passed laws or established court rules that trigger protections for status offenders, parents, and tribes.

* * *

Except as relevant here, those "term or terms shall not include a placement based upon an act which, if committed by an adult would be deemed a crime." Whether juvenile delinquency proceedings are covered by the Act is determined by the placement of the children and the conduct of the parents. As the legislative history explains, "[t]he definition of 'child placement' is intended to include proceedings against juveniles which may lead to foster care and proceedings against status offenders, i.e., juveniles who have not committed an act which would be criminal if they were adults, such as truancy." In 1979, one year after passage of the Act, the BIA Guidelines reiterated the legislative history and stated, "[a]lthough most juvenile delinquency proceedings are not covered by the Act, the Act does apply to status offenses, such as truancy and incorrigibility, which can only be committed by children, and to any juvenile delinquency proceeding that results in termination of the parental relationship."

* * *

Therefore, ICWA analysis for inclusion of status offense proceedings under the Act turns on the question of whether the status offense proceeding may result in out-of-home placement, a voluntary or involuntary foster care placement, guardianship placement, custody placement, or termination of parental rights. It is clear from the text of the Act, the legislative history, and the BIA Guidelines that the Act's protections do not apply when a child is being placed outside the home for committing a crime that would otherwise be considered an adult crime.

* * *

C. The Significance of Legal Protections for Indian Status Offenders

Ensuring legal protections for Indian status offenders is a significant issue. Status offenders are classified as criminal defendants in most states and are detained, adjudicated, and punished in the same manner as juvenile delinquents. According to the Senate Report about the Juvenile Justice and Delinquency Prevention Act (JJDPA), since the 1970s, federal policy had been too focused on the diversion of status offenders incarcerated in juvenile institutions into alternative community-based programs. While the incarceration of status offenders has declined since this time, 4,824 status offenders were incarcerated in public and private juvenile facilities in 2003. Most of the incarcerated youth were classified ungovernable (1,825), followed by runaways (997), and truants (841). These numbers, however, do not represent the full extent to which status offenders are incarcerated. In 1980, Congress amended the JJDPA to allow juvenile courts to incarcerate children "charged with or who have committed a violation of a valid court order." This expanded authority means many of the 14,135 children incarcerated in secure facilities for "technical violations" may be status offenders. For example, in Alabama, Alaska, Hawaii, Illinois, New Jersey, South Carolina, Utah, and Wyoming, at least 25 percent of offenders in custody were in custody for technical violations of probation, parole, or valid court orders. All of these states except New Jersey and Utah have valid court order exceptions. Reports also indicate that status offenders are often relabeled as "delinquent" to keep them housed in secure facilities. Nonetheless, in most adjudicated status offense cases nationally, juvenile court ordered probation/residential placement was the second most-frequent dispositional outcome. Those adjudicated ungovernable were the most likely to be placed in a residential facility, while truants were the most likely of status offenders to be placed on probation.

It is estimated that about one-third of all youth in secure detention facilities are confined, not for delinquent or criminal conduct, but for status offenses or technical probation violations. Furthermore, Indian youth had a higher case rate compared with all other racial categories. For example, in 2005, Indian youth had three times the rate of status offenses compared to Asian youth and twice the rate compared to white juveniles. Indian youth were also more likely to have status offense cases that resulted in adjudication, especially for cases of ungovernability.

As decades of research and best practices in the field have shown, punitive programs that remove youth from their homes and their tribal communities make it harder to address the problems that led to the out-of-home placement in the first place. Without clearly established procedural and jurisdictional safeguards, and ensuring the application of ICWA's protections to status offenders in all states, the purpose of ICWA, which is to keep Indian children with their families and stop the erosion of tribal communities, will be undermined. Given the disproportionate contact of Indian youth with the juvenile justice system, there must be consistent statewide compliance with ICWA combined with comprehensive and culturally sensitive services. Moreover, with such a significant and potentially large number of status offenders still entering secure facilities, much is at stake for an Indian child facing a status offense charge.

Notes

1. Cases where a child is both in a child welfare proceeding and a juvenile delinquency proceeding, sometimes called dual jurisdiction, or dual status, can be the most difficult to work through. The various state courts responsible for both a foster care proceeding and a juvenile criminal matter are not the same. Who sends notice to the child's tribe? What happens when a child is placed by one court because of a status offense, but the tribe doesn't know where? What does this author argue should happen for children charged with status offenses?

2. The commentary to the ICWA federal regulations state:

> The final rule definition of "child custody proceeding" is also updated to make clear that its scope includes proceedings involving status offenses if any part of the proceeding results in the need for out-of-home placement of the child. This reflects the statutory definition of "child-custody proceeding," which is best read to include placements based on status offenses, while explicitly excluding placement[s] based upon an act which, if committed by an adult, would be deemed a crime. See 25 U.S.C. 1903(1).

81 Fed. Reg. 38799.

Unfortunately, that may be the only clear part of the regulations on this issue. There is no additional guidance to states regarding inquiry or notice for status offense cases. Finally, beyond status offenses, most states take a limited view of applying ICWA outside of the status offense arena, even when state statutes may expand the protections of the law.

In re W.B. Jr.

281 P.3d 906 (Cal. 2012)

The minor argues state legislation has expanded ICWA to delinquency proceedings under Welfare and Institutions Code section 602.1. The Courts of Appeal have considered the question with varying results. Here, we determine the federally required scope of ICWA in juvenile delinquency proceedings and whether our

Legislature has expanded those requirements. Consistent with the federal statutes, we hold that California law requires the court to inquire about a child's Indian status at the outset of all juvenile proceedings, but that ICWA's additional procedures are not required in most delinquency cases. A delinquency court must ensure that notice is given and other ICWA procedures are complied with only when (1) exercising "dual status" jurisdiction over an Indian child (See *post*, 144 Cal.Rptr.3d at pp. 852–854, 281 P.3d at pp. 914–915); (2) placing an Indian child outside the family home for committing a "status offense" (§§ 601–602; See *post*, at p. 850, 281 P.3d at p. 912); or (3) placing an Indian child initially detained for "criminal conduct" (§ 602; See *post*, at pp. 850–851, 281 P.3d at pp. 912–913) outside the family home for reasons based entirely on harmful conditions in the home. In this narrow third category, ICWA notice is required when the delinquency court sets a permanency planning hearing to terminate parental rights, or when the court contemplates ordering the ward placed in foster care and announces on the record that the placement is based entirely on abuse or neglect in the family home and not on the ward's delinquent conduct. Without a clear announcement from the court to the contrary, it will be presumed that a placement of a section 602 ward is based on the ward's delinquent conduct, rather than conditions in the home, and thus not subject to ICWA.

* * *

1. Foster Care Placements in Delinquency Proceedings

A temporary or permanent foster care placement typically arises in the context of juvenile dependency proceedings, in which the court determines whether a child's home is unfit. If allegations of parental abuse or neglect are substantiated, the court assumes jurisdiction and removes the child from the family home for the child's own well-being. Such a child is adjudged to be a "dependent" of the court. (§ 300 et seq.) When a dependent child is placed in a foster home, the family generally participates in reunification services, with the goal of the child's safe return to parental custody. Meanwhile, the dependency case proceeds through an intricate system of review hearings. Because family reunification is not always possible, child welfare workers also explore alternatives for a child's permanent placement outside the home through guardianship or adoption. The dependency process culminates in a permanency planning hearing, at which the court determines whether the child can be safely returned home or, if not, whether parental rights must be terminated and the child released to a permanent placement. (§ 366.26.)

Although the great majority of children enter foster care through the dependency process, a child may also enter foster care in a delinquency placement. Foster care placement is one of several dispositional options available to the delinquency court. If the allegations of a section 602 petition are found true, the court may dismiss the petition in the interest of justice (§ 782), place the child on informal probation for up to six months without a declaration of wardship (§ 725, subd. (a)), or declare the child a ward of the juvenile court (§ 725, subd. (b)) and proceed to disposition.

While a delinquent ward may be allowed to remain at home, the grounds for removing a ward from parental custody are established by statute. Removal is warranted only if the court finds: (1) the parent has not or cannot provide "proper maintenance, training, and education" for the child; (2) previous attempts at in-home probation have failed to reform the child; or (3) the child's welfare requires that custody be taken from the parent. (§ 726, subd. (a).) When removed from the family home, the ward comes under the supervision of the probation department. (§ 727, subd. (a).) Depending on the severity of the offense and other rehabilitative considerations, the juvenile court may direct that the ward be placed in a nonsecure home or facility or may order that the ward serve a period of physical confinement, either in a secure local facility (§ 730, subd. (a) [juvenile home, ranch, camp, forestry camp, or juvenile hall]) or in the Department of Corrections and Rehabilitation, Division of Juvenile Facilities (DJF) [formerly the California Youth Authority], which is the most restrictive placement. (§ 731; *In re Eddie M.* (2003) 31 Cal.4th 480, 488, 3 Cal.Rptr.3d 119, 73 P.3d 1115.) If a nonsecure placement is found to be appropriate, the probation department may place a removed ward in the home of a relative, in a licensed community care facility, or in foster care. (§ 727, subd. (a).) A group home is the predominant out-of-home placement chosen for delinquent wards.

* * *

2. "Dual Status" Minors

Delinquency courts follow a system parallel to that used in dependency courts for removing a child from the family home. The dependency and delinquency systems serve overlapping but slightly different aims, however. Whereas the dependency system is geared toward protection of a child victimized by parental abuse or neglect, the delinquency system enforces accountability for the child's own wrongdoing, both to rehabilitate the child and to protect the public. (§ 202, subds. (a), (b).)

* * *

Although California juvenile courts address the needs of dependent and delinquent minors differently, some minors who come before the court seem to fall under both systems. Sociological research has demonstrated a strong link between childhood abuse or neglect and later delinquent behavior. (See, e.g., Judicial Council of Cal., Fact Sheet, Intersection Between Juvenile Dependency and Delinquency: Available Research (June 2005) pp. 2–4 <http://www.courts.ca.gov/documents/Ab129–FactSheetMay05.pdf> [as of Aug. 6, 2012].) Research reveals that dependent children violate criminal laws at a significantly higher rate than children who have not been the subject of dependency petitions. (Dunlap, *Dependents Who Become Delinquents: Implementing Dual Jurisdiction in California Under Assembly Bill 129* (2006) 5 Whittier J. Child & Fam. Advocacy 507, 511–512.) In general, however, California law prohibits a minor from simultaneously being declared a dependent child and a delinquent ward.

In 1989, in response to a Court of Appeal decision that outlined several potential problems with allowing concurrent delinquency and dependency jurisdiction over a minor (*In re Donald S.* (1988) 206 Cal.App.3d 134, 253 Cal.Rptr. 274), the Legislature added section 241.1 to the Welfare and Institutions Code. This statute generally prohibits the juvenile court from assuming dual jurisdiction over minors. Section 241.1, subdivisions (a) through (d) state that when a minor appears to come within the description of both section 300 (dependency) and section 601 or 602 (delinquency), the county probation department and child welfare agency must consult with each other and jointly determine which status will best serve the interests of the minor and the protection of society. Based on this joint assessment, the juvenile court decides whether the child should be treated as a dependent child or a delinquent ward. (*Los Angeles County Dept. of Children & Fam. Services v. Superior Court* (2001) 87 Cal.App.4th 320, 325, 104 Cal.Rptr.2d 425; *In re Marcus G.* (1999) 73 Cal.App.4th 1008, 1013, 87 Cal.Rptr.2d 84.) "Dual jurisdiction is generally forbidden...." (*D.M. v. Superior Court* (2009) 173 Cal.App.4th 1117, 1123, 93 Cal.Rptr.3d 418.)

In 2004, the Legislature created a small exception to the ban on dual jurisdiction. Section 241.1, subdivision (e) allows a minor to be designated a "dual status child," and treated simultaneously under the court's dependency and delinquency jurisdiction, but only in accordance with a precise written protocol. The statute requires that the protocol be developed jointly by the county's probation department and child welfare agency and signed by the heads of these entities as well as the presiding judge of the juvenile court. (§ 241.1, subd. (e).) To avoid duplication of services, county protocols must adopt either an "on-hold" system, in which dependency jurisdiction is suspended while the child is a ward of the delinquency court, or a "lead court/lead agency" system, in which the probation department and social services department decide which agency will take the lead in all case-management and court-related matters. (§ 241.1, subd. (e)(5).)

Few California counties have adopted these joint protocols, however. Currently, eight years after the enactment of section 241.1, subdivision (e), only nine of California's 58 counties have filed dual status protocols with the Judicial Council. (Judicial Council of Cal., Dual Status Children: Protocols for Implementing Assembly Bill 129 <http://www.courts.ca.gov/7989. htm> [as of Aug. 6, 2012].) The reluctance to embrace dual status designation has generated skepticism about the efficacy of section 241.1, subdivision (e)'s approach and led to calls for broader reforms. (See McCulloch, *Still Between a Rock and a Hard Place ... Victim or Delinquent: Dual Status Minors in California—An Illusory Promise?* (2007) 28 J. Juv.L. 118, 132.)

B. Federal Law Regarding Placement of Indian Children

In the juvenile dependency system, children are removed from the family home not as punishment for their own misconduct, but because conditions in the home subject them to abuse or neglect. Additional procedures are required if a child is of Indian heritage. Congress has determined that, as a matter of federal policy, protective steps must be taken before an Indian child may be removed. In 1978, these protections were codified in ICWA. (25 U.S.C. § 1901 et seq.) Dependency courts and social workers are accustomed to complying with ICWA, which applies when an Indian child is removed from parental custody, even temporarily. However, because Congress created a specific exemption for placements based on a child's criminal conduct (25 U.S.C. § 1903(1)), it has long been understood that ICWA's requirements do not apply in most juvenile delinquency cases. (See, e.g., *In re Enrique O.* (2006) 137 Cal.App.4th 728, 40 Cal.Rptr.3d 570.)

* * *

2. California's Statutory Scheme

ICWA's many procedural requirements for juvenile dependency and delinquency cases are found in sections 224 through 224.6 of the Welfare and Institutions Code. We examine these statutes to determine whether, and to what extent, the Legislature extended requirements of the federal Act to delinquency proceedings in California.

* * *

a. Statutory Language

Section 224.3 defines when and how the juvenile court must inquire about a child's possible Indian ancestry. Section 224.3, subdivision (a) states: "The court, county welfare department, and the probation department have an affirmative and continuing duty to inquire whether a child for whom a petition under Section 300, 601, or 602 is to be, or has been, filed is or may be an Indian child in all dependency proceedings and in any juvenile wardship proceedings if the child is at risk of entering foster care or is in foster care." This language is clear. It creates an obligation for the juvenile court, the county welfare department, and the probation department to inquire about the child's Indian status in all dependency proceedings and in any delinquency case involving a child who is already in foster care or who appears to be at risk of entering foster care. "At risk of entering foster care" is a term specifically defined. It "means that conditions within a minor's family may necessitate his or her entry into foster care unless those conditions are resolved." (§ 727.4, subd. (d)(2).) Accordingly, the court or the probation department must ask about Indian status at the outset of any delinquency case involving a child who is currently in foster care. If the child is not currently in foster care, the court and the probation department have a continuing duty to inquire about Indian status if, at any time during the proceedings, it appears that conditions in the child's family may require a foster care placement unless they are resolved. (§§ 224.3, subd. (a), 727.4, subd. (d)(1).)

Once the court has learned that a child under its jurisdiction may have Indian ancestry, the next step ICWA typically requires is notice to the tribe or, if no tribe is identified, to the BIA. (25 U.S.C. § 1912(a).) Obviously, ICWA requirements apply only in those cases that fall under the statutory scheme. Two California statutes describe the notice requirement and when it applies . . . [R]ead together, sections 224.2 and 224.3 require that ICWA notice be provided only when an Indian child is involved in an Indian child custody proceeding. (See *Dyna-Med, Inc. v. Fair Employment & Housing Com.* (1987) 43 Cal.3d 1379, 1387, 241 Cal.Rptr. 67, 743 P.2d 1323; *People v. Pieters* (1991) 52 Cal.3d 894, 899, 276 Cal. Rptr. 918, 802 P.2d 420 [statutory provisions relating to the same subject should be harmonized].)

"Indian child custody proceeding" is a term of art. Section 224.1, subdivision (d) states, in part: "'Indian child custody proceeding' means a 'child custody proceeding' within the meaning of Section 1903 of the Indian Child Welfare Act, including a proceeding for temporary or long-term foster care or guardianship placement, termination of parental rights, preadoptive placement after termination of parental rights, or adoptive placement." California's definition of the child custody proceedings to which ICWA applies thus incorporates, and is coextensive with, the definition in the federal Act. As noted, the definition of "child custody proceeding" in title 25 United States Code section 1903 expressly excludes delinquency proceedings based on an act that would be criminal if committed by an adult.

Section 224.3, subdivision (a) is the only provision in California's ICWA legislation that expressly applies to juvenile delinquency proceedings. (See *R.R. v. Superior Court, supra*, 180 Cal.App.4th at p. 200, 103 Cal.Rptr.3d 110.) All of the other statutes, including the two notice statutes just discussed, extend the rights and protections of ICWA to participants in "an Indian child custody proceeding." (E.g., § 224.4; see also §§ 224.2, subd. (a), 224.5, 224.6, subd. (a).) Because an "Indian child custody proceeding" by definition excludes proceedings to place a child outside the home based on conduct that would be criminal if committed by an adult (§ 224.1, subd. (d); 25 U.S.C. § 1903(1)), it follows that California's ICWA statutes impose no duty of notice, or any other ICWA procedures, in most delinquency cases alleging adult criminal conduct. A narrow exception applies when the court decides to place a delinquent ward outside the home for reasons other than the ward's criminal conduct. Even if the case began as a delinquency matter, circumstances may lead the court to remove a ward from parental custody because of abuse or neglect in the home. In such cases in which a placement is imposed because of dependency concerns and not, even in part, because of the ward's criminal conduct, both California and federal law require that ICWA procedures be followed.

The relevant statutory language indicates that, although the Legislature created a duty of inquiry in all cases involving a potential foster care placement, it did not extend ICWA's notice and enforcement requirements so broadly. Instead, consistent with federal law, the Legislature dictated that the notice and procedural protections of ICWA be provided only in the subset of delinquency cases that meet the federal definition of a "child custody proceeding," i.e., those based on considerations other than the child's criminal conduct.

In sum, from the language of the statutes, we distill the following. In all juvenile delinquency proceedings, including those alleging adult criminal conduct, the court and the probation department have a duty to inquire about Indian status as soon as they determine that the child is in foster care or is at risk of entering foster care due to conditions in the child's home. (§§ 224.3, subd. (a),727.4, subd. (d)(1).) Notice pursuant to ICWA is generally not required in a delinquency proceeding premised on conduct that would be criminal if committed by an adult. However, if, at the disposition stage or at any point in the proceedings, the court contemplates removing an Indian child from the parental home based on concerns about harmful conditions in the home, and not based on the need for rehabilitation or other concerns related to the child's criminal conduct, notice is required and all other ICWA procedures must be followed.

* * *

3. Application of ICWA in Delinquency Cases

We have determined that California's ICWA statutes require the following: In all juvenile court proceedings, both dependency and delinquency, the court, social worker, or probation officer must inquire about the child's Indian status whenever the child is in foster care or conditions in the child's family may potentially require a foster care placement. (§ 224.3, subd. (a).) Notice to the tribes and other ICWA procedures must be provided only if the case is a "child custody proceeding," as defined in 25 U.S.C. section 1903(1). (§ 224.2, subd. (a).) A case qualifies as a "child custody proceeding" if it will involve action taken to terminate parental rights or to place an Indian child in foster care or in an adoptive or preadoptive home or institution. (25 U.S.C. § 1903(1).) Any case involving placement of a child outside the home based upon an act that would be criminal if committed by an adult is not a "'child custody proceeding'" and is thus exempt from ICWA. (25 U.S.C. § 1903(1).)

* * *

Different types of juvenile court cases in California therefore require different levels of ICWA compliance. It is undisputed that all dependency proceedings must be conducted in compliance with ICWA. (See, e.g., *Dwayne P. v. Superior Court* (2002) 103 Cal.App.4th 247, 253, 126 Cal.Rptr.2d 639 ["The ICWA confers on tribes the right to intervene at any point in state court dependency proceedings"].) Delinquency proceedings brought under section 601 also fall within the purview of ICWA because they are based on conduct that would not be criminal if committed by an adult. However, ICWA procedures would be required only in the narrow instance in which a section 601 ward is temporarily or permanently removed from the family home. (See § 601, subd. (b) [expressing legislative intent that truant wards remain in parental custody].)

Whether ICWA applies in a delinquency case brought under section 602 depends, first, on the type of offense alleged in the petition. If the section 602 petition alleges only that the minor committed a status offense (See *ante*, 144 Cal.Rptr.3d at p. 850, 281 P.3d at p. 912), ICWA compliance is required before the minor can be placed outside the home. Like placements under section 601 for truancy or incorrigibility, placements under section 602 based on the minor's commission of a status offense are subject to ICWA because they are not based on criminal conduct. However, if the section 602 petition alleges the minor committed an act that would be a crime if committed by an adult, the proceedings are generally exempt from ICWA. ICWA procedures are ordinarily not required in such proceedings because the placement of a delinquent ward outside the home will almost always be based, at least in part, on the ward's criminal conduct.

In some rare cases, the court may remove a section 602 ward from home for reasons completely unrelated to the ward's offense. Placement of the ward in some type of foster care setting is one option available to the court at a section 602 disposition hearing. (See §§ 727, subd. (a)(3), 727.4, subd. (d)(1), 11402.) In typical delinquency cases, it can be presumed that such placements are made to address the child's misconduct and prevent future wrongdoing. In some rare cases, however, the court may elect to remove a section 602 ward from home and order a foster care placement solely because of parental abuse or neglect. Although a delinquency court cannot assume concurrent dependency jurisdiction over a ward except in a county with an approved dual status protocol (§ 241.1, subd. (d)), the delinquency court does have the power to remove a minor from home if the parent is not providing appropriate care. (§ 726, subd. (a).) These placements may result in termination of parental rights if reunification efforts are unsuccessful. (§ 727.3.) A termination hearing in delinquency court proceeds exactly like a termination hearing in dependency court. (§ 727.31, subd. (a); see § 366.26.)

Under our interpretation of the relevant statutes, ICWA compliance is required in these rare section 602 cases that proceed to a termination of parental rights or that result in a foster care placement motivated solely by concerns about parental abuse or neglect. If the court sets a permanency planning hearing to terminate parental rights over a delinquent ward, or if the court contemplates ordering a delinquent ward placed in foster care and announces on the record that the placement is based entirely on parental abuse or neglect and not on the ward's offense, notice must be sent to the relevant tribes and all other ICWA procedures must be followed. In all other section 602 cases, it will be presumed that a placement outside the home is based upon the minor's criminal offense and thus not subject to ICWA.

A hybrid situation is presented in "dual status" cases. In counties with approved joint protocols, the juvenile court may exercise both dependency and delinquency jurisdiction over a minor who is designated a "dual status child." (§ 241.1, subd. (e); see *ante*, 144 Cal.Rptr.3d at pp. 852–854, 281 P.3d at pp. 914–915.) The same principles we have discussed govern ICWA's application to dual status minors. When the court exercises dependency jurisdiction to terminate parental rights or place a dual status Indian minor in foster care due to harmful conditions in the home, full ICWA compliance is required. However, if the foster care placement of a dual status minor is motivated in part by the minor's delinquent conduct and the need for rehabilitation, the placement is exempt from ICWA.

To summarize, in both dependency and delinquency proceedings, the juvenile court must give notice and comply with other ICWA requirements before it can terminate parental rights over an Indian child or place an Indian child in foster care, or in an adoptive or preadoptive placement, due to abuse or neglect in the child's home. ICWA procedures are thus required for out-of-home placements of dependent children and section 601 and 602 status offenders. Depending on the reasons for the placement, these procedures may also be required when dual status minors are removed from home. ICWA procedures are typically not required for placements of section 602 wards detained for criminal conduct. Unless the delinquency court announces otherwise, on the record, it will be presumed that any placement of a section 602 ward outside the home is based, at least in part, on the ward's criminal conduct. With rare exceptions for dual status minors and status offenders, placements in delinquency proceedings are presumptively exempt from ICWA.

* * *

This was a straightforward juvenile delinquency case. W.B. had committed a string of serious crimes and was ordered to spend time in a controlled setting where he could receive treatment designed to rehabilitate his delinquent behavior. W.B. was not designated a "dual status" minor. The court ordered that he be returned home after a defined period of time, and he was in fact returned home. For the reasons discussed, ICWA does not apply to delinquency placements such as this, which are based on the minor's criminal acts and which do not contemplate an eventual termination of parental rights. Accordingly, assuming the minor was an Indian child, the juvenile court did not err in failing to give notice under ICWA.

Notes

1. This California case addresses a number of issues. How does California handle dual status cases? Are the different goals of dependency or delinquency proceeding really as straightforward as this case states? Are there overlapping goals that could better serve the child? How could the state make it easier for the courts to address the dual status issue?

2. Could a tribe be of assistance if it knew about the criminal charge? For example, some tribes send elders to visit children in detention to talk to them in their language and about their culture. Are there other rehabilitation options for children? If there is a dual status case, could the tribe transfer that portion of the case to tribal court?

Chapter 7

Tribal Practices and Options

The development of many modern tribal courts and legal systems often occurs because of a desire to ensure the tribe's children are protected and well cared for. Along with the passage of child welfare codes, many tribes staff and run their own child welfare departments. These departments, employing tribal members, often do a better job ensuring that tribal cultural norms are followed when working to keep families together and children safe. While ICWA does not apply to tribal governments, tribes have more freedom regarding the standards they create for foster care and adoption placements.

A. Tribal Jurisdiction and ICWA

The anti-extended family bias that ICWA was in part implemented to protect against in county and state courts is not present to the same degree within tribal communities. As ICWA was designed as a remedial statute specifically to address the harmful practices perpetrated upon Indian families, the Act does not apply to tribal child welfare systems. While tribal leaders may be influenced by the best practices found in ICWA, tribal governments do not need to adhere to any of its provisions when designing tribal child welfare systems. Instead, tribal governments can tailor their statutes to the unique needs of the families for which they offer care.

Tribal courts have inherent jurisdiction over all Indian children who reside within their tribal lands. Tribes, in accordance with federal law, delineate their child welfare jurisdiction within their child welfare codes. This jurisdiction sometimes mirrors, and sometimes differs from the jurisdictional provisions found in ICWA. Tribes may extend jurisdiction over tribal member children, non-member Indian children, and even all children living within tribal trust lands. *See* NATIVE NATIONS INSTITUTE, TRIBAL CHILD WELFARE CODES AS SOVEREIGNTY IN ACTION 7 (2016). These provisions can create conflict between state and tribal court judges in the interpretation of ICWA. For children who are tribal members, but reside outside the jurisdiction of the tribe, ICWA details specific requirements for the transfer of those child welfare proceedings to the child's tribal court. *See supra* Chapter 3.

Regardless of whether the tribal child welfare code developed is completely unique, drawn from state law practices, or mirrors ICWA, once a tribal government enacts a child welfare code, it is uniquely tribal law. Tribal judges are not bound by state or federal interpretations of comparable child welfare laws when hearing cases under the codes. While tribal judges, like all judges, may look to persuasive sources in interpreting the child welfare law, they are free to develop tribal specific understandings of child welfare practices.

In the Matter of a Minor Child (L.J.Y. v. T.T.)

8 SWITCA 4, No. 92-008-FMTC (Southwest Intertribal Court of Appeals for the Fort Mojave Tribe, Mar. 3, 1997)

This is an appeal from a final judgment of the trial court removing the minor child from the custody of its mother, appellant L.Y.J., and granting custody of the child to his paternal grandparents, Mr. and Mrs. A.T. This Court concludes . . . that the procedures used by the trial court removed the child from his mother's custody without due process of law, violating the Indian Civil Rights Act. The court below erroneously applied tribal law. . . . However, because the facts in the record below do suggest that the Fort Mojave Indian Tribe Social Services office may have information that would support a petition of child neglect by the mother, it is in the best interests of the minor child that the order in this case be stayed to allow for a petition to be filed a new proceeding to be properly heard. . . .

Proceedings Below

L.J.Y. and T.T. are the natural parents of the minor child. T.T. and the minor child are enrolled members of the Fort Mojave Tribe. L.Y.J. is a member of one of the Colorado River Indian Tribes and now resides on the Colorado River Indian Tribes Reservation. . . .

T.T. filed the petition for custody of his son on November 17, 1995. The grounds given in the petition for removing the child from the custody of its mother were "[w]elfare and safety of my child. I feel that she has caused undue hardship on myself, family, and son." What the petition did not allege, in any manner, was that the minor child was neglected, abused in any way, or otherwise in any danger of harm. . . .

This action was a dispute solely between the two parents. However, during the hearing, the trial court clearly treated the matter as if a charge of negligence had been made against L.Y.J. by the Fort Mojave Tribe. T.T. and his mother were permitted to present allegations of negligence. However, the trial court, based solely on these unsupported allegations, made a determination that there would be a child custody placement pursuant to the Indian Child Welfare Act before L.Y.J. had any opportunity to make any statement to refute the allegations. . . .

. . . An employee of the Fort Mojave Social Services Department appeared at the hearing, and made an on-the-spot recommendation for the placement of the minor child with his paternal grandparents. This recommendation was followed by the court in a temporary custody order entered on that same day, although no motion for a temporary custody placement was made and no evidence was presented to support such a placement. . . .

Legal Analysis

[A.] Tribal Law Violations

To this day, the minor child remains with his paternal grandparents. It was not until L.Y.J. was in court, with no notice sufficient to allow her any opportunity to prepare a response to a petition for custody filed by the natural father of the child, that she learned, for all practical purposes, that the Fort Mojave Tribe was charging her with negligence and removing her son from her custody.... Those orders do not comply with the minimum requirements of due process as required by the Indian Civil Rights Act, apply the Indian Child Welfare Act erroneously, and do not comply with the law of the Fort Mojave Indian Tribe.... Therefore, we must reverse....

When a parent seeks custody of a child under the Fort Mojave Indian Tribe law and order code, the parent must file a petition. Upon a showing of good cause, the court can permit other interested parties to intervene.... However, in the absence of a finding of good cause, the matter is one that is strictly between the parents.... [A] party can seek a temporary custody order. However, the motion for a temporary custody order must be supported by "an affidavit or verified petition setting forth detailed facts supporting the requested order." ... The affidavit or verified petition must be given to all other parties so they can file opposing affidavits.... The trial court "shall deny the motion unless it finds that adequate cause for hearing the motion is established in the pleadings, in which case it shall [hold a hearing]." ... Tribal law also mandates that notice of any child custody proceedings must be given to a child's parent "who may appear, be heard, and file a responsive pleading." ...

In this case, T.T. did not make any motion for the court for a temporary custody order.... Furthermore, even if the initial petition is treated as such a motion, it did not set forth any detailed facts that would support the removal of a child from the custody of the parent.... Even if the petition had set forth adequate facts, Fort Mojave law requires the court to look to the best interests of the child in deciding whether to enter a temporary custody order. All relevant factors may be considered, including (1) the wishes of the child's parents as to his custody; (2) the wishes of the child as to his custodian; (3) the interaction and inter-relationship of the child with his parents, his siblings, and any other person who may significantly affect the child's best interest; (4) the child's adjustment to his home, school and community; (5) the mental and physical health of all individuals involved.... [A]ppellant was denied any notice as to the actual allegations made against her, and she was denied any meaningful opportunity to respond to the unsubstantiated allegations. Therefore, the issuance of the temporary custody order did not comply with tribal law concerning custody disputes between parents of a child....

[B.] Invalid Application of the Indian Child Welfare Act

The Indian Child Welfare Act is a federal law that governs child custody proceedings [under] federal law [in state courts.] ... 25 U.S.C. § 1903. It has been held not to apply to custodial actions between parents.... Thus, it was legally erroneous for the trial court to treat this court action as one arising under the Indian Child Welfare Act.... In some instances tribes have voluntarily adopted the placement preferences in the Act as their own. Here, however, the written law of the tribe has its own preferences for child custody placements pending a hearing on a petition of neglect.... In a proceeding between two parents, if one parent is successful in challenging the custody of the other, the successful parent is awarded custody, not the grandparents....

Conclusion

This Court must conclude that appellant's custodial rights to her minor son, as recognized and protected by the law and order code of the Fort Mojave Indian Tribe, were grievously violated by the trial court. However, as this is a matter that also involves a minor child, and because documentation in the record suggests that the trial court or the tribal social services department may have documentation that would support at least an inquiry as to whether appellant has neglected her minor child, the court must also conclude that it is in the best interests of the minor child that the Tribe, through the tribal court or tribal social services, be given the opportunity to act to protect the child from neglect, and that the minor child not be subject to a change in custody ... [until] the Tribe can determine whether to bring an action alleging neglect....

Notes

1. Why did the tribal judge find that there had been violations of custodial rights, yet choose to leave the child in the non-compliant grandparent placement?

2. Why did the trial court rely on the placement preferences in ICWA when the tribe had its own placement preferences? Do you think this was a situation where the judiciary was inexperienced with child welfare cases, or where the judiciary wanted to err on the side of safety for the minor child?

3. ICWA provides for full faith and credit for tribal court orders in those proceedings that are covered by ICWA. For other types of orders, different states have adopted different ways of extending either full faith and credit or comity. *See* Mich. Ct. R. 2.615; Wash. St. Ct. R. Superior Ct. Civ. R. 82.5 (2016). In addition, while domestic violence and child welfare issues are intertwined, they are often discussed separately. However, the Violence Against Women Act also requires states and tribes to give full faith and credit to be given to state and tribal protection orders. 18 U.S.C. § 2265 (2013).

B. Differences in Tribal Definitions and Practices

The specificities of tribal welfare codes differ according to tribal population, economic health, historical practices, and geographic locations. Disproportionate harms that many tribal communities have to deal with, such as domestic violence and drug use, also influence the particulars of a tribe's child welfare codes. Tribes have a unique freedom to design child welfare remedies and procedures that can both work to correct current issues and reflect a tribe's customary child rearing practices. Tribes can also ensure rights of children are guaranteed in their constitutions and codes, a practice not found in most states.

Little Traverse Bay Bands of Odawa Indians

Constitution
Art. I. Sec. B(5)

[The branches of government shall] assure and promote that children are given opportunities and facilities to develop in a healthy manner and in conditions of freedom and dignity, and that youth and elders are protected against exploitation.

Native Village of Barrow Iñupiat Traditional Government

Tribal Children's Code
4-3-1; 4-3-3

4-3 RESPONSIBILITIES AND RIGHTS REGARDING CHILDREN

4-3-1 RIGHTS OF CHILDREN

4-3-1 A. Right to Life A child has an inherent right to life, survival, and development, and the right to a standard of living adequate to the child's physical, mental, spiritual, moral, and social development and reflective of the traditions and cultural values of that child's people. This right includes the right to nutrition, clothing, shelter, nurturing, and appropriate discipline.

4-3-1 B. Right to Identity A child has the right from birth to acquire and form an identity, including name, tribal affiliation, language, and cultural heritage. A child has the right to learn about and preserve his identity throughout his life, including the right to maintain ties to his birth parents, his extended family, and his village. A child has the right to learn about and benefit from tribal history, culture, language, spiritual traditions, and philosophy.

4-3-1 C. Right to Protection A child has the right to be protected from all forms of physical or mental violence, injury or abuse, neglect or negligent treatment, maltreatment or exploitation, including sexual abuse, while in the care of parents, extended family members, or any other custodian. A child has the right to be free from torture or other cruel, inhuman, or degrading treatment or punishment. A child has the right not to face capital punishment or life imprisonment without possibility of release.

4-3-1 D. Right to Health A child has the right to enjoyment of the highest attainable standard of health and to facilities for the treatment of illness and rehabilitation of health. Mentally or physically disabled children have the right to enjoy a full and decent life in conditions which ensure dignity, promote self-reliance, and facilitate the child's active participation in the community. All children have the right to periodic review of any medical or mental health treatment.

4-3-1 E. Right to Family A child has the right not to be separated from his parents forcibly or against his will, except when competent authorities subject to judicial review determine that such separation is necessary for the best interest of the child. In case such separation is necessary, a child shall have the right wherever possible not to be separated from other members of his immediate and extended family. A child temporarily or permanently deprived of his family environment shall be entitled to special protection and assistance provided by the Tribe, which shall strive to ensure continuity in the child's upbringing and the maintenance of ethnic, cultural, religious, and linguistic heritage.

4-3-1 F. Right to Education A child has the right to education, including academic, physical, and cultural teachings, and training on how to safely undertake subsistence activities and other potentially dangerous work.

4-3-1 G. Right to be Heard A child who is capable of forming his own views has the right to express those views freely in all matters, including judicial proceedings, affecting that child and those views shall be given due weight in accordance with the age and maturity of the child.

4-3-1 H. Right to Due Process A child has the right not to be deprived of his liberty unlawfully or arbitrarily. Every child deprived of liberty shall have the right to challenge the deprivation of liberty and the right to appropriate judicial review. A child shall at all times be treated with humanity and respect for the inherent dignity of the human person, and in a manner which takes into account the needs of a person of his age.

4-3-3 RESPONSIBILITIES AND RIGHTS OF EXTENDED FAMILY MEMBERS
4-3-3 A. Common Responsibility for Children

Extended family members have secondary, common responsibility for the upbringing and development of children in their family. This includes ensuring each child's inherent right to life, survival, and development and to a standard of living adequate to the child's healthy physical, mental, spiritual, moral, and social development and reflective of the traditions and cultural values of that child's people. The best interests of the child shall be their basic concern.

4-3-3 B. Responsibility to Foster Identity Extended family members are responsible for helping children acquire and form identities, including name, tribal affiliation, language, and cultural heritage. 4-3-3 C. Responsibility to Nurture and Discipline Extended family members are secondarily responsible for nurturing children and for administering appropriate discipline to children.

4-3-3 D. Responsibility for Protection Extended family members are responsible for helping to protect children from all forms of physical or mental violence, injury or abuse, neglect or negligent treatment, maltreatment or exploitation, including sexual abuse, torture, or other cruel, inhuman, or degrading treatment or punishment.

4-3-3 E. Responsibility to Assist Extended family members have a responsibility to intervene or assist when necessary to protect a child's rights and well-being, and to ensure the continuity of the child's upbringing and the maintenance of the child's ethnic, cultural, religious, and linguistic heritage.

Notes

1. The Village of Barrow code example comes from the Tribal Law and Policy Institute, *Juvenile Justice: Guide for Drafting or Revising Tribal Juvenile Delinquency and Status Offense Law* (June 2015). More recently, TLPI also released a similar resource for tribes that want to revise their child welfare statutes. In both cases, TLPI collects examples from hundreds of codes for tribes to consider when revising or drafting their own codes. In the Village of Barrow, how does this statute differ from state laws? In 2000, the United States Supreme Court found that parents have a constitutional right to the care, custody, and control of their children—which was interpreted to mean that many grandparent visitation statutes are unconstitutional. *Troxel v. Granville*, 530 U.S. 57 (2000). How might the question of whether a grandparent can have visitation rights be decided under Barrow statutes and tradition? Under the Little Traverse Constitution?

2. The Barrow code allows children to engage in subsistence activities and other "potentially dangerous work." How does this interact with the state cases that weigh the "safety" of a child's placement? How should it?

3. Examining Michigan tribal child welfare codes, attorney Cami Fraser found that ten out of the twelve tribes handled child cases, and while each of the tribes had minor variations in their codes, only two tribes had provisions that were substantially different from the others. Cami Fraser, *Should this ICWA Case be Transferred to Tribal Court?*, 2011 Mich. Child Welfare L.J. 2–3 (2011). The similarities in these tribal codes may reflect the similarities between the Michigan tribes, rather than any influence of ICWA upon the tribes. While the "active efforts" requirement is considered a core provision of ICWA, for example, most of the tribal codes surveyed by Fraser "do not impose ICWA's 'active efforts' requirement upon the social workers." *Id.* at 11.

4. Several tribes have chosen to implement customary adoptions as a unique form of permanence in their communities. These adoptions generally do not permanently sever the biological parents' rights. Parental rights may be suspended, but are not formally terminated, allowing for a reunification to happen at some point in the distant future, while also allowing the child a permanent placement to grow up in. This permanency remedy reflects the realities of many reservation communities. Parents are often not able to parent because of drug and alcohol addictions, but given time and treatment, there are chances of recovery. In reservation communities that are often small and isolated, it can also be nearly impossible to keep a parent separated from her child, or prevent a child from running into his parent while in town. Open adoptions with suspension of parental rights, rather than closed adoptions with termination of parental rights, offer a chance for children to cope with the idea that family relations are fluid throughout time and increasingly complex.

White Earth Band of Ojibwe Judicial Code

Title 4a: Customary Adoption Code

4a-1 B. Declaration of Policy

1. It is the fundamental belief of the White Earth Band of Ojibwe that its children are the sacred responsibility of the Tribe.
2. One of the White Earth Band of Ojibwe's basic inherent sovereign rights is the right to make decisions regarding the best interests of its children including who should provide for the care, custody and control of its children. This code is intended to assure a safe, stable, nurturing and permanent environment for the tribe's children and to provide for the protection of our children, our people and our way of life.
3. The principles that shall guide decisions pursuant to this code are: protection of the child's safety, well-being and welfare and their sense of belonging; preservation of the child's identity as a tribal member and member of an extended family and clan; preservation of the culture, religion, language, values, clan system and relationships of the Tribe.
4. As an exercise of its inherent sovereignty the White Earth Band has the authority and jurisdiction to formally delegate the authority to its Children's Court to adjudicate its own customary practices regarding child rearing and child custody.

4a-12 Certification of a Customary Adoption

1. A customary adoption, conducted in a manner that is a long-established, continued, reasonable process and considered by the people of the White Earth Band to be binding and authentic, based upon the testimony of an expert witness, may be certified by the Children's Court as having the same effect as an adoption order issued by this court so long as it is in the best interests of the child and the child's tribe.
2. A decree certifying a customary adoption has the same effect as a decree or final order of customary adoption issued by this court.

* * *

Pascua Yaqui Tribe of Arizona Title 5 — Civil Code

Chapter 7—Juveniles

Section 440 Open Adoptions (5 PYTC § 7-440)

Adoptions under this subchapter shall be in the nature of "open adoptions." The purpose of such open adoptions is not to permanently deprive the child of connections to, or knowledge of, the child's natural family. The purpose of adoptions shall be to give the adoptive child a permanent home. To this end, the following shall apply and be contained in all adoptive orders and decrees.

(A) The adoptive parents and adoptive child shall be treated under the law as if the relationship was that of a natural child and parent, except as forth herein.

(B) The adoptive child shall have an absolute right, absence a convincing and compelling reason to the contrary, to information and knowledge about his natural family and his tribal heritage.

(C) The adoptive child and members of the child's natural extended family (including parents) may have the right to reasonable visitation, subject to reasonable controls of the adoptive parents, unless otherwise restricted by the Court for a compelling reason.

(D) Adoption shall not serve to prevent an adoptive child from inheriting from a natural parent in the same manner as any other natural child. The natural parents shall not be entitled to inherit from an adoptive child in the same manner as parents would otherwise be entitled to inherit. An adoptive child shall be entitled to inherit from adoptive parents and vice versa in the same manner as if natural parents and child.

Sisseton-Wahpeton Sioux Tribe Codes of Law

Chapter 38—Juvenile Code

38-03-24 Ecagwaya. Or "Traditional Adoption"

Means according to Tribal Custom, the placement of a child by his natural parent(s) with another family but without any Court involvement. After a period of two (2) years in the care of another family, the court, upon petition of the adoptive parents, will recognize that the adoptive parents, in custom or traditional adoption have certain rights over a child even though parental rights of the natural parents have never been terminated. Traditional adoption must be attested to by two (2) reliable witnesses.

The court, in its discretion, on a case by case basis, shall resolve any questions that arise over the respective rights of the natural parent(s) and the adoptive parent(s) in the custom adoption. The decision of the Court shall be based on the best interests of the child and on recognition of where the child's sense of family is. Ecagwaya is to raise or to take in as if the child is a biological child. The Court shall take "Judicial Notice" after proper due process proceedings, that, indeed, Ecagwaya is a custom and tradition of the Tribe.

* * *

Confederated Salish and Kootenai Tribes of the Flathead Reservation CSKT Laws Codified

Title III, Chapter 2—Children

3-1-106. Adoption

(2) Informal or Traditional Adoption. An informal adoption, or traditional adoption, may be created by placement of the child by the natural parent or parents with another person or family, without court involvement.

(a) Such adoption must be voluntarily entered into by the natural parent or parents involved and the custodian, and shall be recognized as a legal adoption. The natural parent or parents consenting to the adoption must do so with knowledge of the permanent nature and effect upon their natural parent right.

* * *

(c) By agreement between the natural parent or parents and the adoptive parent, or by order of the court, certain residual rights may be maintained by the natural parents of the child. The extent and nature of the residual right shall be determined by the agreement of the natural parents and adoptive parent, or by order of the court, in the case of the filing of a petition under this part. Residual rights shall be in accordance with this chapter.

Notes

1. The White Earth Band of Ojibwe Indians, Pascua Yaqui Tribe of Arizona, Sisseton-Wahpeton Sioux Tribe, and the Confederated Salish and Kootenai Tribe have all chosen to include provisions regarding customary or open adoptions within their tribal codes. Do these codes come closer to reproducing how a pre-colonial indigenous community might function?

2. What differences can you identify between the specific vehicles that the above tribes have chosen to accomplish a customary adoption? Do you feel that one method could be more effective than another?

C. Application of Tribal Child Welfare Laws

Once tribal laws have been codified, tribal judges work to ensure they are correctly followed and interpret any unclear provisions. Tribal children are protected by judges who produce sophisticated written opinions to mediate complex situations. The following case is indicative of the level of care found in both tribal child welfare codes and the judicial interpretation of those codes.

In the Welfare of Four Indian Minors

9 NICS App. 105 (Puyallup Tribal Children's Court of Appeals June 2010)

I. Introduction

The Puyallup Tribe appeals the Children's Court orders closing four child dependency cases. The Tribe argues that the court's findings in support of its decision to dismiss the cases were contrary to the evidence presented at the dependency review hearing. We VACATE the Children's Court orders and REMAND the cases for modification of the Family Case Plans consistent with this opinion.

II. Background and Procedural History

This is the second appeal filed in this case. In the first appeal this Court held that the Children's Court erred when it found that the Tribe failed to comply with Puyallup Tribal Law and that the Tribe violated the parents' due process rights when the Tribe changed the children's placement without first obtaining court authorization. *In the Welfare of Five Indian Minors*, 9 NICS App. 61 (Puyallup Tribal Ct. App. 2010). This Court also held that the Children's Court abused its discretion by ordering the children returned to the parents' home for what the Children's Court erroneously determined were due process violations of the parents' rights. *Id.*

The child-in-need-of-care case originally began on September 2, 2008, when the Tribe filed child-in-need-of-care petitions for L.S. and four of her minor siblings. At the initial hearing, the Children's Court found probable cause to believe that:

1. L.S. and her siblings were children in need of proper and effective parental care or control and had no parent, guardian or custodian willing to exercise care or control;
2. The children had not been provided adequate shelter necessary for their health and well being; and
3. The children had been or are likely to be physically and psychologically abused by parents, guardians or custodians.

* * *

On November 20, 2008, the Children's Court issued an Order on Dispositional Hearing in a "Child-In-Need of Care" Proceeding. The order stated that for the children to no longer be deemed children-in-need-of-care and for the case to end, "the parties shall comply with the following Family Case Plan." The order established the mother's ("S.T.S") Family Case Plan requirements as follows:

a. Mother to complete the inpatient treatment program in which she is enrolled as well as follow any/all outpatient recommendations of treatment provider.

b. Mother to enter into individual counseling.

c. Mother to enter into couple counseling with her significant other.

d. Mother to remain clean and sober at all times.

e. Mother to maintain a clean, sober and sanitary house for her children to reside in.

f. Mother to work with the Family Preservation Program within Puyallup Tribe Children Services.

g. Any and all persons who reside in the home or shall care for the children shall pass a criminal background check through Washington State Children's Administration.

h. Any additional services which may be deemed necessary by the assigned caseworker with the approval of the court.

With respect to the children, the Family Case Plan provided that their mother would provide for their daily needs upon her discharge from treatment. Puyallup Tribal Children Services ("PTCS") was ordered to "[e]nsure that the children's needs are being met in any/all respective homes" and to "[a]ssist parents in completion of the case plan."

At the outset of the case, the children were removed from the custody of their parents. By the time of the fourth review hearing on November 29, 2009, the children had been returned to the parents and were in an in-home dependency. Prior to the fourth review hearing, PTCS filed reports with the Children's Court stating that the father was in substantial non-compliance with the court ordered case plan and that the mother was in partial compliance with her court ordered case plan. The report specifically addressed the mother's non-compliance with urinalysis testing (hereinafter "UAs"), non-compliance with couples counseling, concerns about the mother's housing situation and the mother's demonstrated inability to follow through managing the day to day needs for herself and the children. . . .

On January 20, 2010, the Children's Court issued its findings and orders from the fourth review hearing. With respect to the father, the Children's Court found that "at the last review hearing both the Father and Mother stated on record that they are no longer domiciled together." . . . The Children's Court found the mother to be in compliance with the Family Case Plan, rehabilitated and maintaining her family unit. . . . Based on the findings from the fourth review hearing, the Children's Court dismissed all four dependency cases. . . . The relevant text from the order states:

> The court further finds that [mother] is in compliance with the case plan entered November 19, 2009; no positive UA for non-prescription drugs or alcohol; attended alcohol and drug treatment; participated in individual and couples counseling; continued out-patient treatment and random UA's; participated in Family Preservation; and is no longer a victim of domestic violence. [Mother] has maintained a decent family home and the children have attended their entire dental and medical appointments; and supported her oldest daughter during in-patient treatment; and continues to support all the children in school and after school activities.

> WHEREFORE, the court finds that the respondent, [mother] has rehabilitated and is maintaining her family unit; and
>
> THEREFORE, IT is Hereby Ordered, that this entire matter be dismiss [sic] forthwith and with prejudice, the files to be closed and sealed.

* * *

The Tribe appeals the order to dismiss the four dependency cases. The Tribe focused its appeal on the issues of whether the Children's Court made erroneous findings and closed the case against the clear weight of the evidence. The Tribe argues that the mother had not complied with the "no positive UA" requirement when she was a "NO SHOW" for three UAs during the reporting period. The Tribe disputes the finding that the mother participated in couples counseling when she self-terminated counseling without authorization from the court. The Tribe disputes the finding that the mother maintained a decent family home when there was evidence that she might be evicted for non-payment of rent. Finally, the Tribe argues that there is no evidence in the record to support findings that the mother was ensuring that the children were attending dental and medical appointments, supporting the oldest daughter during in-patient treatment, and supporting the children with school activities.

III. Standard of Review

A decision of the trial court will be reversed, modified, or remanded only where there has been an abuse of discretion that prevented a party from receiving a fair trial, or where the decision is contrary to the law and the evidence. PTC 4.16.400 (a), (d) (formerly PTC 4.03.590 (1), (4)). Abuse of discretion occurs if a decision is "manifestly unreasonable or based upon untenable grounds or reasons." *See, e.g., Suquamish Tribe v. Lah-Huh-Bate-Soot*, 4 NICS App 32 at 43 (Suquamish Tribal Ct. App. 1995), citing *Industrial Indem. Co. of N.W., Inc, v. Kallevig,* 114 Wn.2d 907, 926, 792 P.2d 520 (1990); *Davis v. Globe Mach. Mfg. Co.*, 102 Wn.2d 68, 77, 684 P.2d 692 (1984). Substantial evidence is "evidence which would convince an unprejudiced, thinking mind of the truth of a declared premise." *See, e.g., Lower Elwha v. Elofson*, 4 NICS App. 99, 103 (Lower Elwha Tribal Ct. App. 1996), citing *Freeburg v. Seattle*, 71 Wash. App. 367, 859 P.2d 610 (1993). The factual review undertaken by an appellate court is deferential to the trial court, and requires review of the evidence in "the light most favorable to the party who prevailed in the highest forum that exercised fact finding authority." *Id.*

IV. Discussion

There are fundamental procedural problems with this case that start at its beginning. After the initial hearing, the Children's Court did not enter an adjudicatory order, as required by the Puyallup Tribal Code. PTC 7.04.500 (formerly PTC 7.01.1400), *et. seq*. Rather, the first order issued after the initial hearing is entitled "Order on Dispositional Hearing in a 'Child-In-Of Care' Proceeding." In this order, issued on November 20, 2008, the Children's Court states that the child has been "adjudged to be 'children-in-need-of-care' as defined by 7.01.120(6) after . . . an agreed Adjudicatory Hearing." However, there is no separate order regarding the agreed Adjudicatory Hearing, and thus the Court made no specific findings regarding the grounds for the continuing removal of the children from their home, as required by PTC 7.04.580 (formerly PTC 7.01.1450).

This departure from a fundamental procedural requirement at the early stages of the case created problems that compounded as the case moved forward. This is so because it is at the adjudication stage of the proceedings that the determination is made, not only that the children are in need-of-care, but also the grounds for removal. PTC 7.04.580 (formerly PTC 7.01.1450). The purpose of the formal adjudicatory hearing is to have the Children's Court specify in its order the necessary intervention and appropriate steps, if any, the parents must follow to correct the underlying problems. PTC 7.04.590 (formerly PTC 7.01.1455). Because there is no record of, and no order following, an adjudicatory hearing, it is unclear whether the parties agreed to all of the allegations in the original petition, or something else.

If the Children's Court finds the allegations of the child/family protection petition to be true, as it did in this case, and out of home placement necessary, which took place at the outset of this case, then "with the accomplishment of specified action by the parent(s) . . . the child may be returned absent good cause to the contrary." PTC 7.04.600 (formerly PTC 7.01.1460). The Children's Court is required to issue an order that specifies the actions, and the time frames for such actions, that the parents must accomplish before the child is returned. *Id.* Finally, the Children's Court is required to issue a written order specifying the facts, grounds, and code sections upon which it relied to make its decision. PTC 7.04.620 (formerly PTC 7.01.1470).

In this case, based on the Family Case Plan, we are left to assume that the problems that led to the child-in-need-of-care petition were alcohol and drug abuse, poor housekeeping to the point of unhealthiness, lack of stable housing, and domestic violence. We assume this because the "Order on Dispositional Hearing" attempts to address these issues, presumably to comply with the requirements of PTC 7.04.590 (formerly PTC 7.01.1455). However, there is another problem: the Family Case Plan ("case plan") adopted in the disposition order does not address some of the issues in a manner that could reasonably allow the court to determine whether the intervention and required "steps" resulted in a correction of the "underlying problems" that presumably led to the initial decision to take the children into care. For example, the case plan requires Mother to "enter into individual counseling" and to "enter into couple counseling". How would simply "entering into" counseling address the problems of domestic violence, unstable housing and lack of adequate parenting of the children? In these examples the case plan is missing "outcome" provisions and timeframes for accomplishing requirements, and thus any provision by which the Children's Court could measure progress, completion, or determine whether the ordered interventions were successful.

The two failures described above, the failure to specify the grounds for removal in an adjudicatory order, and the failure to adopt a carefully crafted case plan to address the underlying problems in the family, led, perhaps inevitably, to the confusing and disjointed court review resulting in the order on appeal.

The Puyallup Children's Code provides that after adjudication, the Children's Court must review the status of all children who are "subject to the Children and Family Protection Code" within 90 days following the adjudicatory hearing and at least every six months thereafter. PTC 7.04.740 (formerly PTC 7.01.1700). After such review, a child must be returned home "unless the Court finds that a reason for removal as set forth in PTC 7.04.580 still exists." PTC 7.04.750 (formerly PTC 7.01.1710). If the Court finds "unresolved problems in the home", court intervention and supervision may be continued. *Id.* Written findings are required if the court determines after review that continued court intervention is necessary. PTC 7.04.760 (formerly PTC 7.01.1720). Because the order on appeal dismisses the matter, the dismissal means that the Children's Court found that all of the reasons for removal had been remedied, and that none of the reasons set out in PTC 7.04.580 existed at that time.

Because the relevant tribal code refers to all reasons for removal set out in PTC 7.04.580, we shall use both the general provisions of PTC 7.04.580 and the case plan adopted by the court, including the modifications to the plan included in the Order on 3rd Review Hearing, to determine whether the Children's Court decision in the Order on 4th Review Hearing was contrary to the evidence.

A. UAs

The first Children's Court finding at issue concerns the mother's compliance with Urine Analysis ("UA") testing. The basis for the UA requirements were initially ordered in the November 20, 2008 Family Case Plan, and also more specifically in the Order on 3rd Review Hearing issued on August 21, 2009.... The specific requirement from the Family Case Plan states, "Mother to remain clean and sober at all times." The Order on 3rd Review Hearing requires, "Mother shall submit to random UAs upon notification that she is required to do so." ...

The evidence provided to the Children's Court for the fourth review hearing indicated that the mother was a "NO SHOW" at three UA appointments during the reporting period.... The mother did not attend UA appointments on August 26, 2009, October 2, 2009 and October 29, 2009. *Id.* The Tribe argues that a "NO SHOW" is considered a positive result. The mother did not provide the Children's Court with evidence to support her reasons for missing the UA appointments.

In the January 20, 2010, Order on 4th Review Hearing, the Children's Court found the mother to be in compliance with the Family Case Plan. With respect to UA's, the Children's Court found "no positive UA for non-prescription drugs or alcohol"....

The Children's Court findings with respect to the UAs are contrary to the evidence presented at the fourth review hearing. The reason the mother had "no positive UA..." tests, was due to her failure to appear for UA testing, which she was required to do in the Order on 3rd Review Hearing.... The mother was clearly in non-compliance with the requirement to submit to random UA's. Further, it is reasonable to presume that failure to attend a UA or avoiding a UA may be due to the donor's concern that the result may be unfavorable. If the mother had good cause grounds for failing to attend the UA's, then the Children's Court should have taken that evidence and made the appropriate findings. However, failing to attend three UAs during a reporting period, even if there was good cause, should not be treated as having "no positive UA." Taking into consideration the whole purpose of the dependency case, to remedy the problems leading to the dependency, the Children's Court should treat such situations as an unresolved problem and continue court intervention until there are sufficient UAs administered to satisfy the court that the mother is clean and sober. The Children's Court had ample grounds to continue court intervention due to the mother not participating in court ordered UA requirements, when she failed to attend three UA appointments during the reporting period. PTC 7.04.760(e) (formerly PTC 7.01.1720 (5)).

B. Counseling

The next issue was whether the Children's Court properly found that the mother was in compliance with the couples counseling requirement. The November 20, 2008, Family Case Plan required, "Mother to enter into couple [sic] counseling with her significant other."

At the third review hearing held on August 20, 2009, the Children's Court found, "Mother's attendance frequency needs to be documented to show Mother is attending and participating in the counseling sessions on a regular basis, i.e., as the counselor recommends." . . . The evidence presented to the Children's Court indicated that, "The couple informed CW on 9/17/09 that they have decided to separate and see no reason to continue couple counseling." . . . The findings from the Order on 3rd Review Hearing as to Father, held on August 27, 2009, were that the Children's Court denied the PTCS motion to remove the father from the residence he lived in with the mother, the child and the child's siblings until he was able to "demonstrate long-term stability and sobriety". . . . The Family Preservation Status Report dated November 4, 2009, indicated that as of October 4, 2009, the mother and father were evicted from their house and were going to be sharing a residence until the mother could obtain suitable housing. . . . The evidence shows that less than a month after the Children's Court found the mother to be in partial compliance, she self-terminated future couples counseling without authorization from the Court.

The Children's Court ruled in the Order on 4th Review Hearing that the mother, "participated in individual and couples counseling." . . . Technically, the Children's Court is correct, the mother did participate in couples counseling. Unfortunately, the language used in drafting the initial Family Case Plan is not very helpful, because it states "mother to enter into couple [sic] counseling with her significant other." A well-drafted Family Case Plan should be designed to fit the particular needs of the individual and should be written to provide sufficient notice for someone to understand when they have fully complied with a requirement. Carefully drafted case plan requirements aid the family, the court and service providers know what constitutes satisfactory compliance.

Notwithstanding the poorly drafted case plan requirement and the Children's Court finding that the mother participated in couples counseling, the clear weight of the evidence shows that the mother had not satisfied the couples counseling requirement. The mother was only in partial compliance at the third review hearing on August 20, 2009. . . . Less than one month later, she self-terminated couples counseling. Only the Children's Court has the authority to relieve a party from a court ordered Family Case Plan requirement. If the mother had cause to be relieved from the couples counseling requirement, the proper procedure would be for her to file a motion with the court. The Children's Court could then evaluate the evidence and make the appropriate determination. Without having been granted relief from the couples counseling requirement by the court, her decision to terminate couples counseling is *per se* non-compliance.

In reviewing whether court ordered Family Case Plan requirements have been satisfied, the Children's Court must analyze the evidence of parental compliance by taking into consideration the initial reason for ordering the requirement, the overall goals of the case, the intent and purpose of the Children's Code and whether the parent's efforts in fulfilling the requirement have resulted in helping create a safe and stable environment for the child. Therefore, there must be some finding by the Children's Court that the intent and purpose of the requirement has been fulfilled and the problem necessitating the requirement has been resolved. That was not done for this requirement.

C. Housing

The third issue raised by the Tribe is whether the Children's Court properly found that the mother satisfied the requirement to "maintain a clean, sober, and sanitary house for her children to reside in." With respect to this requirement, the Children's Court found that the "[Mother] has maintained a decent family home . . ." . . .

At the fourth review hearing, the Tribe argued that the mother's housing situation was tenuous. The Tribe's position was supported by evidence that, "She [mother] is on a waiting list for housing since her ex-boyfriend was evicted from their apartment on 10/9/09." . . . The Family Preservation Status Report dated November 4, 2009, indicated that as of October 4, 2009, the mother and father were evicted from their house by Puyallup Tribal Housing Authority and were going to be sharing a residence until the mother could obtain suitable housing. . . .

On December 8, 2009, the mother's attorney filed a Motion to Dismiss Case. . . . In the motion, the mother's attorney alleges that the mother filed proof with the Court on November 30, 2009 that she is leasing a four bedroom house through the Puyallup Housing Authority. The court file contains a Rental Agreement between the mother and Puyallup Tribal Housing Authority for a dwelling located in Tacoma. CP 149. The rental agreement is dated December 1, 2009. . . .

On January 4, 2010, Puyallup Tribe Children Services Caseworker Laura Ducolon filed a declaration with the Children's Court stating that the mother had not paid rent for January 2010, which she was required to do because she was late on the December 2009 rent payment. . . . The declaration stated that, "Freda has begun the eviction process due to [mother's] failure to pay rent on-time and to have a garbage can." *Id.* On January 14, 2010, counsel for mother filed a response stating that as of that date no eviction was pending. . . . The Children's Court issued its Order on 4th Review Hearing on January 20, 2010. . . .

A prerequisite to maintaining a decent family home is to have a dwelling in which the threat of eviction is not an imminent possibility. The term "maintain" in this context means preserve from lapse, decline, failure or cessation. Black's Law Dictionary, Sixth Edition, pg. 953. In the same month that the Children's Court issued its order that found, "[Mother] has maintained a decent family home", the parties were filing court documents concerning the possibility of the mother being evicted from the house in which she had signed a rental agreement only six weeks prior. . . . Even if the mother avoided eviction in January 2010, more time than a few weeks must be given to allow for the housing situation to stabilize. Successes in dependency cases are marked by long-term stability in maintaining compliance with court ordered family case plan requirements. When there is not a specific timeframe established in the family case plan, then the length of time required to determine stability for any given requirement depends on the nature of the requirement and should be considered in totality with all of the other requirements of the family case plan necessary to accomplish the overall goals of solving the problems that caused the case to be initiated. In light of the evidence presented at the fourth review hearing and thereafter, the Children's Court decision finding the mother had maintained a decent family home was contrary to the evidence.

D. Appointments and General Support for Children's Activities

The Tribe challenged the Children's Court findings that "the children have attended their entire dental and medical appointments; and supported her oldest daughter during in-patient treatment; and continues to support all the children in school and after school activities." . . . The initial Family Case Plan issued on November 20, 2008, did not require these provisions. Although, the Order on 3rd Review Hearing did require that the, "Mother shall notify PTCS of the name/s of any other agency besides Puyallup Tribal Health Authority that she has had or will have any of the children brought to for medical, dental or other health reasons . . ." CP 128, pg. 6. Because the Children's Court believed the mother's participation in these activities were important enough to take into consideration in deciding to dismiss the cases, we will review whether the evidence supported these findings.

The specific findings from the Order on 4th Review Hearing state:

> [Mother] is no longer a victim of domestic violence. [Mother] has maintained a decent family home and the children have attended their entire dental and medical appointments; and supported her oldest daughter during in-patient treatment; and continues to support all the children in school and after school activities.

* * *

In the mother's Response and Objection to Petitioner's Motion and Proposed Order Received 12/22/2009, filed on December 29, 2009, in language similar to that later used by the Children's Court in its findings, her attorney argues that the mother is in compliance as follows:

> She has not been a victim of further Domestic Violence. Her children have not been abused. She maintains a decent home, and her children attended all of their medical and dental appointments. She supported her teenage daughter through in-patient treatment this past summer, and supported her other children in school and after school activities.

* * *

These arguments made by the mother's attorney were not supported by an affidavit or declaration. Arguments of legal counsel are not evidence.

The Tribe argues that the part of the order regarding the "children have attended their entire dental and medical appointments" and "continues to support all the children in school and after school activities" is not supported by the evidence. We agree. In fact, the evidence indicates that the mother was struggling with meeting daily needs for her and the children. The Report For 4th Review Hearing In Case No. PUY-CW-09/08-064, filed on November 6, 2009, states the following:

> [Mother] has demonstrated the inability to follow through managing the day to day needs of the children and her. She needs reminders to follow through with appointments for the children and her. [Mother] recently had her 6th child and multitasking all of her children's school needs, health care needs, and housing appears to be overwhelming.

* * *

The Tribe next argues that there is no evidence in the record that the mother "supported her oldest daughter during in-patient treatment." We agree. There is no evidence in the record that shows the mother's efforts to support her daughter during in-patient treatment. The Tribe's evidence during the reporting period covered by the 4th Review Hearing refers to a previous incident in which the mother had a CPS referral for giving her daughter unprescribed Oxycodone "due to not knowing what else to do since [daughter] was in pain and crying." . . .

Argument of legal counsel is not evidence and the Children's Court cannot base findings of fact on the statements of the mother's attorney. We conclude that the findings by the Children's Court were contrary to the evidence available to the Court at the fourth review hearing.

E. The Father

The father had requirements to fulfill under the Family Case Plan issued on November 20, 2008. There was no indication in the record that the father was previously dismissed from the case or relieved of his requirements to comply with the Family Case Plan. Yet, the father's compliance was not addressed in the order that ultimately dismissed the case. The only reference to the father was found in paragraph six of the Order on 4th Review Hearing:

> At the last review hearing both the Father and Mother stated on record that they are no longer domiciled together.

* * *

This finding as to the domiciliary status of the parents is contradicted by the Family Preservation Status Report dated November 4, 2009.... The Report indicated that as of October 4, 2009, the mother and father were evicted from their house by Puyallup Tribal Housing Authority and were going to be sharing a residence until the mother could obtain suitable housing.... This information indicates that the mother and father lived together after the August 27, 2009 third review hearing.

The finding is further contradicted by the Order on 3rd Review Hearing as to Father:

> At the August 27, 2009 hearing concerning the father, PTCS requested removal of the father from the residence he lives in with the mother, the child and the child's siblings. PTCS specifically asked that the father leave the home and "demonstrate long-term stability and sobriety" before being allowed to live back in the home.
>
> The Court denies that motion because this presiding judge does not find that evidence has been presented to show any immediate danger to the child and or her siblings that would warrant removal of the father from the home.

* * *

This determination by the Children's Court in the Order on 3rd Review Hearing as to the father is inconsistent with the findings relied upon for dismissing the case, in regards to the domiciliary status of the parents at the third review hearing.

Even if the father and mother were no longer domiciled together, it can be reasonably presumed that the father would continue to have visitation with the children and contact with the mother. Based on the initial probable cause determination that the children were in need of care, because "the children had been or are likely to be physically and psychologically abused by parents", there should have been findings and an order to address visitation or restrictions to protect the children. Compliance with the Family Case Plan is necessary to help resolve the problems that impair the father's ability to be a safe and stable caregiver.

We conclude that the Children's Court finding regarding the father's domiciliary status with the mother was contrary to the evidence available to the Children's Court at the fourth review hearing.

V. Conclusion: Holding and Order

This Court holds that the Children's Court decisions were contrary to the evidence available prior to issuing its January 20, 2010, Orders on 4th review hearing. Those orders are hereby VACATED and these cases are REMANDED to the Children's Court to modify the Family Case Plans to specify the actions the parents must take to resolve the family problems, as they currently exist, that led to the dependency cases, and set forth time frames to accomplish such actions before the cases can be closed based on findings made in a manner consistent with this opinion.

Notes

1. The case above offers a detailed review of enacted tribal law. *In re the K. Children*, 7 SWITCA 6 (Southwest Intertribal Court of Appeals for the Fort Mojave Indian Tribe 1996), is another example of a tribal court applying tribal law, rather than the federal ICWA, to determine the required burden of proof and necessary findings in a termination of parental rights case. After you read the below excerpt, consider how Fort Mojave tribal law on termination of parental rights differs from the standards set out in ICWA.

> The second challenge to the trial court's findings was made at oral argument. Mrs. K. stated that she could not determine the basis for the trial court's decision to terminate her parental rights. A review of the trial court's order, in light of Fort Mojave Law governing termination of parental rights, supports this challenge to the adequacy of [the] trial court's order.
>
> Under Fort Mojave law, parental rights can only be terminated for very specific statutory grounds. Grounds to support termination of parental rights are stated in Section 436 of the Fort Mojave Indian Tribe Law and Order Code:
>
> > The rights of the parents may be terminated if the court finds:
> >
> > a. The parent or parents are unfit and incompetent by reason of conduct or condition seriously detrimental to the child; or
> >
> > b. That the parent or parents have abandoned the child[,] . . . ; or
> >
> > c. That for a period of time, during which the child was kept in his own home under protective supervision, or during which the child was allowed to live in his own home, the parent or parents substantially and continuously refused or failed to give the child proper parental care and protection, or to exercise appropriate control of the child. *Fort Mojave Tribe Law and Order Code, Art. IV, Section 436.*
>
> * * *
>
> We are mindful of the need for resolution in the lives of these children. At oral argument the guardian *ad litem* for the children urged us not to ignore the children's need for permanency for the sake of the parents' rights. That position of course ignores the fact that parental rights is legal shorthand for the rights of the children and as well as that of the parents to some form of relationship. The rights at issue are of value to both the children and the parents. For the Tribe to permanently sever these rights, it is essential that

> the facts show severance to be in accordance with the Tribe's law, no matter how strongly a case may tug at the heart. The trial court's order does not do that. Due to our extensive review of the record in this case, we note that there may be no need for the trial court to conduct any further hearings in this matter. There may well be facts in the voluminous record to support all aspects of its order. The need of any such supplemental hearing should be determined by the trial court in the first instance.

2. Relatedly, the court in *In the Matter of I.R.C.*, No. 99-001-A, 2 Am. Tribal Law 46, 49–50 (Cheyenne River Sioux Tribal Court of Appeals, July 6, 1999), analyzes both provisions of ICWA and tribal law to determine which authority is the appropriate precedent to be used in the case, where a provision of ICWA has been incorporated into tribal law.

> The "Consent to termination of parental rights" form signed by Appellant is invalid for two overlapping yet complementary reasons. Appellant correctly argues that Section 10.02(B) of the Cheyenne River Sioux Tribe's Children's Code governs placements outside the Cheyenne River Sioux Reservation as in the case at bar and it provides in relevant part:
>
> > Where placement outside the Cheyenne River Sioux Reservation is contemplated, a consent of relinquishment shall conform with the provisions of the Indian Child Welfare Act, 25 U.S.C. § 1913.
>
> 25 U.S.C. § 1913(a) specifically states:
>
> > Where any parent or Indian custodian voluntarily consents to a foster care placement or to termination of parental rights, such consent shall not be valid unless executed in writing and recorded before a judge of a court of competent jurisdiction and accompanied by the presiding judge's certificate that the terms and consequences of the consent were fully explained in detail and were fully understood by the parent or Indian custodian. The court shall also certify that either the parent or Indian custodian fully understood the explanation in English or that it was interpreted into a language that the parent or Indian custodian understood. Any consent given prior to, or within ten days after, birth of the Indian child shall not be valid.
>
> Appellant's "consent" in this matter—as acknowledged by both parties—was not "executed in writing before a judge of a court of competent jurisdiction and accompanied by the presiding judge's certificate that the terms and consequences of the consent were fully explained in detail and were fully understood by the parent or Indian custodian." It is therefore void and inoperable as a matter of law.
>
> While the above analysis is dispositive, there is a somewhat overlapping yet complementary issue presented by Section 11.02(G) of the Cheyenne River Sioux Children's Code which provides:

> A consent to adoption may be withdrawn at any time prior to entry of an Order of Adoption, and only upon permission of the Court for the reason that the best interests of the child will be served by such withdrawal. However, if within six (6) months from the date of consent it can be shown beyond a reasonable doubt that the consent to adoption was given as a result of fraud, coercion, or duress, such consent may be withdrawn during such period.

Unlike 25 U.S.C. § 1913, the provisions of section 11.02(G) of the Children's Code appear to grant the Children's Court some discretion to decline withdrawal of consent where not in the best interests of the child. Thus, an interesting statutory interpretation question is posed as to whether proceedings, like this one, contemplating placement of a minor child outside the reservation are governed by section 11.02(G) of the Children's Code or pursuant to section 10.02(B) of the Children's Code by the provisions of section 25 U.S.C. § 1913.

Fortunately, this Court need not to resolve this particular question of statutory construction since it finds that the "Voluntary Consent to Termination of Parental Rights" signed by Elena Condon Dupris was invalid from the beginning. There is no dispute that the form was signed by Elena Condon Dupris before a notary public as suggested on the form itself. The problem with this procedure is that section 11.02(F) of the Cheyenne River Sioux Children's Code expressly provides:

> Consent of a parent [to termination of parental rights and adoption] shall be taken by the Court and shall be accomplished by signing a consent form to be provided by the Court which explains the consequences of consenting to the adoption. The Court shall certify that the parent fully understood the explanation in English or that it was interpreted into a language that the parent understood. For parents residing outside the Reservation, the consent form shall be executed before a Notary Public who must certify that the consent of the parent appears to be freely given in order for such consent to be valid.

There is no dispute that at all times relevant to this proceeding Elena Condon Dupris was and is an enrolled member of the Cheyenne River Sioux Tribe and a resident of the Cheyenne River Sioux Reservation. Thus, under the clear language of section 11.02(F), her consent to termination of her parental rights and to adoption had to be taken before the Children's Court, not by a notary public. Furthermore, for the consent to be valid the Children's Court was required to certify that she fully understood the consequences of her consent in either English or in her native language.

3. In many tribal nations, the termination of parental rights is considered a particularly heinous aspect of western child welfare. Often a tribal child welfare code

will provide for alternatives to termination, including suspension of parental rights, or a long term guardianship.

In re the Guardianship of a Tulalip Minor

13 NICS App. 12 (Tulalip Tribal Court of Appeals March 2015)

Background

The child who is the subject of this guardianship proceeding was the subject of a Youth in Need of Care case opened in November, 2011. The child was originally placed in the temporary custody of his maternal grandmother on November 3, 2011. On November 8, 2011, beda?chelh [the Tulalip Tribe's social services department] filed a Declaration of Emergency Change of Placement and on the next day the child was placed with his paternal grandparents because they lived on the Tulalip reservation and the maternal grandmother did not. GAL Report p. 3. The maternal grandmother had no visitation rights until December 22, 2011 when the court issued an order establishing a visitation schedule for four specific days. An incident occurred on December 27, 2011, in which the paternal grandparents took the child to his parents' residence in their car. The paternal grandparents attempted to get the child's mother to leave with them before the police arrived to investigate the domestic violence that had occurred there. GAL p. 5. As a result, the child was placed with his maternal grandmother again where he remained for the next 18 months. In August, 2013, the child was removed from the maternal grandmother's custody because she allowed the parents to have a supervised visit with the child and the child was placed again with the paternal grandparents. Although it was later reported to beda?chelh that the paternal grandparents had allowed the child's father to be with his son in June, 2013, beda?chelh did not change the placement.

* * *

Both the maternal grandmother and paternal grandparents petitioned for guardianship. A Guardian ad Litem (GAL) was appointed by order of the court on September 12, 2013, and was charged with recommending which of the parties should be appointed as guardian. The GAL's eighteen page sealed report and six page public report were submitted on December 2, 2013. It was the conclusion of the GAL that the child should be placed with the maternal grandmother, and that the paternal grandparents be granted visitation one weekend per month. After a trial that began on December 18, 2013 and concluded on February 12, 2014, the court granted both petitions and divided custody between the parties. Findings of Fact, Conclusions of Law and Order on Guardianship (hereinafter also "FFCL"), March 10, 2014.

The maternal grandmother appeals from the court's order.

* * *

The Best Interests of the Child

The appointment of a guardian shall be governed by the best interests of the youth who is the subject of the guardianship. [Tulalip Tribal Code] TTC 4.05.370(1)(b)(v).

This is the primary criteria to be applied when deciding who shall be appointed guardian of a child notwithstanding other factors, including those listed in TTC 4.05.370(1)(b)(i). While this "order of preference for appointing a guardian" subsection precedes the mandate that the appointment be governed by the best interests of the child, it does not supersede it. Therefore, reliance by the trial court upon the "order of preference" factors as decisive, including the on reservation residence of the paternal grandparents and off reservation residence of the maternal grandmother, is misplaced. The trial court stated that its decision would be based upon the best interests of the child even though implying that would not be the case if the petitioners did not both have some factors in their favor.

"Although in summary fashion, it should be noted that some factors weigh in favor of each Petitioner so the deciding factor will be the best interests of the minor child." FFCL and Order on Guardianship Petitions, p. 3. However, the trial court reached its decision contrary to the only independent evidence before it regarding the best interests of the child.

Guardian ad Litem (GAL)

The function and purpose of a Guardian ad Litem (GAL) is ". . . to represent a child, for the protection of the best interests of the child . . ." TTC 4.05.020(24). It would usually be the function of beda?chelh to advise the trial court which placement of a child would be in the best interests of that child. TTC 4.05.370(4)(c). For whatever reason, beda?chelh refused to do that in this case, reporting only that both parties were "eligible." We are not persuaded by beda?chelh's argument on reconsideration that reporting that both of the competing petitioners were "eligible" constitutes a "recommendation regarding the legal guardianship" for purposes of TTC 4.05.370(4)(c). Where there are competing petitions, "either" is not a recommendation. We conclude that in the case of competing petitions, TTC 4.05.370(4)(c) requires beda?chelh to recommend which of the competing petitions for guardianship would best serve the interests of the child and explain its reasoning, regardless of whether it is an easy choice or a close call.

The GAL was appointed in this case for the specific purpose of recommending who should be appointed as guardian because the court had to make a choice without the benefit of a recommendation from beda?chelh. Order on Hearing, September 12, 2013. The GAL report, dated December 2, 2013, is detailed and identifies all of the people contacted and interviewed, all of the factors that went into her recommendation that the maternal grandmother be made the child's guardian, and recommendations for follow-up for the benefit of the child.

The trial court chose to disregard the GAL recommendation without any discussion or acknowledgement of the content of the GAL report

* * *

Appellant argued before the trial court that the GAL report should be accorded the substantial legal weight accorded to beda?chelh by the TTC. The trial court disagreed, stating that "The Court disagrees with granting this substantial favor to a party NOT necessarily representing the Tribe or the Tribe's interest." FFCL&Order, p.3 (emphasis in original). In so stating, the trial court disregards the facts that the base criteria for its decision is the best interest of the child, that the sole function of the GAL is to represent those interests and that the GAL was appointed because beda?chelh, the agency charged with representing the best interests of the child, abdicated its obligation under TTC 4.05.370(4)(c) to make a recommendation. The trial court's reference to the GAL as a "party" is telling. The GAL is not a "party." Pursuant to TTC 4.05.020(24), the GAL is the child's legal representative. We need not resolve the question [whether] the GAL's recommendation should have been accorded the same weight as one from beda?chelh. The trial court was clearly not at liberty to disregard the facts and recommendations submitted by the child's legal representative.

* * *

Conclusion

We agree with the dissent in regards to the respective roles of the Court of Appeals and the trial court, and the deference due to the trial court's determinations of witness credibility and findings of fact. However, just as a guardian ad litem is not a "party," neither is a guardian ad litem a "witness." Therefore, the command of TTC 2.20.090(3) that we defer to the trial court's determination of witness credibility as a finding of fact is inapplicable here. Likewise, the command of TTC 2.20.090(1) that we sustain a finding of fact by the trial court unless it is clearly erroneous is not the applicable standard here because our concern is that the trial court's failure to address the evidence and recommendations presented by the GAL overrides whatever findings the trial court did make. The applicable standard of review here is set forth at TTC 2.20.090(8), where we are instructed to sustain a matter within the discretion of the trial court only if the trial court applied the appropriate legal standard to the facts. We hold that because the trial court did not apply the appropriate legal standard to the GAL's report and recommendations, the trial court abused its discretion.

The trial court erred by disregarding and dismissing the GAL report and recommendations on the grounds that it was not entitled to the same weight as a recommendation from beda?chelh would be given. While we do not decide whether the GAL's recommendation is entitled to the same weight as one from beda?chelh, we do hold that the GAL's recommendations deserved substantially more weight than they were given by the trial court. The trial court further erred by disregarding the only independent evidence of what constituted the best interests of the child. The trial court also erred by granting guardianship without making written findings as to whether there is clear and convincing evidence that the guardianship is in the best interests of the child. TTC 4.05.370(7). The decision of the trial court placing guardianship with the paternal grandparents is reversed and this matter remanded back to the trial court for further proceedings consistent with this opinion.

Notes

1. Both this case and the one before it were heard in the Northwest Intertribal Court System (NICS). Tribes in the northwest established NICS to assist with both tribal trial courts and appeals from tribal courts. As tribal court systems have grown, especially those in tribes with significant resources, some of those tribes no longer use NICS. The Tulalip Tribe now has its own appellate court system. The Tulalip Tribal court is a large court, with multiple trial judges, a large child welfare system, a juvenile justice diversion system, and an adult healing to wellness court.

2. The Tulalip Tribal Code is specific when it comes to guardianships, especially since that is the preferred long term solution when a child cannot go home. Usually beda?chelh has a large role in recommending a guardianship placement and reviewing that placement. While it is unclear in this case why beda?chelh did not make a recommendation, the tribal appellate court made clear the trial court must consider a GAL report when determining a guardianship placement. This case is an example of the way tribal courts also weigh reports from the tribal social services department *and* from those representatives of individuals. Many times in state court, there is a monolithic understanding of "the tribe" as a unit with one opinion. In fact, most tribes have separate tribal social service departments, which make recommendations for the tribal court to consider—*under tribal law.* The Appellate Court here spends considerable time addressing what the Tulalip Tribal Code requires in this situation.

D. Child Support in Tribal Child Welfare Cases

Enforcing child support orders in tribal courts, especially when the order to be enforced is originally from a non-tribal court, the defendant's employer is located off the reservation, or the defendant's only source of income is a monetary payment from the tribe, raises unique issues of jurisdiction.

State ex rel. Maney v. Maney

No. CV 99-558, 2005 WL 6438072
(Supreme Court of the Eastern Band of Cherokee Indians May 10, 2005)

The record discloses the following:

1. On September 23, 1999, plaintiff commenced this action against defendant for child support for the two minor children of plaintiff and defendant, born April 8, 1993 and September 19, 1994. Defendant and the two children are enrolled members of the Eastern Band of Cherokee Indians.
2. The verified complaint was personally served on defendant October 6, 1999.
3. Defendant, represented by counsel, filed a verified answer on December 15, 1999.

4. This case was originally filed in the Cherokee Court of Indian Offenses and was transferred to the Cherokee Court on April 1, 2000.
5. On April 19, 2000, the Cherokee Court entered an order, consented to by the parties, ordering defendant to pay $50.00 per month to the Clerk of the Court as child support and ordered defendant's per capita distribution check garnished to pay $1800.00 child support arrearage. Defendant was represented by counsel.
6. Plaintiff filed divorce proceedings against defendant in the District Court, Jackson County, North Carolina on July 19, 2000, and the parties were subsequently divorced.
7. After July 19, 2000, defendant was convicted in the Superior Court of North Carolina of first-degree sex offense against his minor female child and defendant has been confined in the custody of the North Carolina Department of Corrections, since March 19, 2004, or earlier, serving a sentence of at least 20–25 years imprisonment.
8. On March 19, 2004, plaintiff filed a motion for distribution of defendant's per capita, pursuant to Cherokee Code Sec. 110–2A (b)(3).
9. On April 8, 2004, the Cherokee Court entered an order finding facts and conclusions of law, and denied defendant's motion to dismiss the proceeding and defendant's motion to suppress. The hearing on the merits was scheduled for April 16, 2004.
10. After hearing on April 16, 2004, the Cherokee Court filed an order May 4, 2004 allowing the motion for distribution pursuant to Cherokee Code Sec. 110–2A (b)(3).
11. Defendant gave notice of appeal in open court and the court entered a stay order pending this appeal.

At the outset, we note that the Tribal Council on January 6, 2005 amended Chapter 110–2A (b)(3) by deleting the last sentence beginning "additionally," and added the following sentence: "Additionally, when the responsible parent is incarcerated for a period that is expected to last one year or more, the Court may order that his or her child support obligation be set at an amount not to exceed 75% of his or her per capita distribution." So, this appeal may be, as Justice Holmes observed, "like a railroad ticket, good for this trip and this train only."

Our task is to construe Cherokee Code 110–2A (b)(3) as of May 4, 2004. In so doing, beyond considering the literal words, the Court considers the history, culture, traditions of the Tribe, and the purposes and consequences of the ordinance.

Chapter 110–2A establishes the purposes of the ordinance are to provide support for the children of the Tribe for their reasonable needs of health, education, shelter and maintenance, having due regard for the estate, earnings and standard of living of the child and the responsible parent, and other facts of the case.

In Section 110–2A (b)(3), the Tribal Council considered the role of the responsible parent's per capita distribution from gaming in meeting the above purposes. First, it included such per capita distribution in the income calculations of the responsible parent in determining monthly child support payments. Then, in addition to monthly child support, the ordinance established that if the responsible parent was incarcerated serving a sentence expected to last one year or more, the Court may order the distribution of his entire per capita share for the support of his minor children during the period of incarceration. Thus, to achieve the purposes of the child support ordinance, the Tribal Council in Section (b)(3) made the per capita fund available in two ways:

1. It was always included in the income of the responsible parent; and,
2. If the parent was incarcerated as required, the Court could order the entire per capita distributed for child support purposes.

By adopting Cherokee Code 110–2A (b)(3) the Tribal Council added another method to provide child support under the limited conditions of incarceration set out. Under this statute, upon a finding the defendant was a "responsible parent ... incarcerated for a period that is expected to last one year or more" the court could order defendant's per capita distribution to be distributed, in whole or in part, for child support. An order of garnishment is not necessary to apply this remedy; the judge is authorized to distribute a defendant's per capita without an underlying order of child support.

Thus, in this case the consent order of support dated April 19, 2000, remains in effect unchanged by the order appealed. Additional support for defendant's children is secured by the court's per capita distribution older pursuant to Chapter 110–2A (b)(3). This ordinance does not authorize a garnishment of defendant's per capita distribution; garnishment is already authorized by Chapter 16C–5 (d) of the Cherokee Code. The order appealed does not order a garnishment of defendant's per capita distribution. It is a separate, additional method of securing child support under these limited conditions.

The cases of *Conrad v. Conrad*, 239 S.E.2d 862 (1978) and *Sampson County v. Bolton*, 377 S.E.2d 88 (1989), concern modifying a support order by a subsequent garnishment proceeding. Here, the court expressly does not modify the consent support order and does not order a garnishment. Conrad and Bolton are not applicable to this appeal.

Defendant contends that Cherokee Code 110–2A (b)(3) violates the Indian Civil Rights Act, (ICRA) 25 U.S.C. 1302 (1968) with respect to equal protection of the laws and impairing his rights under a contract. The Indian Civil Rights Act states that no Indian tribe in exercising powers of self-government shall "(8) deny to any person within its jurisdiction the equal protection of its laws or deprive any person of liberty or property without due process of laws;" 25 USC 1302.

We conclude that Cherokee Code 110–2A (b)(3) does not create a suspect class, *White v. Pate*, 304 S.E.2d 199 (1983), nor a quasi-suspect class. *Cleburne v. Cleburne*

Living Center, Inc. 473 U.S. 432 (1985). No fundamental right of defendant is impaired, such as the right to vote or rear children. See *Troxel v. Granville,* 530 U.S. 57 (2000). Such right as defendant may have a per capita distribution is one granted by the Tribal Council and can be amended by that body, as occurred with the passage of Cherokee Code 110–2A (b)(3).

Thus the rational basis test is the standard of review on this issue. Under this test the challenged ordinance is presumed to be valid and will be sustained if the classification is rationally related to a legitimate governmental interest. Surely, the Eastern Band of Cherokee Indians has a legitimate governmental interest in requiring responsible parents to provide for the support and welfare of their minor children. Granting to a judge of the Cherokee Court the authority to order the distribution of an incarcerated parent's per capita for the support of his children is rationally related to this governmental interest. The class is small, made up with those responsible parents who are incarcerated serving a prison sentence of more than one year.

The Tribal Council was aware that the per capita distribution for the enrolled members is an important part of their incomes and used for food, clothing, shelter, education, transportation and medical needs. The Tribal Council was also aware that prisoners serving prison sentences greater than a year were provided with these necessities without expense to the prisoners. Many other benefits (e.g., books, institutions, skills, legal services) are provided prisoners. Thus, the Tribal Council wisely decided that a judge of the Cherokee Court, after a plenary hearing, should have the authority to decide the best use of the per capita in fulfilling the purposes of the Tribe in providing support for Indian children.

We hold that Cherokee Code 110–2A (b)(3) does not violate the Indian Civil Rights Act.

Defendant further contends that Cherokee Code 110–2A (b)(3) violates Article I, Section 10, of the United States Constitution. This section prohibits states from impairing the obligation of contracts. Indian tribes are not "states" within the meaning of the United States Constitution. Nor do we find any prohibition against Indian tribes impairing the obligation of contract in the Indian Civil Rights Act (ICRA). Defendant has failed to provide evidence of a contract between the Eastern Band of Cherokee Indians and himself. There is no allegation of a contract. We reject this argument.

We hold that Cherokee Code 110–2A (b)(3), as of May 04, 2004, did not violate the Indian Civil Rights Act or impair the obligation of any contract of defendant, and was a valid ordinance of the Eastern Band of Cherokee Indians.

This decision is in accord with the culture and traditions of the Eastern Band of Cherokee Indians in securing support for the Tribe's children, especially where a responsible parent by a deliberate criminal act has impaired or destroyed support for a child.

The Master said, "Suffer the little children to come unto me. . . ." St. Mark 10:14. Surely, this Court can do no less.

The order of the Cherokee Court of May 04, 2004, is affirmed.

Notes

1. The above case illustrates how a benefit of tribal membership can be used to enforce compliance with a child support order. At the end of the case, however, the tribal judge incorporates a quote from the Christian Bible regarding the care of tribal children. Is this quote something you would expect to see in a tribal court opinion? What does it reveal about the history of Native American and Euro-American relations, especially considering the role that religious institutions played in removing Native children from their families?

2. As a stream of income not dependent on a tribal parent's employment status, other tribes have also enacted provisions subjecting tribal per capita payments to garnishment when child support payments are in arrears. *See Cramer v. Greene*, 6 Am. Tribal Law 454 (Mohegan Tribal Trial Court Nov. 1, 2005):

> Resolution No.2004–12 ("Resolution") was adopted by the legislative body of the Mohegan Tribe on April 7, 2004 to "provide for recognition and enforcement of valid child support orders from courts of other jurisdictions against non-paying Mohegan Tribal Members." Preamble, Resolution No.2004–12.
>
> The Resolution provides in pertinent part as follows:
>
> "The Mohegan Tribal Court shall recognize as the law of the Mohegan Tribe, any valid child support order from any court of competent jurisdiction that has been entered against a Mohegan Tribal Member." . . .
>
> "Once the Court has deemed a child support order to be valid, the Court shall consider evidence from a petitioning party of chronic, persistent non-payment of such child support, and shall make a finding regarding whether arrearages exist that are due to the petitioner for the support of Mohegan Tribal Children." . . .
>
> "If the Court finds that chronic, persistent non-payment of child support has resulted in arrearages, the Court shall order the withholding of per capita distribution benefits from the Tribal Member and such per capita distribution benefits shall be distributed by the Tribe to the party identified in the child support order for the benefit of the Mohegan Tribal children until such time as the arrearages are paid in full." . . .

3. Child support payments in tribal communities also bring up issues not normally seen in state courts. In *Anderson v. Keevama*, 4 Am. Tribal Law 410 (Appellate Court of the Hopi Tribe Apr. 15, 2002), the father of two children was in arrears of his required child support payments because of an inter-tribal dispute between a local

village and the tribal council. While supportive of the father's good faith efforts, the Hopi Tribal Court recognized that the protection and support of children was an overarching policy concern.

> Trial Court appeared to give considerable weight to the fact that Appellee was continuing to work as a Community Service Administrator ("CSA") for the Village of Mishongnovi, although he was not receiving any pay because of a dispute between the Village of Mishongnovi and the Tribal Council. The Tribal Court noted that it is Appellee's hope that he can help to resolve the dispute so that the Tribal Council will release the frozen funds. However, Appellee did not show that there was progress being made toward a resolution of the village-tribal conflict. He did not show that the conflict was likely to be concluded and funds released.
>
> However much the Tribal Court sympathizes with the need to resolve the conflict between Mishongnovi and the Tribal Council, it is also a need that Mr. Keevama's children be financially supported. The question of whether or not the Appellee is doing a "societal good" by remaining at his CSA job, though laudable does not end Mr. Keevama's duties toward his children.

4. *Sharpe v. Sharpe*, 366 P.3d 66 (Alaska 2016), illustrates why it is important for tribal courts to be involved in all aspects of cases involving tribal members. In this case, the non-custodial mother, a Yup'ik tribal member, moved from Anchorage to the native village of Stebbins, to reconnect with her tribal culture and traditional subsistence lifestyle. Because of this change, she had a reduced income, and requested a reduction in the amount of child support owed from the state superior court that had awarded custody and support, but was denied. After reading the following excerpt, do you think the case would have turned out differently had it been heard in a Yup'ik tribal court? Do the lower court's comments trivialize the value of a tribal subsistence lifestyle?

> Jolene argues that the superior court "direct[ed] nearly total focus on [her] past income history" and gave short shrift to Jolene's religious and cultural needs. It is true that "the parents' needs" is one of the factors the superior court must consider in evaluating the totality of the circumstances. But the superior court did adequately consider Jolene's needs, and after considering these needs it found that they did not outweigh other concerns, including her daughter's need for financial support:
>
>> [Jolene] finds that [living in Stebbins] is sort of rehabilitative for her from the standpoint of her eliminating . . . some of the poisons of urban life. . . . She is finding sort of a spiritual reawakening or reconnecting with Native dance, Native culture, subsistence lifestyle, all of which is . . . admirable in an abstract sense.
>>
>> Then again . . . she effectively is . . . taking a vacation from the financial responsibilities that she assumed when she had a child, and the result of her not working and providing financial assistance is that it's going to

> impose . . . a greater burden on [Jyzyk], but, more importantly, it's going to have an impact over time on the opportunities . . . and resources that are available to take care of [the parties' daughter].
>
> Now, I don't know whether it's realistic to continue child support at [$]120,000 a year, . . . but given her background and her previous earnings I do not agree that it should be that she does not have any income capacity simply because she chose to relocate to the village of Stebbins and earn nothing. . . .
>
> . . . I do find it a difficult choice in this case because [Jolene] does seem to derive some very valid benefits from being in Stebbins, and I'm sure that for the summers [her daughter] derives some benefits there, too, but then there's the other nine months of the year when [the parties' daughter] lives in Anchorage and she'd be getting $50 a month, if that, instead of . . . $1500 a month, which could go a long way toward providing for necessities and also toward . . . providing for her future needs, educational needs, and to help give her a good start in life.

The record thus reflects that the superior court adequately considered Jolene's personal needs when it determined that her voluntary unemployment was unreasonable.

Despite this consideration, the dissent worries that the superior court "trivialize[s] Alaska Natives' way of life" and "devalues Alaska Natives' cultural, spiritual, and religious connections to their villages and their subsistence lifestyle." Yet in reality the dissent's desired outcome would have enormous financial implications for Alaska Native children. "The primary purpose of Rule 90.3 is to ensure that child support orders are adequate to meet the needs of children, subject to the ability of parents to pay." Granting either parent absolute freedom to exit the workforce would undermine this purpose.

366 P. 3d 66, 74.

For further discussion of this case and how it intersects with the best interest of the child, see Chapter Two.

Some tribes do not have specific statutes governing child support payments. In that case, the tribal court often provides the guidance for how those payments are to be assessed.

In re L.M.D.

13 Am. Tribal Law 441 (Ft. Peck Court of Appeals 2016)

This matter came before the Fort Peck Appellate Court on a Notice of Appeal, filed October 13, 2015 by Appellant Raymond Lamb. Appellant Lamb appears to be challenging paternity regarding the above-named minor child, challenging the award of child support by the lower court on September 28, 2015, and alleging a possible due process violation due to his unavailability to attend the scheduled hearing. Appellee Heather Daniels filed a responsive pleading on March 1, 2016.

On September 22, 2015, a child support hearing was held regarding the above-named minor child. Appellee Daniels appeared at the hearing. Appellant Lamb did not appear. The record reflects that notice of an order granting a continuance for a previously scheduled hearing, along with the date and time of the re-scheduled hearing was served on Appellant Lamb by court process server on August 26, 2015.

After the September 22, 2015 hearing, the court issued an order on September 28, 2015 requiring Appellant Lamb to pay $300 per month in child support.

Statement of Jurisdiction

The Fort Peck Appellate Court has jurisdiction to review all final orders from the Fort Peck Tribal Court when a timely appeal is made. II CCOJ § 202. The order entered on September 28, 2015 is a final order and this appeal is deemed timely filed.

Issues

1. Did the lower court violate due process requirements when it held the hearing on September 22, 2015?

2. Did the lower Court improperly find Appellant Lamb to be the father of the child?

3. Did the lower court abuse it discretion when it awarded $300 per month for child support given the information contained in the lower court record?

Standard of Review

This Court has long recognized that it will not disturb lower court factual findings if such findings are supported by substantial evidence. Nor will it overturn a lower court decision if the lower court does not abuse its discretion when making a final determination in custody and child support matters. Title II CCOJ § 202. See generally *In the Matter of D.R.B.*, FPCOA #327 (2001) and *In the Matter of B.R.Y.*, FPCOA #419 (2003). Questions of law, however, are reviewed de novo. Title II CCOJ § 202.

Discussion

The record in this matter reflects that Appellant Lamb was served notice of the continuance and re-scheduled hearing date on August 26, 2015. Appellant argues that he was gone to training when the re-scheduled hearing was held. Although Appellant could have filed a request for a continuance of the September 22, 2015 hearing, the only request for a continuance in the record relates to an August 2015 hearing. Absent an official request for a continuance by a party, the lower court has no basis for changing the date of a court hearing once it has been scheduled and notice served on the parties.

The imposition of child support is an obligation imposed on parents of minor children to insure a child's needs are adequately met. In situations where the parents were not married, the court must evaluate the issue of paternity prior to imposing child support. The birth certificate for the minor child, admitted at the time of hearing, lists Raymond Lamb as the father. In addition, the evidence submitted to the lower court included an acknowledgement of paternity document signed by Appellant Lamb on June 5, 2015. This document is a notarized statement certifying that the information being provide is true and that the parties understand the responsibilities and consequences arising from signing the acknowledgement. Based on the record, there was sufficient reliable evidence submitted for both the lower court and this Court to determine that Appellant Raymond Lamb is the biological father of the minor child as a matter of law.

Child support is mentioned in Titles 8, 9 and 10 of the Fort Peck Comprehensive Code of Justice, however, there is virtually no guidance provided regarding what factors should be used when determining an appropriate child support amount. Given the lack of any substantive tribal legislation guiding child support calculation matters, the lower court cannot be found to have abused its discretion when determining appropriate child support so long as the lower court record can support the final child support award based on judicially accepted calculation methods. *Redstone v. Tolefson*, FPCOA #357 (2001). Any specific limits on this discretion must be dictated through the tribal legislative process and not imposed by this Court.

Appellant indicates he cannot afford the child support imposed by the lower court. Determinations regarding the abilities of a parent to provide a specific amount of child support must be made by a trial court. Even though Appellant was not present at the lower court hearing, that court still had to base its child support determination on the information provided at the time of scheduled hearing. This Court will not set aside a finding by the lower court arising from a valid hearing unless the record indicates the court abused its discretion in some manner when awarding child support.

Although the lower court record does not articulate the precise reasons for imposing the amount of child support it did, there is nothing in the record to indicate that the imposed child support is unreasonable based on the alleged income of the non-custodial parent. Certainly, modification of a child support award can occur when a trial court finds current circumstances justify changing the amount of the support award. Appellant is free to file a motion requesting modification of the support order with the lower court or to reach an agreement with Appellee regarding child support which can be submitted to the lower court for approval. Appellant can also make a request to the lower court for parenting time with his minor child if the parties cannot mutually agree upon the frequency and length of time for any contact between him and his child. This Court, however, does not have the power to unilaterally modify a child support award or impose parenting time.

Based on the above reasoning, this Court finds no due process violations, errors in application of law or abuse of discretion by the lower court in connection with its determination of child support in its September 28, 2015 order.

Order

The lower court child support order issued September 28, 2015 is hereby AFFIRMED.

SO ORDERED.

Notes

1. Under ICWA, state courts must grant tribal court orders involving "Indian child custody proceedings" full faith and credit. 25 U.S.C. § 1911(d). Whether this would include child support orders is unclear. Presumably, the "child custody proceedings" would be those defined in the federal law. However, some states have provisions to recognize tribal court orders (and vice versa). For example, Michigan's court rule 2.615 provides a protected comity analysis, where if the tribal court recognizes the state court orders, the state court will recognize tribal court orders. This means that state child support orders can be brought to tribal court and enforced, even if the parent works and lives on the reservation.

2. The Alaska Supreme Court has a series of cases that extends tribal jurisdiction and enforcement of orders beyond that defined in ICWA and into other areas of child welfare generally. In holding that the Central Council of Tlingit and Haida Indian Tribe of Alaska had jurisdiction to issue child support orders over both member *and* non-member parents, the Court stated,

> The holding we announce today comports with our previous decisions on the inherent, non-territorial subject matter jurisdiction of tribal courts. In *John I* we held that "[a] tribe's inherent sovereignty to adjudicate internal domestic custody matters depends on the membership or eligibility for membership of the child." Whether the children whose custody was at issue were in fact eligible for tribal membership was contested, and we determined that their eligibility was "a critical fact that must be determined by the superior court on remand." On remand, the superior court "concluded that the children were eligible for membership." In our view, the superior court "correctly determined that [the tribe] had subject matter jurisdiction."
>
> * * *
>
> We are sympathetic to the concerns that nonmember parents may have about contesting their child support rights and obligations in a court system that may be less familiar to them than the state courts. But tribal courts that take on this responsibility share the goals of state courts and parents everywhere: They are, as Central Council's child support enforcement agency states in the first sentence of its governing policy guide, "motivated and dedicated to bettering the future of our children." And what was true in 1999, when *John I* was decided, remains true today: "Recognizing the ability and power of tribes to resolve internal disputes in their own forums, while preserving the right of access to state courts, can only help in the administration of justice for all."

State v. Central Council of Tlingit and Haida Indian Tribes of Alaska, 371 P. 3d 255, 274–5 (Alaska 2016).

E. Family Wellness Courts

Tribes are also extending alternatives to the western-court model in Indian child welfare cases. Family wellness courts are one such alternative. These courts are distinct from juvenile justice courts, healing to wellness courts, peacemaking circles, family group conferencing, and drug courts, because they involve the entire family in the process, including the child who is at risk of abuse or neglect. Family wellness courts create a streamlined process pulling together services to address the multiple issues with which a family struggles. With this coordination, substance abuse, mental health, job loss, and inadequate parenting skills can all be remedied in the same system to create a reunified, healthy family.

What follows is an information sheet that explains the Ho-Chunk Nation's Family Wellness Court as it currently operates, created for the 2016 National Indian Child Welfare Association annual conference. Portions of this information were taken directly from the Participant's Handbook, given to participants of the Family Wellness Court to explain the goals and expectations of the program.

Ho-Chunk Nation Family Wellness Court

Vision Statement: The Ho-Chunk Nation Family Wellness Court strives to prevent the out-of-home placement of Ho-Chunk children resulting from abuse and neglect related to alcohol and other drug abuse and to actively support community members by encouraging healthy, spiritual, and sober lifestyles that will result in positive role models for future generations.

Mission Statement: The Ho-Chunk Nation Family Wellness Court is committed to the well-being and healthy lifestyles of families affected by substance abuse. Family members are provided individualized therapeutic programs designed to strengthen individuals, families, and the community through Ho-Chunk traditional values and spiritual healing.

About the FWC: The Family Wellness Court is a comprehensive alternative court designed to improve child safety and well-being by providing parents access to drug and alcohol treatment, frequent judicial monitoring of their sobriety, and individualized services to support the whole family unit. Participation is 100% voluntary.... Each parent begins at Phase 1 and moves through each phase according to their individual progress made until they complete Phase 5 and graduate. Each participant is evaluated on a case-by-case basis. Failure to make progress and/or graduate may result in children being placed in long term guardianship.

Collaborative Team Approach:

- HCN [Ho-Chunk Nation] Behavioral Health
  - To provide tools required to get into recovery and stay in recovery
- HCN Social Services

  - To receive progress case plan reports and referrals based upon the identified needs and strengths of each individual family
- Vocational Rehabilitation for Native Americans
  - To support participants in their efforts to lead independent lives through employment
- HCN Traditional Court and Clan Mothers
  - To provide cultural knowledge, resources, and perspective when dealing with Ho-Chunk families
- HCN Department of Justice
  - To hold participants accountable to the rules and requirements of the program
- Parent Counsel
  - To represent the parent's interests and advocate for their rights during staff updates and the in the courtroom

Key Aspects and Benefits:

- Immediate intervention
- Comprehensive, holistic assessments
- Frequent informal court interactions with the judge and team
- Graduated responses (sanctions) and incentives (awards) to promote healthy behaviors
- Promotion of participant accountability
- Team approach to supporting treatment
- Being with other similarly situated families
- Services for health care, education, and vocational training
- Individualized treatment plans
- Child and parent focused
- Five phases, each developed with recovery in mind
- Short-term goal setting

Notes

1. What are some benefits to bringing together substance abuse treatment with resources to improve parenting skills?

2. What problems might result from tying together a parent's custody rights with their success in a substance abuse treatment program? Would any expected problems be mitigated by the fact that one team of dedicated individuals is overseeing the progress in both areas?

Chapter 8

International Law

International indigenous child welfare has received a paucity of attention from scholars in the American legal field. Expanding students' and practitioners' horizons on international treatment of indigenous children is a worthwhile endeavor that can offer context and a deeper understanding of ICWA's enforcement methods. Although important information is often located only in foreign language sources, this should not stop students and practitioners from understanding that indigenous peoples all over the world are struggling for the right to raise their children to perpetuate their cultures into the future.

> [A]lthough breaking down the limitations of a legal system dominated by the self-interest of states can be difficult and frustrating, recent attempts at norm creation in the field of indigenous rights have brought together a rich variety of perspectives and ideas on the right to self-determination that can now be constructively employed to forward the domestic debate.... Despite the difficult historical relationship between international law and indigenous peoples, international law now promises to deliver a restructuring of state, group and individual relations that remains much more faithful to the fundamental link between the right to self-determination and decolonization.

Sonia Harris-Short, Aboriginal Child Welfare, Self-Government and the Rights of Indigenous Children 17 (2012).

This chapter will first explore tenets of global laws intended to protect against the involuntary removal of indigenous children from their families. The chapter will then detail the practices of several countries in protecting indigenous children, including practices in Canada, Australia, New Zealand, South America, and Scandinavia. The fight to protect the rights of indigenous peoples to raise their children is not unique to the United States, Canada, Australia, and New Zealand. These four countries often receive the most attention in international indigenous child welfare discourse because of the relatively recent impact of the assimilative effects of colonization on the indigenous populations, and the ease of identifying the countries' indigenous peoples. Identifying indigenous peoples is often a politically charged, complex, and fluid task. *See* Indigenous Peoples and Demography: The Complex Relation Between Identity and Statistics (Per Axelsson & Peter Skold eds., 2011); Rashwet Shrinkhal, *Problems in Defining "Indigenous Peoples" Under International Law*, 7 Chotanagpur L.J. 187 (2014). This chapter aims to give a broader context to the issue of indigenous child welfare.

A. Global Protections

In recent years, a child's right to remain within his family unit has become a necessary inclusion in any work on or for international indigenous peoples. The nineteenth and twentieth centuries were full of "those in power" removing children from the indigenous peoples within their newly created power lines. This has created perpetual cycles of family disruption and child loss that current policy-makers are finding it difficult to rectify in countries across the world. The removal of children from their families not only destroys the fabric of the family and eviscerates any chance for indigenous parents to learn how to become more effective parents, but it threatens the very existence of the indigenous cultural groups as a whole. Without children, there is no one to teach tribal culture and language to into the future, meaning that when the current generation is gone, vast swaths of traditional knowledge disappear. While children are considered important and cherished in many communities around the world, for the indigenous groups that hold their children as sacred, the loss of children can lead to the breakdown of religions, kinship and traditional governing structures, and important ties to the land and place that the indigenous groups maintain. Without appropriate protections for children, indigenous groups can quite literally vanish.

The 2007 passage of the United Nations Declaration on the Rights of Indigenous Peoples (UNDRIP) was a tremendous win for all aspects of indigenous peoples' rights. Activists, scholars, and politicians now have a uniform document, supported by an influential political body, to point to when calling for protections and rights for indigenous peoples. While the non-binding nature of the document lessens its force in American jurisprudence, UNDRIPs existence recognizes the need for all United Nations member countries to consider indigenous peoples in all governmental decisions. *See* Sonia Harris-Short, Aboriginal Child Welfare, Self-Government and the Rights of Indigenous Children, Chpt. 6 (2012). Article 7 of UNDRIP specifically protects against the removal of indigenous children from their families and communities.

> Indigenous peoples have the collective right to live in freedom, peace and security as distinct peoples and shall not be subjected to any act of genocide or any other act of violence, including forcibly removing children of the group to another group.

G.A. Res. 61/295, annex art. 7(2), United Nations Declaration on the Rights of Indigenous Peoples, U.N. Doc. A/RES/61/295 (Oct. 2, 2007).

The first major international document of the modern era focusing on indigenous peoples was the International Labour Conference's (ILO) Convention No. 169 of 1989. This document was a revision of the ILO's earlier Indigenous and Tribal Populations Convention of 1957. ILO Convention No. 169 was the first to recognize "the right of [indigenous] peoples to be involved in the decision-making process as it affects them." Lee Swepston, *A New Step in the International Law on Indigenous and Tribal Peoples: ILO Convention No. 169 of 1989*, 15 Okla. City U. L. Rev. 677,

690 (1990). Article 28 of Convention No. 169 specifically recognizes the right that children have to be raised in the culture of their communities as it relates to literacy: "Children belonging to the peoples concerned shall, wherever practicable be taught to read and write in their own indigenous language or in the language most commonly used by the group to which they belong." International Labour Conference [ILO] Convention No. 169, art. 28(1).

The linking of children and culture is at the forefront of the United Nations Convention on the Rights of the Child, which has been signed and ratified by every nation-state member of the United Nations except the United States. Article 30 of the CRC ensures that "a child . . . who is indigenous shall not be denied the right, in community with other members of his or her group, to enjoy his or her own culture, to profess and practice his or her own religion, or to use his or her own language." United Nations Convention on the Rights of the Child art. 30, Nov. 20, 1989 1577 U.N.T.S. 3. The CRC's language is reflective of Article 27 of the International Covenant on Civil and Political Rights, which protects the rights of indigenous peoples, "in community with the other members of their group, to enjoy their own culture, to profess and practice their own religion, or to use their own language." International Covenant on Civil and Political Rights art. 27, Dec. 19, 1966, 999 U.N.T.S. 171. Neither this, nor the mandate in the CRC, is possible unless indigenous children are kept in their own communities, with their families or kinship relations, who can ensure the child will be raised in his or her own culture.

For more information on the growing number of international laws that support the rights of indigenous children to live within their families and communities, see Kristen A. Carpenter & Lorie M. Graham, *Human Rights to Culture, Family, and Self-Determination: The Case of Adoptive Couple v. Baby Girl, in* Indigenous Rights in International Law (Stefan Kirchner & Joan Policastri eds., *forthcoming*); *see also* Sonia Harris-Short, Aboriginal Child Welfare, Self-Government and the Rights of Indigenous Children (2012).

B. Canada

Canada's atrocious treatment of indigenous children has spanned more than two centuries and still continues today. Through forced geographic removal, boarding schools, sterilizations, and massive underfunding of social services and educational systems, indigenous children in Canada, often classified as either First Nations, Inuit, or Métis, and often falling within the term aboriginal, have continually been separated from their families. In the years of 2000–2002, 40% of children living in care in Canada were First Nations, Inuit, or Métis. Nico Trocmé, Della Knoke & Cindy Blackstock, *Pathways to the Overrepresentation of Aboriginal Children in Canada's Child Welfare System*, 78 Soc. Serv. Rev. 577, 577–78 (2004) (citing Cheryl Farris-Manning & Marietta Zandstra, *Children in Care in Canada: A Summary of Current Issues and Trends with Recommendations for Future Research*, Child Welfare League of Canada 2003). Some reports indicate that indigenous children "comprise nearly 80 percent of children living in out-of-home care." *Id.* at 578. With less than 5% of children in Canada identifying as aboriginal, this is a vast and disturbing disparity. *Id.*

Canada does not have a national policy for First Nations children equivalent to the United States' Indian Child Welfare Act. Although there have been strides of movement in the direction of recognizing the need for First Nations children to be raised by First Nations parents, for many years, the controlling decision by the Canadian Supreme Court in child welfare deemphasized a child's culture as a factor in placement after removal.

> [W]hen the test to be met is the best interests of the child, the significance of cultural background and heritage as opposed to bonding abates over time. The closer the bond that develops with the prospective parents the less important the racial element becomes.

Racine v. Woods [1983] 2 S.C.R. 173, 183 (Can.).

1. Residential Schools

Canada's indigenous populations suffered from some of the longest-running, most tortious residential (boarding) schools. Canada's residential schools have been accused of some of the worst physical, sexual, and emotional abuse in recorded history, continuing into the 1970s.

> It can start with a knock on the door one morning. It is the local Indian agent, or the parish priest, or, perhaps, a Mounted Police officer. The bus for residential school leaves that morning. It is a day the parents have been long dreading. Even if the children have been warned in advance, the morning's events are still a shock. The officials have arrived and the children must go.
>
> For tens of thousands of Aboriginal children for over a century, this was the beginning of their residential schooling. They were torn from their parents, who often surrendered them only under threat of prosecution. Then, they were hurled into a strange and frightening place, one in which their parents and culture would be demeaned and oppressed.

Truth & Reconciliation Commission of Canada, Honouring the Truth, Reconciling for the Future: Summary of the Final Report of the Truth & Reconciliation Commission of Canada 37 (2015), *available at* http://www.trc.ca/websites/trcinstitution/File/2015/Honouring_the_Truth_Reconciling_for_the_Future_July_23_2015.pdf. Appropriately addressing the criminal acts perpetrated on children takes far more space than allocated in this textbook. For resources that properly address the sphere of abuses, see Celia Haig-Brown, Resistance and Renewal: Surviving the Indian Residential School (1988); Agnes Grant, Finding My Talk: How Fourteen Canadian Native Women Reclaimed Their Lives After Residential School (2005); Behind Closed Doors: Stories from the Kamloops Indian Residential School (2006);

Brent Stonefish, Moving Beyond: Understanding the Impacts of the Residential Schools (2007).

Announced in 2006 and implemented in 2007, the Canadian federal government agreed to a $2 billion plan to compensate survivors of the residential school children.[1] The settlement contained five separate areas of relief. First, it allocated $1.9 billion to a Common Experience Payment Fund to allocate lump sum payments to survivors of the residential school system. Second, it set additional money aside as part of an Independent Assessment Process, to offer more compensation to those who suffered severe physical or sexual abuses. Third, the fund allocated $125 million to the Aboriginal Healing Foundation to fund programs to help former students and their families with emotional, spiritual, and physical healing. Fourth, the settlement required the creation of a Truth and Reconciliation Commission and allocated $60 million to its mission (discussed below). Finally, the settlement allocated $20 million towards a Commemoration Fund, dedicated towards creating national and community projects to remember and bring awareness to the residential school system. *See* Indian Residential Schools Settlement Agreement 22–24, 43–53 (May 8, 2006), *available at* http://www.residentialschoolsettlement.ca/english.html.

As mandated in the settlement agreement, the Truth and Reconciliation Commission was established to address, in a non-monetary way, the impacts of Canada's residential schools. The Commission was a five year mandated process to collect stories, statements, documents, and other materials relating to the indigenous experience in residential boarding schools, and to disseminate that information with all of Canada, so that Canadians are aware of what has happened in their country's recent history. *Schedule N*, Indian Residential Schools Settlement Agreement 1-2 (May 8, 2006), *available at* http://www.residentialschoolsettlement.ca/SCHEDULE_N.pdf. The chair of the Commission , Justice Murray Sinclair, was the first Aboriginal judge in Manitoba prior to his appointment to the Truth and Reconciliation Commission. *See Meet the Commissioners*, Truth and Reconciliation Commission of Canada, http://www.trc.ca/websites/trcinstitution/index.php?p=5 (last accessed May 24, 2016).

The six volume report was released in 2015, capturing testimonies from nearly 7,000 witnesses, including 1,300 hours of oral history and countless records from the residential schools, the churches that ran them, and the governments that were charged with supervision of the residential schools. Truth and Reconciliation Commission of Canada, *TRC Final Report*, Truth and Reconciliation Commission of Canada (2015), http://www.trc.ca/websites/trcinstitution/index.php?p=890. The report collects the history of residential schools; stories of survivors and the impact that the residential schools had on their lives; and the lingering impact that remains on the country of Canada. Culminating with seven national events held by the

---

1. This class action excluded residential schools located in Newfoundland and Labrador, as well as individuals who were educated through the residential schools, but in a day-school format. Ongoing class actions are attempting to provide relief and compensation to these victims.

Truth and Reconciliation Commission to encourage national conversations about the residential schools, the report contains 94 separate calls to action to continue the reconciliation process and make a positive change in the lives of Canada's aboriginal peoples. *Calls to Action*, Truth and Reconciliation Commission of Canada (2015), http://www.trc.ca/websites/trcinstitution/File/2015/Findings/Calls_to_Action_English2.pdf. The very first set of calls to action center on child welfare:

1. We call upon the federal, provincial, territorial, and Aboriginal governments to commit to reducing the number of Aboriginal children in care by:
   i. Monitoring and assessing neglect investigations.
   ii. Providing adequate resources to enable Aboriginal communities and child-welfare organizations to keep Aboriginal families together where it is safe to do so, and to keep children in culturally appropriate environments, regardless of where they reside.
   iii. Ensuring that social workers and others who conduct child-welfare investigations are properly educated and trained about the history and impacts of residential schools.
   iv. Ensuring that social workers and others who conduct child-welfare investigations are properly educated and trained about the potential for Aboriginal communities and families to provide more appropriate solutions to family healing.
   v. Requiring that all child-welfare decision makers consider the impact of the residential school experience on children and their caregivers.
2. We call upon the federal government, in collaboration with the provinces and territories, to prepare and publish annual reports on the number of Aboriginal children (First Nations, Inuit, and Métis) who are in care, compared with non-Aboriginal children, as well as the reasons for apprehension, the total spending on preventive and care services by child-welfare agencies, and the effectiveness of various interventions.
3. We call upon all levels of government to fully implement Jordan's Principle.[2]

---

2. [Editor's footnote] Jordan's Principle was established to guide determinations regarding whether the federal or provincial governments must pay for the at-home care of status First Nation's children living on reserves in Canada. Jordan River Anderson, a Norway House Cree Nation child, was born with special needs and was required to spend the first two years of his life in the hospital. Once he was healthy enough to return home, a funding dispute broke out between the federal and provincial governments regarding which was required to pay for his extensive at home medical care. Jordan died in the hospital while awaiting the result. In 2007, the House of Commons passed Motion 296, which requires that First Nation's children be provided any necessary care first, with discussion of payment between the federal and provincial governments coming only after services have been provided. There remains an ongoing reluctance on the part of Canadian governments to fully implement Jordan's Principle. *See Jordan's Principle—Timeline and Documents*, First Nations Child & Family Caring Society of Canada, https://fncaringsociety.com/jordans-timeline (last visited May 23, 2016).

4. We call upon the federal government to enact Aboriginal child-welfare legislation that establishes national standards for Aboriginal child apprehension and custody cases and includes principles that:
   i. Affirm the right of Aboriginal governments to establish and maintain their own child-welfare agencies.
   ii. Require all child-welfare agencies and courts to take the residential school legacy into account in their decision making.
   iii. Establish, as an important priority, a requirement that placements of Aboriginal children into temporary and permanent care be culturally appropriate.
5. We call upon the federal, provincial, territorial, and Aboriginal governments to develop culturally appropriate parenting programs for Aboriginal families.

Id. at 1. The widely-distributed executive summary of the report is available at http://www.trc.ca/websites/trcinstitution/File/2015/Honouring_the_Truth_Reconciling_for_the_Future_July_23_2015.pdf. The summary covers the role of the Commission, the history and enduring legacy of the residential schools, the complex challenge of reconciliation in Canada, and the detailed calls to action from the government and citizens of Canada. The intergenerational trauma stemming from Canada's boarding school history will linger far into the future, but Canada is beginning to take important steps to rectify the wrongs of that history.

2. Sixties Scoop

Canada continues to deal with a crisis involving the rearing of its current children. Beginning with the "Sixties' Scoop," First Nations, Inuit, and Métis children were removed from their homes to be raised in non-indigenous communities. The following case illustrates how this systemic removal developed and the current remedial efforts.

Brown v. Canada (Attorney General)

2010 ONSC 3095 (Ontario Superior Court of Justice May 26, 2010)

Perell, J.:

The aboriginal communities in Ontario refer to it as the "Sixties' Scoop." For a time, and particularly for a nineteen-year period between 1965 and 1984, welfare authorities in Ontario removed many Indian and aboriginal children from their families and communities and placed them with foster or adoptive parents that were non-aboriginals. It is alleged that many of the "scooped" children lost their identity as aboriginal persons and suffered mentally and physically. The aboriginal communities describe the effects of the Sixties Scoop as horrendous, destructive, devastating, and tragic.

Marcia Brown and Roberta Commanda are aboriginals of Ojibway ancestry, and they were scooped children. In this proposed class action, which was commenced on February 9, 2009, notably they do not sue the Ontario welfare authorities. They sue only the Federal Crown. They accuse the Federal Crown of a systemic assimilation policy purposely designed to destroy First Nations families and communities. They bring their action on behalf of approximately 16,000 aboriginals who, they allege, were the victims of a deliberate program of "identity genocide of children" that occurred in Ontario between December 1, 1965 and December 31, 1984. Their litigation is supported by a resolution of the Chiefs of Ontario adopted on November 20, 2008.

Ms. Brown and Mr. Commanda allege that during the 19 years between December 1, 1965 and December 31, 1984, when new child welfare legislation came into force in Ontario, the Federal Crown wrongfully delegated its exclusive responsibility as guardian, trustee, protector, and fiduciary of aboriginal persons by entering into an agreement with Ontario that authorized a child welfare program that systemically eradicated the aboriginal culture, society, language, customs, traditions, and spirituality of the children.

Ms. Brown and Mr. Commanda allege that they personally suffered from Ontario's child protection program; they experienced psychological problems associated with a loss of culture, self-esteem, and identity. They claim damages of $50,000 per class member and a declaration that the Federal Crown breached its non-delegable fiduciary obligation and duty of care to protect aboriginal rights and did commit the actionable wrong of "identity genocide."

Ms. Brown and Mr. Commanda make a motion to have their action certified as a class action. The Federal Crown makes a motion to have their action dismissed as disclosing no reasonable cause of action.

On both sides, there are some very powerful emotive and rhetorical forces at work. On the side of Ms. Brown and Mr. Commanda, there is the primal emotions shared by individuals and communities to love, to cherish, to care, and to protect their children, and there is the primal fear that their children will be taken away by an enemy. There is the communal fear of extinction as a community, culture, and race. On the side of the Federal Crown there is the outrage, the embarrassment, and the indignity of being accused of racist and colonial acts of the gravest moral turpitude and criminality and the sentiment that the accusations are slanderous, unfair, and false. The dignity and pride of both sides is offended.

It is necessary that these forces be acknowledged so that passion does not overcome reason. It is also necessary to acknowledge that Ms. Brown's and Mr. Commanda's action involves the implicit submission that the courts of Ontario were complicit in perpetrating a great evil and that the Federal Crown's defence to the action and to the motion now before the court involves the explicit counter-submission that during the years of the Sixties Scoop, the courts were acting properly, honourably, and in the best interests of the aboriginal children that were the subject of their orders. . . .

The legitimate target or focus of the certifiable class action that emerges is that of answering a complex, difficult but largely legal question. The question is:

> In Ontario, between December 1, 1965 and December 31, 1984, when an aboriginal child was placed in the care of non-aboriginal foster or adoptive parents who did not raise the child in accordance with the child's aboriginal customs, traditions, and practices, did the federal Crown have and breach a fiduciary or common law duty of care to take reasonable steps to prevent the aboriginal child from losing his or her aboriginal identity?

If this question were answered in the negative at a common issues trial, 16,000 potential claims would be dismissed. If this question were answered in the positive, then there would have to be individual trials to determine whether or not any individual class member can prove identification as an aboriginal, causation, damages, and the quantum of compensation. Both the common issue and the individual issues trials will be difficult, particularly the matter of causation, but Ms. Brown and Mr. Commanda and any others like them should have their day in court to attempt to prove an entitlement to compensation, as should the Federal Crown have its day in court to refute the allegations made against it. . . .

Social worker Mr. Richard deposed that there were a large number of aboriginal children who were removed from their families and that these removals have come to be known in the aboriginal community as the "Sixties Scoop." It was his opinion that the survivors of the Sixties Scoop had lost touch with their culture, customs, traditions, language, and spirituality. In his opinion, they experienced a loss of self esteem, identity crisis, and were socially dysfunctional requiring therapy and counseling. He stated:

> In my experience, it does not matter how "attached" or "bonded" were the children to their non-native and non-Indian homes, or even how benign an environment it may have been provided that wherever they were placed, they lost touch or connection with their particular indigenous Indian or native culture, customs, traditions, language and spirituality. This is a common effect of the "Sixties Scoop." It presents problems independent of whatever particular level of care and comfort, or lack of care and comfort the Indian or native person experienced as a child.

Psychologist Dr. Bodnor deposed that the loss of culture was a matter of great concern to First Nations individuals and communities. She deposed that for aboriginals, the loss of cultural identity caused low self-esteem, depression, anxiety, suicidal ideation, suicide, physical illnesses without clear causes, difficulties in parenting, difficulties in maintaining positive relationships, substance abuse and violence. She deposed that for communities, loss of culture caused loss of traditional economic viability, loss of self-government, loss of language, loss of land base and land based teachings, loss of traditional spiritual and religious practices, loss of life cycle teachings and rituals, and loss of integrity and self-esteem.

Dr. Bodnor deposed that recovering one's culture had clinical benefits leading to increased self-esteem, reduced substance abuse, less suicide, reduced anxiety, the development of a sense of pride and a positive sense of belonging in the world.

It was Dr. Bodnor's opinion that since the individual aboriginal's suffering and loss of identity affected the whole community, the process for recovery would be more effective as a collective experience. I understand that this opinion was advanced in support of the argument that a class proceeding would be the preferable procedure for the resolution of the claims of the class.

Vernon Harper, who is employed by the Aboriginal Services Program Center for Addiction and Mental Health in Toronto, is an "Urban Elder." He deposed that much of the therapeutic work that he does involved treating Indians who had a breakdown in their relationship with the non-Indians who had raised them. He deposed that the loss of identity emerged as the trauma of trying to re-claim one's identity and the culture, traditions, and spirituality that comprised that identity.

Psychiatrist, Dr. Armstrong, who among other things was the chairperson of the Canadian Psychiatric Association Section on Native Mental Health for many years and who directed a University of Toronto program that provided mental health services to about 15,000 Cree and Ojibway people deposed that the First Nations people of Ontario "experienced intentional and inadvertent culture/identity genocide."

It was Dr. Armstong's opinion that:

> In the early part of the 20th century, Canada applied a policy of cultural extermination when officials seized thousands of native children from their homes on the reserve and committed them to residential schools that not only deprived them of the experience of living in an aboriginal family, but punished them for expressing their Indian customs, traditions and languages.
>
> That in the 1960s, 70s and 80s, ill-informed child welfare workers in Ontario, who did not know enough about native communities and their resources to parent and protect the community's children, removed children and placed them with non-Indian caregivers with the same intention as of the residential school experience, albeit in the context of a replacement family rather than a residential school setting.
>
> This was a misguided policy based on the belief that the answer to the Indian problem was to assimilate the Indian children into mainstream culture.
>
> The effect of this policy was loss of culture, loss of language, loss of ability to parent as an aboriginal person, loss of identity, increased rate of psychopathology, confused identity formulation, psychiatric disorders, substance

abuse, emotional isolation, violence, unemployment, feelings of betrayal, and extreme lack of emotional attachment.

Notes

1. The court above went on to conditionally approve class action status in the above lawsuit. However, that decision was later reversed by *Brown v. Canada (Attorney General)*, 2011 ONSC 7712 (Ont. Div. Ct., Dec. 28, 2011), and the reversal was affirmed by *Brown v. Canada (Attorney General)*, 2013 ONCA 18 (Ont. Ct. App. Jan. 17, 2013).

2. The Court in *Brown v. Canada* centers its discussion around the claim and concept of an "identity genocide of children" that occurred during the "Sixties' Scoop." Should an "identify genocide" be considered under the same rubric in international law as a "genocide"? What remedy can a court offer for "identity genocide"?

3. As with the cyclical problem of children removal in the United States, the "Sixties' Scoop" has led to high numbers of children in care in Canada. The following section details the current issues that children in care face, along with some of the progress that has been made to ensure that First Nations, Inuit, and Métis children can remain safely with their families.

3. Current Children in Care

Aboriginal Canadian children still suffer from a gross disproportionality of placements in the child care system. There are an estimated three times more First Nations, Inuit, and Métis children in care now than were in residential schools at any one time. *See, e.g.*, Cindy Blackstock, *Residential Schools: Did They Really Close or Just Morph into Child Welfare?* 6 Indigenous L.J. 71, 74 (2007) (citing Assembly of First Nations, Leadership Action Plan on First Nations Child Welfare (2006)). For more statistics on the disproportionality of Aboriginal children in care in Canada, see Ashley Quinn, *Reflections on Intergenerational Trauma: Healing as a Critical Intervention*, 3 First Peoples Child & Fam. Rev. 72 (2007).

In an attempt to remedy this disproportionality, First Nations are beginning to develop their own child and family services systems. These First Nations Child and Family Services Agencies are funded through Program Directive 20.1, which requires the First Nations to enter into a funding agreement based on data with the Canadian federal government, and into agreements with the local provincial government regarding the FNCFSA's authority, jurisdiction, and transfer provisions within the program. The administration of Program Directive 20.1 and FNCFSAs were recently the subject of a major decision by the Canadian Human Rights Tribunal. The Tribunal exposed the massive disparities in the funding granted to FNCFSAs versus the local child and family services systems, up to 22% less per child in some cases. The Tribunal also uncovered other issues with the funding scheme, such as only allowing reimbursement for services after a child is removed from the home, denigrating the incentive for an agency to keep a child with their family.

See Sarah Clarke, *Ending Discrimination and Protecting Equality: A Challenge to the INAC Funding Formula of First Nations Child and Family Service Agencies*, 6 Indigenous L.J. 79, 81 (2007).

First Nations Child and Family Caring Society of Canada v. Attorney General of Canada

No. T1340/7008, 2016 Canadian Human Rights Tribunal 2 (Jan. 26, 2016),

. . .

At issue are the activities of Indian and Northern Affairs Canada (INAC), known at the time of the hearing as Aboriginal Affairs and Northern Development Canada (AANDC), in managing the First Nations Child and Family Services Program (the FNCFS Program), its corresponding funding formulas and a handful of other related provincial and territorial agreements that provide for child and family services to First Nations living on reserve and in the Yukon Territory. Pursuant to the FNCFS Program and other agreements, child and family services are provided to First Nations on-reserve and in the Yukon by First Nations Child and Family Services Agencies (FNCFS Agencies) or by the province/territory in which the community is located. In either situation, the child and family services legislation of the province/territory in which the First Nation is located applies. AANDC funds the child and family services provided to First Nations by FNCFS Agencies or the province/territory.

Pursuant to section 5 of the Canadian Human Rights Act (the CHRA), the Complainants, the First Nations Child and Family Caring Society of Canada (the Caring Society) and the Assembly of First Nations (the AFN), allege AANDC discriminates in providing child and family services to First Nations on reserve and in the Yukon, on the basis of race and/or national or ethnic origin, by providing inequitable and insufficient funding for those services (the Complaint). On October 14, 2008, the Canadian Human Rights Commission (the Commission) referred the Complaint to this Tribunal for an inquiry. . . .

In the context of this Complaint, under section 5 of the CHRA, the Complainants must demonstrate (1) that First Nations have a characteristic or characteristics protected from discrimination; (2) that they are denied services, or adversely impacted by the provision of services, by AANDC; and, (3) that the protected characteristic or 7 characteristics are a factor in the adverse impact or denial (see *Moore v. British Columbia (Education)*, 2012 SCC 61 at para. 33 [*Moore*]).

The first element is relatively simple in this case: race and national or ethnic origin are prohibited grounds of discrimination under section 3 of the CHRA. There was no dispute that First Nations possess these characteristics.

The second element requires the Complainants to establish that AANDC is actually involved in the provision of a "service" as contemplated by section 5 of the CHRA; and, if so, to demonstrate that First Nations are denied services or adversely impacted by AANDC's involvement in the provision of those services.

For the third element, the Complainants have to establish a connection between elements one and two. . . .

It is through this lens, and with these principles in mind, that the Panel examined the evidence and arguments advanced by the parties in this case. For the reasons that follow, the Panel finds AANDC is involved in the provision of child and family services to First Nations on reserves and in the Yukon; that First Nations are adversely impacted by the provision of those services by AANDC, and, in some cases, denied those services as a result of AANDC's involvement; and; that race and/or national or ethnic origin are a factor in those adverse impacts or denial. . . .

The FNCFS Program, corresponding funding formulas and other related provincial/territorial agreements intend to provide funding to ensure the safety and well-being of First Nations children on reserve by supporting culturally appropriate child and family services that are meant to be in accordance with provincial/territorial legislation and standards and be provided in a reasonably comparable manner to those provided off -reserve in similar circumstances. However, the evidence above indicates that AANDC is far from meeting these intended goals and, in fact, that First Nations are adversely impacted and, in some cases, denied adequate child welfare services by the application of the FNCFS Program and other funding methods.

Under the FNCFS Program, Directive 20-1 has a number of shortcomings and creates incentives to remove children from their homes and communities. Mainly, Directive 20-1 makes assumptions based on population thresholds and children in care to fund the operations budgets of FNCFS Agencies. These assumptions ignore the real child welfare situation in many First Nations' communities on reserve. Whereas operations budgets are fixed, maintenance budgets for taking children into care are reimbursable at cost. If an FNCFS Agency does not have the funds to provide services through its operations budget, often times the only way to provide the necessary child and family services is to bring the child into care. For small and remote agencies, the population thresholds of Directive 20-1 significantly reduce their operations budgets, affecting their ability to provide effective programming, respond to emergencies and, for some, put them in jeopardy of closing. . . .

AANDC incorporated some of the same shortcomings of Directive 20-1 into the EPFA, such as the assumptions about children in care and population levels, along with the fixed streams of funding for operations and prevention. Despite being aware of these shortcomings in Directive 20-1 based on numerous reports, AANDC has not followed the recommendations in those reports and has perpetuated the main shortcoming of the FNCFS Program: the incentive to take children into care—to remove them from their families. . . .

The provision of child and family services under the FNCFS Program and the other provincial agreements are specifically aimed at First Nations living on reserve. Under the Yukon Agreement, the services are aimed at all First Nations living in the territory. That is, the determination of the public to which the services are offered is based uniquely on the race and/or ethnic origin of the service recipients. Pursuant to the application of the FNCFS Program, corresponding funding formulas and the other provincial/territorial agreements, First Nations people living on reserve and in the Yukon are prima facie adversely differentiated and/or denied services because of their race and/or national or ethnic origin in the provision of child and family services.

AANDC argues there is no evidence that any changes to the FNCFS Program and corresponding funding formulas or the other related provincial/territorial agreements would lead to better outcomes for First Nations children and families. Therefore, it argues the Complainants have failed to establish a prima facie case of discrimination. In any event, the question of whether federal funding is sufficient to meet a perceived need is beyond the scope of an investigation into discrimination under section 5 of the CHRA.

The prima facie discrimination analysis is not concerned with proposed outcomes. It is concerned with adverse impacts and whether a prohibited ground is a factor in any adverse impacts. Proposed outcomes only come into play if the complaint is substantiated and an order from the Tribunal is required to rectify the discrimination under section 53(2) of the CHRA. The Panel also disagrees that the question of whether funding is sufficient to meet a perceived need is beyond the scope of an investigation into discrimination under the CHRA. That question and evidence related thereto informs the ultimate determination to be made in this case: whether First Nations children and families residing on-reserve have an opportunity equal with other individuals in accessing child and family services. That is, it addresses the issue of substantive equality. . . .

In providing the benefit of the FNCFS Program and the other related provincial/territorial agreements, AANDC is obliged to ensure that its involvement in the provision of child and family services does not perpetuate the historical disadvantages endured by Aboriginal peoples. If AANDC's conduct widens the gap between First Nations and the rest of Canadian society rather than narrowing it, then it is discriminatory (see A at para. 332; and, *Eldridge* at para. 73).

The evidence in this case not only indicates various adverse effects on First Nations children and families by the application of AANDC's FNCFS Program, corresponding funding formulas and other related provincial/territorial agreements, but also that these adverse effects perpetuate historical disadvantages suffered by Aboriginal peoples, mainly as a result of the Residential Schools system.

Please note that the information below contains graphic facts about Residential Schools. If this information causes distress, especially for survivors and their families, a 24-hour Indian Residential Schools Crisis Line has been set up to provide support, including emotional and crisis referral services: 1-866-925-4419 . . .

During the Residential Schools era, Aboriginal children were removed from their homes, often forcibly, and brought to residential schools to be "civilized". Living conditions in many cases were appalling, giving place to disease, hunger, stress, and despair. Children were often cold, overworked, shamed and could not speak their native language for fear of severe punishment, including some students who had needles inserted into their tongues. Many children were verbally, sexually and/or physically abused. There were instances where students were forced to eat their own vomit. Some children were locked in closets, cages, and basements. Others managed to run away, but some of those who did so during the winter months died in the cold weather. Many children committed suicide as a result of attending a Residential School.

Overall, a large number of Aboriginal children under the supervision of the Residential Schools system died while "in -care" (see A National Crime at p. 51). Many of those who managed to survive the ordeal are psychologically scarred as a result. In addition to the impacts on individuals, Dr. Milloy also explained how the Residential Schools affected First Nations communities as a whole. In losing future generations to the Residential Schools, the culture, language and the very survival of many First Nations communities was put in jeopardy. . . .

Residential Schools operated as a "school system" from the 1880's until the 1960's, when it became a marked component of the child welfare system. In about 1969, the Church's involvement in the Residential Schools system ceased, and the federal government took over sole management of the institutions. At around the same time, new regulations came into effect outlining who could attend Residential Schools, placing an emphasis on orphans and "neglected" children. The primary role of many Residential Schools changed from a focus on "education" to a focus on "child welfare". Despite this, many children were not sent home, because their parents were assessed as not being able to assume the responsibility for the care of their children (see A National Crime at pp. 211–212; and, testimony of Dr. Milloy, Transcript Vol. 34 at pp. 19–20).

Over a 50-year period, between the 1930's to the 1980's, the number of schools declined steadily from 78 schools in 1930 down to 12 schools in 1980. The last school closed in 1986. The FNCFS Program is then implemented in 1990. . . .

Dr. Bombay explained how Residential Schools fits into the larger traumatic history that Aboriginal peoples have been exposed to[.]

> . . . for indigenous groups in Canada and worldwide, colonialism has comprised multiple collective traumas [. . .] these include things like military conquest, epidemic diseases and forced relocation.
>
> So Indian residential schools is really just one example of one collective trauma which is part of a larger traumatic history that aboriginal peoples have already been exposed to.
>
> (Transcript Vol. 40 at p. 94)

According to Dr. Bombay, these collective traumas have had a cumulative effect over time, namely on individual and community health (see Transcript Vol. 40 at

p. 83). In her words: "these collective effects are greater than the sum of the individual effects" (Transcript Vol. 40 at p. 82). Similar effects have been shown in other populations and in other groups who have undergone similar collective traumas, such as Holocaust survivors, Japanese Americans subjected to internment during World War II, and survivors of the Turkish genocide of Armenians (see Transcript Vol. 40 at pp. 111–112). To measure and describe the fact that some groups have undergone this chronic exposure to collective traumas, Dr. Maria Yellow Horse Brave Heart of the University of New Mexico coined the term "historical trauma", which is defined as ". . . the cumulative emotional and psychological wounding over the lifespan across generations emanating from massive group trauma" (see testimony of Dr. Bombay, Transcript Vol. 40 at pp. 94–95).

For Residential School survivors, Dr. Bombay indicated that they are more likely to suffer from various physical and mental health problems compared to Aboriginal adults who did not attend. For example, Residential School survivors report higher levels of psychological distress compared to those who did not attend, and they are also more likely to be diagnosed with a chronic physical health condition (see Transcript Vol. 40 at pp. 109–110). . . .

Generationally, the above noted impacts could descend from the Residential School survivor, to their children and then to their grandchildren. In this regard, Dr. Bombay indicated, relying on the 2002–2003 Regional Health Survey, that 43% of First Nations adults on-reserve perceived that their parents' attendance at Residential School negatively affected the parenting that they received while growing up; 73.4% believed that their grandparents' attendance at Residential School negatively affected the parenting that their parents received; 37.2% of First Nations adults whose parents attended Residential School had contemplated suicide in their life versus 25.7% whose parents did not; and, the grandchildren of survivors were also at an increased risk for suicide as 28.4% had attempted suicide versus only 13.1% of those whose grandparents did not attend Residential School (see Transcript at Vol. 40 pp. 110–11, 114–115). . . .

Similar to the Residential Schools era, today, the fate and future of many First Nations children is still being determined by the government, whether it is through the application of restrictive and inadequate funding formulas or through bilateral agreements with the provinces. The purpose of having a First Nation community deliver child and family services, and to be involved through a Band Representative, is to ensure services are culturally appropriate and reflect the needs of the community. This in turn may help legitimize the child and family services in the eyes of the community, increasing their effectiveness, and ultimately help rebuild individuals, families and communities that have been heavily affected by the Residential Schools system and other historical trauma.

In this regard, it should be noted again that the federal government is in a fiduciary relationship with Aboriginal peoples and has undertaken to improve outcomes for First Nations children and families in the provision of child and family services. On this basis, more has to be done to ensure that the provision of child and family services on First Nations reserves is meeting the best interest of those communities and, in the particular context of this case, the best interest of First Nations children. This also corresponds to Canada's international commitments recognizing the special status of children and Indigenous peoples.

[The Tribunal undertook a lengthy discussion of the applicable international human rights laws that supported its judgment.] . . .

The international instruments and treaty monitoring bodies referred to above view equality to be substantive and not merely formal. Consequently, they consider that specific measures, including of a budgetary nature, are often required in order to achieve substantive equality. These international legal instruments also reinforce the need for due attention to be paid to the unique situation and needs of children and First Nations people, especially the combination of those two vulnerable groups: First Nations children.

The concerns expressed by international monitoring bodies mirror many of the issues raised in this Complaint. The declarations made by Canada in its periodic reports to the various monitoring bodies clearly show that the federal government is aware of the steps to be taken domestically to address these issues. Canada's statements and commitments, whether expressed on the international scene or at the national level, should not be allowed to remain empty rhetoric.

Substantive equality and Canada's international obligations require that First Nations children on-reserve be provided child and family services of comparable quality and accessibility as those provided to all Canadians off-reserve, including that they be sufficiently funded to meet the real needs of First Nations children and families and do not perpetuate historical disadvantage.

In light of the above, the Panel finds the Complainants have presented sufficient evidence to establish a prima facie case of discrimination under section 5 of the CHRA. Specifically, they prima facie established that First Nations children and families living on reserve and in the Yukon are denied [s. 5(a)] equal child and family services and/or differentiated adversely [s. 5(b)] in the provision of child and family services. . . .

Despite being aware of the adverse impacts resulting from the FNCFS Program for many years, AANDC has not significantly modified the program since its inception in 1990. Nor have the schedules of the 1965 Agreement in Ontario been updated since 1998. Notwithstanding numerous reports and recommendations to address the adverse impacts outlined above, including its own internal analysis and evaluations, AANDC has sparingly implemented the findings of those reports. While efforts have been made to improve the FNCFS Program, including through the EPFA and other additional funding, those improvements still fall short of addressing the service gaps, denials and adverse impacts outlined above and, ultimately, fail to meet the goal of providing culturally appropriate child and family services to First Nations children and families living on-reserve that are reasonably comparable to those provided off-reserve.

This concept of reasonable comparability is one of the issues at the heart of the problem. AANDC has difficulty defining what it means and putting it into practice, mainly because its funding authorities and interpretation thereof are not in line with provincial/territorial legislation and standards. Despite not being experts in the area of child welfare and knowing that funding according to its authorities is often insufficient to meet provincial/territorial legislation and standards, AANDC insists that FNCFS Agencies somehow abide by those standards and provide reasonably comparable child and family services. Instead of assessing the needs of First Nations children and families and using provincial legislation and standards as a reference to design an adequate program to address those needs, AANDC adopts an ad hoc approach to addressing needed changes to its program.

This is exemplified by the implementation of the EPFA. AANDC makes improvements to its program and funding methodology, however, in doing so, also incorporates a cost-model it knows is flawed. AANDC tries to obtain comparable variables from the provinces to fit them into this cost-model, however, they are unable to obtain all the relevant variables given the provinces often do not calculate things in the same fashion or use a funding formula. By analogy, it is like adding support pillars to a house that has a weak foundation in an attempt to straighten and support the house. At some point, the foundation needs to be fixed or, ultimately, the house will fall down. Similarly, a REFORM of the FNCFS Program is needed in order to build a solid foundation for the program to address the real needs of First Nations children and families living on reserve.

Not being experts in child welfare, AANDC's authorities are concerned with comparable funding levels; whereas provincial/territorial child and family services legislation and standards are concerned with ensuring service levels that are in line with sound social work practice and that meet the best interest of children. It is difficult, if not impossible, to ensure reasonably comparable child and family services where there is this dichotomy between comparable funding and comparable services. Namely, this methodology does not account for the higher service needs of many First Nations children and families living on reserve, along with the higher costs to deliver those services in many situations, and it highlights the inherent problem with the assumptions and population levels built into the FNCFS Program.

AANDC's reasonable comparability standard does not ensure substantive equality in the provision of child and family services for First Nations people living on reserve. In this regard, it is worth repeating the Supreme Court's statement in *Withler*, at paragraph 59, that "finding a mirror group may be impossible, as the essence of an individual's or group's equality claim may be that, in light of their distinct needs and circumstances, no one is like them for the purposes of comparison". This statement fits the context of this complaint quite appropriately. That is, human rights principles, both domestically and internationally, require AANDC to consider the distinct needs and circumstances of First Nations children and families living on-reserve—including their cultural, historical and geographical needs and circumstances—in order to ensure equality in the provision of child and family services to them. A strategy premised on comparable funding levels, based on the application of standard funding formulas, is not sufficient to ensure substantive equality in the provision of child and family services to First Nations children and families living on-reserve.

As a result, and having weighed all the evidence and argument in this case on a balance of probabilities, the Panel finds the Complaint substantiated.

The Panel acknowledges the suffering of those First Nations children and families who are or have been denied an equitable opportunity to remain together or to be reunited in a timely manner. We also recognize those First Nations children and families who are or have been adversely impacted by the Government of Canada's past and current child welfare practices on reserves.

Notes

1. The order in this case included the following remedies:

A) Findings of discrimination;

B) Cease the discriminatory practice and take measures to redress and prevent it;

C) Compensation;

D) Costs for obstruction of process; and

E) Retention of jurisdiction.

2. Prior to the above decision from the Canadian Human Rights Tribunal, a Canadian court had repeatedly emphasized that there was no recognized treaty right in Canada for specific funding for children in foster care, making it extremely difficult to improve indigenous-focused child and family services. In *Winnipeg Child & Family Services (Southeast Area) v. Canada (Attorney General)*, Manitoba Court of Queen's Bench, July 24, 1997 (1997 CarswellMan 370) [*Southeast Child and Family Services v. Canada (Attorney General)* [1997] M.J. No. 385 [QL] [Southeast]], the deciding court held:

> In my view, there is nothing which obligates Canada to provide Services to Families Funding. There is no aboriginal or treaty right which so provides. While clearly there is a fiduciary relationship between Canada and aboriginal people which creates certain obligations upon Canada with respect to Indian children and families, this fiduciary relationship does not obligate Canada to pay any specific amount of funding, or for any specific purpose.

The case challenged the decision made by Canada to suddenly stop providing Services to Families Funding to Manitoba First Nation reserve organizations authorized to provide services, and instead solely receive funding from the Canadian government. This abrupt loss in funding, even though it was the only First Nation organizations receiving the funding, caused a considerable drop in ability for the organizations to provide needed services.

3. The inequality in Canada for First Nations children extends beyond underfunded social services. In *Children of the Broken Treaty*, Charlie Angus explores the youth-led human rights movement in Canada to ensure a quality education for First Nations children. The youth movement was led, until her early death, by Shannen Koostachin, a Cree teenager who refused to accept her education in Attawapiskat that was taking place in "broke-down portables on a toxic site" where children "were getting sick and losing hope." Charlie Angus, Children of the Broken Treaty, xii (2015). In the two short years of her activism, Shannen brought a proper school to Attawapiskat, but she also inspired a national, youth-led movement to bring schools to all First Nations children that culminated in the passage of "Shannen's Dream," a parliamentary motion in the House of Commons that called on the Canadian government to adequately provide for the education of First Nations children, as promised by a multitude of treaties. *Id.* at xv-xvi.

4. Finally, the issues with Canada's child welfare treatment of First Nations children existed long before they are ever born. In *An Act of Genocide*, Karen Stote examines the horrific sterilization, birth control, and abusive abortions practiced on First Nations women in Canada. Gathering statistics on these practices is incredibly difficult, but Stote has collected data indicating over five hundred First Nations women were sterilized between the years of just 1971 and 1974. Karen Stote, An Act of Genocide 79 (2015). In one data set, 12–21% of First Nations women of childbearing age were sterilized because of "multiparity," or the condition of having more than two children. *Id.* at 81. These numbers are just one drop of the larger problem that Stote examines—a history of the colonial government of Canada refusing to allow First Nations women the chance to have and raise their own children, encompassing eugenics, involuntary sterilization, birth control, forced abortions, and genocide.

C. South America

Encompassing similar concerns as the United States and Canada, the child welfare systems in South America has been heavily criticized:

> The care and socialization of the sons and daughters of the wealthy have essentially been a private matter, and the rearing of middle-class children has proceeded in a similar fashion, although with ample support from the state, in the form of diverse subsidies in housing, health and education. In sharp contrast, it is the families living in poverty that are exposed to a direct and intrusive state intervention. The professionals and institutions of the child welfare system are entrusted with the mission of determining

what families are fit to keep their children and what type of substitute care is in the best interest of children considered at risk.

Francisco J. Pilotti, *The Historical Development of the Child Welfare System in Latin America*, 6 Childhood 408, 408–09 (1999). The indigenous children of Latin America have been removed from their homes and families at the direction of non-indigenous governments. There have been some successes in the region; by the 1990s, what had once been one of the world's leading regions for international adoptions had transformed itself so that only two countries were in the top ten leading nations for international adoptions in 2004—Guatemala and Colombia. Laura Briggs, Somebody's Children: The Politics of Transnational and Transracial Adoption 223.

In Brazil, the centuries of deprivation and assimilation of the many indigenous groups has also affected indigenous children. Issues surrounding indigenous child welfare in Brazil often surface in the form of legal child trafficking, where laws, policies, and procedures make it possible for indigenous children to be adopted internationally with little protection for the indigenous Brazilian family. For more information regarding international adoption of Latin American children, see *id* at 127.

The indigenous people of Brazil come from a large number of ethnic groups, making up 0.2% of Brazil's total population. UNICEF Innocenti Research Centre, Ensuring the Rights of Indigenous Children 8 (2003). Through a series of organizations, children's codes, and constitutional reform, Brazil has made efforts to care for the rights of its indigenous children. The Fundação Nacional do Índio is a governmental organization established to ensure the protection of Brazil's indigenous population. *Fundação Nacional do Índio*, Brasil, available at http://www.funai.gov.br/ (last visited April 1, 2016). In 1988, the Brazilian Constitution specifically recognized protections for Brazil's indigenous population, including their traditional "social organization." Constituição Federal [C.F.] [Constitution] 1988, ch. VIII, art. 231(0) (Braz.). In 1990, Brazil passed the Estatuto da Criança e Adolescente, a strong children's code dedicated to wholesale reform of the Brazilian childcare system. Decreto No. 8069, de 13 de Julho de 1990, Diário Oficial da União [D.O.U.] de 16 de Julho de 1990 (Braz.). However, one scholar has declared that there remains a wide gap between the protections the law requires and the actual behavior of Brazilian citizens. Claudia Fonseca, *Inequality Near and Far: Adoption as Seen from the Brazilian Favelas*, 36 Law & Soc'y Rev. 397 (2002).

The battle between misunderstood indigenous child-rearing practices and governmental legislation in Brazil recently gained world-wide attention after the release of the movie *Hakani: A Survivor's Story* in 2008. The movie told the purportedly true story of a young indigenous child who had been the victim of an attempted infanticide. The producers of the film claim it was necessary to expose the harmful child-rearing practices in some indigenous communities in Brazil. Critics of the film and representatives of several Brazilian indigenous groups claim it was produced by missionaries only in an attempt to pass the "Muwaji Law," and that the issue of infanticide is no more a problem for the indigenous peoples of Brazil than it is for any community in the world, but it is being used as a rhetoric to distract from the issues of indigenous rights to land and resources. *"Hakani" and Paving a Road to Hell*, Survival International, available at http://assets.survivalinternational.org/static/files/background/hakani-qanda.pdf (accessed Sept. 5, 2018). The "Muwaji Law," or Project of Law 1057/2007, would allow the removal of Brazilian indigenous children from their families based on reports, rather than evidence, of harmful cultural practices. After eight years of making its way through the Brazilian legislature, it is currently awaiting confirmation in the Senate. *See* PL 1057/2007, CÂmara Dos Deputados, http://www.camara.gov.br/proposicoesWeb/fichadetramitacao?idProposicao=351362.

D. Australia

Australia has a long and heartbreaking history of atrocity in indigenous child welfare, spanning from the late eighteenth century to the adoption of the Children and Young Persons Act of 1989, which finally formally adopted principles of Aboriginal child placement into the youth law of the country.

The governmental policies of Australia with regards to its Aboriginal peoples closely mimicked the policies of the United States, with a greater presence of violence. Each Australian state and territory adopted laws that varied, but a similar progression of events occurred in each area: Aboriginal people were removed from their territorial lands after conflict to reserves; Aboriginal children were forcefully removed from their parents pursuant to laws that cast them as wards of the state under policies of "protection"; taken children, from the "Stolen Generations," were placed in educational institutions run by charitable and missionary organizations, where they were subject to physical, emotional, and sexual abuse; discriminatory absolution, assimilation, and protectionist laws were repealed, but a reluctance exists to formally apologize and provide restitutionary measures for the wrongs experienced by generations of Aboriginal families. *See* Human Rights and Equal Opportunity Commission, Bringing Them Home: National Inquiry into the Separation of Aboriginal and Torres Strait Islander Children from Their Families (1997), https://www.humanrights.gov.au/sites/default/files/content/pdf/social_justice/bringing_them_home_report.pdf.

The following case illustrates the lingering effects from Australia's removal policy on Aboriginal children, including the reluctance of some in the country's judiciary to accept the sustained effects the policies have had on Aboriginal children and families.

B v. R and Separate Representative

Family Court of Australia, Full Court
27 June 1995, 27 September 1995, 127 FLR 438

Introduction

[The two and a half year-old C in this case was placed in the custody of her father, with her mother receiving visitation rights. The mother appealed the custody order.] . . .

The mother is an Aboriginal who was born in Western Australia in 1963. She spent her early years in Western Australia but now lives in Portland, Victoria, as does her mother.

The father is a white Australian who was born in 1960 in eastern Australia and now lives in Burnie, Tasmania, with C. A number of members of his family also live in the Burnie area.

The parties commenced to live together in 1989, first in Tasmania, subsequently in Queensland and, for the latter part of their relationship, in Victoria. C was born on 21 December 1992 in Victoria.

The evidence indicated that the parties' relationship was characterised by heavy drinking by each of them and domestic violence. . . .

In December 1993 the mother entered a drug and alcohol rehabilitation centre in Melbourne as a full-time resident whilst the child remained living with the father in Melbourne. In February 1994, without the mother's consent, the husband took C to Burnie where they have lived to the present time. Shortly after that the mother commenced custody proceedings in this Court. In April 1994 the parties attempted a reconciliation in Tasmania but it was unsuccessful. In May 1994 the mother returned to Melbourne and re-entered the rehabilitation centre where she remained until September 1994. Since that time she has been living in Portland. . . .

On 19 January 1995 the mother gave birth to a second child, R. That child lives with her. At the trial the father neither admitted nor denied that he was the father but has had no contact with this child.

That background is sufficient to enable us to turn to the two major issues with which this judgment is concerned.

1. Aboriginality

(a) At trial

At the commencement of the trial, Mrs Mandelert, who appeared for the separate representative, sought to file an affidavit by Mr Peter Rotumah. He had for nine years been employed at the Victorian Aboriginal Child Care Agency. His evidence was constituted by a report which he had prepared for the Agency relating to the placement of Aboriginal children with non-Aboriginal families, that is, placement in the sense of adoption, foster care or other long term care. Having regard to the rulings which the trial judge made relating to this evidence, it is unnecessary for present purposes to set out the report in full. The substance of it is sufficiently summarised from the following extracts from Mr Rotumah's report (appeal book, vol 1 at 180) as follows:

> "The Social Welfare Department, as it was called then, began to acknowledge that placement of Aboriginal children in non-Aboriginal families failed to address the needs of those children. In many cases these children suffered disastrous physical and emotional trauma. . . .
>
> "There were a number of factors that contributed to the placement breakdowns but the major factor was the inability of non-Aboriginal caregivers to address the issues of racism and cultural differences that an Aboriginal child would inevitably face in his or her developing years. In fact there is evidence that many non-Aboriginal caregivers used to convey negative notions of the Aboriginal culture and their families to the children. More often than not this type of tactic produced severe psychological and emotional trauma for the children concerned. In some cases Aboriginal children had attempted extraordinary measures, both physically and emotionally, to deny their Aboriginality. . . .
>
> "Although I have portrayed a rather negative picture, there have been non-Aboriginal caregivers who viewed Aboriginal culture in a positive light and made attempts to ensure that their foster or adoptive child had access to their culture. But even in situations where caregivers are supportive, the child can still experience severe emotional trauma because of issues relating to their Aboriginality and the inability of the non-Aboriginal caregiver in addressing those needs. . . .
>
> "Whether the placement of an Aboriginal child is with non-Aboriginal foster-care or adoptive parents or within their non-Aboriginal extended family is of no consequence. The issues surrounding their Aboriginality will still be the same. Because of the negative attitudes towards Aborigines that still exist in our community, it is inevitable that an Aboriginal child will to be subjected to racial taunts by their peers and, if that child is isolated from Aboriginal family and community supports, it is most likely that he or she will develop psychological and emotional problems, that will take a very long time, if ever, to heal. And these problems will surface regardless of what colour skin the child has or whether he or she is not physically regarded as 'being Aboriginal'. Since colonisation of this continent it is quite reasonable to assume that a child borne out of mixed parentage have never been categorised, if one could say that, as 'part-white' or 'part-European'. Thus once it is known that a child has an Aboriginal parent, he or she is seen by the wider community as an Aborigine and will be subject to racist and other negative attitudes experienced by Aborigines. In order to cope with these issues, and others surrounding his or her

> Aboriginal identity, it is of paramount importance that the child remain or be placed in an Aboriginal family, preferably the natural or extended family. The child will be with people who have experienced the problems that he or she will inevitably face and be able to address them effectively. Thus, apart from the normal needs of children, the needs pertaining to his cultural heritage and identity will also be addressed."

* * *

What the separate representative was seeking to do was to place evidence of this historic experience before the trial judge as one of the matters which it was relevant to consider in determining where the best interests of this child would be served. The relevance of the evidence lay in its illustration of the common experiences of aboriginal and part-aboriginal children raised in non-aboriginal environments. To the extent that history has repeatedly demonstrated the tragic consequences that may arise from such situations, the evidence was argued to be relevant to any assessment of the possible effects of such a placement on the child in the present case, a consideration itself a factor relevant to the welfare of the child.

When this material was raised the trial judge showed a marked reluctance to treat it as having any evidentiary value and refused to admit it. . . .

> HIS HONOUR [Trial Judge]: Well yes, but this must not be out of proportion, this case, you know. It would not matter, any person, any Australian citizen coming before this Court be they black, yellow or have an origin and other country, I will not be looking at it in any different way.
>
> MRS MANDELERT: No, your Honour, it is purely and simply as one of the parties is Aboriginal and one is not.
>
> HIS HONOUR: Yes.
>
> MRS MANDELERT: The difficulties that Mr Rotumah in his experience with Aboriginal children and so forth, can just help your Honour and assist you in terms of being made aware of some of those problems.
>
> HIS HONOUR: But this is just a case between mother and father, after all, is it not, as to the question of custody of the child?
>
> MRS MANDELERT: Certainly, your Honour, but it does—
>
> HIS HONOUR: Why is it any different from any other case like this?
>
> MRS MANDELERT: Well, your Honour, in my respectful submission, where there is an element in this case where one of the parties is Aboriginal with a little girl who is still very young and may have some difficulties if she remains, for instance in this case, with the father, there are problems that she may face which your Honour, in my respectfully submission, should hear about and know about.
>
> HIS HONOUR: What problem would they be?
>
> MRS MANDELERT: Well, in terms of, effectively—

> HIS HONOUR: I mean, first of all, she has a white father, has she not?
>
> MRS MANDELERT: Yes, she does.
>
> HIS HONOUR: And she has a black mother?
>
> MRS MANDELERT: Yes, yes, and there may be some difficulty in terms of relationships with other people and so forth.
>
> HIS HONOUR: Oh dear, that is getting it out of proportion, is it not, really? Again, I repeat, this is a normal custody case between two parents, both of whom who are Australian citizens. . . .
>
> HIS HONOUR: Would we be calling Greek experts to say just, you know, how this child might feel in a Greek community, you know, I mean we do not want to allow ourselves to get involved with political influences, Mrs Mandelert. . . .

One of the major grounds of appeal of the mother was that the trial judge was wrong in his rulings in relation to the evidence of this witness and that as a consequence he refused to allow evidence to be given upon an issue which may have been important in this case. Those submissions were supported by the separate representative. The purpose of the evidence was to place before the trial judge material of the now well-known negative consequences for many Aboriginal children placed in non-Aboriginal care, and then to suggest that those consequences, or some of them, may also occur in a case like the present if the Aboriginal child is in the custody of the non-Aboriginal parent. That is, that those consequences were brought about not solely by the trauma of removal of those children from familiar surroundings but also by subsequently living in environments which did not adequately reflect, respond to, or validate their Aboriginal identity. Finally, it would then be a matter of evaluating that issue with all of the other issues in order to determine the custody dispute between the child's parents. . . .

This overall issue was referred to only briefly by his Honour in his judgment. Towards the end of the judgment, after he had examined the other issues which he identified as relevant, he said (appeal book, vol 1 at 24):

> "There remains only one other factor for consideration and that is, the child's 'Aboriginality'. In this 'multi-cultural' nation of Australia, as it is often described, it is obviously desirable that a child of parents of ethnic origin do not lose sight of it and are encouraged to learn about their parent's culture. Equally it seems to me it is desirable for a child whose parent or parents are Aboriginal that the child is encouraged to learn about the Aboriginal culture. I believe that the father is very conscious of this responsibility as a parent of the child and that he is genuine in his assurance given in his evidence that he will carry out that responsibility. According to information given by the husband to Dr Kenny, there is an Aboriginal community in the Burnie area."

(b) Discussion of issues

Thus, his Honour addressed, although rather briefly, the relevance of the child's Aboriginality in broad cultural terms. To his Honour, it was important for this child, as for any other child, to know and to be comfortable with her cultural heritage. That is a right recognised in the *United Nations Convention on the Rights of the Child*, which was ratified by the Commonwealth Executive on 17 December 1990 and entered into force for Australia on 16 January 1991.

Article 30 of the Convention states:

> "In those States in which ethnic, religious or linguistic minorities or persons of indigenous origin exist, a child belonging to such a minority or who is indigenous shall not be denied the right, in community with other members of his or her group, to enjoy his or her own culture, to profess and practise his or her own religion, or to use his or her own language."

While we strongly agree with the importance to be attached to these rights, it appears to us that to regard the relevance of Aboriginality as confined only to its connection with such general rights is to adopt too narrow a view of the significance of the child's Aboriginality as advanced in this case. The evidence which was sought to be adduced in this case focused on the effects on aboriginal children of being raised in a white environment, in which the lack of reinforcement of their identity contributed to severe confusions of that identity and profound experiences of alienation. Though obviously connected to Aboriginal culture and heritage, it appears to us that the point which this evidence seeks to make is either separate and distinct from the more general cultural issue, or at least a much deeper illustration of it. . . .

It is not just that Aboriginal children should be encouraged to learn about their culture, and to take pride in it in the manner in which any other child might be so encouraged. What this issue directs our minds to is the particular problems and difficulties confronted throughout Australian history, and at the present time, by Aboriginal Australians in mainstream Australian society. The history of Aboriginal Australians is a unique one, as is their current position in Australian life. The struggles which they face in a predominantly white culture are, too, unique. Evidence which makes reference to these types of experiences and struggles travels well beyond any broad "right to know one's culture" assertion. It addresses the reality of Aboriginal experience, relevant as that experience is to any consideration of the welfare of the child in the present case, a reality far deeper and more profound than the type of traditionally broad statements of principle referred to by the trial judge.

It appears to us that in this case his Honour failed to appreciate the significance of this deeper, unique, issue and that his approach was fundamentally wrong in principle and out of step with a number of decisions in Australia and overseas.

The first step in the admissibility of this type of evidence is, we think, now beyond controversy. This is the devastating long-term effect on thousands of Aboriginal children arising from their removal from their Aboriginal family and their subsequent upbringing within a white environment.

In *Mabo v Queensland (No 2)* (1992) 175 CLR 1, Deane and Gaudron JJ spoke of the dispossession of aboriginals from their land "as a conflagration of oppression and conflict which was, over the (19th) century, to spread across the continent to dispossess, degrade and devastate the aboriginal peoples and leave a national legacy of unutterable shame" (at 104); and that it represented "the darkest aspect of the history of this nation" (at 109). There can, in our view, be little doubt that on a more directly personal level the policy of colonial, and later State, administrations in Australia to systematically remove aboriginal children from their parents and place them in institutions or other care and the consequences of that can be described in equally strong terms.

From at least 1814 when Governor Macquarie established the Native Home for young aboriginal children in Parramatta (see J C Woolmington, *Aboriginals in Colonial Society* 1788–1850 (1973)) through to the early 1970s a systematic policy was carried into effect of removing Aboriginal and especially part Aboriginal children, usually of tender years, from their parents and placing them in institutions or in other white care. In the earlier years there was little public discussion about these actions or the policy behind them. It was seen by many as an inevitable, perhaps welcome, step in the process of assimilation and in furtherance of the belief that the indigenous people of this country would die out and their young children would be better served by occupying (lowly) places in a dominant white society. Many acted from what they regarded as benevolent motives—the removal of young children from what were seen as poor standards of health and lifestyle and the provision instead of what were regarded as superior standards in those areas. These issues, like many other Aboriginal issues, could and should have been addressed in other ways. Tragically this policy left many Aboriginals in childhood, adolescence and adulthood adrift in a white society which treated them as inferior and in which they lost fundamental connections with family and culture.

The 1921 report of the New South Wales Aborigines Protection Board stated that "the continuation of this policy of disassociating the children from camp life must eventually solve the aboriginal problem". Its 1938 report spoke of "the ultimate object of assisting the lighter caste aboriginals to merge into the white population". The 1941 report stated that Aboriginals must "strive to attain the whiteman's standard" and that the white population "must help the darker skinned brethren to a more purposeful view of life". This was reflected in the policy and practices of the other States. For example, legislation in Victoria in 1886 required "full bloods" to be kept on reserves whilst those of "mixed race" were to be integrated into the community. In Queensland, Western Australia and the Northern Territory virtually complete control by the department over the lives of Aboriginals continued into the 1970s. For example, the *Aboriginals Ordinance 1918* (NT) enabled the chief protector to "remove Aboriginal and half-caste children" from their families where he considered it "necessary or desirable" to do so. In each State the children were removed by legislation and practice which it would be impossible to justify or even contemplate today. Alongside this, missions were established to assist Aboriginals, particularly in earlier years, for the purpose of instilling Christian virtues and practices but which often resulted in the denigration of Aboriginal beliefs and attachments. . . .

The history of these events can no longer be a matter of serious controversy. Numerous writings, especially in recent times, both personal and by way of research, attest to this policy and its consequences. We have been assisted in this aspect not only by the material placed before us by the parties in this case but also by the research of scholars and the searing personal recollections of Aboriginals who were the subject of this policy. . . .

The Australian Law Reform Commission in its Report No 31, The Recognition of Aboriginal Customary Laws (1986) par 345 stated that "during the period 1883 to 1969, in New South Wales alone, it has been estimated that over 5,500 Aboriginal children were removed from their parents. This represents approximately one in six Aboriginal children being taken from their parents during this period . . .".

The constant themes from the writings referred to above and from daily Aboriginal experience include the following:

(A) In Australia a child whose ancestry is wholly or partly indigenous is treated by the dominant white society as "black", a circumstance which carries with it widely accepted connotations of an inferior social position. Racism still remains a marked aspect of Australian society. Daily references in the media demonstrate this. Aboriginal people are often treated as inferior members of the Australian society and regularly face discriminatory conduct and behaviour as part of their daily life. This is likely to permeate their existence from the time they commence direct exposure to the outside community and continues through experiences such as commencing school, reaching adolescence, forming relationships, and seeking employment and housing.

(B) The removal of an Aboriginal child from his/her environment to a white environment is likely to have a devastating effect upon that child, particularly if it is coupled with a long-term upbringing in that environment, and especially if it results in exclusion from contact with his/her family and culture.

(C) Generally an Aboriginal child is better able to cope with that discrimination from within the Aboriginal community because usually that community actively reinforces identity, self-esteem and appropriate responses. Racism is a factor which Aboriginal children may confront every day. Because non-Aboriginals are largely oblivious of that, they are less able to deal with it or prepare Aboriginal children for it.

(D) Aboriginal children often suffer acutely from an identity crisis in adolescence, especially if brought up in ignorance of or in circumstances

> which deny or belittle their Aboriginality. This is likely to have a significant impact upon their self-esteem and self-identity into adult life.

However, the task of this Court is not to redress those historic wrongs....

The first positive public affirmation of the need for a change in approach was the statement of the First National Conference on Adoption in 1976 that:

> Any aboriginal child growing up in Australian society today will be confronted by racism. His best weapons against entrenched prejudice are pride in his aboriginal identity and cultural heritage, and a strong support from other members of the aboriginal community.

It supported an explicit policy of child placement preference in the adoption or other placement of Aboriginal children. That is, a policy of preference for placing Aboriginal children in Aboriginal households.

Those views were supported in the following year (1977) by the report of the Royal Commission on Human Relationships (vol 4 at 127): see also Sommerland, *Aboriginal Children Belong to Aboriginal Community: Changing Practices in Adoption* (1977) 12(3) Australian Journal of Social Studies 167.

Further support for this approach was provided in the report of the Australian Law Reform Commission, The Recognition of Aboriginal Customary Laws in 1986. The commission supported the concept of an Aboriginal child placement preference principle in adoption and placement areas and extensively discussed equivalent legislation in the United States: *Indian Child Welfare Act 1978* (US)....

In the meantime, in 1984 a working party of social welfare administrators recommended the adoption of an Aboriginal child placement principle in relation to adoption and foster care. Since that time this has generally been accepted in the States and Territories either by specific legislation (for example, *Adoption Act 1984* (Vic), s 50) or as part of established practice.

Finally, the Reports of the Royal Commission Into Aboriginal Deaths in Custody (1991) provide most compelling evidence of the tragic outcomes to many Aboriginal people brought about, at least partly, by policies of removal with the consequent loss of identity and loss of self-esteem....

(f) Conclusions

It follows from what we have said that we are of the view that the ruling of the trial judge to reject this evidence was wrong in principle and inconsistent with a number of cases in this and other courts over the last two decades.

Evidence of the type sought to be called in this case raised a relevant and potentially important issue in the determination of the best interests or welfare of this child. It adds a further dimension to the delicate and important task of the adjudication of disputes between parents about the future custody of their children....

It appears that the trial judge regarded the question of Aboriginality as separate from the issue of the welfare of the child and as inconsistent with the provisions of the *Family Law Act*. However, it is specifically because the matters to which we have referred may impact on the welfare of the child that they are relevant in cases of this nature. Considering them in making a decision about the child results in a more complete evaluation of that child's best interests. . . .

Whilst many of the matters to which we have referred above are now so notorious that it would be expected that a trial judge would take judicial notice of them, nevertheless, we think that in future cases involving the custody of an Aboriginal child it would be expected that these issues would be explored and evidence provided, especially about their significance in the particular case. We do not consider that a matter such as this should be decided on the basis of the general, more personal, views and experience of the judge in question. This is a specific issue in the custody of Aboriginal children which requires delicate and professional handling to ensure that all aspects of it are considered and that the interests of the child, especially long-term, are taken into account. This material is partly constituted by readily accessible public information of which it would be expected that a trial judge would inform himself or herself, but it would also be important, at least for the predictable future, for the detail and thrust of that material to be marshalled and presented to the court by an appropriately qualified expert so as to avoid the risk that the case may turn upon varying degrees of individual knowledge. . . .

Consequently, in such cases it would be expected that a separate representative would be appointed at an early stage and that one of the responsibilities of the separate representative would be to examine these issues and ensure that all relevant evidence and submissions are placed before the court. That is not to say that the task lies exclusively or even primarily with the separate representative or that the parties should not be expected to put forward evidence relating to this. However, it is obviously a matter which goes to a central aspect of the separate representative's role in a case like this and it would need to be approached in that way. . . .

2. The role of the separate representative

In this matter a separate representative was appointed to act on behalf of the child and instructed counsel at the trial and also before us. The separate representative supported the mother both at trial and on appeal. . . .

In our opinion the circumstances in which a separate representative ought be appointed have been settled. In *Re K* (1994) 117 FLR 63 the Full Court (at 81–86), set out guidelines as to the circumstances in which a separate representative should normally be appointed. . . .

The Full Court also said (at 85) that the guidelines are not exhaustive and that there may well be other circumstances calling for the appointment of a separate representative. In our opinion, in cases in which the Aboriginality of a child and its significance are issues, because of the importance of these issues in Australia and the complexity which they ordinarily involve, a separate representative should be appointed. . . .

It has been suggested by some commentators (Eidelson and Papaleo, 10(2) Australian Family Lawyer 36) that the true importance of *Re K* is that it elevates the child's case to a level which requires independent advocacy and that it acknowledges, by implication, that only by having available to it independent advocacy of the child's case, can the Court truly give effect to the mandatory provisions of s 64(1)(a) of the Act and to the requirements of the *United Nations Convention on the Rights of the Child*. . . .

Conclusions

We concluded that the incorrect approach of the trial judge to both of the issues discussed above required a re-trial of this matter.

Notes

1. The trial judge in this case referenced the Aboriginal child's rights to be in connection with the child's heritage only as all children have a right to appreciate their heritage. The author of this opinion, however, quotes Article 30 of the United Nations Convention on the Rights of the Child, which Australia has ratified, to support its decision requiring additional evidence on the necessity of placement within an Aboriginal environment. To what extent does the use of international law in domestic decisions increase its usefulness as a document? Does the use of international law in other colonizing countries increase the likelihood that it will be adopted in United States courts?

2. The *B v. R* opinion notes at one point that the "task of this Court is not to redress historic wrongs." In issuing its decision, the court goes on to require re-trial of the case with consideration of the effect of placing an Aboriginal child with a non-Aboriginal parent. Is this reconsideration an action towards redressing the historic wrongs against Aboriginal children, regardless of what the opinion declares?

3. The movies *Rabbit Proof Fence* (2002) and *Australia* (2008) brought awareness of the Stolen Generations to mainstream culture in both Australia and around the world. *Australia* was released just months after the Australian government issued a formal apology to Aboriginal peoples for its past treatment, and the removal of Aboriginal and Torres Strait Islander children from their families in particular. Is education through cinema an appropriate replacement for institutional education of this history, particularly in countries other than that which it occurred? What benefits come from cinematic portrayals of the 1880–1960 time period, where indigenous children were being removed from their families around the world? What issues can arise when the only story many people know is the one they learned about in popular culture?

4. The indigenous peoples of New Zealand, the Maori, have experienced a unique history of colonial influence on their traditions. In 1988, the Maori Perspective Advisory Committee issued a formal report regarding the deficiencies in New Zealand's Department of Social Welfare. "Te Puao-te-Ata-tu," or the Daybreak Report,

inquired into Maori children and young adults receiving inadequate services from the Department of Social Welfare, leading to disproportionalities in the number of Maori in penal institutions and out-of-home care. The Puao-te-Ata-tu report exposed the institutionalized racism within the Department of Social Welfare and the country of New Zealand. The Puao-te-Ata-tu report included a number of recommendations, including reformation of the existing Children and Young Persons Act of 1974 to better align with the needs of Maori children and families.

> The Maori child is not to be viewed in isolation, or even as part of a nuclear family, but as a member of a wider kin group or hapu community that has traditionally exercised responsibility for the child's care and placement. The technique . . . must be to reaffirm the hapu bonds and capitalize on the traditional strengths of the wider group.
>
> This needs emphasis. The guiding principle in the current legislation is that the welfare of the child shall be regarded as the first and paramount consideration. There need be no inherent conflict between that and the customary preference for the maintenance of children within the hapu. The current principle is seen in practice as negating the right of the group to care for its own or to be heard in the proceedings.
>
> The Committee heard several complaints of children placed with foster parents outside of the kin group to meet the child's immediate and material needs but without any (or any adequate) attempt to find foster parents within the hapu.
>
> The Committee was told the hapu was rarely consulted, sometimes as an omission, but more usually through a positive opinion that the hapu had no right to be involved, or because of an exaggerated emphasis on "confidentiality".
>
> The Committee considers these practices in urgent need of review. An affirmative statement of the hapu principle in the governing legislation is now needed. The physical, social and spiritual wellbeing of a Maori child is inextricably related to the sense of belonging to a wider whanau group.

New Zealand Dep't Social Welfare, Te Puao-te-Atu-tu: Report of the Ministerial Advisory Committee on a Maori Perspective for the Dep't of Social Welfare 29–30 (1988). The Children, Young Persons, and Their Families Act of 1989 formally institutionalized many of the recommendations from the Puao-te-Atu-tu Report.

> In determining the welfare and interests of a child or young person, the court . . . must be guided by the principle that children and young people must be protected from harm and have their rights upheld, . . . as well as the following principles:
>
> * * *

(b) the principle that the primary role in caring for and protecting a child or young person lies with the child's or young person's family, whanau, hapu, iwi, and family group, and that accordingly—

(i) a child's or young person's family, whanau, hapu, iwi, and family group should be supported, assisted, and protected as much as possible; and

(ii) intervention into family life should be the minimum necessary to ensure a child's or young person's safety and protection[.]

* * *

(d) where a child or young person is considered to be in need of care or protection, the principle that, wherever practicable, the necessary assistance and support should be provided to enable the child or young person to be cared for and protected within his or her own family, whanau, hapu, iwi, and family group[.]

(e) the principle that a child or young person should be removed from his or her family, whanau, hapu, iwi, and family group only if there is a serious risk of harm to the child or young person[.]

Children, Young Persons and Their Families Act of 1989, Pt 2, § 13(2). The Act also formally established the use of the Family Group Conference (FGC) as an alternative to traditional courtroom procedures for children and youth who are the subject of neglect or abuse proceedings, or who have offended. *Id.* § 20–38. FGCs bring together a child's immediate and extended family, community, and legal and mental health professionals to create a solution to ensure the safety and wellbeing of the child. *Id.* § 22. An application for a declaration that a child or young person is in need of care or protection may be made only after a FGC has been held and any plan made; a court may not declare a child in need of care or protection unless the FGC plan either did not work or was not practicable or appropriate. *Id.* § 70(1); 73(1). Recently, Whānau Ora has emerged as a methodology for family health in New Zealand, placing the whanau at the center of social service deliveries, rather than the individual. *See* New Zealand Productivity Commission, More Effective Social Services, Appx. C Case Study: Whānau Ora (2015), https://www.productivity.govt.nz/sites/default/files/social-services-final-report-appendix-c.pdf.

E. Scandinavia

In Scandinavia, the Sami people are an ethnic minority group that retain their own cultures and traditions, much as American Indian and Alaska Native peoples do in the United States. The Sami People 11 (Aage Solbaak ed., 1990). Because *Sápmi*, the existing land base for Sami people, spans across Russia, Norway, Sweden, and Finland, it is difficult to identify any comprehensive child welfare policy to ensure Sami children are raised in their families and communities. As with other indigenous peoples around the world, the Sami people were routinely ousted to the margins of society. In the early colonization of the Nordic countries, this marginalization took the form of prohibitory taxes laid upon the reindeer and other animals that the Sami relied upon for sustenance and economic survival. Mattias Ahren, *Indigenous Peoples' Culture, Customs, and Traditions and Customary Law—The Saami People's Perspective*, 21 Ariz. J. Int'l & Comp. L. 63, 73–75 (2004). As part of a complicated history between the Scandinavia nation-states and the Sami, as late as the 1980s, Sami children were sent to boarding schools that did not teach Sami culture or history.

> While there was no explicit, written policy in any of the Nordic countries intending to assimilate and 'civilize' the Sami by taking children away from their families, the consequences of forcing Sami children to attend the public school system alongside with Finnish, Swedish, and Norwegian children was, however, in many ways very similar to those in North America, resulting in commonalities of low self-esteem, alienation from one's cultural background, and difficulties in integrating and adapting in society, whether one's own or the dominant.

Rauna Kuokkanen, *Survivance in Sami and First Nations Boarding School Narratives*, 27 Am. Indian Q. 697, 707 (2003).

Today, the Nordic countries are taking steps to ensure that Sami children can grow up within their family households and surrounded by their traditional language and cultural traditions. In Norway, Sweden, and Finland, Sami children living within designated Sami areas have the right to receive education in the Sami languages. Special Rapporteur on the Rights of Indigenous Peoples, *The Situation of the Sami People in the Sápmi Region of Norway, Sweden and Finland*, Human Rights Council, ¶ 67, U.N. Doc. A/HRC/18/35/Add.2 (June 6, 2011). Sami families living within the Russian Federation face a much more difficult battle in obtaining recognized rights for their families, communities, and broader culture, in part because the Russian government does not recognize any Sami political group. *See* Mikkel Berg-Nordlie, *Striving to Unite: The Russian Sámi and the Nordic Sámi Parliament Model*, 2 Arctic Rev. L. & Pol. 52 (2011).

After its ratification of the Convention on the Rights of the Child, Sami children in Norway have the right to enjoy the community, culture, religion, and language of the Sami people. Ministry of Children and Equality, Norway's Fourth Periodic Report to the U.N. Committee on the Rights of the Child 143 (2008), https://www.regjeringen.no/globalassets/upload/bld/rapporter/2008/the_rights_of_the_child.pdf. Practically, this is accomplished through provisions in the Barnehager Act, which ensures that early child care centers in areas with high concentrations of Sami people are based on Sami language and culture. Act No. 64, Ch. 3, § 8 (Norway 2005). For children and parents who live within the officially designated "Sami language administrative districts," Sami children and parents have the right to use Sami language when meeting with representatives of child welfare services. The Sami Act, §§ 3-2, 3-3 (Norway 1987).

If a Sami child is removed from his home and placed into foster care, Norwegian law requires that his ethnic, religious, and language background is taken into consideration. Regulations on Foster Care, § 4, Ministry of Children, Equality, and Social Inclusion (Norway 2003), https://lovdata.no/dokument/SF/forskrift/2003-12-18-1659. When removed, Sami children have the right to continue to use and learn the Sami language and culture in foster homes and in care institutions. *Id.* § 8; *see also* Regulations Relating to Supervision of Children in Care Institutions for Care and Treatment, § 7, Ministry of Children, Equality, and Social Inclusion (Norway 2003), https://lovdata.no/dokument/SF/forskrift/2003-12-11-1564. In involuntary removal cases, Sami families that live within a Sami language administrative district are offered a spokesperson that speaks Sami and is aware of Sami culture to guide them through the process. Regulations on Child Spokesperson in Matters to be Considered by the County Board for Child Welfare and Social Affairs, § 3, Ministry of Children, Equality, and Social Inclusion (Norway 2013), https://lovdata.no/dokument/SF/forskrift/2013-02-18-203.

In Sweden, where the Sami have been recognized as indigenous peoples since 1977, Sami children have a right to be educated in the Sami language if at least one parent is Sami. Ombudsmannen Mot Etnisk Diskriminering, Discrimination of the Sami: The Rights of the Sami From a Discrimination Perspective 14–15 (2008), http://www2.ohchr.org/english/issues/indigenous/ExpertMechanism/3rd/docs/contributions/SwedishEqualityOmbudsman_2.pdf. However, an Equality Ombudsman report notes that this mandate often only materializes if there is an available Sami language teacher in the area, and the child already has a basic understanding of Sami language. *Id.*

The minor successes that Sami people have been able to obtain regarding their children are often at odds with a Nordic view of society.

> That is, as the Sami pursue their collective right to local autonomy and social equality they come into conflict with the practical and legal implications of the Nordic welfare states' tendency to extend entitlement solely to the individual. And furthermore, just as the individual is the responsibility of society-as-a-whole, the responsibility of the individual is first and foremost to society-as-a-whole. Nordic governments thus find the Sami's cultural and collective rights orientation very difficult and uncomfortable to accept politically, and hence tend largely to ignore it or make a pretense of accepting it, on the one hand, or, on the other hand, attempt to control it by means of instituting controversial policy measures.

Sven E. Olsson & Dave Lewis, *Welfare Rules and Indigenous Rights: The Sami People and the Nordic Welfare States, in* Social Welfare with Indigenous Peoples 141, 142–43 (John Dixon & Robert P. Scheurell eds., 1994).

Appendix

Indian Child Welfare Act

25 U.S.C. 1901 et seq

§ 1901. Congressional findings

Recognizing the special relationship between the United States and the Indian tribes and their members and the Federal responsibility to Indian people, the Congress finds—

(1) that clause 3, section 8, article I of the United States Constitution provides that "The Congress shall have Power * * * To regulate Commerce * * * with Indian tribes" and, through this and other constitutional authority, Congress has plenary power over Indian affairs;

(2) that Congress, through statutes, treaties, and the general course of dealing with Indian tribes, has assumed the responsibility for the protection and preservation of Indian tribes and their resources;

(3) that there is no resource that is more vital to the continued existence and integrity of Indian tribes than their children and that the United States has a direct interest, as trustee, in protecting Indian children who are members of or are eligible for membership in an Indian tribe;

(4) that an alarmingly high percentage of Indian families are broken up by the removal, often unwarranted, of their children from them by nontribal public and private agencies and that an alarmingly high percentage of such children are placed in non-Indian foster and adoptive homes and institutions; and

(5) that the States, exercising their recognized jurisdiction over Indian child custody proceedings through administrative and judicial bodies, have often failed to recognize the essential tribal relations of Indian people and the cultural and social standards prevailing in Indian communities and families.

§ 1902. Congressional declaration of policy

The Congress hereby declares that it is the policy of this Nation to protect the best interests of Indian children and to promote the stability and security of Indian tribes and families by the establishment of minimum Federal standards for the removal of Indian children from their families and the placement of such children in foster or adoptive homes which will reflect the unique values of Indian culture, and by providing for assistance to Indian tribes in the operation of child and family service programs.

§ 1903. Definitions

For the purposes of this chapter, except as may be specifically provided otherwise, the term—

(1) "child custody proceeding" shall mean and include—

(i) "foster care placement" which shall mean any action removing an Indian child from its parent or Indian custodian for temporary placement in a foster home or institution or the home of a guardian or conservator where the parent or Indian custodian cannot have the child returned upon demand, but where parental rights have not been terminated;

(ii) "termination of parental rights" which shall mean any action resulting in the termination of the parent-child relationship;

(iii) "preadoptive placement" which shall mean the temporary placement of an Indian child in a foster home or institution after the termination of parental rights, but prior to or in lieu of adoptive placement; and

(iv) "adoptive placement" which shall mean the permanent placement of an Indian child for adoption, including any action resulting in a final decree of adoption.

Such term or terms shall not include a placement based upon an act which, if committed by an adult, would be deemed a crime or upon an award, in a divorce proceeding, of custody to one of the parents.

(2) "extended family member" shall be as defined by the law or custom of the Indian child's tribe or, in the absence of such law or custom, shall be a person who has reached the age of eighteen and who is the Indian child's grandparent, aunt or uncle, brother or sister, brother-in-law or sister-in-law, niece or nephew, first or second cousin, or stepparent;

(3) "Indian" means any person who is a member of an Indian tribe, or who is an Alaska Native and a member of a Regional Corporation as defined in 1606 of title 43;

(4) "Indian child" means any unmarried person who is under age eighteen and is either (a) a member of an Indian tribe or (b) is eligible for membership in an Indian tribe and is the biological child of a member of an Indian tribe;

(5) "Indian child's tribe" means (a) the Indian tribe in which an Indian child is a member or eligible for membership or (b), in the case of an Indian

child who is a member of or eligible for membership in more than one tribe, the Indian tribe with which the Indian child has the more significant contacts;

(6) "Indian custodian" means any Indian person who has legal custody of an Indian child under tribal law or custom or under State law or to whom temporary physical care, custody, and control has been transferred by the parent of such child;

(7) "Indian organization" means any group, association, partnership, corporation, or other legal entity owned or controlled by Indians, or a majority of whose members are Indians;

(8) "Indian tribe" means any Indian tribe, band, nation, or other organized group or community of Indians recognized as eligible for the services provided to Indians by the Secretary because of their status as Indians, including any Alaska Native village as defined in section 1602 (c) of title 43;

(9) "parent" means any biological parent or parents of an Indian child or any Indian person who has lawfully adopted an Indian child, including adoptions under tribal law or custom. It does not include the unwed father where paternity has not been acknowledged or established;

(10) "reservation" means Indian country as defined in section 1151 of title 18 and any lands, not covered under such section, title to which is either held by the United States in trust for the benefit of any Indian tribe or individual or held by any Indian tribe or individual subject to a restriction by the United States against alienation;

(11) "Secretary" means the Secretary of the Interior; and

(12) "tribal court" means a court with jurisdiction over child custody proceedings and which is either a Court of Indian Offenses, a court established and operated under the code or custom of an Indian tribe, or any other administrative body of a tribe which is vested with authority over child custody proceedings.

SUBCHAPTER I: Child Custody Proceedings

§ 1911. Indian tribe jurisdiction over Indian child custody proceedings

(a) Exclusive jurisdiction

An Indian tribe shall have jurisdiction exclusive as to any State over any child custody proceeding involving an Indian child who resides or is domiciled within the reservation of such tribe, except where such jurisdiction is otherwise vested in the State by existing Federal law. Where an Indian child is a ward of a tribal court, the Indian tribe shall retain exclusive jurisdiction, notwithstanding the residence or domicile of the child.

(b) Transfer of proceedings; declination by tribal court

In any State court proceeding for the foster care placement of, or termination of parental rights to, an Indian child not domiciled or residing within the reservation of the Indian child's tribe, the court, in the absence of good cause to the contrary, shall transfer such proceeding to the jurisdiction of the tribe, absent objection by either parent, upon the petition of either parent or the Indian custodian or the Indian child's tribe: Provided, That such transfer shall be subject to declination by the tribal court of such tribe.

(c) State court proceedings; intervention

In any State court proceeding for the foster care placement of, or termination of parental rights to, an Indian child, the Indian custodian of the child and the Indian child's tribe shall have a right to intervene at any point in the proceeding.

(d) Full faith and credit to public acts, records, and judicial proceedings of Indian tribes

The United States, every State, every territory or possession of the United States, and every Indian tribe shall give full faith and credit to the public acts, records, and judicial proceedings of any Indian tribe applicable to Indian child custody proceedings to the same extent that such entities give full faith and credit to the public acts, records, and judicial proceedings of any other entity.

§ 1912. Pending court proceedings

(a) Notice; time for commencement of proceedings; additional time for preparation

In any involuntary proceeding in a State court, where the court knows or has reason to know that an Indian child is involved, the party seeking the foster care placement of, or termination of parental rights to, an Indian child shall notify the parent or Indian custodian and the Indian child's tribe, by registered mail with return receipt requested, of the pending proceedings and of their right of intervention. If the identity or location of the parent or Indian custodian and the tribe cannot be determined, such notice shall be given to the Secretary in like manner, who shall have fifteen days after receipt to provide the requisite notice to the parent or Indian custodian and the tribe. No foster care placement or termination of parental rights proceeding shall be held until at least ten days after receipt of notice by the parent or Indian custodian and the tribe or the Secretary: Provided, That the parent or Indian custodian or the tribe shall, upon request, be granted up to twenty additional days to prepare for such proceeding.

(b) Appointment of counsel

In any case in which the court determines indigency, the parent or Indian custodian shall have the right to court-appointed counsel in any removal, placement, or termination proceeding. The court may, in its discretion, appoint counsel for the child upon a finding that such appointment is in the best interest of the child. Where State law makes no provision for appointment of counsel in such proceedings, the court shall promptly notify the Secretary upon appointment of counsel, and the Secretary, upon certification of the presiding judge, shall pay reasonable fees and expenses out of funds which may be appropriated pursuant to section 13 of this title.

(c) Examination of reports or other documents

Each party to a foster care placement or termination of parental rights proceeding under State law involving an Indian child shall have the right to examine all reports or other documents filed with the court upon which any decision with respect to such action may be based.

(d) Remedial services and rehabilitative programs; preventive measures

Any party seeking to effect a foster care placement of, or termination of parental rights to, an Indian child under State law shall satisfy the court that active efforts have been made to provide remedial services and rehabilitative programs designed to prevent the breakup of the Indian family and that these efforts have proved unsuccessful.

(e) Foster care placement orders; evidence; determination of damage to child

No foster care placement may be ordered in such proceeding in the absence of a determination, supported by clear and convincing evidence, including testimony of qualified expert witnesses, that the continued custody of the child by the parent or Indian custodian is likely to result in serious emotional or physical damage to the child.

(f) Parental rights termination orders; evidence; determination of damage to child

No termination of parental rights may be ordered in such proceeding in the absence of a determination, supported by evidence beyond a reasonable doubt, including testimony of qualified expert witnesses, that the continued custody of the child by the parent or Indian custodian is likely to result in serious emotional or physical damage to the child.

§ 1913. Parental rights; voluntary termination

(a) Consent; record; certification matters; invalid consents

Where any parent or Indian custodian voluntarily consents to a foster care placement or to termination of parental rights, such consent shall not be valid unless executed in writing and recorded before a judge of a court of competent jurisdiction and accompanied by the presiding judge's certificate that the terms and consequences of the consent were fully explained in detail and were fully understood by the parent or Indian custodian. The court shall also certify that either the parent or Indian custodian fully understood the explanation in English or that it was interpreted into a language that the parent or Indian custodian understood. Any consent given prior to, or within ten days after, birth of the Indian child shall not be valid.

(b) Foster care placement; withdrawal of consent

Any parent or Indian custodian may withdraw consent to a foster care placement under State law at any time and, upon such withdrawal, the child shall be returned to the parent or Indian custodian.

(c) Voluntary termination of parental rights or adoptive placement; withdrawal of consent; return of custody

In any voluntary proceeding for termination of parental rights to, or adoptive placement of, an Indian child, the consent of the parent may be withdrawn for any reason at any time prior to the entry of a final decree of termination or adoption, as the case may be, and the child shall be returned to the parent.

(d) Collateral attack; vacation of decree and return of custody; limitations

After the entry of a final decree of adoption of an Indian child in any State court, the parent may withdraw consent thereto upon the grounds that consent was obtained through fraud or duress and may petition the court to vacate such decree. Upon a finding that such consent was obtained through fraud or duress, the court shall vacate such decree and return the child to the parent. No adoption which has been effective for at least two years may be invalidated under the provisions of this subsection unless otherwise permitted under State law.

§ 1914. Petition to court of competent jurisdiction to invalidate action upon showing of certain violations

Any Indian child who is the subject of any action for foster care placement or termination of parental rights under State law, any parent or Indian custodian from whose custody such child was removed, and the Indian child's tribe may petition any court of competent jurisdiction to invalidate such action upon a showing that such action violated any provision of sections 1911, 1912, and 1913 of this title.

§ 1915. Placement of Indian children

(a) Adoptive placements; preferences

In any adoptive placement of an Indian child under State law, a preference shall be given, in the absence of good cause to the contrary, to a placement with

(1) a member of the child's extended family;

(2) other members of the Indian child's tribe; or

(3) other Indian families.

(b) Foster care or preadoptive placements; criteria; preferences

Any child accepted for foster care or preadoptive placement shall be placed in the least restrictive setting which most approximates a family and in which his special needs, if any, may be met. The child shall also be placed within reasonable proximity to his or her home, taking into account any special needs of the child. In any foster care or preadoptive placement, a preference shall be given, in the absence of good cause to the contrary, to a placement with—

(i) a member of the Indian child's extended family;

(ii) a foster home licensed, approved, or specified by the Indian child's tribe;

(iii) an Indian foster home licensed or approved by an authorized non-Indian licensing authority; or

(iv) an institution for children approved by an Indian tribe or operated by an Indian organization which has a program suitable to meet the Indian child's needs.

(c) **Tribal resolution for different order of preference; personal preference considered; anonymity in application of preferences**

In the case of a placement under subsection (a) or (b) of this section, if the Indian child's tribe shall establish a different order of preference by resolution, the agency or court effecting the placement shall follow such order so long as the placement is the least restrictive setting appropriate to the particular needs of the child, as provided in subsection (b) of this section. Where appropriate, the preference of the Indian child or parent shall be considered: Provided, That where a consenting parent evidences a desire for anonymity, the court or agency shall give weight to such desire in applying the preferences.

(d) **Social and cultural standards applicable**

The standards to be applied in meeting the preference requirements of this section shall be the prevailing social and cultural standards of the Indian community in which the parent or extended family resides or with which the parent or extended family members maintain social and cultural ties.

(e) **Record of placement; availability**

A record of each such placement, under State law, of an Indian child shall be maintained by the State in which the placement was made, evidencing the efforts to comply with the order of preference specified in this section. Such record shall be made available at any time upon the request of the Secretary or the Indian child's tribe.

§ 1916. Return of custody

(a) **Petition; best interests of child**

Notwithstanding State law to the contrary, whenever a final decree of adoption of an Indian child has been vacated or set aside or the adoptive parents voluntarily consent to the termination of their parental rights to the child, a biological parent or prior Indian custodian may petition for return of custody and the court shall grant such petition unless there is a showing, in a proceeding subject to the provisions of section 1912 of this title, that such return of custody is not in the best interests of the child.

(b) **Removal from foster care home; placement procedure**

Whenever an Indian child is removed from a foster care home or institution for the purpose of further foster care, preadoptive, or adoptive placement, such placement shall be in accordance with the provisions of this chapter, except in the case where an Indian child is being returned to the parent or Indian custodian from whose custody the child was originally removed.

§ 1917. Tribal affiliation information and other information for protection of rights from tribal relationship; application of subject of adoptive placement; disclosure by court

Upon application by an Indian individual who has reached the age of eighteen and who was the subject of an adoptive placement, the court which entered the final decree shall inform such individual of the tribal affiliation, if any, of the individual's biological parents and provide such other information as may be necessary to protect any rights flowing from the individual's tribal relationship.

§ 1918. Reassumption of jurisdiction over child custody proceedings

(a) Petition; suitable plan; approval by Secretary

Any Indian tribe which became subject to State jurisdiction pursuant to the provisions of the Act of August 15, 1953 (67 Stat. 588), as amended by title IV of the Act of April 11, 1968 (82 Stat. 73, 78), or pursuant to any other Federal law, may reassume jurisdiction over child custody proceedings. Before any Indian tribe may reassume jurisdiction over Indian child custody proceedings, such tribe shall present to the Secretary for approval a petition to reassume such jurisdiction which includes a suitable plan to exercise such jurisdiction.

(b) Criteria applicable to consideration by Secretary; partial retrocession

(1) In considering the petition and feasibility of the plan of a tribe under subsection (a) of this section, the Secretary may consider, among other things:

(i) whether or not the tribe maintains a membership roll or alternative provision for clearly identifying the persons who will be affected by the reassumption of jurisdiction by the tribe;

(ii) the size of the reservation or former reservation area which will be affected by retrocession and reassumption of jurisdiction by the tribe;

(iii) the population base of the tribe, or distribution of the population in homogeneous communities or geographic areas; and

(iv) the feasibility of the plan in cases of multitribal occupation of a single reservation or geographic area.

(2) In those cases where the Secretary determines that the jurisdictional provisions of section 1911 (a) of this title are not feasible, he is authorized to accept partial retrocession which will enable tribes to exercise referral jurisdiction as provided in section 1911 (b) of this title, or, where appropriate, will allow them to exercise exclusive jurisdiction as provided in section 1911 (a) of this title over limited community or geographic areas without regard for the reservation status of the area affected.

(c) Approval of petition; publication in Federal Register; notice; reassumption period; correction of causes for disapproval

If the Secretary approves any petition under subsection (a) of this section, the Secretary shall publish notice of such approval in the Federal Register and shall notify the affected State or States of such approval. The Indian tribe concerned shall reassume jurisdiction sixty days after publication in the Federal Register of notice of approval. If the Secretary disapproves any petition under subsection (a) of this section, the Secretary shall provide such technical assistance as may be necessary to enable the tribe to correct any deficiency which the Secretary identified as a cause for disapproval.

(d) Pending actions or proceedings unaffected

Assumption of jurisdiction under this section shall not affect any action or proceeding over which a court has already assumed jurisdiction, except as may be provided pursuant to any agreement under section 1919 of this title.

§ 1919. Agreements between States and Indian tribes

(a) Subject coverage

States and Indian tribes are authorized to enter into agreements with each other respecting care and custody of Indian children and jurisdiction over child custody proceedings, including agreements which may provide for orderly transfer of jurisdiction on a case-by-case basis and agreements which provide for concurrent jurisdiction between States and Indian tribes.

(b) Revocation; notice; actions or proceedings unaffected

Such agreements may be revoked by either party upon one hundred and eighty days' written notice to the other party. Such revocation shall not affect any action or proceeding over which a court has already assumed jurisdiction, unless the agreement provides otherwise.

§ 1920. Improper removal of child from custody; declination of jurisdiction; forthwith return of child: danger exception

Where any petitioner in an Indian child custody proceeding before a State court has improperly removed the child from custody of the parent or Indian custodian or has improperly retained custody after a visit or other temporary relinquishment of custody, the court shall decline jurisdiction over such petition and shall forthwith return the child to his parent or Indian custodian unless returning the child to his parent or custodian would subject the child to a substantial and immediate danger or threat of such danger.

§ 1921. Higher State or Federal standard applicable to protect rights of parent or Indian custodian of Indian child

In any case where State or Federal law applicable to a child custody proceeding under State or Federal law provides a higher standard of protection to the rights of the parent or Indian custodian of an Indian child than the rights provided under this subchapter, the State or Federal court shall apply the State or Federal standard.

§ 1922. Emergency removal or placement of child; termination; appropriate action

Nothing in this subchapter shall be construed to prevent the emergency removal of an Indian child who is a resident of or is domiciled on a reservation, but temporarily located off the reservation, from his parent or Indian custodian or the emergency placement of such child in a foster home or institution, under applicable State law, in order to prevent imminent physical damage or harm to the child. The State authority, official, or agency involved shall insure that the emergency removal or placement terminates immediately when such removal or placement is no longer necessary to prevent imminent physical damage or harm to the child and shall expeditiously initiate a child custody proceeding subject to the provisions of this subchapter, transfer the child to the jurisdiction of the appropriate Indian tribe, or restore the child to the parent or Indian custodian, as may be appropriate.

§ 1923. Effective date

None of the provisions of this subchapter, except sections 1911 (a), 1918, and 1919 of this title, shall affect a proceeding under State law for foster care placement, termination of parental rights, preadoptive placement, or adoptive placement which was initiated or completed prior to one hundred and eighty days after November 8, 1978, but shall apply to any subsequent proceeding in the same matter or subsequent proceedings affecting the custody or placement of the same child.

SUBCHAPTER II: Indian Child And Family Programs

§ 1931. Grants for on or near reservation programs and child welfare codes

(a) Statement of purpose; scope of programs

The Secretary is authorized to make grants to Indian tribes and organizations in the establishment and operation of Indian child and family service programs on or near reservations and in the preparation and implementation of child welfare codes. The objective of every Indian child and family service program shall be to prevent the breakup of Indian families and, in particular, to insure that the permanent removal of an Indian child from the custody of his parent or Indian custodian shall be a last resort. Such child and family service programs may include, but are not limited to—

(1) a system for licensing or otherwise regulating Indian foster and adoptive homes;

(2) the operation and maintenance of facilities for the counseling and treatment of Indian families and for the temporary custody of Indian children;

(3) family assistance, including homemaker and home counselors, day care, afterschool care, and employment, recreational activities, and respite care;

(4) home improvement programs;

(5) the employment of professional and other trained personnel to assist the tribal court in the disposition of domestic relations and child welfare matters;

(6) education and training of Indians, including tribal court judges and staff, in skills relating to child and family assistance and service programs;

(7) a subsidy program under which Indian adoptive children may be provided support comparable to that for which they would be eligible as foster children, taking into account the appropriate State standards of support for maintenance and medical needs; and

(8) guidance, legal representation, and advice to Indian families involved in tribal, State, or Federal child custody proceedings.

(b) Non-Federal matching funds for related Social Security or other Federal financial assistance programs; assistance for such programs unaffected; State licensing or approval for qualification for assistance under federally assisted program

Funds appropriated for use by the Secretary in accordance with this section may be utilized as non-Federal matching share in connection with funds provided under titles IV–B and XX of the Social Security Act [42 U.S.C. 620 et seq., 1397 et seq.] or under any other Federal financial assistance programs which contribute to the purpose for which such funds are authorized to be appropriated for use under this chapter. The provision or possibility of assistance under this chapter shall not be a basis for the denial or reduction of any assistance otherwise authorized under titles IV–B and XX of the Social Security Act or any other federally assisted program. For purposes of qualifying for assistance under a federally assisted program, licensing or approval of foster or adoptive homes or institutions by an Indian tribe shall be deemed equivalent to licensing or approval by a State.

§ 1932. Grants for off-reservation programs for additional services

The Secretary is also authorized to make grants to Indian organizations to establish and operate off-reservation Indian child and family service programs which may include, but are not limited to—

(1) a system for regulating, maintaining, and supporting Indian foster and adoptive homes, including a subsidy program under which Indian adoptive children may be provided support comparable to that for which they would be eligible as Indian foster children, taking into account the appropriate State standards of support for maintenance and medical needs;

(2) the operation and maintenance of facilities and services for counseling and treatment of Indian families and Indian foster and adoptive children;

(3) family assistance, including homemaker and home counselors, day care, afterschool care, and employment, recreational activities, and respite care; and

(4) guidance, legal representation, and advice to Indian families involved in child custody proceedings.

§ 1933. Funds for on and off reservation programs

(a) Appropriated funds for similar programs of Department of Health and Human Services; appropriation in advance for payments

In the establishment, operation, and funding of Indian child and family service programs, both on and off reservation, the Secretary may enter into agreements with the Secretary of Health and Human Services, and the latter Secretary is hereby authorized for such purposes to use funds appropriated for similar programs of the Department of Health and Human Services: Provided, That authority to make payments pursuant to such agreements shall be effective only to the extent and in such amounts as may be provided in advance by appropriation Acts.

(b) Appropriation authorization under section 13 of this title

Funds for the purposes of this chapter may be appropriated pursuant to the provisions of section 13 of this title.

§ 1934. "Indian" defined for certain purposes

For the purposes of sections 1932 and 1933 of this title, the term "Indian" shall include persons defined in section 1603 (c) 1 of this title.

SUBCHAPTER III: Recordkeeping, Information Availability, and Timetables

§ 1951. Information availability to and disclosure by Secretary

(a) Copy of final decree or order; other information; anonymity affidavit; exemption from Freedom of Information Act

Any State court entering a final decree or order in any Indian child adoptive placement after November 8, 1978, shall provide the Secretary with a copy of such decree or order together with such other information as may be necessary to show—

(1) the name and tribal affiliation of the child;

(2) the names and addresses of the biological parents;

(3) the names and addresses of the adoptive parents; and

(4) the identity of any agency having files or information relating to such adoptive placement.

Where the court records contain an affidavit of the biological parent or parents that their identity remain confidential, the court shall include such affidavit with the other information. The Secretary shall insure that the confidentiality of such information is maintained and such information shall not be subject to the Freedom of Information Act (5 U.S.C. 552), as amended.

(b) Disclosure of information for enrollment of Indian child in tribe or for determination of member rights or benefits; certification of entitlement to enrollment

Upon the request of the adopted Indian child over the age of eighteen, the adoptive or foster parents of an Indian child, or an Indian tribe, the Secretary shall disclose such information as may be necessary for the enrollment of an Indian child in the tribe in which the child may be eligible for enrollment or for determining any rights or benefits associated with that membership. Where the documents relating to such child contain an affidavit from the biological parent or parents requesting anonymity, the Secretary shall certify to the Indian child's tribe, where the information warrants, that the child's parentage and other circumstances of birth entitle the child to enrollment under the criteria established by such tribe.

§ 1952. Rules and regulations

Within one hundred and eighty days after November 8, 1978, the Secretary shall promulgate such rules and regulations as may be necessary to carry out the provisions of this chapter.

SUBCHAPTER IV: Miscellaneous Provisions

§ 1961. Locally convenient day schools

(a) Sense of Congress

It is the sense of Congress that the absence of locally convenient day schools may contribute to the breakup of Indian families.

(b) Report to Congress; contents, etc.

The Secretary is authorized and directed to prepare, in consultation with appropriate agencies in the Department of Health and Human Services, a report on the feasibility of providing Indian children with schools located near their homes, and to submit such report to the Select Committee on Indian Affairs of the United States Senate and the Committee on Interior and Insular Affairs of the United States House of Representatives within two years from November 8, 1978. In developing this report the Secretary shall give particular consideration to the provision of educational facilities for children in the elementary grades.

§ 1962. Copies to the States

Within sixty days after November 8, 1978, the Secretary shall send to the Governor, chief justice of the highest court of appeal, and the attorney general of each State a copy of this chapter, together with committee reports and an explanation of the provisions of this chapter.

§ 1963. Severability

If any provision of this chapter or the applicability thereof is held invalid, the remaining provisions of this chapter shall not be affected thereby.

Federal Regulations

For the reasons stated in the preamble, the Department of the Interior, Bureau of Indian Affairs, amends part 23 in Title 25 of the Code of Federal Regulations as follows:

Part 23—Indian Child Welfare Act

1. The authority citation for part 23 continues to read as follows: 5 U.S.C. 301; 25 U.S.C. 2, 9, 1901–1952.

§ 23.2 Definitions.

* * * * *

Active efforts means affirmative, active, thorough, and timely efforts intended primarily to maintain or reunite an Indian child with his or her family. Where an agency is involved in the child-custody proceeding, active efforts must involve assisting the parent or parents or Indian custodian through the steps of a case plan and with accessing or developing the resources necessary to satisfy the case plan. To the maximum extent possible, active efforts should be provided in a manner consistent with the prevailing social and cultural conditions and way of life of the Indian child's Tribe and should be conducted in partnership with the Indian child and the Indian child's parents, extended family members, Indian custodians, and Tribe. Active efforts are to be tailored to the facts and circumstances of the case and may include, for example:

(1) Conducting a comprehensive assessment of the circumstances of the Indian child's family, with a focus on safe reunification as the most desirable goal;

(2) Identifying appropriate services and helping the parents to overcome barriers, including actively assisting the parents in obtaining such services;

(3) Identifying, notifying, and inviting representatives of the Indian child's Tribe to participate in providing support and services to the Indian child's family and in family team meetings, permanency planning, and resolution of placement issues;

(4) Conducting or causing to be conducted a diligent search for the Indian child's extended family members, and contacting and consulting with extended family members to provide family structure and support for the Indian child and the Indian child's parents;

(5) Offering and employing all available and culturally appropriate family preservation strategies and facilitating the use of remedial and rehabilitative services provided by the child's Tribe;

(6) Taking steps to keep siblings together whenever possible;

(7) Supporting regular visits with parents or Indian custodians in the most natural setting possible as well as trial home visits of the Indian child

during any period of removal, consistent with the need to ensure the health, safety, and welfare of the child; (8) Identifying community resources including housing, financial, transportation, mental health, substance abuse, and peer support services and actively assisting the Indian child's parents or, when appropriate, the child's family, in utilizing and accessing those resources;

(9) Monitoring progress and participation in services;

(10) Considering alternative ways to address the needs of the Indian child's parents and, where appropriate, the family, if the optimum services do not exist or are not available;

(11) Providing post-reunification services and monitoring.

Child-custody proceeding means and includes any action, other than an emergency proceeding, that may culminate in one of the following outcomes:

(1) *Foster-care placement,* which is any action removing an Indian child from his or her parent or Indian custodian for temporary placement in a foster home or institution or the home of a guardian or conservator where the parent or Indian custodian cannot have the child returned upon demand, but where parental rights have not been terminated;

(2) *Termination of parental rights,* which is any action resulting in the termination of the parent-child relationship;

(3) *Preadoptive placement,* which is the temporary placement of an Indian child in a foster home or institution after the termination of parental rights, but prior to or in lieu of adoptive placement; or

(4) *Adoptive placement,* which is the permanent placement of an Indian child for adoption, including any action resulting in a final decree of adoption.

An action that may culminate in one of these four outcomes is considered a separate child-custody proceeding from an action that may culminate in a different one of these four outcomes. There may be several child-custody proceedings involving any given Indian child. Within each child-custody proceeding, there may be several hearings. If a child is placed in foster care or another out-of-home placement as a result of a status offense, that status offense proceeding is a child-custody proceeding.

* * * * *

Continued custody means physical custody or legal custody or both, under any applicable Tribal law or Tribal custom or State law, that a parent or Indian custodian already has or had at any point in the past. The biological mother of a child has had custody of a child.

Custody means physical custody or legal custody or both, under any applicable Tribal law or Tribal custom or State law. A party may demonstrate the existence of custody by looking to Tribal law or Tribal custom or State law.

Domicile means:

(1) For a parent or Indian custodian, the place at which a person has been physically present and that the person regards as home; a person's true, fixed, principal, and permanent home, to which that person intends to return and remain indefinitely even though the person may be currently residing elsewhere.

(2) For an Indian child, the domicile of the Indian child's parents or Indian custodian or guardian. In the case of an Indian child whose parents are not married to each other, the domicile of the Indian child's custodial parent.

Emergency proceeding means and includes any court action that involves an emergency removal or emergency placement of an Indian child.

Extended family member is defined by the law or custom of the Indian child's Tribe or, in the absence of such law or custom, is a person who has reached age 18 and who is the Indian child's grandparent, aunt or uncle, brother or sister, brother-in-law or sister-in-law, niece or nephew, first or second cousin, or stepparent.

* * * * *

Hearing means a judicial session held for the purpose of deciding issues of fact, of law, or both.

* * * * *

Indian child means any unmarried person who is under age 18 and either: (1) is a member or citizen of an Indian Tribe, or (2) is eligible for membership or citizenship in an Indian Tribe and is the biological child of a member/citizen of an Indian Tribe.

Indian child's Tribe means:

(1) The Indian Tribe in which an Indian child is a member or eligible for membership; or

(2) In the case of an Indian child who is a member of or eligible for membership in more than one Tribe, the Indian Tribe described in § 23.109.

Indian custodian means any Indian who has legal custody of an Indian child under applicable Tribal law or custom or under applicable State law, or to whom temporary physical care, custody, and control has been transferred by the parent of such child. An Indian may demonstrate that he or she is an Indian custodian by looking to Tribal law or Tribal custom or State law.

Indian foster home means a foster home where one or more of the licensed or approved foster parents is an "Indian" as defined in 25 U.S.C. 1903(3).

Involuntary proceeding means a child-custody proceeding in which the parent does not consent of his or her free will to the foster-care, preadoptive, or adoptive placement or termination of parental rights or in which the parent consents to the foster-care, preadoptive, or adoptive placement under threat of removal of the child by a State court or agency.

* * * * *

Parent or *parents* means any biological parent or parents of an Indian child, or any Indian who has lawfully adopted an Indian child, including adoptions under Tribal law or custom. It does not include an unwed biological father where paternity has not been acknowledged or established.

Reservation means Indian country as defined in 18 U.S.C 1151 and any lands, not covered under that section, title to which is held by the United States in trust for the benefit of any Indian Tribe or individual or held by any Indian Tribe or individual subject to a restriction by the United States against alienation.

Secretary means the Secretary of the Interior or the Secretary's authorized representative acting under delegated authority.

* * * * *

Status offenses mean offenses that would not be considered criminal if committed by an adult; they are acts prohibited only because of a person's status as a minor (e.g., truancy, incorrigibility).

* * * * *

Tribal court means a court with jurisdiction over child-custody proceedings and which is either a Court of Indian Offenses, a court established and operated under the code or custom of an Indian Tribe, or any other administrative body of a Tribe vested with authority over child-custody proceedings.

* * * * *

Upon demand means that the parent or Indian custodian can regain custody simply upon verbal request, without any formalities or contingencies.

* * * * *

Voluntary proceeding means a child-custody proceeding that is not an involuntary proceeding, such as a proceeding for foster-care, preadoptive, or adoptive placement that either parent, both parents, or the Indian custodian has, of his or her or their free will, without a threat of removal by a State agency, consented to for the Indian child, or a proceeding for voluntary termination of parental rights.

3. Revise § 23.11.

The revision reads as follows:

§ 23.11 Notice.

(a) In any involuntary proceeding in a State court where the court knows or has reason to know that an Indian child is involved, and where the identity and location of the child's parent or Indian custodian or Tribe is known, the party seeking the foster-care placement of, or termination of parental rights to, an Indian child must directly notify the parents, the Indian custodians, and the child's Tribe by registered or certified mail with return receipt requested, of the pending child-custody proceedings and their right of intervention. Notice must include the requisite information identified in§ 23.111 of these regulations, consistent with the confidentiality requirement in § 23.111(a)(2)(I). Copies of these notices must be sent to the appropriate Regional Director listed in paragraphs (b)(1) through (12) by registered or certified mail with return receipt requested or by personal delivery and must include the information required by § 23.111 of these regulations.

(b)(l) For child-custody proceedings in Alabama, Connecticut, Delaware, District of Columbia, Florida, Georgia, Kentucky, Louisiana, Maine, Maryland, Massachusetts, Mississippi, New Hampshire, New Jersey, New York, North Carolina, Pennsylvania, Rhode Island, South Carolina, Tennessee, Vermont, Virginia, West Virginia, or any territory or possession of the United States, notices must be sent to the following address: Eastern Regional Director, Bureau of Indian Affairs, 545 Marriott Drive, Suite 700, Nashville, Tennessee 37214.

(2) For child-custody proceedings in Illinois, Indiana, Iowa, Michigan, Minnesota, Ohio, or Wisconsin, notices must be sent to the following address: Minneapolis Regional Director, Bureau of lndian Affairs, 331 Second Avenue South, Minneapolis, Minnesota 55401-2241.

(3) For child-custody proceedings in Nebraska, North Dakota, or South Dakota, notices must be sent to the following address: Aberdeen Regional Director, Bureau of Indian Affairs, 115 Fourth Avenue, SE, Aberdeen, South Dakota 57401.

(4) For child-custody proceedings in Kansas, Texas (except for notices to the Ysleta del Sur Pueblo of El Paso County, Texas), or the western Oklahoma counties of Alfalfa, Beaver, Beckman, Blaine, Caddo, Canadian, Cimarron, Cleveland, Comanche, Cotton, Custer, Dewey, Ellis, Garfield, Grant, Greer, Harmon, Harper, Jackson, Kay, Kingfisher, Kiowa, Lincoln, Logan, Major, Noble, Oklahoma, Pawnee, Payne, Pottawatomie, Roger Mills, Texas, Tillman, Washita, Woods or Woodward, notices must be sent to the following address: Anadarko Regional Director, Bureau of lndian Affairs, P.O. Box 368, Anadarko, Oklahoma 73005. Notices to the Ysleta del Sur Pueblo must be sent to the Albuquerque Regional Director at the address listed in paragraph (b)(6).

(5) For child-custody proceedings in Wyoming or Montana (except for notices to the Confederated Salish and Kootenai Tribes of the Flathead Reservation, Montana), notices must be sent to the following address: Billings Regional Director, Bureau of lndian Affairs, 316 N. 26th Street, Billings, Montana 59101. Notices to the Confederated Salish and Kootenai Tribes of the Flathead Reservation, Montana, must be sent to the Portland Regional Director at the address listed in paragraph (b)(11).

(6) For child-custody proceedings in the Texas counties of El Paso and Hudspeth or in Colorado or New Mexico (exclusive of notices to the Navajo Nation from the New Mexico counties listed in paragraph (b)(9)), notices must be sent to the following address: Albuquerque Regional Director, Bureau of Indian Affairs, 615 First Street, P.0. Box 26567, Albuquerque, New Mexico 87125. Notices to the

Navajo Nation must be sent to the Navajo Regional Director at the address listed in paragraph (b)(9).

(7) For child-custody proceedings in Alaska (except for notices to the Metlakatla Indian Community, Annette Island Reserve, Alaska), notices must be sent to the following address: Juneau Regional Director, Bureau of Indian Affairs, 709 West 9th Street, Juneau, Alaska 99802-1219. Notices to the Metlakatla Indian Community, Annette Island Reserve, Alaska, must be sent to the Portland Regional Director at the address listed in paragraph (b)(11).

(8) For child-custody proceedings in Arkansas, Missouri, or the eastern Oklahoma counties of Adair, Atoka, Bryan, Carter, Cherokee, Craig, Creek, Choctaw, Coal, Delaware, Garvin, Grady, Haskell, Hughes, Jefferson, Johnson, Latimer, LeFlore, Love, Mayes, McCurtain, McClain, Mcintosh, Murray, Muskogee, Nowata, Okfuskee, Okmulgee, Osage, Ottawa, Pittsburg, Pontotoc, Pushmataha, Marshall, Rogers, Seminole, Sequoyah, Stephens, Tulsa, Wagoner, or Washington, notices must be sent to the following address: Muskogee Regional Director, Bureau of Indian Affairs, 101 North Fifth Street, Muskogee, Oklahoma 74401.

(9) For child-custody proceedings in the Arizona counties of Apache, Coconino (except for notices to the Hopi Tribe of Arizona and the San Juan Southern Paiute Tribe of Arizona) or Navajo (except for notices to the Hopi Tribe of Arizona); the New Mexico counties of McKinley (except for notices to the Zuni Tribe of the Zuni Reservation), San Juan, or Socorro; or the Utah county of San Juan, notices must be sent to the following address: Navajo Regional Director, Bureau of lndian Affairs, P.O. Box 1060, Gallup, New Mexico 87301. Notices to the Hopi and San Juan Southern Paiute Tribes of Arizona must be sent to the Phoenix Regional Director at the address listed in paragraph (b)(10). Notices to the Zuni Tribe ofthe Zuni Reservation must be sent to the Albuquerque Regional Director at the address listed in paragraph (b)(6).

(10) For child-custody proceedings in Arizona (exclusive of notices to the Navajo Nation from those counties listed in paragraph (b)(9)), Nevada, or Utah (exclusive of San Juan County), notices must be sent to the following address: Phoenix Regional Director, Bureau of lndian Affairs, 1 North First Street, P.O. Box 10, Phoenix, Arizona 85001.

(11) For child-custody proceedings in Idaho, Oregon, or Washington, notices must be sent to the following address: Portland Regional Director, Bureau of Indian Affairs, 911 NE 11th Avenue, Portland, Oregon 97232. All notices to the Confederated Salish and Kootenai Tribes of the Flathead Reservation, located in the Montana counties of Flathead, Lake, Missoula, and Sanders, must also be sent to the Portland Regional Director.

(12) For child-custody proceedings in California or Hawaii, notices must be sent to the following address: Sacramento Regional Director, Bureau oflndian Affairs, Federal Office Building, 2800 Cottage Way, Sacramento, California 95825.

(c) Upon receipt of the notice, the Secretary will make reasonable documented efforts to locate and notify the child's Tribe and the child's parent or Indian custodian. The Secretary will have 15 days, after receipt of the notice, to notify the child's Tribe and parents or Indian custodians and to send a copy of the notice to the court. If within the 15-day period the Secretary is unable to verify that the child meets the criteria of an Indian child as defined in § 23.2, or is unable to locate the parents or Indian custodians, the Secretary will so inform the court and state how much more time, if any, will be needed to complete the verification or the search. The Secretary will complete all research efforts, even if those efforts cannot be completed before the child-custody proceeding begins.

(d) Upon request from a party to an Indian child-custody proceeding, the Secretary will make a reasonable attempt to identify and locate the child's Tribe, parents, or Indian custodians to assist the party seeking the information.

4. Revise§ 23.71 as follows:

Subpart G- Administrative Provisions

§ 23.71 Recordkeeping and information availability.

(a) The Division of Human Services, Bureau of lndian Affairs (BIA), is authorized to receive all information and to maintain a central file on all State Indian adoptions. This file is confidential and only designated persons may have access to it.

(b) Upon the request of an adopted Indian who has reached age 18, the adoptive or foster parents of an Indian child, or an Indian Tribe, BIA will disclose such information as may be necessary for purposes of Tribal enrollment or determining any rights or benefits associated with Tribal membership. Where the documents relating to such child contain an affidavit from the biological parent or parents requesting anonymity, BIA must certify to the Indian child's Tribe, where the information warrants, that the child's parentage and other circumstances entitle the child to enrollment under the criteria established by such Tribe.

(c) BIA will ensure that the confidentiality of this information is maintained and that the information is not subject to the Freedom of Information Act, 5 U.S.C. 552, as amended.

5. Add subpart I to read as follows:

Subpart I—Indian Child Welfare Act Proceeding

General Provisions

Sec.

23.101 What is the purpose of this subpart?

23.102 What terms do I need to know?

23.103 When does ICWA apply?

General Provisions

§ 23.101 What is the purpose of this subpart?

These regulations clarify the minimum Federal standards governing implementation of the Indian Child Welfare Act (ICWA) to ensure that ICWA is applied in all States consistent with the Act's express language, Congress's intent in enacting the statute, and to promote the stability and security of Indian tribes and families.

§ 23.102 What terms do I need to know?

The following terms and their definitions apply to this subpart. All other terms have the meanings assigned in § 23.2.

Agency means a nonprofit, for-profit, or governmental organization and its employees, agents, or officials that performs, or provides services to biological parents, foster parents, or adoptive parents to assist in the administrative and social work necessary for foster, preadoptive, or adoptive placements.

Indian organization means any group, association, partnership, corporation, or other legal entity owned or controlled by Indians or a Tribe, or a majority of whose members are Indians.

§ 23.103 When does ICWA apply?

(a) ICWA includes requirements that apply whenever an Indian child is the subject of:

(1) A child-custody proceeding, including:

(i) An involuntary proceeding;

(ii) A voluntary proceeding that could prohibit the parent or Indian custodian from regaining custody of the child upon demand; and

(iii) A proceeding involving status offenses if any part of the proceeding results in the need for out-of-home placement of the child, including a foster-care, preadoptive, or adoptive placement, or termination of parental rights.

(2) An emergency proceeding. (b) ICWA does not apply to: (1) A Tribal court proceeding;

(2) A proceeding regarding a criminal act that is not a status offense;

(3) An award of custody of the Indian child to one of the parents including, but not limited to, an award in a divorce proceeding; or

(4) A voluntary placement that either parent, both parents, or the Indian custodian has, of his or her or their free will, without a threat of removal by a State agency, chosen for the Indian child and that does not operate to prohibit the child's parent or Indian custodian from regaining custody of the child upon demand.

(c) If a proceeding listed in§ 23.103(a) concerns a child who meets the statutory definition of "Indian child," then ICWA will apply to that proceeding. In determining whether ICWA applies to a proceeding, the State court may not consider factors such as the participation of the parents or the Indian child in Tribal cultural, social, religious, or political activities, the relationship between the Indian child and his or her parents, whether the parent ever had custody of the child, or the Indian child's blood quantum.

(d) If ICWA applies at the commencement of a proceeding, it will not cease to apply simply because the child reaches age 18 during the pendency of the proceeding.

§ 23.104 What provisions of this subpart apply to each type of child-custody proceeding?

The following table lists what sections of this regulation apply to each type of child-custody proceeding identified in § 23.103(a):

Section	Type of Proceeding
23.101–23.106 (General Provisions)	Emergency, Involuntary, Voluntary
Pretrial Requirements	—
23.107 (How should a State court determine ifthere is reason to know the child is an Indian child?)	Emergency, Involuntary, Voluntary
23.108 (Who makes the determination as to whether a child is a member whether a child is eligible for membership, or whether a biological parent is a member of a Tribe?)	Emergency, Involuntary, Voluntary
23.109 (How should a State court determine an Indian child's Tribe when the child may be a member or eligible for membership in more than one Tribe?)	Emergency, Involuntary, Voluntary
23.110 (When must a State court dismiss an action?)	Involuntary, Voluntary
23.111 (What are the notice requirements for a child-custody proceeding involving an Indian child?)	Involuntary (foster-care placement and termination of parental rights)
23.112 (What time limits and extensions apply?)	Involuntary (foster-care placement and termination of parental rights)
23.113 (What are the standards for emergency proceedings involving an Indian child?)	Emergency
23.114 (What are the requirements for determining improper removal?)	Involuntary
Petitions to Transfer to Tribal Court	—
23.115 (How are petitions for transfer of a proceeding made?)	Involuntary, Voluntary (foster-care placement and termination of parental rights)
23.116 (What happens after a petition for transfer is made?)	Involuntary, Voluntary (foster-care placement and termination of parental rights)
23.117 (What are the criteria for ruling on transfer petitions?)	Involuntary, Voluntary (foster-care placement and termination of parental rights)
23.118 (How is a determination of "good cause" to deny transfer made?)	Involuntary, Voluntary (foster-care placement and termination of parental r ights)
23.119 (What happens after a petition for transfer is granted?)	Involuntary, Voluntary (foster-care placement and termination of parental rights)

(continued)

Section	Type of Proceeding
Adjudication of Involuntary Proceedings	—
23.120 (How does the State court ensure that active efforts have been made?)	Involuntary (foster-care placement and termination of parental rights)
23.121 (What are the applicable standards of evidence?)	Involuntary (foster-care placement and termination of parental rights)
23.122 (Who may serve as a qualified expert witness?)	Involuntary (foster-care placement and termination of parental rights)
23.123 Reserved.	N/A
Voluntary Proceedings	—
23.124 (What actions must a State court undertake in voluntary proceedings?)	Voluntary
23.125 (How is consent obtained?)	Voluntary
23.126 (What information must a consent document contain?)	Voluntary
23.127 (How is withdrawal of consent to a foster-care placement achieved?)	Voluntary
23.128 (How is withdrawal of consent to a termination of parental rights or adoption achieved?)	Voluntary
Dispositions	—
23.129 (When do the placement preferences apply?)	Involuntary, Voluntary
23.130 (What placement preferences apply in adoptive placements?)	Involuntary, Voluntary
23.131 (What placement preferences apply in foster-care or preadoptive placements?)	Involuntary, Voluntary
23.132 (How is a determination of"good cause" to depart from the placement preferences made?)	Involuntary, Voluntary
Access	—
23.133 (Should courts allow participation by alternative methods?)	Emergency, Involuntary
23.134 (Who has access to reports and records during a proceeding?)	Emergency, Involuntary
23.135 Reserved.	N/A
Post-Trial Rights & Responsibilities	—
23.136 (What are the requirements for vacating an adoption based on consent having been obtained through fraud or duress?)	Involuntary (if consent given under threat of removal), voluntary
23.137 (Who can petition to invalidate an action for certain ICWA violations?)	Emergency (to extent it involved a specified violation), involuntary, voluntary
23.138 (What are the rights to information about adoptees' Tribal affiliations?).	Emergency, Involuntary, Voluntary

(continued)

Section	Type of Proceeding
23.139 (Must notice be given of a change in an adopted Indian child's status?)	Involuntary, Voluntary
Recordkeeping	
23.140 (What information must States furnish to the Bureau of Indian Affairs?)	Involuntary, Voluntary
23.141 (What records must the State maintain?)	Involuntary, Voluntary
23.142 (How does the Paperwork Reduction Act affect this subpart?)	Emergency, Involuntary, Voluntary
Effective Date	—
23.143 (How does this rule apply to pending proceedings?)	Emergency, Involuntary, Voluntary
Severability	—
23.144 (What happens if some portion of this rule is held to be invalid by a court of competent jurisdiction?)	Emergency, Involuntary, Voluntary

For purposes of this table, status-offense child-custody proceedings are included as a type of involuntary proceeding.

§ 23.105 How do I contact a Tribe under the regulations in this subpart?

To contact a Tribe to provide notice or obtain information or verification under these regulations, you should direct the notice or inquiry as follows:

(a) Many Tribes designate an agent for receipt of ICWA notices. The BIA publishes a list of Tribes' designated Tribal agents for service of ICWA notice in the Federal Register each year and makes the list available on its website at www .bia.gov.

(b) For a Tribe without a designated Tribal agent for service of ICWA notice, contact the Tribe to be directed to the appropriate office or individual.

(c) If you do not have accurate contact information for a Tribe, or the Tribe contacted fails to respond to written inquiries, you should seek assistance in contacting the Indian Tribe from the BIA local or regional office or the BIA's Central Office in Washington, D.C. (see www.bia.gov).

§ 23.106 How does this subpart interact with State and Federal laws?

(a) These regulations provide minimum Federal standards to ensure compliance with ICWA.

(b) Under § 1921 of ICWA, where applicable State or other Federal law provides a higher standard of protection to the rights of the parent or Indian custodian than the protection accorded under the Act, ICWA requires the State or Federal court to apply the higher State or Federal standard.

Pretrial Requirements

§ 23.107 How should a State court determine if there is reason to know the child is an Indian child?

(a) State courts must ask each participant in an emergency or voluntary or involuntary child-custody proceeding whether the participant knows or has reason to know that the child is an Indian child. The inquiry is made at the commencement of the proceeding and all responses should be on the record. State courts must instruct the parties to inform the court if they subsequently receive information that provides reason to know the child is an Indian child.

(b) If there is reason to know the child is an Indian child, but the court does not have sufficient evidence to determine that the child is or is not an "Indian child," the court must:

(1) Confirm, by way of a report, declaration, or testimony included in the record that the agency or other party used due diligence to identify and work with all of the Tribes of which there is reason to know the child may be a member (or eligible for membership), to verify whether the child is in fact a member (or a biological parent is a member and the child is eligible for membership); and

(2) Treat the child as an Indian child, unless and until it is determined on the record that the child does not meet the definition of an "Indian child" in this part.

(c) A court, upon conducting the inquiry required in paragraph (a) of this section, has reason to know that a child involved in an emergency or child-custody proceeding is an Indian child if:

(1) Any participant in the proceeding, officer of the court involved in the proceeding, Indian Tribe, Indian organization, or agency informs the court that the child is an Indian child;

(2) Any participant in the proceeding, officer of the court involved in the proceeding, Indian Tribe, Indian organization, or agency informs the court that it has discovered information indicating that the child is an Indian child;

(3) The child who is the subject of the proceeding gives the court reason to know he or she is an Indian child;

(4) The court is informed that the domicile or residence of the child, the child's parent, or the child's Indian custodian is on a reservation or in an Alaska Native village;

(5) The court is informed that the child is or has been a ward of a Tribal court; or

(6) The court is informed that either parent or the child possesses an identification card indicating membership in an Indian Tribe.

(d) In seeking verification of the child's status in a voluntary proceeding where a consenting parent evidences, by written request or statement in the record, a desire for anonymity, the court must keep relevant documents pertaining to the inquiry required under this section confidential and under seal. A request for anonymity does not relieve the court, agency, or other party from any duty of compliance with ICWA, including the obligation to verify whether the child is an "Indian child." A Tribe receiving information related to this inquiry must keep documents and information confidential.

§ 23.108 Who makes the determination as to whether a child is a member, whether a child is eligible for membership, or whether a biological parent is a member of a Tribe?

(a) The Indian Tribe of which it is believed the child is a member (or eligible for membership and of which the biological parent is a member) determines whether the child is a member of the Tribe, or whether the child is eligible for membership in the Tribe and a biological parent of the child is a member of the Tribe, except as otherwise provided by Federal or Tribal law.

(b) The determination by a Tribe of whether a child is a member, whether a child is eligible for membership, or whether a biological parent is a member, is solely within the jurisdiction and authority of the Tribe, except as otherwise provided by Federal or Tribal law. The State court may not substitute its own determination regarding a child's membership in a Tribe, a child 's eligibility for membership in a Tribe, or a parent's membership in a Tribe.

(c) The State court may rely on facts or documentation indicating a Tribal determination of membership or eligibility for membership in making a judicial determination as to whether the child is an "Indian child." An example of documentation indicating membership is a document issued by the Tribe, such as Tribal enrollment documentation.

§ 23.109 How should a State court determine an Indian child's Tribe when the child may be a member or eligible for membership in more than one Tribe?

(a) If the Indian child is a member or eligible for membership in only one Tribe, that Tribe must be designated as the Indian child's Tribe.

(b) If the Indian child meets the definition of "Indian child" through more than one Tribe, deference should be giv.en to the Tribe in which the Indian child is already a member, unless otherwise agreed to by the Tribes.

(c) If an Indian child meets the definition of "Indian child" through more than one Tribe because the child is a member in more than one Tribe or the child is not a member of but is eligible for membership in more than one Tribe, the court must provide the opportunity in any involuntary child-custody proceeding for the Tribes to determine which should be designated as the Indian child's Tribe.

(1) If the Tribes are able to reach an agreement, the agreed-upon Tribe should be designated as the Indian child's Tribe.

(2) If the Tribes are unable to reach an agreement, the State court designates, for the purposes of ICWA, the Indian Tribe with which the Indian child has the more significant contacts as the Indian child's Tribe, taking into consideration:

(i) Preference of the parents for membership of the child;

(ii) Length of past domicile or residence on or near the reservation of each Tribe;

(iii) Tribal membership of the child's custodial parent or Indian custodian;

(iv) Interest asserted by each Tribe in the child-custody proceeding;

(v) Whether there has been a previous adjudication with respect to the child by a court of one of the Tribes; and

(vi) Self-identification by the child, if the child is of sufficient age and capacity to meaningfully self-identify.

(3) A determination of the Indian child's Tribe for purposes of ICWA and these regulations do not constitute a determination for any other purpose.

§ 23.110 When must a State court dismiss an action?

Subject to 25 U.S.C. 1919 (Agreements between States and Indian Tribes) and§ 23.113 (emergency proceedings), the following limitations on a State court's jurisdiction apply:

(a) The court in any voluntary or involuntary child-custody proceeding involving an Indian child must determine the residence and domicile of the Indian child. If either the residence or domicile is on a reservation where the Tribe exercises exclusive jurisdiction over child- custody proceedings, the State court must expeditiously notify the Tribal court of the pending dismissal based on the Tribe's exclusive jurisdiction, dismiss the State-court child-custody proceeding, and ensure that the Tribal court is sent all information regarding the Indian child-custody proceeding, including, but not limited to, the pleadings and any court record.

(b) If the child is a ward of a Tribal court, the State court must expeditiously notify the Tribal court of the pending dismissal, dismiss the State-court child-custody proceeding, and ensure that the Tribal court is sent all information regarding the Indian child-custody proceeding, including, but not limited to, the pleadings and any court record.

§ 23.111 What are the notice requirements for a child-custody proceeding involving an Indian child?

(a) When a court knows or has reason to know that the subject of an involuntary foster- care-placement or termination-of-parental-rights proceeding is an Indian child, the court must ensure that:

(1) The party seeking placement promptly sends notice of each such child-custody proceeding (including, but not limited to, any foster-care placement or any termination of parental or custodial rights) in accordance with this section; and

(2) An original or a copy of each notice sent under this section is filed with the court together with any return receipts or other proof of service.

(b) Notice must be sent to:

(1) Each Tribe where the child may be a member (or eligible for membership if a biological parent is a member) *(see* § 23.105 for information on how to contact a Tribe);

(2) The child's parents; and

(3) If applicable, the child's Indian custodian.

(c) Notice must be sent by registered or certified mail with return receipt requested. Notice may also be sent via personal service or electronically, but such alternative methods do not replace the requirement for notice to be sent by registered or certified mail with return receipt requested.

(d) Notice must be in clear and understandable language and include the following:

(1) The child's name, birthdate, and birthplace;

(2) All names known (including maiden, married, and former names or aliases) of the parents, the parents' birthdates and birthplaces, and Tribal enrollment numbers if known;

(3) If known, the names, birthdates, birthplaces, and Tribal enrollment information of other direct lineal ancestors of the child, such as grandparents;

(4) The name of each Indian Tribe in which the child is a member (or may be eligible for membership if a biological parent is a member);

(5) A copy of the petition, complaint, or other document by which the child-custody proceeding was initiated and, if a hearing has been scheduled, information on the date, time, and location of the hearing;

(6) Statements setting out:

(i) The name of the petitioner and the name and address of petitioner's attorney;

(ii) The right of any parent or Indian custodian of the child, if not already a party to the child-custody proceeding, to intervene in the proceedings.

(iii) The Indian Tribe's right to intervene at any time in a State-court proceeding for the foster-care placement of or termination of parental rights to an Indian child.

(iv) That, if the child's parent or Indian custodian is unable to afford counsel based on a determination of indigency by the court, the parent or Indian custodian has the right to court-appointed counsel.

(v) The right to be granted, upon request, up to 20 additional days to prepare for the child-custody proceedings.

(vi) The right of the parent or Indian custodian and the Indian child's Tribe to petition the court for transfer of the foster-care-placement or termination-of-parental-rights proceeding to Tribal court as provided by 25 U.S.C. 1911 and § 23.115.

(vii) The mailing addresses and telephone numbers of the court and information related to all parties to the child-custody proceeding and individuals notified under this section.

(viii) The potential legal consequences of the child-custody proceedings on the future parental and custodial rights of the parent or Indian custodian.

(ix) That all parties notified must keep confidential the information contained in the notice and the notice should not be handled by anyone not needing the information to exercise rights under ICWA.

(e) If the identity or location of the child's parents, the child's Indian custodian, or the Tribes in which the Indian child is a member or eligible for membership cannot be ascertained, but there is reason to know the child is an Indian child, notice of the child-custody proceeding must be sent to the appropriate Bureau of Indian Affairs Regional Director (see www.bia.gov). To establish Tribal identity, as much information as is known regarding the child's direct lineal ancestors should be provided. The Bureau of Indian Affairs will not make a determination of Tribal membership but may, in some instances, be able to identify Tribes to contact.

(f) If there is a reason to know that a parent or Indian custodian possesses limited English proficiency and is therefore not likely to understand the contents of the notice; the court must provide language access services as required by Title VI of the Civil Rights Act and other Federal laws. To secure such translation or interpretation support, a court may contact or direct a party to contact the Indian child's Tribe or the local BIA office for assistance in locating and obtaining the name of a qualified translator or interpreter.

(g) If a parent or Indian custodian of an Indian child appears in court without an attorney, the court must inform him or her of his or her rights, including any applicable right to appointed counsel, right to request that the child-custody proceeding be transferred to Tribal court, right to object to such transfer, right to request additional time to prepare for the child-custody proceeding as provided in § 23.112, and right (if the parent or Indian custodian is not already a party) to intervene in the child-custody proceedings.

§ 23.112 What time limits and extensions apply?

(a) No foster-care-placement or termination-of-parental-rights proceeding may be held until at least 10 days after receipt of the notice by the parent (or Indian custodian) and by the Tribe (or the Secretary). The parent, Indian custodian, and Tribe each have a right, upon request, to be granted up to 20 additional days from the date upon which notice was received to prepare for participation in the proceeding.

(b) Except as provided in 25 U.S.C. 1922 and§ 23.113, no child-custody proceeding for foster-care placement or termination of parental rights may be held until the waiting periods to which the parents or Indian custodians and to which the Indian child's Tribe are entitled have expired, as follows:

(1) 10 days after each parent or Indian custodian (or Secretary where the parent or Indian custodian is unknown to the petitioner) has received notice of that particular child-custody proceeding in accordance with 25 U.S.C. 1912(a) and§ 23.111;

(2) 10 days after the Indian child's Tribe (or the Secretary if the Indian child's Tribe is unknown to the party seeking placement) has received notice of that particular child-custody proceeding in accordance with 25 U.S.C. 1912(a) and§ 23.111;

(3) Up to 30 days after the parent or Indian custodian has received notice of that particular child-custody proceeding in accordance with 25 U.S.C. 1912(a) and§ 23.111, if the parent or Indian custodian has requested up to 20 additional days to prepare for the child-custody proceeding as provided in 25 U.S.C. 1912(a) and§ 23.111; and

(4) Up to 30 days after the Indian child's Tribe has received notice of that particular child-custody proceeding in accordance with 25 U.S.C. 1912(a) and§ 23.111, if the Indian child's Tribe has requested up to 20 additional days to prepare for the child-custody proceeding.

(c) Additional time beyond the minimum required by 25 U.S.C. 1912 and § 23.111 may also be available under State law or pursuant to extensions granted by the court.

§ 23.113 What are the standards for emergency proceedings involving an Indian child?

(a) Any emergency removal or placement of an Indian child under State law must terminate immediately when the removal or placement is no longer necessary to prevent imminent physical damage or harm to the child.

(b) The State court must:

(1) Make a finding on the record that the emergency removal or placement is necessary to prevent imminent physical damage or harm to the child;

(2) Promptly hold a hearing on whether the emergency removal or placement continues to be necessary whenever new information indicates that the emergency situation has ended; and

(3) At any court hearing during the emergency proceeding, determine whether the emergency removal or placement is no longer necessary to prevent imminent physical damage or harm to the child.

(4) Immediately terminate (or ensure that the agency immediately terminates) the emergency proceeding once the court or agency possesses sufficient evidence to determine that the emergency removal or placement is no longer necessary to prevent imminent physical damage or harm to the child.

(c) An emergency proceeding can be terminated by one or more of the following actions:

(1) Initiation of a child-custody proceeding subject to the provisions of ICWA;

(2) Transfer of the child to the jurisdiction of the appropriate Indian Tribe; or

(3) Restoring the child to the parent or Indian custodian.

(d) A petition for a court order authorizing the emergency removal or continued emergency placement, or its accompanying documents, should contain a statement of the risk of imminent physical damage or harm to the Indian child and any evidence that the emergency removal or placement continues to be necessary to prevent such imminent physical damage or harm to the child. The petition or its accompanying documents should also contain the following information:

(1) The name, age, and last known address of the Indian child;

(2) The name and address of the child's parents and Indian custodians, if any

(3) The steps taken to provide notice to the child's parents, custodians, and Tribe about the emergency proceeding;

(4) If the child's parents and Indian custodians are unknown, a detailed explanation of what efforts have been made to locate and contact them, including contact with the appropriate BIA Regional Director (see www.bia.gov);

(5) The residence and the domicile of the Indian child;

(6) If either the residence or the domicile of the Indian child is believed to be on a reservation or in an Alaska Native village, the name of the Tribe affiliated with that reservation or village;

(7) The Tribal affiliation of the child and of the parents or Indian custodians;

(8) A specific and detailed account of the circumstances that led the agency responsible for the emergency removal of the child to take that action;

(9) If the child is believed to reside or be domiciled on a reservation where the Tribe exercises exclusive jurisdiction over child-custody matters, a statement of efforts that have been made and are being made to contact the Tribe and transfer the child to the Tribe's jurisdiction; and

(10) A statement of the efforts that have been taken to assist the parents or Indian custodians so the Indian child may safely be returned to their custody.

(e) An emergency proceeding regarding an Indian child should not be continued for more than 30 days unless the court makes the following determinations:

(1) Restoring the child to the parent or Indian custodian would subject the child to imminent physical damage or harm;

(2) The court has been unable to transfer the proceeding to the jurisdiction of the appropriate Indian Tribe; and

(3) It has not been possible to initiate a "child-custody proceeding" as defined in § 23.2.

§ 23.114 What are the requirements for determining improper removal?

(a) If, in the course of any child-custody proceeding, any party asserts or the court has reason to believe that the Indian child may have been improperly removed from the custody of his or her parent or Indian custodian, or that the Indian child has been improperly retained (such as after a visit or other temporary relinquishment of custody), the court must expeditiously determine whether there was improper removal or retention.

(b) If the court finds that the Indian child was improperly removed or retained, the court must terminate the proceeding and the child must be returned immediately to his or her parent or Indian custodian, unless returning the child to his parent or Indian custodian would subject the child to substantial and immediate danger or threat of such danger.

Petitions to Transfer to Tribal Court

§ 23.115 How are petitions for transfer of a proceeding made?

(a) Either parent, the Indian custodian, or the Indian child's Tribe may request, at any time, orally on the record or in writing, that the State court transfer a foster-care or termination-of-parental-rights proceeding to the jurisdiction of the child's Tribe.

(b) The right to request a transfer is available at any stage in each foster-care or termination-of-parental-rights proceeding.

§ 23.116 What happens after a petition for transfer is made?

Upon receipt of a transfer petition, the State court must ensure that the Tribal court is promptly notified in writing of the transfer petition. This notification may request a timely response regarding whether the Tribal court wishes to decline the transfer.

§ 23.117 What are the criteria for ruling on transfer petitions?

Upon receipt of a transfer petition from an Indian child's parent, Indian custodian, or Tribe, the State court must transfer the child-custody proceeding unless the court determines that transfer is not appropriate because one or more of the following criteria are met:

(a) Either parent objects to such transfer;

(b) The Tribal court declines the transfer; or

(c) Good cause exists for denying the transfer.

§ 23.118 How is a determination of "good cause" to deny transfer made?

(a) If the State court believes, or any party asserts, that good cause to deny transfer exists, the reasons for that belief or assertion must be stated orally on the record or provided in writing on the record and to the parties to the child-custody proceeding.

(b) Any party to the child-custody proceeding must have the opportunity to provide the court with views regarding whether good cause to deny transfer exists.

(c) In determining whether good cause exists, the court must not consider:

(1) Whether the foster-care or termination-of-parental-rights proceeding is at an advanced stage if the Indian child's parent, Indian custodian, or Tribe did not receive notice of the child-custody proceeding until an advanced stage;

(2) Whether there have been prior proceedings involving the child for which no petition to transfer was filed;

(3) Whether transfer could affect the placement of the child;

(4) The Indian child's cultural connections with the Tribe or its reservation; or

(5) Socioeconomic conditions or any negative perception of Tribal or BIA social services or judicial systems.

(d) The basis for any State-court decision to deny transfer should be stated orally on the record or in a written order.

§ 23.119 What happens after a petition for transfer is granted?

(a) If the Tribal court accepts the transfer, the State court should expeditiously provide the Tribal court with all records related to the proceeding, including, but not limited to, the pleadings and any court record.

(b) The State court should work with the Tribal court to ensure that the transfer of the custody of the Indian child and of the proceeding is accomplished smoothly and in a way that minimizes the disruption of services to the family.

Adjudication of Involuntary Proceedings

§ 23.120 How does the State court ensure that active efforts have been made?

(a) Prior to ordering an involuntary foster-care placement or termination of parental rights, the court must conclude that active efforts have been made to prevent the breakup of the Indian family and that those efforts have been unsuccessful.

(b) Active efforts must be documented in detail in the record.

§ 23.121 What are the applicable standards of evidence?

(a) The court must not order a foster-care placement of an Indian child unless clear and convincing evidence is presented, including the testimony of one or more qualified expert witnesses, demonstrating that the child's continued custody by the child's parent or Indian custodian is likely to result in serious emotional or physical damage to the child.

(b) The court must not order a termination of parental rights for an Indian child unless evidence beyond a reasonable doubt is presented, including the testimony of one or more qualified expert witnesses, demonstrating that the child's continued custody by the child's parent or Indian custodian is likely to result in serious emotional or physical damage to the child.

(c) For a foster-care placement or termination of parental rights, the evidence must show a causal relationship between the particular conditions in the home and the likelihood that continued custody of the child will result in serious emotional or physical damage to the particular child who is the subject of the child-custody proceeding.

(d) Without a causal relationship identified in paragraph (c) of this section, evidence that shows only the existence of community or family poverty, isolation, single parenthood, custodian age, crowded or inadequate housing, substance abuse, or nonconforming social behavior does not by itself constitute clear and convincing evidence or evidence beyond a reasonable doubt that continued custody is likely to result in serious emotional or physical damage to the child.

§ 23.122 Who may serve as a qualified expert witness?

(a) A qualified expert witness must be qualified to testify regarding whether the child's continued custody by the parent or Indian custodian is likely to result in serious emotional or physical damage to the child and should be qualified to testify as to the prevailing social and cultural standards of the Indian child's Tribe. A person may be designated by the Indian child's Tribe as being qualified to testify to the prevailing social and cultural standards of the Indian child's Tribe.

(b) The court or any party may request the assistance of the Indian child's Tribe or the BIA office serving the Indian child's Tribe in locating persons qualified to serve as expert witnesses.

(c) The social worker regularly assigned to the Indian child may not serve as a qualified expert witness in child-custody proceedings concerning the child.

§ 23.123 **[Reserved.]**

Voluntary Proceedings

§ 23.124 What actions must a State court undertake in voluntary proceedings?

(a) The State court must require the participants in a voluntary proceeding to state on the record whether the child is an Indian child, or whether there is reason to believe the child is an Indian child, as provided in § 23.107 of these regulations.

(b) If there is reason to believe the child is an Indian child, the State court must ensure that the party seeking placement has taken all reasonable steps to verify the child's status. This may include contacting the Tribe of which it is believed the child is a member (or eligible for membership and of which the biological parent is a member) to verify the child's status. As described in§ 23.107, where a consenting parent requests anonymity, a Tribe receiving such information must keep relevant documents and information confidential.

(c) State courts must ensure that the placement for the Indian child complies with §§ 23.129–23.132.

§ 23.125 How is consent obtained?

(a) A parent's or Indian custodian's consent to a voluntary termination of parental rights or to a foster-care, preadoptive, or adoptive placement must be executed in writing and recorded before a court of competent jurisdiction.

(b) Prior to accepting the consent, the court must explain to the parent or Indian custodian:

(1) The terms and consequences of the consent in detail; and

(2) The following limitations, applicable to the type of child-custody proceeding for which consent is given, on withdrawal of consent:

(i) For consent to foster-care placement, the parent or Indian custodian may withdraw consent for any reason, at any time, and have the child returned; or

(ii) For consent to termination of parental rights, the parent or Indian custodian may withdraw consent for any reason, at any time prior to the entry of the final decree of termination and have the child returned; or

(iii) For consent to an adoptive placement, the parent or Indian custodian may withdraw consent for any reason, at any time prior to the entry of the final decree of adoption, and have the child returned.

(c) The court must certify that the terms and consequences of the consent were explained on the record in detail in English (or the language of the parent or Indian custodian, if English is not the primary language) and were fully understood by the parent or Indian custodian.

(d) Where confidentiality is requested or indicated, execution of consent need not be made in a session of court open to the public but still must be made before a court of competent jurisdiction in compliance with this section.

(e) A consent given prior to, or within 10 days after, the birth of an Indian child is not valid.

§ 23.126 What information must a consent document contain?

(a) If there are any conditions to the consent, the written consent must clearly set out the conditions.

(b) A written consent to foster-care placement should contain, in addition to the information specified in paragraph (a) of this section, the name and birthdate of the Indian child; the name of the Indian child's Tribe; the Tribal enrollment number for the parent and for the Indian child, where known, or some other indication of the child's membership in the Tribe; the name, address, and other identifying information of the consenting parent or Indian custodian; the name and address of the person or entity, if any, who arranged the placement; and the name and address of the prospective foster parents, if known at the time.

§ 23.127 How is withdrawal of consent to a foster-care placement achieved?

(a) The parent or Indian custodian may withdraw consent to voluntary foster-care placement at any time.

(b) To withdraw consent, the parent or Indian custodian must file a written document with the court or otherwise testify before the court. Additional methods of withdrawing consent may be available under State law.

(c) When a parent or Indian custodian withdraws consent to a voluntary foster-care placement, the court must ensure that the Indian child is returned to that parent or Indian custodian as soon as practicable.

§ 23.128 How is withdrawal of consent to a termination of parental rights or adoption achieved?

(a) A parent may withdraw consent to voluntary termination of parental rights at any time prior to the entry of a final decree of termination.

(b) A parent or Indian custodian may withdraw consent to voluntary adoption at any time prior to the entry of a final decree of adoption.

(c) To withdraw consent prior to the entry of a final decree of adoption, the parent or Indian custodian must file a written document with the court or otherwise testify before the court. Additional methods of withdrawing consent may be available under State law.

(d) The court in which the withdrawal of consent is filed must promptly notify the person or entity who arranged any voluntary preadoptive or adoptive placement of such filing, and the Indian child must be returned to the parent or Indian custodian as soon as practicable.

Dispositions

§ 23.129 When do the placement preferences apply?

(a) In any preadoptive, adoptive, or foster-care placement of an Indian child, the placement preferences specified in § 23.130 and§ 23.131 apply.

(b) Where a consenting parent requests anonymity in a voluntary proceeding, the court must give weight to the request in applying the preferences.

(c) The placement preferences must be applied in any foster-care, preadoptive, or adoptive placement unless there is a determination on the record that good cause under § 23.132 exists to not apply those placement preferences.

§ 23.130 What placement preferences apply in adoptive placements?

(a) In any adoptive placement of an Indian child under State law, where the Indian child's Tribe has not established a different order of preference under paragraph (b) of this section, preference must be given in descending order, as listed below, to placement of the child with:

(1) A member of the Indian child's extended family;

(2) Other members of the Indian child's Tribe; or

(3) Other Indian families.

(b) If the Indian child's Tribe has established by resolution a different order of preference than that specified in ICWA, the Tribe's placement preferences apply.

(c) The court must, where appropriate, also consider the placement preference of the Indian child or Indian child's parent.

§ 23.131 What placement preferences apply in foster-care or preadoptive placements?

(a) In any foster-care or preadoptive placement of an Indian child under State law, including changes in foster-care or preadoptive placements, the child must be placed in the least-restrictive setting that:

(1) Most approximates a family, taking into consideration sibling attachment;

(2) Allows the Indian child's special needs (if any) to be met; and

(3) Is in reasonable proximity to the Indian child's home, extended family, or siblings.

(b) In any foster-care or preadoptive placement of an Indian child under State law, where the Indian child's Tribe has not established a different order of preference under paragraph (c) of this section, preference must be given, in descending order as listed below, to placement of the child with:

(1) A member of the Indian child's extended family;

(2) A foster home that is licensed, approved, or specified by the Indian child's Tribe;

(3) An Indian foster home licensed or approved by an authorized non-Indian licensing authority; or

(4) An institution for children approved by an Indian Tribe or operated by an Indian organization which has a program suitable to meet the child's needs.

(c) If the Indian child's Tribe has established by resolution a different order of preference than that specified in ICWA, the Tribe's placement preferences apply, so long as the placement is the least-restrictive setting appropriate to the particular needs ofthe Indian child, as provided in paragraph (a) of this section.

(d) The court must, where appropriate, also consider the preference of the Indian child or the Indian child's parent.

§ 23.132 How is a determination of "good cause" to depart from the placement preferences made?

(a) If any party asserts that good cause not to follow the placement preferences exists, the reasons for that belief or assertion must be stated orally on the record or provided in writing to the parties to the child-custody proceeding and the court.

(b) The party seeking departure from the placement preferences should bear the burden of proving by clear and convincing evidence that there is "good cause" to depart from the placement preferences.

(c) A court's determination of good cause to depart from the placement preferences must be made on the record or in writing and should be based on one or more of the following considerations:

(1) The request of one or both of the Indian child's parents, if they attest that they have reviewed the placement options, if any, that comply with the order of preference;

(2) The request of the child, if the child is of sufficient age and capacity to understand the decision that is being made;

(3) The presence of a sibling attachment that can be maintained only through a particular placement;

(4) The extraordinary physical, mental, or emotional needs of the Indian child, such as specialized treatment services that may be unavailable in the community where families who meet the placement preferences live;

(5) The unavailability of a suitable placement after a determination by the court that a diligent search was conducted to find suitable placements meeting the preference criteria, but none has been located. For purposes of this analysis, the standards for determining whether a placement is unavailable must conform to the prevailing social and cultural standards of the Indian community in which the Indian child's parent or extended family resides or with which the Indian child's parent or extended family members maintain social and cultural ties.

(d) A placement may not depart from the preferences based on the socioeconomic status of any placement relative to another placement.

(e) A placement may not depart from the preferences based solely on ordinary bonding or attachment that flowed from time spent in a non-preferred placement that was made in violation of ICWA.

Access

§ 23.133 Should courts allow participation by alternative methods?

If it possesses the capability, the court should allow alternative methods of participation in State-court child-custody proceedings involving an Indian child, such as participation by telephone, videoconferencing, or other methods.

§ 23.134 Who has access to reports and records during a proceeding?

Each party to an emergency proceeding or a foster-care-placement or termination-of-parental-rights proceeding under State law involving an Indian child has a right to timely examine all reports and other documents filed or lodged with the court upon which any decision with respect to such action may be based.

§ 23.135 [Reserved.]

Post-Trial Rights & Responsibilities

§ 23.136 What are the requirements for vacating an adoption based on consent having been obtained through fraud or duress?

(a) Within two years after a final decree of adoption of any Indian child by a State court, or within any longer period of time permitted by the law of the State, the State court may invalidate the voluntary adoption upon finding that the parent's consent was obtained by fraud or duress.

(b) Upon the parent's filing of a petition to vacate the final decree of adoption of the parent's Indian child, the court must give notice to all parties to the adoption proceedings and the Indian child's Tribe and must hold a hearing on the petition.

(c) Where the court finds that the parent's consent was obtained through fraud or duress, the court must vacate the final decree of adoption, order the consent revoked, and order that the child be returned to the parent.

§ 23.137 Who can petition to invalidate an action for certain ICWA violations?

(a) Any of the following may petition any court of competent jurisdiction to invalidate an action for foster-care placement or termination of parental rights under state law where it is alleged that 25 U.S.C. 1911, 1912, or 1913 has been violated:

(1) An Indian child who is or was the subject of any action for foster-care placement or termination of parental rights;

(2) A parent or Indian custodian from whose custody such child was removed; and

(3) The Indian child's Tribe.

(b) Upon a showing that an action for foster-care placement or termination of parental rights violated any provision of 25 U.S.C. 1911, 1912, or 1913, the court must determine whether it is appropriate to invalidate the action.

(c) To petition for invalidation, there is no requirement that the petitioner's rights under ICWA were violated; rather, a petitioner may challenge the action based on any violations of 25 U.S.C. 1911, 1912, or 1913 during the course of the child-custody proceeding.

§ 23.138 What are the rights to information about adoptees' Tribal affiliations?

Upon application by an Indian who has reached age 18 who was the subject of an adoptive placement, the court that entered the final decree of adoption must inform such individual of the Tribal affiliations, if any, of the individual's biological parents and provide such other information necessary to protect any rights, which may include Tribal membership, resulting from the individual's Tribal relationship.

§ 23.139 Must notice be given of a change in an adopted Indian child's status?

(a) If an Indian child has been adopted, the court must notify, by registered or certified mail with return receipt requested, the child's biological parent or prior Indian custodian and the Indian child's Tribe whenever:

(1) A final decree of adoption of the Indian child has been vacated or set aside; or

(2) The adoptive parent has voluntarily consented to the termination of his or her parental rights to the child.

(b) The notice must state the current name, and any former name, of the Indian child, inform the recipient of the right to petition for return of custody of the child, and provide sufficient information to allow the recipient to participate in any scheduled hearings.

(c) A parent or Indian custodian may waive his or her right to such notice by executing a written waiver of notice and filing the waiver with the court.

(1) Prior to accepting the waiver, the court must explain the consequences of the waiver and explain how the waiver may be revoked.

(2) The court must certify that the terms and consequences of the waiver and how the waiver may be revoked were explained in detail in English (or the language

of the parent or Indian custodian, if English is not the primary language), and were fully understood by the parent or Indian custodian.

(3) Where confidentiality is requested or indicated, execution of the waiver need not be made in a session of court open to the public but still must be made before a court of competent jurisdiction in compliance with this section.

(4) The biological parent or Indian custodian may revoke the waiver at any time by filing with the court a written notice of revocation.

(5) A revocation of the right to receive notice does not affect any child-custody proceeding that was completed before the filing of the notice of revocation.

Recordkeeping

§ 23.140 What information must States furnish to the Bureau of Indian Affairs?

(a) Any State court entering a final adoption decree or order in any voluntary or involuntary Indian-child adoptive placement must furnish a copy of the decree or order within 30 days to the Bureau of Indian Affairs, Chief, Division of Human Services, 1849 C Street NW Mail Stop 4513 MIB, Washington, DC 20240, along with the following information, in an envelope marked "Confidential":

(1) Birth name and birthdate of the Indian child, and Tribal affiliation and name of the Indian child after adoption;

(2) Names and addresses of the biological parents;

(3) Names and addresses of the adoptive parents;

(4) Name and contact information for any agency having files or information relating to the adoption;

(5) Any affidavit signed by the biological parent or parents asking that their identity remain confidential; and

(6) Any information relating to Tribal membership or eligibility for Tribal membership of the adopted child.

(b) If a State agency has been designated as the repository for all State-court adoption information and is fulfilling the duties described in paragraph (a) of this section, the State courts in that State need not fulfill those same duties.

§ 23.141 What records must the State maintain?

(a) The State must maintain a record of every voluntary or involuntary foster-care, preadoptive, and adoptive placement of an Indian child and make the record available within 14 days of a request by an Indian child's Tribe or the Secretary.

(b) The record must contain, at a minimum, the petition or complaint, all substantive orders entered in the child-custody proceeding, the complete record of the placement determination (including, but not limited to, the findings in the court record and the social worker's statement), and, if the placement departs from the placement preferences, detailed documentation of the efforts to comply with the placement preferences.

(c) A State agency or agencies may be designated to be the repository for this information. The State court or agency should notify the BIA whether these records are maintained within the court system or by a State agency.

§ 23.142 How does the Paperwork Reduction Act affect this subpart?

The collection of information contained in this part have been approved by the Office of Management and Budget under 44 U.S.C. 3501 et seq. and assigned the OMB Control Number 1076-0186. Response is required to obtain a benefit. A Federal agency may not conduct or sponsor, and you are not required to respond to, a collection of information unless the form or regulation requesting the information displays a currently valid OMB Control Number. Send comments regarding this collection of information, including suggestions for reducing the burden, to the Information Collection Clearance Officer- Indian Affairs, 1849 C Street, NW., Washington, DC 20240.

Effective Date

§ 23.143 How does this rule apply to pending proceedings?

None of the provisions of this rule affects a proceeding under State law for foster-care placement, termination of parental rights, preadoptive placement, or adoptive placement that was initiated prior to December 12, 2016, but the provisions of this rule apply to any subsequent proceeding in the same matter or subsequent proceedings affecting the custody or placement of the same children

Severability

§ 23.144 What happens if some portion of this rule is held to be invalid by a court of competent jurisdiction?

If any portion of this rule is determined to be invalid by a court of competent jurisdiction, the other portions of the rule remain in effect. For example, the Department has considered separately whether the provisions of this rule apply to involuntary and voluntary proceedings; thus, if a particular provision is held to be invalid as to one type of proceeding, it is the Department's intent that it remains valid as to the other type of proceeding.

Guidelines for
Implementing the Indian Child Welfare Act

December 2016

U.S. Department of the Interior
Office of the Assistant Secretary—Indian Affairs
Bureau of Indian Affairs

Guidelines for Implementing the Indian Child Welfare Act

Purpose of These Guidelines

These guidelines are intended to assist those involved in child custody proceedings in understanding and uniformly applying the Indian Child Welfare Act (ICWA) and U.S. Department of the Interior (Department) regulations (also referred to as a "rule"). All such parties—including the courts, state child welfare agencies, private adoption agencies, Tribes, and family members—have a stake in ensuring the proper implementation of this important Federal law designed to protect Indian children, their parents, and Indian Tribes.

ICWA is a statute passed by Congress and codified in the United States Code (U.S.C.). The Department promulgated ICWA regulations to implement the statute; the regulations were published in the Federal Register and will be codified in the Code of Federal Regulations (CFR).

ICWA, the statute: Codified in the United State Code (U.S.C.) at 25 U.S.C. 1901 *et seq.*

ICWA regulations: Published at 81 FR 38864 (June 14, 2016) and codified at 25 CFR part 23.

The regulations apply to any child custody proceeding initiated on or after December 12, 2016, even if the child has already undergone child custody proceedings prior to that date to which the regulation did not apply. The statute defines a "child-custody proceeding" as a foster-care placement, a termination of parental rights (TPR), a preadoptive placement, or an adoptive placement; so, if any one of these types of proceedings is initiated on or after December 12, 2016, the rule applies to that proceeding.[1]

While not imposing binding requirements, these guidelines provide a reference and resource for all parties involved in child custody proceedings involving Indian children. These guidelines explain the statute and regulations and also provide examples of best practices for the implementation of the statute, with the goal of encouraging greater uniformity in the application of ICWA. These guidelines replace the 1979 and 2015 versions of the Department's guidelines.

Reader's Tip: Under each heading of these guidelines is a regulatory provision (if there is one) and then guidelines to provide guidance, recommended practices, and suggestions for implementation. The text of the regulation is included as part of these guidelines for ease of reference and also because it reflects the Department's guidance on ICWA's requirements.

Context for ICWA, the Regulations, and These Guidelines

Congress enacted ICWA in 1978 to address the Federal, State, and private agency policies and practices that resulted in the "wholesale separation of Indian children from their families."[2] Congress found "that an alarmingly high percentage of Indian families are broken up by the removal, often unwarranted, of their children from them by nontribal public and private agencies and that an alarmingly high percentage of such children are placed in non-Indian foster and adoptive homes and institutions . . . ."[3] Although the crisis flowed from multiple causes, Congress found that non-Tribal public and private agencies had played a significant role, and that State agencies and courts had often failed to recognize the essential Tribal relations of Indian people and the cultural and social standards prevailing in Indian communities and families.[4] To address this failure, ICWA establishes minimum Federal standards for the removal of Indian children from their families and the placement of these children in foster or adoptive homes, and confirms Tribal jurisdiction over child-custody proceedings involving Indian children.[5]

Following ICWA's enactment, the Department issued regulations in July 1979 addressing notice procedures for involuntary child custody proceedings involving Indian children, as well as governing the provision of funding for and administration of Indian child and family service programs as authorized by ICWA.[6] Those reg-

1. *See* 25 U.S.C. 1903(1); 25 CFR § 23.2.
2. H.R. Rep. No. 95-1386, at 9 (1978), reprinted in 1978 U.S.C.C.A.N. 7530, 7531.
3. 25 U.S.C. 1901(4).
4. 25 U.S.C. 1901(4)-(5).
5. 25 U.S.C. 1902.
6. See 25 CFR part 23.

ulations did not address the specific requirements and standards that ICWA imposes upon State court child custody proceedings, beyond the requirements for contents of the notice. Also, in 1979, the Department published guidelines for State courts to use in interpreting many of ICWA's requirements in Indian child custody proceedings.[7] In 2014, the Department invited public comments to determine whether to update its guidelines to address inconsistencies in State-level ICWA implementation that had arisen since 1979 and, if so, what changes should be made. The Department held several listening sessions, including sessions with representatives of federally recognized Indian Tribes, State-court representatives (e.g., the National Council of Juvenile and Family Court Judges (NCJFCJ) and the National Center for State Courts' Conference of Chief Justices Tribal Relations Committee), the National Indian Child Welfare Association, and the National Congress of American Indians. The Department received comments from those at the listening sessions and also received written comments, including comments from individuals and additional organizations. The Department considered these comments and subsequently published updated Guidelines (2015 Guidelines) in February 2015.[8]

Many commenters on the 2015 Guidelines requested not only that the Department update its ICWA guidelines but that the Department also issue binding regulations addressing the requirements and standards that ICWA provides for State-court child-custody proceedings. Recognizing the need for such regulations, the Department engaged in a notice-and-comment process to promulgate formal ICWA regulations. The Department issued a proposed rule on March 20, 2015.[9] After gathering and reviewing comments on the proposed rule, the Department issued a final rule on June 14, 2016.[10] When it issued those regulations, the Department noted that it planned to issue updated guidelines, which it is doing with these guidelines.[11] These guidelines replace both the 2015 and the 1979 versions of the Department's guidelines.

The Department has found that, since ICWA's passage in 1978, implementation and interpretation of the Act has been inconsistent across States and sometimes can vary greatly even within a State. This has led to significant variation in applying ICWA's statutory terms and protections. This variation means that an Indian child and her parents in one State can receive different rights and protections under Federal law than an Indian child and her parents in another State. This disparate application of ICWA based on where the Indian child resides creates significant gaps in ICWA protections and is contrary to the uniform minimum Federal standards intended by Congress.

---

7. 44 FR 67584 (Nov. 26, 1979).
8. See 80 FR 10146 (Feb. 25, 2015).
9. 80 FR 14480 (Mar. 20, 2015).
10. 81 FR 38778 (June 14, 2016).
11. Id. at 38780.

The need for consistent minimum Federal standards to protect Indian children, families, and Tribes still exists today. The special relationship between the United States and the Indian Tribes and their members upon which Congress based the statute continues in full force, as does the United States' direct interest, as trustee, in protecting Indian children who are members of or are eligible for membership in an Indian Tribe.[12] Native American children, however, are still disproportionately more likely to be removed from their homes and communities than other children.[13] In addition, some State court interpretations of ICWA have essentially voided Federal protections for groups of Indian children to whom ICWA clearly applies. And commenters provided numerous anecdotal accounts where Indian children were unnecessarily removed from their parents and extended families; where the rights of Indian children, their parents, or their Tribes were not protected; or where significant delays occurred in Indian child-custody proceedings due to disputes or uncertainty about the interpretation of the Federal law.

For these reasons, and to promote the consistent application of ICWA across the United States, the Department issued the June 2016 regulations and is issuing these guidelines.

A. General Provisions

A.1 Federal ICWA and ICWA regulations and other Federal and State law

Regulation

§ 23.106 How does this subpart interact with State and Federal laws?

(a) The regulations in this subpart provide minimum Federal standards to ensure compliance with ICWA.

(b) Under section 1921 of ICWA, where applicable State or other Federal law provides a higher standard of protection to the rights of the parent or Indian custodian than the protection accorded under the Act, ICWA requires the State or Federal court to apply the higher State or Federal standard.

12. 25 U.S.C. 1901, 1901(2).

13. See, e.g., Attorney General's Advisory Committee on American Indian and Alaska Native Children Exposed to Violence, Ending Violence So Children Can Thrive 87 (Nov. 2014); National Council of Juvenile and Family Court Judges, Disproportionality Rates for Children of Color in Foster Care, Fiscal Year 2013 (June 2015).

Guidelines

ICWA establishes the minimum procedural and substantive standards that must be met, regardless of State law. The regulations provide a binding, consistent, nationwide interpretation of ICWA's minimum standards. ICWA displaces State laws and procedures that are less protective.[14]

Many States have their own laws applying to child welfare proceedings involving Indian children that establish protections beyond the minimum Federal standards. In those instances, the more protective State law applies. For example, the Federal ICWA does not require notice requirements in voluntary child custody proceedings (although such notice is a recommended practice). Some States have passed laws that do require notice in voluntary proceedings and that higher standard of protection would apply.

A.2 Tribal-State ICWA agreements

Regulation

(The statute (at 25 U.S.C 1919) specifies that the Tribe and State may enter into an agreement. The regulation makes clear that the mandatory dismissal provisions in § 23.110 are "[s]ubject to 25 U.S.C. 1919 (Agreements between States and Indian Tribes).")

Guidelines

Some States and Tribes have entered into negotiated Tribal-State agreements that establish specific procedures to follow in Indian child custody proceedings. The Department strongly encourages both Tribes and States to enter into these cooperative agreements. The statute makes clear these agreements can address the "care and custody of Indian children and jurisdiction over child custody proceedings" and specifically can include agreements that provide for the orderly transfer of jurisdiction on a case-by-case basis and agreements that provide for concurrent jurisdiction between States and Indian tribes. 25 U.S.C. 1919. The regulation provides, for example, that the mandatory dismissal provisions in § 23.110 do not apply if the State and Tribe have an agreement regarding the jurisdiction whereby the Tribes choose to refrain from asserting jurisdiction. Such agreements can also address how States notify Tribes in emergency removal and initial State hearings, financial arrangements between the Tribe and State regarding care of children, mechanisms for identifying and recruiting appropriate placements and other similar topics.

14. See, e.g., In re Adoption of M.T.S., 489 N.W. 2d 285, 288 (Minn. Ct. App. 1992) (ICWA preempted Minnesota State law because State law did not provide higher standard of protection to the rights of the parent or Indian custodian of Indian child).

A.3 Considerations in providing access to State court ICWA proceedings

Regulation

§ 23.133 Should courts allow participation by alternative methods?

If it possesses the capacity, the court should allow alternative methods of participation in the State-court child custody proceedings involving an Indian child, such as participation by telephone, videoconferencing, or other methods.

Guidelines

Section 23.133 encourages State courts to permit alternative means of participation in Indian child-custody proceedings, such as by phone or video. This enables the court to receive all relevant information regarding the child's circumstances, and also minimizes burdens on Tribes and other parties. Several State court systems permit the use of video-conferencing in various types of proceedings.[15] The Department notes that requesting statements under oath, even by teleconference, as to who is present may provide sufficient safeguards to maintain control over who is present on the teleconference for the purposes of confidentiality. A service such as Skype would be included in "other methods."

This issue may be particularly relevant to a Tribe's participation in a case. A Tribe's members may live far from the Tribal reservation or headquarters and the Indian child's Tribe may not necessarily be located near the State court Indian child custody proceeding. As such, it may be difficult for many Tribes to participate in State court proceedings, particularly where those actions take place outside of the Tribe's State. Allowing alternative methods of participation in a court proceeding can help alleviate that burden.

Another barrier to Tribal participation in State court proceedings is that the Tribe may not have an attorney licensed to practice law in the State in which the Indian child custody proceeding is being held. Many tribes have limited funds to hire local counsel. The Department encourages all State courts to permit Tribal representatives to present before the court in ICWA proceedings regardless of whether they are attorneys or attorneys licensed in that State, as a number of State courts have already done.[16]

---

15. *See, e.g.*, National Center for State Courts Video Technologies Resource Guide (available at www.ncsc.org/Topics/Technology/Video-Technologiesw/Resource-Guide.aspx).

16. *See, e.g.*, *J.P.H. v. Fla. Dep't of Children & Families*, 39 So.3d 560 (Fla. Dist. Ct. App.2010) (per curiam); *State v. Jennifer M. (In re Elias L.)*, 767 N.W.2d 98, 104 (Neb. 2009); *In re N.N.E.*, 752 N.W. 2d 1, 12 (Iowa 2008); *State ex rel. Juvenile Dep't of Lane Cty. v. Shuey*, 850 P.2d 378 (Or. Ct. App. 1993).

B. Applicability & Verification

It is important to determine at the outset of any State court child custody proceeding whether ICWA applies. Doing so promotes stability for Indian children and families and conserves resources by reducing the need for delays, duplication, appeals, and attendant disruptions. There are two questions to ask in determining whether ICWA applies:

1. Does ICWA apply to this child?
2. Does ICWA apply to the proceeding?

B.1 Determining whether the child is an "Indian child" under ICWA

Regulation

---

§ 23.2 *Indian child* means any unmarried person who is under age 18 and either:

(1) Is a member or citizen of an Indian Tribe; or

(2) Is eligible for membership or citizenship in an Indian Tribe and is the biological child of a member/citizen of an Indian Tribe.

§ 23.107 How should a State court determine if there is reason to know the child is an Indian child?

(a) State courts must ask each participant in an emergency or voluntary or involuntary child-custody proceeding whether the participant knows or has reason to know that the child is an Indian child. The inquiry is made at the commencement of the proceeding and all responses should be on the record. State courts must instruct the parties to inform the court if they subsequently receive information that provides reason to know the child is an Indian child.

(b) If there is reason to know the child is an Indian child, but the court does not have sufficient evidence to determine that the child is or is not an "Indian child," the court must:

(1) Confirm, by way of a report, declaration, or testimony included in the record that the agency or other party used due diligence to identify and work with all of the Tribes of which there is reason to know the child may be a member (or eligible for membership), to verify whether the child is in fact a member (or a biological parent is a member and the child is eligible for membership); and

(2) Treat the child as an Indian child, unless and until it is determined on the record that the child does not meet the definition of an "Indian child" in this part.

(c) A court, upon conducting the inquiry required in paragraph (a) of this section, has reason to know that a child involved in an emergency or child-custody proceeding is an Indian child if:

(1) Any participant in the proceeding, officer of the court involved in the proceeding, Indian Tribe, Indian organization, or agency informs the court that the child is an Indian child;

(2) Any participant in the proceeding, officer of the court involved in the proceeding, Indian Tribe, Indian organization, or agency informs the court that it has discovered information indicating that the child is an Indian child;

(3) The child who is the subject of the proceeding gives the court reason to know he or she is an Indian child;

(4) The court is informed that the domicile or residence of the child, the child's parent, or the child's Indian custodian is on a reservation or in an Alaska Native village;

(5) The court is informed that the child is or has been a ward of a Tribal court;

or

(6) The court is informed that either parent or the child possesses an identification card indicating membership in an Indian Tribe.

(d) In seeking verification of the child's status in a voluntary proceeding where a consenting parent evidences, by written request or statement in the record, a desire for anonymity, the court must keep relevant documents pertaining to the inquiry required under this section confidential and under seal. A request for anonymity does not relieve the court, agency, or other party from any duty of compliance with ICWA, including the obligation to verify whether the child is an "Indian child." A Tribe receiving information related to this inquiry must keep documents and information confidential.

Guidelines

Definition of "Indian child"

The rule reflects the statutory definition of "Indian child," which is based on the child's political ties to a federally recognized Indian Tribe, either by virtue of the child's own citizenship in the Tribe, or through a biological parent's citizenship and the child's eligibility for citizenship. ICWA does not apply simply based on a child or parent's Indian ancestry. Instead, there must be a political relationship to the Tribe.

Most Tribes require that individuals apply for citizenship and demonstrate how they meet that Tribe's membership criteria. Congress recognized that there may not have been an opportunity for an infant or minor child to become a citizen of a Tribe prior to the child-custody proceeding, and found that Congress had the power to act for those children's protection given the political tie to the Tribe through parental citizenship and the child's own eligibility.[17]

Inquiry

Even if a party fails to assert that ICWA may apply, the court has a duty to inquire as to ICWA's applicability to the proceeding.

Timing of inquiry. The applicability of ICWA to a child-custody proceeding turns on the threshold question of whether the child in the case is an "Indian child." It is, therefore, critically important that there be inquiry into that threshold issue by courts, State agencies, and participants to the proceedings as soon as possible. If this inquiry is not timely, a child-custody proceeding may not comply with ICWA and thus may deny ICWA protections to Indian children and their families or, at the very least, cause inefficiencies. The failure to timely determine if ICWA applies also can generate unnecessary delays, as the court and the parties may need to redo certain processes or findings under the correct standard. This is inefficient for courts and parties, and can create delays and instability in placements for the Indian child.

Subsequent discovery of information. Recognizing that facts change during the course of a child-custody proceeding, courts must instruct the participants to inform the court if they subsequently learn information that provides "reason to know" the child is an "Indian child." Thus, if the State agency subsequently discovers that the child is an Indian child, for example, or if a parent enrolls the child in an Indian Tribe, they will need to inform the court so that the proceeding can move forward in compliance with the requirements of ICWA.

Inquiry each proceeding. The rule does not require an inquiry at each hearing within a proceeding; but, if a new child-custody proceeding (such as a proceeding to terminate parental rights or for adoption) is initiated for the same child, the court must make a finding as to whether there is "reason to know" that the child is an Indian child. In situations in which the child was not identified as an Indian child in the prior proceeding, the court has a continuing duty to inquire whether the child is an Indian child.[18]

---

17. See, e.g., H.R. Rep. No. 95-1386, at 17. This is consistent with other contexts in which the citizenship of a parent is relevant to the child's political affiliation to that sovereign. See, e.g., 8 U.S.C. 1401 (providing for U.S. citizenship for persons born outside of the United States when one or both parents are citizens and certain other conditions are met); id. 1431 (child born outside the United States automatically becomes a citizen when at least one parent of the child is a citizen of the United States and certain other conditions are met).

18. *See, e.g., In re Isaiah W.,* 1 Cal.5th 1 (2016).

Reason to Know

If the court has "reason to know" that a child is a member of a Tribe, then certain obligations under the statute and regulations are triggered (specifically, the court must confirm that due diligence was used to: (1) identify the Tribe; (2) work with the Tribe to verify whether the child is a citizen or a biological parent is a citizen and the child is eligible for citizenship; and (3) treat the child as an Indian child, unless and until it is determined that the child is not an Indian child).

The regulation lists factors that indicate a "reason to know" the child is an "Indian child." State courts and agencies are encouraged to interpret these factors expansively. When in doubt, it is better to conduct further investigation into a child's status early in the case; this establishes which laws will apply to the case and minimizes the potential for delays or disrupted placements in the future. States or courts may choose to require additional investigation into whether there is a reason to know the child is an Indian child.

When one or more factors is present. If there is "reason to know" the child is an "Indian child," the court needs to ensure that due diligence was used to identify and work with all of the Tribes of which there is a reason to know the child may be a member or eligible for membership, to verify whether the child is in fact a member (or a biological parent is a member and the child is eligible for membership). In order to provide the information that the court needs, the State agency or other party seeking placement should ask the child, parents, and potentially extended family which Tribe(s) they have an affiliation with and obtain genealogical information from the family, and contact the Tribe(s) with that information.

When none of the factors is present. If there is no "reason to know" the child is an "Indian child," the State agency (or other party seeking placement) should document the basis for this conclusion in the case file.

Verification or documentation of a factor. The rule provides that the court has a "reason to know" the child is an "Indian child" if it is informed that either parent or the child possesses an identification card indicating membership in an Indian Tribe. This provision reflects that there may already be sufficient documentation available to demonstrate that the Tribe has concluded that a parent or child is a citizen of the Tribe. However, for the court's determination as to whether the child is an Indian child, the best source is a contemporaneous communication from the Tribe.

Due Diligence to Work with Tribes to Verify

The determination of whether a child is an "Indian child" turns on Tribal citizenship or eligibility for citizenship. The rule recognizes that these determinations are ones that Tribes make in their sovereign capacity and requires courts to defer to those determinations. The best source for a court to use to conclude that a child or parent is a citizen of a Tribe (or that a child is eligible for citizenship)[19] is a contemporaneous communication from the Tribe documenting the determination.

See section B.7 of these guidelines for more information on verification and when a State court determination is appropriate.

Treating the Child as an Indian Child, Unless and Until Determined Otherwise

This requirement (triggered by a "reason to know" the child is an "Indian child") ensures that ICWA's requirements are followed from the early stages of a case and that harmful delays and duplication resulting from the potential late application of ICWA are avoided. For example, it makes sense to place a child that the court has reason to know is an Indian child in a placement that complies with ICWA's placement preferences from the start of a proceeding, rather than having to consider a change a placement later in the proceeding once the court confirms that the child actually is an Indian child. Notably, the early application of ICWA's requirements—which are designed to keep children, when possible, with their parents, family, or Tribal community—should benefit children regardless of whether it turns out that they are Indian children as defined by the statute. If, based on feedback from the relevant Tribe(s) or other information, the court determines that the child is not an "Indian child," then the State may proceed under its usual standards.

B.2 Determining whether ICWA applies

Regulation

---

§ 23.103 When does ICWA apply?

(a) ICWA includes requirements that apply whenever an Indian child is the subject of:

(1) A child-custody proceeding, including:

(i) An involuntary proceeding;

(ii) A voluntary proceeding that could prohibit the parent or Indian custodian from regaining custody of the child upon demand; and

(iii) A proceeding involving status offenses if any part of the proceeding results in the need for out-of-home placement of the child, including a foster-care, preadoptive, or adoptive placement, or termination of parental rights.

(2) An emergency proceeding.

(b) ICWA does not apply to:

(1) A Tribal court proceeding;

(2) A proceeding regarding a criminal act that is not a status offense;

---

19. These guidelines use the terms "member" and "citizen" interchangeably.

(3) An award of custody of the Indian child to one of the parents including, but not limited to, an award in a divorce proceeding; or

(4) A voluntary placement that either parent, both parents, or the Indian custodian has, of his or her or their free will, without a threat of removal by a State agency, chosen for the Indian child and that does not operate to prohibit the child's parent or Indian custodian from regaining custody of the child upon demand.

(c) If a proceeding listed in paragraph (a) of this section concerns a child who meets the statutory definition of "Indian child," then ICWA will apply to that proceeding. In determining whether ICWA applies to a proceeding, the State court may not consider factors such as the participation of the parents or the Indian child in Tribal cultural, social, religious, or political activities, the relationship between the Indian child and his or her parents, whether the parent ever had custody of the child, or the Indian child's blood quantum.

(d) If ICWA applies at the commencement of a proceeding, it will not cease to apply simply because the child reaches age 18 during the pendency of the proceeding.

Guidelines

ICWA has provisions that apply to "child-custody proceedings." *See* the definition of "child-custody proceeding" and associated guidelines in section L of these guidelines. Child-custody proceedings include both involuntary proceedings and voluntary proceedings involving an "Indian child," regardless of whether individual members of the family are themselves Indian. Thus, for example, a non-Indian parent may avail himself or herself of protections provided to parents by ICWA if her child is an "Indian child."

Involuntary Proceedings

If the child may be involuntarily removed from the parents or Indian custodian or the child may be involuntarily placed, then ICWA applies to the proceeding. If the parent or Indian custodian does not agree to the removal or placement, or agrees only under threat of the child's removal, then the proceeding is involuntary.

Voluntary Proceedings

If the parents or Indian custodian voluntarily agrees to removal or placement of the Indian child, then certain provisions of ICWA still apply. Voluntary proceedings require a determination of whether the child is an Indian child and compliance with ICWA and the regulation's provisions relating to the placement preferences. *See* section B.3 of these guidelines for a list of which regulatory provisions apply to each type of proceeding.

A proceeding is voluntary only if the parent or Indian custodian voluntarily agrees to placement, of his or her own free will, without threat of removal.

Voluntary Placements Where Custody of the Child Can Be Regained "Upon Demand"

If the parent or Indian custodian has voluntarily placed the child (upon his or her own free will without threat of removal) and can regain custody "upon demand," meaning without any formalities or contingencies, then ICWA does not apply. These excepted voluntary placements are typically done without the assistance of a child welfare agency. An example is where a parent arranges for a relative or neighbor to care for their child while they are out of town for a period of time. If a child welfare agency is involved, it is recommended that placement intended to last for an extended period of time be memorialized in written agreements that explicitly state the right of the parent or Indian custodian to regain custody of the child upon demand without any formalities or contingencies.

The distinction between a voluntary and involuntary placement can be nuanced and depends on the facts. For example:

- If parent wishes to enter a drug treatment and places the child while in treatment, but can get the child back upon demand even if treatment is not completed, then that is likely a voluntary placement.
- If parent is told they will lose the child unless they enter a drug treatment program during which child is placed elsewhere, that is not a voluntary placement.
- If a parent wishes to enter drug treatment and places the child while in treatment, and is told that they can only get child back if treatment is successfully completed, that is not a voluntary placement.

Placements Resulting from a Child's Status Offense

ICWA also applies to placements resulting from a child's status offense. Status offenses are offenses that would not be considered criminal if committed by an adult, and are prohibited only because of a person's status as a minor (such as truancy or incorrigibility). If the child is being removed because he or she committed a status offense, then ICWA applies.

Guardianships/Conservatorships

ICWA also applies to placements with a guardian or conservator, because ICWA includes guardianships in the definition of "foster care placement."

Intra-Family Custody Disputes

The statute and rule exclude custody disputes between parents, but can apply to other types of intra- family disputes—including disputes with grandparents, stepparents, or other family members—assuming that such disputes otherwise meet the statutory and regulatory definitions.

Placement with Parent

Placement with a parent is generally not an "Indian child-custody proceeding" because it is not included as a "foster-care placement." While the Act specifically exempts from ICWA's applicability awards of custody to one of the parents "in divorce proceedings," the exemption necessarily includes awards of custody to one of the parents in other types of proceedings as well. However, if a proceeding seeks to terminate the parental rights of one parent, that proceeding falls within ICWA's definition of "child-custody proceeding" even if the child will remain in the custody of the other parent or a step-parent.

Factors that May Not Be Considered

If a child-custody proceeding concerns a child who meets the statutory definition of "Indian child," then the court may not determine that ICWA does not apply based on factors such as the participation of the parents or the Indian child in Tribal cultural, social, religious, or political activities, the relationship between the Indian child and his or her parents, whether the parent ever had custody of the child, or the Indian child's blood quantum (sometimes known as the "Existing Indian Family" exception). These factors are not relevant to the inquiry of whether the statute applies. Rather, ICWA applies whenever an "Indian child" is the subject of a "child-custody proceeding," as those terms are defined in the statute. In addition, Congress expressly recognized that State courts and agencies often failed to recognize the essential Tribal relations of Indian people and the cultural and social standards prevailing in Indian communities and families. A standard that requires the evaluation of the strength of these social or cultural ties frustrates ICWA's purpose to provide more objective standards for Indian child-custody proceedings.[20]

Application Even if Child Reaches Age 18

Where State and/or Federal law provides for a child-custody proceeding to extend beyond an Indian child's 18th birthday, ICWA would not stop applying to the proceeding simply because of the child's age. This is to ensure that a set of laws apply consistently throughout a proceeding, and also to discourage strategic behavior or delays in ICWA compliance in circumstances where a child's 18th birthday is near.

B.3 Determining which requirements apply based on type of proceeding

Regulation

§ 23.104 What [rule] provisions . . . apply to each type of child-custody proceeding?

The following table lists what sections of this subpart apply to each type of child-custody proceeding identified in § 23.103(a):

20. *See* 81 FR 38801-38802 (June 14, 2016).

Regulatory Section	Type of Proceeding
23.101—23.106 (General Provisions)	Emergency, Involuntary, Voluntary
Pretrial Requirements	
23.107 (How should a State court determine if there is reason to know the child is an Indian child?)	Emergency, Involuntary, Voluntary
23.108 (Who makes the determination as to whether a child is a member whether a child is eligible for membership, or whether a biological parent is a member of a Tribe?)	Emergency, Involuntary, Voluntary
23.109 (How should a State court determine an Indian child's Tribe when the child may be a member or eligible for membership in more than one Tribe?)	Emergency, Involuntary, Voluntary
23.110 (When must a State court dismiss an action?)	Involuntary, Voluntary
23.111 (What are the notice requirements for a child-custody proceeding involving an Indian child?)	Involuntary (foster-care placement and TPR)
23.112 (What time limits and extensions apply?)	Involuntary (foster-care placement and TPR)
23.113 (What are the standards for emergency proceedings involving an Indian child?)	Emergency
23.114 (What are the requirements for determining improper removal?)	Involuntary
Petitions to Transfer to Tribal Court	
23.115 (How are petitions for transfer of a proceeding made?)	Involuntary, Voluntary (foster-care placement and TPR)
23.116 (What happens after a petition for transfer is made?)	Involuntary, Voluntary (foster-care placement and TPR)
23.117 (What are the criteria for ruling on transfer petitions?)	Involuntary, Voluntary (foster-care placement and TPR)
23.118 (How is a determination of "good cause" to deny transfer made?)	Involuntary, Voluntary (foster-care placement and TPR)
23.119 (What happens after a petition for transfer is granted?)	Involuntary, Voluntary (foster-care placement and TPR)
Adjudication of Involuntary Proceedings	
23.120 (How does the State court ensure that active efforts have been made?)	Involuntary (foster-care placement and TPR)
23.121 (What are the applicable standards of evidence?)	Involuntary (foster-care placement and TPR)
23.122 (Who may serve as a qualified expert witness?)	Involuntary (foster-care placement and TPR)
23.123 Reserved.	N/A

(*continued*)

Regulatory Section	**Type of Proceeding**
Voluntary Proceedings	
23.124 (What actions must a State court undertake in voluntary proceedings?)	Voluntary
23.125 (How is consent obtained?)	Voluntary
23.126 (What information must a consent document contain?)	Voluntary
23.127 (How is withdrawal of consent to a foster-care placement achieved?)	Voluntary
23.128 (How is withdrawal of consent to a termination of parental rights or adoption achieved?)	Voluntary
Dispositions	
23.129 (When do the placement preferences apply?)	Involuntary, Voluntary
23.130 (What placement preferences apply in adoptive placements?)	Involuntary, Voluntary
23.131 (What placement preferences apply in foster-care or preadoptive placements?)	Involuntary, Voluntary
23.132 (How is a determination of "good cause" to depart from the placement preferences made?)	Involuntary, Voluntary
Access	
23.133 (Should courts allow participation by alternative methods?)	Emergency, Involuntary
23.134 (Who has access to reports and records during a proceeding?)	Emergency, Involuntary
23.135 Reserved.	N/A
Post-Trial Rights & Responsibilities	
23.136 (What are the requirements for vacating an adoption based on consent having been obtained through fraud or duress?)	Involuntary (if consent given under threat of removal), Voluntary
23.137 (Who can petition to invalidate an action for certain ICWA violations?)	Emergency (to extent it involved a specified violation), Involuntary, Voluntary
23.138 (What are the rights to information about adoptees' Tribal affiliations?)	Emergency, Involuntary, Voluntary
23.139 (Must notice be given of a change in an adopted Indian child's status?)	Involuntary, Voluntary
Recordkeeping	
23.140 (What information must States furnish to the Bureau of Indian Affairs?)	Involuntary, Voluntary
23.141 (What records must the State maintain?)	Involuntary, Voluntary
23.142 (How does the Paperwork Reduction Act affect this subpart?)	Emergency, Involuntary, Voluntary

(*continued*)

Regulatory Section	Type of Proceeding
Effective Date	
23.143 (How does this rule apply to pending proceedings?)	Emergency, Involuntary, Voluntary
Severability	
23.144 (What happens if some portion of this rule is held to be invalid by a court of competent jurisdiction?)	Emergency, Involuntary, Voluntary

Note: For purposes of this table, status-offense child-custody proceedings are included as a type of involuntary proceeding.

Guidelines

As discussed above, ICWA has provisions that apply to both involuntary proceedings and voluntary proceedings involving an "Indian child," regardless of whether individual members of the family are themselves Indian. ICWA also includes a separate category for "emergency" proceedings, which are described in section C of these guidelines, below.

This chart is intended as a quick-reference tool to provide an overview of what regulatory provisions apply to what types of proceedings. For specifics on how each regulatory provision applies, please refer directly to the regulatory provision and appropriate section of these guidelines.

B.4 Identifying the Tribe

Guidelines

Sometimes, the child or parent may not be certain of their citizenship status in an Indian Tribe, but may indicate they are somehow affiliated with a Tribe or group of Tribes. In these circumstances, State agencies and courts should ask the parent and, potentially, extended family what Tribe or Tribal ancestral group the parent may be affiliated with.

If a specific Tribe is indicated, determine if that Tribe is listed as a federally recognized Indian Tribe on the BIA's annual list, viewable at www.bia.gov. Some Tribes are recognized by States but not recognized by the Federal Government. The Federal ICWA applies only if the Tribe is a federally recognized Indian Tribe and therefore listed on the BIA list.

If only the Tribal ancestral group (e.g., Cherokee) is indicated, then we recommend State agencies or courts contact each of the Tribes in that ancestral group (*see* section B.6 of these guidelines regarding the published list of ICWA designated agents) to identify whether the parent or child is a member of any such Tribe. If the State agency or court is unsure that it has contacted all the relevant Tribes, or needs other assistance in identifying the appropriate Tribes, it should contact the BIA Regional Office. Ideally, State agencies or courts should contact the BIA Regional Office for the region in which the Tribe is located, but if the State agency or court is not aware of the appropriate BIA Regional Office, it may contact any BIA Regional Office for direction.

B.5 Identifying the Tribe when there is more than one Tribe

Regulation

---

§ 23.109 How should a State court determine an Indian child's Tribe when the child may be a member or eligible for membership in more than one Tribe?

(a) If the Indian child is a member or eligible for membership in only one Tribe, that Tribe must be designated as the Indian child's Tribe.

(b) If the Indian child meets the definition of "Indian child" through more than one Tribe, deference should be given to the Tribe in which the Indian child is already a member, unless otherwise agreed to by the Tribes.

(c) If an Indian child meets the definition of "Indian child" through more than one Tribe because the child is a member in more than one Tribe or the child is not a member of but is eligible for membership in more than one Tribe, the court must provide the opportunity in any involuntary child-custody proceeding for the Tribes to determine which should be designated as the Indian child's Tribe.

(1) If the Tribes are able to reach an agreement, the agreed-upon Tribe should be designated as the Indian child's Tribe.

(2) If the Tribes are unable to reach an agreement, the State court designates, for the purposes of ICWA, the Indian Tribe with which the Indian child has the more significant contacts as the Indian child's Tribe, taking into consideration:

(i) Preference of the parents for membership of the child;

(ii) Length of past domicile or residence on or near the reservation of each Tribe;

(iii) Tribal membership of the child's custodial parent or Indian custodian; and

(iv) Interest asserted by each Tribe in the child-custody proceeding;

(v) Whether there has been a previous adjudication with respect to the child by a court of one of the Tribes; and

(vi) Self-identification by the child, if the child is of sufficient age and capacity to meaningfully self-identify.

(3) A determination of the Indian child's Tribe for purposes of ICWA and the regulations in this subpart do not constitute a determination for any other purpose.

Guidelines

If a child meets the definition of "Indian child" through more than one Tribe, it is a best practice to communicate with both (or all) of the Tribes regarding any upcoming actions regarding the child. The Tribes must be informed that the child may be a member or eligible for membership in multiple Tribes, and must be given reasonable opportunity to agree on which Tribe will be designated as the Indian child's Tribe for the purposes of the child-custody proceeding. If the Tribes are unable to reach an agreement, the State court will designate a Tribe, after considering the factors identified in the regulation. It is a best practice to conduct a hearing regarding designation of the Indian child's Tribe so that the court can gather the information about the factors identified in the regulation.

B.6 Contacting the Tribe

Regulation

---

§ 23.105 How do I contact a Tribe under the regulations in this subpart?

To contact a Tribe to provide notice or obtain information or verification under the regulations in this subpart, you should direct the notice or inquiry as follows:

(a) Many Tribes designate an agent for receipt of ICWA notices. The BIA publishes a list of Tribes' designated Tribal agents for service of ICWA notice in the Federal Register each year and makes the list available on its website at www.bia.gov.

(b) For a Tribe without a designated Tribal agent for service of ICWA notice, contact the Tribe to be directed to the appropriate office or individual.

(c) If you do not have accurate contact information for a Tribe, or the Tribe contacted fails to respond to written inquiries, you should seek assistance in contacting the Indian Tribe from the BIA local or regional office or the BIA's Central Office in Washington, D.C. (see www.bia.gov).

Guidelines

Although the regulation focuses on written contact, it is recommended that, in addition, State agencies contact, by telephone and/or email, the Tribal ICWA agent, as listed in BIA's most recent list of designated Tribal agents for service of ICWA notice (available on www.bia.gov and published annually in the Federal Register). This facilitates open communication and enables the State and Tribal social workers to coordinate on services that may be available to support the family. State agencies should document their conversations with Tribal agents. If, for some reason, the State agency cannot reach the Tribal agent listed in the most recent list on www.bia.gov or in the Federal Register, we recommend contacting the BIA.

B.7 Verifying Tribal membership

Regulation

§ 23.108 Who makes the determination as to whether a child is a member, whether a child is eligible for membership, or whether a biological parent is a member of a Tribe?

(a) The Indian Tribe of which it is believed the child is a member (or eligible for membership and of which the biological parent is a member) determines whether the child is a member of the Tribe, or whether the child is eligible for membership in the Tribe and a biological parent of the child is a member of the Tribe, except as otherwise provided by Federal or Tribal law.

(b) The determination by a Tribe of whether a child is a member, whether a child is eligible for membership, or whether a biological parent is a member, is solely within the jurisdiction and authority of the Tribe, except as otherwise provided by Federal or Tribal law. The State court may not substitute its own determination regarding a child's membership in a Tribe, a child's eligibility for membership in a Tribe, or a parent's membership in a Tribe.

(c) The State court may rely on facts or documentation indicating a Tribal determination of membership or eligibility for membership in making a judicial determination as to whether the child is an "Indian child." An example of documentation indicating membership is a document issued by the Tribe, such as Tribal enrollment documentation.

***See, also,* § 23.107(b)(1) in section B.1 of these guidelines, above.**

Guidelines

Tribes, as sovereign governments, have the exclusive authority to determine their political citizenship and their eligibility requirements. A Tribe is, therefore, the authoritative and best source of information regarding who is a citizen (or member) of that Tribe and who is eligible for citizenship of that Tribe. Thus, the rule defers to Tribes in making such determinations and makes clear that a court may not substitute its own determination for that of a Tribe regarding a child's citizenship or eligibility for citizenship in a Tribe.

If the court has "reason to know" the child is an "Indian child" (*see* section B.1 of these guidelines, above), agencies must use due diligence to work with the relevant Tribe(s) to obtain verification regarding whether the child is a citizen or a biological parent is a citizen and the child is eligible for citizenship. The Department encourages agencies to contact Tribes informally, in addition to providing written notice, to seek such verification. The regulation requires that the agency's efforts to identify and work with those Tribes be documented in the court record. It is a best practice for these efforts to be maintained in agency files as well.

Form of Verification

While written verification from the Tribe(s) is an appropriate method for such verification, other methods may be appropriate. A Tribal representative's testimony at a hearing regarding whether the child is a citizen (or a biological parent is a citizen and the child is eligible for citizenship) is an appropriate method of verification by the Tribe.

Information in Request for Tribe's Verification

The Department encourages State courts and agencies to include enough information in the requests for verification to allow the Tribes to readily determine whether the child is a Tribal citizen (or whether the parent is a Tribal citizen and the child is eligible for citizenship). The request for verification is a meaningful request only if it provides sufficient information to the Tribe to make the determination as to whether the child is a citizen (or the parent is a citizen and the child is eligible for citizenship). Providing as much information as possible facilitates earlier identification of an Indian child and helps prevents delays and disruptions. Section 23.111(d) includes categories of information that must be provided in the notice to a Tribe in involuntary foster-care placement or TPR proceedings. Such information may be helpful to provide a Tribe to assist in verification of whether the child an Indian child. It is also important that names, birthdates, and other relevant information be reported accurately to the Tribe, as misspellings or other incorrect information can generate inaccurate or delayed responses.

A primary reason for courts mistakenly not being aware that a child is an Indian child is that the request for verification lacks the information necessary (or lacks accurate information) for the Tribe to make a determination as to membership or eligibility for membership. We therefore recommend parties include as much information as is available regarding the child in order to help the Tribe identify whether the child or the child's parent is a member. If possible, include the following information:

- Genograms or ancestry/family charts for both parents;
- All known names of both parents (maiden, married and former names or aliases), including possible alternative spellings;
- Current and former addresses of the child's parents and any extended family;
- Birthdates and places of birth (and death, if applicable) of both parents;
- All known Tribal affiliation (or Indian ancestry if Tribal affiliation not known) for individuals listed on the ancestry/family charts; and
- The addresses for the domicile and residence of the child, his or her parents, or the Indian custodian and whether this is on an Indian reservation or in an Alaska Native village.

Court's Determination

While a Tribe is the authoritative and best source regarding Tribal citizenship information, the court must ultimately determine whether the child is an Indian child for purposes of the child-custody proceeding. Ideally, that determination would be based on information provided by the Tribe, but may need to be based on other information if, for example, the Tribe(s) fail(s) to respond to verification requests.

The Department encourages prompt responses by Tribes, but if a Tribe fails to respond to multiple requests for verification regarding whether a child is in fact a citizen (or a biological parent is a citizen and the child is eligible for citizenship), and the agency has sought the assistance of the Bureau of Indian Affairs (BIA) in contacting the Tribe, a court may make a determination regarding whether the child is an Indian child for purposes of the child-custody proceeding based on the information it has available. A finding that a child is an "Indian child" applies only for the purposes of the application of ICWA to that proceeding, and does not establish that child's membership in a Tribe or eligibility for any Federal programs or benefits for any other purpose. If new evidence later arises, the court will need to consider it and should alter the original determination if appropriate.

It is recommended the agency document the requests to the Tribe to obtain information or verification of a child's or parent's Tribal citizenship and provide this information for the court file.

BIA Assistance

BIA does not make determinations as to Tribal citizenship or eligibility for Tribal citizenships except as otherwise provided by Federal or Tribal Law, but BIA can help route the notice to the right place.

B.8 Facilitating Tribal membership

Guidelines

In many cases, Tribal citizenship would make more services and programs available to the child. Even where it is not clear that Tribal services and programs would assist the child, there are both immediate and long-term benefits to being a Tribal citizen. It is thus a recommended practice for the social worker (or party seeking placement in a voluntary adoption) to facilitate the child becoming a member, such as by assisting with the filing of a Tribal membership application or otherwise.

C. Emergency Proceedings

C.1 Emergency proceedings in the ICWA context

Regulation

§23.2 *Emergency proceeding* means and includes any court action that involves an emergency removal or emergency placement of an Indian child.

Guidelines

The statute and regulations recognize that emergency proceedings may need to proceed differently from other proceedings under ICWA.[21] Specifically, section 1922 of ICWA was designed to "permit, under applicable State law, the emergency removal of an Indian child from his parent or Indian custodian or emergency placement of such child in order to prevent imminent physical harm to the child notwithstanding the provisions of" ICWA.[22] While States use different terminology (e.g., preliminary protective hearing, shelter hearing) for emergency hearings, the regulatory definition of emergency proceedings is intended to cover such proceedings as may be necessary to prevent imminent physical damage or harm to the child.

Both the legislative history and the decisions of multiple courts support the conclusion that ICWA's emergency proceedings provisions apply to both: (1) Indian children who are domiciled off of the reservation and (2) Indian children domiciled on the reservation, but temporarily off of the reservation.[23]

C.2 Threshold for removal on an emergency basis

Regulation

... necessary to prevent imminent physical damage or harm to the child. *See* § 23.113(b)(1), above.

Guidelines

ICWA allows for removal of a child from his or her parents or Indian custodian, as part of an emergency proceeding only if the child faces "imminent physical damage or harm." The Department interprets this standard as mirroring the

21. *See* 25 U.S.C. 1922.

22. H.R. Rep. No. 9501386; 25 U.S.C. 1922.

23. *See* 81 FR 38794-38795 (June 14, 2016).

constitutional standard for removal of *any* child from his or her parents without providing due process.

As a general rule, before any parent may be deprived of the care or custody of their child without their consent, due process—ordinarily a court proceeding resulting in an order permitting removal—must be provided.[24] A child may, however, be taken into custody by a State official without court authorization or parental consent only in emergency circumstances. Courts have defined emergency circumstances as "circumstances in which the child is immediately threatened with harm," including when there is an immediate threat to the safety of the child, when a young child is left without care or adequate supervision, or where there is evidence of serious ongoing abuse and the officials have reason to fear imminent recurrence.[25] The same standards and protections apply when an Indian child is involved. And those standards and protections are reflected in section 1922 of ICWA, which addresses emergency proceedings involving Indian children.

C.3 Standards and processes for emergency proceedings

Regulation

§ 23.113 What are the standards for emergency proceedings involving an Indian child?

(a) Any emergency removal or placement of an Indian child under State law must terminate immediately when the removal or placement is no longer necessary to prevent imminent physical damage or harm to the child.

(b) The State court must:

(1) Make a finding on the record that the emergency removal or placement is necessary to prevent imminent physical damage or harm to the child;

(2) Promptly hold a hearing on whether the emergency removal or placement continues to be necessary whenever new information indicates that the emergency situation has ended; and

(3) At any court hearing during the emergency proceeding, determine whether the emergency removal or placement is no longer necessary to prevent imminent physical damage or harm to the child.

(4) Immediately terminate (or ensure that the agency immediately terminates) the emergency proceeding once the court or agency possesses sufficient evidence to determine that the emergency removal or

---

24. *See, e.g., Tenenbaum v. Williams,* 193 F.3d 581 (2d Cit. 1999); *Doe v. Kearney,* 329 F.3d 1286 (11th Cir. 2003).

25. *Hurlman v. Ric,* 927 F.2d 74, 80–81 (2d Cir. 1991 (citing cases).

placement is no longer necessary to prevent imminent physical damage or harm to the child.

(c) An emergency proceeding can be terminated by one or more of the following actions:

(1) Initiation of a child-custody proceeding subject to the provisions of ICWA; (2) Transfer of the child to the jurisdiction of the appropriate Indian Tribe; or

(3) Restoring the child to the parent or Indian custodian.

. . .

Guidelines

Timing of hearing. If any child (including a non-Indian child) is removed from her parents by State officials without court authorization or parental consent, the State must generally provide a meaningful hearing promptly after removal.[26] States may call these proceedings by different names, such as "protective custody," "emergency custody," "shelter care," or "probable cause," among others, but they typically take place within a short time frame after the removal, such as 48 or 72 hours. These hearings should provide parents with a meaningful opportunity to be heard. If the agency determines the emergency has ended, State procedures will dictate whether the agency may return the child without the need for a hearing.

Termination of Emergency Removal. If a child was removed from the home on an emergency basis because of a temporary threat to his or her safety, but the threat has been removed and the child is no longer at risk, the State should terminate the removal, either by returning the child to the parent or transferring the case to Tribal jurisdiction. This comports with standards that apply to all child-welfare cases, and protects the "fundamental liberty interest" that parents have in the care and custody of their children.[27] If circumstances warrant, however, the State agency may instead initiate a child-custody proceeding to which the full set of ICWA protections would apply.

- **Restoring the child to the parent or Indian custodian.** If the agency determines the emergency has ended, State procedures will dictate whether the agency may return the child without the need for a hearing. A safety plan may be a solution to mitigate the situation that gave rise to the need for emergency removal and placement and allow the State to terminate the emergency proceeding. If the State court finds that the implementation of a safety plan means that emergency removal or placement is no longer necessary to prevent imminent physical damage or harm to the child, the child should be returned to the parent or

---

26. *Swipies v. Kofka,* 419 F.3d 709, 715 (8th Cir. 2005).
27. *See Troxel v. Granville,* 530 U.S. 57 (2000).

custodian. The State may still choose to initiate a child-custody proceeding, or may transfer the case to the jurisdiction of the Tribe.

- **Transferring the proceeding to Tribal jurisdiction.** The agency may terminate the emergency proceeding by transferring the child to the jurisdiction of the Tribe. Transfer of a proceeding is discussed below in section F of these guidelines.
- **Initiating a "child custody proceeding."** To initiate a full "child custody proceeding" (as defined in 25 CFR § 23.2), the State agency should set the hearing date and send out notice by registered or certified mail, return receipt requested, to the parent or Indian custodian and Tribe in accordance with ICWA's required timeframes (see section D.7 of these guidelines).

Termination of the emergency proceeding does not necessarily mean that the actual placement of the child must change. If an Indian child cannot be safely returned to the parents or custodian, the child must either be transferred to the jurisdiction of the appropriate Indian Tribe, or the State must initiate a child-custody proceeding to which the full set of ICWA protections would apply. Under this scenario, the child may end up staying in the same placement, but such placement will not be under the emergency proceeding provisions authorized by section 1922. Instead, that placement would need to be pursuant to Tribal law (if the child is transferred to the jurisdiction of the Tribe) or comply with the relevant ICWA statutory and rule provisions for a child-custody proceeding (if the State retains jurisdiction) ICWA and the rule emphasize that an emergency proceeding under ICWA section 1922 needs to be as short as possible and include provisions that are designed to achieve that result. ICWA requires that State officials "insure" that Indian children are returned home (or transferred to their Tribe's jurisdiction) as soon as the threat of imminent physical damage or harm has ended, or that State officials "expeditiously" initiate a child-custody proceeding subject to all ICWA protections.[28] The rule requires that an emergency removal or placement of an Indian child must "terminate immediately" when it is no longer necessary to prevent imminent physical damage or harm to the child.

C.4 Contents of petition for emergency removal

Regulation

---

§ 23.113 What are the standards for emergency proceedings involving an Indian child?

. . . (d) A petition for a court order authorizing the emergency removal or continued emergency placement, or its accompanying documents, should contain a statement of the risk of imminent physical damage or harm to the

28. 25 U.S.C. 1922.

Indian child and any evidence that the emergency removal or placement continues to be necessary to prevent such imminent physical damage or harm to the child. The petition or its accompanying documents should also contain the following information:

(1) The name, age, and last known address of the Indian child;

(2) The name and address of the child's parents and Indian custodians, if any; (3) The steps taken to provide notice to the child's parents, custodians, and

Tribe about the emergency proceeding;

(4) If the child's parents and Indian custodians are unknown, a detailed explanation of what efforts have been made to locate and contact them, including contact with the appropriate BIA Regional Director (see www.bia.gov);

(5) The residence and the domicile of the Indian child;

(6) If either the residence or the domicile of the Indian child is believed to be on a reservation or in an Alaska Native village, the name of the Tribe affiliated with that reservation or village;

(7) The Tribal affiliation of the child and of the parents or Indian custodians;

(8) A specific and detailed account of the circumstances that led the agency responsible for the emergency removal of the child to take that action;

(9) If the child is believed to reside or be domiciled on a reservation where the Tribe exercises exclusive jurisdiction over child-custody matters, a statement of efforts that have been made and are being made to contact the Tribe and transfer the child to the Tribe's jurisdiction; and

(10) A statement of the efforts that have been taken to assist the parents or Indian custodians so the Indian child may safely be returned to their custody.

. . .

Guidelines

The contents listed in this section of the regulation are strongly recommended, but not required (as indicated by the word "should" rather than "must"). A failure to include any of the listed information should not result in denial of the petition if the child faces imminent physical damage or harm.

C.5 Outer limit on length of emergency removal

Regulation

---

§ 23.113 What are the standards for emergency proceedings involving an Indian child?

. . . (e) An emergency proceeding regarding an Indian child should not be continued for more than 30 days unless the court makes the following determinations:

(1) Restoring the child to the parent or Indian custodian would subject the child to imminent physical damage or harm;

(2) The court has been unable to transfer the proceeding to the jurisdiction of the appropriate Indian Tribe; and

(3) It has not been possible to initiate a "child-custody proceeding" as defined in § 23.2.

Guidelines

Emergency proceedings—which generally do not include the full suite of due process or ICWA protections for parents and children—must not extend for longer than necessary to prevent imminent physical damage or harm to the child. If there is sufficient evidence of abuse or neglect, the State should promptly initiate a proceeding that provides the full suite of due process and ICWA protections. State laws vary in their handling of emergency proceedings and the initiation of foster-care proceedings, and it may not always be easy to ascertain when the "emergency proceeding" is concluded. The intent of the presumptive outer bound on the length of an emergency proceeding (30 days) is to ensure the safeguards of the Act cannot be evaded by use of long-term emergency proceedings.

States should adapt the regulation to their own procedures, with the goal of ensuring that proceedings (beyond the emergency custody, shelter care, or otherwise named initial hearing) that include the full suite of due process and ICWA protections are commenced within 30 days of any emergency removal. While there may be State-specific types of emergency proceedings with separate timeframes, all of the State requirements may be followed, so long as a proceeding with the full suite of due process and ICWA protections is underway within 30 days, absent extenuating circumstances.

Should the court need the emergency proceeding of an Indian child to last longer than 30 days, however, it may extend the emergency proceeding if it makes all three of the specific findings listed at § 23.113(e). Allowing a court to extend an emergency proceeding if it makes those findings provides appropriate flexibility for a court that finds itself facing unusual circumstances.[29]

C.6 Emergency placements

Regulation

See § 23.113, above.

Guidelines

As a matter of general best practice in child welfare, State agencies should try to identify extended family or other individuals with whom the child is already familiar as possible emergency placements. If the child is an Indian child, agencies should strive to provide an initial placement for the child that meets ICWA's (or the Tribe's) placement preferences. This will help prevent subsequent disruptions if the child needs to be moved to a preferred placement once a child-custody proceeding is initiated.

State agencies should also determine if there are available emergency foster homes already licensed by the State or the child's Tribe.

If the Indian child is placed on an emergency basis in a non-preferred placement because a preferred placement is unavailable or has not yet met background check or licensing requirements, State agencies should have a concurrent plan for placement as soon as possible with a preferred placement.

C.7 Identifying Indian children in emergency situations

Regulation

See § 23.113, above.

Guidelines

It is recommended that the State agency ask the family and extended family whether the child is a Tribal member or whether a parent is a Tribal member and the child is eligible for membership as part of the emergency removal and placement process. If the State agency believes that the child may be an Indian child, it is recommended that it let the Tribe know the child has been removed on an emergency

29. *See* 81 FR 38817 (June 14, 2016).

basis, and begin coordination with the Tribe regarding services and placements. If there is still uncertainty regarding who is the Indian child's Tribe, it is recommended that the State agency continue to investigate the applicability of ICWA and document findings.

C.8 Active efforts in emergency situations

Guidelines

We recommend that State agencies work with Tribes, parents, and other parties as soon as possible, even in an emergency situation, to begin providing active efforts to reunite the family.

C.9 Notice in emergency situations

Regulation

No regulatory requirements for notice by registered or certified apply in emergency proceedings; however, § 23.113(c) requires agencies to report to the court on their efforts to contact the parents, Indian custodian, and Tribe for the emergency proceeding.

Guidelines

Neither the statute nor rule requires notice prior to an emergency removal because of the short timeframe in which emergency proceedings are conducted to secure the safety of the child (although there may be relevant State or due process requirements). In order to protect the parents', Indian custodians', and Tribes' due process and other rights in these situations, however, it is a recommended practice for the agency to take all practical steps to contact them. This likely includes contact by telephone or in person and may include email or other written forms of contact.

D. Notice

D.1 Requirement for notice

Regulation

§ 23.11 Notice.

(a) In any involuntary proceeding in a State court where the court knows or has reason to know that an Indian child is involved, and where the identity and location of the child's parent or Indian custodian or Tribe is known, the party seeking the foster-care placement of, or termination of parental rights to, an Indian child must directly notify the parents, the Indian custodians, and the child's Tribe by registered or certified mail with return receipt requested, of the pending child-custody proceedings and their right of intervention. Notice must include the requisite information identified in § 23.111, consistent with the confidentiality requirement in § 23.111(d)(6)(ix). Copies of these notices must be sent to the appropriate Regional Director listed in paragraphs (b)(1) through (12) of this section by registered or certified mail with return receipt requested or by personal delivery and must include the information required by § 23.111.

(b) [See Appendix 1]

(c) Upon receipt of the notice, the Secretary will make reasonable documented efforts to locate and notify the child's Tribe and the child's parent or Indian custodian. The Secretary will have 15 days, after receipt of the notice, to notify the child's Tribe and parents or Indian custodians and to send a copy of the notice to the court. If within the

15-day period the Secretary is unable to verify that the child meets the criteria of an Indian child as defined in § 23.2, or is unable to locate the parents or Indian custodians, the Secretary will so inform the court and state how much more time, if any, will be needed to complete the verification or the search. The Secretary will complete all research efforts, even if those efforts cannot be completed before the child-custody proceeding begins.

(d) Upon request from a party to an Indian child-custody proceeding, the Secretary will make a reasonable attempt to identify and locate the child's Tribe, parents, or Indian custodians to assist the party seeking the information.

§ 23.111 What are the notice requirements for a child-custody proceeding involving an Indian child?

(a) When a court knows or has reason to know that the subject of an involuntary foster-care-placement or termination-of-parental-rights proceeding is an Indian child, the court must ensure that:

(1) The party seeking placement promptly sends notice of each such child-custody proceeding (including, but not limited to, any foster-care placement or any termination of parental or custodial rights) in accordance with this section; and

(2) An original or a copy of each notice sent under this section is filed with the court together with any return receipts or other proof of service.

(b) Notice must be sent to:

(1) Each Tribe where the child may be a member (or eligible for membership if a biological parent is a member) (see § 23.105 for information on how to contact a Tribe);

(2) The child's parents; and

(3) If applicable, the child's Indian custodian.

Guidelines

Prompt notice of a child-custody proceeding is vitally important because it gives the parent, Indian custodian, and Tribe the opportunity to respond to any allegations in the case, to intervene, or to seek transfer jurisdiction to the Tribe. In addition, prompt notice facilitates the early identification of preferred placements as well as the provision of Tribal services to the family.

Notice by registered or certified mail, return receipt requested, to the parents, Indian custodian(s), and Indian child's Tribe is required for:

- Any involuntary foster-care proceeding; or
- Any TPR proceeding.

Notice is required for a TPR proceeding, even if notice has previously been given for the child's foster- care proceeding.

This notice is required in addition to the informal contacts made with the Tribe, such as those to verify Tribal membership and open the lines of communication.

Notice by registered or certified mail, return receipt requested is not required for voluntary proceedings, pre-adoptive proceedings, or adoptive proceedings (all of which are defined by the rule), but is a recommended practice.

While not required by the Act or rule, we recommend that State agencies and/or courts provide notice to Tribes and parents or Indian custodians of:

- Each individual hearing within a proceeding;
- Any change in placement—the statute provides rights to parents, Indian custodians and Tribes (e.g., right to intervene) and a change in circumstances resulting from a change in placement may prompt an individual or Tribe to invoke those rights, even though they did not do so before;
- Any change to the child's permanency plan or concurrent plan—a change in the ultimate goal may prompt an individual or Tribe to invoke their rights, even though they did not do so before;
- Any transfer of jurisdiction to another State or receipt of jurisdiction from another State.

D.2 Method of notice (registered or certified mail, return receipt requested)

Regulation

§ 23.111 What are the notice requirements for a child-custody proceeding involving an Indian child?

. . . (c) Notice must be sent by registered or certified mail with return receipt requested. Notice may also be sent via personal service or electronically, but such alternative methods do not replace the requirement for notice to be sent by registered or certified mail with return receipt requested.

Guidelines

The Act requires notice be provided by registered mail, return receipt requested. The regulation also allows for notice to be provided by certified mail, return receipt requested, as a less expensive option that better meets the underlying goal of effecting notice.[30]

If State law requires actual notice or personal service, that may be a higher standard for protection of the rights of the parent or Indian custodian of an Indian child than is provided for in ICWA. In that case, meeting that higher standard would be required.[31] Even in this case, it is a best practice to also provide notice by registered or certified mail, return receipt requested, because the return receipt provides documentation for the record that notice was received.

We encourage States to act proactively in contacting parents, custodians, and Tribes by phone, email, and through other means, in addition to sending registered or certified mail, so parties can begin gathering documents and making necessary decisions as early as practicable in the process. Tribes may agree to waive their right to challenge the adequacy of notice if the notice to the Tribe was sent by a means other than registered or certified mail (e.g., by e-mail), but may not waive or affect the statutory rights of parents or other parties to the case.

The statute and regulations require notice to the parents; a "parent" includes an unwed father that has established or acknowledged paternity. If, at any point, it is discovered that someone is a "parent," as that term is defined in the regulations, that parent would be entitled to notice.

30. *See* 81 FR 38810-38811 (June 14, 2016).
31. *See* 25 U.S.C. 1921.

D.3 Contents of notice

Regulation

§ 23.111 What are the notice requirements for a child-custody proceeding involving an Indian child?

. . . (d) Notice must be in clear and understandable language and include the following:

(1) The child's name, birthdate, and birthplace;

(2) All names known (including maiden, married, and former names or aliases) of the parents, the parents' birthdates and birthplaces, and Tribal enrollment numbers if known;

(3) If known, the names, birthdates, birthplaces, and Tribal enrollment information of other direct lineal ancestors of the child, such as grandparents;

(4) The name of each Indian Tribe in which the child is a member (or may be eligible for membership if a biological parent is a member);

(5) A copy of the petition, complaint, or other document by which the child-custody proceeding was initiated and, if a hearing has been scheduled, information on the date, time, and location of the hearing;

(6) Statements setting out:

(i) The name of the petitioner and the name and address of petitioner's attorney;

(ii) The right of any parent or Indian custodian of the child, if not already a party to the child-custody proceeding, to intervene in the proceedings.

(iii) The Indian Tribe's right to intervene at any time in a State-court proceeding for the foster-care placement of or termination of parental rights to an Indian child.

(iv) That, if the child's parent or Indian custodian is unable to afford counsel based on a determination of indigency by the court, the parent or Indian custodian has the right to court-appointed counsel.

(v) The right to be granted, upon request, up to 20 additional days to prepare for the child-custody proceedings.

(vi) The right of the parent or Indian custodian and the Indian child's Tribe to petition the court for transfer of the foster-care-placement or termination-of-parental-rights proceeding to Tribal court as provided by 25 U.S.C. 1911 and § 23.115.

(vii) The mailing addresses and telephone numbers of the court and information related to all parties to the child-custody proceeding and individuals notified under this section.

(viii) The potential legal consequences of the child-custody proceedings on the future parental and custodial rights of the parent or Indian custodian.

(ix) That all parties notified must keep confidential the information contained in the notice and the notice should not be handled by anyone not needing the information to exercise rights under ICWA.

Guidelines

The rule specifies the information to be contained in the notice in order for the recipients of a notice to be able to exercise their rights in a timely manner.

While notice and verification of Tribal membership are separate concepts (see section B.7 for verification), they can be accomplished through the same communication or separate communications. The BIA has a sample notice form posted at www.bia.gov as an example for States to consider if they are combining their notice and verification.

Confidentiality

While a petition may contain confidential information, providing a copy of the petition with notice to Tribes is a government-to-government exchange of information necessary for the government agencies' performance of duties. *See* 81 FR 38811. The petition is necessary to provide sufficient information to allow the parents, Indian custodian and Tribes to effectively participate in the proceeding.

D.4 Notice to the Bureau of Indian Affairs

Regulation

§ 23.11 Notice

(a) . . . . Copies of these notices must be sent to the appropriate Regional Director listed in paragraphs (b)(1) through (12) of this section by registered or certified mail with return receipt requested or by personal delivery and must include the information required by § 23.111.

Guidelines

Notice to the BIA may be provided by personal delivery in lieu of registered or certified mail with return receipt requested. To determine the appropriate BIA office to send the copy to, see the list of regional offices at § 23.11(b) (available at

Appendix 1). A copy of the notice must be sent to the BIA Regional Director even when the identity of the child's parents, Indian custodian, and Tribes can be ascertained. No notices, except for final adoption decrees, are required to be sent to the BIA Central Office in Washington, DC.

D.5 Documenting the notice with the court

Regulation

§ 23.111 What are the notice requirements for a child-custody proceeding involving an Indian child?

(a) . . . .

. . . (2) An original or a copy of each notice sent under this section is filed with the court together with any return receipts or other proof of service.

Guidelines

If the agency or other party seeking placement voluntarily chooses to provide notice in other Indian child welfare proceedings where notice is not required by law, it is helpful to file a copy of the notice with the court so that the court record is as complete as possible.

D.6 Unascertainable identity or location of the parents, Indian custodian, or Tribes

Regulation

§ 23.111 What are the notice requirements for a child-custody proceeding involving an Indian child?

. . . (e) If the identity or location of the child's parents, the child's Indian custodian, or the Tribes in which the Indian child is a member or eligible for membership cannot be ascertained, but there is reason to know the child is an Indian child, notice of the child-custody proceeding must be sent to the appropriate Bureau of Indian Affairs Regional Director (see www.bia.gov). To establish Tribal identity, as much information as is known regarding the child's direct lineal ancestors should be provided. The Bureau of Indian Affairs will not make a determination of Tribal membership but may, in some instances, be able to identify Tribes to contact.

§ 23.11 Notice.

. . . (c) Upon receipt of the notice, the Secretary will make reasonable documented efforts to locate and notify the child's Tribe and the child's parent or Indian custodian. The Secretary will have 15 days, after receipt of the notice, to notify the child's Tribe and parents or Indian custodians and to send a copy of the notice to the court. If within the 15-day period the Secretary is unable to verify that the child meets the criteria of an Indian child as defined in § 23.2, or is unable to locate the parents or Indian custodians, the Secretary will so inform the court and state how much more time, if any, will be needed to complete the verification or the search. The Secretary will complete all research efforts, even if those efforts cannot be completed before the child-custody proceeding begins.

(d) Upon request from a party to an Indian child-custody proceeding, the Secretary will make a reasonable attempt to identify and locate the child's Tribe, parents, or Indian custodians to assist the party seeking the information.

Guidelines

The party seeking foster-care placement or TPR has responsibility for providing notice. If that party cannot ascertain the identity or location of the parents, Indian custodian, or Tribes, it should contact the BIA Region and provide BIA with as much information as possible regarding potential Tribal affiliations. If the Region cannot assist the party, it can also contact the BIA's central office in Washington, DC. *See* Appendix 1 for a list of BIA regional offices.

D.7 Time limits for notice

Regulation

---

§ 23.112 What time limits and extensions apply?

(a) No foster-care-placement or termination-of-parental-rights proceeding may be held until at least 10 days after receipt of the notice by the parent (or Indian custodian) and by the Tribe (or the Secretary). The parent, Indian custodian, and Tribe each have a right, upon request, to be granted up to 20 additional days from the date upon which notice was received to prepare for participation in the proceeding.

(b) Except as provided in 25 U.S.C. 1922 and § 23.113, no child-custody proceeding for foster-care placement or termination of parental rights may be held until the waiting periods to which the parents or Indian custodians and to which the Indian child's Tribe are entitled have expired, as follows:

(1) 10 days after each parent or Indian custodian (or Secretary where the parent or Indian custodian is unknown to the petitioner) has received notice of that particular child-custody proceeding in accordance with 25 U.S.C. 1912(a) and § 23.111;

(2) 10 days after the Indian child's Tribe (or the Secretary if the Indian child's Tribe is unknown to the party seeking placement) has received notice of that particular child-custody proceeding in accordance with 25 U.S.C. 1912(a) and § 23.111;

(3) Up to 30 days after the parent or Indian custodian has received notice of that particular child-custody proceeding in accordance with 25 U.S.C. 1912(a) and § 23.111, if the parent or Indian custodian has requested up to 20 additional days to prepare for the child-custody proceeding as provided in 25 U.S.C. 1912(a) and § 23.111; and

(4) Up to 30 days after the Indian child's Tribe has received notice of that particular child-custody proceeding in accordance with 25 U.S.C. 1912(a) and § 23.111, if the Indian child's Tribe has requested up to 20 additional days to prepare for the child-custody proceeding.

(c) Additional time beyond the minimum required by 25 U.S.C. 1912 and § 23.111 may also be available under State law or pursuant to extensions granted by the court.

Guidelines

These time limitations ensure that parents, Indian custodians, and the Tribe have time to determine whether a child is an Indian child and respond to and prepare for the proceeding.

Minimum time limit. As the rule states, no foster-care-placement or termination-of-parental-rights proceeding may be held until at least 10 days after receipt of the notice by the parent (or Indian custodian) and by the Tribe (or the Secretary).

Extensions. The parent, Indian custodian, and Indian child's Tribe are entitled to one extension of up to 20 days for each proceeding. Any extension beyond the initial extension up to 20 days is subject to the State court's rules and discretion.

Informal notification. Although the rule sets out the required elements of an ICWA notice, in order to ensure that the proceeding is held promptly, we encourage agencies to contact the Tribe and the parents as soon as there is sufficient information to identify a child who may be a member of or eligible for membership in that Tribe. While the timelines set out in the rule do not begin to run until the service of formal notice as required by the rule, the initial notification may nevertheless be helpful to allow the Tribe to confirm that the child is an Indian child and begin to gather information about the case.

D.8 Translation or interpretation

Regulation

---

§ 23.111 What are the notice requirements for a child-custody proceeding involving an Indian child?

. . . (f) If there is a reason to know that a parent or Indian custodian possesses limited English proficiency and is therefore not likely to understand the contents of the notice, the court must provide language access services as required by Title VI of the Civil Rights Act and other Federal laws. To secure such translation or interpretation support, a court may contact or direct a party to contact the Indian child's Tribe or the local BIA office for assistance in locating and obtaining the name of a qualified translator or interpreter.

Guidelines

If the parent or Indian custodian requires translation or interpretation in a Native language, it is recommended that the court or party contact the Indian child's Tribe or BIA for assistance.

D.9 Right to an attorney

Regulation

---

§ 23.111 What are the notice requirements for a child-custody proceeding involving an Indian child?

. . . (g) If a parent or Indian custodian of an Indian child appears in court without an attorney, the court must inform him or her of his or her rights, including any applicable right to appointed counsel, right to request that the child-custody proceeding be transferred to Tribal court, right to object to such transfer, right to request additional time to prepare for the child-custody proceeding as provided in § 23.112, and right (if the parent or Indian custodian is not already a party) to intervene in the child-custody proceedings.

Guidelines

This provision recognizes that parents may not have appointed counsel at early hearings in the case, and helps ensure that parents are notified of their rights under Federal law.

It is a recommended practice, where possible, to appoint the same counsel for the entirety of the trial court case (throughout all proceedings), to ensure parents' rights are addressed consistently throughout the trial court case, rather than appointing different representatives at each stage.

D.10 Lack of response to notice

Regulation

See § 23.11 and § 23.111 requiring notice of each proceeding.

Guidelines

If the Tribe does not respond to the notice, or responds that it is not interested in participating in the proceeding, the court or agency must still send the Tribe notices of subsequent proceedings for which notice is required (i.e., a subsequent TPR proceeding). In cases where the Tribe does not confirm receipt of the required notice or otherwise does not respond, the Department recommends following up telephonically. The Tribe may decide to intervene or otherwise participate at a later point even if it has previously indicated it is not interested in participating.

E. Active Efforts

E.1 Meaning of "active efforts"

Regulation

§ 23.2 *Active efforts* means affirmative, active, thorough, and timely efforts intended primarily to maintain or reunite an Indian child with his or her family . . .

Guidelines

ICWA requires the use of "active efforts" to provide remedial services and rehabilitative programs designed to prevent the breakup of the Indian family.[32] The statute does not define "active efforts," but the regulation does in § 23.2. The "active efforts" requirement in ICWA reflects Congress' recognition of the particular history of the treatment of Indian children and families. Many Indian children were

32. 25 U.S.C. 1912(d).

removed from their homes because of poverty, joblessness, substandard housing, and other situations that could be remediated through the provision of social services. The "active efforts" requirement helps ensure that parents receive the serves that they need so that they can be safely reunified with their children. The "active efforts" requirement is designed primarily to ensure that services are provided that would permit the Indian child to remain or be reunited with her parents, whenever possible, and helps protect against unwarranted removals by ensuring that parents who are, or may readily become, fit parents are provided with services necessary to retain or regain custody of their child. This is viewed by some child-welfare organizations as part of the "gold standard" of what services should be provided in all child-welfare proceedings, not just those involving an Indian child.[33]

Other Federal and State laws require that child-welfare agencies make at least "reasonable efforts" to provide services that will help families remedy the conditions that brought the child and family into the child-welfare system. And some courts and States understand "active efforts" and "reasonable efforts" as relative to each other, where "active efforts" is higher on the continuum of efforts required and "reasonable efforts" is lower on that continuum.[34] Some courts and States consider "active efforts" to be essentially the same as "reasonable efforts."[35] Instead of focusing on such a comparison, the rule defines "active efforts" by focusing on the quality of the actions necessary to constitute "active efforts" (affirmative, active, thorough, and timely) and providing examples and clarification as to what constitutes "active efforts."

ICWA requires "active efforts" prior to foster-care placement of or TPR to an Indian child, regardless of whether the agency is receiving Federal funding.

What constitutes sufficient "active efforts" will vary from case-to-case, and courts have the discretion to consider the facts and circumstances of the particular case before it when determining whether the definition of "active efforts" is met.

Active efforts should be:

- Affirmative;
- Active;
- Thorough; and
- Timely.

---

33. *See* 81 FR 38813-388-14.
34. *See, e.g., In re Nicole B.*, 927 A.2d 1194, 1206–07 (Md. Ct. Spec. App. 2007)
35. *See, e.g., In re C.F.*, 230 Ca. App. 4th 227 (2014); *In re Michael G.*, 63 Cal. App. 4th 700 (1998).

E.2 Active efforts and the case plan

Regulation

§ 23.2 . . . Where an agency is involved in the child-custody proceeding, active efforts must involve assisting the parent or parents or Indian custodian through the steps of a case plan and with accessing or developing the resources necessary to satisfy the case plan.

Guidelines

Because active efforts must involve assisting the parents or Indian custodian through the steps of the case plan, and with accessing or developing resources necessary to satisfy the case plan, the State agency may need to take an active role in connecting the parent or Indian custodian with resources. By its plain and ordinary meaning, "active" cannot be merely "passive."

E.3 Active efforts consistent with prevailing social and cultural conditions of Tribe

Regulation

§ 23.2 . . . To the maximum extent possible, active efforts should be provided in a manner consistent with the prevailing social and cultural conditions and way of life of the Indian child's Tribe and should be conducted in partnership with the Indian child and the Indian child's parents, extended family members, Indian custodians, and Tribe.

Guidelines

The rule indicates that, to the maximum extent possible, active efforts should be provided in a manner consistent with the prevailing social and cultural conditions of the Indian child's Tribe, and in partnership with the child, parents, extended family, and Tribe. This is consistent with congressional direction in ICWA to conduct Indian child-custody proceedings in a way that reflects the cultural and social standards prevailing in Indian communities and families. There is also evidence that services that are adapted to the client's cultural backgrounds are better.[36]

Determining the appropriate active efforts may entail discussions with Tribal leadership, elders, or religious figures or academics with expertise concerning a

36. *See.* 81 FR 38790-38791 (June 14, 2016).

given Tribe as to the type of culturally appropriate services that could be provided to the family.

Culturally appropriate services in the child welfare context could include trauma-informed therapy that incorporates best practices in addressing Native American historical and intergenerational trauma, pastoral counseling that incorporates a Native American holistic approach and focus on spirituality, and Tribal/Native faith healers or medicine/holy men or women within the Tribe who utilize prayers, ceremonies, sweat lodge and other interventions. Another example is the use of Positive Indian Parenting curriculum, which is based on Native American beliefs and customs, and provided to clients to improve their parenting skills with a strong culture-based background. These are examples only and not an exhaustive list.

E.4 Examples of active efforts

Regulation

§ 23.2 . . . Active efforts are to be tailored to the facts and circumstances of the case and may include, for example:

(1) Conducting a comprehensive assessment of the circumstances of the Indian child's family, with a focus on safe reunification as the most desirable goal;

(2) Identifying appropriate services and helping the parents to overcome barriers, including actively assisting the parents in obtaining such services;

(3) Identifying, notifying, and inviting representatives of the Indian child's Tribe to participate in providing support and services to the Indian child's family and in family team meetings, permanency planning, and resolution of placement issues;

(4) Conducting or causing to be conducted a diligent search for the Indian child's extended family members, and contacting and consulting with extended family members to provide family structure and support for the Indian child and the Indian child's parents;

(5) Offering and employing all available and culturally appropriate family preservation strategies and facilitating the use of remedial and rehabilitative services provided by the child's Tribe;

(6) Taking steps to keep siblings together whenever possible;

(7) Supporting regular visits with parents or Indian custodians in the most natural setting possible as well as trial home visits of the Indian child during any period of removal, consistent with the need to ensure the health, safety, and welfare of the child;

> (8) Identifying community resources including housing, financial, transportation, mental health, substance abuse, and peer support services and actively assisting the Indian child's parents or, when appropriate, the child's family, in utilizing and accessing those resources;
>
> (9) Monitoring progress and participation in services;
>
> (10) Considering alternative ways to address the needs of the Indian child's parents and, where appropriate, the family, if the optimum services do not exist or are not available;
>
> (11) Providing post-reunification services and monitoring.

Guidelines

The examples of active efforts provided in the ICWA regulations reflect best practices in the field of Indian child welfare, but are not meant to be an exhaustive list. Active efforts must be tailored to each child and family within each ICWA case and could include additional efforts by the agency working with the child and family. The minimum actions required to meet the "active efforts" threshold will depend on unique circumstances of the case. It is recommended that the State agency determine which active efforts will best address the specific issues facing the family and tailor those efforts to help keep the family together. This will help active efforts to respond to the unique facts and circumstances of the case. For example, if one of the child's parents has a problem with alcohol abuse, active efforts might include assisting that parent with enrollment in an alcohol treatment program and helping to coordinate transportation to and from meetings. If substance abuse is not an issue, active efforts would not need to include this kind of assistance.

As the examples illustrate, the State agency should actively connect Indian families with substantive services and not merely make the services available. Agency workers and courts should ask whether they have truly taken "active" steps (i.e., affirmative, proactive, thorough, and timely efforts) to provide services and programs to the family, recognizing that resource constraints will always exist.

E.5 Providing active efforts

Regulation

> **§ 23.120 How does the State court ensure that active efforts have been made?**
>
> (a) Prior to ordering an involuntary foster-care placement or termination of parental rights, the court must conclude that active efforts have been made to prevent the breakup of the Indian family and that those efforts have been unsuccessful. . . .

Guidelines

The statute and rule provide that the State court must conclude that active efforts were provided and were unsuccessful prior to ordering an involuntary foster-care placement or TPR.[37] Thus, if a detention, jurisdiction, or disposition hearing in an involuntary child-custody proceeding includes a judicial determination that the Indian child must be placed in or remain in foster care, the court must first be satisfied that the active-efforts requirement has been met. In order to satisfy this requirement, active efforts should be provided at the earliest point possible.

If reunification with one parent is not possible (e.g., where the parent has severely abused a child or will be incarcerated for a long period of time), the court should still consider whether active efforts could permit reunification of the Indian child with the other parent.

Active efforts are required to prevent the breakup of the Indian child's family, regardless of whether individual members of the family are themselves Indian. The child's family is an "Indian family" because the child meets the definition of an "Indian child."

Checking on status of active efforts. The regulations reflect that the court must conclude that active efforts were made prior to ordering foster-care placement or TPR, but does not require such a finding at each hearing.[38] It is, however, a recommended practice for a court to inquire about active efforts at every court hearing and actively monitor compliance with the active efforts requirement. This will help avoid unnecessary delays in achieving reunification with the parent, or other permanency for the child. The court should not rely solely on past findings regarding the sufficiency of active efforts, but rather should routinely ask as part of a foster-care or TPR proceeding whether circumstances have changed and whether additional active efforts have been or should be provided.

How long to provide active efforts. There are no specific time limits on active efforts, and what is required will depend on the facts of each case. State agencies should keep in mind that the State court must make a finding that active efforts were provided in order to make a foster-care placement or order TPR to an Indian child. Even if a finding was made that sufficient active efforts were made to support the foster-care placement, circumstances may have changed such that the court may require additional active efforts prior to ordering TPR. For example, if a parent initially refused alcohol treatment despite an agency's active efforts to provide services, a court could find that these efforts satisfied the requirement for purposes of the foster-care placement. But, if the parent subsequently completes alcohol treatment and needs additional services to regain custody (such as parenting skills training), the court will need to consider whether active efforts were made to provide these services. The requirement to conduct active efforts necessarily ends at the TPR because,

---

37. *See* 25 U.S.C. 1912(d); 25 CFR § 23.120.
38. *See* 25 CFR § 23.120.

after that point, there is no service or program that would prevent the breakup of the Indian family. If a child-custody proceeding is ongoing, even after return of the child, then active efforts would be required before there may be a subsequent foster-care placement or TPR.

Applying for Tribal membership. There is no requirement to conduct active efforts to apply for Tribal citizenship for the child. In any particular case, however, it may be appropriate to assist the child or parents in obtaining Tribal citizenship for the child, as this may make more services and programs available to the child. Securing Tribal citizenship may have long-term benefits for an Indian child, including access to programs, services, benefits, cultural connections, and political rights in the Tribe. It may be appropriate, for example, to assist in obtaining Tribal citizenship where it is apparent that the child or its biological parent would become enrolled in the Tribe during the course of the proceedings, thereby aiding in ICWA's efficient administration.

E.6 Documenting active efforts

Regulation

---

§ 23.120 How does the State court ensure that active efforts have been made?

. . . (b) Active efforts must be documented in detail in the record.

Guidelines

The active-efforts requirement is a key protection provided by ICWA, and it is important that compliance with the requirement is documented in the court record. The rule therefore requires the court to document active efforts in detail in the record.

State agencies also need to help ensure that there is sufficient documentation available for the court to use in reaching its conclusions regarding the provision of active efforts. Although the court itself determines what level of documentation it will require, the Department recommends that the State agency include the following in its documentation of active efforts, among any other relevant information:

- The issues the family is facing that the State agency is targeting with the active efforts (these should be the same issues that are threatening the breakup of the Indian family or preventing reunification);
- A list of active efforts the State agency determines would best address the issues and the reasoning for choosing those specific active efforts;
- Dates, persons contacted, and other details evidencing how the State agency provided active efforts;

- Results of the active efforts provided and, where the results were less than satisfactory, whether the State agency adjusted the active efforts to better address the issues.

While ICWA does not establish a standard of evidence for review of whether active efforts have been provided, the Department favorably views cases that apply the same standard of proof for the underlying action to the question of whether active efforts were provided (i.e., clear and convincing evidence for foster care placement and beyond a reasonable doubt for TPR).

F. Jurisdiction

F.1 Tribe's exclusive jurisdiction

Regulation

§ 23.110 When must a State court dismiss an action?

Subject to 25 U.S.C. 1919 (Agreements between States and Indian Tribes) and §

23.113 (emergency proceedings), the following limitations on a State court's jurisdiction apply:

(a) The court in any voluntary or involuntary child-custody proceeding involving an Indian child must determine the residence and domicile of the Indian child. If either the residence or domicile is on a reservation where the Tribe exercises exclusive jurisdiction over child-custody proceedings, the State court must expeditiously notify the Tribal court of the pending dismissal based on the Tribe's exclusive jurisdiction, dismiss the State-court child-custody proceeding, and ensure that the Tribal court is sent all information regarding the Indian child-custody proceeding, including, but not limited to, the pleadings and any court record.

(b) If the child is a ward of a Tribal court, the State court must expeditiously notify the Tribal court of the pending dismissal, dismiss the State-court child-custody proceeding, and ensure that the Tribal court is sent all information regarding the Indian child-custody proceeding, including, but not limited to, the pleadings and any court record.

Guidelines

With limited exceptions, ICWA provides for Tribal jurisdiction "exclusive as to any State" over child-custody proceedings involving an Indian child who resides or is domiciled within the reservation of such Tribe.[39] ICWA also provides for exclusive Tribal jurisdiction over an Indian child who is a ward of a Tribal court, notwithstanding the residence or domicile of the child. If the child's domicile[40] or residence is on an Indian reservation or the child is a ward of Tribal court, then the Tribe has exclusive jurisdiction over the proceeding, unless "such jurisdiction is otherwise vested in the State by existing Federal law."[41] To ensure the well-being of the child, State officials should continue to work on the case until the State court officially dismisses the case from State jurisdiction.[42]

The mandatory dismissal provisions in §23.110 apply "subject to" §23.113 (emergency proceedings) so that the State may take action through an emergency proceeding when necessary to prevent imminent physical damage or harm to the child. Likewise, the mandatory dismissal provisions do not apply if the State and Tribe have an agreement regarding jurisdiction because, in some cases, Tribes choose to refrain from asserting jurisdiction. *See* section A.5 of these guidelines.

Contacting court prior to determining whether dismissal is necessary. In determining whether dismissal is necessary, the State court may need to contact the Tribal court and/or Tribal child-welfare agency to:

- Confirm the child's status as a ward of that court; and
- Determine whether jurisdiction over child-custody proceedings for that Tribe is otherwise vested in the State by existing Federal law.[43]

If the State court does not have contact information for the Tribal court, the Tribe's designated ICWA agent may provide that information. The BIA publishes, on an annual basis, a list of contacts designated by each Tribe for receipt of ICWA notices in the Federal Register and makes the list available at www.bia.gov. Each Tribe's ICWA designated contact will have information on whether the Tribe exercises exclusive jurisdiction.

Coordination of dismissal and transfer. State and Tribal courts and State and Tribal child-welfare agencies are encouraged to work cooperatively to ensure that dismissal and transfer of information proceeds expeditiously and that the welfare of the Indian child is protected. The rule requires the court to transmit all information in its possession regarding the Indian child-custody proceeding to the Tribal court. Such information would include all the information within the court's possession regarding the Indian child-custody proceeding, including the pleadings and any

39. 25 U.S.C. 1911(a).

40. *See* definition of "domicile"

41. 25 U.S.C. 1911(a); Certain courts have interpreted the 'existing federal law' clause as granting state courts in Public Law 280 states concurrent jurisdiction over cases in which jurisdiction would otherwise remain exclusively with the tribe. *See, e.g., Doe v. Mann,* 415 F.3d 1038(9th Cir. 2005).

42. *See* 25 CFR §23.110 at Appendix 6.

43. *See* 25 U.S.C. 1911(a).

court record.[44] In order to best protect the welfare of the child, State agencies should also work to share information that is not contained in the State court's records but that would assist the Tribe in understanding and meeting the Indian child's needs.

Safety investigative services. The rule does not affect State authority to provide safety investigative services when a child is domiciled on reservation but located off reservation.

See also the definition of "reservation."

F.2 State's and Tribe's concurrent jurisdiction

Regulation

---

§ 23.115 How are petitions for transfer of a proceeding made?

(a) Either parent, the Indian custodian, or the Indian child's Tribe may request, at any time, orally on the record or in writing, that the State court transfer a foster-care or termination-of-parental-rights proceeding to the jurisdiction of the child's Tribe.

(b) The right to request a transfer is available at any stage in each foster-care or termination-of-parental-rights proceeding.

Guidelines

Section 1911(b) of ICWA provides for the transfer of any State court proceeding for the foster-care placement, or TPR to, an Indian child not domiciled or residing within the reservation of the Indian child's Tribe. This provision and § 23.115 recognize that Indian Tribes maintain concurrent jurisdiction over child-welfare matters involving Tribal children, even off of the reservation.

Applicable proceedings. Provisions addressing transfer apply to both involuntary and voluntary foster-care and TPR proceedings. This includes TPR proceedings that may be handled concurrently with adoption proceedings.

Other proceedings. Parties may request transfer of preadoptive and adoptive placement proceedings, but the standards for addressing such motions are not dictated by ICWA or the regulations. Tribes possess inherent jurisdiction over domestic relations, including the welfare of child citizens of the Tribe, even beyond that authority confirmed in ICWA. Thus, it may be appropriate to transfer preadoptive and adoptive proceedings involving children residing outside of a reservation to Tribal jurisdiction in particular circumstances.[45]

---

44. *See* 25 CFR § 23.110.

45. *See* 81 FR 38821 for additional information on how Congress has repeatedly sought to strengthen Tribal courts.

Availability at any stage. The rule provides that the right to request a transfer is available at any stage in each foster-care or TPR proceeding. Transfer to Tribal jurisdiction, even at a late stage of a proceeding, will not necessarily entail unwarranted disruption of an Indian child's placement. The Tribe or parent may have reasons for not immediately moving to transfer the case (e.g., because of geographic considerations, maintaining State-court jurisdiction appears to hold out the most promise for reunification of the family).[46]

F.3 Contact with Tribal court on potential transfer

Regulation

§ 23.116 What happens after a petition for transfer is made?

Upon receipt of a transfer petition, the State court must ensure that the Tribal court is promptly notified in writing of the transfer petition. This notification may request a timely response regarding whether the Tribal court wishes to decline the transfer.

Guidelines

It is important for the State court to contact the Tribal court upon receipt of the transfer petition to alert the Tribal court (usually reachable by first contacting the Tribe's designated ICWA agent) and provide it with the opportunity to determine whether it wishes to decline jurisdiction. It is recommended that, in addition to the required written notification, State court personnel contact the Tribe by phone as well.

F.4 Criteria for ruling on a transfer petition

Regulation

§ 23.117 What are the criteria for ruling on transfer petitions?

Upon receipt of a transfer petition from an Indian child's parent, Indian custodian, or Tribe, the State court must transfer the child-custody proceeding unless the court determines that transfer is not appropriate because one or more of the following criteria are met:

(a) Either parent objects to such transfer;

(b) The Tribal court declines the transfer; or

(c) Good cause exists for denying the transfer.

46. *See* 81 FR 38823 for information on why the rule does not establish a deadline or time limit for requesting transfer.

Guidelines

A keystone of ICWA is its recognition of a Tribe's exclusive or concurrent jurisdiction over child-custody proceedings involving Indian children. When the State and Tribe have concurrent jurisdiction, ICWA establishes a presumption that a State must transfer jurisdiction to the Tribe upon request. The rule reflects ICWA section 1911(b)'s requirement that a child-custody proceeding be transferred to Tribal court upon petition of either parent or the Indian custodian or the Indian child's Tribe, except in three circumstances: (1) where either parent objects; (2) where the Tribal court declines the transfer; or (3) where there is good cause for denying the transfer.

Either Parent Objects

The rule mirrors the statute in respecting a parent's objection to transfer of the proceeding to Tribal court. As Congress noted, "[e]ither parent is given the right to veto such transfer."[47] However, if a parent's parental rights have been terminated and this determination is final, they would no longer be considered a "parent" with a right under these rules to object.

While, this criterion addresses the objection of either parent, nothing prohibits the State court from considering the objection of the guardian ad litem or child himself under the third criteria (good cause to deny transfer), where appropriate.

Tribe Declines

If the Tribal court explicitly states that it declines jurisdiction, the State court may deny a transfer motion. It is recommended that the State court obtain documentation of the Tribal court's declination to include in the record.

Good Cause Exists

This exception is not defined in the statute, and in the Department's experience, has in the past been used to deny transfer for reasons that frustrate the purposes of ICWA. The legislative history indicates that this provision is intended to permit a State court to apply a modified doctrine of forum non conveniens, in appropriate cases, to insure that the rights of the child as an Indian, the Indian parents or custodian, and the Tribe are fully protected. State courts may exercise case-by-case discretion regarding the "good cause" finding, but this discretion should be limited and animated by the Federal policy to protect the rights of the Indian child, parents, and Tribe, which can often best be accomplished in Tribal court. Exceptions cannot be construed in a manner that would swallow the rule.

---

47. H.R. Rep. No. 95-1386, at 21.

F.5 Good cause to deny transfer

Regulation

---

§ 23.118 How is a determination of "good cause" to deny transfer made?

(a) If the State court believes, or any party asserts, that good cause to deny transfer exists, the reasons for that belief or assertion must be stated orally on the record or provided in writing on the record and to the parties to the child-custody proceeding.

(b) Any party to the child-custody proceeding must have the opportunity to provide the court with views regarding whether good cause to deny transfer exists.

(c) In determining whether good cause exists, the court must not consider:

(1) Whether the foster-care or termination-of-parental-rights proceeding is at an advanced stage if the Indian child's parent, Indian custodian, or Tribe did not receive notice of the child-custody proceeding until an advanced stage;

(2) Whether there have been prior proceedings involving the child for which no petition to transfer was filed;

(3) Whether transfer could affect the placement of the child;

(4) The Indian child's cultural connections with the Tribe or its reservation; or

(5) Socioeconomic conditions or any negative perception of Tribal or BIA social services or judicial systems.

(d) The basis for any State-court decision to deny transfer should be stated orally on the record or in a written order.

Guidelines

While the statute and the rule provide State courts with the discretion to determine "good cause" based on the specific facts of a particular case, the rule does mandate certain procedural protections if a court is going to conduct a good cause analysis. It also identifies a limited number of considerations that should not be part of the good-cause analysis because there is evidence Congress did not wish them to be considered, they have been shown to frustrate the purposes of ICWA, or would otherwise work a fundamental unfairness. The regulation's limitations on what may be considered in the "good cause" determination do not limit State judges from considering some exceptional circumstance as the basis of good cause. However, the "good cause" determination whether to deny transfer to Tribal court should address which court is best positioned to adjudicate the child-custody proceeding, not predictions about the outcome of that proceeding.

Standard of Evidence

Neither the statute nor the rule establishes a Federal standard of evidence for the determination of whether there is good cause to transfer a proceeding to Tribal court. There is, however, a strong trend in State courts to apply a clear and convincing standard of evidence.[48] The Department notes that the strong trend in State court decisions on this issue is compelling and recommends that State courts follow that trend.

Prohibited Considerations

Advanced stage if notice was not received until an advanced stage. The rule prohibits a finding of good cause based on the advanced stage of the proceeding, if the parent, Indian custodian, or Indian child's Tribe did not receive notice of the proceeding until an advanced stage. This protects the rights of the parents and Tribe to seek transfer where ICWA's notice provisions were not complied with, and thus will help to promote compliance with these provisions. It also ensures that parties are not unfairly advantaged or disadvantaged by noncompliance with the statute. Parents, custodians, and Tribes who were disadvantaged by noncompliance with ICWA's notice provisions should still have a meaningful opportunity to seek transfer.

The rule also clarifies that "advanced stage" refers to the proceeding, rather than the case as a whole. Each individual proceeding will culminate in an order, so "advanced stage" is a measurement of the stage within each proceeding. This allows Tribes to wait until the TPR proceeding to request a transfer to Tribal court, because the parents, Indian custodian, and Tribe must receive notice of each proceeding. It is often at the TPR stage that factors that may have dissuaded a Tribe from taking an active role in the case (such as the State's efforts to reunite a child with her nearby parent) change in ways that may warrant reconsidering transfer of the case.

Prior proceedings for which no petition to transfer was filed. As just discussed, the rule clarifies that "advanced stage" refers to the proceeding, rather than the case as a whole. ICWA clearly distinguishes between foster-care and TPR proceedings, and these proceedings have significantly different implications for the Indian child's parents and Tribe. There may be compelling reasons to not seek transfer for a foster-care proceeding, but those reasons may not be present for a TPR proceeding.

Effect on placement of the child. The rule provides that the State court must not consider, in its decision as to whether there is good cause to deny transfer to the Tribal court, whether the Tribal court could change the child's placement. This is not an appropriate basis for good cause because the State court cannot know or accurately predict which placement a Tribal court might consider or ultimately order. A transfer to Tribal court does not automatically mean a change in placement; the Tribal court will consider each case on and individualized basis and determine what is best for that child. Like State courts, Tribal courts and agencies

48. *See* 81 FR 38827 (June 14, 2016) for additional information on States' application of this standard of evidence.

seek to protect the welfare of the Indian child, and would consider whether the current placement best meets that goal.

Cultural connections to the Tribe or reservation. The regulations prohibit a finding of good cause based on the Indian child's perceived cultural connections with the Tribe or reservation. Congress enacted ICWA in express recognition of the fact that State courts and agencies were generally ill-equipped to recognize the essential tribal relations of Indian people and the cultural and social standards prevailing in Indian communities and families.[49] As such, State courts must not evaluate the sufficiency of an Indian child's cultural connections with a Tribe or reservation in evaluating a motion to transfer.

Negative perceptions of Tribal or BIA social services or judicial systems. The regulations prohibit consideration of any perceived inadequacy of Tribal or BIA social services or judicial systems. This is consistent with ICWA's strong recognition of the competency of Tribal fora to address child-custody matters involving Tribal children. It is also consistent with section 1911(d)'s requirement that States afford full faith and credit to public acts, records, and judicial proceedings of Tribes to the same extent as any other entity.

Socioeconomic conditions within the Tribe or reservation. The regulations prohibit consideration of the perceived socioeconomic conditions within a Tribe or reservation. Congress found that misplaced concerns about low incomes, substandard housing, and similar factors on reservations resulted in the unwarranted removal of Indian children from their families and Tribes. These factors can introduce bias into decision-making and should not come into play in considering whether transfer is appropriate.

State courts retain the ability to determine "good cause" based on the specific facts of a particular case, so long as they do not base their good cause finding on one or more of these prohibited considerations. If a State court considers the distance of the parties from the Tribal court, it must also weigh any available accommodations that may address the potential hardships caused by the distance.

For additional information on the basis for the parameters for "good cause," *see* 81 FR 38821–38822 (June 14, 2016).

F.6 Transferring to Tribal court

Regulation

§ 23.119 What happens after a petition for transfer is granted?

(a) If the Tribal court accepts the transfer, the State court should expeditiously provide the Tribal court with all records related to the proceeding, including, but not limited to, the pleadings and any court record.

49. 25 U.S.C. 1901(5).

(b) The State court should work with the Tribal court to ensure that the transfer of the custody of the Indian child and of the proceeding is accomplished smoothly and in a way that minimizes the disruption of services to the family.

Guidelines

Once the State court determines that it must transfer to Tribal court, the State court and Tribal court should communicate to agree to procedures for the transfer to ensure that the transfer of the proceeding minimizes disruptions to the child and to services provided to the family.

If the State court does not have contact information for the Tribal court, the court should contact the Tribe's ICWA officer. If this occurs, State court personnel should work with the Tribal court and agency to transfer or provide copies of all records in the Indian child's case file so that the Tribal court and agency may best meet the child's needs. State agencies should share records with Tribal agencies as they would other governmental jurisdictions, presumably at no charge.

G. Adjudication of Involuntary Proceedings

G.1 Standard of evidence for foster-care placement and TPR proceedings

Regulation

§ 23.121 What are the applicable standards of evidence?

(a) The court must not order a foster-care placement of an Indian child unless clear and convincing evidence is presented, including the testimony of one or more qualified expert witnesses, demonstrating that the child's continued custody by the child's parent or Indian custodian is likely to result in serious emotional or physical damage to the child.

(b) The court must not order a termination of parental rights for an Indian child unless evidence beyond a reasonable doubt is presented, including the testimony of one or more qualified expert witnesses, demonstrating that the child's continued custody by the child's parent or Indian custodian is likely to result in serious emotional or physical damage to the child.

(c) For a foster-care placement or termination of parental rights, the evidence must show a causal relationship between the particular conditions in the home and the likelihood that continued custody of the child will result in serious emotional or physical damage to the particular child who is the subject of the child-custody proceeding.

(d) Without a causal relationship identified in paragraph (c) of this section, evidence that shows only the existence of community or family poverty, isolation, single parenthood, custodian age, crowded or inadequate housing, substance abuse, or nonconforming social behavior does not by itself constitute clear and convincing evidence or evidence beyond a reasonable doubt that continued custody is likely to result in serious emotional or physical damage to the child.

Guidelines

ICWA and the rule require that a court may not order a foster-care placement of an Indian child or a TPR unless there is a showing that the continued custody of the child by the parent or Indian custodian is likely to result in serious emotional or physical damage to the child. The court's determination must be supported by clear and convincing evidence, in the case of a foster-care placement, or by evidence beyond a reasonable doubt, in the case of a TPR. The evidence supporting the determination must also include the testimony of a qualified expert witness.

The rule requires there be a causal relationship between the particular conditions in the home and risk of serious emotional or physical damage to the child. Put differently, the evidence must show the existence of particular conditions in the home that are likely to result in serious emotional or physical damage to the particular child who is the subject of the proceeding.

The rule prohibits relying on **any one** of the factors listed in paragraph (d), **absent the causal connection** identified in (c), **as the sole basis** for determining that clear and convincing evidence or evidence beyond a reasonable doubt support a conclusion that continued custody is likely to result in serious emotional or physical damage to the child. This provision addresses the types of situations identified in the statute's legislative history where Indian children are removed from their home based on subjective assessments of home conditions that, in fact, are not likely to cause the child serious emotional or physical damage.

"Nonconforming social behavior" may include behaviors that do not comply with society's norms, such as dressing in a manner that others perceive as strange, an unusual or disruptive manner of speech, or discomfort in or avoidance of social situations.

These provisions recognize that children can thrive when they are kept with their parents, even in homes that may not be ideal in terms of cleanliness, access to nutritious food, or personal space, or when a parent is single, impoverished, or a substance abuser. Rather, there must be a demonstrated correlation between the conditions of the home and a threat to the specific child's emotional or physical well-being.

G.2 Qualified expert witness

Regulation

§ 23.122 Who may serve as a qualified expert witness?

(a) A qualified expert witness must be qualified to testify regarding whether the child's continued custody by the parent or Indian custodian is likely to result in serious emotional or physical damage to the child and should be qualified to testify as to the prevailing social and cultural standards of the Indian child's Tribe. A person may be designated by the Indian child's Tribe as being qualified to testify to the prevailing social and cultural standards of the Indian child's Tribe.

(b) The court or any party may request the assistance of the Indian child's Tribe or the BIA office serving the Indian child's Tribe in locating persons qualified to serve as expert witnesses.

(c) The social worker regularly assigned to the Indian child may not serve as a qualified expert witness in child-custody proceedings concerning the child.

Guidelines

Qualified expert witnesses must have particular expertise. The rule requires that the qualified expert witness must be qualified to testify regarding whether the continued custody of the child by the parent or Indian custodian is likely to result in serious emotional or physical damage to the child. This requirement flows from the language of the statute requiring a determination, supported by evidence, including testimony of qualified expert witnesses, that the continued custody of the child by the parent or Indian custodian is likely to result in serious emotional or physical damage to the child.[50] Congress noted that "[t]he phrase 'qualified expert witness' is meant to apply to expertise beyond normal social worker qualifications."[51]

Qualified expert witness should have knowledge of prevailing social and cultural standards of the Tribe. In addition, the qualified expert witness should have specific knowledge of the prevailing social and cultural standards of the Indian child's Tribe. In passing ICWA, Congress wanted to make sure that Indian child-welfare determinations are not based on "a white, middle-class standard which, in many cases, forecloses placement with [an] Indian family."[52] Congress recognized that States have failed to recognize the essential Tribal relations of Indian people

50. 25 U.S.C. 1912(e), (f).
51. H.R. Rep. No. 95-1386, at 22.
52. *Holyfield,* 490 U.S. at 36 (citing H.R. Rep. No. 95-1386, at 24).

and the cultural and social standards prevailing in Indian communities and families.[53] Accordingly, expert testimony presented to State courts should reflect and be informed by those cultural and social standards. This ensures that relevant cultural information is provided to the court and that the expert testimony is contextualized within the Tribe's social and cultural standards. Thus, the question of whether the continued custody of the child by the parent or Indian custodian is likely to result in serious emotional or physical damage to the child is one that should be examined in the context of the prevailing cultural and social standards of the Indian child's Tribe.

The rule does not, however, strictly limit who may serve as a qualified expert witness to only those individuals who have particular Tribal social and cultural knowledge. The rule recognizes that there may be certain circumstances where a qualified expert witness need not have specific knowledge of the prevailing social and cultural standards of the Indian child's Tribe in order to meet the statutory standard. For example, a leading expert on issues regarding sexual abuse of children may not need to know about specific Tribal social and cultural standards in order to testify as a qualified expert witness regarding whether return of a child to a parent who has a history of sexually abusing the child is likely to result in serious emotional or physical damage to the child. Thus, while a qualified expert witness should normally be required to have knowledge of Tribal social and cultural standards, that may not be necessary if such knowledge is plainly irrelevant to the particular circumstances at issue in the proceeding. A more stringent standard may, of course, be set by State law.

Separate expert witnesses may be used to testify regarding potential emotional or physical damage to the child and the prevailing social and cultural standards of the Tribe.

A person testifying to the prevailing social and cultural standards of the Indian child's Tribe must be knowledgeable and experienced in the Tribe's society and culture. The Indian child's Tribe may designate a person as being qualified to testify to the prevailing social and cultural standards of the Indian child's Tribe.

Assistance in locating a qualified expert witness. The rule encourages the court or any party to request the assistance of the Indian child's Tribe or the BIA office serving the Indian child's Tribe in locating persons qualified to serve as expert witnesses. The rule also allows a Tribe to designate a person as being qualified to testify as to the prevailing social and cultural standards of the Indian child's Tribe.

Social worker regularly assigned to the child. The qualified expert witness should be someone who can provide a culturally informed, outside opinion to the court regarding whether the continued custody by the parent is likely to result in serious emotional or physical harm to the child. By imposing the requirement for a

53. *See* 25 U.S.C. 1901(5).

qualified expert witness, Congress wanted to ensure that State courts heard from experts other than State social workers seeking the action before placing an Indian child in foster care or ordering the TPR. Therefore, the regulation provides that the social worker regularly assigned to the Indian child (i.e., the State agency seeking the action) may not serve as a qualified expert witness in child-custody proceedings concerning the child. If another social worker, Tribal or otherwise, serves as the qualified expert witness, that person must have expertise beyond the normal social worker qualifications.[54]

Citizen of Tribe. There is no requirement that the qualified expert witness be a citizen of the child's Tribe. The witness should be able to demonstrate knowledge of the prevailing social and cultural standards of the Indian child's Tribe or be designated by a Tribe as having such knowledge. In some instances, it may be appropriate to accept an expert with knowledge of the customs and standards of closely related Tribes. Parties may also contact the BIA for assistance.

Number of expert witnesses. ICWA and the rule do not limit the number of expert witnesses that may testify. The court may accept expert testimony from any number of witnesses, including from multiple qualified expert witnesses.

Familiarity with the child. It is also recommended that the qualified expert witness be someone familiar with that particular child. If the expert makes contact with the parents, observes interactions between the parent(s) and child, and meets with extended family members in the child's life, the expert will be able to provide a more complete picture to the court.

See 81 FR 38829–38832 (June 14, 2016) for additional information on qualified expert witnesses.

H. Placement Preferences

H.1 Adoptive placement preferences

Regulation

---

§ 23.130 What placement preferences apply in adoptive placements?

(a) In any adoptive placement of an Indian child under State law, where the Indian child's Tribe has not established a different order of preference under paragraph (b) of this section, preference must be given in descending order, as listed below, to placement of the child with:

(1) A member of the Indian child's extended family; (2) Other members of the Indian child's Tribe; or

54. *See* H.R. Rep. No. 95-1386, at 22.

(3) Other Indian families.

(b) If the Indian child's Tribe has established by resolution a different order of preference than that specified in ICWA, the Tribe's placement preferences apply.

(c) The court must, where appropriate, also consider the placement preference of the Indian child or Indian child's parent.

Guidelines

In ICWA, Congress expressed a strong Federal policy in favor of keeping Indian children with their families and Tribes whenever possible, and established preferred placements that it believed would help protect the needs and long-term welfare of Indian children and families, while providing the flexibility to ensure that the particular circumstances faced by individual Indian children can be addressed by courts.

Order. Each placement should be considered (without being skipped) in that order; the preferences are in the order of most preferred to least preferred.

Tribe's order of preference. State agencies should determine if the child's Tribe has established, by resolution, an order of preference different from that specified in ICWA. If so, then apply the Tribe's placement preferences. Otherwise, apply ICWA's placement preferences as set out in § 23.131.

The statute requires that a Tribal order of preference be established by "resolution." While different Tribes act through different types of actions and legal instruments, the Department understands that a Tribal "resolution," for this purpose, would be a legally binding statement by the competent Tribal authority that lays out an objective order of placement preferences.

If a Tribal-State agreement on ICWA establishes the order of preference, that would constitute an order of preference established by "resolution," as required by the rule. Such a document would be a legally binding statement by the competent Tribal authority that lays out an objective order of placement preferences. In addition, the statute specifically authorizes Tribal-State agreements respecting care and custody of Indian children.

Consideration of child's or parent's preference. The rule reflects the language of the statute. This language does not require a court to follow a child's or parent's preference, but rather requires that it be considered where appropriate.

H.2. Foster-care placement preferences

Regulation

§ 23.131 What placement preferences apply in foster-care or preadoptive placements?

(a) In any foster-care or preadoptive placement of an Indian child under State law, including changes in foster-care or preadoptive placements, the child must be placed in the least-restrictive setting that:

(1) Most approximates a family, taking into consideration sibling attachment; (2) Allows the Indian child's special needs (if any) to be met; and

(3) Is in reasonable proximity to the Indian child's home, extended family, or siblings.

(b) In any foster-care or preadoptive placement of an Indian child under State law, where the Indian child's Tribe has not established a different order of preference under paragraph (c) of this section, preference must be given, in descending order as listed below, to placement of the child with:

(1) A member of the Indian child's extended family;

(2) A foster home that is licensed, approved, or specified by the Indian child's Tribe;

(3) An Indian foster home licensed or approved by an authorized non-Indian licensing authority; or

(4) An institution for children approved by an Indian Tribe or operated by an Indian organization which has a program suitable to meet the child's needs.

(c) If the Indian child's Tribe has established by resolution a different order of preference than that specified in ICWA, the Tribe's placement preferences apply, so long as the placement is the least-restrictive setting appropriate to the particular needs of the Indian child, as provided in paragraph (a) of this section.

(d) The court must, where appropriate, also consider the preference of the Indian child or the Indian child's parent.

Guidelines

The placement preferences included in ICWA and the rule codify the generally accepted best practice to favor placing the child with extended family. Congress recognized that this generally applicable preference for placing children with family is even more important for Indian children and families, given that one of the factors leading to the passage of ICWA was the failure of non-Indian child welfare workers to understand the role of the extended family in Indian society. In many cases, the placement preferences have special force and effect for Indian children, since, as Congress recognized, there are harms to individual children and parents caused by disconnection with their Tribal communities and culture, and also harms to Tribes caused by the loss of their children.

While it may be the practice in some jurisdictions for judges to defer to State agencies to issue placement orders, the statute contemplates court review of placements of Indian children. For this reason, there must be a court determination of the placement and, if applicable, an examination of whether good cause exists to depart from the placement preferences.

Least restrictive setting. The foster-care placement includes the additional requirement that the placement be the least restrictive setting, which means the setting that most approximates a family. The placement decision must take into consideration sibling attachment and the proximity to the child's home, extended family, and/or siblings. If for some reason it is not possible to place the siblings together, then the Indian child should be placed, if possible, in a setting that is within a reasonable proximity to the sibling. In addition, if the sibling is age 18 or older, that sibling is extended family and would qualify as a preferred placement. The placement should also be one that allows the Indian child's special needs, if any, to be met.

Order. Each placement should be considered (without being skipped) in that order; the preferences are in the order of most preferred to least preferred.

Tribe's order of preference. *See* section H.1 of these guidelines on how to account for the Tribe's order of preference, but note that, for foster-care placements, the Tribe's placement preferences should be applied as long as the placement is the least-restrictive setting appropriate to the particular needs of the Indian child.

Consideration of child's or parent's preference. The rule reflects the language of the statute. This language does not require a court to follow a child or parent's preference, but rather requires that it be considered where appropriate.

See 81 FR 38838–38843 for additional information on placement preferences.

H.3 Finding preferred placements

Regulation

[*See* §§ 23.130 and 23.131, above].

Guidelines

The Department recommends that the State agency or other party seeking placement conduct a diligent search for placements that comply with the placement preferences. The diligent search should be thorough, ongoing and in compliance with child welfare best practices. A diligent search should also involve:

- Asking the parents for information about extended family, whether members of an Indian Tribe or not;
- Contacting all known extended family, whether members of an Indian Tribe or not;
- Contacting all Tribes with which the child is affiliated for assistance in identifying placements;
- Conducting diligent follow-up with all potential placements;
- Contacting institutions for children approved or operated by Indian Tribes if other preferred placements are not available.

It is recommended that the State agency (or other party seeking placement) document the search, so that it is reflected in the record.

Guidance and assistance for families wishing to serve as placements. As a recommended practice for State agencies, the State agency should provide the preferred placements with enough information about the proceeding so they can avail themselves of the preference. As a recommended practice, State courts should treat any individual who falls into a preferred placement category and who has expressed a desire to adopt (or provide foster care to) the Indian child as a potential preferred placement. The courts should not find that no preferred placement is available simply because the individual has not timely completed the formal steps required, such as filing a petition for adoption. Agencies and courts should be aware that a family member may wish to be a foster-care or adoptive placement for an Indian child but may not know how to file a petition for adoption, may have language or education barriers, or may live far from the State court. As a best practice, States may establish that actions such as testifying in court regarding the desire to adopt, or sending a statement to that effect in writing, may substitute for a formal petition for adoption for purposes of applying the placement preferences. If a State does not have formal requirements regarding how to qualify as a preferred placement, these should be made clear to potential placements.

Availability of preferred placements. The Department encourages States and Tribes to collaborate to increase the availability of Indian foster homes. Organizations such as the National Resource Center for Diligent Recruitment at AdoptUSKids provide tools and resources for recruiting Indian homes. See, e.g., National Resource Center for Diligent Recruitment, For Tribes: Tool and Resources (last visited Apr. 27, 2016), www.nrcdr.org/for-tribes/tools-and-resources.

Preferred placements in State. The fact that a no federally recognized Tribe is located within a State where the proceeding is occurring does not mean that there are no family members or members of Tribes residing or domiciled in that State. It is also important to note that a preferred placement may not be excluded from consideration merely because the placement is not located in the State where the proceeding is occurring.

Cooperation with the Tribe. The State agency should cooperate with the Tribe in identifying placement preferences. If a child is ultimately placed in a non-preferred placement, the Tribe may request that the foster or adoptive parent take actions, such as securing membership for the child, to maintain the child's Tribal affiliation.

H.4 Good cause to depart from the placement preferences

Regulation

§ 23.129 When do the placement preferences apply?

. . . (c) The placement preferences must be applied in any foster-care, pre-adoptive, or adoptive placement unless there is a determination on the record that good cause under § 23.132 exists to not apply those placement preferences.

§ 23.132 How is a determination of "good cause" to depart from the placement preferences made?

(a) If any party asserts that good cause not to follow the placement preferences exists, the reasons for that belief or assertion must be stated orally on the record or provided in writing to the parties to the child-custody proceeding and the court.

(b) The party seeking departure from the placement preferences should bear the burden of proving by clear and convincing evidence that there is "good cause" to depart from the placement preferences.

(c) A court's determination of good cause to depart from the placement preferences must be made on the record or in writing and should be based on one or more of the following considerations:

(1) The request of one or both of the Indian child's parents, if they attest that they have reviewed the placement options, if any, that comply with the order of preference;

(2) The request of the child, if the child is of sufficient age and capacity to understand the decision that is being made;

(3) The presence of a sibling attachment that can be maintained only through a particular placement;

(4) The extraordinary physical, mental, or emotional needs of the Indian child, such as specialized treatment services that may be unavailable in the community where families who meet the placement preferences live;

(5) The unavailability of a suitable placement after a determination by the court that a diligent search was conducted to find suitable placements

meeting the preference criteria, but none has been located. For purposes of this analysis, the standards for determining whether a placement is unavailable must conform to the prevailing social and cultural standards of the Indian community in which the Indian child's parent or extended family resides or with which the Indian child's parent or extended family members maintain social and cultural ties.

Guidelines

Congress determined that a placement with the Indian child's extended family or Tribal community will serve the child's best interest in most cases. A court may deviate from these preferences, however, when good cause exists.

A determination that good cause exists to deviate from the placement preferences must be made on the record by the court. It is recommended that the court state the reasons for finding good cause and incorporate agency documentation (required by § 23.141) of its search for placement preferences and other information regarding the child's needs and available placements.

This good cause standard applies to requests to deviate from both the Federal placement preferences and any applicable Tribal-specific preferences being applied in lieu of the Federal preferences.

If a party believes that good cause not to comply with the placement preferences exists because one of the factors in § 23.132(c) applies, the party must provide documentation of the basis for good cause.

Standard of evidence for "good cause" determination. While not mandatory, it is recommended that the documentation meet the "clear and convincing" standard of proof. Courts that have grappled with the issue have almost universally concluded that application of the clear and convincing evidence standard is required as it is most consistent with Congress's intent in ICWA to maintain Indian families and Tribes intact. Widespread application of this standard will promote uniformity of the application of ICWA. It will also prevent delays in permanency that would otherwise result from protracted litigation over what the correct burden of proof should be.

A court evidentiary hearing may not be required to effect a placement that departs for good cause from the placement preferences, if such a hearing is not required under State law and if the requirements of 25 U.S.C. 1912(d)-(e) have been met. Regardless of the level of court involvement in the placement, however, the basis for an assertion of good cause must be stated in the record or in writing and a record of the placement must be maintained.

Where a party to the proceeding objects to the placement, however, the rule establishes the parameters for a court's review of whether there is good cause to deviate from the placement preferences and requires the basis for that determination to be on the record. While the agency may place a child prior to or without any determination by the court, the agency does so knowing that the court reviews the placement to ensure compliance with the statute.

Congress established preferred placements in ICWA that it believed would help protect the long-term health and welfare of Indian children, parents, families, and Tribes. ICWA must be interpreted as providing meaningful limits on the discretion of agencies and courts to remove Indian children from their families and Tribes, since this is the very problem that ICWA was intended to address. Accordingly, the rule identifies specific factors that should provide the basis for a finding of good cause to deviate from the placement preferences.

Paragraph (c) of § 23.132 provides specific factors that can support a "good cause determination. Congress intended "good cause" to be a limited exception to the placement preferences, rather than a broad category that could swallow the rule.

Factors that may form the basis for good cause. The rule's list of is not exhaustive. The State court has the ultimate authority to consider evidence provided by the parties and make its own judgment as to whether the moving party has met the statutory "good cause" standard. In this way, the rule recognizes that there may be extraordinary circumstances where there is good cause to deviate from the placement preferences based on some reason outside of the five specifically-listed factors. The rule thereby retains discretion for courts and agencies to consider any unique needs of a particular Indian child in making a good cause determination.

Flexibility to find there is no good cause even when one or more factors are present. The court retains the discretion to find that good cause does not exist (and apply the placement preferences) even where one or more of the listed factors for good cause is present. Such a finding may be appropriate if other circumstances lead the court to conclude that there is not good cause. For example, if one parent consents and one does not, the court is not mandated to deviate from the preferences—rather it should be able to listen to the arguments of both sides and then decide.

Request of parent. The statute provides that, where appropriate, preference of the parent must be considered.[55] The rule therefore reflects that the request of the parent may provide a basis for a "good cause" determination, if the court agrees. The rule requires that the parent or parents making such a request must attest that they have reviewed the placement options that comply with the order of preference. The rule uses the term "placement options" to refer to the actual placements, rather than just the categories.

Request of child. The statute provides that, where appropriate, preference of the Indian child must be considered.[56] The rule adds that the child must be of "sufficient age and capacity to understand the decision that is being made" but leaves it to the fact-finder to make the determination as to age and capacity.

---

55. *See* 25 U.S.C. 1915(c).
56. *See* 25 U.S.C. 1915(c).

Sibling attachment. The rules governing placement preferences recognize the importance of maintaining biological sibling connections. The sibling placement preference makes clear that good cause can appropriately be found to depart from ICWA's placement preferences where doing so allows the "Indian child" to remain with his or her sibling. This allows biological siblings to remain together, even if only one is an "Indian child" under the Act.

Extraordinary needs. The rule retains discretion for courts and agencies to consider any extraordinary physical, mental, or emotional needs of a particular Indian child.

Unavailability of suitable placement. The rule provides that the unavailability of a suitable placement may be the basis for a good cause determination. It also requires that, in order to determine that there is good cause to deviate from the placement preferences based on unavailability of a suitable placement, the court must determine that a diligent search was conducted to find placements meeting the preference criteria. This provision is required because the Department understands ICWA to require proactive efforts to determine if there are extended family or Tribal community placements available. It is also consistent with the Federal policy for all children—not just Indian children—that States are to exercise "due diligence" to identify, locate, and notify relatives when children enter the foster care system. *See* 81 FR 38839 (June 14, 2016) for additional explanation for why the State must provide documented efforts to comply with the preferences. *See* section H.3 of these guidelines for additional guidance on what a diligent search involves.

The rule requires that, if the agency relies on unavailability of placement preferences as good cause for deviating from the placement preferences, it must be able to demonstrate to the court on the record that it conducted a diligent search. This showing would occur at the hearing in which the court determines whether a placement or change in placement is appropriate.

The determination of whether a "diligent search" has been completed is left to the fact-finder and will depend on the facts of each case. As a best practice, a diligent search will require a showing that the agency made good-faith efforts to contact all known family members to inquire about their willingness to serve as a placement, as well as whether they are aware of other family members that might be willing to serve as a placement. A diligent search will also generally require good-faith efforts to work with the child's Tribe to identify family-member and Tribal-community placements. If placements were identified but have not yet completed a necessary step for the child to be placed with them (such as filing paperwork or completing a background check), the fact-finder will need to determine whether sufficient time and assistance has been provided.

Safety of placement. While the standards for determining whether a placement is unavailable must conform to the prevailing social and cultural standards of the Indian community, nothing in the rule eliminates other requirements under State or Federal law for ensuring that placements will protect the safety of the Indian child.

H.5 Limits on good cause

Regulation

---

§ 23.132 How is a determination of "good cause" to depart from the placement preferences made?

. . . (d) A placement may not depart from the preferences based on the socioeconomic status of any placement relative to another placement.

(e) A placement may not depart from the preferences based solely on ordinary bonding or attachment that flowed from time spent in a non-preferred placement that was made in violation of ICWA.

Guidelines

The rule identifies certain factors that may not be the basis for a finding of good cause to depart from the preferences. These limits focus on those factors that there is evidence Congress did not wish to be considered, or that have been shown to frustrated the application of 25 U.S.C. 1911(b). State courts retain discretion to determine "good cause," so long as they do not base their good cause finding on one or more of these prohibited considerations.

Socioeconomic status. The fact that a preferred placement may be of a different socioeconomic status than a non-preferred placement may not serve as the basis for good cause to depart from the placement preferences.

Ordinary bonding with a non-preferred placement that flowed from time spent in a non-preferred placement that was made in violation of ICWA. If a child has been placed in a non-preferred placement in violation of ICWA and the rule, the court should not base a good-cause determination solely on the fact that the child has bonded with that placement.

A placement is "made in violation of ICWA" if the placement was based on a failure to comply with specific statutory or regulatory mandates. The determination of whether there was a violation of ICWA will be fact-specific and tied to the requirements of the statute and this rule. For example, failure to provide the required notice to the Indian child's Tribe for a year, despite the Tribe having been identified earlier in the proceeding, would be a violation of ICWA. By comparison, placing a child in a non-preferred placement would not be a violation of ICWA if the State agency and court followed the statute and applicable rules in making the placement, including by properly determining that there was good cause to deviate from the placement preferences.

As a best practice, in all cases, State agencies and courts should carefully consider whether the fact that an Indian child has developed a relationship with a non-preferred placement outweighs the long-term benefits to a child that can arise from maintaining connections to family and the Tribal community. Where a child is in a non-preferred placement, it is a best practice to facilitate connections between the Indian child and extended family and other potential preferred placements. For example, if a child is in a non-preferred placement due to geographic considerations and to promote reunification with the parent, the agency or court should promote connections and bonding with extended family or other preferred placements who may live further away. In this way, the child has the opportunity to develop additional bonds with these preferred placements that could ease a transition to that placement.

I. Voluntary Proceedings

I.1 Inquiry and verification in voluntary proceedings

Regulation

---

§ 23.124 What actions must a State court undertake in voluntary proceedings?

(a) The State court must require the participants in a voluntary proceeding to state on the record whether the child is an Indian child, or whether there is reason to believe the child is an Indian child, as provided in § 23.107.

(b) If there is reason to believe the child is an Indian child, the State court must ensure that the party seeking placement has taken all reasonable steps to verify the child's status. This may include contacting the Tribe of which it is believed the child is a member (or eligible for membership and of which the biological parent is a member) to verify the child's status. As described in § 23.107, where a consenting parent requests anonymity, a Tribe receiving such information must keep relevant documents and information confidential.

. . .

Guidelines

The rule provides minimum requirements for State courts to determine whether a child in a voluntary proceeding is an "Indian child" as defined by statute. That determination is essential in order to assess the State court's jurisdiction and what law applies in voluntary proceedings. The determination of whether the child is an "Indian child" is a threshold inquiry; it affects the jurisdiction of the State court and what law applies to the matter before it.

In some cases, it may be undisputed that the child is an Indian child, such as where the parents attest to this fact. If, however, there is reason to believe (i.e., reason to know) that the child is an "Indian child," but this cannot be confirmed based on the evidence before the State court, it must ensure that the party seeking placement has taken all reasonable steps to confirm the child's status. This includes seeking verification of the Indian child's status with the Tribes of which the child might be a citizen. Tribes, like other governments, are equipped to keep such inquiries confidential, and the rule requires this of Tribes.

The regulation's use of the language "reason to believe" echoes, and is intended to be substantively the same as, the statutory language "reason to know."

I.2 Placement preferences in voluntary proceedings

Regulation

§ 23.124 What actions must a State court undertake in voluntary proceedings?

... (c) State courts must ensure that the placement for the Indian child complies with §§ 23.129—23.132.

Guidelines

This provision explains that the regulatory provisions addressing the application of the placement preferences apply with equal force to voluntary proceedings. The Act and rule require application of the placement preferences in both voluntary and involuntary placements.

As discussed in section H.4 of these guidelines, above, the judge may consider as a basis for good cause to depart from the placement preferences the request of one or both of the parents, if they attest that they have reviewed the placement options, if any, that comply with the order of preference. This good cause provision allows birth parents to express their preference for an adoptive family that does not fall within ICWA's placement preferences. It is important, however, for birth parents to be made aware of ICWA's preferences and whether there are available placements within the extended family or Tribal community. This balances the interest of the parent with the other interests protected by ICWA.

Situations in which a step-parent seeks to adopt the child would fall within the first placement preference because step-parents are included in the definition of "extended family member."

I.3 Notice in voluntary proceedings

Guidelines

The Department recommends that the Indian child's Tribe be provided notice of voluntary proceedings involving that child to allow the Tribe's participation in identifying preferred placements and to promote the child's continued connections to the Tribe. As discussed above, communication with the Tribe may be required in order to verify the child's status as an Indian child. States may choose to require notice to Tribes and other parties in voluntary proceedings.

I.4 Effect of a request for anonymity on verification

Regulation

§ 23.107 How should a State court determine if there is reason to know the child is an Indian child?

... (d) In seeking verification of the child's status in a voluntary proceeding where a consenting parent evidences, by written request or statement in the record, a desire for anonymity, the court must keep relevant documents pertaining to the inquiry required under this section confidential and under seal. A request for anonymity does not relieve the court, agency, or other party from any duty of compliance with ICWA, including the obligation to verify whether the child is an "Indian child." A Tribe receiving information related to this inquiry must keep documents and information confidential.

Guidelines

In voluntary proceedings where the consenting parent requests, in writing, to remain anonymous, it is recommended that the party seeking placement notify the Tribe of the request for anonymity; the Tribe is required to keep information related to the verification inquiry confidential.

I.5 Effect of a request for anonymity on placement preferences

Regulation

§ 23.129 When do the placement preferences apply?

... (b) Where a consenting parent requests anonymity in a voluntary proceeding, the court must give weight to the request in applying the preferences.

Guidelines

If the consenting parent requests anonymity, it is recommended that the agency work with the Tribe to identify placement preferences that protect the parent's anonymity. The rule does not mandate contacting extended family members to identify potential placements.

I.6 Parent's or Indian custodian's consent

Regulation

§ 23.125 How is consent obtained?

(a) A parent's or Indian custodian's consent to a voluntary termination of parental rights or to a foster-care, preadoptive, or adoptive placement must be executed in writing and recorded before a court of competent jurisdiction.

(b) Prior to accepting the consent, the court must explain to the parent or Indian custodian:

(1) The terms and consequences of the consent in detail; and

(2) The following limitations, applicable to the type of child-custody proceeding for which consent is given, on withdrawal of consent:

(i) For consent to foster-care placement, the parent or Indian custodian may withdraw consent for any reason, at any time, and have the child returned; or

(ii) For consent to termination of parental rights, the parent or Indian custodian may withdraw consent for any reason, at any time prior to the entry of the final decree of termination and have the child returned; or

(iii) For consent to an adoptive placement, the parent or Indian custodian may withdraw consent for any reason, at any time prior to the entry of the final decree of adoption, and have the child returned.

(c) The court must certify that the terms and consequences of the consent were explained on the record in detail in English (or the language of the parent or Indian custodian, if English is not the primary language) and were fully understood by the parent or Indian custodian.

(d) Where confidentiality is requested or indicated, execution of consent need not be made in a session of court open to the public but still must be made before a court of competent jurisdiction in compliance with this section.

(e) A consent given prior to, or within 10 days after, the birth of an Indian child is not valid.

Guidelines

An individual parent's consent is valid only as to himself or herself.

The rule provides that the consent must be "recorded" before a court; this must be accomplished by providing a written document to the court.

I.7 Contents of consent document

Regulation

---

§ 23.126 What information must a consent document contain?

(a) If there are any conditions to the consent, the written consent must clearly set out the conditions.

(b) A written consent to foster-care placement should contain, in addition to the information specified in paragraph (a) of this section, the name and birthdate of the Indian child; the name of the Indian child's Tribe; the Tribal enrollment number for the parent and for the Indian child, where known, or some other indication of the child's membership in the Tribe; the name, address, and other identifying information of the consenting parent or Indian custodian; the name and address of the person or entity, if any, who arranged the placement; and the name and address of the prospective foster parents, if known at the time.

Guidelines

A State may choose to include or require the inclusion of additional information, beyond what is required in § 23.126.

The BIA has a sample form for consent posted at www.bia.gov as an example for States to consider.

I.7 Withdrawal of consent

Regulation

---

§ 23.127 How is withdrawal of consent to a foster-care placement achieved?

(a) The parent or Indian custodian may withdraw consent to voluntary foster-care placement at any time.

(b) To withdraw consent, the parent or Indian custodian must file a written document with the court or otherwise testify before the court. Additional methods of withdrawing consent may be available under State law.

(c) When a parent or Indian custodian withdraws consent to a voluntary foster-care placement, the court must ensure that the Indian child is returned to that parent or Indian custodian as soon as practicable.

§ 23.128 How is withdrawal of consent to a termination of parental rights or adoption achieved?

(a) A parent may withdraw consent to voluntary termination of parental rights at any time prior to the entry of a final decree of termination.

(b) A parent or Indian custodian may withdraw consent to voluntary adoption at any time prior to the entry of a final decree of adoption.

(c) To withdraw consent prior to the entry of a final decree of adoption, the parent or Indian custodian must file a written document with the court or otherwise testify before the court. Additional methods of withdrawing consent may be available under State law.

(d) The court in which the withdrawal of consent is filed must promptly notify the person or entity who arranged any voluntary preadoptive or adoptive placement of such filing, and the Indian child must be returned to the parent or Indian custodian as soon as practicable.

Guidelines

A parent may withdraw consent to a TPR any time before the final decree for that TPR is entered, and a parent may withdraw consent to an adoption any time before the final decree of adoption is entered. However, note that if a parent's or Indian custodian's parental rights have already been terminated, then the parent or Indian custodian may no longer withdraw consent to the adoption, because they no longer legally qualify as a parent or Indian custodian.

The written withdrawal of consent filed with the court (or testimony before the court) is not intended to be an overly formalistic requirement. Parents involved in pending TPR or adoption proceedings can be reasonably expected to know that there are court proceedings concerning their child, and the rule balances the need for a clear indication that the parent wants to withdraw consent with the parent's interest in easily withdrawing consent. States may have additional methods for withdrawing consent that are more protective of a parent's rights that would then apply.

Under the rule, whenever consent has been withdrawn, court must contact the party by or through whom any preadoptive or adoptive placement has been arranged. In most cases this will be the agency, whether public or private. The agency is expected to have the contact information for the placement.

The BIA has a sample form for withdrawal of consent posted at www.bia.gov as an example for States to consider.

J. Recordkeeping & Reporting

J.1 Record of every placement

Regulation

§ 23.141 What records must the State maintain?

(a) The State must maintain a record of every voluntary or involuntary foster-care, preadoptive, and adoptive placement of an Indian child and make the record available within 14 days of a request by an Indian child's Tribe or the Secretary.

(b) The record must contain, at a minimum, the petition or complaint, all substantive orders entered in the child-custody proceeding, the complete record of the placement determination (including, but not limited to, the findings in the court record and the social worker's statement), and, if the placement departs from the placement preferences, detailed documentation of the efforts to comply with the placement preferences.

(c) A State agency or agencies may be designated to be the repository for this information. The State court or agency should notify the BIA whether these records are maintained within the court system or by a State agency.

Guidelines

The statute and the rule require that the State maintain a record of each placement, under State law, of an Indian child. The files may be originals or may be true copies of the originals.

The rule ensures States have the flexibility to determine the best way to maintain their records to ensure that they can comply with the 14-day timeframe.

Paragraph (b) of § 23.141 directly addresses only court records because the court records must include all evidence justifying the placement determination. States may require that additional records be maintained.

It is recommended that the record include any documentation of preferred placements contacted and, if any were found ineligible as a placement, an explanation as to the ineligibility.

It is recommended that State agencies coordinate with State courts and private agencies to identify who is best positioned to fulfill this duty.

J.2 Transmission of every final adoption decree

Regulation

§ 23.140 What information must States furnish to the Bureau of Indian Affairs?

(a) Any State court entering a final adoption decree or order in any voluntary or involuntary Indian-child adoptive placement must furnish a copy of the decree or order within 30 days to the Bureau of Indian Affairs, Chief, Division of Human Services, 1849 C Street NW., Mail Stop 4513 MIB, Washington, DC 20240, along with the following information, in an envelope marked "Confidential":

(1) Birth name and birthdate of the Indian child, and Tribal affiliation and name of the Indian child after adoption;

(2) Names and addresses of the biological parents; (3) Names and addresses of the adoptive parents;

(4) Name and contact information for any agency having files or information relating to the adoption;

(5) Any affidavit signed by the biological parent or parents asking that their identity remain confidential; and

(6) Any information relating to Tribal membership or eligibility for Tribal membership of the adopted child.

(b) If a State agency has been designated as the repository for all State-court adoption information and is fulfilling the duties described in paragraph (a) of this section, the State courts in that State need not fulfill those same duties.

Guidelines

Providing the information to BIA for each final adoption decree and order allows BIA to serve as a resource for Indian children who, when they become adults, seek information on their adoption.

It is recommended that State agencies coordinate with State courts and private agencies to identify who is best positioned to fulfill this duty.

J.3 Adoptions that are vacated or set aside

Regulation

§ 23.139 Must notice be given of a change in an adopted Indian child's status?

(a) If an Indian child has been adopted, the court must notify, by registered or certified mail with return receipt requested, the child's biological parent or prior Indian custodian and the Indian child's Tribe whenever:

(1) A final decree of adoption of the Indian child has been vacated or set aside; or

(2) The adoptive parent has voluntarily consented to the termination of his or her parental rights to the child.

(b) The notice must state the current name, and any former name, of the Indian child, inform the recipient of the right to petition for return of custody of the child, and provide sufficient information to allow the recipient to participate in any scheduled hearings.

(c) A parent or Indian custodian may waive his or her right to such notice by executing a written waiver of notice and filing the waiver with the court.

(1) Prior to accepting the waiver, the court must explain the consequences of the waiver and explain how the waiver may be revoked.

(2) The court must certify that the terms and consequences of the waiver and how the waiver may be revoked were explained in detail in English (or the language of the parent or Indian custodian, if English is not the primary language), and were fully understood by the parent or Indian custodian.

(3) Where confidentiality is requested or indicated, execution of the waiver need not be made in a session of court open to the public but still must be made before a court of competent jurisdiction in compliance with this section.

(4) The biological parent or Indian custodian may revoke the waiver at any time by filing with the court a written notice of revocation.

(5) A revocation of the right to receive notice does not affect any child-custody proceeding that was completed before the filing of the notice of revocation.

Guidelines

If an adoption is vacated or set aside, or the adoptive parent voluntarily consents to TPR, then the State agency should work with the State court to ensure that the notice requirements of § 23.139 are fulfilled.

This notice is required because, in the particular circumstances where an adoption is vacated or set aside, or the adoptive parent voluntarily consents to TPR, the statute provides certain rights to the biological parent or prior Indian custodian.[57] The notice enables the biological parent or prior Indian custodian to avail himself or herself of those rights.

This section of the rule addresses waiver of notice for two particular situations:

- Where an adoption of an Indian child is subsequently vacated or set aside; or
- Where the adoptive parents decide to voluntarily terminate their parental rights. In those cases, the biological parent or prior Indian custodian may waive notice of these actions.

---

57. *See* 25 U.S.C. 1916(a).

J.4 Adult adoptees' access to information about their Tribal affiliation

Regulation

§ 23.138 What are the rights to information about adoptees' Tribal affiliations?

Upon application by an Indian who has reached age 18 who was the subject of an adoptive placement, the court that entered the final decree of adoption must inform such individual of the Tribal affiliations, if any, of the individual's biological parents and provide such other information necessary to protect any rights, which may include Tribal membership, resulting from the individual's Tribal relationship.

Guidelines

ICWA provides Indian adult adoptees with specific rights to information on Tribal, as reflected in the above rule provision. States may provide additional rights to adoptees.

Some States have registries that allow individuals to obtain information on siblings for purposes of reunification.

It is recommended that the State agency work with the State court to ensure that, with each adoptive placement, there is sufficient information in the record regarding the individual's Tribal relationship to allow the court to meet its requirements under § 23.138 for the protection of any rights that may result from the individual's Tribal membership.

BIA is also adding information to its website (www.bia.gov) to assist adult adoptees who are looking to reconnect with their Tribes.

J.5 Parties' access to the case documents

Regulation

§ 23.134 Who has access to reports and records during a proceeding?

Each party to an emergency proceeding or a foster-care-placement or termination-of-parental-rights proceeding under State law involving an Indian child has a right to timely examine all reports and other documents filed or lodged with the court upon which any decision with respect to such action may be based.

Guidelines

Parties to emergency, foster-care-placement, or TPR proceedings are entitled to receipt of documents upon which a decision may be based.

States cannot refuse to provide a party to an ICWA proceeding, including a Tribe that is a party, access to information about the proceedings.

K. Improper Removal, Consent Obtained through Fraud or Duress, Other ICWA Violations

Both the State agency and the court have an independent responsibility under Federal law to follow ICWA. The following addresses regulatory provisions setting out how an Indian child, parent, Indian custodian, or the Tribe can seek redress for certain actions made in violation of ICWA.

K.1 Improper removal

Regulation

---

§ 23.114 What are the requirements for determining improper removal?

(a) If, in the course of any child-custody proceeding, any party asserts or the court has reason to believe that the Indian child may have been improperly removed from the custody of his or her parent or Indian custodian, or that the Indian child has been improperly retained (such as after a visit or other temporary relinquishment of custody), the court must expeditiously determine whether there was improper removal or retention.

(b) If the court finds that the Indian child was improperly removed or retained, the court must terminate the proceeding and the child must be returned immediately to his or her parent or Indian custodian, unless returning the child to his parent or Indian custodian would subject the child to substantial and immediate danger or threat of such danger.

Guidelines

This regulatory provision implements section 1920 of the statute. It requires that, where a court determines that a child has been improperly removed from custody of the parent or Indian custodian or has been improperly retained in the custody of a petitioner in a child-custody proceeding, the court should return the child to his/her parent or Indian custodian unless returning the child to his/her parent or custodian would subject the child to a substantial and immediate danger or threat of such danger.

K.2 Consent obtained through fraud or duress

Regulation

§ 23.136 What are the requirements for vacating an adoption based on consent having been obtained through fraud or duress?

(a) Within two years after a final decree of adoption of any Indian child by a State court, or within any longer period of time permitted by the law of the State, the State court may invalidate the voluntary adoption upon finding that the parent's consent was obtained by fraud or duress.

(b) Upon the parent's filing of a petition to vacate the final decree of adoption of the parent's Indian child, the court must give notice to all parties to the adoption proceedings and the Indian child's Tribe and must hold a hearing on the petition.

(c) Where the court finds that the parent's consent was obtained through fraud or duress, the court must vacate the final decree of adoption, order the consent revoked, and order that the child be returned to the parent.

Guidelines

The two-year statute of limitations applies only to invalidation of adoptions based on parental consent having been obtained through fraud or duress. If a State's statute of limitations exceeds two years, then the State statute of limitations may apply; the two-year statute of limitations is a minimum timeframe.

K.3 Other ICWA violations

Regulation

§ 23.137 Who can petition to invalidate an action for certain ICWA violations?

(a) Any of the following may petition any court of competent jurisdiction to invalidate an action for foster-care placement or termination of parental rights under state law where it is alleged that 25 U.S.C. 1911, 1912, or 1913 has been violated:

(1) An Indian child who is or was the subject of any action for foster-care placement or termination of parental rights;

(2) A parent or Indian custodian from whose custody such child was removed;

and

(3) The Indian child's Tribe.

(b) Upon a showing that an action for foster-care placement or termination of parental rights violated any provision of 25 U.S.C. 1911, 1912, or 1913, the court must determine whether it is appropriate to invalidate the action.

(c) To petition for invalidation, there is no requirement that the petitioner's rights under ICWA were violated; rather, a petitioner may challenge the action based on any violations of 25 U.S.C. 1911, 1912, or 1913 during the course of the child-custody proceeding.

Guidelines

The court of competent jurisdiction referenced in this rule provision may be a different court from the court where the original proceedings occurred.

A party may assert violations of ICWA requirements that may have impacted the ICWA rights of other parties (e.g., a parent can assert a violation of the requirement for a Tribe to receive notice under section 1912(a)). One party cannot waive another party's right to seek to invalidate such an action. Additionally, parties may have other appeal rights under State or other Federal law in addition to the rights established in ICWA.

A petition to invalidate an action does not necessarily affect only the action that is currently before the court. For example, an action to invalidate a TPR may affect an adoption proceeding.

The rule does not require the court to invalidate an action, but requires the court to determine whether it is appropriate to invalidate the action under the standard of review under applicable law.

L. Definitions

L.1 Active Efforts

Regulation

§ 23.2

. . . *Active efforts* means affirmative, active, thorough, and timely efforts intended primarily to maintain or reunite an Indian child with his or her family. Where an agency is involved in the child-custody proceeding, active efforts must involve assisting the parent or parents or Indian custodian through the steps of a case plan and with accessing or developing the resources necessary to satisfy the case plan. To the maximum extent possible, active efforts should be provided in a manner consistent with the prevailing social and cultural conditions and way of life of the Indian child's

Tribe and should be conducted in partnership with the Indian child and the Indian child's parents, extended family members, Indian custodians, and Tribe. Active efforts are to be tailored to the facts and circumstances of the case and may include, for example:

(1) Conducting a comprehensive assessment of the circumstances of the Indian child's family, with a focus on safe reunification as the most desirable goal;

(2) Identifying appropriate services and helping the parents to overcome barriers, including actively assisting the parents in obtaining such services;

(3) Identifying, notifying, and inviting representatives of the Indian child's Tribe to participate in providing support and services to the Indian child's family and in family team meetings, permanency planning, and resolution of placement issues;

(4) Conducting or causing to be conducted a diligent search for the Indian child's extended family members, and contacting and consulting with extended family members to provide family structure and support for the Indian child and the Indian child's parents;

(5) Offering and employing all available and culturally appropriate family preservation strategies and facilitating the use of remedial and rehabilitative services provided by the child's Tribe;

(6) Taking steps to keep siblings together whenever possible;

(7) Supporting regular visits with parents or Indian custodians in the most natural setting possible as well as trial home visits of the Indian child during any period of removal, consistent with the need to ensure the health, safety, and welfare of the child;

(8) Identifying community resources including housing, financial, transportation, mental health, substance abuse, and peer support services and actively assisting the Indian child's parents or, when appropriate, the child's family, in utilizing and accessing those resources;

(9) Monitoring progress and participation in services;

(10) Considering alternative ways to address the needs of the Indian child's parents and, where appropriate, the family, if the optimum services do not exist or are not available;

(11) Providing post-reunification services and monitoring.

Guidelines

See section E of these guidelines.

L.2 Agency

Regulation

§ 23.102

. . . *Agency* means a private State-licensed agency or public agency and their employees, agents or officials involved in and/or seeking to place a child in a child custody proceeding.

Guidelines

The rule defines "agency" as an organization that performs, or provides services to biological parents, foster parents, or adoptive parents to assist in, the administrative and social work necessary for foster, preadoptive, or adoptive placements. The definition includes non-profit, for-profit, or governmental organizations including those who may assist in the administrative or social work aspects of seeking placement. An "agency" may also be assisting in the legal aspects of seeking placement, but the definition does not include attorneys or law firms, standing alone, because as used in the rule, "agencies" are presumed to have some capacity to provide social services. Attorneys and others involved in court proceedings are addressed separately in various provisions in the rule. This comports with the statute's broad language imposing requirements on "any party" seeking placement of a child or TPR.

L.3 Child-custody proceeding

Regulation

§ 23.2

. . . *Child-custody proceeding.*

(1) "Child custody proceeding" means and includes any action, other than an emergency proceeding, that may culminate in one of the following outcomes:

(i) Foster-care placement, which is any action removing an Indian child from his or her parent or Indian custodian for temporary placement in a foster home or institution or the home of a guardian or conservator where the parent or Indian custodian cannot have the child returned upon demand, but where parental rights have not been terminated;

(ii) Termination of parental rights, which is any action resulting in the termination of the parent-child relationship;

(iii) Preadoptive placement, which is the temporary placement of an Indian child in a foster home or institution after the termination of parental rights, but prior to or in lieu of adoptive placement; or

(iv) Adoptive placement, which is the permanent placement of an Indian child for adoption, including any action resulting in a final decree of adoption.

(2) An action that may culminate in one of these four outcomes is considered a separate child-custody proceeding from an action that may culminate in a different one of these four outcomes. There may be several child-custody proceedings involving any given Indian child. Within each child-custody proceeding, there may be several hearings. If a child is placed in foster care or another out-of-home placement as a result of a status offense, that status offense proceeding is a child-custody proceeding.

Guidelines

ICWA requirements apply to an action that may result in one of the placement outcomes, even if it ultimately does not. For example, ICWA would apply to an action where a court was considering a foster-care placement of a child, but ultimately decided to return the child to his parents. Thus, even though the action did not result in a foster-care placement, it may have culminated in such a placement and, therefore, should be considered a "child-custody proceeding" under the statute. The definition further makes clear that a child-custody proceeding that may culminate in one outcome (e.g., a foster-care placement) would be a separate child-custody proceeding from one that may culminate in a different outcome (e.g., a TPR), even though the same child may be involved in both proceedings.

This definition explicitly excludes emergency proceedings from the scope of a child-custody proceeding, as emergency proceedings are addressed separately.

This definition includes proceedings involving status offenses if any part of the proceeding results in the need for out-of-home placement of the child.

Adoptions that do not involve TPR, for example, Tribal customary adoptions, are included within the definition of "child-custody proceeding" as either a "foster-care placement" or an "adoptive placement," because these terms, as defined, do not require TPR. *See* 25 U.S.C. 1903.

See § 23.103 and <u>section B.2</u> of these guidelines. *See, also,* 81 FR 38799 (June 14, 2016) for additional information on this definition.

L.4 Continued custody and custody

Regulation

---

§ 23.2

... *Continued custody* means physical custody or legal custody or both, under any applicable Tribal law or Tribal custom or State law, that a parent or Indian custodian already has or had at any point in the past. The biological mother of a child has had custody of a child.

Custody means physical custody or legal custody or both, under any applicable Tribal law or Tribal custom or State law. A party may demonstrate the existence of custody by looking to Tribal law or Tribal custom or State law.

Guidelines

The definition of "continued custody" includes custody the parent or Indian custodian "has or had at any point in the past" as there is no evidence that Congress intended temporary disruptions (e.g., surrender of the child to another caregiver for a period) not to be included in "continued custody." The definition also clarifies that the parent or custodian may have physical and/or legal custody under any applicable Tribal law or Tribal custom or State law.

These definitions clarify that physical and/or legal custody may be defined by applicable Tribal law or custom, or by State law, but do not establish an order of preference among Tribal law, Tribal custom, and State law because custody may be established under any one of the three sources.

L.5 Domicile

Regulation

§ 23.2

. . . *Domicile* means:

(1) For a parent or Indian custodian, the place at which a person has been physically present and that the person regards as home; a person's true, fixed, principal, and permanent home, to which that person intends to return and remain indefinitely even though the person may be currently residing elsewhere.

(2) For an Indian child, the domicile of the Indian child's parents or Indian custodian or guardian. In the case of an Indian child whose parents are not married to each other, the domicile of the Indian child's custodial parent.

Guidelines

This definition reflects the common-law definition, which acknowledges that a person may reside in one place but be domiciled in another.

Note that, while the rule does not define "residing" or "residence," the Department interprets "residence" to mean the location where an individual is currently living but which is not their permanent, fixed home to which they intend to return—for example, a child might be domiciled with his or her parents but residing at a boarding school or university, or with family members while his or her parents are away for an extended period of time.

L.6 Emergency proceeding

Regulation

---

§ 23.2

. . . *Emergency proceeding* means and includes any court action that involves an emergency removal or emergency placement of an Indian child.

Guidelines

See section C of these guidelines.

L.7 Extended family member

Regulation

---

§ 23.2

. . . *Extended family member* is defined by the law or custom of the Indian child's Tribe or, in the absence of such law or custom, is a person who has reached age 18 and who is the Indian child's grandparent, aunt or uncle, brother or sister, brother-in-law or sister-in-law, niece or nephew, first or second cousin, or stepparent.

Guidelines

Additional categories of individuals may be included in the meaning of the term if the law or custom of the Indian child's Tribe includes them.

"Extended family member" is not limited to Tribal citizens or Native American individuals.

L.8 Hearing

Regulation

---

§ 23.2

. . . *Hearing* means a judicial session held for the purpose of deciding issues of fact, of law, or both.

Guidelines

In order to demonstrate the distinction between a hearing and a child-custody proceeding, the definition of "child-custody proceeding" explains that there may be multiple hearings involved in a single child-custody proceeding.

L.9 Indian

Regulation

§ 23.2

. . . *Indian* means any person who is a member of an Indian tribe, or who is an Alaska Native and a member of a Regional Corporation as defined in section 7 of the Alaska Native Claims Settlement Act, 43 U.S.C. 1606.

Guidelines

Note that this term includes only those individuals who are members of "Indian Tribes" (i.e., federally recognized Tribes) and members of Alaska Native Claims Settlement Act regional corporations.

L.10 Indian child's Tribe

Regulation

§ 23.2

. . . *Indian child's Tribe* means:

(1) The Indian Tribe in which an Indian child is a member or eligible for membership;

or

(2) In the case of an Indian child who is a member of or eligible for membership in more than one Tribe, the Indian Tribe described in § 23.109.

Guidelines

Note that while a child may meet the definition of "Indian" through more than one Tribe, ICWA establishes that one Tribe must be designated as the "Indian child's Tribe" for the purposes of the Act.

L.11 Indian custodian

Regulation

§ 23.2

... *Indian custodian* means any Indian who has legal custody of an Indian child under applicable Tribal law or custom or under applicable State law, or to whom temporary physical care, custody, and control has been transferred by the parent of such child. An Indian may demonstrate that he or she is an Indian custodian by looking to Tribal law or Tribal custom or State law.

Guidelines

This definition allows for consideration of Tribal law or custom.

L.12 Indian foster home

Regulation

§ 23.2

... *Indian foster home* means a foster home where one or more of the licensed or approved foster parents is an "Indian" as defined in 25 U.S.C. 1903(3).

Guidelines

Note that a foster home does not meet the definition of an "Indian foster home" merely by virtue of an Indian child being present in the home; rather, one of the foster parents must meet the definition of "Indian."

L.13 Indian organization

Regulation

§ 23.102

... *Indian organization* means any group, association, partnership, corporation, or other legal entity owned or controlled by Indians or a tribe, or a majority of whose members are Indians.

Guidelines

This term is used in § 23.107(c), regarding reason to know the child is an Indian child, and § 23.131, regarding foster-care placement preferences (the last preferred placement is an institution for children approved by an Indian Tribe or operated by an Indian organization which has a program suitable to meet the child's needs).

L.14 Indian tribe

Regulation

---

§ 23.2

... *Indian tribe* means any Indian tribe, band, nation, or other organized group or community of Indians federally recognized as eligible for the services provided to Indians by the Secretary because of their status as Indians, including any Alaska Native village as defined in section 3(c) of the Alaska Native Claims Settlement Act, 43 U.S.C. 1602(c).

Guidelines

Note that "Indian Tribe" under ICWA includes only federally recognized Tribes. States may have a more inclusive definition of "Indian Tribe" that includes State-recognized or other groups; however, the Federal ICWA statute and rule do not apply to those groups.

L.15 Involuntary proceeding

Regulation

---

§ 23.2

... *Involuntary proceeding* means a child-custody proceeding in which the parent does not consent of his or her free will to the foster-care, preadoptive, or adoptive placement or termination of parental rights or in which the parent consents to the foster-care, preadoptive, or adoptive placement under threat of removal of the child by a State court or agency.

Guidelines

See discussion in section B of these guidelines regarding ICWA's applicability to involuntary proceedings.

L.16 Parent or parents

Regulation

---

§ 23.2

... *Parent or parents* means any biological parent or parents of an Indian child, or any Indian who has lawfully adopted an Indian child, including adoptions under Tribal law or custom. It does not include an unwed biological father where paternity has not been acknowledged or established.

Guidelines

Note that the rule does not provide a Federal standard for acknowledgment or establishment of paternity. Many State courts have held that, for ICWA purposes, an unwed father must make reasonable efforts to establish paternity, but need not strictly comply with State laws.[58]

L.17 Reservation

Regulation

---

§ 23.2

... *Reservation* means Indian country as defined in 18 U.S.C 1151 and any lands, not covered under that section, title to which is held by the United States in trust for the benefit of any Indian Tribe or individual or held by any Indian Tribe or individual subject to a restriction by the United States against alienation.

Guidelines

Note that this definition includes land that is held in trust but not officially proclaimed a "reservation." Indian country generally includes lands within the boundaries of an Indian reservation, dependent Indian communities, Indian allotments, and any lands that are either held by the United States in trust for the benefit of any Indian tribe or individual or held by any Indian tribe or individual subject to a restriction by the United States against alienation. This definition does not include Alaska Native Villages unless they fall within one of these categories.

---

58. *See* 81 FR 38796 (June 14, 2016) for a discussion of case law articulating a constitutional standard regarding the rights of unwed fathers.

L.18 Status offenses

Regulation

§23.2

. . . *Status offenses* mean offenses that would not be considered criminal if committed by an adult; they are acts prohibited only because of a person's status as a minor (e.g., truancy, incorrigibility).

Guidelines

See also the definition of "child custody proceeding," which includes proceedings where a child is placed in foster care or another out-of-home placement as a result of a status offense.

If the placement is based upon a status offense, ICWA provisions apply, regardless of whether the State is a PL-280 State.

A placement, including juvenile detention, resulting from status offense proceedings meets the statutory definition of "foster-care placement" and such placement is therefore subject to ICWA.

L.19 Tribal court

Regulation

§23.2

. . . *Tribal court* means a court with jurisdiction over child-custody proceedings and which is either a Court of Indian Offenses, a court established and operated under the code or custom of an Indian Tribe, or any other administrative body of a Tribe vested with authority over child-custody proceedings.

Guidelines

Note that the definition includes any other administrative body of a tribe vested with authority over child-custody proceedings in recognition that a Tribe may have other mechanisms for making child-custody decisions (e.g., the Tribal council may preside over child-custody proceedings).

L.20 Upon demand

Regulation

§ 23.2

. . . *Upon demand* means that the parent or Indian custodian can regain custody simply upon verbal request, without any formalities or contingencies.

Guidelines

This definition is important for determining whether a placement is a "foster-care placement" (because the parent cannot have the child returned upon demand) under § 23.2, and therefore subject to requirements for involuntary proceedings for foster-care placement. Placements where the parent or Indian custodian can regain custody of the child upon demand are not subject to ICWA.

Examples of formalities or contingencies are formal court proceedings, the signing of agreements, and the repayment of the child's expenses.

L.21 Voluntary proceeding

Regulation

§ 23.2

. . . *Voluntary proceeding* means a child-custody proceeding that is not an involuntary proceeding, such as a proceeding for foster-care, preadoptive, or adoptive placement that either parent, both parents, or the Indian custodian has, of his or her or their free will, without a threat of removal by a State agency, consented to for the Indian child, or a proceeding for voluntary termination of parental rights.

Guidelines

The rule refers to "both parents" to allow for situations where both parents are known and reachable. If a parent refuses to consent to the foster-care, preadoptive, or adoptive placement or TPR, the proceeding would meet the definition of an "involuntary proceeding." Nothing in the statute indicates that the consent of one parent eliminates the rights and protections provided by ICWA to a non-consenting parent.

The definition specifies that placements where the parent agrees to the placement only under threat of losing custody is not "voluntary," by including the phrase "without a threat of removal by a State agency." The rule also specifies that a voluntary proceeding must be of the parent's or Indian custodian's free will to clarify that a proceeding in which the parent agrees to an out-of-home placement of the child under threat that the child will otherwise be removed is not "voluntary."

The distinguishing factor for a "voluntary proceeding" is the parent(s) or Indian custodian's consent, not whether they personally "chose" the placement for their child.

L.22 Other definitions

Regulation

§ 23.2

. . . *Act* means the Indian Child Welfare Act (ICWA), Pub. L. 95-608, 92 Stat. 3069, 25 U.S.C. 1901 et seq.

Assistant Secretary means the Assistant Secretary—Indian Affairs, the Department of the Interior.

Bureau of Indian Affairs (BIA) means the Bureau of Indian Affairs, the Department of the Interior.

Secretary means the Secretary of the Interior or the Secretary's authorized representative acting under delegated authority.

State court means any agent or agency of a state, including the District of Columbia or any territory or possession of the United States, or any political subdivision empowered by law to terminate parental rights or to make foster care placements, preadoptive placements, or adoptive placements.

Tribal government means the federally recognized governing body of an Indian tribe.

Guidelines

Note that while the regulation often refers to the "Secretary" of the Interior, generally, the Secretary has delegated authority for day-to-day matters arising under ICWA to BIA officials (e.g., BIA ICWA Specialist, BIA social services workers).

M. Additional Context for Understanding ICWA

M.1 ICWA's standards and the "best interests of the child" standard

In a child-custody proceeding, a party might argue that an aspect of ICWA or the rule is in tension with what is in the "best interests of the child." In most cases, this argument lacks merit. First, ICWA was specifically designed by Congress to protect the best interests of Indian children. In order to achieve that general goal, Congress established specific minimum Federal standards for the removal of Indian children from their families that are designed to protect children and their relationship with their parents, extended family, and Tribe.

One of the most important ways that ICWA protects the best interests of Indian children is by ensuring that, if possible, children remain with their parents and that, if they are separated, that support for reunification is provided. This is entirely consistent with the "best interests" standard applied in state courts, which recognizes the importance of family integrity and the preference for avoiding removal of a child from his or her home. If a child does need to be removed from her home, ICWA's placement preferences continue to protect her best interests by favoring placements within her extended family and Tribal community. Other ICWA provisions also serve to protect a child's best interests by, for example, ensuring that a child's parents have sufficient notice about her child-custody proceeding and an ability to fully participate in the proceeding (25 U.S.C. 1912(a),(b),(c)) and helping an adoptee access information about her Tribal connections (25 U.S.C. 1917).

Congress enacted ICWA specifically to address the problems that arose out of the application of subjective value judgments about what is "best" for an Indian child. Congress found that the unfettered subjective application of the "best interests" standard often failed to consider Tribal cultural practices or recognize the long-term advantages to children of remaining with their families and Tribes.[59] By providing courts with objective rules that operate above the emotions of individual cases, Congress was facilitating better State-court practice on these issues and the protection of Indian children, families, and Tribes.[60]

ICWA and the regulations provide objective standards that are designed to promote the welfare and short- and long-term interests of Indian children. However, the regulations also provide flexibility for courts to appropriately consider the particular circumstances of the individual children and to protect those children.

N. Additional Resources

The Department encourages States and Tribes to collaborate to advance ICWA implementation and suggests looking to some of the tools developed by States to aid in implementation of ICWA. For example:

- New York has published a State guide to ICWA (see A Guide to Compliance with the Indian Child Welfare Act published by the New York Office of Children and Family Services at *http://ocfs.ny.gov/main/publications/pub4757guidecompliance.pdf*)

---

59. H.R. Rep. No. 95-1386 at 19.

60. See National Council of Juvenile and Family Court Judges, Adoption and Permanency Guidelines: Improving Court Practice in Child Abuse and Neglect Cases 14 (2000).

- Washington has established a State evaluation of ICWA implementation, which it performs in partnership with Tribes (see 2009 Washington State Indian Child Welfare Case Review at *https://www.dshs.wa.gov/sites/default/files/SESA/oip/documents/Region%202%20ICW%20CR%20report.pdf*)
- Michigan has established a "bench card" as a tool for judges implementing ICWA and the State counterpart law (see 2014 Michigan Indian Family Preservation Act (MIFPA) Bench Card (last visited Apr. 27, 2016), *http://courts.mi.gov/Administration/SCAO/OfficesPrograms/CWS/CWSToolkit/Documents/BC_ICWA_M IFPA.pdf*)
- Several States have established State-Tribal forums to discuss child-welfare policy and practice issues (see Montana, North Dakota, Oklahoma, Oregon, Utah, and Washington)
- Several States have established State-Tribal court forums where court system representatives meet regularly to improve cooperation between their jurisdictions (see California, Michigan, New Mexico, New York, and Wisconsin).

In addition, several non-governmental entities offer tools for ICWA implementation, such as the National Council of Juvenile and Family Court Justices, National Indian Child Welfare Association, and Native American Rights Fund.

Appendix 1: BIA regional office addresses

§ 23.11 Notice.

(b)(1) For child-custody proceedings in Alabama, Connecticut, Delaware, District of Columbia, Florida, Georgia, Kentucky, Louisiana, Maine, Maryland, Massachusetts, Mississippi, New Hampshire, New Jersey, New York, North Carolina, Pennsylvania, Rhode Island, South Carolina, Tennessee, Vermont, Virginia, West Virginia, or any territory or possession of the United States, notices must be sent to the following address: Eastern Regional Director, Bureau of Indian Affairs, 545 Marriott Drive, Suite 700, Nashville, Tennessee 37214.

(2) For child-custody proceedings in Illinois, Indiana, Iowa, Michigan, Minnesota, Ohio, or Wisconsin, notices must be sent to the following address: Minneapolis Regional Director, Bureau of Indian Affairs, 331 Second Avenue South, Minneapolis, Minnesota 55401-2241.

(3) For child-custody proceedings in Nebraska, North Dakota, or South Dakota, notices must be sent to the following address: Aberdeen Regional Director, Bureau of Indian Affairs, 115 Fourth Avenue, SE, Aberdeen, South Dakota 57401.

(4) For child-custody proceedings in Kansas, Texas (except for notices to the Ysleta del Sur Pueblo of El Paso County, Texas), or the western Oklahoma counties of Alfalfa, Beaver, Beckman, Blaine, Caddo, Canadian, Cimarron, Cleveland, Comanche, Cotton, Custer, Dewey, Ellis, Garfield, Grant, Greer, Harmon, Harper,

Jackson, Kay, Kingfisher, Kiowa, Lincoln, Logan, Major, Noble, Oklahoma, Pawnee, Payne, Pottawatomie, Roger Mills, Texas, Tillman, Washita, Woods or Woodward, notices must be sent to the following address: Anadarko Regional Director, Bureau of Indian Affairs, P.O. Box 368, Anadarko, Oklahoma 73005. Notices to the Ysleta del Sur Pueblo must be sent to the Albuquerque Regional Director at the address listed in paragraph (b)(6).

(5) For child-custody proceedings in Wyoming or Montana (except for notices to the Confederated Salish and Kootenai Tribes of the Flathead Reservation, Montana), notices must be sent to the following address: Billings Regional Director, Bureau of Indian Affairs, 316 N. 26th Street, Billings, Montana 59101. Notices to the Confederated Salish and Kootenai Tribes of the Flathead Reservation, Montana, must be sent to the Portland Regional Director at the address listed in paragraph (b)(11).

(6) For child-custody proceedings in the Texas counties of El Paso and Hudspeth or in Colorado or New Mexico (exclusive of notices to the Navajo Nation from the New Mexico counties listed in paragraph (b)(9)), notices must be sent to the following address: Albuquerque Regional Director, Bureau of Indian Affairs, 615 First Street, P.O. Box 26567, Albuquerque, New Mexico 87125. Notices to the Navajo Nation must be sent to the Navajo Regional Director at the address listed in paragraph (b)(9).

(7) For child-custody proceedings in Alaska (except for notices to the Metlakatla Indian Community, Annette Island Reserve, Alaska), notices must be sent to the following address: Juneau Regional Director, Bureau of Indian Affairs, 709 West 9th Street, Juneau, Alaska 99802-1219. Notices to the Metlakatla Indian Community, Annette Island Reserve, Alaska, must be sent to the Portland Regional Director at the address listed in paragraph (b)(11).

(8) For child-custody proceedings in Arkansas, Missouri, or the eastern Oklahoma counties of Adair, Atoka, Bryan, Carter, Cherokee, Craig, Creek, Choctaw, Coal, Delaware, Garvin, Grady, Haskell, Hughes, Jefferson, Johnson, Latimer, LeFlore, Love, Mayes, McCurtain, McClain, McIntosh, Murray, Muskogee, Nowata, Okfuskee, Okmulgee, Osage, Ottawa, Pittsburg, Pontotoc, Pushmataha, Marshall, Rogers, Seminole, Sequoyah, Stephens, Tulsa, Wagoner, or Washington, notices must be sent to the following address: Muskogee Regional Director, Bureau of Indian Affairs, 101 North Fifth Street, Muskogee, Oklahoma 74401.

(9) For child-custody proceedings in the Arizona counties of Apache, Coconino (except for notices to the Hopi Tribe of Arizona and the San Juan Southern Paiute Tribe of Arizona) or Navajo (except for notices to the Hopi Tribe of Arizona); the New Mexico counties of McKinley (except for notices to the Zuni Tribe of the Zuni Reservation), San Juan, or Socorro; or the Utah county of San Juan, notices must be sent to the following address: Navajo Regional Director, Bureau of Indian Affairs, P.O. Box 1060, Gallup, New Mexico 87301. Notices to the Hopi and San Juan Southern Paiute Tribes of Arizona must be sent to the Phoenix Regional Director at the

address listed in paragraph (b)(10). Notices to the Zuni Tribe of the Zuni Reservation must be sent to the Albuquerque Regional Director at the address listed in paragraph (b)(6).

(10) For child-custody proceedings in Arizona (exclusive of notices to the Navajo Nation from those counties listed in paragraph (b)(9)), Nevada, or Utah (exclusive of San Juan County), notices must be sent to the following address: Phoenix Regional Director, Bureau of Indian Affairs, 1 North First Street, P.O. Box 10, Phoenix, Arizona 85001.

(11) For child-custody proceedings in Idaho, Oregon, or Washington, notices must be sent to the following address: Portland Regional Director, Bureau of Indian Affairs, 911 NE 11th Avenue, Portland, Oregon 97232. All notices to the Confederated Salish and Kootenai Tribes of the Flathead Reservation, located in the Montana counties of Flathead, Lake, Missoula, and Sanders, must also be sent to the Portland Regional Director.

(12) For child-custody proceedings in California or Hawaii, notices must be sent to the following address: Sacramento Regional Director, Bureau of Indian Affairs, Federal Office Building, 2800 Cottage Way,

Sacramento, California 95825.

* * *

Index

G

J